I0198367

THE BRETTON WOODS TRANSCRIPTS

The Bretton Woods Transcripts

Edited by

Kurt Schuler
and
Andrew Rosenberg

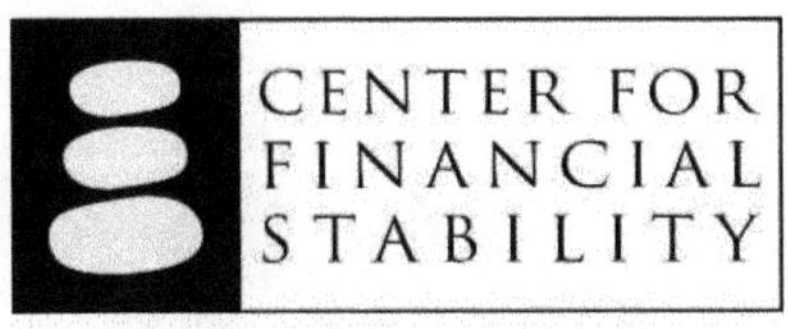

Dialog • Insight • Solutions

NEW YORK

Copyright 2012 by Kurt Schuler and Andrew Rosenberg. All rights reserved. Until 2023, no part of this book may be reproduced or transmitted in any form without written permission from the authors. Send requests to Kurt Schuler, <kschuler@the-cfs.org>. Starting in 2023, the authors permit anyone to reproduce the English language electronic edition of the book, provided that there is no alteration to the original content and that distribution to readers is free. The authors continue to reserve all other rights, including the rights to the English language print edition and to all foreign language editions.

E-book published 2012, print edition published 2013 by the Center for Financial Stability, 1120 Avenue of the Americas, 4th floor, New York, NY 10036, <http://www.the-cfs.org>

Suggested Cataloging Data

Schuler, Kurt

The Bretton Woods transcripts / edited by Kurt Schuler and Andrew Rosenberg ; preface by Jacques de Larosière and Steve H. Hanke.

xviii, 680 p. ; 24 cm.

New York : Center for Financial Stability, 2013.

Includes bibliographical references and index. Online companion files.

ISBN 978-1-941801-01-7 (hbk.), 978-1-941801-00-0 (e-book)

1. United Nations Monetary and Financial Conference (1944: Bretton Woods, N.H.) 2. International Monetary Fund 3. World Bank

I. Rosenberg, Andrew II. Title

Library of Congress Control Number : 2013933612

(Call numbers will be available from Library of Congress Web site)

Contents

PART II
COMMITTEES OF COMMISSION I

Committee 2: Operations of the Fund

Committee 3: Organization and Management of the Fund

Committee 4: Form and Status of the Fund

PART III
COMMISSIONS II AND III
WORLD BANK; OTHER MEANS OF COOPERATION

APPENDICES

ONLINE COMPANION FILES (at <http://www.the-cfs.org>)

Preface

by Jacques de Larosière and Steve H. Hanke

It has been almost seventy years since Bretton Woods, New Hampshire hosted one of the world's most important financial conferences. The Bretton Woods conference was a star-studded affair—one in which the postwar rules of the game for a new monetary order were hammered out, and one that gave birth to the International Monetary Fund and the World Bank. It is, therefore, remarkable that the Bretton Woods transcripts have never seen the light of day.

Indeed, for decades the transcripts had gone unnoticed, collecting dust in the library of the U.S. Treasury, until they were uncovered by Kurt Schuler. We owe him a debt of gratitude for this discovery, and for his painstaking work. Schuler, along with his coeditor, Andrew Rosenberg, has done a superb job in putting this treasure trove in shape for publication. Even though there have been thousands and thousands of pages written about the Bretton Woods conference, nothing beats the transcripts for a first-hand feel of what transpired.

In a matter of three short weeks, in July 1944, an enormous amount of high-quality output was produced. The transcripts tell the tale. What they don't tell is that a great deal of preparation preceded Bretton Woods. Indeed, the conference and its output did not just appear out of thin air.

In 1941, John Maynard Keynes of the United Kingdom and Harry Dexter White of the United States produced drafts of their respective visions for a postwar international monetary order. These were each revised and published, in 1943. Then, in consultation with other experts, a "Joint Statement" was issued in 1944, prior to the Bretton Woods conference. Importantly, a preparatory conference was held in Atlantic City, New Jersey, during the last half of June 1944, just before Bretton Woods. When the delegates, who represented 44 countries, arrived at Bretton Woods, the substantive ground had been well prepared. No organizational or staffing detail had been overlooked, either.

The conference was divided into three commissions. Commission I dealt with the International Monetary Fund. It was chaired by White, who was impressively assisted by Edward Bernstein from the U.S. Treasury. Commission II, chaired by Keynes, was responsible for the World Bank. Commission III focused on other means of international cooperation and was chaired by Eduardo Suárez of Mexico.

The assignments of the delegates and staffs were carefully thought out in advance, resulting in a well-oiled, efficient conference. The atmosphere was collegial, with about half of the countries represented participating quite actively. When it came to the 178 delegates, the "80-20 rule" prevailed, with only about 20 percent of the delegates providing 80 percent of the substantive contributions. It should be noted that a number of those represented the relatively small countries of Belgium, Cuba, New Zealand, and Norway. Also active were three representatives from India, which still had a colonial status. Another colony, the Philippine Commonwealth, was also represented. France—actually the *Gouvernement provisoire de la République française* (GPRF), which was formed right before Bretton Woods, but not recognized by the Allies until October 1944—was actively represented by Pierre Mendès-France, who went on to become France's prime minister. So, there was a wide range of representation.

There was also a great deal of leadership on display by the host country. The United States counted twelve delegates, and four of the twelve were quite active. In addition, the U.S. technical staff numbered 33—by far the largest at the Conference. And, unlike those from any other country, five members of the U.S. technical team were active conference participants. If that wasn't enough, the 39 members of the conference secretariat were all Americans. In addition to preparation, staffing, and organization, America's leadership role was enhanced by the fact that the United States held almost 60 percent of the world's monetary gold at the time.

The organization of the conference facilitated a fast pace. The chairmen of the commissions, with their intelligent use of the committee structure, placed a premium on speed and took every opportunity to use it. Nowhere was this more evident than in Commission II, chaired by Keynes. He presided over very brisk meetings, in which matters were voted on rapidly, or dispatched to committees for further work, before time was wasted on premature discussion.

That said, the conference was punctuated by vigorous and substantive debate. For example, there was considerable discussion about whether the International Monetary Fund would be engaged in facilitating the settlement of war debts; led by the United States and the United Kingdom, the conference ultimately rejected this idea. Another example involved the USSR, which was opposed to reporting requirements for gold holdings and a number of other economic statistics. Again, led by the United States and the United Kingdom, transparency and full reporting won the day. The USSR was also opposed to the idea that "moderate immigrant remittances for family living expenses" would be free from capital controls; China made the most eloquent arguments against the Soviet position, and immigrant remittances remained unimpeded by controls.

Certain debates were, by today's light, quite modern. Many of what today would be described as emerging-market countries wanted larger quotas (more voting power), and they also wanted to have their gold contribution reduced from 75 percent of their obligations to 50 percent (a lower entry fee). These proposals were actively debated, and eventually voted down, as was a proposal put forward by Egypt to establish regions, such as the Middle East and Latin America, which would have their own executive directors within the International Monetary Fund. *Plus ça change, plus c'est la même chose.*

In reading *The Bretton Woods Transcripts,* we were struck by the fact that the deliberations were not simply driven by the events of the day. Indeed, the conference and its participants proceeded like a well-balanced river approaching a well-defined delta. Many of the distinguished conference personalities moved seamlessly from Bretton Woods to the highest ranks at the International Monetary Fund and the World Bank. For example, the Fund's first Managing Director, Camille Gutt (Belgium) was a Bretton Woods veteran, and he was not alone. Over 35 high positions at the International Monetary Fund were filled, at one time or another, by Bretton Woods veterans, and the World Bank eventually counted 30 conference veterans in its highest ranks. These men presided over an international monetary order, established at Bretton Woods, that endured for more than a quarter of a century.

Bretton Woods was the result of a perfect storm: some big problems; a set of ideas that attracted a consensus; a group of prepared and capable participants; and a leader, namely the United States, that was prepared to lead. Today, we don't see such a perfect storm on the horizon. But, then again, we don't claim to be weather forecasters, either.

September 2012

Jacques de Larosière was Managing Director of the International Monetary Fund from 1978 to 1987. He was also formerly Undersecretary of Monetary Affairs in the French Treasury (1974–1978), Governor of the Banque de France (1987-1993), and President of the European Bank for Reconstruction and Development (1993–1998). He is currently Chairman of Eurofi in Paris. Steve H. Hanke is Professor of Applied Economics at The Johns Hopkins University in Baltimore and Special Counselor at the Center for Financial Stability in New York.

About the Editors

Kurt Schuler is an economist in the Office of International Affairs at the U.S. Department of the Treasury in Washington, D.C. In his spare time he is Senior Fellow in Financial History of the Center for Financial Stability. He is the editor of the Center's Historical Financial Statistics, a free online database. He has written many books and essays on monetary theory, policy, and history. Before joining the Treasury he worked as an economic consultant and as a senior economist at the Joint Economic Committee of the U.S. Congress. His research during that time on currency boards and dollarization influenced successful monetary reforms in Estonia, Lithuania, Bosnia, Bulgaria, and Ecuador.

Andrew Rosenberg is a research associate of the Center for Financial Stability. During his initial work on this volume, he worked as an intern at the Cato Institute in Washington, D.C. for Steve H. Hanke, who is a Senior Fellow there. He has a B.A. in economics from Washington University in St. Louis.

The views here are ours alone and should not be attributed to the institutions we are connected with.

1

Introduction

The United Nations Monetary and Financial Conference at Bretton Woods, New Hampshire in 1944 began an era of international economic cooperation that endures today. The chief business of the conference was to arrive at agreements to govern the International Monetary Fund (IMF) and the International Bank for Reconstruction and Development (IBRD or World Bank), which remain important in the world financial system. Because of its impact, the Bretton Woods conference continues to offer food for thinkers and fodder for writers in economics, history, political science, and politics.[1]

Despite all that has been written on the conference, its transcripts have passed almost unnoticed until now. Kurt Schuler discovered copies of the transcripts in 2010 while browsing through a selection of uncatalogued material in the library of the U.S. Department of the Treasury, where he works. He knew he had made a significant find when he saw some pages with remarks by John Maynard Keynes that had never been published.

The transcripts were never intended for release. The rules of the conference specified that printed minutes of conference meetings would not attribute positions to particular country delegations except by request of the delegations. The printed minutes, released to the public in 1948, are much shorter than the transcripts of the same meetings, and they omit or downplay disagreements in the interest of harmony. The transcripts offer a rare verbatim record of what delegates to a major international conference said in a situation where they expected most of their remarks to remain private.

The transcripts document a turning point in international relations. Even when severely tested, most member countries of the IMF and World Bank, especially those of greatest importance to the world financial system, have not repeated the disastrous turning inward, economically and politically, that marked the 1930s and culminated in World War II.

[1] Several books have been recently published or are forthcoming on Bretton Woods: Steil (2013), Conway (2014), Helleiner (forthcoming), and Rauchway (forthcoming). (All references are at the end of the introduction.)

One reason they have not is that at Bretton Woods, they found workable procedures for safeguarding the interests of large and small nations alike in the common pursuit of prosperity. Readers of the transcripts should keep in mind that underlying story when they encounter passages where delegates to the conference seem merely to be debating details of the IMF and World Bank agreements. To the delegates, the shape of the postwar world was at stake. The details mattered greatly because the IMF and World Bank embodied a new approach to international organizations. As an American delegate said of the agreement on the IMF, "this document is an attempt to marry, to mingle and to blend the political aspects of this agency with the practical business aspects of the agency, the economic aspects. Institutions in the past have been established on more or less completely commercial lines. Others have been established on completely political lines. This whole document is an attempt to blend those two concepts."[2]

Neither the IMF nor the World Bank now performs its initial main role. The IMF ceased supervising an international system of pegged exchange rates in 1973, when the system experienced its final collapse; it responded by enlarging its role as a provider of advice and aid to countries in financial crisis. The World Bank concerned itself with the postwar reconstruction of Europe only for a few years, and ever since has concentrated on the "development" part of its full name. The transcripts of the Bretton Woods conference help us understand why the IMF and World Bank have proved so durable and remained so important despite their changing missions: they facilitate international economic cooperation in a way hard to reproduce in other organizations or in informal understandings. Their organizational structure balancing the interests of large and small economies, and their practice of arriving at decisions by consensus rather than by formal voting wherever possible—both of which came out of the Bretton Woods conference—have contributed to their unusual adaptability. Despite a huge increase in their membership since Bretton Woods, resulting from decolonization and the end of the Cold War, the IMF and World Bank have remained capable of acting quickly and decisively.

That the Bretton Woods conference arrived at agreements for not just one, but two important international organizations made it a high-water mark in diplomacy. Periodic calls for a "new Bretton Woods" invoke its

---

[2] Ansel Luxford, in chapter 27. Some organizational features of the IMF and World Bank were like those of the abortive Inter-American Bank proposed in 1940 but not ratified by the U.S. Congress (Horsefield 1969, v. 1: 10-11).

name because they dream of imitating its success. Anyone who thinks the world requires a new Bretton Woods needs to study the transcripts of the original, which show the spirit, the organizational techniques, and the particular compromises that made it successful. It is also vital to remember that Bretton Woods was not a self-contained conference, but the end of three years of thought, debate, and negotiation. The transcripts refer to the long nights that bleary-eyed delegates spent hashing out details at the conference, but the details existed within a framework established before the conference.

Background to the conference

While World War II was still in an early phase, British and American government officials began thinking about arrangements for postwar international economic cooperation.[3] They wished to prevent the "unrestrained economic fighting of the 1930s,"[4] in which economic crisis and lack of international cooperation had led countries to take steps that were politically popular in the short term but destructive to international trade and, in the long term, to domestic markets. They also wished to spur postwar economic rebuilding.

Independently, Harry Dexter White of the U.S. Department of the Treasury and John Maynard Keynes of the British Treasury originated plans in mid 1941 for an international monetary organization. Both had first thought about the subject years earlier. Keynes first saw a revised draft of White's plan in July 1942 and White saw a revised draft of Keynes's plan a month later. After further changes, both plans were published in April 1943.[5] The Keynes plan proposed an International Clearing Union as a central bank to the world's national central banks. Unlike a typical central bank, the Clearing Union would impose charges on member countries that were large creditors as well as on those that were large debtors. Keynes's goal was to place part of the burden of adjustment to the balance of payments on creditor countries, such as the United States, and to reduce the burden on debtor countries, such as the

---

[3] This section and the next draw on Horsefield (1969, v. 1: 3-113), Mason and Asher (1973: 12-33), UNMFC (1948, v. 1: v-vii); van Dormael (1978: 29-167); and Young (1950). Horsefield (1969, v. 3: 3-214) contains several of the documents we mention in this section.

[4] Harry Dexter White's phrase in his opening speech to the Bretton Woods commission on the IMF, in Document 59 of the conference (UNMFC 1948, v. 1: 97).

[5] Federal Reserve (1943).

United Kingdom. The White plan envisioned a United Nations Stabilization Fund, an international loan fund rather than an international central bank. It was less generous to debtors than the Keynes plan, imposed no charges on large creditors, and therefore involved a much lower prospective outlay of resources by the United States. Besides the Keynes and White plans, there were also Free French and Canadian plans. The Free French plan was more modest than the Keynes or White plans. It was written by André Istel, who would become a delegate at Bretton Woods, and Hervé Alphand, the former French financial attaché in Washington. The Canadian plan was conceived as a compromise between the Keynes and White plans. It was written by Louis Rasminsky, who would become a delegate at Bretton Woods.

Discussion between American experts led by White and British experts led by Keynes, and consultation with other governments, resulted in a "Joint Statement by Experts on the Establishment of an International Monetary Fund," also known as the Joint Statement of Principles or simply the Joint Statement.[6] It was published simultaneously in the United States and several other Allied countries on April 21, 1944. The Joint Statement was closer to the White plan than to the Keynes plan, reflecting that the United States, as the world's largest economy and largest creditor, would set the terms of any agreement of which it would be the major financier. The United Kingdom had little choice but to acquiesce, especially given that it was seeking further wartime loans from the United States in negotiations that would not conclude until after the Bretton Woods conference.

On May 25, 1944, the U.S. government invited most of the world's independent countries except those belonging to the Axis to send

---

[6] Reproduced in Appendix IV, part 7 of the conference proceedings (UNMFC 1948, v. 2: 1629-1636). The discussions leading to the Joint Statement were at first contentious. Keynes generally disliked Americans and Jews, so it annoyed him that many American officials who dealt with international finance were Jews, including Secretary of the Treasury Henry Morgenthau, Jr.; Harry Dexter White (of Jewish parentage, but not religiously observant); and White's assistant, Edward Bernstein. After one meeting with the Americans, Keynes ranted, "Bernstein is a regular little rabbi, a reader of the Talmud, to Harry's grand political high rabbidom....The chap knows every rat run in his local ghetto, but it is difficult to persuade him to come out for a walk with us on the high ways of the world" (Keynes 1980b: 364). Bernstein later remarked that if the U.S. Treasury had known of Keynes's remark, it would have ceased discussions with Keynes (Black 1991: 39-40). For a summary of Keynes's attitudes toward Jews, including episodes that show a better side of him, see Chandavarkar (2000).

representatives to an international monetary conference, "for the purpose of formulating definite proposals for an International Monetary Fund and possibly a Bank for Reconstruction and Development."[7] (The word "International" was only added to the Bank's title late in the conference. We will generally call the bank the World Bank, its more commonly used name today.) The U.S. government also invited a smaller group of countries to send experts to a preliminary conference in Atlantic City, New Jersey, to develop preliminary draft proposals for the Bretton Woods conference. The Atlantic City conference was held from June 15-30, 1944, although because of travel delays, not all delegations were present for the whole conference. The conference worked mainly on ideas for the IMF, producing a series of alternatives to provisions in the Joint Statement that, with the Joint Statement itself, formed the basis of discussion on the IMF at Bretton Woods.

Before the Bretton Woods conference, far less work was done on the Bank for Reconstruction and Development. In November 1943 the U.S. Treasury sent to other governments a draft of a proposal for the bank. The British government did not comment on it until April 1944. On the British delegation's boat trip to the United States for the Atlantic City conference, though, Keynes supervised a British draft on the subject. The British and American drafts were close enough that the two governments concluded that an agreement was feasible. The Atlantic City conference devoted two days to discussing the Bank, and by the time the delegates were ready to proceed to Bretton Woods, a draft agreement for the Bank existed.[8]

The International Monetary and Financial Conference of the United and Associated Nations, as it was officially called, took place at the Mount Washington Hotel in Bretton Woods, New Hampshire, from July 1 to

---

[7] The letter should not be confused with a 1943 letter from Secretary of the Treasury Henry Morgenthau, Jr. to finance ministers of 37 countries, reproduced in Appendix IV, part 3 of the conference proceedings (UNMFC 1948, v. 2: 1573-1574). The earlier letter contained a version of the White plan for the IMF. The 1944 invitation went to 42 countries (United States Department of State 1944: 498). The principal independent countries not invited were the major Axis powers (Germany, Italy, and Japan); their co-belligerents (Bulgaria, Finland, Hungary, Romania, and Thailand); and some neutral countries (Argentina, Ireland, Portugal, Spain, Sweden, Switzerland, and Turkey). India and the Philippines, although colonies, sent their own delegations, and the Indian delegation boldly advocated views on some points opposed to those of the United Kingdom.

[8] Document 169 (UNMFC 1948, v. 1: 191-215), issued on July 6.

July 22, 1944. There were several reasons for choosing Bretton Woods as the location of the conference. The summer climate was temperate, a key consideration because air conditioning was not yet widespread. ("For God's sake do not take us to Washington in July, which would surely be a most unfriendly act," Keynes had written to White in May 1944.[9]) The remote location offered greater security and seclusion than would have been possible in a large city. Unlike many other resort hotels of the time, the Mount Washington Hotel accepted Jews as guests, and many staff and delegates at the conference were Jews. Finally, the Democratic administration of President Franklin Roosevelt sought bipartisan support for any agreement that would arise from the conference. Senator Charles Tobey of New Hampshire was the senior Republican on the Senate Committee on Banking and Currency, whose approval would be vital for the agreement. Tobey, who was facing an opponent in the Republican primary election, suggested holding the conference in New Hampshire as a way of showing the people of his state that he was influential. The Roosevelt administration accepted Tobey's suggestion as a way of winning his favor for the agreement.[10] Originally the conference was scheduled to end on July 19, but it was extended for three days to complete its work.[11] Delegates from 44 nations plus a representative of Denmark and observers from several international organizations attended.[12]

From the vantage point of nearly seventy years later, it is easy to forget how bleak the world's recent monetary experience had been and how strongly the countries attending the conference wanted to signal a break with it. The financial strains of World War I had disrupted the largely stable prewar world monetary system based on gold. The 1920s had seen hyperinflations in central Europe and lesser but still painful problems elsewhere in returning to the gold standard. The 1930s had seen a worldwide depression, the collapse of the international gold standard, and the imposition of exchange controls that hampered international trade. The economic calamity of the 1930s had created the political conditions leading to World War II. The European delegations at Bretton Woods, other than those of the Union of Soviet Socialist Republics (USSR) and the United Kingdom, all represented exile governments of countries

[9] Keynes (1980: 27).

[10] De Vries (1996: 9).

[11] Document 433 (UNMFC 1948, v. 2: 1184).

[12] Delegates attended from all the invited countries mentioned in a previous footnote, plus Bolivia and of course the United States itself. Denmark did not attend as a full participant because it had no government in exile.

under German occupation, while the Philippines was under Japanese occupation. Keynes vividly expressed their situation when he observed, "[T]he various members of this alliance have suffered in mind, body and estate through the exhaustion of war, through which we are differing in kind and degree. These sacrifices cannot be weighed one against the other. Those of us who are most directly threatened and were nevertheless able to remain in the fight, such as the USSR and the United Kingdom, have fought this war on the principle of unlimited liability and with a more reckless disregard to economic consequences. Others are more fortunately placed. We do not need information in the larger fields of human affairs. Nothing could be less prudent than hesitation or careful counting of the cost. But as a result, there has been inevitably no equality of financial sacrifice."[13]

Conference organization

The highest body of the Bretton Woods conference was its **plenary session.** Plenary sessions met only in the first and last days of the conference and were more for show than for work, existing mainly to confirm decisions reached by other bodies of the conference. The conference conducted its major work through three **commissions.**

Commission I dealt with the IMF and was chaired by Harry Dexter White, Assistant to the Secretary of the U.S. Treasury and the chief American negotiator at the conference. The early part of the conference focused on Commission I. A table at the end of this introduction shows how the Commission divided its work among its four main committees, in terms of the sections of the preliminary draft IMF agreement that each committee handled and the corresponding parts of the final Articles of Agreement. Tables in Appendix E, and a spreadsheet on the page for this book at the Web site of the Center for Financial Stability, show the correspondence between the preliminary draft and the final agreement section by section instead of just article by article, for both the IMF and World Bank agreements.

The core working document on the IMF was Document 32 of the conference.[14] It contained the Joint Statement plus alternatives (amendments) proposed at the Atlantic City conference. After the delegates had made some progress on specifying how the IMF would work, the Drafting Committee of Commission I compiled the results to

---

[13] In chapter 4.

[14] Document 32 (UNMFC 1948, v. 1: 21-60).

date in an intermediate draft, Document 321.[15] The final Articles of Agreement for the IMF were published in Document 492.[16]

Commission II dealt with the International Bank for Reconstruction and Development (World Bank), and was chaired by John Maynard Keynes. Keynes's unassuming title of economic adviser to the British Chancellor of the Exchequer (minister of finance) belied his central role in British war finance, which included being the chief British negotiator at the conference. After a perfunctory initial meeting on July 3, 1944, Commission II did not meet again until July 11. In the meantime, the committees of Commission I finished most of their assigned work. Many matters of governance, legal status, and the like were similar for the IMF and the World Bank. Commission II took advantage of the work that delegates had done on the IMF agreement by borrowing the wording they had hammered out and using it, with minor changes, to apply to the World Bank agreement. The saving of time involved, nimble chairmanship by John Maynard Keynes, and the extension of the conference beyond its original end date enabled Commission II to complete its work despite a late start. The first preliminary draft agreement for the World Bank, published as Document 169 of the conference, was issued on July 6.[17] By the time of Commission II's second meeting, when it began its work in earnest, Document 169 it had been superseded by Document 245, issued on July 10.[18] Document 245 therefore became the core document of the World Bank agreement. The final Articles of Agreement for the World Bank were published in Document 492 along with those for the IMF.

Commission III dealt with other means of international financial cooperation and was chaired by Eduardo Suárez, Mexico's minister of finance and the leader of the Mexican delegation.[19] Commission III was a venue for ideas that did not fall under the other two commissions. It was less important than they were, so it held fewer meetings than they did. Its recommendations, described in more detail below, left no lasting impact because the commission neither established a new international

---

[15] Document 321 (UNMFC 1948, v. 1: 518-537).

[16] Document 492 (UNMFC 1948: 927-1015).

[17] Document 169 (UNMFC 1948, v. 1: 191-215).

[18] Document 245 (UNMFC 1948, v. 1: 365-402).

[19] The after-hours gatherings of delegates in the hotel nightclub were jokingly termed "Commission IV" (Mikesell 1994: 42). Regrettably, no transcripts were made of its proceedings, but there does exist a mock charter for an "International Ballyhoo Fund" in the papers of the conference president, Henry Morgenthau, Jr. (McJimsey 2008: 428-430).

organization nor significantly changed any existing organization. Its core working document was Document 235 of the conference, the report of its Agenda Committee on the proposals various national delegations had submitted.[20]

Each commission had a number of **committees.** Commission I, for instance, had

- four standing (main) committees dealing with particular aspects of the IMF;
- eight ad hoc committees on special topics;
- a Drafting Committee to resolve questions purely of language;
- a Special Committee on Unsettled Problems; and
- subcommittees appointed by the committees.

Every country represented at the conference was entitled to send delegates to all meetings of the commissions and standing committees, but subcommittees and other groups had restricted membership to allow them to work more efficiently. Appendix A shows all the committees and committee members listed in the published conference volumes. Appendix B shows the schedule of meetings. As is evident from the schedule, delegates to the conference worked hectically on many issues in parallel.

The transcripts

The U.S. Department of the Treasury, aided by the U.S. Department of State, was the host of the Bretton Woods conference. To record the conference, the Treasury employed a number of stenographers. Stenographers were not numerous enough to record every meeting of all the main committees, much less the ad hoc committees and subcommittees, but they generated hundreds of pages of material. The stenographers' notes were typed and corrected. The Treasury made an unknown but apparently small number of Photostat copies and distributed the copies in bound covers to senior officials.

As we mentioned, Kurt Schuler discovered copies of the transcripts in a selection of uncatalogued material in the Treasury Library. A catalog number on the spines indicates that the volumes had been catalogued at some point before the catalog switched from cards to an electronic database, but they were unknown to the current librarians.[21] Subsequent

[20] Document 235 (UNMFC 1948, v. 1: 326-333).

[21] Later, Schuler found the transcripts listed in Treasury Library (1997: 6).

research revealed that Schuler was not the first person to discover the transcripts, but the last, in the sense that now they will never need to be rediscovered. Several references to the transcripts exist in previous writings. The official history of the IMF's early years mentions the transcripts briefly, describing them as "unofficial verbatim reports, but the incomplete and provisional nature of these reports makes them of uncertain value."[22] The transcripts are incomplete, but they are still extensive, and they seem to be as faithfully transcribed as the stenographers and typists could make them. For the major proceedings, they are as good a record as one could expect short of a recording.[23] Henry Bittermann, who attended the conference, makes a passing reference to the transcript of the July 11 meeting of Commission II.[24] A publication in Norwegian on Norway and the Bretton Woods conference also cites the transcripts.[25] The Web site of the IMF archives has also for some years mentioned the transcript volumes,[26] but judging by the lack of references to them, researchers have failed to notice.

What seems to be an original version of the transcripts exists at the National Archives in College Park, Maryland. It consists of sheets of loose paper. Like the Treasury Library, the IMF Archives in Washington, D.C. has a set of Photostat copies of the transcripts. The Photostat copies are divided into four bound volumes. Commission I (the IMF), is in three volumes: the meetings of the full Commission; Committees 1 and 2; and Committees 3 and 4. Commissions II and III are combined in a single volume. The Treasury Library set has the notation "H. D. White" written in pen in the flyleaves, indicating that it belonged to Harry Dexter White. We relied mainly on the Treasury Library set to compile this book because it was most accessible to us. The catalog listing for the IMF Archives set indicates that it belonged to Edward Bernstein, who as executive secretary (chief technical adviser) of the American delegation was White's deputy at the Bretton Woods conference, and who later became the first director of the IMF's Research Division.

---

22 Horsefield (1969, v. 1: 93). The official histories of the World Bank's early years contain no reference to the transcripts (Mason and Asher 1973: 21-33; Kapur and others 997: 58-62).

23 Yves-André Istel, son of the French delegate André Istel, has read the sections of the transcripts containing remarks by his father and has commented that they sound perfectly compatible with his father's modes of expression.

24 Bittermann (1971: 70 n. 14).

25 Halvorsen (1982: 130-131, nn. 9, 10, 20, 21, 31).

26 IMF (2007).

The sets at the Treasury Library and IMF Archives contain no markings indicating when they were copied or distributed. That the Treasury Library has White's set suggests that they were distributed before White joined the IMF on April 30, 1946, as its first Executive Director representing the United States. The copies are sometimes hard to read: photocopying technology was still in its infancy and the original typescripts were not always clear, having been typed on manual typewriters and corrected by hand in places. Because members of the IMF executive board and IMF staff sometimes referred to the transcripts during early board meetings, the IMF had a clean copy typed of the transcripts of the meetings of Commission I.[27] The IMF made a limited number of copies for internal use; they were not intended for outside circulation. While we were in the last stages of preparing this book, the IMF Archives posted an electronic file of the clean copy on its Web site, along with electronic files of many other documents related to the Bretton Woods conference.

What we call "the transcripts" in the broad sense includes transcripts in the narrow sense, summaries, and draft minutes. The bulk of the material is transcripts in the narrow sense—attempts to record meetings word for word, identifying the speakers wherever possible. Summaries identify speakers, but summarize their remarks rather than trying to record them word for word. Draft minutes are briefest: they typically do not identify speakers, instead reviewing only the overall course of discussion during meetings.

The coverage of the transcripts varies. It is extensive for the full commission and some committee meetings of Commission I. The transcripts contain less material on Commissions II and III because they were lower priorities for the conference and received less coverage from the pool of stenographers. Sometimes so many committee meetings were happening that the stenographers could not cover them all. For instance, a typed note inserted in the transcripts by an unknown person says, "Commission I—Committee 2[:] Miss Bourneuf [Alice Bourneuf, Assistant Secretary of the committee] told me September 6, 1944 that about July 6 the stenographic pool was unable to send stenos. [stenographers] to take verbatim minutes of the meetings and that is why her committee along with other committees do not have full minutes of the meetings. I checked what I have with her copies and these were all that were taken."

---

[27] IMF (1951).

Insights from the transcripts

Numerous summaries of the Bretton Woods conference exist.[28] Rather than revisit ground that is already well trod and lengthen an already long book, we limit our observations about insights from the transcripts to some brief remarks.

- The United States and United Kingdom had the greatest influence at the conference, in accord with their economic strength, key roles in world finance, and dominant share of the world's leading economists, but Bretton Woods was a genuinely multilateral negotiation. The other large and medium-size countries also shaped the conference, especially though their membership on multiple ad hoc committees. Talented delegates from Belgium, Cuba, Czechoslovakia, Greece, and Norway played important roles out of proportion to the small size of their countries.
- Debate on IMF quotas was contentious, even bitter.[29] About one-third of the countries present wanted higher quotas, which would have given them greater voting power. France and India felt particularly slighted at being assigned proposed quotas that they considered not to reflect their importance in the world economy. Agreements intended to be so important to the world financial system were inherently political. The Quota Committee was chaired by Fred Vinson of the United States, who had an unusual combination of high-level experience as a legislator, judge, and bureaucratic administrator, but even his political acumen was insufficient to prevent the eruption of anger over quotas that many delegations expressed.
- The development of the Bretton Woods international monetary system as based in practice on the U.S. dollar, and only indirectly on gold, arose because in 1944, the dollar was the only currency with some degree of convertibility into gold that was widely held internationally. Hence when the question arose of defining "gold convertible" exchange for the IMF Articles of Agreement, an

---

[28] See especially Horsefield (1969, v. 1: 89-110), Mason and Asher (1973: 21-33), Oliver (1975: 182-210), Schild (1995: 107-127), and van Dormael (1978: 168-233). Rauchway (forthcoming) also has an account.

[29] See chapter 8. Mikesell (1994: 35-38) gives a further first-hand account of the debate on quotas, including events in the Committee on Quotas, whose proceedings are not in the transcripts.

American delegate (perhaps Edward Bernstein) said, "On the practical side, there seems to be no difference of opinion, and it is possible for the monetary authorities of other countries to purchase gold freely in the United States for dollars. There are a number of other currencies which can be used to purchase dollars without restriction, and these dollars in turn [can be] used to purchase gold. The definition of gold convertible currency might include such currencies, but the practical importance of holdings of the countries represented here is so small that it has been felt it would be easier for this purpose to regard the United States dollar as what was intended when we speak of gold convertible exchange."[30] Here is the seed of what French finance minister Valéry Giscard d'Estaing would in the 1960s term the dollar's "exorbitant privilege" as an international reserve currency.

- As is evident from Appendix A, which lists biographical tidbits about the conference delegates and secretariat, among the Americans at the conference were several Communists who spied for the USSR. Harry Dexter White was not a Communist or formally a spy, but was sympathetic to the USSR and passed classified information to American Communists who were spies. He made his first direct contact with an operative of the Soviet spy agency in July 1944, that is, possibly during the Bretton Woods conference.[31] Soviet success in spying availed naught, though, because the USSR decided not to join the IMF and World Bank. Reluctance to divulge its economic statistics was likely one of the factors that led it not to join. (Attending the Bretton Woods conference and signing its final agreement did not commit countries to join the IMF and World Bank; it merely indicated that their governments would consider the matter, on the terms the agreement established.) Russia only joined in 1992, after Soviet communism and the USSR itself had ended.[32]
- The delegates were an extraordinarily promising group. They included future prime ministers of Canada, France, Greece, New Zealand, and Peru; future presidents of Colombia and Iceland; future finance ministers and central bank governors of many

---

[30] See chapter 5.

[31] Haynes and Klehr (1999: 129-145); Craig (2004: 83-112); Haynes and others (2009: 260).

[32] Chapter 4; see also Bernstein (1993).

countries; and key officials of the IMF and World Bank, including the IMF's first Managing Director, its top official.[33]

- The global influence of the American university system is apparent. Many of the non-U.S. delegates who were most active in the conference debates had studied economics at U.S. universities or at the time of the conference were professors at American universities. Many members of the American delegation had doctorates in economics and quite a few had been at some point been professors of economics; Appendix A offers a partial list.
- As in other international meetings of the era, few women held high positions. There seems to have been only two female delegates: Mabel Newcomer of the United States and a Mrs. L. Gouseva of the USSR, who was so obscure we could not even find her full first name. A few women held important positions in the conference secretariat, which was staffed by employees of the U.S. government.

Overview of the transcripts

Before wading into the transcripts, readers may find it useful to have a narrative overview of the material they cover. The transcripts cover only some of the formal meetings at the Bretton Woods conference, and none of the informal discussions, so our overview of the transcripts is not a full overview of the conference.

Many segments of the transcripts are dull. As editors, we felt a duty to be thorough, to spare future scholars the effort of retracing our steps. Readers have no parallel duty to read every word we transcribed. Readers who are easily bored should feel free to treat the book as one to be dipped into rather than read cover to cover. More patient readers may want to read the dull segments not so much for their surface content as for the subtext of the Bretton Woods conference as a study in successful international negotiation.

Commission I, on the IMF, chaired by Harry Dexter White of the United States, was the most important part of the conference. If the conference accomplished nothing else, it was expected to arrive at a final agreement on the IMF. As with the other commissions and some of the committees, the first meeting of Commission I was consumed by a

[33] Edward Bernstein, who made the most important contributions to the conference other than White and Keynes, described the delegates as "technicians moving up in the hierarchy" (Black 1991: 47).

speech by the chairman and organizational matters, rather than discussion of substantive issues by delegates. The second meeting was devoted to further organizational matters and hearing the initial reports of committees, again precluding discussion of the issues. The major issues the committee covered in its remaining seven meetings are easier to understand if described in logical rather than chronological order, since discussion of some issues spanned multiple meetings.

The most fundamental issue was what ***the IMF's purposes*** should be. How much should it focus on economic development, including full employment in rich countries and the improvement of living standards in poor countries, in addition to the more narrowly monetary problems of smoothing adjustment in the balance of payments and addressing financial crises? The delegates agreed to modest changes to Article I of the draft IMF agreement, listing the purposes of the organization, but not to bigger changes advocated notably by India and Australia. In compensation, Commission II changed the draft World Bank agreement to lay greater emphasis on economic development.

There was also a question whether the IMF should be involved with ***the debt legacy of World War II.*** The United Kingdom in particular owed large amounts to countries that had supplied it with war materiel. India and Egypt were emphatic in stating that after the war, they wished to be able to use the pounds sterling they had been paid to buy goods that at present they could not, because of British exchange controls. The term they used for this issue at the conference was "multilateral clearing." Leading the opposition to involving the IMF in wartime debts were the United Kingdom, for obvious reasons; France, which operated a French franc zone similar to the sterling area; and the United States, which did not want to weaken the capabilities of two of its major allies. They argued that the IMF already had enough to do, and involving it in settling wartime debts might overload it. Commission I accepted their argument, but as a palliative, the United Kingdom issued public statements assuring India and Egypt that it would try to resolve problems related to the sterling balances soon after the war.

To promote better understanding of the world economy and its potential trouble spots, the draft IMF agreement specified various categories of ***statistics*** that members would be obligated to supply to the IMF. The delegates understood that some statistics would initially be imprecise or nonexistent for many countries. The League of Nations already collected some financial statistics, but member countries were under no obligation to supply them to it. John Maynard Keynes was keen on having statistics; he claimed that "There is hardly any greater service the Fund can do than provide up-to-date barometers of the monetary problems of the world."[34] The USSR, on the other hand, wished to minimize the statistics it would have to divulge to the IMF, in keeping with its policy of secrecy about many kinds of economic data. The USSR made several proposals to limit the collection and publication of statistics, which failed to gain the approval of other countries.

The experience of the years between the two world wars had convinced many people that fully convertible currencies, without exchange controls, could be dangerous because they might permit destabilizing flows of speculative capital. The IMF agreement therefore obliged members to pledge to work toward ***convertibility of their currencies for current-account payments,*** such as those for imported goods, but not capital-account payments, defined as those for the purpose of transferring capital. Countries depended heavily on remittances by emigrants for foreign exchange, such as China, Greece, and India, wanted to ensure that the IMF agreement classified remittances as current-account payments. After extended debate, they largely succeeded. For many occupied countries, it was apparent that the politics of achieving current-account convertibility and other aspects of monetary order after liberation would be time-consuming. Commission I therefore approved provisions in the IMF agreement to make matters easier for occupied countries. Article XIV of the final agreement remains relevant today. It permits a transitional period during which countries may delay the obligation to allow current-account convertibility. Some countries have remained in this supposedly temporary status for decades.

Even countries that had not suffered war damage worried whether the postwar international financial system would be liberal enough to encourage exports, or whether wartime restrictions on finance, which affected the financing of international trade and investment, would hinder exports. Delegates with experience in finance reassured such countries that the IMF would not be the only source of credit for financing trade transactions the postwar international financial system. Private-sector credit would also be available, and for most countries most of the time, the private sector rather than the IMF would be the main source of credit. For small economies such as the Netherlands or New Zealand, the matter was of the utmost importance: without a postwar liberalization of world trade and finance, they would not recover their prewar standard of living because they relied on the proceeds of exports to pay for the many goods their economies were too small to produce efficiently at home.

---

[34] In chapter 4.

An issue that ran through many of the topics Commission I discussed was ***how to balance the interests of large and small economies.*** The large economies, particularly the United States, would supply most of the IMF's resources, while the small economies were more numerous. The IMF could not work unless each group felt that the other would not take advantage of it. To achieve balance, Commission I agreed to provisions weighting IMF voting partly but not entirely by economic size; requiring supermajorities for quorums and important decisions; and requiring the Board of Governors, the IMF's highest body, to convene whenever requested by at least five countries or one-quarter of the voting power.

Beyond the formal provisions in the IMF agreement, delegates developed an informal understanding that the IMF (and the World Bank) would make its decisions to a large extent by ***consensus*** rather than by voting. The conference itself operated by consensus rather than by voting, as much as was compatible with its tight schedule. Former officials of the IMF and World Bank who have read this book have remarked on how important the practice of seeking consensus has been in enabling the organizations to remain influential and effective.

The most important factor determining countries' influence in the IMF was ***quotas,*** IMF jargon for the subscriptions of members to the organization's capital. Not surprisingly, the issue was heatedly debated. Had quotas had been allocated strictly according to economic size, the United States would have had more than half of the total. Recognizing that such a degree of dominance was the temporary result of wartime conditions and that it would be unacceptable to other countries, the United States was willing to sacrifice some of its quota. The final agreement gave the United States 31.25 percent of the total. Negotiators led by the United States worked for months before the conference trying to devise a consensus formula for allocating quotas. No easily calculated set of criteria found general acceptance. Ultimately the United States forced though a set of allocations through some admittedly arbitrary decisions in backroom negotiations. The allocations were acceptable to enough countries to gain approval, despite protests from countries that thought they had been short-changed. Given that later reallocations of quotas have been equally contentious, it is hard to see how else Commission I could have arrived at a decision on the subject.

Although quotas were the most importance factor determining influence in the IMF, ***voting power*** did not depend on quotas alone. Each member received a uniform number of base votes as well as votes proportioned to its quota. The United States thereby further sacrificed some voting power to the small economies, though it and the other largest economies retained enough voting power to ensure that they would be able to block important decisions they opposed. The largest economies also retained a degree of symbolic control of the IMF's resources by being specified as the places where the IMF would deposit the great bulk of its gold and other assets.

The IMF's Board of Governors was to contain appointed representatives from every country. For supervising the IMF's day-to-day operations, a group of more than forty countries would be too clumsy, so the Board of Governors would delegate those decisions a smaller group, the ***Executive Directors.*** There was general agreement, or at least acceptance, that each of the five countries with the largest quotas—the United States, United Kingdom, USSR, China, and France—should each appoint its own director. (The charter of the United Nations, agreed upon the year after Bretton Woods, contains a parallel in its provision for the same five countries to have permanent seats on the Security Council.) The other directors would be elected by coalitions of countries. It remained to be decided how many other directors there should be; whether they should be elected within regions or by potentially cross-regional coalitions of countries; whether there should be a provision to prevent the Executive Directorate from becoming a "debtors' club" that favored debtors over creditors unfairly and unsustainably; and what the relationship between Executive Directors and their alternates should be. The outcome was a set of compromises. Initially there were to be at least additional seven directors. To satisfy Latin American countries, which were the most numerous contingent at the conference, two Executive Directors were reserved to them. The remaining directors did not have to be elected from within specified regions. If the appointed directors did not include the two countries that had made the largest recent net additions to IMF credit, those countries would be entitled to appoint directors. (Amendments to the IMF Articles of Agreement in later years dropped the regional directors for Latin America and from creditor countries.) Alternates were to chosen by the Executive Directors rather than separately elected.

The IMF was, as we have noted, a mixed economic and political body. One issue that came up in regard to the mixture was how the IMF should treat borrowing ("purchases," in IMF jargon), and what ***fees and interest rates*** it should charge. The IMF was intended to offer credit to member governments in situations where the private sector might offer it only at high interest rates or not at all. The delegates did not wish to stigmatize borrowing to the extent that it would discourage countries in need, but they did not want the IMF to be so generous as to encourage borrowing by countries that had no real need. Experience has shown that they struck the balance they sought. The oversight that accompanies loans from the IMF has been sufficient to deter countries from requesting large loans simply because the interest rates are generally below market rates.

The final issue Commission I considered that is worth mentioning here is ***changes in par values*** (parities), the exchange rates with gold that member countries pledged to maintain. Delegates wanted to avoid the large surprise devaluations of the 1930s that had created tensions in financial markets and trade politics. They allowed countries to change par values within a limited range without consulting the IMF, but required consultation for larger changes. In addition, they created an escape hatch from 1930s-style worldwide deflation, or worldwide inflation, by agreeing to a procedure for changing par values of all currencies against gold by a uniform percentage.

Commission I had four main committees. Whereas the Commission has a complete set of transcripts (in the narrow sense of word-for-word records) for its meetings, no committee has a complete set. For Committees 1, 2, and 3, transcripts or summaries exist for the earlier meetings, but only draft minutes exist for the later meetings. For Committee 4, no transcripts or summaries exist, only draft minutes.

Committee 1, on "Purposes, Policies, and Quotas of the Fund," was chaired by the Chinese diplomat Tingfu Tsiang. Transcripts or detailed summaries exist for the first four of its six meetings. The committee spent a large share of its time considering proposals on the IMF's statement of purposes. Differences of opinion within the committee were so strong that it referred the most significant proposals to Commission I rather than arriving at its own consensus on them. The committee also discussed the payment of quotas, although it did not determine the amounts of quotas, which was the province of a special ad hoc committee of Commission I. The committee decided that there would be a regular review of quotas at least every five years to determine if they needed adjustment. The committee also clarified that countries that held gold were obligated to use part of it to fulfill their quota subscriptions, but countries holding their reserves exclusively in foreign exchange, such as many countries in the sterling area, could pay exclusively in foreign exchange rather than having to scramble for gold. The other major issue the committee discussed was the obligations of member countries, especially with respect to current-account payments. There was an understanding that the IMF agreement would not commit members to remove exchange controls on capital-account payments, but committee members had different ideas about what should count as current-account payments, so the chairman referred the matter to Commission I. The committee also agreed that members would cooperate to enforce one another's exchange controls.

Committee 2, on "Operations of the Fund," was nominally chaired by Pavel Maletin, deputy minister of finance of the USSR, but actually run by the vice chairman, the Canadian finance official William Mackintosh. "Operations" included the all-important matters of declaring and changing par values (exchange rates) with gold, and outlining the terms on which the IMF would lend. Transcripts exist for the first three of the committee's eight meetings. In those meetings, the committee was unable to reach a consensus about how liberal the terms should be for member governments that wanted to borrow from the IMF. Australia, Brazil, and New Zealand, which all depended for export revenue on commodities whose prices fluctuated substantially, argued for more liberal conditions than the United States, United Kingdom, and some other countries preferred. The committee also began to consider "scarce currencies," meaning those whose stock at the IMF was exhausted, constituting a barrier to international payments. The committee concluded its discussion of these issues in later meetings for which no transcripts exist. It developed agreement on the principles concerning charges for borrowers, though not on all the details, and approved a provision allowing members to discriminate against currencies that had become scarce. In addition, the committee handled other issues not discussed in the first three meetings.

Committee 3, on "Organization and Management of the Fund," was chaired by Artur de Souza Costa, Brazil's minister of finance. Transcripts exist for the first three of its seven meetings. In those meetings, the committee agreed on a compromise allowing either five countries or countries with at least 25 percent of total votes to call a meeting of the Board of Governors. Similarly, it agreed that a quorum for the Board of Governors should include both two-thirds of votes and half of the member countries. To further protect small economies, the committee agreed to give each country a uniform number of base votes. Debate occurred on whether the Executive Directors should be in permanent residence at the IMF's headquarters, but the issue was not resolved in the first three meetings. In later meetings, the committee resolved issues related to the Executive Directors and considered certain other matters.

Committee 4, on "Form and Status of the Fund," was chaired by Manuel Llosa, a top Peruvian legislator. Its work was mainly about how the piece of paper that was the IMF agreement would work, rather than about how the IMF as an organization would work. No transcripts of its meetings exist. We have included the draft minutes so that readers can follow events in the committee, but the minutes are so lacking in detail that they offer little opportunity for adding color. The subjects seemingly discussed at greatest length were restrictions on member countries' power to tax the IMF and its staff; the IMF's relationship to other international organizations; provisions specifying what would happen if member countries quit the IMF; miscellaneous powers of the IMF; and the article on interpretation of the IMF agreement.

Commission II, on the International Bank for Reconstruction and Development (World Bank), chaired by John Maynard Keynes of the United Kingdom, was the big question mark of the conference. It existed because the extent of harmony at the Atlantic City, New Jersey conference preceding Bretton Woods had created hope that the Bretton Woods conference might be able to reach a final agreement on the World Bank as well as on the IMF. To allow the conference to focus on the IMF agreement, Commission II and its committees did no work until the conference was half finished. Because Commission II was secondary to Commission I, the conference secretariat sent stenographers to Commission I when there were not enough to cover both commissions. Consequently, there is only a transcript for the second meeting of Commission II, and no transcripts of its meetings of its committees. In the meeting, Keynes led a first run-through of the draft agreement on the World Bank. The Commission assigned to its committees clauses that gave major difficulty; reserved for the Commission itself those that gave intermediate difficulty; and assigned to the Drafting Committee those that gave no difficulty, with the idea that the Drafting Committee would polish the language and present the result to the Commission later for only a brief discussion before final approval.

Commission III, on "other means of financial cooperation," chaired by Eduardo Suárez of Mexico, was a forum for ideas that did not fit in the other two commissions. It seems to have been intended more to offer recommendations than to reach final agreement for action on the topics proposed to it. It held three meetings: a short organizational meeting; a meeting to review the proposals submitted to it; and a meeting to hear the recommendations of its committees and approve or disapprove the proposals. No transcripts exist for meetings of the committees of Commission III. The Commission approved proposals on further study of the possible use of silver in the international monetary system; liquidation of the Bank for International Settlements as redundant given that the IMF would exist; measures to return property looted by Axis armies of occupation; and holding one or more international conferences on commodities, trade, and employment. The most significant recommendation was to liquidate the Bank for International Settlements in Basel, Switzerland, a sort of central banker's club that was accused of helping Germany loot assets from Allied countries during World War II. Liquidation never occurred because American hostility toward the bank softened after its two most powerful critics left the U.S. Treasury. Treasury Secretary Henry Morgenthau, Jr., who had been the president of the Bretton Woods conference, resigned in July 1945 to return to private life; Harry Dexter White resigned in May 1946 to become the first U.S. Executive Director at the IMF.

Keynes in the transcripts

John Maynard Keynes is a much smaller presence in the transcripts than he was at the Bretton Woods conference. Stenographers transcribed only one of the nine meetings of Commission II, which Keynes chaired, as opposed to all nine meetings of Commission I, which Harry Dexter White chaired. Even on the basis of the sole meeting of Commission II, the contrast between Keynes's and White's styles is evident. White proceeded methodically, at a pace the delegates could follow. Keynes proceeded with lightning speed, hop-scotching across the provisions of the draft World Bank agreement, because he was able to hold all of its provisions in his mind in a way that probably no other delegate could. Henry Bittermann, the secretary of Committee 2 of Commission II, later remarked that other delegates found Keynes's style as chairman confusing.[35]

Keynes also appears in the first, second, and third meetings of Commission I. It is possible as well that Keynes made some of the remarks by delegates of the United Kingdom where the transcripts do not specify the delegates' names.

Our editorial changes to the transcripts

We have tried to produce a version of the transcripts that is both faithful to the original text and easy to read. Andrew Rosenberg used dictation software to create a word processing file from the Treasury Library copy of the transcripts. Kurt Schuler then proofread the file, comparing it to the Treasury Library copy. Where the Treasury Library copy was unclear we compared the word processing file to the National Archives copy. We

[35] Bittermann (1971: 69).

both then read every part of the file again at least three times and added footnotes and appendices.

Our general rule has been to make unimportant changes silently but to identify important changes by brackets or footnotes. We have corrected obvious errors of punctuation and spelling, changed punctuation from the original where necessary for clarity, and written in full some words abbreviated in the original typescripts. In long speeches, we have often inserted paragraph breaks where the typescripts run on for pages at a time without them. Especially for delegates who were not native speakers of English, we have sometimes made minor changes to their wording to make their speech more grammatical, such as silently correcting their use of prepositions where the meaning they wished to convey was obvious.

We have adopted a uniform style for identifying conference meetings, delegations, and participants. For instance, the typescripts identify Free French delegates by personal name only, or variously call the delegation "France," "French delegation," "Free French delegation," "French National Committee," "French Committee," and "French Comité," because its official name was the *Comité français de la Libération nationale* (French Committee of National Liberation). In the bold lettering that identifies speakers and their countries, we always write "France" even though it is not entirely correct. At the time of the Bretton Woods conference, the Free French government controlled Corsica and all French overseas possessions except Indochina, but Allied forces had only just begun to retake mainland France. The Free French government declared itself the provisional government of France on June 3, 1944, but the other major Allies continued to recognize the Vichy government instead until October 1944.

We identify chairmen by name and country the first time they appear in a meeting, then refer them only by position. We identify delegates by country, then list personal names in parentheses. Sometimes it is only possible to identify the country, because the stenographers did not know the name of the delegate or because multiple delegates from a country attended a meeting and in the activity of the moment it was hard to distinguish among them. Occasionally the stenographers who took the original notes could not tell who was speaking; in such cases we write "Unidentified." Where delegates were acting as officers of a committee rather than as representatives of their countries, we list their names first, with their positions on the committee in parentheses.

We have made the following types of additions to the transcripts:

(1) Summary headings of the topics each meeting covered, in bold italics at the start of chapters.

(2) Short narrative summaries of many meetings, identifying the key issues and speakers, in italics at the start of chapters. We have included narrative summaries for meetings described by transcripts or summaries, but have omitted them for most meetings that are described only by brief minutes.

(3) Material in single square brackets, indicating places where we have made insertions to clarify the text or to fill in passages where we are highly confident that we are correct. The typescripts often omit the full text of passages where delegates were reading from prepared material that appeared as published conference documents. We were usually able to locate the material in the published conference proceedings, and have used it fill in passages. The additions are often lengthy, but without them it would be hard to understand what the delegates are debating. We were also able in many cases to infer the names of delegates where the transcripts only identify their countries. In some cases the chairman or other delegates referred to speakers by name, while for some smaller countries, the lists of delegates in the conference documents specify that only one delegate was to be present at a meeting of a particular committee. In the main text, page numbers in brackets such as "[p. 12]" identify pages in the unpublished typescripts. In Appendix F (only available in the electronic versions of the book) they identify pages in the published conference proceedings.

(4) Material in double brackets, thus: [[and]], indicating passages we have filled in where ellipsis points, blank spaces, or other notations indicate that the stenographer could not follow what the speaker was saying. In such cases we make our insertions with less confidence than for material in single brackets.

(5) Footnotes, which we have used mainly to identify the documents the conference delegates discussed. In the set of versions of this book for portable electronic reading devices, the footnotes are hyperlinked to the documents, enabling readers to consult the documents easily.

Conference documents cited in the transcripts

In the transcripts, delegates often make remarks that assume knowledge of the conference's system for organizing documents. Each document had a number. Some documents also had a combination letter-number code indicating their place in the conference agenda. Document 32, the core working document on the IMF, was sometimes also termed document SA/1, "SA" meaning "Secretariat Agenda."[36] Document 32 consisted of the Joint Statement by Experts on the Establishment of an International Monetary Fund published in April 1944 plus alternatives (amendments) proposed at the Atlantic City conference in June. (A minor source of confusion is that delegates sometimes referred to the whole of Document 32 as the Joint Statement, not distinguishing between the original statement and the Atlantic City alternatives.) The Joint Statement contained ten articles, compared to twenty in the final IMF Articles of Agreement. Each article was divided into sections, and some sections were further divided into subsections, also called paragraphs or items. Articles had Roman numerals; sections within articles had Arabic numerals; and alternatives had capital letters.

At the start of the conference, delegates received a loose-leaf binder, informally termed the conference "bible." During the conference, delegations submitted further alternatives, which were printed and distributed for inclusion in the binders so that delegates could read them before debating and voting on them. Alternatives submitted during the conference were printed as individual documents. They had document numbers for easy identification and page numbers to indicate their relation to Document 32 (or, in the case of alternatives about the World Bank, Document 245). So, for example, Article IV, Section 1 was on page 16 of Document 32, and Alternative B to the section was printed as Document 177, numbered page 16a.

After delegates had made some progress on the IMF agreement, the Drafting Committee of Commission I compiled the results to date in an intermediate draft, Document 321.[37] Delegates sometimes called it the "New Testament" to distinguish it from the "Old Testament" of Document 32.

To enable readers to follow the discussions of various conference documents in the transcripts, Appendix F (only available in the electronic versions of the book) contains almost all those documents. Clicking on hyperlinks to footnotes and then on hyperlinks in the footnotes to documents will take readers to, or a little above, the passage discussed in the main text.

---

[36] Document 32 of the conference (UNMFC 1948, v. 1: 21-60).

[37] Document 321 of the conference (UNMFC 1948, v. 1: 518-537).

Versions of this book

We are issuing this book in three versions. One version, or more precisely set of versions, is for portable electronic reading devices. It has reflowable text adaptable to various formats. The electronic version is really two volumes in one: the edited conference transcripts, and additional conference documents cited in the transcripts, contained in Appendix F and hyperlinked to the transcripts. Although the electronic reader version is equivalent to a 1400-page book, it costs no more than a mass-market paperback.

The second version of the book is a PDF file. The PDF file, which we expect to issue later in 2013, includes the concordances of the IMF and World Bank agreements in Appendix E, which the versions for portable electronic reading devices omit because the formatting is awkward.

The third version of the book is this paper edition. To keep it to a manageable size and reduce printing costs, it omits the documents in Appendix F, which are available elsewhere in print and online.

Because the page numbers of the various versions of the book may differ, we suggest that scholars who wish to cite page numbers of the transcripts use the commission or committee number, date, and typescript page numbers. The typescript page numbers appear in the transcripts within brackets. In some cases, the typescript for a meeting comprises two sets of typed pages, numbered separately rather than continuously. In such cases we have numbered pages of the second set with their own set numbers first, followed in parentheses by the numbers of a consecutive ordering. So, "[p. 3 (14)]" indicates that the page number in the typescript is 3 and that the page is the 14th page for the meeting in question, implying that the first 11 pages belong to a separately numbered set.

To ensure that the edited transcripts will be free of the copyright problems that keep some important scholarly books out of print for decades before they pass into the public domain, we have limited our claim of copyright for the electronic edition to ten years. The expanded content of the electronic edition, use of internal hyperlinks to allow readers to check references, low price, free dissemination of related documents, and voluntary limitation of copyright to far less than the 70-plus years that American law currently grants are practices that we hope other economists and historians will imitate.

Other publications of and about the conference

Until now, the only really detailed original source publication on the Bretton Woods conference has been two volumes of conference proceedings issued in 1948 by the U.S. Department of State with the help of the IMF and World Bank.[38] At the conference, about 500 official documents were issued to delegates or to the press. Conference documents included drafts of the agreements to establish the IMF and World Bank, proposed alternative clauses, committee reports, and press releases. The conference secretariat published a daily journal to keep delegates informed of meeting schedules and of the results of the deliberations of the commissions and major committees. Appendix C contains a list of conference documents. The 1948 volumes reprinted all the conference documents judged likely to have lasting historical significance.

The conference documents not published in 1948, while of lower significance, offer some useful tidbits of background. We therefore examined and photographed all that we found at the National Archives in College Park, Maryland, and at the Library of Congress and the U.S. Treasury Library in Washington, D.C. The copies at the National Archives are sheets of loose paper. The copies at the Library of Congress and the Treasury Library are bound volumes, issued by the Treasury.[39] As described below, both the published and unpublished documents are available online.

Besides the published conference documents, the other main source of first-hand information about the conference that previous researchers have used is the reminiscences of participants. More than a dozen participants wrote unpublished letters or memos that were eventually archived; later published essays or chapters in memoirs; or gave interviews about the conference. John Maynard Keynes's letters and memos on the conference, many of which were published in his *Collected Writings,* are the best-known material in this category.[40]

---

[38] UNMFC (1948).

[39] United States Department of the Treasury (1944).

[40] Acheson (1969: 81-84); Beyen (1949: 169-180); Bittermann (1971: 69-83); Black (1991: 35-49); Blum (1967: 257-278); Cornish (1993: 447-450); Harrod (1951: 577-584); Crombois (2011: 105-108); Harry S. Truman Library and Museum [2012]; Howson (2011: 524-532); Keynes (1980b: 72-112); Kirshner (1996: 19-51); Madan (1969); Mikesell (1994; 2000: 42-61); Moggridge (1992: 712-755); Morgenthau (2007: v. 749-757); Robbins in Robbins and Meade (1981: 166-193); Skidelsky (2001: 347-356); World Bank Archives Oral History Program

Online companion files

The Web site of the Center for Financial Stability contains a free Web page on this book. There, readers can consult extensive online companion files containing the previously published conference proceedings; photographs of the original typewritten transcripts; other documents prepared for the conference but not published as part of the conference proceedings; and certain extra documents related to the conference. The combined extent of the companion files is roughly 3,000 pages.

To repeat, the U.S. Department of State published two volumes of conference proceedings in 1948. Whereas Appendix F of the electronic versions of this book reprints only the documents from the volumes that delegates refer to in the transcripts, the Web page has PDF files of the full volumes.

To allow interested readers to compare our edited version of the transcripts to the original typescripts, we have made digital photographs of the typescripts and converted them into PDF files, one file per chapter.

The conference proceedings published in 1948 excluded some documents not considered of sufficient general interest to justify the cost of printing. Today, the low cost of digital photography and data storage argues for making the documents available even though they may interest only a handful of readers. The Web page therefore contains PDF files of digital photographs of all the previously unpublished official conference documents we found. Most are new bulletins for delegates or notices of the conference secretariat about logistics, including conference telephone directories.

Finally, we have also made available online certain extra documents related to the conference.[41]

Because the typescripts, other previously unpublished conference documents, and the previously published conference proceedings are

---

[2012]; and Young (1950). In addition, there are unpublished papers that may be useful, such as those of Edward M. Bernstein at the Louis Round Wilson Special Collections Library of the University of North Carolina; John Maynard Keynes in the Modern Archives at King's College, University of Cambridge; and Harry Dexter White at the Mudd Manuscript Library of Princeton University. Sources for official material include the British National Archives, U.S. National Archives, IMF Archives, World Bank Archives, and the Federal Reserve Bank of St. Louis's online database, FRASER (Federal Reserve Archival System for Economic Research). Keynes's Treasury papers are collected in Keynes (undated).

[41] The documents include Acsay (2000) and Federal Reserve [1946].

products of the U.S. government, they themselves are not copyrighted.[42]. Our edited version of the transcripts *is* copyrighted, however, as are our photographs in the electronic companion files just described. Persons who wish to make copies of the content in the electronic companion files may lawfully do so by seeking out and photographing the original documents, as we did, but may not copy our files without our permission.

Acknowledgments

We thank Zac Twining and Andy Young of the U.S. Treasury Library for help with its copies of the Bretton Woods transcripts. Carole Brookins, Benjamin Jerry Cohen, Barry Eichengreen, Eric Rauchway, Stephen Schuker, and Benn Steil made helpful comments on drafts. For the preface, we thank Jacques de Larosière and Steve H. Hanke. Roger Farley offered revealing advice on marketing. For extensive help with bringing the book to publication and with the online companion files to the book, we thank at the Center for Financial Stability Jeff van den Noort, LeAnn Yee, and especially Lawrence Goodman.

[42] United States Code, Title 17, Section 105, as of October 2012.

Table. Assignments of Committees of Commission I (IMF)
Preliminary draft (Document 51) → final agreement (Document 492)

Committee 1: Purposes, Policies, and Quotas of the Fund

Article I, Purpose and Policies of the Fund → Article I, Purposes

Article II, Subscription to the Fund → Article II, Membership; Article III, Quotas and Subscriptions; *and* Schedule A, Quotas

Article IX, Sections 1-4, Obligations of Member Countries (exchange rates) → Article VIII, General Obligations of Members *and* Schedule B, Provisions with Respect to Repurchase by a Member of Its Currency Held by the Fund

Committee 2: Operations of the Fund

Article III, Transactions with the Fund → Article V, same title

Article IV, Par Values of Member Currencies → Article IV, Par Values of Currencies

Article V, Capital Transactions → Article VI, Capital Transfers

Article VI, Apportionment of Scarce Currencies → Article VII, Scarce Currencies

Article X, Transitional Arrangements → Article XIV, Transitional Period

Committee 3: Organization and Management of the Fund

Article VII, Management of the Fund → Article XII, Organization and Management; Article XIII, Offices and Depositories; *and* Schedule C, Election of Executive Directors

Article VIII, Withdrawal from the Fund → Article XV, Withdrawal from Membership *and* Schedule D, Settlement of Accounts with Members Withdrawing

Committee 4: Form and Status of the Fund

Article IX, Sections 5-7, Obligations of Member Countries (immunities of the Fund) → Article IX, Status, Immunities and Privileges

Article X, Relations with Other International Organizations → Article XI, Relations with Non-Member Countries

Article XI, Amendments → Article XVII, same title

Article XII, Interpretation of the Agreement → Article XVIII, Interpretation *and* Article XIX, Explanation of Terms

Article XIII, [Final Provisions] → Article XVI, Emergency Provisions; Article XX, Final Provisions; *and* Schedule E, Administration of Liquidation

References

The references emphasize first-hand accounts of the Bretton Woods conference or writings that use first-hand accounts and original documents extensively. A much larger body of writing exists that discusses the Bretton Woods agreements and their consequences. For a bibliography on the agreements close to the time they were written, see Federal Reserve (1946); for a later bibliography, see Joint Bank-Fund Library (2004b); for the latest research, see Helleiner (forthcoming) and Rauchway (forthcoming). The electronic versions of this book include hyperlinks for many references. Here we omit most citations of hyperlinks. Hyperlinks were valid as of April 5, 2013.

Acheson, A.L. K[eith], J[ohn] F. Chant, [and] M[artin] F.J. Prachowny. 1972. *Bretton Woods Revisited; Evaluations of the International Monetary Fund and the International Bank for Reconstruction and Development. Papers Delivered at a Conference at Queen's University, Kingston, Canada.* Toronto: University of Toronto Press. (See "Canadian Views": 34-47.)

Acsay, Peter Josef. 2000. "Planning for Postwar Economic Cooperation: The U.S. Treasury, the Soviet Union, and Bretton Woods 1933-1946." Ph.D. dissertation, St. Louis University.

Acheson, Dean. 1969. *Present at the Creation: My Years in the State Department.* New York: W.W. Norton and Company.

Bernstein, Edward M[orris]. 1993. "General Discussion: The Soviet Union and Bretton Woods." In Michael D[avid] Bordo and Barry Eichengreen, editors, *A Retrospective on the Bretton Woods System: Lessons for International Monetary Reform:* 195-198. Chicago: University of Chicago Press.

Beyen, Johan W[illem]. 1949. *Money in a Maelstrom.* New York: Macmillan.

Bittermann, Henry J. 1971. "Negotiation of the Articles of Agreement of the International Bank for Reconstruction and Development." *International Lawyer,* v. 5, no. 1: 59-88.

Black, Stanley W. 1991. *A Levite Among the Priests: Edward Bernstein and the Origins of the Bretton Woods System.* Boulder, Colorado: Westview Press. (Interviews with Bernstein.)

Blum, John Morton. 1967. *From the Morgenthau Diaries: Years of War, 1941-1945.* (Volume 2 of 3.) Boston: Houghton Mifflin.

Boskey, Shirley. 1957. "Bretton Woods Recalled." *International Bank Notes* (World Bank), July.

Chandavarkar, Anand. 2000. "Was Keynes Anti-Semitic?" *Economic and Political Weekly* (Bombay), May 6: 1619-1624.

Conway, Edmund. 2014 (forthcoming). *The Summit.* New York: Little, Brown and Company.

Cornish, Selwin. 1993. "Sir Leslie Melville: An Interview." *Economic Record,* v. 69, no. 267, December: 437-457.

Craig, R. Bruce. 2004. *Treasonable Doubt: The Harry Dexter White Spy Case.* Lawrence, Kansas: University Press of Kansas.

Crombois, Jean F. 2011. *Camille Gutt and Postwar International Finance.* London: Pickering and Chatto.

Dam, Kenneth W. 1982. *The Rules of the Game: Reform and Evolution in the International Monetary System.* Chicago: University of Chicago Press.

De Vries, Margaret Garritsen. 1996. "The Bretton Woods Conference and the Birth of the International Monetary Fund." In Orrin Kirshner, editor, *The Bretton Woods-GATT System: Retrospect and Prospect after Fifty Years:* 3-18. Armonk, New York: M.E. Sharpe.

Dormael, Armand van. 1978. *Bretton Woods: Birth of a Monetary System.* London: Macmillan.

Eckes, Alfred E. 1975. *A Search for Solvency: Bretton Woods and the International Monetary System.* Austin: University of Texas Press.

Federal Reserve. 1943. United States. Board of Governors of the Federal Reserve System. "Postwar International Monetary Stabilization," *Federal Reserve Bulletin,* v. 29, no. 6, June: 501-521.

Federal Reserve. [1946.] United States. Board of Governors of the Federal Reserve System. Library. *Bretton Woods Agreements: A Bibliography, April 1943-December 1945.* Washington, D.C.: Library, Board of Governors of the Federal Reserve System.

Gardner, Richard N. 1980. *Sterling-Dollar Diplomacy in Current Perspective: The Origins and Prospects of Our International Economic Order,* revised edition. New York: Columbia University Press.

Halvorsen, Dag. 1982. *Norge og grunnleggelsen av Bretton Woods-systemet: Norges tilslutning til det Internasjonale valutafond og Verdensbanken 1943-46.* (Norway and the Establishment of the Bretton Woods System: Norway's Adherence to the International Monetary Fund and World Bank 1943-46.) Oslo: Norsk Utenrikspolitisk Institutt.

Harrod, Roy [Forbes]. 1951. *The Life of John Maynard Keynes.* New York: Harcourt, Brace and Company.

Harry S. Truman Library and Museum. [2012]. "Oral History Interviews." In <http://www.trumanlibrary.org/oralhist/oral_his.htm>. (Contains interviews with the following people who attended the Bretton Woods conference: Emilio Collado, Elbridge Durbrow, J. Burke Knapp, August Maffry, Leroy D. Stinebower, Ivan B. White, Arthur N. Young, and John Parke Young.)

Haynes, John Earl, Harvey Klehr, and Alexander Vassiliev. 2009. *Spies: The Rise and Fall of the KGB in America.* New Haven: Yale University Press.

Haynes, John Earl, and Harvey Klehr. 1999. *Venona: Decoding Soviet Espionage in America.* New Haven: Yale University Press.

Helleiner, Eric. Forthcoming. *The International Development of Bretton Woods: North-South Dialogue in the Making of the Postwar Order.*

Horsefield, J[ohn] Keith. 1969. *The International Monetary Fund 1945-1965: Twenty Years of International Monetary Cooperation,* 3 v. *Volume I: Chronicle; Volume II: Analysis,* by Margaret G[arritsen] de Vries and J[ohn] Keith Horsefield; *Volume III: Documents.* Washington, D.C.: International Monetary Fund.

Howson, Susan. 2011. *Lionel Robbins.* Cambridge: Cambridge University Press.

IMF. Undated [1950s?]. International Monetary Fund. "Bibliography—Bretton Woods." <http://adlib.imf.org/digital_assets/wwwopac.ashx?command=getcontent&server=webdocs&value=\BWC\BWC1319-05.pdf>.

IMF. 1951. International Monetary Fund. "Informal Minutes, Commission I, United Nations Monetary and Financial Conference at Bretton Woods, July 1944." Typescript mimeographed for limited internal distribution. IMF Archives, Washington, D.C., Bretton Woods Conference (BWC) files, File 57/479, Box 25. Also at <http://adlib.imf.org/digital_assets/wwwopac.ashx?command=getcontent&server=webdocs&value=\BWC\BWC1556-01.pdf>.

IMF. [2007]. International Monetary Fund. Archives. "IMF Archives Catalog > Bretton Woods Conference Collection," reference number 8391, and "IMF Archives Catalog > Bretton Woods Conference Collection > Bretton Woods Conference Files," reference number 1261. At <http://www.imf.org/external/np/arc/eng/archive.htm>. Previously "IMF Archives: Finding Aids > Bretton Woods Conference Collection: Bretton Woods Conference Files," <http://www.imf.org/external/np/arc/eng/fa/bwc/s4.htm>; the earliest appearance of that Web page in the "Wayback Machine" of the Internet Archive, at <http://www.archive.org>, is July 6, 2007. See the descriptions of Files 52/474 (index to conference documents), 52-53/475 and 52-53/475 (conference documents), 56/477 and 56/478 (transcripts), and 57/479 (retyped minutes of Commission I transcripts).

James, Harold. 1996. *International Monetary Co-operation Since Bretton Woods.* Washington, D.C. and New York: International Monetary Fund and Oxford University Press.

Joint Bank-Fund Library (International Monetary Fund and World Bank). 2004a. "Bretton Woods 60th Anniversary Virtual Exhibition 1944-2004." <http://jolis.worldbankimflib.org/Bwf/>.

Joint Bank-Fund Library (International Monetary Fund and World Bank). 2004b. "Bretton Woods Bibliography." <http://jolis.worldbankimflib.org/Bwf/60thbibliography.htm>.

Kapur, Devesh, John P. Lewis, and Richard Webb. 1997. *The World Bank: Its First Half-Century.* Washington, D.C.: Brookings Institution Press.

Keynes, John Maynard. 1980a. *Activities 1940-1944: Shaping the Post-War World: The Clearing Union. The Collected Writings of John Maynard Keynes,* v. 25. Edited by Donald Moggridge. London: Macmillan / New York: Cambridge University Press.

Keynes, John Maynard. 1980b. *Activities 1941-1946: Shaping the Post-War World: Bretton Woods and Reparations. The Collected Writings of John Maynard Keynes,* v. 26. Edited by Donald Moggridge. London: Macmillan / New York: Cambridge University Press.

Keynes, John Maynard. Undated. "Treasury Papers Series Two: Treasury Papers of John Maynard Keynes (Public Record Office Class T 247 - Papers relating to International Finance and the Chancellor of the Exchequer's Consultative Committee, 1940-1946)." Microfilm. London: Adam Matthew Publications. (Table of contents at <http://www.ampltd.co.uk/digital_guides/treasury_papers_series_2_jmk/detailed-listing.aspx>; we have not viewed the microfilm rolls.)

Kirshner, Orrin, editor. 1996. *The Bretton Woods-GATT System: Retrospect and Prospect after Fifty Years.* Armonk, New York: M.E. Sharpe.

Madan, B[al] K[rishna]. 1969. "Echoes of Bretton Woods." *Finance and Development,* June: 30-38.

Mason, Edward S[agendorph], and Robert E. Asher. 1973. *The World Bank Since Bretton Woods.* Washington, D.C.: Brookings Institution.

McJimsey, George [T.], editor. 2008. *Documentary History of the Franklin D. Roosevelt Presidency. Volume 40: The Bretton Woods Conference.* [Bethesda, Maryland: University Publications of America] / LexisNexis.

Mikesell, Raymond F[rench]. 1994. *The Bretton Woods Debates: A Memoir.* Essays in International Finance No. 192, March. Princeton, New Jersey: International Finance Section, Department of Economics, Princeton University.

Mikesell, Raymond F[rench]. 2000. *Foreign Adventures of an Economist.* Eugene, Oregon: University of Oregon Press.

Moggridge, D[onald] E[dward]. 1992. *John Maynard Keynes: An Economist's Biography.* London: Routledge.

Morgenthau, Jr., Henry. 2007. *The Morgenthau Diaries: World War II and Postwar Planning, 1943–1945.* Microform. Project coordinator, Robert E. Lester. Accompanied by Charles E. Smith and Robert E. Lester, *A Guide to the Microfilm Edition of the Morgenthau Diaries.* Guide at <http://cisupa.proquest.com/ksc_assets/catalog/9693.pdf>. Bethesda, Maryland: LexisNexis.

Oliver, Robert W[arner]. 1975, 1996. *International Economic Co-Operation and the World Bank,* original edition, revised edition. London: Macmillan.

Plumptre, A[rthur] F[itzWalter] W[ynne]. 1977. *Three Decades of Decision: Canada and the World Monetary System, 1944-75.* Toronto: McClelland and Stewart.

Rauchway, Eric. Forthcoming. *The Money-Makers: The Invention of Prosperity from Bullion to Bretton Woods.* New York: Simon and Schuster.

Robbins, Lionel, and James [Edward] Meade. 1981. *The Wartime Diaries of Lionel Robbins and James Meade, 1943-45.* Edited by Susan Howson and Donald Moggridge. New York: St. Martin's Press.

Schild, Georg [Manfred]. 1995. *Bretton Woods and Dumbarton Oaks: American Economic and Political Postwar Planning in the Summer of 1944.* New York: St. Martin's Press.

Skidelsky, Robert [Jacob Alexander]. 2001. *John Maynard Keynes. Volume 3: Fighting for Freedom, 1937-1946.* New York: Viking Penguin.

Steil, Benn. 2013. *The Battle of Bretton Woods: John Maynard Keynes, Harry Dexter White, and the Making of a New World Order.* Princeton, New Jersey: Princeton University Press.

Treasury Library. 1997. United States. Department of the Treasury. Library. *Inventory of Historic Research Materials.* Washington, D.C.: Department of the Treasury, Departmental Offices, Treasury Library.

UNFMC. 1944a. United Nations Monetary and Financial Conference (1944: Bretton Woods, New Hampshire). "Transcript of Minutes of Meetings of United Nations Monetary and Financial Conference," 3 v. in 4. "Commission 1, Part 1: Meetings of Full Commission," v. 1, part 1; "Commission 1, Part 2: Committees 1 and 2," v. 1, part 2; "Commission 1, Part 3: Committees 3 and 4," v. 1, part 3; and "Commission 2 and Commission 3," v. 2. Mimeographed. (All volumes are available at the International Monetary Fund Archives, Washington, D.C., Bretton Woods Conference (BWC) files, Files 56/477 and 5/478, Box 24, and the United States Treasury Library, Washington, D.C. Treasury Library copies have "H.D. White" written in the flyleaf. Call number JX1999.A2 Conf. 1944a, v. 1, pt. 1; v. 1, pt. 2; v. 1, pt. 3; v. 2. Loose-leaf pages of the material exist in the United States National Archives, College Park, Maryland, in National Archives identifier number 632487).

UNMFC. 1944b. United Nations Monetary and Financial Conference (1944: Bretton Woods, New Hampshire). *Doc[uments] No. [1]-547,* 4 v. Typescript. (At the Library of Congress, Washington, D.C., call number HG205 1944.A3A2. Also at the United States Treasury Library, Washington, D.C., as United States Department of the Treasury, *Bretton Woods Conference,* 10 v. in 5. V. 1, parts 1-5; v. 2, parts 1-2; v. 3; v. 4; v 5. Call number Treas. JX 1977.A2 Conf. 1944. Also in loose sheets at the United States National Archives, College Park, Maryland. These typescripts are the source documents of the published conference proceedings, UNMFC 1948, as opposed to the source documents of the previously unpublished transcripts in this book. They also contain some documents of lesser importance not published in the conference proceedings.)

UNMFC. 1948. United Nations Monetary and Financial Conference (1944: Bretton Woods, New Hampshire). *Proceedings and Documents of the United Nations Monetary and Financial Conference, Bretton Woods, New Hampshire, July 1-22, 1944,* 2 v. United States, Department of State, Office of Public Affairs, Division of Publications, publication no. 2866, International Organization and Conference Series I, 3. Washington, D.C.: Government Printing Office. (Page numbers in volumes are consecutive.) Also on FRASER (Federal Reserve Archival System for Economic Research, Federal Reserve Bank of St. Louis), <http://fraser.stlouisfed.org/publication/?pid=430>.

United States. Department of State. 1944. "United Nations Monetary and Financial Conference." *Department of State Bulletin,* May 27: 498.

Van Dormael. *See* Dormael.

World Bank Archives. [2012a] "Bretton Woods Conference." <http://web.worldbank.org/WBSITE/EXTERNAL/EXTABOUTUS/EXTARCHIVES/0,,contentMDK:64054691~menuPK:64319211~pagePK:36726~piPK:36092~theSitePK:29506,00.html>.

World Bank Archives. [2012b]. "Reference Collection on World Bank History." <http://web.worldbank.org/WBSITE/EXTERNAL/EXTABOUTUS/EXTARCHIVES/0,,contentMDK:20263656~menuPK:7212347~pagePK:36726~piPK:437378~theSitePK:29506~isCURL:Y~isCURL:Y,00.html>.

World Bank Archives. Oral History Program. [2012]. <http://web.worldbank.org/WBSITE/EXTERNAL/EXTABOUTUS/EXTARCHIVES/0,,contentMDK:20033284~menuPK:35061~pagePK:36726~piPK:36092~theSitePK:29506,00.html>.

Young, John Parke. 1950. "Developing Plans for an International Monetary Fund and a World Bank." *Department of State Bulletin,* November 13: 778-790.

PART I

COMMISSION I:

INTERNATIONAL MONETARY FUND

2

Commission I
International Monetary Fund
First meeting: transcript
July 3, 1944, 2:00 p.m.[43]

Convening of the Commission and naming of officers • Chairman's opening speech • Division of the Commission into committees • Work schedule • Press relations • Delegates' suggestions about work schedule

The ideas that led to the Bretton Woods conference originated with American and British government officials. The U.S. vision dominated in the end because the United States was the world's largest creditor nation, while the United Kingdom was a debtor dependent on credit from the United States during World War II and likely to remain somewhat dependent after the war. The highest goal of the conference was to establish an agreement for the International Monetary Fund (IMF); until shortly before the conference began, it was uncertain whether sufficient consensus existed to reach an agreement for the International Bank for Reconstruction and Development (World Bank, as it is now more commonly called). The United States, as the world's largest economy, received the chairmanship of Commission I, whose subject was the IMF. The United Kingdom received the chairmanship of Commission II, whose subject was the World Bank.

The chairman of Commission I was Harry Dexter White, a former professor of economics who had worked at the U.S. Treasury for a decade by the time of the

---

[43] Summarized in Document 58, pp. 96-97 of the conference proceedings. To help readers, we now switch from the footnote style of the introduction, which requires consulting the reference section for full information, to a more self-contained style. In the footnotes that follow, all mentions of document and appendix numbers, and their associated page numbers, refer to United Nations Monetary and Financial Conference, *Proceedings and Documents of the United Nations Monetary and Financial Conference, Bretton Woods, New Hampshire, July 1-22, 1944*, 2 v. (Washington, D.C.: Government Printing Office, 1948). Pages up through 1126 are in volume 1 of the conference proceedings; subsequent pages are in volume 2.

Bretton Woods conference. As Assistant to the Secretary of the Treasury he directed American involvement in international monetary matters, including being the chief negotiator on the subject during World War II.

The first meetings of Commissions I, II, and III follow a common pattern: the chairman is introduced; he makes a speech; the group discusses organizational matters; then it adjourns, leaving substantive debate for subsequent meetings. Warren Kelchner, a U.S. Department of State official who acted as the Secretary General, meaning that he was in charge of conference logistics, introduces White, who makes a speech contrasting the conflicting international economic policies of the 1930s with the more harmonious policies he hopes the conference will inaugurate. White then offers proposals on dividing the work of the Commission into committees and organizing the committee schedules. He informs the delegates that journalists will enjoy access to a considerable amount of conference material "on background," embargoed until conference officials gave approval for publication. Journalists were barred from attending commission and committee meetings, though.

Secretary General (Warren Kelchner, United States): Commission I of United Nations Monetary and Financial Conference is hereby convened.

At the Plenary Session this morning it was decided to establish a Commission I to consider International Monetary Funds. At the same session, the following officials were elected: chairman, the representative of the United States; vice chairman, the representative of Venezuela; for recording [reporting] delegate, the representative of Canada. I have been informed the representative of the United States to act as chairman of this committee[44] is Mr. Harry D. White. For vice president [vice chairman], the chairman of the Venezuela delegation, Mr. Rodolfo Rojas, will serve for Venezuela. I have been informed that the representative of Canada to serve as the reporting delegate will be Mr. L[ouis] Rasminsky. I now turn over the chair to the chairman of Commission I, Mr. White.

Chairman (Harry Dexter White, United States): I am informed that according to the rules and regulations adopted at the conference this morning[45] that the Commission meetings are held in executive session. If there are any persons present who are not entitled to be present at an executive meeting, will they please leave. During the next meetings the members will have to show a pass upon entrance.

---

[44] Participants in the conference sometimes used the term "committee" in a procedural sense to refer to any body of delegates at the conference, whether officially termed a commission, committee, or subcommittee.

[45] Document 14, pp. 9-17.

I would like to take the opportunity to introduce your Secretary, Mr. Leroy Stinebower, who is adviser of the Office of Economic Affairs of the Department of State, and his assistant, Mrs. Eleanor Dulles of the Office of Financial and Monetary Affairs of the Department of State. They are here to help you in every possible way. If you have any questions at all in connection with the meetings, or if there is any material that you would want in preparation for subsequent meetings or that relate to any of the meetings that [p. 2] have already been held, if you contact them they will be ready to serve you in every way possible.

Each of the United and Associated Nations[46] [has as a fundamental objective the creation of as full production and employment as is possible in its own country. This is the only practical way to improve the standard of living in the peace-loving nations. But this objective is attainable only if there is the fullest trade among the nations based on the interest of all. It cannot be achieved if military warfare is followed by economic warfare—if each country, to the disregard of the interest of other countries, battles solely for its own short-range economic interests. The unrestrained economic fighting of the 1930s points clearly to the conclusion that such economic warfare is neither in the best interest of the particular country nor in the general interest of all countries. Unrestrained economic warfare, if allowed to continue in the future, will again disrupt production and employment by destroying international trade and injuring national markets. It will undermine one of the foundation stones for a secure peace.

Some examples from the United States may illustrate what I mean. The condition of the American cotton, tobacco, and other agricultural producers depends upon the ability of European and other countries to buy substantial portions of their crops. If Europe is not prosperous and the proper mechanisms of trade are not used, these American producers will not be able to export as much of their produce. At the same time, the prosperity of the other parts of the world and of the United States depends on the importation of raw materials from foreign countries. The higher the production levels in the United States and the more efficient the trade mechanisms, the more raw materials we import from abroad. Both the United States and other countries are thus benefited. A unilateral or bilateral approach to our trade problems cannot produce the

[46] After this point, the transcript merely says, "(speech read by Dr. White)," and ceases to transcribe his remarks because he was reading from a prepared speech. The speech was published as Document 59, pp. 97-98, from which we have reproduced the portion in brackets.

highest benefits for the peace-loving nations. The approach must be multilateral.

The proposal for an International Monetary Fund which we are to consider in this Commission is designed to promote the development of international markets by providing a permanent institution for international monetary cooperation. It would promote exchange rate stability; assure multilateral payment facilities; help lessen international disequilibrium; and give confidence to member countries. Only by developing the necessary machinery to maintain multilateral nondiscriminatory trading among nations can we hope to avoid resort to exchange restrictions, quotas, and other devices which inevitably cause a contraction of trade and production. The proposed Fund, which is before you for consideration, would be an important influence toward stability in international monetary and economic relations.]

Clearly it is going to be a difficult task to get over all the ground that we would hope to accomplish before the end of the conference. It can only be obtained if we concentrate on the job and cooperate to the fullest possible extent. In order to facilitate consideration of the various problems, it has been the proposal [i.e., proposed] to divide the work of the committee [conference] up and [to divide] the Commission up into four committees.

You have before you a mimeograph sheet[47] containing the titles of the four committees and a brief word about the subject matter that each one of the committees is to consider. Committee A deals with purposes and policies and quotas of the Fund; Committee B with the operation of the Fund; Committee C with organization and management; Committee D with the form and status of the Fund.[48]

You will find on your discussion in the committee meetings that some of the material you will have to deal with relates to subject matter contained in the titles of the other committees. Obviously there is an interdependency between many of the points discussed in Committee A and to some extent under Committee C and Committee B. Where it is possible, we would expect that the committees confine themselves to the particular subject matter of their committees. Where it is necessary to include in your discussions matter which is also being considered in other committees, you will, of course, do so. There will be placed before you when you leave—these are already distributed—documents which will

---

[47] Apparently Document 7, pp. 5-7.

[48] Elsewhere, the committees of Commission I are called 1, 2, 3, and 4 instead of A, B, C, and D.

constitute the working basis for the work of this Commission and the work of the committees.[49] The Secretary informs me that they have not had an opportunity to complete the document. You now have [p. 3] been given some twenty pages. The remainder, I understand, will be ready for you tomorrow.

There is explanatory material on [i.e., in] the first part of the document which we need not review at this time. It is expected that each committee will select those portions of the draft document which is before you which relates to their particular subject matter. In most cases you will find that the material that is to be considered by Committee A is the first part of the document. Committee B will be found in the sections that follow the work of Committee A, and C and D, etc. That does not hold true throughout, but in general that is the situation.

The document, as you know, includes the amendments of the various proposals and suggested alterations that have been handed in by the delegates of the various countries. There will, of course, appear new suggestions, new amendments, new provisions which will be submitted to the Secretary and will be incorporated in revised drafts of the document that is before you. By having the Statement of Principles taken from the Joint Statement of Principles agreed upon by the technicians[50] followed by the various alternate provisions which have been suggested and others that will be suggested, you will be able to concentrate on a particular part in your committee discussions before going to subsequent material.

The thought was that we would have the committees work concurrently with the commissions. In other words, the committees will meet tomorrow—the four committees. We tried to stagger committee meetings, and we have been able to do that partly, so that two committees will meet at one time. The committees will discuss the material. They will then present to this Commission when it next meets the tentative conclusion[s] which they have arrived at in the discussions. In many cases, they will find that there is unanimity of opinion with respect to the desirability of [p. 4] some provisions. In that event, they will so report. In some cases, doubtless, there will be differences of opinion. Such differences will be expressed in alternative provisions. These alternative provisions will likewise be submitted to this Commission for discussion.

---

[49] Apparently Document 32, pp. 21-60.

[50] Document 32 contains the Joint Statement of Principles issued in April 1944 plus alternatives (amendments) that had been proposed up to the time the document was printed. The bare Joint Statement of Principles is in Appendix IV, part 7 of the conference proceedings, pp. 1629-1636.

Because of the short time we have here and because of the amount of material we have to cover, we thought it would be unwise to wait until each committee had considered all material and reported to this Commission before this Commission considered it. We therefore deem it advisable that the committees make as much progress as they can in the next two meetings that they will have, and then report to this Commission on such work as they have already covered. Some committees will make more rapid progress than others, but in any event, the Commission will have an opportunity for longer discussion for many of the points than would be the case were the committees to consider all of the material they had and then present a report this Commission. After all, there are four committees. Each one is covering a great deal of subject matter, so that the amount of work that each committee will be able to do in the two or three sessions which will take place between meetings of the Commission will, we believe, motivate ample material to keep this Commission occupied during the rest of its meetings. If we find that the committees are proceeding more rapidly than we had expected, then we can make the meetings of this Commission less frequent. If we find that the committee meetings are raising points about which there is very considerable difference, then we may have to meet more frequently in order to permit this Commission to discuss adequately the various drafts which are placed before you.

So, our preliminary program is flexible; we may change it later. The proposal is to have Committees A, B, C, and D [p. 5] meet tomorrow, and each committee will meet twice a day. I think the plan is to have two committees meet at 9 o'clock—from 9:00 to 11:00—and two committees from 11:00 to 1:00. Then the thought is to have no formal committees meeting between 1:00 and 4:00. Then at 4:00 there will be two committees meeting until 5:30, and from 5:30 to 7:00 two other committees. Of course, the committees will appoint ad hoc subcommittees to consider specific matters. Such subcommittees will meet at such times as they may. There will be no schedule made for subcommittees. That program will continue until Wednesday [July 5]. On Wednesday morning this Commission will meet at—we don't know yet, it will be posted—and we will then determine whether any modification in our procedure is warranted.

I said the committees will meet at 9 o'clock each morning. Tomorrow we would like to make an exception because there have been a number of group meetings which have already been scheduled, so the first two committees will meet tomorrow at 10:00 instead of 9:00, but this is only true tomorrow. The second two committees will meet at 11:00. In other words, the first two committees will have only one hour instead of the usual two. We may modify that by one-half hour. In any case, the exact hour and rooms of meeting will be included in the mimeographed sheet that will be available to you and distributed from the usual sources either tonight or tomorrow. We have hesitated to ask the committees to meet twice a day, but we felt only in that way could we make sufficient progress. If we find progress is more rapid than we anticipated then we [p. 6] can modify the schedule.

The Secretariat requests me to ask that the members give their name and country when rising to speak so they will be able to make proper notes. The Secretariat also asked me to note that it is important that each delegate submit their names, indicating their membership on this Commission and on the four committees. They would like to obtain that today. This should be presented at the Secretary General's office, which is Room 136, or to the Secretary of the delegation [Commission], which is Room 156.

The draft document which you will have before you, I need not remind you, is strictly confidential, and is not to be given to anybody for official release or for any other use. After saying that, I am going to inform you that the document is going to be distributed to the press this afternoon, but the press will not be able to publish the material until it is to be officially released. They are on their honor. This has been done, I gather, in part before. If there are any infractions it cannot be helped, but in view of the fact that all the delegations would have the document and all advisers would have the document and many of the technicians would have the document, it was thought that this was a more appropriate way to handle it.

The press will be given the document, and at the same time there will be an attempt made to explain briefly the material which is being currently discussed at the committees and at the Commission. We are going to attempt to keep them informed of what is going on. Each day or every second day, depending upon the amount of progress that is made, the press will be informed on what meeting, what articles or sections 1 to 3 or 5 or pages 1 to 6 may be released, so that they will release portions from time to time. The press conference will also provide an opportunity for the press [p. 7] to raise questions about the material which is being discussed at the committee meetings. Explanation will be given as far as it is appropriate and as far as it is possible to help them understand what the provisions mean, and also to give them some idea of the different views as expressed by the ultimate provisions. Nothing will be said to them as to what country has presented what alternative; that they will have to accumulate in their usual fashion. The expectation is that the press, by being informed, will be able to handle the material much more intelligently and will bother the delegates much less. Just how that will work out, we don't know. I understand from our press relations man that this is a novel attempt. We are hoping that it will facilitate our work and inform the public of what is being done here.

Now, are there any questions or comments? [p. 8]

Greece (Kyriakos Varvaressos): May I suggest, Mr. President, that Committees Nos. 1 and 2 will probably require considerable time. Is it possible that some arrangements may be made so that these two committees will not meet at the same time? Could Committees 1 ["Purposes, Policies, and Quotas of the Fund"] and 3 ["Organization and Management of the Fund"] or 4 ["Form and Status of the Fund"] meet at 9:00, and Committees 2 ["Operations of the Fund"] and 3 or 4 at 11 o'clock?

Chairman: That sounds like an excellent proposal, in view of our subject matter. Unless there is some objection, I will ask the Secretary to arrange it that way.

United Kingdom (John Maynard Keynes): Since Committees A and B are so closely related, some delegates might wish to attend both meetings, so I suggest that A and C meet from 10:00 to 11:00 and B and D from 11:00 to 1:00. That would seem to me a suitable distribution.

Chairman: That was the suggestion of Mr. Varvaressos, and unless there is some objection, we will make that arrangement.

Are there any other questions?

If not, the meeting is adjourned.

(2:45 p.m.)

3

Commission I
International Monetary Fund
Second meeting: transcript
July 5, 1944, 10:30 a.m.[51]

Reports of committees • Division of labor between Commission and committees • Procedures for making the Commission's work efficient

This meeting consists mainly of reports of the four committees that Commission I established to report to it. Each committee is represented by a reporter, also sometimes called the reporting delegate, who summarizes what the committee discussed. The reporters were chosen in part for their intellect, and it is evident from the transcripts that they were influential in the Commission's debates as members of their national delegations, not only as reporters.

Kyriakos Varvaressos gives the report of Committee 1, "Purposes, Policies, and Quotas of the Fund." Varvaressos had been the governor of Greece's central bank, when the German invasion of Greece occurred in 1941. The occupation government fired him and he went into exile. The committee decided to set aside the questions of quotas (capital subscriptions) until a paper being prepared on the subject was ready for distribution. It turned to Article I of the draft IMF agreement, on the purposes of the IMF, and made a modest beginning in its deliberations on the subject.

Robert Mossé gives the report of Committee 2, "Operations of the Fund." The committee's focus was rules for exchange rates and exchange controls. Before World War II, Mossé had been a professor of law (what today might be called law and economics) in France. After the German occupation of France, he was fired because he was a Jew. To avoid further persecution he fled the country, eventually becoming a professor of economics at the New School for Social Research in New York, a haven for many European exiles. Committee 2 deliberated on a number of provisions of Article III, "Transactions with the Fund." It reached agreement on provisions stating through what agencies member governments should deal with the IMF; conditions under which members could purchase the currencies of other members (in other words,

[51] Summarized in Document 132, pp. 145-146.

borrow from the IMF); conditions governing purchases for capital transfers; declaring members ineligible to use the IMF's resources; limitations on the IMF's operations; and, for the most part, a section on preventing currencies from becoming scarce. There was a wide difference of opinion, however, on a clause that the IMF could require countries to sell a certain amount of gold to it at the end of its financial year if their holdings of gold and gold-convertible exchange had increased during the year.

Ervin Hexner gives the report of Committee 3, "Organization and Management of the Fund." Before World War II, Hexner had been a lawyer, university lecturer, and specialist on cartels in Czechoslovakia, on whose delegation he served at the conference. He immigrated to the United States in 1939, eventually becoming a professor of economics and political science at the University of North Carolina. He reports that the committee reached broad agreement that the Board of Governors, the IMF's highest body, with representatives from all member countries, should delegate most of its supervisory responsibilities to a smaller Executive Committee, and that among the Executive Directors, several would be appointed by the member countries with the largest quotas, while others would be elected by groups of members with smaller quotas.

Wilhelm Keilhau gives the report of Committee 4, "Form and Status of the Fund." The committee's focus was the legal status of the IMF's relationship with member countries and legal provisions of the draft IMF agreement on matters such as interpretation and amendment. Before World War II, Keilhau had been a lawyer and professor of economics in Norway, writing a number of publications on monetary policy. After the German invasion of Norway in 1940, he fled, becoming part of the exile government in London as director in exile of the Norway's central bank. He reports that the committee did not meet because the material for discussion was not available.

After the reports of the committees, Commission chairman Harry Dexter White explains how he hopes that, to improve the chance of reaching a final agreement on the IMF, delegates will confine their discussions to essential points and forego long speeches. Then White and the delegates, especially John Maynard Keynes of the United Kingdom, discuss the scheduling of committee meetings before the next Commission meeting.

Chairman (Harry Dexter White, United States): The meeting will please come to order. Will the Secretary please note any absentees for the record. He might call out the absentees.

Secretary ([Leroy Stinebower, United States]): Those who seem to be absent are Ecuador, Honduras, and Nicaragua.

Chairman: The first item on the order of business is a report by Mr. Varvaressos from Committee 1.

[Kyriakos Varvaressos, Greece, Reporter, Committee 1]:[52] [Mr. Chairman, your Committee 1 on "Purposes, Policies, and Quotas of the Fund" held two meetings on July 4; the first at 10 a.m. and the second at 4 p.m.

A document (Document No. 51[53]) containing the committee assignments has been distributed to the members of the Committee at its first meeting. In determining the objects which should come within its jurisdiction, the Committee has been guided by the suggestions contained in the document.

With regard to the procedure to be followed, the Chairman proposed and the Committee accepted that whenever there are several alternatives to be considered, those involving substantial changes of the provisions of the Joint Statement would be considered first.

On the other hand, it has been moved and accepted by the Committee that, in order to expedite matters, a small Drafting Subcommittee[54] be appointed, and that alternatives involving no substantial changes of the Joint Statement provisions be referred to this committee by the Chairman, with the approval in each case of the Committee.

A subcommittee has accordingly been constituted to that effect.

At the beginning of the first meeting, it was suggested that the principal question which comes within the jurisdiction of the Committee is the question of the determination of the quotas of member countries referred to in Article II, Section 7 of the Joint Statement.[55] It was argued that this question was of the highest importance to the member countries, and that a procedure ought to be established for determining such quotas. The Committee, being in the meantime informed that a paper referring to this subject was being prepared for distribution to its members, has decided to postpone temporarily the discussion of quotas until such paper has been distributed.

During the further discussions of the specific subjects of the Committee, it was suggested that it would be desirable in so far as possible to eliminate voting and that, where a fundamental difference of opinion was evident and a rapprochement of the different views was

---

[52] The transcript merely says, "(Report read)." We have reproduced the report from Document 125, pp. 134-136. It summarizes deliberations in chapters 11 and 12.

[53] Document 51, pp. 88-91.

[54] Also called the Drafting Committee.

[55] Apparently Alternative B to Article II, Section 3 of the Joint Statement (Document 32, p. 27), which proposed to reduce initial gold payments for member countries that had been occupied during World War II.

unattainable, the Chairman, with the consent of the Committee, would refer the matter to your Commission with a record of the different opinions represented.

The Committee then proceeded to discussion of Article I of the Joint Statement, referring to the purposes and policies of the Fund, and of the numerous alternatives submitted by members.

The Committee has not been able to make substantial progress in arriving at an agreement in the first day of its meetings.

Three subjects involving questions of principle have been reviewed, which absorbed the time allowed for the two meetings. The first of these three subjects was Alternative C, Section 2, of Article I.[56] The purpose of this alternative, which was explained to the Committee, was to state explicitly that one of the purposes of the Fund was "to assist in the fuller utilization the resources of economically underdeveloped countries and to contribute there by the maintenance in the world as a whole of a high level of employment and real income, [which must be a primary objective of economic policy]." It was thought by the proposer [India] that the wording of Section 2 as it stands now was stressing unduly the position of highly industrialized countries while it made no reference to underdeveloped agricultural countries. Alternative C has been seconded by several members, while others expressed very serious doubts on the advisability of adopting wording which would be interpreted as enlarging the purpose of the Fund in a way which was out of proportion with the means at its disposal, and attributing to it objectives which were appropriately those of the Bank for Reconstruction and Development.

In discussion, however, there developed a consensus that the *attainment* of a high level of employment and real income as well as their *maintenance* was intended to be included among the purposes, and that the addition of appropriate words to that effect would be desirable.

At the conclusion of the discussion, the Chairman referred Alternative C to the Drafting Committee on the understanding that the intent of the amendment was not to enlarge the purposes of the Fund, but merely to make them more explicit.

The second subject involving a question of principle was Alternatives B, D, and E of Article I, Section 4, which relates to exchange stability.

---

[56] All the alternatives Varvaressos discusses in his report are in Document 32, pp. 23-24. Article I in the draft agreement remained Article I in the final agreement, Document 492. The delegates often call the subdivisions of Article I "sections," and we follow this usage, but unlike the case for other articles, at no stage does the IMF agreement itself ever term them "sections."

The discussion on these alternatives revealed but the wording of this section of the purposes and policies of the Fund was closely connected with Article IV of the Joint Statement, dealing with par values of member countries and providing for changes in these par values.

It has been accordingly decided that the subject be referred to the Drafting [Sub]committee on the understanding that it would not make its report until later stage when the provisions of Article IV of the plan have been agreed upon.

The third subject was Alternative G, which would include among the purposes of the Fund "to promote and facilitate the settlement of abnormal indebtedness arising out of the war." The sponsors of the proposal [India] stressed the vital importance of the problem for the countries directly concerned, and indicated the necessity of including the subject in a scheme of postwar international monetary corporation. In the discussion, the dangers and difficulties of burdening the Fund with the immense problem of settlement of balances is accumulated in wartime were emphasized. It has been suggested that the Committee should refer the matter to your Commission.

Other alternatives to the sections of Article I of the Joint Statement, which do not involve substantial changes, have been referred by the Committee to the Drafting Subcommittee, which will report to the Committee in due time.]

Chairman: Thank you, Mr. Varvaressos. It would appear that for the first business meeting of the Commission, we might hear all the reporters[57] first, before opening the meeting for a discussion or any views. [Or] we may not: even if that practice is followed at the first meeting at the pleasure of the Commission, it need not be followed later on. We may find that for the next meeting it is desirable to discuss in detail the report of each committee after it is presented, but for the first meeting it might be preferable to hear all the reports first. Unless there is an objection to that procedure, I propose that it be followed. Is there any objection to that procedure for this morning alone?

---

[57] In the transcripts, the world "reporters" always means reporting delegates, who were designated to summarize the discussions and conclusions of committee meetings, and never means journalists. To clarify roles, in our identifications of delegates in bold type, we reserve the term "reporting delegate" for the commission officers who reported to the plenary session of the conference; we call all reporting delegates of committees and subcommittees "reporters."

Apparently, there is not, and I will, therefore, call upon Professor Mossé of the French Comité[58] on the work of Committee 2. I am going to ask Professor Mossé to step up to the microphone.

Robert Mossé (France, Reporter, Committee 2):[59] [I am reporting to you on the work of Committee No. 2 of Commission I, which deals with the "Operations of the Fund." I shall cover both the morning and afternoon meetings held on July 4. I will keep the following order:

1. I shall offer some remarks on the procedure of our Committee.

2, I shall enumerate the items which have obtained a general agreement.

3. Finally, I shall report to you more fully about one point in which wide differences of opinion have appeared.

Concerning the procedure, it had been generally accepted that committees should not take a formal vote, but that they should try to iron out differences of opinion.

In order to do so, the Committee authorized the Chairman to appoint a small Asterisk Committee—so called because it will study the texts which are marked with an asterisk in Document F-1 [another name for Document 32]. This Asterisk Committee will be limited to questions which do not involve wide differences, and are chiefly questions of language.[60]

Committee 2 also decided that the Chairman should invite objections; when no objection is made, the Chairman shall declare that there is a general agreement, and the Reporting Delegate shall so report to the Committee. However, any delegate [delegation] may go on record for any opinion, if it so desires, and this will be reported by the Reporting Delegate.

When there are wide differences of opinion, the Reporter will so report to the Commission. But the Chair stated that it will always welcome suggestions from the floor designed to adjust differences. Any delegate may suggest devices which may serve to reconcile conflicting views—for instance, an ad hoc committee or unofficial conversations among delegates. So much for the question of procedure.

---

[58] The Free French Comité français de la Libération nationale.

[59] The transcript merely says, "(Report read)." We have reproduced the report from Document 128, pp. 139-141. It summarizes deliberations in chapters 17 and 18.

[60] In the initial draft agreement for the IMF (Document 32, pp. 21-60), an asterisk indicated that a proposed alternative contained no substantial change from the corresponding provision of the Joint Statement.

I am now glad to report that Committee No. 2 has covered Article III ["Transactions with the Fund," Sections] 1, 2, 3. If you refer to Document No. 51,[61] on committee assignments, the Committee has covered Section 1, Section 2, Section 2a, Section 3, Section 4, and, in part, Section 5. With the exception of one question, there has been general agreement on substance on all questions. I shall name them in order, according to Document No. 32. May in invite you, gentlemen, to take Document 32, or F-1, page 5.[62]

On page 5, with reference to Joint Statement [Article] III, [Section] 1 ["Agencies Dealing with the Fund"], there has been general agreement on Alternative A, with, however, a suggestion for the lawyers to ensure harmony between this Alternative A and Alternative A [of Article III], Section 5, on page 8 ["Operations for the Purpose of Preventing Currencies from Becoming Scarce"], concerning borrowing by the Fund from any other source. The minutes of the meeting of Committee 2 of Commission I at 11:30 a.m. on July 4 (Document No. 104[63]) should be corrected accordingly to include this suggestion.

Section 2, page 6a, Alternative A ["Conditions upon which Any Member May Purchase Currencies of Other Members"], has been accepted by common agreement, with the exception of paragraph (2), which was reserved for later discussion, and of paragraph (3), upon which I shall speak later. Now, although there was general agreement on the wording, I am not sure that there is agreement on the interpretation; some countries believe that buying is a right, while others believe that a certain amount of elbow room is left to the Fund.

There has been general agreement on Section 2a, on "Conditions Governing Purchases for Capital Transfers," but an important question was raised by the delegates of Greece and Czechoslovakia. They asked whether the country of which the currency is requested for capital transfer is obliged to accept imports of capital. Let me take an illustration of this point. Under certain conditions, which have been fully agreed and understood by the members of the Committee, Canada might purchase [Greek] drachmas in order to make capital investments in Greece.

---

[61] Document 51, pp. 88-91.

[62] The items referred to in the rest of Mossé's remarks are in Document 32, pp. 27-31. When delegates mention page numbers in the meetings of Commission I and its committees, they are usually to pages in loose-leaf binders whose numbering is keyed to Document 32.

[63] Document 104, pp. 119-120.

Normally, Greece is required to accept drachmas for current[64] payments, but is she obliged to accept them for capital investments in Greece by Canadian interests? The delegates of Canada gave the answer that any country could refuse imports of capital. In other words, the consent of the nation of which the currency is purchased will be required in practice. This answer was deemed satisfactory, and it is with this implication that the section has been generally accepted.

Section 3, page 6b, concerning ineligibility of members to use the resources of the Fund, has been generally accepted, but with the suppression of the words "and policies" at the end of the second line. The Committee recognized that Alternative A is more mindful of the dignity of the country members; as Mr. [Ned] Brown (USA) said, "It is better to limit the use of the Fund or to declare a nation ineligible rather than to suspend it with a connotation of blame."

Section 4, Alternative A, page 7, "Limitation on the Operations of the Fund," has been generally approved without objection.

Section 5, Alternative A, page 8, on "Operations for the Purpose of Preventing Currencies from Becoming Scarce," has been generally agreed, with the exception of paragraph (2), which has not yet been discussed. However, there are in paragraph (1) of this section some minor problems of drafting, and this section has been turned over to the Asterisk Committee.

To summarize, Committee 1 has achieved a general agreement on Sections 1, 2, 2a, and 4, with the exception of paragraphs (2) and (3) in Section 2.

I think that I am not going beyond the assignment of a Reporting Delegate in saying that Committee 2 recommends that this Commission approve these articles.

Now I come to the only point in which there were wide differences of opinion, namely [Article] III, [Section] 2(c) of the Joint Statement [on the IMF requiring countries to sell gold to it]. Before doing so, I want to ask, what is your pleasure? If the Commission decides to put the question on its order of the day right away, it is appropriate that I should report to you the discussion which took place in Committee No. 2 If, on the other hand, you decide to postpone the discussion on this rather ticklish question, I respectfully submit that my report be postponed until such time as the Commission may select.]

---

[64] In the transcripts, "current" is often a shorthand for "current-account," that is, payments for goods and services, as opposed to capital (capital-account) payments for financial assets or other investments.

Chairman: Thank you, Mr. Mossé, for a most excellent report.

The Chair recognizes the Judge Vinson of the United States delegation. [p. 2]

United States (Fred Vinson): Mr. Chairman, I move that this item be referred to Committee 2 for reconsideration.

Chairman: There is a motion that this item be referred to Committee 2 for reconsideration.

The Chair recognizes the delegate from Mexico.

Mexico (Antonio Espinosa de los Monteros): I second that motion.

Chairman: Does anyone care to comment on that?

If not, the Chair will assume that the Commission approves.

I will now call upon Dr. Hexner of Czechoslovakia to report on the committee work of Committee 3.

Ervin Hexner (Czechoslovakia, Reporter, Committee 3): The Committee on the Organization and Management of the Fund has held two meetings on July 4.[65] Although no general discussion in the formal sense took place, there became crystallized one or two fundamental principles. The most important was that what may be called economic statesmanship should prevail in the management. Though it was clear that consultation will be the principal means of cooperation, the Committee realized that the management of the Fund has to be prepared to deal with possible or potential conflicts of interest which ultimately may have to be voted upon. There was no doubt that in the management of the Fund large countries should have a stronger representation and certain privileges, and also no disagreement was expressed about the implementing of the organization to give adequate protection to small countries.

The discussion was based on the draft presented to the Committee. The Committee discussed Article VII, [Sections] 1 and 2 of the Joint Statement ["Structure of the Fund" and "Voting"].[66] It was an envisaged that there will be an agency called [the] Board of Governors, consisting of the representatives of all member countries. [p. 3]

Chairman: I am going to ask the reporters to refer clearly to the article and the page number and the section before discussion of any particular subject. It is a little easier to follow if the delegates have an

---

65 For the reports of Committee 3, see Document 103, pp. 118-119, and Document 113, pp. 125-126. The reports summarize deliberations in chapters 25 and 26.

66 In Document 32, pp. 42-43.

opportunity to turn to the appropriate section. So, if you don't mind, Dr. Hexner, I will do it for you. Dr. Hexner is now discussing the article on page 24—page 24 in the draft statement.

Ervin Hexner (Reporter, Committee 3): These representatives serve at the pleasure of their governments and can be recalled and replaced according to the discretion of the member countries. The same relates to their alternates, who may participate in the meetings.

All powers, as far as not specifically assigned to other agencies, are concentrated in the Board of Governors. It was agreed upon that this agency may delegate its power to other agencies within the Fund as far as such delegation is not excluded expressly by the statutes of the Fund. I am referring to [sub]section (b) of [Article] VII, [Section] 1 ["Structure of the Fund"].

A small change was made in two points. First, Alternative B was accepted because five countries made up the meeting of the governing board.[67] It means that the Board of Governors has to be called whenever requested by one or the other of them. Meetings of this Board shall be convened whenever requested by members representing one-quarter of the aggregate votes or by five member countries. [Second,] the Committee did not accept the provision of the draft that annual meetings shall not be held in the same country more than once in five years. Thus no limitation was placed in this regard on the management.

The Board of Governors will have a Chairman; however, no particular discussion took place about the powers of this presiding officer. It was assumed that the voting in the Board of Governors will be conducted according to quotas unless [p. 4] otherwise provided for. There was general agreement about those items which the Board of Governors cannot delegate to other agencies.

The discussion was not finished concerning the jurisdiction and election of agencies other than the Board of Governors and its Chairman. There was general agreement about the items which should be delegated to the Executive Committee. This is again [Article] VII, [Section] 1(b).

Now I am passing to [Article] VII, [Section] 2 ["Voting"], where there are two alternatives.[68] The opinions were not even crystallized on the point whether a fruitful discussion on the structure of the Executive Committee may take place before the quotas are agreed upon. It may

---

[67] That is, under Alternative B the Board of Governor would meet whenever requested by at least five member countries, while under Alternative A the threshold was one-quarter of all member countries or one-quarter of all votes.

[68] In Document 32, pp. 43-46.

perhaps be wise to indicate some difference of opinion concerning the structure and jurisdiction of the Executive Committee as contained in Alternatives A and B to VII-2.

[Sub]section (a): There was general agreement that the Executive Committee shall consist of two types of members: of representatives of large countries, which are designated by the large countries, and of representatives of smaller countries, elected by those smaller countries. No agreement was reached and no provision is contained in both alternatives [either alternative] whether the members of the Executive Committee serve at the pleasure of their governments or not. This makes some complications with the members of the Executive Committee who were elected because it isn't clear what happens—whether new elections should be ordered or not.

There was no agreement whether countries should be elected or persons [should instead be elected] to the Executive Committee.

No agreement was reached in regard to whether members of the Executive Committee should be necessarily members of the Board of Governors or whether outsiders should be invited to serve as members of the Executive Committee.

Concerning the [p. 5] Chairman of the Executive Committee, no agreement was reached as to whether Alternative A should be accepted, which provides the Managing Director should be automatically Chairman of the Executive Committee, or whether Alternative B should be accepted, that a Chairman with strong jurisdiction should be specifically elected, who may be the same person as the Chairman of the Board of Governors or may not be the same person.

No agreement was reached about the function and jurisdiction of the Executive Committee. Alternative A provides for a very extensive jurisdiction of the Executive Committee without particularly strong jurisdiction for its Chairman. Alternative B provides for a very strong Chairman of the Executive Committee with large functions, without particularly prominent functions assigned to the Executive Committee.

No agreement was reached whether the Executive Committee should be in permanent session according to Alternative A, or whether it should be called into session according to expediency.

I am emphasizing these disagreements, though they were not in reality disagreements because the discussion was not finished. I am emphasizing that in order to give something of a snapshot of how we finished the discussion yesterday. Generally, there was a visible trend to make [it] possible to establish a framework which could serve the purposes indicated in the Joint Statement.

Chairman: Thank you, Dr. Hexner.

I should like now to call upon Mr. Keilhau of Norway to report on the work of Committee No. 4.

Wilhelm Keilhau (Norway, Reporter, Committee 4): You will allow me to speak from here [rather than from a microphone] because my report is very brief.

Chairman: And your voice is very good.

Wilhelm Keilhau (Reporter, Committee 4):[69] [After the opening remarks of the Chairman at the first meeting of Committee 4 of Commission I on July 4, he announced that the material to be used by the Committee would not be available for distribution until the afternoon. Because of this, discussion was postponed until the regular meeting scheduled for July 5. There is nothing further to report.] [p. 6]

Chairman: The Secretariat regrets that the material was not ready.

You have heard the reports from the reporters of the four committees. There are several alternatives open to this Commission with respect to the discussion that may follow. We either can begin the discussion on the report of Committee 1 until there is no further discussion called for and then proceed to the work of Committee 2 and of 3 and of 4, or we might treat this first meeting rather in the nature of an opportunity to obtain a progress report on the part of the committees and to postpone any more definitive discussion until the next session of the Commission. The advantages of the second procedure for your consideration might be that the committees have not gotten into the work to a sufficient extent possible to warrant further discussion before this Commission. I think that the committees have done very well considering that it has been—that there have passed only two days. Certainly Committee 4 is not responsible for not having made any progress, since they did not have the necessary documents.

Those of you who have attended international conferences in the past—as I look around the room and note the names of some of the persons, I suppose there is nobody is here that hasn't attended at least one, and many of you have attended twenty or thirty to my recollection—not that I have been there, but I've read about it. You all appreciate that the first few days are naturally taken up with settling down, general discussions, some essential speech-making, getting some things off our chest that we have been waiting a long time to say, and in general getting prepared to get down to real business. I think probably the delegates have

[69] The transcript merely says, "(Report read)." We have reproduced the report from Document 127, p. 138. It summarizes deliberations in chapter 32.

arrived at the point where they are ready now to concentrate on the business in hand.

This conference is like all conferences to the extent that we can't stay indefinitely. [p. 7] It is unlike other conferences, most other conferences that I know of, in two respects. First, we have got to get out of here by the 20th [of July] because the hotel won't let us stay beyond that. That was the only understanding upon which we could get the use of this hotel. We tried our best to leave some flexible date beyond that because we were quite uncertain as to the extent of the progress to be made, but the hotel was adamant. Coupled with the beautiful scenery and the fact that there was no other hotel available, we had to accept their conditions. So we have to get out by the 20th. That means that the next couple of days can be cut out for regular business, plenary sessions, and one thing or another. We have already reached the 5th [of July], so there is actually a little less than two weeks that this conference can meet, and, as you know, the days pass awfully quickly. Moreover, we would hope that the delegates would have some opportunity—I speak now for Senator Tobey of New Hampshire[70]—to enjoy the country around here. That means that you have very little time.

This conference [also] differs in a second respect: namely, that we are trying to end up, if possible, with some definite formulation on two very different areas. You have the Fund. You will remember that in the letter of the President [Franklin D. Roosevelt]—in the invitation of the President—he stated that we would discuss the Fund at this conference and possibly the Bank.[71] Whether that possibility will become an actuality depends entirely upon the progress that will be made by this committee [Commission] in discussions of the Fund. You are fully cognizant of the fact that the Fund is a complicated subject. There are a lot of provisions. Each provision is pregnant with various interpretations and many provisions containing important material. The Bank likewise has many important provisions and many difficult provisions. If there is [p. 8] to be any hope of getting over the ground, we must constantly have in mind the shortness of the period and the difficulty of the subject. We must therefore restrain our very legitimate and natural desire to discuss in full by the Commission and by the committees and by the subcommittees each provision. But [i.e., because] if we do that, gentlemen, we are not going to get through with even a part of the Fund, let alone the whole or a part of the Bank.

---

70 Charles Tobey, an American delegate.

71 The text of the letter of invitation is in Document 6, pp. 3-5.

Therefore, in your consideration as to what to do before this Commission and in your procedure that is followed in the committees, we would strongly urge that you constantly have in mind the two factors which I have pointed out, and that means, gentlemen, that you try as much as possible to confine yourselves to the essential points delegated to the subcommittees. The clarification, as I understand from the reports, two of the committees have already done and it seems like a very excellent procedure, and if you will also forego, shall I say both the pleasure and possibly, in some mind, the desirability of discussing any one point too long, after it is very evident that you have made your point clear, I think that certainly in the committees and subcommittees, that is enough. You will have another opportunity at the Commission, when everybody will appreciate the amount of business and will curtail the length of the talks, and will avoid insofar as possible repetition.

I am going to set a good example and I am going to stop talking on that point now, and ask for views of the Commission whether or not it would be desirable, in the light of what I have said, to forego any further discussion on the reports of the committees and wait until the next Commission meeting, at which time the committees will have made more comprehensive and more definite progress and members of the Commission would have an opportunity to examine more carefully the findings of the committees. [p. 9] Do I hear any comment?

United Kingdom (John Maynard Keynes): Mr. Chairman, I have one or two modest suggestions to make further the objectives which you been putting before us. First, I suggest the reporters of each committee circulate their reports in writing, and that there should be generally just enough time for delegates to have seen those reports before they are discussed at the Commission.

Chairman: Lord Keynes has suggested that the report circulate their written reports with sufficient time prior to the Commission meetings so that the members will have an opportunity to study them and be prepared to express such views as they wish to prior to coming to the meeting.

Unidentified: I second that motion.

Chairman: All those who approve, say "aye."

Delegates: Aye.

Chairman: And so be it. And so from now on, Mr. Secretary, will you make certain that the various reporters circulate the reports. I know that is an additional burden on the reporters, but I am sure that under the circumstances, they will gladly undertake it.

United Kingdom (John Maynard Keynes): After that is adopted, there is a further reason for following your advice that the next meeting of the Commission is, for the moment, deferred. When the time for that meeting comes, we shall have before us, I hope, in writing, the reports we have already received today, together with the results of perhaps one or two meetings by the several committees. That would mean that if they meet this evening and tomorrow morning, we could have reports by tomorrow evening of what they have done up to the end of tomorrow morning, to be considered by the Commission on the following day. Meanwhile, the committees could have met again tomorrow afternoon without our attempting to have reports of that before the Commission on the [p. 10] following day, if I make myself clear.

Chairman: If I understand you correctly, you are suggesting that the committees meet this afternoon and will meet tomorrow morning; and that there will be in the hands of the various delegates the written reports of those two meetings, in addition to the reports which have been presented this morning; and that the delegates will then be in a position to discuss those reports at the meeting of the Commission, which would take place the following morning. Do I understand you correctly?

United Kingdom (John Maynard Keynes): That is right, and that need not interfere with the committees meeting again tomorrow afternoon to make further progress, but no attempt need be made to bring the results of that meeting before the Commission on the following day.

Chairman: Before considering that, there is just one point you might wish to also evaluate. We thought that we might leave the question of the time of the next meeting of the Commission flexible and defer it until we see the amount of progress. Now, it looks very likely that the amount of progress that will have been made by the day after tomorrow—that is, two days after tomorrow—

United Kingdom (John Maynard Keynes): Day after tomorrow.

Chairman: That would make Saturday morning the next meeting of the Commission.

United Kingdom (John Maynard Keynes): Friday morning.

Chairman: There probably will be enough work done by the committees to justify the meeting on Friday morning. But I am wondering whether it might not be preferable to leave that decision to the Chair after he has made inquiries with respect to the amount of progress made in the committees. You must realize that when the committees meet, the Commission does not. It is not a question of merely whether the committee shall meet. Every time the Commission meets, the [p. 11] committees do less work, so it might be that progress has not been adequate to justify a Commission meeting, so if the Commission will kindly grant that share of the authority to determine whether the meeting shall be Friday or Saturday morning, I think it might be helpful, particularly when taken together with one other fact. There have been a number of suggestions made which I was going to set before you—not to have the committees meet twice a day, but to have them meet for a longer period and once a day. That would enable the various delegations to discuss the various matters among themselves, and also have an opportunity for the subcommittees to do their work. It was thought that there would be more progress made in the committees if they met once a day and if the periods were longer.

Now, with that before you, I should like to hear an expression of views.

United Kingdom (John Maynard Keynes): Mr. Chairman, I doubt the advisability of the one meeting a day, just at first. It seems to me to have little short meetings of an hour and a half twice a day would leave enough time for other groups, and some progress would then be made. If there is only one meeting a day, [p. 1 (12)][72] we shall not get the prospectus of the committees. I would submit that for the time being we should drive the committees very hard indeed.

Chairman: We would be driving them harder to meet once a day than twice. I will be glad to hear any suggestions.

Norway ([Wilhelm Keilhau?]): It has happened in three of the committees where I have had the pleasure to be present that discussions have had to be interrupted at very fatal moments just because the room should be taken by another committee. It has made the discussions rather nervous because we knew that in that meeting we [would] have to go out of the room at a definite time. If two committees could meet before lunch and two after lunch, that would make it easier for smaller delegations.

Chairman: We are interested in merely obtaining better results. I am going to call on one other delegate.

Ecuador: I would suggest that we have meetings from 3:00 to 7:00 in the afternoon—Committee 1 and Committee 2, two hours each.

Chairman: The view has been expressed that it would be [p. 2 (13)] desirable to have meetings in the afternoon. Unless there is any objection, the Chairman is going to decide.

---

[72] Here one typescript ends and we pick up from another, which appears near the end of the same bound volume of the copy of the typescripts at the U.S. Treasury Library, instead of following directly after the first typescript.

There will be one meeting in the morning and the delegates will have an opportunity to discuss outside of the meeting what might be more preferable procedure. Tomorrow there will be one meeting in the morning, and we hope it will last as long as the delegates can sit it—stand it.

Is there any other business before this Commission?

Belgium ([Camille Gutt]): I would like to know whether there will be tomorrow one meeting of the four committees at the same time. That would be very difficult.

Chairman: It is the intention to stagger two meetings, as before. That raises an interesting question. I had hoped that the meetings would last long, but how we can stagger them and have them last long, too, is a question. There will be a bulletin posted in the usual place in the dining room indicating the time and place of the meeting. We may modify it later. The four committees will meet at the staggered hours as have been indicated yesterday. Tonight at dinner there will be a mimeographed sheet indicating the hours at which their committees will meet tomorrow morning.

United States: May I ask the reconsideration of the decision made by the Chairman in respect of the four meetings being held tomorrow morning? [p. 3 (14)]

Chairman: Reconsideration has been asked of the decision to hold four meetings in the morning. Does the delegate have some other suggestion?

United States: Two meetings in the morning and two in the afternoon.

Chairman: I detect acquiescence and general approval of that suggestion, and the Chair will alter his previous statement. There will be two meetings in the morning and two in the afternoon. And which [ones] will be in the morning and [which in the] afternoon, I hope you will leave to the Chair and Secretariat, and they will be posted.

(2:45 p.m.)

4

Commission I
International Monetary Fund
Third meeting: transcript
July 10, 1944, 11:30 a.m.[73]

Appointment of Drafting Committee • Foreign exchange balances accumulated in wartime • Exchange controls • Voting on uniform changes in par values of currencies • Obligation of members to furnish information to the IMF • Executive Directors and alternates • Depositories

Commission chairman Harry Dexter White opens with the optimistic wish that the Commission will finish its work after the next (fourth) meeting; it would actually hold nine meetings. He then appoints a Drafting Committee to handle all matters on which the Commission has reached agreement, but where the language may need changes to be conform to accepted standards for international agreements.

Turning to the draft IMF agreement, India's A.D. Shroff, an industrialist, proposes to include among the purposes of the IMF the facilitation of multilateral settlement of foreign exchange accumulated during the war. Although posed as a general goal, India's proposal originates from its particular circumstances. The United Kingdom was paying India in pounds sterling for war materiel, but because of wartime exchange controls, the funds were only readily usable to buy goods from the "sterling area"—the countries that used the pound sterling as their anchor currency. India wants assurance that after the war, the United Kingdom will loosen exchange controls, allowing India to use its sterling balances to buy goods from outside the sterling area. The United Kingdom, United States, and France all oppose India's proposal as ill suited for the IMF because it is a matter for bilateral rather than multilateral negotiation. The proposal fails. Edward Bernstein makes his first appearance in the transcripts. Bernstein was Assistant Director of Monetary Research at the U.S. Treasury and executive secretary of the American delegation. He was the American delegate most deeply involved with the details of drafting the IMF agreement, and as such was the most important person for the Bretton Woods conference other than White

---

[73] Summarized in Document 267, pp. 432-433.

and Keynes. He had an unmatched understanding of the technical details of the agreement.

The Commission then refers back to committee some proposals on the definition of exchange controls and uniform changes in par values of currencies (a uniform devaluation or revaluation against gold). After that, it debates what economic data member countries should be obligated to provide to the IMF. The USSR, in accord with its longstanding practice under the Communist rule of revealing little economic data, wishes to minimize the data members must divulge. To meet this and other concerns, the Commission refers the matter back to committee.

The next topic is whether for Executive Directors who represent more than one country, the director himself or the group of countries he represents should choose his alternate. The Commission decides that the director shall choose his alternate.

Finally, the Commission discusses the extent to which the IMF agreement should specify where the IMF may hold its assets. After some delegates criticize the current proposal as too rigid, the chairman proposes appointing an ad hoc committee to explore the issue in more detail.

Chairman (Harry Dexter White, United States): The meeting will please come to order.

You all have before you the reports of the four committees, and in addition to the reports of the four committees the Secretariat has prepared a summary of the status of the committee assignments.[74] If you gentlemen will please pick that particular sheet up and place it before you, I should like to call your attention to certain matters. It is hoped that we will be able to finish the work of this Commission at the next meeting. Owing to the fact that some of the matters that will come before you have not yet been completed, we propose to have the next meeting of the Commission on Thursday morning [July 13]. The committees of this Commission will have the work completed by Wednesday and will report to the commission the following day, which is on Thursday. You will find that in the last column of the sheet before you, headed "No Action, or Decision Deferred." All the items that are listed under the column are matters for the committees and their subcommittees to complete in time to report to this Commission on Thursday. In column 1, you will find listed the provisions which have already been acted upon and which the language has been accepted. The next step would be to refer to those listed in that first column to a Drafting Committee to be appointed by the Commission, if that be the will of the Commission. The Chair would like

[74] "Commission I: Status of Committee Assignments," Document 240 (202), pp. 352-360.

permission of the Commission to appoint a Drafting Committee who will report back to this Commission at our next meeting. [p. 2]

New Zealand: I should like to move according to suggestion.

Chairman: It has been moved and seconded that a Drafting Committee be appointed by the Chair and report to this Commission. Any objection?

We will assume that that is the will of the Commission. I will announce the Drafting Committee immediately after this meeting. Unless there are objections, I propose to refer to that Drafting Committee all of the provisions which are listed in the first column. The first column, you will remember, are provisions which the various committees have discussed and accepted the language thereof. Do I hear any objection to referring to the Drafting Committee all of the provisions which are listed in the first column?

Since there is no objection, we will so order it.

With respect to the items in the second column, headed "Referred to Drafting or Other Subcommittees," we are not ready to discuss them at this meeting of the Commission. The items listed in that column will therefore be delayed for consideration at this Commission meeting until next meeting. The committees will complete their work on the items in that column by Wednesday and they will report on Thursday. That applies to the fourth column, as I have said before.

We then have left the provisions which are listed under the third column, which have been referred to the Commission without decision. Those provisions will now be placed before this Commission for discussion. The first ones on the list are Alternatives G and H, Section 6 of Article I ["Purpose and Policies of the Fund"]. If you will turn to Article I, Section 6, Alternatives G and H, you [p. 3] will find the matter that is open for discussion now. The pages in the earlier discussion are 1c and 1d.[75]

India ([A.D. Shroff]): I now find that the Commission is to take into consideration some provisions of Section 6. I would like to have your

[75] For Alternative G (in Document 32, p. 24), see the main text a few paragraphs below. Alternative H (Document 109, p. 122), offered by Egypt, proposed to add the words "To promote the multilateral settlement of foreign credit balances accumulated during the war." Alternative K (Document 216, p. 278), mentioned just below and offered by India, proposed to add the words "To facilitate the multilateral settlement of a reasonable potion of the foreign credit balances accumulated amongst the member countries during the war to as to promote the purposes referred to in Subdivision 2, without placing undue strain on the resources of the Fund."

ruling on one point, Mr. Chairman: on Article I, Section 2,[76] the Indian delegation has reserved its right to raise the question to this Commission, and I would like to know what is exactly the scope of the work of this Commission [and?] when I will be permitted to raise this point.

Chairman: The delegate from India asks what will be the procedure if Section 2 of Article I is raised in the next Commission meeting. The view of our procedure is that any delegate will be free to discuss any of the measures which are reported back to the Commission by the Drafting Committee. We are merely attempting to facilitate the work and let the Drafting Committee handle the work and let it be placed before this Commission, and then any delegate will be free to discuss that particular provision and take any position that he sees fit. Alternative G, which you presumably have before you, reads, ["To promote and facilitate the settlement of abnormal indebtedness arising out of the war."] That alternative is now before the Commission for discussion.

India ([A.D. Shroff]): Mr. Chairman, at the outset I should like to have your ruling on one matter which would probably facilitate discussion and proposal of this item. In Committee 1 of Commission I, we discussed on two separate occasions Alternatives G and H.[77] As the result of these discussions, the Indian delegation has tabled Alternative K, which has not yet been discussed by Committee 1. I suggest, sir, for your consideration [that] Alternatives G, H, and K may all be [p. 4] discussed together.

Chairman: The speaker has the permission of the Chair to consider in his discussion Alternatives G, H, and K in view of the fact that they are so closely interrelated.

India ([A.D. Shroff]):[78] With this ruling, I will now place before Commission I Alternative A, tabled by our delegation, which reads as follows:

["The purposes of the International Monetary Fund are:

"1. To promote international monetary co-operation by providing permanent machinery for consultation on international monetary problems.

---

[76] Referred to as "Subdivision (ii)" in the index to the conference proceedings, p. 1643. The subdivisions of Article I ("Purposes") had Arabic numbers in the preliminary draft, but the final agreement replaced them with lower-case Roman numerals. "Section 2," then, refers to what was later called subdivision (ii).

[77] See the second and third meetings of Committee 1, in chapters 12 and 13.

[78] This speech was also published with minor changes as Press Release No. 25, Document 259, pp. 1171-1173.

"2. To facilitate the expansion and balanced growth of international trade and to contribute thereby to the promotion and maintenance of high levels of employment and real income, as a primary objective of economic policy.

"3. To give confidence to member countries by making the Fund's resources available to them under adequate safeguards, thus giving them time to correct maladjustments in their balance of payments without resort to measures destructive of national or international prosperity.

"4. To promote exchange stability, to maintain orderly exchange arrangements among member countries, and to avoid competitive exchange depreciation.

"5. To assist in the establishment of a multilateral system of payments in respect of current transactions between members and in the elimination of foreign exchange restrictions which hamper the growth of world trade.

"6. In accordance with the above, to shorten the periods and lessen the degree of disequilibrium in the international balances of payments of members.

"The Fund shall be guided in all its decisions by the purposes set forth above."]

At the time we discussed [Alternatives] G and H in Committee 1, two principal objections were raised. The delegate from the United States opposed either of these alternatives on the ground that inclusion of this item will overload the Fund. From the very start when we placed our alternative for consideration before this conference, we were absolutely clear in our minds, and when I spoke at one of the meetings of the Committee 1, I endeavored to clear up that misunderstanding that we never intended the International Monetary Fund, when it was set up, to take over straightaway in one lump sum the entire accumulated balances during the war. In explaining particularly the situation of India, I also made it clear that considering the very close ties between the United Kingdom and India, it is more than likely that a very large proportion of the sterling balances we have accumulated in London will over a period of years be used in our buying goods of both categories—consumer and capital goods—from the United Kingdom.

At the same time, I pointed out that if we were going to be realists, we must consider the actual situation in the United Kingdom today and in the postwar period. I refer, for instance, to the unfortunate loss of very valuable investments of the United Kingdom, and I may add today that the necessity [exists] for rehabilitation of some of the industries in the United Kingdom, the necessity of at least reducing some of the tremendous [p. 5] privations which are being borne by the population of the United Kingdom, during the last four and one-half years. All these factors will tend to reduce the capacity of the United Kingdom to give us goods which we badly want.

That being so, our position is this: that the underlined [words "as a primary objective of economic policy" should be adopted?] in clause [Section] 2—and I repeat that we attach very great importance to the definition of the primary objective. Now, [regarding] the maintenance of a high level of employment and income—attaching [the] importance that we do in this primary objective, taking into consideration [the in]ability of the United Kingdom at least for a fairly long period from now onwards to meet our requirement of capital goods—I submit to this conference that if the country is situated as we are, is enthusiastic in international collaboration, then some means has to be devised by which multilateral activity [i.e., clearing, in the sense of convertibility] would be given at least to a certain proportion of the large balances we have accumulated in London. I understand the argument that the International Monetary Fund can be unduly overloaded if this item was included among the purposes of the Fund. We are met here at the instance of the sponsors of this conference to tackle a very big problem. I ask you to be realistic enough in undertaking to tackle this problem if you are going to permit billions of accumulated balances abroad. As I said in Committee 1, you are going to stack up simultaneous with the establishment of the Fund a sort of rival fund [i.e., the World Bank], and I asked whether it would be conducive to the maintenance of the main objectives of the Fund if you complete [i.e., achieve] the loss of large balances abroad.

My answer [p. 6] to the contention of the USA delegation [is]: I say you are starting to make a dreadful mistake, yet you are not having [the] resources of [for] battling this problem adequately. It appears to me you are just sending out a jellyfish to tackle a whale if your argument is that International Monetary Fund is not adequately equipped to deal with this problem in its totality. What we ask for is the settlement of a reasonable portion. If this Commission is prepared to accept the principle of our amendment, then I see no reason in involving a concrete formula by which the purposes set out in our amendment could be easily matched. The purposes set out in our amendment are two: to secure multilateral activity for a visible portion of our balances and, secondly, that that proportion which could be put in a formula could be so devised as not to place undue strain on the resources of the Fund.

I think, sir, talking amongst friends, it may well be to speak frankly about this question. We haven't disguised from the very outset a very strong feeling in our country on this question. I am sure the sponsors of this conference are seeking collaboration from all countries of the world known as United and Associated Nations. It may be unfortunate that situated as we are politically, perhaps the "big guns" in the conference may not attach that great importance to a country like India. But I am bound to point out this, if you are prepared to ignore a country of the size of India, 400 million population with natural resources in my judgment thought not incomparable to the natural resources of some of the biggest powers on this Earth, you do not expect that contribution to the strengthening of the resources of the Fund which you will otherwise get. [p. 7]

Suppose you don't accept our position. You are placing us in a situation which I compare to the position of a man with a $1 million balance in the bank but not enough sufficient cash to pay his taxi fare. That is the position you put us in, if you consider closely the objectives of this plan. You want to facilitate the expansion and balance of international trade. You, incidentally, want to help build up a higher level of employment and income throughout the world as a whole. Mr. Morgenthau, in his very fine opening address, said poverty is a menace wherever it is found in the country.[79] Do you expect to fulfill the main objectives of this Fund if you allow large countries to be festered with this sort of poverty? I would like this Commission to face this question in a very realistic spirit. I am sure everybody here needs collaboration of everybody else, but if that collaboration has to be obtained unrealistically, you will make it impossible for all countries in the world to be associated with you. I beg of you, Commission, to deal very dispassionately—to deal with the problem I put before you. Thank you very much.

Chairman: Does anyone wish the floor to continue discussion on this matter?

United States (Edward Bernstein): We are all cognizant of the importance of the problem presented by the delegate of India. We are confident that the problem he is presenting can be settled. We doubt the advisability of attempting to settle this problem through the Fund. We must be sure that the success of the International Monetary Fund is not made more difficult by burdening it with facts which it cannot undertake [to act upon?] and for which it is not particularly well suited. It was

[79] Document 40, p. 81. Henry Morgenthau, Jr., Secretary of the U.S. Department of the Treasury, was the president of the Bretton Woods conference. His precise words were, "Poverty, wherever it exists, is menacing to us all and undermines the well-being of each of us."

recognition [p. 8] of this fundamental principle that led the technical experts who have participated in the discussions to recommend that the Fund should not be used for the purposes of relief for reconstruction or for meeting indebtedness arising out of the war. The Fund can contribute most effectively to the solution of postwar monetary and exchange problems if it confines itself to the specialized task for which it is designed.

While the Fund cannot deal directly with indebtedness arising out of a war, we are confident that its operations will facilitate the development ordinarily of inviolable and stable exchange rates free from exchange restrictions that hamper world trade. Wartime indebtedness can be amicably settled by the countries directly concerned. The Fund can do a good deal in this way. It is all the Fund can be sure to do. [To] ask it to do more is to impose upon the Fund the necessity of doing too little in meeting the task for which is particularly suited. The U.S. delegation hopes that the Alternatives [G, H, and K] will not be pressed, and that the delegate from India will seek the other way of direct settlement of the problem of abnormal war balances.

United Kingdom (John Maynard Keynes):[80] Mr. Chairman, since the United Kingdom is the only country here represented which has incurred large-scale war debt to our allies and associates, also here present, these three alternative amendments must be assumed, as indeed Mr. Shroff made clear, to relate primarily to her. Mr. Chairman, the various members of this alliance have suffered in mind, body and estate through the exhaustion of war, through which we are differing in kind and degree. These sacrifices cannot be weighed one against the other. Those [p. 9] of us who are most directly threatened and were nevertheless able to remain in the fight, such as the USSR and the United Kingdom, have fought this war on the principle of unlimited liability and with a more reckless disregard to economic consequences. Others are more fortunately placed. We do not need information in the larger fields of human affairs. Nothing could be less prudent than hesitation or careful counting of the cost. But as a result, there has been inevitably no equality of financial sacrifice.

In respect to overseas assets, the end of the war will find the United Kingdom greatly impoverished and other of the United Nations considerably enriched at our expense. We make no complaint to this provided that the resulting situation is accepted for what it is. On the

---

80 This speech was also published with minor changes as Press Release No. 24, Document 258, pp. 1169-1170.

contrary, we are grateful to those allies, particularly to our [Indian][81] friends, who put their resources at our disposal without stint, and themselves suffered from privation as result. Our efforts would have been gravely, perhaps critically, embarrassed if they had held back from helping us so wholeheartedly and on so great a scale. We will appreciate the moderate, friendly and realistic statement to the problem which Mr. Shroff has put before you today. Nevertheless, the settlement of these debts must be, in our clear and settled judgment, a matter between those directly concerned. When the end is reached and we can see our way into the daylight, we will take it up without any delay to settle honorably what was honorably and generously given. But we do not intend to ask assistance in this matter from the International Monetary Fund beyond the fact, as Mr. Bernstein has just pointed out, that the existence of the Fund and the general assistance it will give to stability, and expansion of trade may be expected to improve indirectly our [p. 10] ability to meet other obligations. We concur entirely with the view that has just been expressed by Mr. Bernstein on behalf of the American delegation that the Fund is not intended to deal directly with war indebtedness.

Now, since we do not intend either to ask for or to avail ourselves of any special treatment from the Fund, it appears to the United Kingdom delegation that this amendment could be of no practical effect, and it is therefore better to discard it if misunderstanding is to be avoided about the role which the Fund can be expected to play.

Chairman: Are there any other delegates who wish to discuss this provision?

France ([André Istel]):[82] It [my comment] is very short, Mr. Chairman, and I will attempt to speak from here [rather than go to a microphone]. The delegate from France [Pierre Mendès-France] listened with great interest to the remarkable speech of the Indian delegate, but he wishes to support entirely the position taken by the United States and the United Kingdom. Although France and other occupied countries have accumulated huge war balances against Germany, they do not request that the Fund should be concerned with these because they consider that it is not the Fund's business. The very argument given by the Indian delegate as to the time which will take for India to obtain goods against their blocked balances shows that the transaction completed is not of a current

[81] The typescript says "English," which the context suggests is an error by the speaker or the stenographer. The printed version (see the preceding footnote) says "Indian."

[82] This speech was also published with minor changes as Press Release No. 26, Document 260, pp. 1173-1174.

nature, and also not in conformity with the purpose of the Fund. We certainly do not ignore India. But we consider that the question raised by the Indian delegate should not be addressed the Fund, but to some other organization. [p. 11]

Chairman: The delegate from the French Comité has stated his reasons for supporting the views as expressed by the delegates of the United States and the United Kingdom. Is there any other delegate who wishes to be heard on this amendment?

If not, it appears to be the will of this Commission that the amendments [Alternatives] G, H, and K be not accepted, and unless there is an objection to that ruling, the Secretary will please know that G, H, and K have not been accepted by the Commission.

We then turn to the next item, which is Alternatives B and C, Article II, Section 3 ["Time and Place of Payment"]. You will find it on pages 2a and 4a of the draft.[83] I should like to call upon Mr. Varvaressos to briefly explain to the Commission the matter.

[Kyriakos Varvaressos] (Greece, Reporter, Committee 1): Mr. Chairman, I think that all three alternatives on page 2a and 4a have been really referred to the Ad Hoc Committee [on the Problems of Liberated Areas] because they referred to liberated countries, and I think that it might be more advisable for this Commission to wait up until the time before discussion [i.e., to wait until the committee has discussed the alternatives].

Chairman: The view has been discussed that the material appropriately belongs in the discussion of the Ad Hoc Committee. Inasmuch as the Committee on Liberated Areas is, I understand, not prepared to render this report to the Commission at this time, and unless there is any objection, we will pass to the next point.

The next item is on the reverse side of the first page of Section 4 ["Exchange Controls on Current Payments"], under Article IX ["Obligations of Member Countries"], on page 40 of your draft.[84] I should like to ask Mr. Varvaressos to explain that amendment.

[Kyriakos Varvaressos] (Reporter, Committee 1): I have put in my report[85] a few words about this. On page 6 of my second report I have put some words about this opinion of the Committee. During the

---

[83] In Document 32, pp. 25-27. Page 2a is Alternative B to Article II, Section 1, "Quotas."

[84] In Document 32, p. 55.

[85] Document 238, pp. 335-345. The report summarizes deliberations in chapters 13, 14, and 15.

discussion of this section, it has been recognized [p. 12] that a distinction must be made between exchange controls and exchange restrictions. However, as the discussion developed, some uncertainty [arose] as to the character of the restrictions which member countries obligate themselves to eliminate under this section, [so] the Committee decided to request Commission I to clarify the matter and to postpone further consideration of that until Committee 2 also discussed the question. Now, there was a feeling of this Committee that also the subject was connected with some subjects which have been assigned to Committee 2, and I think that this decision has two intentions. First, to postpone any definite decision before something has been considered by Committee 2, and then to ask this Commission for clarification about the nature of the restrictions to which the countries are asked to abolish.

Chairman: The Reporter has indicated that the subject matter in this amendment is related to the subject matter of another committee. The Chair suggests the most efficacious way of handling that would be to appoint an ad hoc committee to include members of Committees 1 and 2 and have that ad hoc committee report directly to this Commission. Unless there is an objection, that will be done.

The next item is Section 5 ["Uniform Changes in Par Value"], Article IV ["Par Values of Member Currencies"], and the page [is] no. 18 of your draft.[86]

[Robert Mossé] (France, [Reporter, Committee 2]): The issue was about the way in which it should be voted [i.e., the way in which voting should be made] on this question. There are three main elements [options] which may be taken into consideration for voting. One is to vote by countries, each country with one vote. The second [p. 13] possibility is to vote according to the voting power: that means according to the quotas. And a third factor [option] is to give more influence to the countries having [at least] 10 percent of their [i.e., the total] quota. I think that one way to handle this matter might be to refer it to Committee 3, which deals with voting matters. This has been included in my report.[87]

Chairman: The recommendation is that this provision be referred back to Committee 3.

[Robert Mossé[88]] ([Reporter, Committee 2]): This was dealt with in Committee 2, and the suggestion made by the Reporter was that

---

[86] In Document 32, p. 38.

[87] The report is Document 234, pp. 309-325. It summarizes deliberations in chapters 19, 20, 21, and 22.

[88] Identified in the typescript only as "Mr. M."

Committee 3 deal with other voting arrangements. This [i.e., they?] might give consideration to this particular voting question, but it is not referred back to them. It came from Committee 2, and his suggestion is it might be given to Committee 3.

Chairman: [The Chair proposes] an ad hoc committee composed of members of Committees 2 and 3 to which this will be referred, and they will report back to the next Commission meeting. Any objection?

The next item is at the top of page 6,[89] Article III ["Transactions with the Fund"], Section 11 ["Furnishing Information"], and pages 14c, 14d and 14e.[90] The Chair will call upon the Reporter from Committee 3, Dr. Hexner.

[Ervin Hexner] (Czechoslovakia, Reporter, Committee 3): Mr. Chairman, Committee 3 considered this provision only according to Alternative C. This is Document 182 and Alternative D, because Alternative E was replaced by Alternative C. That's why Alternatives C and D were considered only. The report on [of the] Special Committee on Furnishing Information of the Agenda Committee condensed the discussion on this point.[91] No agreement was reached because the member countries introducing Alternative D [were] sharply opposed [p. 14] to the extent of the meaning of the information as enumerated in items 1 to 12 in Alternative C. That is why Committee 3 referred this item for decision to Commission I.

Chairman: The amendment is now before the Commission for discussion. Does any delegate wish to speak?

USSR [Mrs. L. Gouseva?]: Mr. Chairman, we don't object against the general principle contained in the proposition of the U.S. delegation. But it seems to us that it would be unreasonable to endeavor to enumerate [in] the status [statutes] of the International Monetary Fund a detailed list of data which may be necessary for carrying out its preparations. Some of the data inserted in the list—old Alternative C—will concern only some countries. One part of this information would be probably impossible to furnish [for] the other countries because they don't possess some of the statistical data required in this list. In the opinion of the Soviet delegation, the obligatory information to be furnished to the Fund should be limited to [the] indispensable minimum

[89] Page 6 in the original printing of Document 240 (202), in p. 357 of the conference proceedings.

[90] In Document 32, p. 36; Document 182, pp. 224-225; and Document 203, p. 267.

[91] Document 129, pp. 141-143, a pre-conference document dated June 28, 1944.

of data absolutely necessary to the Fund for carrying out its operations resulting from the provisions of the Fund.

The Soviet delegation proposes therefore to reduce the obligatory information which the member countries should furnish the Fund to the following data: (1) Gold holdings of the central bank and Treasury. [(2) Gold convertible exchange holdings of the central bank and Treasury. (3) Movement of capital. (4) Foreign trade data. (5) Other items of the balance of payments. (6) Rates of exchange and their changes.] Further information which the Fund may need shall be obtained by arrangement between the Fund and the respective member countries. That is the proposal of the Soviet delegation.

Chairman: The view of the Soviet delegation is that they are in sympathy with the necessity for obtaining information, but they feel that many countries do not have the statistical material which would enable them to supply [p. 15] the data which is specified in Alternative C. Therefore, they believe that the most feasible way would be to require a minimum of essential data. They believe that that minimum of essential data is included in their proposed Alternative D. For your convenience, we will call attention to the fact that the first two items which are in Alternative C and which are not in Alternative B, [are] nos. 3 and 4 ["Production of gold" and "Gold exports and imports according to countries of destination and origin"]. And there are some other items on the second page. The amendment is before you for discussion.

United States (August Maffry): Mr. Chairman, the proposal in Alternative C is put forward first on general grounds and second on specific grounds. First, with regard to the general basis of this proposal, it goes without saying that in the view of the U.S. delegation, the Fund must be possessed of adequate statistical and other information for carrying out its operations. This would seem obvious from the fact that the Fund will have little or no knowledge of individual transactions, and that it must depend therefore very largely upon its knowledge of trends and tendencies to the international transactions of member countries. Now, with regard to the specific grounds, I believe that every item in the enumeration in Alternative C, with one possible exception, is directly related to a specific provision of the draft agreement. If the Chair wishes, I shall be glad to identify the specific provisions of the draft agreement [Document 32] to which each of these enumerated items directly relate.

Chairman: I think it would be helpful to the Commission if you indicated the numbers of those items which are included in draft suggestion [i.e., Alternative] C and not in D, or vice versa. [p. 16]

United States (August Maffry): I think it would save time if I went down the list. I don't have the items that way. Items 1 and 2, in Alternative C, [are] believed to [be] require[d] under the specific provisions of Article III, Section 7 ["Acquisition by Members of the Currencies of Other Members"], dealing with the repurchase of member countries' currencies, and to be related also to the provision of additional Article XII, Section 2 ["Definitions"].

Chairman: I understand that the point you are making is that the execution of certain provisions in the suggested draft [agreement] required information which is listed in [items] 1 and 2.

United States (August Maffry): That is correct.

Chairman: And without such information it would not be possible to execute those provisions.

United States (August Maffry): This list is not theoretical list, but is based upon specific provisions of the draft agreement which cannot be carried out by the Fund in the absence of such information. I passed over for a moment item 3, the production of gold, included in the shorter list. Items 4, 5, 6 and 7, dealing with gold movement, responsibilities and imports of merchandise, balance of payments data, and international investment data, would seem to be required under the Agreement as a whole, but it would be required especially under the terms of Article III, Sections 2 ["Conditions upon which Any Member May Purchase Currencies of Other Members"] and 6, ["Multilateral International Clearing"] and Article V ["Capital Transactions"]. I must pause to say that [words perhaps not recorded].

Chairman: Might the Chair request Mr. Maffry to restrict his comments to those points which are not common to both alternatives? Would you agree that items 4 and 5 of the Soviet proposal, on foreign trade data or other items of international balances, would not include many of the items you suggest? If it were possible to really confine your comments to those items [p. 17] which are not common to the draft [agreement], it might save some time.

United States (August Maffry): Article VII—[or rather,] item 7, dealing with international investment data, is not, I believe, included in the shorter list by the USSR delegation, but such information, where available, would seem to be extremely important to the Fund in tracing movements of capital between member countries. Items 8 and 9, which are also omitted on the shorter list, can be shown to be required under the terms of Article IV ["Par Values of Member Currencies"], which sets forth the circumstances under which the Fund may object or may not object to a proposed change in par values. Item 10 is not in controversy.

Item 11 seems to be required clearly under the provisions of Article IX, Section 4 ["Exchange Controls on Current Payments,"] of the draft agreement, dealing with permissible exchange controls, as well as to the provisions of Article X, Section 2 ["Nature of Transitional Period"], dealing with exchange controls during the transition period. Item 12, dealing with delays in transfers, would seem to be required under the terms of Article V, Section 2 ["Limitations on Controls of Capital Movements"], which provides that there shall not be undue delays in the commitments arising from control restrictions on capital transfers.

Mr. Chairman, I would submit further that the position of countries whose statistical services are less well developed than those of others are fully safeguarded in the preamble to Alternative C, which says that the Fund shall take into consideration the ability to furnish the data asked for. Under this safeguarding clause, a country may plead inability to supply. With regard to production of gold, it is perhaps true that information on gold production cannot be directly related to any specific agreement of the draft agreement unless it be [related] to par values to which the [p. 18] production of gold is directed. It is also true that if a member furnishes information on gold movements, gold production may be inferred, although with a considerable margin of errors in some cases. This item should be included on the list because it would seem to be very useful to the Fund and to have direct relation to gold.

Chairman: The view of the American delegate is that the information listed in Alternative C is either essential to the carrying out of the various provisions or is desirable in order for intelligent decisions to be made by the Executive Committee. He also pointed out that there is a clause in the preamble of the first paragraph of the Alternative C amendment which takes out those countries which do not have or cannot have the statistical data available. Are there any other views?

United Kingdom (John Maynard Keynes): The United Kingdom delegation very much hopes that Alternative C, advocated by the U.S. delegation, will be adopted. We, like you, are great believers in the beneficent influence of knowledge on these problems. There is hardly any greater service the Fund can do than provide up-to-date barometers of the monetary problems of the world. We hope that the very greatest importance will be given to the statistical branch of the Fund and that they will be encouraged to make reports [for] the instruction and benefit of all of us on a scale that has never been possible heretofore. At the same time, we are well aware that [a] full degree of completeness would only be approached. That is set forth quite clearly in the preamble to the alternative, where, Mr. Maffry [p. 19] has explained, every latitude [is] allowed countries not in a position to provide it for themselves.

I would therefore argue with the delegation of the USSR that they should not—I will not say stand in the way, but they will not minimize the importance of the statistical knowledge in this connection. In fact, as Mr. Maffry has explained, this information differs very little except in details of complexity from the information in the previous lists, and I suppose that unless they put into effect the preamble of [Article III,] Section 11 ["Furnishing Information"]—that seems to me to be valuable because that seems to put in the list what we are aiming at. I do not believe that if the USSR is unable to provide more than what is set forth in that alternative that anything in Alternative C would stand in their way.

It would be rather unfortunate if this bare list was put out to the world as something we are aiming at. We must have something full in detail, although we must be well aware that [in] the early years [we] will not [with] the best will [in] the world fully attain [it].

Chairman: Is there anyone that hasn't been able to hear that comment?

USSR ([Aleksei Smirnov]): Mr. Chairman, the delegation of the USSR has already said what are the reasons for inserting in the list of information all of these data which are enumerated in Alternative C. But we must point out that it is not [our] principal disagreement[92] with this list [and with the data] which are enumerated there. When it was mentioned that the data enumerated in our proposal do not include the movement of gold and the export and import of gold, we [in contrast] understood that they *are* included in the data. In addition, [p. 20] when she [our delegate] proposed this limited amount of information, she had in mind to give such information by every country which every country is able at this time to furnish the Fund, but it is not the principal objection against other data enumerated in the Alternative C. Therefore, the delegation of USSR proposed to submit this question, the Alternatives C and D, to a subcommittee of Committee 3 dealing with this matter, in order to try to prepare such a list of information data which would be acceptable to all the delegations.

Chairman: The Chair recognizes the delegate from India.

India ([A.D. Shroff?]): The government of India is opposed to Alternative C, but in doing so wants to emphasize the extreme desirability

---

[92] The meaning of this passage, which seems garbled because of the delegate's imperfect command of English and the difficulty the stenographer had transcribing, may be that the USSR had no disagreement in principle with the list.

of the protective clause which has now been inserted into the introductory remarks. We have the greatest possible hesitation in putting forward statistics which in certain cases, at any rate, would be nothing more than the merest guesswork, and we would like to enter into the arena of statistical information on subjects on which we know very little. We must express her view that under present circumstances in India, it would not be possible for us to furnish anything except the guesswork on item no. 6, while items nos. 7 and 8, we would not be able to furnish at all.

New Zealand: Everyone would hope that the proposal set out by Smirnov will be accepted and [that we] will go back again and reconsider the two alternatives. I think it would be right to say that members of the Fund feel that they have the information or the Fund has the information and every one of them have full confidence in the Fund. It would be impossible for the Fund to operate anywhere near as effectively as we hoped it would operate unless we have confidence. In [p. 21] the long run, it means maximum publicity, so that the smaller as well as the larger nations and competent persons will know why the decisions of the Fund are so made, and if it is to operate along the lines which have been proposed in the various reports up to now, it is imperative to obtain the information if it is available. The Soviet Union obviously wants to supply the information to enable the Fund to operate. If they feel they are capable of supplying it, they will cooperate. It is good to get suggestions that this should be considered, but I hope that when it is considered, it will be considered on the basis of giving every member country fuller confidence in the Fund's decisions. Unless we get that, we will have outside parties publishing wrong information. If the right information is not known, then the wrong information in many cases will be received as right and the Fund's objective will not be reached.

Chairman: In view of the fact that there may be some misunderstanding in the meaning of some of the items enumerated, the Chair believes that it would be helpful if the matter were referred back to the committee [Committee 3], as the delegate of the Soviet Union suggests, and they would report their findings at the next Commission meeting.

If there is no objection, it is so ordered.

The next item on the agenda is Document 212 [on the Executive Directors of the IMF], coming after page 26g. The alternative to that amendment is contained on page 26d, paragraph 3.[93] Mr. Hexner, would you please indicate the summary of those two items.

[Ervin Hexner] (Reporter, Committee 3): The final alternative submitted by the [sub]committee was approved by Committee 3 except two or three provisions.[94] One of them is the problem of electing [p. 22] Executive Directors. This is [being] discussed now in an ad hoc committee of Commission I, and this committee will probably report one small disagreement, and this is that according to the final alternative submitted to Committee 3, alternates [alternate Executive Directors] should be appointed by the elected members of the Executive Committee. One of the delegations submitted an alternative according to which alternates should be elected the same way as Executive Directors should be elected. There is another provision in that alternative that alternates meet alone, but this second statement in the alternative isn't important, because it is obviously implied in the final statement, so that this Commission should discuss and decide only the following issues: Should an Executive Director who is elected, not just appointed,[95] have the right to appoint his alternate, or should alternates be elected in the same way as Executive Directors are elected?

Chairman: The issue resolves itself to the question of whether or not [each of] the Executive Directors—the elected directors—may appoint his alternate, or [whether] the alternate of the elected Executive Director should be elected. Is there any discussion?

United States: I should like to point out that perhaps the question as to whether you elect the alternate is perhaps a very significant one. For this reason, the whole theory of electing Executive Directors is on the premise that the countries participating in the naming of a particular man will choose a man that represents their point of view. Now, if on the other hand an alternate is elected to be the substitute, you have the question as to whether that alternate will represent the same point of view. [p. 23] We have felt all through the discussion that the Executive Director should be elected by a group of countries, and he alone should bear the full responsibility; that he represents the views of the countries, [hence] he should have the right to name the alternate, so if he [the alternate] does not represent his [the Executive Director's] view, he [the Executive Director] will have the right to pick another alternate. But it

[93] Document 212, pp. 275-277, and Document 237, p. 334.

[94] Chapter 30.

[95] An elected Executive Director means one who represents a group of countries; an appointed Executive Director means one who represents only a single country.

must stand on the proposition of having an alternate that can work in close cooperation with the Executive Director. Failing that, you will have a conflict in your meetings of the Executive Directors between the Executive Director and the alternate, which would be unfortunate situation, since they both participate in the meetings. You would have two voices for one group of countries, and that is exactly what you are attempting to avoid.

Netherlands: The Netherlands delegation supports strongly the view expressed by the representative of the United States. The situation that might occur if the alternate were elected would indeed the most regrettable. The alternate should represent, and know that he represents, the Executive Director, and he should not have a separate status. Apart from that, the Netherlands delegation doesn't see why there is so much objection in certain parts [i.e., quarters] against the fact that the Executive Director should nominate his alternate. In cases where countries have to agree on the [person] they will elect as an Executive Director, it is quite possible for them to agree informally on persons whom the Executive Director might nominate as an alternate. We don't see any reason for this method, and think it is dangerous to follow it. We know there is only [p. 24] one way a director can work with an alternate: when there is a measure of confidence between them that makes possible for him to leave his work to be done by somebody else. We strongly support the views of the U.S. delegation.

Norway: Mr. Chairman, the delegate who can speak on the subject has been called out, but if you will allow me, I can state briefly the Norwegian point of view. When we are voting for a director, we are voting for a person and not for a country, and we think, in our opinion, we should also be allowed to vote for the alternate. During the discussion in Committee 3 on this subject, it has been suggested that the country in question should agree whether the candidate [is] for director or alternate. But we think that small countries, for example like Norway, have a very small share in one director. It would be very difficult for us to agree with the director or the alternate. That is why we would like an opportunity to elect the alternate for our director.

Chairman: The delegate from Norway expresses the view of his country [that] in electing representatives, is electing the man and not the country, and they would, therefore, like to have the privilege of electing an alternate rather than have the alternate appointed by the director. Are there any comments?

United Kingdom (John Maynard Keynes): This matter, sir, was discussed fully at the committee meeting. The importance of the point raised by the delegate from Norway was appreciated, but the United Kingdom delegate agrees completely with the views expressed by the delegate of the United States and from the Netherlands about the practical working. A group of countries are in effect choosing [p. 25] two people. They are choosing teams of the director and the right to elect the alternate. It seems much more likely that there will be good relations between the director and his alternate, and therefore either of them would discharge the responsibilities to countries very much better if they were regarded as a team of two to be chosen, rather than risk the chance of an alternate who would not see eye to eye with the director. I think Netherlands pointed out the very serious difficulties which would arise if that situation occurs. We feel that this is a matter which can work itself out more satisfactorily than providing for cumbersome doubling of all the voting system.

Chairman: The delegate of the United Kingdom supports the views of delegates from the United States and Netherlands.

France: France also wishes to agree with the expression of the United States and the United Kingdom.

Belgium ([Camille Gutt]): Belgium supports the views of the Netherlands.

Chairman: The Chair concludes that the consensus of this Commission is to accept the amendment of Section 3 in Document 212. Unless there are any objections, that will be the decision.

The next item is Alternative A, on page 29 [Article VII, Section 6, "Depositories"]. There are three different alternatives: [the others are] Alternative B on page 29a, Alternative C on page 29b.[96]

[Ervin Hexner] (Reporter, Committee 3): Committee 3 discussed three alternatives which have been presented in reading form and one alternative which has been presented orally. The problem is about depositories with reference to other deposits of local currencies. One of the members found acceptable [p. 26] Alternative A. It means [i.e., specifies] that at least half of the gold and other assets which are not local currencies should be placed in that country which has the largest quota. The rest may be placed with other depositories, but there is emphasized in the first place for member countries.[97] One of the second proposals [i.e., proposers of an alternative?] was satisfied with this Amendment A, however, if the four countries [designated in the amendment as depositories for IMF gold and other assets] would be changed to five or

[96] In Document 32, pp. 49-50.

[97] The original wording, reproduced here, seems garbled.

more countries. Another alternative, D, is rather strict in this regard and gives the Fund almost no discretion. And this Alternative D[98] says that at least one-half of the holdings of gold of the Fund shall be shared in the designated depository in the member country in which the Fund has its principal office. Forty percent of holdings of gold of the Fund shall be held in depositories of the remaining three members. It means the alternative strictly defines where 90 percent of the gold and other assets should be held. There are four alternatives which should be decided upon by this committee [Commission].

Netherlands: Mr. Chairman, I can't quite agree with the delegate of the United Kingdom, [that] these others are just small items. And I suggest that you follow your original proposal and adjourn the meeting.

Chairman: In view of the fact that this is the only item left and in view of the fact that we hoped that the committees would wind up their work by Wednesday, I am wondering whether we might not see whether it cannot be cleared up in five or ten minutes. If that were so, it would save another meeting. Would the delegate care to consider this suggestion? [p. 27]

Netherlands: Mr. Chairman, in that case, I feel free from the responsibility of keeping you all from your luncheon by saying a few words on the subject. I only want to repeat what I said in the committee, that it seems to be unwise to give any strict rules to the Executive Directors about where they should place their gold. It seems to me there are only two considerations that have to be taken in this respect. One is safety of the place where the gold is held, and the other the convenien[ce of the] place. It seems to me that it is frightfully difficult to see beforehand now, for a period let us hope of at least twenty or thirty years, what would be the wisest decision in this respect. If we accept the principle that the largest part of the gold would be in the head office or it would only be put into rigid rule which in practice would naturally be gold.[99] But if we put that rigid rule in, it would be quite natural that other rules going much further than that would be brought forward. I only want you to imagine what would happen if we accept the rule on 90 percent. In the first place, as soon as you sell gold anywhere, you have to shift the whole thing to get the percentage right again, and if we follow the all the rules that the gold remains in a certain proportion all the time

[98] Document 181, p. 223.

[99] The original wording, reproduced here, seems garbled. What the delegate seems to be saying is that the alternatives specify a rigid distribution of gold holdings among the depositories.

with the countries who have prescribed [subscribed] it, that practical objection would only be worse. Therefore, Mr. Chairman, I would strongly suggest that the directorate will consist of people with a sense of responsibility and judgment. That they will therefore discuss amongst each other and among all the countries who are mentioned in the particular alternative. I would strongly suggest that we leave them [p. 28] to judge where the gold should be held.

Chairman: Is there any other delegate who wishes to comment on this amendment?

South Africa: I would like to support the view which has just been placed by the delegate from the Netherlands. I think it is a quite unusual thing, even in the articles of association of companies, to lay down any such rigid provisions as are suggested. The only point here seems to be that the gold should be held in some of the bigger countries—say, inside the management of the Fund—to get it put there if they want it there. I think we could tie it down in discussing the management. I think we are making a very bad start.

Chairman: The delegate of the Union of South Africa believes that there is already sufficient flexibility in the deciding as to where the gold should be held, and that the large countries would have sufficient voice to determine the appropriate place.

USSR: The delegation of the USSR is of the opinion that it would be advisable to proceed with further discussion in this matter and, therefore, the delegation of the USSR wants to propose to refer to this question to the Third Committee again, and to ask Committee 3 to establish a special committee to try to discuss the situation and to make a final proposal.

Chairman: In view of the lateness of time, would the delegate from the USSR wish to modify his proposal to suggest that the Chair appoint an ad hoc committee which would consist of the same committee that discussed that before, but would report back to the Commission?

Unless there is an objection to that, the meeting is adjourned, and we will not meet this afternoon.

5

Commission I
International Monetary Fund
Fourth meeting: transcript
July 13, 1944, 2:30 p.m.[100]

Report of Drafting Committee • Report of Ad Hoc Committee on Exchange Controls on Current Payments • Exchange controls • Report of Ad Hoc Committee on Voting Arrangements and Executive Directors • Executive Directors and geographical representation • Relations of IMF members with nonmember countries • Report of Ad Hoc Committee on Uniform Changes in Par Value • Report of Committee 1 • Matters referred to Special Committee on Unsettled Problems • Report of Committee 2 • Charges and commissions

Louis Rasminsky reads the report of the Drafting Committee. Rasminsky was an official at Canada's central bank and the alternate chairman of Canada's Foreign Exchange Control Board. As the reporting delegate of Commission I, his role was to keep track of the proceedings of the Commission. He was also the chairman of the Drafting Committee, which had two jobs. One was to ensure that sections of the draft IMF agreement approved by committees were expressed in appropriate legal language and were consistent with other sections, to enable Commission I to focus on the main features of various proposals rather than on grammatical or legal details. The other job was to assemble sections approved by Commission I into a coherent final agreement. Rasminsky submits the table of contents and a revised draft of the IMF agreement and proposed alternatives as they exist so far.

Yee-Chung Koo, chairman of the Ad Hoc Committee on Exchange Controls on Current Payments, reads its report. Koo was China's vice minister of finance. As a young man, Koo had studied economics, accounting, and business in the United States. The committee was appointed to bring together scattered provisions related to exchange controls. The committee proposes a new section to the draft agreement incorporating

---

[100] Summarized in Document 370, pp. 597-599, and Document 370 (Correction), p. 600.

these provisions. The delegates then discuss a number of points related to the provisions. India's A.D. Shroff again presses the point of whether India's sterling balances will be convertible into other currencies after the war. The Commission then approves several sections of the draft agreement dealing with exchange controls.

Artur de Souza Costa, Brazil's minister of finance and chairman of the Ad Hoc Committee on Voting Arrangements and Executive Directors, reports that the committee was unable to reach agreement on the basis for appointing the IMF's Executive Directors, the body charged with day-to-day supervisory responsibilities over the IMF's management. The issue is highly controversial because it determines who will have the most influence over the IMF, so it is unsurprising that it requires the full Commission for an airing and a resolution. The delegates debate whether elected Executive Directors (those representing multiple countries) should be elected on a regional basis or by coalitions of countries that may cut across regions. They conclude that the question is strongly connected to the assignment of quotas (capital subscriptions), and defer further discussion until the Committee on Quotas makes its recommendations about how large each prospective member's quota should be.

Wilhelm Keilhau of Norway, chairman of the Ad Hoc Committee on Relations with Nonmember Countries, reports that the committee recommends the IMF agreement contain a section specifying that member countries shall not undertake transactions with nonmembers contrary to the purposes of the IMF. The provision is sent to the Drafting Committee for polishing.

André Istel, chairman of the Ad Hoc Committee on Uniform Changes in Par Value, reports that the committee has just recently made progress on the issue it is charge with. Istel was a technical counselor to the Free French Department of Finance and about a year before the Bretton Woods conference had coauthored a Free French proposal for international monetary cooperation. Before World War II he had been a prominent banker. Commission chairman Harry Dexter White defers further consideration until the next meeting to give the committee time to prepare a written report.

Kyriakos Varvaressos of Greece, the reporter for Committee 1 ("Purposes, Policies, and Quotas of the Fund"), reports on the committee's conclusions regarding the share of quota payments that countries should make in gold; the permissible margin that exchange rates may deviate from their declared parities (par values); and the legality of foreign-exchange transactions outside a member's territory in which exchange rates exceed the permissible margins of deviation. The Commission chairman refers some knotty matters connected with these points to what would be called the Special Committee on Unsettled Problems, a powerful committee chaired by Edward Bernstein of the United States.

Robert Mossé of France, the reporter for Committee 2 ("Operations of the Fund"), relates four matters the committee discussed: carryover of the right to draw from quotas (a country's ability to borrow against its capital subscription to the IMF); an

Australian proposal on enlargement of the early increments of drawings from quotas; a Mexican proposal on the role of silver; and a Cuban proposal on warehouse receipts.

Finally, the Commission considers a section on the IMF's charges and commission fees to members for borrowing, which Committee 2 had been unable to resolve. Walter Nash, New Zealand's minister of finance, expresses concern that the charges are too punitive, especially if creditor countries impose trade barriers to the exports of debtor countries. Ned Brown, an American delegate who was president of a large Chicago bank and president of an advisory council to the Federal Reserve Board of Governors, replies that they are necessary to prevent excessive borrowing from the IMF, which the United States envisions as an organization for stabilizing currencies, not to finance fluctuations in the balance of payments. The Commission then adjourns.

Chairman (Harry Dexter White, United States): The meeting will come to order.

The material on practically all sections of the Fund has been circulated, and except for material which has just come out, the various committees have completed most of their work. Such of the work as was completed by noon yesterday and some, though not all, that has been completed since has been incorporated in the new draft which has been circulated and which is now before you. The most urgent piece of business is to clean up all material on which the various committees are prepared to report, and as the Drafting Committee continues its labors, the material can be incorporated into the revised draft.

I probably need not inform the group here—you already know—that the Drafting Committee has been working terribly hard, until 2:00 and 3:00 in the morning, and that the committees and subcommittees have been working at all hours. That accounts for the fact that so much progress has been made and that the Drafting Committee got along as well as it has.

I am going to first call on the chairman of the Drafting Committee to report on the work of his committee, but we will postpone consideration of the draft until after the various committees and ad hoc committees have reported.

Mr. Rasminsky.

Louis Rasminsky (Canada, Chairman, Drafting Committee):[101] [Your Drafting Committee, which consists of representatives of the following delegations: Canada (Chairman), China, French Committee of

[101] The transcript merely says, "(Mr. Rasminsky read the first five paragraphs of Document 342, the report of the Drafting Committee)." We have reproduced the paragraphs, in pp. 571-572.

National Liberation, Mexico, Netherlands, Union of Soviet Socialist Republics, United Kingdom, and United States of America, has met several times since it was appointed on July 10, and we are able to submit today a report covering all the articles which have been cleared for the various committees of Commission I, including the special ad hoc committees, by yesterday noon, and some which had been cleared through these committees later in the day.

Your Drafting Committee has been obliged to work under considerable pressure, and we are aware that the documents submitted to you this morning require polishing and improvement. We therefore request the authority of the Commission to make such changes as appear to us desirable in matters of pure form, and to eliminate any internal inconsistencies or duplications which may become apparent on more leisurely examination, and to insert cross-references where necessary.

We are placing two documents before you. The first, Document No. 320,[102] is referred to as Annex I of our report, and consists of an outline or table of contents of the articles and sections of the Fund Agreement. An examination of this document will enable members of the Commission to see the order in which we have seen fit to arrange the subject matter. At the end of each heading on this table of contents, members will find references to various pages of Document SA/1, the so-called loose-leaf "bible" [whose core is Document 32]. The sections referred to are those which were approved by your committees, and by comparing these sections with the corresponding sections of our report, members of the Commission will be able to see what changes we have made in language.

Against certain sections of Annex I of our report, Document No. 320, members will find an asterisk. An asterisk indicates that the relevant section has either not yet been cleared through the appropriate committee, or that it was cleared too late for us to incorporate in this report. Your Drafting Committee takes the liberty of pointing out that it cannot make further progress in its work until the sections marked with an asterisk have been cleared.

The main body of our report has been distributed as Annex II, Document No. 321.[103] It consists of our draft of the Articles of Agreement of the International Monetary Fund insofar as these have been agreed by your committees.]

---

[102] Document 320, pp. 515-518.

[103] Document 321, pp. 518-537.

I should point out that in four or five cases we have made rather major changes in the wording. Page 7 of Document 321,[104] paragraph (b) of [Article IV,] Section 9 ["Maintenance of Gold Value of the Fund's Assets"], should read: [p. 2] "Whenever [(i) the] par value of a member's currency should be reduced, [or (ii)] the foreign exchange value of a member's currency [has, in the opinion of the Fund, depreciated to a significant extent within that member's territories, the member shall compensate the Fund by paying to the Fund with a reasonable time an amount of its currency equal to the reduction in the gold value of the currency held by the Fund]."

On page 24 of the same document, under Article XIV, "Withdrawal from Membership," Section 2, "Compulsory Withdrawal,"[105] the words beginning on the second line of small paragraph (a), "in a manner which is contrary to the purposes of the Fund," should be struck out, so that section [paragraph] (a) reads: "if a member fails to fulfill any of its obligations under this agreement, the Fund will declare [the member ineligible to use the resources of the Fund. Nothing in this Section [shall be deemed to affect the provisions of Article IV, Section 7, or Article V, Section 5]."

Page 27 of the same document [Article XVII, "Interpretation"],[106] at the end of the first sentence on that page, "by the President of the Permanent Court of International Justice": please insert the following words, "or such other authority as may have been prescribed by regulations adopted by the Board of Governors."

I have been asked to report those words which are to be inserted at the end of the first sentence on page 27, "or such authority as may have been prescribed by regulation adopted by the Board of Governors."

The final change which is of sufficient substance for me to mention it now is on page 28, [Article XIX], Section 2, "Entry into Force."[107] That section should read as follows: "As soon as"—and strike out the words "this agreement has been signed on behalf of"—" as soon as governments having 65 percent of the aggregate of the quotas set forth in Schedule A"—please add the following words: "have signed this agreement and deposited the instrument referred to in Section 1 (d) above."

---

[104] In Document 321, p. 522.
[105] In Document 321, p. 534.
[106] In Document 321, p. 535.
[107] In Document 321, p. 536.

I am going to repeat that paragraph as it now reads: "As soon as governments having 65 percent of the aggregate of the quotas set forth in Schedule A have signed this agreement and deposited the instrument referred to in Section 1(d) above, this agreement," etc.

Other changes have been made, [p. 3] but they are not of sufficient consequence to report at this time. The Drafting Committee in submitting the text of Article IX, Section 10, dealing with immunities from taxation, desires to place on record certain assumptions regarding its interpretation of the intention underlying this article. These assumptions are as follows:

(a) The Fund is not entitled to import goods free of customs duty without any restriction on their subsequent sale in the country to which they were imported;

(b) The Fund enjoys no exemption from duties or taxes which form part of the price of goods sold;

(c) The Fund enjoys no exemption from taxes or duties which are in fact no more than charges for services rendered.

The Drafting Committee desires further to place on its record its understanding that the phrase "territory of members" or "territories of members," where it appears in Article IX, on "Status, Immunities and Privileges of the Fund" (our numeration), is to be construed sufficiently widely to include the political subdivisions of members and, where relevant, their taxing authorities.

The Drafting Committee wishes to add the following to Article XIX, Section 1 ["Signature"] on page 28 of its report:[108]

"(g) In the case of governments whose metropolitan territories have been under enemy occupation, the deposit of the instrument referred to in (d) above may be delayed until _____ months after the date on which these territories have been liberated. If, however, it is not deposited before the expiration of this period by any such government, the signatures affixed in its behalf shall become void and the portion [p. 4] of the subscription paid under (f) above shall be returned to it.

"(h) Paragraphs (f) and (g) shall come into force with regard to each signatory government as from the date of its signature."

The Drafting Committee understands that, in the discussion of certain sections in the committees of the Commission, various delegations reserve their right, in cases where the consensus of the committee was contrary to the views they expressed, to make declarations to that effect

[108] In Document 321, p. 536.

before the Commission. Your Committee has not regarded it as part of its duty to make reference in its report to such reservations.

Chairman: You have heard the chairman of the [Drafting] Committee request that this Commission empower them to make such changes in matters of pure form and to eliminate any inconsistencies or duplications. Unless I hear objections, the Chair will assume that this commission readily grants that authority to its Drafting Committee.

(No objection voiced.)

As I said before, we are going to postpone the examination of the detailed report of the Drafting Committee until after the reports of the various committees.

For the first report I want to call on the Ad Hoc Committee on Exchange Controls on Current Payments. Mr. Koo of China is chairman. The document which Mr. Koo will discuss is Document 329, and also page 40 of the loose-leaf Fund document. If you have that document before you while Mr. Koo is making his report, it will facilitate hearing him.

Mr. Koo.

Yee-Chung Koo (China, Chairman, Ad Hoc Committee on Exchange Controls on Current Payments):[109] [The Committee met on Wednesday, July 12 at 6 p.m., with the following represented: China, Chairman; Canada, Uruguay, French Delegation, Iran, United Kingdom, and United States.

The Committee considered the proposed language for provisions which bring together under one article of the Agreement obligations which member countries assume with regard to the convertibility of their currencies as members of the Fund. The material which [it] is now proposed to include as Article IX, Sections 4 ["Exchange Controls on Current Payments"], 5, and 6, is presented in Document SA/1 [whose core is Document 32] as Article III, Section 6 (["Multilateral International Clearing"], page 9) and Article IX, Section 4 (["Exchange Controls on Current Payments"], page 40).[110]

The Committee considered Alternative D on Article IX, Section 4 ["Exchange Controls on Current Payments"], which appears on page 40b of Document SA/1,[111] and after full discussion it takes the view that the objectives which Alternative D is intended to safeguard are fully

[109] The transcript merely says, "(Read Document 329)." We have reproduced Document 329, pp. 544-546.

[110] In Document 32, p. 55.

[111] Document 219, pp. 279-280.

protected under the proposed language. In particular, was brought out in discussion that the proposed provisions did not contain any language which commits a member country to pursue any given commercial policy, and [the language] is confined strictly to the question of exchange restrictions on transactions on current account, and to discriminatory and multiple currency practices. No specific reservations were made by any of the delegations present on the language of the proposed provisions.

A question was raised as to whether the obligations of a member under the proposed Article IX, Section 4 to buy balances of its currency held by another member with the currency of that member, or with gold, would cease when the member was no longer entitled to buy foreign exchange from the Fund under any provisions of the Agreement, or when it had exhausted its quota. The view of the Committee was that the language clearly intends that the obligation should cease when the member is no longer able to draw on the Fund under any of its provisions. One of the delegates felt that some clarification of the language would be desirable to make this perfectly clear.

The question was raised concerning the application of the provisions of the Agreement for discriminatory currency arrangements or multiple currency practices prevailing in member countries the time the Agreement is signed and which are not wartime measures. The Committee agreed to add the sentence beginning "A member country in which such practices" at the end of Article IX, Section 6 ["Discriminatory or Multiple Currency Practices"].[112]

Convertibility [proposed amendment to the IMF Articles of Agreement]

[Article] IX, [Section] 4. Each member shall buy balances of its currency held by another member with currency of that member or, at the option of the member buying, with gold, if the member selling represents given that the balances in question having been currently acquired or that their conversion is needed for making current payments which are consistent with the provisions of the Fund. This obligation shall not relate to transactions involving:

(a) capital transfers; or

(b) holdings of currency which have accumulated as a result of transactions effected before the removal by a member of restrictions on multilateral clearing maintained or imposed under X.1 below; or

(c) the provision of a currency which has been declared scarce under VI above; or

---

[112] In Document 329, p. 546.

(d) holdings of the currency acquired contrary to the exchange regulations of the member which is asked to buy such currency;

nor shall it apply to a member which has ceased to be entitled to buy currencies of other members from the Fund in exchange for its own currency.

IX.5. Subject to the provisions of Article VI and Article X no member shall impose restrictions on the making of payments and transfers for current international transactions without the approval of the Fund.

IX.6. No member shall engage in any discriminatory currency arrangements or multiple currency practices except as authorized under this Agreement, or approved by the Fund. A member country in which such practices and arrangements are in effect at the time of this Agreement is signed shall consult with the Fund as to their progressive removal, unless such practices and arrangements are covered by Article X.] [p. 5]

Chairman: I think you have heard the report of Mr. Koo. Is there anyone who wishes to comment on the report?

The delegate from New Zealand.

New Zealand: I wonder if I can ask a direct question here. The country that controls its exchange entirely and makes provision for all the money necessary for its current transactions would not be in any way contravening the provisions of this agreement?

Chairman: The question has been asked whether any country that makes all the foreign exchange necessary for its transactions available would not contravene this agreement. Did I interpret your statement correctly?

New Zealand: The starting point—a country controlling its exchange in its entirety, controlling the whole exchange obtained from the sale of its commodities or in any other way, and at the same time making full provision for the funds necessary to meet its current transactions, would that country by controlling its exchange in any way contravene the provisions of this agreement?

Chairman: The question has been asked whether any country that completely controls foreign exchange and yet makes exchange available for its transactions, would it be contravening the provisions in the statement of Section 9 [i.e., Article IX, "Obligations of Member Countries"]. What does Section 9 [Article IX] say?

The delegate from the United States.

United States (Edward Bernstein): It is impossible to write into a document every possible technique that may be used for controlling or restricting transactions in foreign exchange. It is quite clear to the technicians that have discussed this problem that the use of authorized dealer for the purchase and sale of exchange, that the concentration of exchange [p. 6] dealings in some authority, is not a contravention of the purposes of this agreement. Until some specific type of transaction or some specific type of restriction is before the Fund, it would be impossible to say whether or not it is a violation of the obligations under the article that this committee has put before us.

Chairman: I gather the speaker makes a distinction between exchange control and exchange restrictions, and that the question involved the category of complete exchange control, whereas the delegate from the United States pointed out that this provision applies to possible restrictions and not control.

The delegate from New Zealand.

New Zealand: Could we get that a little clearer? Exchange control is not in any way barred, then, by this agreement? Not in any way whatever?

Chairman: That would be the Chair's interpretation. Does anyone disagree with that interpretation?

(No disagreement voiced.)

The delegate from South Africa.

South Africa: I take it in what you have just said that he has implied the condition that that exchange control does not work in a discriminatory meaning [manner] as between members of the Fund.

Chairman: I thought that that was not the question in point. That relates, I think, to another provision, which will doubtless come before us for discussion, if I understood the remarks of the delegate from New Zealand and the response by the delegates from the United States.

Then, we clearly have before us the distinction between exchange control and exchange restrictions. Exchange controls [p. 7] are not in violation of any one of the provisions, but if an exchange control is so operated as to in effect restrict transactions of a kind which are permitted in the draft document, then that would constitute a violation, and I think the delegate from the United States pointed out that before one could tell whether such restriction is in violation one would have to know the particular transaction or study the particular prohibitions which are enumerated in here. Does that answer the delegate from New Zealand?

New Zealand: I still want to get it cleared, if possible. There is no question that this agreement, if ratified, would be prohibitive in the long run of discriminatory practices in connection with the exchange. Two points: one, is exchange control in order? The answer apparently is yes. Exchange restriction in any way antagonistic to current transactions in trade is not in order.

Could I finish that, Mr. Chairman, then?

Chairman: Yes.

New Zealand: If, then, a country in some form or another entirely controlled its foreign exchange and inside its own rules made for provision for every current transaction that is carried out, that could be carried out under normal trade, then at that point that country would not be in any way restricting the availability of exchange for current transactions and would be quite inside of the provisions of this agreement.

Chairman: That would be my understanding.

New Zealand: And providing all the exchange for current transactions.

Chairman: That would be my understanding, Mr. Chairman.[113] But is there anyone who feels that a different interpretation is in any way warranted by any phraseology in this document? [p. 8] Does anyone disagree with the interpretation of the Chair?

(After a pause.) If not, then we will accept that as the interpretation. Is there any other comment?

The delegate from India.

India (A.D. Shroff): Under [Article] IX, [Section] 5 ["Avoidance of Restrictions on Current Payments"][114]—

Chairman: A little louder, Mr. Shroff, if you please.

India (A.D. Shroff): With reference to IX.5—

Chairman: IX, 5 of the document before us.

India (A.D. Shroff): I should like to have an interpretation of this clause from the delegation from the United Kingdom as to how it will work between member countries who are ordinarily accustomed to carry on their trade in terms of the United Kingdom currency.

Chairman: Were you through with the question?

India (A.D. Shroff): I should like to have an interpretation from the United Kingdom delegation as to how this provision will affect foreign trade transactions between member countries who are ordinarily accustomed to carry on their foreign trade in terms of sterling.

Chairman: The delegate from India requests an interpretation from the delegate of the United Kingdom as to how this provision would affect the transactions of the country that is accustomed to carrying on its

---

[113] Harry Dexter White is apparently addressing Yee-Chung Koo, the Chairman of the Ad Hoc Committee on Exchange Controls on Current Payments.

[114] In Document 329, p. 546.

foreign trade transactions in terms of sterling. If the United Kingdom delegate would prefer to answer that in a few moments, we will pass that question and give the delegate from the United Kingdom the floor when he requests it a little later. Is the delegate from the United Kingdom prepared to answer that now?

United Kingdom ([Dennis Robertson]): I think I can answer that. My understanding is that sterling acquired as a result of current transactions would be really convertible either into [p. 9] rupees or into any other currency. That, of course, applies only to sterling which at the time is being currently acquired as the results of current transactions.

Chairman: The delegate from India clearly heard the answer?

India (A.D. Shroff): Yes. There is only one point. Do I understand that this provision will have that interpretation as soon as the Fund starts operations?

Chairman: The question has been asked whether or not this provision will have applicability as soon as the Fund starts operation.

United Kingdom ([Dennis Robertson]): No. The whole of this clause refers to normal operations of the Fund after the member concerned has accepted the obligation of convertibility. None of that applies during the transitional period before such obligation is accepted.

Chairman: Has the reply been heard and understood?

India (A.D. Shroff): The reply has been heard and understood, but unfortunately it is not very satisfactory.

(General laughter.)

Chairman: I gather from the response of the committee [Commission] that they heard with the delegate from India said. Is there any other comment?

The delegate from France.

France: Mr. Chairman, I would like to have clarification concerning Article IX, [Section] 4 ["Exchange Controls on Current Payments."][115] Is that in order?

Chairman: Any request for clarification is in order.

France: The three last lines of IX, 4 read as follows: "nor should it apply to a member which has ceased to be entitled to buy currency of other members from the Fund in exchange for its own currency." Do the words "have ceased to be entitled to buy [p. 10] currency" apply to each instance where the country cannot buy currency from the Fund? I mean, for instance, [does it apply] if its yearly quota, if its yearly allowance, 25

[115] In Document 329, pp. 545-546.

percent, has been exhausted, or does it apply only in [the] case where 200 percent of the quota has been reached?

Chairman: The question has been asked as to the interpretation of the last three lines of IX, 4. The specific question was as to whether or not this applies to a country that has reached its maximum quota. Did I understand your question correctly?

France: It might be interpreted as applying exclusively to a country which has reached its limit of drawing, which is about 200 percent of the quota, or it might apply, also, to a country which has not reached 200 percent but has used in the previous month more than—in the previous 12 months more than—25 percent of its quota and, therefore, which is not entitled anymore for the time being to acquire foreign exchange from the Fund.

Chairman: I see. Your question was whether in the event that a country utilized its current rate during the earlier part of the year, and there was a part of the year left during which it might be construed that it shall not be entitled to buy—the question is whether during that period which is left, it was free of the obligation.

France: Exactly, Mr. Chairman.

Chairman: The delegate of the United States.

United States (Edward Bernstein): That provision, as I understand it, is intended to cover the fact that a country does not have access to the Fund. It, therefore, applies in the case of a country that has exhausted the 25 percent of its quota for any 12-month period. It applies to a country that [p. 11] has exhausted the whole of its quota when the Fund's holdings have reached 200 percent of its quota. It applies to a country which has been declared ineligible for use of the Fund's resources because of its actions contrary to the purposes of the Fund. It applies to every other case where a member is for some other reason declared ineligible to use the resources of the Fund.

Chairman: The Chair is in some doubt as to the appropriate interpretation of that clause, and feels that it may need a little clarification and discussion. Therefore, the Chair would like to refer to that particular section or the last lines of that section to a special committee which the Chair will appoint, and the committee which the Chair will appoint will consider not only that question, but any other question that comes up at the Commission meeting which, in the opinion of the Chair or the Commission, needs either further clarification or further discussion.[116]

---

[116] The committee came to be called the Special Committee on Unsettled Problems.

The Chair, then, rules that the interpretation as applying to these last three sentences be postponed until that special committee reports.

Any further comment?

(After a pause.) If there is no comment—is there any view that any member cares to express of approval or disapproval?

(After a pause.) If not, the Chair will call for a vote of "ayes" and "nays" on that part of the session up to [Article IX, Section 4, paragraph] (c), and the reason the Chair is doing that is that we want to get as much done as possible and leave for later Commission meetings only those particular sentences or phrases about which there is either doubt or further discussion to be called for; or, unless there is something in the particular phrase which may affect the earlier part, in which case we [p. 12] will do for the whole section. I do not think that is true of this section and, therefore, I should like to call for a voice vote on it.

Mr. Gutt, the delegate from Belgium. [(Upon realizing that the delegate is not Mr. Gutt.)] Mr. Chlepner.

Belgium (Ben Chlepner): I should like to say a word about [Article IX, Section 4, paragraph] (a), "Capital Transfers," in the document that we have discussed.[117] Certain capital transfers had been allowed: "those transfers that are required for the expansion of exports in the ordinary course…of other business." Should not the general obligation by which this clause does not relate to transactions involving capital transfer exclude those special transfers not authorized by the document?

Chairman: The question which has been raised seems very appropriate. The question is as to whether or not the obligation indicated in [paragraph] (a) should not contain an exception of those transactions which are permitted in other parts of the document.

The delegate from the United States.

United States (Edward Bernstein): Mr. Chairman, the provisions that the representative from Belgium referred to under "authorized capital transactions" represent transactions which the Fund may not forbid. There is no obligation on a member country to permit such capital transactions, if in its judgment it is necessary to control them. Therefore, in the sense that the country, the member, retains the full control over the regulation of capital transfers, it would be authorized to restrict this multilateral clearing provision when applied in the case of capital transfers.

---

[117] In Document 329, p. 546. The proposed paragraph stated that IMF members were not required to buy their currency held by other members if the holdings arose from transactions related to capital transfers.

Chairman: Does the reply satisfy the delegate from Belgium, or would he like to give the matter further consideration?

[Belgium (Ben Chlepner)]: (Inaudible reply.) [p. 13]

Chairman: Inasmuch as the delegate from Belgium would like to further consider the significance of that point, the Chair is going to rule that the whole section be referred to the Clearing Committee[118] and that an opportunity be provided for the delegate from Belgium to discuss the matter with the appropriate committee.

We, then, pass to [Article] IX, [Section] 5 ["Avoidance of Restrictions on Current Payments"].[119] Are there any comments to be made on that point beyond those which have already been made by way of interpretation?

(After a pause.) Do any delegates want to express any approval or disapproval on this matter?

(No response.)

Then the Chair will call for a voice vote. All those in favor of section [Article] IX, please say "aye."

Delegates: Aye.

Chairman: That is, section [Article] IX, [Section] 5, please say "aye."

Delegates: Aye.

Chairman: All those opposed?

(None.)

Chairman: Then, it is passed.

[Article IX,] Section 6 ["Avoidance of Discriminatory Currency Practices"].[120] "No member shall engage in any discriminatory practices," etc., you have already. It is not necessary to read it again. Any comment on that provision?

(No comment.)

I call for a voice vote. All those in favor of IX, Section 6, say "aye."

Delegates: Aye.

Chairman: All those opposed?

(None.)

It is passed.

The Chair will now call upon the next ad hoc committee [p. 13] to report, which is the Ad Hoc Committee on the Executive Committee and Voting Arrangements. The chairman, Dr. de Souza Costa.

---

[118] Perhaps this means the Standing Committee of Commission I.

[119] Became Article VIII, Section 2 in the final agreement.

[120] Became Article VIII, Section 3 in the final agreement.

Artur de Souza Costa (Brazil, Chairman, Ad Hoc Committee on Voting Arrangements and Executive Directors):[121] [The Committee met at 9 p.m. in Room B. Dr. de Souza Costa [Brazil] presided; and representatives of Belgium, Brazil, Canada, China, Cuba, Czechoslovakia, Egypt, France, Netherlands, Poland, United Kingdom, USSR, and the United States were present.

The Committee approved Alternative G (SA/1/44; Document No. 237; page 26g [Article VII, Section 2, "Executive Directors," provisions on vacancies]).[122]

The Committee discussed at length the provisions and problems presented by Alternative J (SA/1/54; Document No. 310; page 26j [Article VII, Section 2, "Executive Directors," provisions on appointed and elected directors),[123] and Alternative E (SA/1/55; Document No. 315; page 25h [on the same subject]).[124] While several delegations express themselves as favorable to Alternative J in principle, although a few with minor reservations, an almost equal number expressed complete reservation or reservation pending knowledge of quotas; and one additional delegation expressed the thought that after allocating membership on the Executive Directorate to "*ex officio* members, the remainder should be allotted equitably between economic and a geographical areas."

A new proposal was introduced as a substitute for paragraph (2) of Alternative J cited above. This proposal is to be submitted as Alternative K, page 2m. It was discussed by the Committee with general sympathy; but the Committee took no action regarding it, and it was referred to Commission I for decision.

The Committee also discussed paragraphs (a) and (b) of Alternative A (SA/1; Document No. 32; [Article VII, Section 3, "Voting,"] page 26[125]), related to voting. No decision was reached, and the matter is before the Commission.]

Chairman: You have heard the report of the chairman of the Ad Hoc Committee on Executive Directors and Voting Arrangements. The

[121] The transcript merely says, "(The report was read)." We have reproduced the report from Document 334, pp. 558-559.

[122] Document 237, p. 334.

[123] Document 310, pp. 502-504.

[124] Document 315, pp. 506-507.

[125] In Document 32, p. 47.

committee first approved Alternative [G]. We call it G; in Brazil they call it J, but the Secretary will read it to make sure no one misunderstands.[126]

Read the first few sentences so that there will be no question.

Secretary (Leroy Stinebower, United States): Alternative G on page 26g of the loose-leaf "bible," Document 237.[127] The following material is suggested as an addition to the combined Alternatives A and B for Joint Statement [Article] VII, [Sections] 1, 2 and 3, and additional material on page 27 of Document SA/1.[128]

This now begins the text: "Paragraph (a): Add to Section 2: 'Directors shall continue in office until their successors are appointed or elected.' Paragraph (b), 'Add as a new section under Section 3.' Section 4,"—

Chairman:—Which need not be read. Is there anyone who would wish to comment on that particular section?

Delegate from Egypt.

Egypt: (Inaudible comment.)

May I be allowed, Mr. Chairman, to say just a few words in connection with Alternative G presented by the Cuban delegation?

(Chorus of "noes.")

Chairman: I think the speaker is not commenting on the particular provision that is before this Commission. Am I correct, Mr. de Souza Costa? I think your comments applied to the latter part of the [earlier] report. I was first trying to get this part out of the way. [p. 15]

If there are no objections to this section [Alternative] G, the Chair will consider it approved.[129]

There is now before us the other subject matter of the report, and I would call on the delegate from Egypt.

Egypt: Mr. Chairman, may I be allowed to say just a few words in connection with Alternative G. That was the alternative presented by the Cuban delegation. We have no quarrel with that proposal. In fact, we view it favorably. The grouping together of countries into economic areas for units for the purpose of allotting seats appears to be a sound principle. It seems to be the principle which has inspired this alternative. This alternative recognized Latin America as an economic unit and allotted it to seats on the strength of that recognition. But we would like only to point out that the proper application of the principle underlying

[126] The Chairman is referring to the fact that when spelling individual letters, the English pronunciation for G sounds like the Portuguese pronunciation for J.

[127] Document 237, p. 334.

[128] In Document 32, p. 43.

[129] Became part of Article XII, Section 3 in the final agreement.

that alternative must necessarily entail its extension to all economic areas, not Latin America alone. This would eliminate the inconsistency that would arise from applying the principle exclusively to Latin America. In its present form, it is difficult to believe that the proposal does not discriminate against countries other than Latin America and the Big Five.[130]

We are prepared to back the Latin American proposal. In fact, we support it. But we should like to see the principle consistently applied. In the revised draft of the Egyptian delegation, there we claim, and claim rightly, that the Middle East, which is undoubtedly and unquestionably an economic unit, should on this ground be allotted at least one seat. A financial conference for the Middle East countries was held in Cairo last April.[131] The United Kingdom and the United States of America were represented. This is an instance where full recognition was provided for an [p. 16] economic grouping which, for purposes of trade, money, and exchange, you cannot very well afford to ignore.

Chairman: The delegate from Egypt has indicated his complete support for the proposal by Cuba and the recommendation of the committee that the Latin American countries be assigned to delegates. However, in view of the economic importance of the Middle East, he feels that the same principle should be extended to the Middle East and that the Middle East area be accorded one delegate.

I recognize the gentleman from India.

India ([A.D. Shroff]): On a point of order: I would like to know whether this committee can carry on a really useful discussion about the nature of the Executive Directors, their number and manner of election nomination, before this Commission has got full knowledge of how the position stands regarding the question of quotas. At this stage it is not possible for the Indian delegation to express a definite opinion whether they would favor the original allocation of seats. We have had various alternatives before us in which the Latin American republics are mentioned. The Far East comes probably ex-officially; the Middle East wants additional representation; and we want to see in which area do we come. I submit that it would not be possible to continue useful discussion of the subject, which I know is of vital importance to all the countries concerned, before we have some information regarding the question of

130 The five major World War II Allies: China, France, the USSR, the United Kingdom, and the United States.

131 The Middle East Financial Conference, held at the American University, Cairo, April 24-29, 1944.

quotas, and I would like your ruling, sir, whether the committee [Commission] is going to be honored to discuss the question straightaway.

Chairman: The delegate of India would like to know in which geographical area India might be considered.

(Chorus of "noes.")

India (A.D. Shroff): That is not so. [p. 17]

Chairman: Would the delegate of India briefly summarize his point? I am not sure that everyone heard it and I am not certain that I fully followed it.

India (A.D. Shroff): The delegation from India will not be in a position to express a definite opinion either in favor of regional representation or not without knowing the position regarding quotas. So far as the alternatives that now stand on order are concerned, I find various classifications of the world and I am not sure in which classification India would come.

Chairman: I think it depends on which way you are looking. But I get your point. The delegate feels that they are in no position to comment on the proposal until they have been informed of the entire quota classifications.

The delegate from Belgium.

Belgium (Camille Gutt): Gentlemen, I was going to move the same resolution as has just been proposed by the delegate for India. That is to say, to postpone the discussion of their [Egypt's] question until there is an agreement on quotas. If there is a general feeling in this Commission in favor of that proposal, I will not comment upon it. If there were an argument needed, I would ask leave to comment upon it afterwards.

United States (Ansel Luxford): Mr. Chairman.

Chairman: The delegate from the United States.

United States (Ansel Luxford): The Ad Hoc Committee that considered the various proposals on Executive Directors was deeply conscious of the point raised by the delegate from India and the delegate from Belgium.[132] The problem confronting [p. 18] the Ad Hoc Committee—and, I might say, confronting this Commission—is whether it is possible to move forward at all until you have determined quotas. There was a general feeling on the part of a number of members of the Ad Hoc Committee that as a practical matter, we should attempt to move forward with full recognition; however, that after the quotas are released, it may be necessary to re-examine the application of this provision to

---

132 Luxford apparently sat on the committee.

specific quotas. Nevertheless, if you accept that reservation, it still may be worthwhile to push forward on the work of this Commission by discussing this thing with that reservation.

Egypt: I defer—

Chairman: The delegate from Egypt.

Egypt: Will you allow me to add an addition to the proposal of my friend [[the delegate from India?]][133] If you once make a principle of regionalization, as seems to be admitted in the Cuban proposal, I think you must be logical and carry it out to its logical conclusion. That is, you must have a full regionalization of all the countries represented. So, I would suggest that if—that is, supposing there are twelve Executive Directors and five of the seats are allocated to the principal powers—I would suggest that the remaining countries be distributed into seven regions, as nearly as possible all identical economic relations, and that the seven remaining seats than be distributed amongst the seven different regions. In that way, no region could feel that they are left out in the cold. Sometimes there have been cases in Geneva where a country has felt that it has been slighted and left in the cold by the distribution of seats on the Board of the League of Nations; consequently, the League of Nations has been disturbed. Therefore, I would [p. 19] suggest that the whole of the original members minus the five be divided into seven regions, and that the seven remaining seats on the executive board be distributed amongst the seven.

Chairman: The delegate from Egypt indicates that once the door is opened to the principle of regionalism that it calls forth in allocation of the seats on the basis of geographic regions and he suggests that there be seven regions created, in which each shall have representation by virtue of its geographical position.

The delegate from Iraq.

Iraq: Sir, as a point of order has been raised, how can the discussion usefully proceed until the Chair has decided the point of order?

Chairman: The point of order being what?

Iraq: The point of order was raised by the Indian delegation and was supported by the delegate from Belgium, whether this discussion should proceed at all—

---

[133] Recall that double brackets indicate that we are somewhat speculatively interpolating material into passages where the typescript notes that a speaker was inaudible or where ellipsis points indicate that the stenographer could not follow the speaker.

Chairman: The view expressed by the delegate from India was an expression of opinion. I didn't understand that he was raising a point of order. It was an opinion to the effect that this question could not be intelligently discussed until the quotas were settled. Apparently, there were contrary views and we were listening to the various views. If the delegate from India raises it as a question of order, the Chair would defer reply until there are comments from a few more of the delegates.

India (A.D. Shroff): But in that case, shouldn't the comments be restricted to the point raised in the point of order, and not deal with the substantive merits of the amendment which is before us?

Chairman: The delegate from Iraq. [p. 20]

Iraq: The delegation from Iraq supports the motion raised by the—

Chairman: You are going to confine your remarks to the subject matter raised by the question of order?

Iraq: I have no comment on the question of order. I am only commenting on the merit of the case.

Chairman: I am sorry; the Chair will have to declare you out of order for the moment. We will call on you later. The question before the Commission is whether or not it is necessary to know the quotas in order to discuss appropriately the question of representation.

The delegate from Belgium.

Belgium (Camille Gutt): On the point of order, I would only like to point out that the suggestion made this afternoon by the representative for the United States was made yesterday evening at the Ad Hoc Committee [on Executive Directors and Voting Arrangements]; that is to say, that we would, leaving aside the question of substance and the question of quotas, try to approach this matter as the discussion of a practical matter of a practical procedure. And I want to point out that the Ad Hoc Committee tried during two hours to follow the suggestion and failed. So I am quite sure that the whole Commission would fail this afternoon, because at every corner we came up against this question of quotas. We couldn't escape from it; the Commission couldn't escape from it.

Chairman: The delegate from United Kingdom. [p. 21]

United Kingdom: Mr. Chairman, I rise to support the point of order raised by the Indian delegation and the delegation from Belgium. I participated in all of the discussions that have taken place on this subject, and at each of these discussions we have started out exactly the same way trying to decide this question of principle. About halfway through the discussion we got onto the quotas and stuck in the quotas from there on until the chairman would release us. I suggest we reserve this question until quotas are determined.

Chairman: Inasmuch as the Chair does not wish to place any obstacles [to progress], the Chair takes the point of order [as] well taken and will appoint a Committee on Quotas, who will report back to the Commission and inform the various delegates of their findings before the Commission so they will be enabled to discuss the matter intelligently.

Canada: May I say a word of explanation, but not relating to the point of order that has just been raised. I have been told that there is a reference in the report of the Ad Hoc [Committee on Executive Directors and Voting Arrangements] considered by the committee and reported without decision. This was technically important. While geographically, no account has been taken of the very important consideration of division of those countries which might be creditors of the Fund and those which might be, in a sense, debtors. We suggest therefore that there ought to be a provision [[providing representation?]] for those countries which at all times will be creditors. I wish to say there that [we] urged this as a technical provision in the interest of the Fund. We urged in the interest of the Fund—

Chairman: The Chairman will now call upon the chairman of Ad Hoc Committee on Relations with Nonmember Countries. [p. 22]

[Wilhelm Keilhau] (Norway, Chairman, Ad Hoc Committee on Relations with Nonmember Countries): Mr. Chairman, the question of relations to nonmember countries might have raised many difficult problems. In the present draft before us, the Fund is restricted to actions taken on the initiative of member countries. That is to say, their relations to nonmember countries will not appear during the daily transactions of the Fund. The only thing which we really have to look after is this: to prevent nonmember countries to engage, as well as we can do, in practices that may be dangerous to the policies of the Fund. We have no jurisdiction over a nonmember country. The only thing we can do is to impose some duties on member countries concerning their relations with nonmember countries. We have placed before the Commission clauses contained in Document 311.[134] I will pause just a moment until everyone has found 311.

We propose here a new section to be added to Article IX ["Obligations of Member Countries"], and I will say in advance when I introduce it that this suggestion, or this proposal, which I have, is clear in

134 Document 311, p. 505.

its language although it is not beautiful in its language, but I should prefer the clear language.

["Each member country agrees:

"(a) Not to undertake any transactions with a nonmember country which would be contrary to the purposes and provisions of the Fund, and not to allow its agencies with the Fund to undertake such transactions,

"(b) Not to cooperate with nonmember countries in practices which are against the purposes and provisions of the Fund,

"(c) To cooperate with the Fund in order to apply appropriate measures to prevent transactions with nonmember countries in practices which are contrary to the purposes and provisions of the Fund."]

I will just add one thing more, which has nothing to do with that clause. This Committee received a letter from the Danish minister[135] asking some questions concerning the position of Denmark, which is a nonmember country. We did not find that within the scope of the mandate of this Commission, but I think as chairman I may draw the attention of the Steering Committee to the fact that the Danish minister has been invited here by America in a very special way, and I think there ought to be some possibilities for Denmark to join this Fund, as it has been allowed to join some other associations in an easier way than other nonmembers. [p. 23]

Chairman: The Commission has before it, first, the recommendation of the Ad Hoc Committee on Relations with Nonmember Countries; and then, the suggestion that the Steering Committee consider the possibility of membership of Denmark. Is there anyone who wishes to comment on the recommendation of the committee?

[Iraq[136]]: May I ask what "agency with the Fund" means in paragraph (a): "allow its agencies with the Fund"?

[Wilhelm Keilhau] (Chairman, Ad Hoc Committee on Relations with Nonmember Countries): Mr. Chairman, it would not be a member country, as such, which acts with the Fund, but it should appoint a central bank or some other agency to represent the member country towards the Fund, and that is this agency which is meant.

---

[135] The Danish minister (ambassador) in Washington, Henrik de Kauffmann. Unlike other German-occupied countries at the conference, Denmark had no formal government in exile, so de Kauffmann attended the Bretton Woods conference in a personal capacity at the invitation of the U.S. government rather than as a delegate sent by the Danish government.

[136] The typescript says "Iran," but in view of the exchange between the Chairman and Iraq just below, we think it is mistaken.

Chairman: Is there a possibility that there might be some misunderstanding that you failed to indicate—"to the countries and its agencies"? If there [is] such an ambiguity, would Dr. Keilhau be willing to accept the suggestion that if the Drafting Committee should see fit, would it be so incorporated?

Norway: I don't think there is any such ambiguity. In the first sentence it says, "Not to undertake any transactions with a nonmember country which would be contrary to the purposes and provisions of the Fund," and in the next part of the sentence it says that it should not "allow its agencies with the Fund to undertake such transactions." I think both cases are clear.

Chairman: Does that please the delegate from Iraq?

Iraq: I think so. [p. 24]

Chairman: Any other comment?

If not, the Chair considers this ready for drafting. The Chair will now call [on the] Ad Hoc Committee on Uniform Changes in Par Value. Mr. Istel, have you any oral report to make? There has been no written report submitted.

André Istel (France, Chairman, Ad Hoc Committee on Uniform Changes in Par Value): Mr. Chairman, I just received a report that notwithstanding differences which arose at the Ad Hoc Committee in its meeting of yesterday evening, that now there seems to be substantial agreement between the members on Alternative C, which reads as follows:

["Article IV, Section 5. Uniform Changes in Par Values.

"Notwithstanding the provisions of Section 2 of this Article, the Fund may make uniform proportionate changes in the par values of all the members, provided each such change is approved (a) by a majority vote and (b) by at least one-third of the members, and (c) by every member which as 10 percent or more of the aggregate votes. Such uniform changes shall be excluded from consideration in applying the provisions of Sections 4(3) and (4) of this Article."]

Chairman: Document 164, page 18b, Section 5.[137] Do I understand, Mr. Istel, that agreement was reached practically on a provision which is like Alternative C but [is] not Alternative C?

André Istel (Chairman, Ad Hoc Committee on Uniform Changes in Par Value): Not "practically" [Alternative C]: the last report is that it *is* Alternative C.

[137] Document 164, p. 184.

Chairman: The Chair is going to rule that we give the Ad Hoc Committee time to prepare a written report and prepare it by the next meeting. Would that be satisfactory?

André Istel (Chairman, Ad Hoc Committee on Uniform Changes in Par Value): Yes, Mr. Chairman.

Chairman: So be it.

I have been reminded that the question raised by Dr. Keilhau with respect to the Danish minister was not put before the Commission for comment. Does anyone wish to comment? The question is that the Steering Committee consider the possibility of inviting Denmark as a member.

If there are no comments, then the question will be referred to the Steering Committee.

I call on the Ad Hoc Committee on Special Problems of Liberated Areas, which I understand has held no meeting because of the existence of so many other subcommittees.

We will then turn to the reports of standing committees of the Commission. [p. 25] The reports have been available in writing and in view of the time, we may dispose of the reading of the written reports, but call upon the reports and comments.

[Kyriakos Varvaressos] (Greece, Reporter, Committee 1): Mr. Chairman, I want to—Document 343[138]—I want to draw attention of the Commission to the three points that came before the Committee. The first is connected with Section 5 ["Initial Payments"] of Alternative A of Part [Article] II ["Subscription to the Fund"], at [the] top of page 2 of my report. There, our Commission has asked to fill [in] the day on which the holdings of gold and collateral exchange by member countries should be established as provided in this document. As you remember, we have agreed on the proposals of the Committee with regard to this section. (Reads:) "Each member shall pay in gold as a maximum either (a) 25 percent of its quota or (b) 10 percent of its official holdings." [As for] the day on which the holdings of the members will be established, the Committee was not able to fix any day, and it is a matter for the Commission. That is the first point.

The second point is similar. It deals with Section 3 ["Foreign Exchange Dealings Based on Par Values"] of Article IX, page 39,

---

[138] Document 343, pp. 573-576. This passage is from p. 575; paragraph (c) in brackets below is from pp. 575-576. The report summarizes deliberations in chapter 16.

Document SA/1.[139] We have also accepted the [Drafting] Committee's proposal, which is as follows:

["(a) The Fund shall prescribe a uniform maximum margin not exceeding _____ percent, by which rates for transactions in the currencies if members may differ from parity. In exceptional circumstances the Fund may authorize a member country to establish a wider margin for transactions in its currency."][140]

The Committee, while accepting in principle this wording, thought that it relates closely to problems discussed by Committee 2, and decided therefore to refer to the suggestion to the Commission. The Committee refers the discussion which is taking place to Committee 2, about the commission [fee] which the Fund requires from each member to pay on the application of its dealings in foreign exchange. Now, we thought the percentage which ought to be proposed here must depend on the percentage which this Committee [i.e., Committee 2] will fix. The members, in discussing the matter, recommend to Committee 2 that [a] percentage between ½ [percent] and 1 percent ought to be raised by the bank [Fund]. It [p. 26] depends on the percentage which shall be accepted in this case—what percentage would be established for this purpose.

The third question applies to Section 3, paragraph (c) of Alternatives A and B, page 39 or 39a of Document SA/1. The Committee has referred this question to the Drafting Committee and the Drafting Committee reported there are three alternatives, Alternative A, Alternative B, and the new provisions proposed by the Drafting Committee. The new drafting is worded as follows:

["(c) Exchange transactions in the territory of one member involving the currency of any other member which are outside the prescribed variation from parity set forth in (a) above, shall not be enforceable in the territory of any member country.

"Each member agrees to cooperate with other members in their efforts to effectuate exchange regulations prescribed by such members in accordance with this agreement."]

Now, the difference between the first two alternatives (A and B) and the proposal is this: Alternative A declares not enforceable any transaction holding currency of a member country which voids or avoids changes of relation, and declares not enforceable any transaction which tries to evade or avoid [exchange regulations] of another member. The

[139] In Document 32, p. 54.

[140] This proposal concerns the maximum margins by which exchange rates may differ from their par values.

second alternative, B—this wording, which has been pressed by one delegation, declares those transactions not enforceable [for anyone] who has [committed] an offense, and the wording proposed by the Drafting Committee declares not enforceable any transaction described by [the] issue. Now, I may add that the delegation of [the] United Kingdom, while expressing its preference for Alternative B, declared their willingness to concede their position if Alternative [A][141] were accepted. On the contrary, [the] United States decided on the language of the Drafting Committee. That is why our Committee decided to defer the matter to the Commission. I think the three principal points which have been deferred by the Committee to this Commission can be seen. [p. 27]

Chairman: The first question raised by the committee for your consideration is that of the date on which the holdings of gold and gold convertible exchange of member countries shall be established as provided in this cause. The committee made no recommendation. Is there anyone who wishes to discuss that point?

India ([A.D. Shroff?]): Before this Commission makes its decision on fixing the date, I think it is high time that the USA delegation give us a definition of gold and gold convertible exchange. We have discussed this proposal and the several other proposals. Those words "gold" and "convertible exchange" are subject to definition, and I don't know if the U.S. delegation is now prepared to give us a definition of gold and convertible exchange as used in this provision.

Chairman: Delegation from India has requested a definition of gold and convertible exchange as used in this provision.

United Kingdom ([Dennis Robertson?]): The question was addressed to the United States, but I think that it is not in any way their fault that the furnishing of this definition has been so long delayed. I would like to propose an amendment to the text which is before us, according to which the criteria of payment of official gold subscription should be expressed as official holdings of gold and United States dollars. That involves a change of page 3 of the new document, [Article III,] Section 3(b), and also involves a change on the following page in Section 4(a).[142] I don't know if I need to say anything further in connection with the explanation of the change, except that the concept of gold convertible exchange is a difficult one to give an exact definition to, and our own feeling is that the balance of advantage so far as the [p. 28] payment of

---

141 The typescript says "B," but Document 343, p. 576, makes it clear that "A" is meant.

142 In Document 321, pp. 519-520.

additional subscription goes [[is on the side of the country whose reserves consist of gold and United States dollars]].[143] This has nothing to do with the recapture provision which occurs when the Fund is functioning in the later stage, but so far as the gold element in the original subscription goes, the balance of advantage is on the side of the country being the country holding all gold and United States dollars, and nothing else.

Chairman: Delegate from United States.

United States ([Edward Bernstein?]): Mr. Chairman, it might be possible to give a definition of gold convertible exchange which would be satisfactory to everyone here, but it would involve a long discussion. On the practical side, there seems to be no difference of opinion, and it is possible for the monetary authorities of other countries to purchase gold freely in the United States for dollars. There are a number of other currencies which can be used to purchase dollars without restriction, and these dollars in turn [can be] used to purchase gold. The definition of gold convertible currency might include such currencies, but the practical importance of holdings of the countries represented here is so small that it has been felt it would be easier for this purpose to regard the United States dollar as what was intended when we speak of gold convertible exchange.

Chairman: Unless there are any objections, this question will be referred to the special committee. Any objection?

Then we pass to the next problem raised by Committee 1, and that is [Article IX,] Section 3 ["Foreign Exchange Dealings Based on Par Values"]. The Committee indicated that it was not prepared to specify the exact percentage which would constitute the range at which exchange could be permitted to move, and referred the question, therefore, to the Commission. Are there any views by any member delegate on this point?

If not, that question will be deferred to the special committee. [p. 29]

Norway ([Wilhelm Keilhau]): Mr. Chairman, may I in that connection suggest that the decision might be left to the Fund, because from time to time it may not be certain that the same rates would be practical, and it would save us very much work in this conference if such a question could be left to the Fund. I think the Fund will get as good a Board and Executive Committee that with full confidence we could leave it to the Fund, and simply say a margin not exceeding—

Greece ([Kyriakos Varvaressos]): Mr. Chairman, we have discussed this in the Drafting Committee and Committee 1, and someone proposed

143 The only way we are able to make sense of this sentence is by adding the phrase in double brackets.

to word this as follows: "The Fund shall prescribe a uniform maximum margin by which rates may differ from parities." This would limit the Fund within a percentage which will be fixed in this document, to leave [i.e., leaving] at the discretion of the Fund the question of margins in which member countries shall freely move; but we felt that it was a general idea of a majority of members that it would be better to fix a limit even to this discretion of the Fund to fix margins.

Chairman: The question will be considered by the special committee, and in consideration of that question, the special committee will take due note that any limitation placed upon the range must be considered in the light of the possibility of violating or making ineffective the central thread that runs through this whole measure by having a range of variations that is wide. They will have in mind that the Commission may doubt the wisdom of extending that degree of flexibility in the authorization of the Fund.

Does the delegate from the United States wish to speak?

If not, the matter will be referred to the special committee.

The next point is Section 3, paragraph (c) [p. 30] on the next page [on the enforceability of exchange transactions exceeding prescribed margins from parity]. There are several alternatives enumerated in the question before us.

Delegate from United States.

United States ([Edward Bernstein?]): Mr. Chairman, in glancing over the proposed subparagraph (c), it seems to me that it has to a very substantial extent changed at least what was contemplated by paragraph (c), Alternative A, and is now, in fact, overlapping the principle of [paragraph] (b) of Alternative A. Under (b) of Alternative A, countries undertake appropriate measures, including the use of gold, to maintain rates of exchange. As I now read the proposed [paragraph] (c) of the Ad Hoc Committee, they are instead making it a question for law. In other words, you are going to have a legal requirement that rates of exchange may not vary in the various countries. I think that changes entirely the meaning and purpose of [paragraph] (c) as it was originally introduced. I think that further than that it places an undue burden on each country. As originally drafted, it was contemplated that while you might not permit black-market operations, we might render such transactions unenforceable. You did not have to go further than that. I believe this goes considerably further than that and I suggest that it be recommended to the special committee.

Chairman: The suggestion is made that this be recommitted to the special committee. Are there any objections?

If not, we will so recommit it. That completes the matters raised by Mr. Varvaressos, chairman [Reporter] of Committee 1. [p. 31]

[Kyriakos Varvaressos] (Greece, Reporter, Committee 1): Mr. Chairman, there is another question on page 2, Article IX, Alternative A, Section 2, page 38 of SA/1 ["Gold Purchases Based on Parity Prices"].[144] The question deals with transactions in gold. The Committee proposes that "The Fund shall prescribe [for] transactions in gold by member countries [a permissible margin above and below the agreed parity. No member country shall buy gold at a price above the prescribed range, or sell gold at a price below that range.]" Under this clause, member countries are permitted to buy gold below the exchange [rate parity] and sell the gold above the exchange [rate parity]. On the other hand, they are not prevented from following a domestic policy of encouragement by means other than paying a higher price for gold.

Chairman: Delegate from United States.

United States ([Edward Bernstein?]): This provision was referred to the Drafting Committee. I might say I see no objection to the substance of what they are driving at. There is a very distinct difficulty in the language, which the Drafting Committee, I believe, is working out. There is no objection to the principle here enunciated. It is the way it has been worded, and the Drafting Committee has that problem [under consideration] already.

Chairman: The Drafting Committee is now considering that problem, and therefore is not necessary to consider it at this meeting until the Drafting Committee has attempted—or is it already included in the draft?

United States ([Edward Bernstein?]): That is right.

Chairman: You mean the Drafting Committee has the problem before them and have suggested the draft which we will come to?

United States ([Edward Bernstein?]): That is right.

Chairman: Then if there is no objection, we will postpone further discussion on this point until we come to the Drafting Committee provision bearing on this point.

I now call on the Reporter from Committee 2, Professor Robert Mossé. [p. 32]

Robert Mossé (France, Reporter, Committee 2): Mr. Chairman, I am referring to [the] report of Committee 2, which is Document 333, with the symbols C1/2, page 3.[145] Committee 2 has completed its study of

[144] Again, Document 343, p. 575.

[145] Document 333, pp. 554-558. The report summarizes deliberations in chapters 23 and 24.

[Article III,] Section 2, "Conditions Confronting Purchases of Currencies of Other Members" ["Conditions under which Any Member May Purchase Currencies of Other Members"]. This Committee was faced with four questions, embodied in different alternatives or proposals. There was the question of the carryover. You remember this question, which has already been discussed, whether or not a country which has not used during one twelve-month period its 25 percent [right to draw] would be allowed to carry over its remaining purchasing power to another period. Then there was the Australian alternative concerning the enlargement of the early increments allowed. Then there was a Mexican proposal referring to silver, to be brief, and other relative matters. And there was a Cuban proposal referring to warehouse receipts.

Concerning the first—the two first—questions, an ad hoc committee[146] has studied the question and proposed to Committee 2 a compromise. According to this compromise, the carryover proposal would be dropped and also the Australian proposal, but instead some moderate satisfaction would be given the members wishing those possibilities by introducing, or rather by modifying, the waiver provisions at the end of the section; and according to this compromise, which you have under your eyes, I hope, there would be a kind of instruction given to the Fund or a possibility given to the Fund to allow members in avoiding long or continuous use of the resources, allowing the Fund to give them a little more than the normal yearly increment. Also this compromise included this sentence: that in such cases the Fund would consider political or exceptional requirements of members. Now, the Czechoslovakian delegation suggested another alternative, which simply reversed the order of the terms and, to be brief, [p. 33] says, "First the waiver will be according to needs, and secondly the waiver will be according to the good behavior or small use." Now, the Committee approved the text as presented by the Ad Hoc Committee. There are a couple of mistakes, but in order to be fair I must say that the Czechoslovakian alternative obtained in our Committee received a very substantial support, and I also have to say that the Australian delegation expressed [[a reservation?]].

Now also, the question of purchases. We have two questions, which I can dispose of very quickly. The second proposal was adopted. This proposal authorized the Fund to take as collateral gold and other securities or other acceptable assets. Now, the Cuban suggestion referred

[146] Apparently the Ad Hoc Committee on Article III, Section 2, [Paragraph] (3), concerning the purchase of currencies.

to warehouse receipts and also suggested that these warehouse receipts should be accepted as collateral. Now, it was the view of the Committee that it was not necessary, and here there is a mistake in the report. At the end of the paragraph before the last suggestion by the Cuban delegation were [the words] "thought not necessary." Our Committee felt that it was not necessary to include the words as suggested by the Cuban delegation, because the Mexican alternative also included the same by the use of the words "or other acceptable assets." These acceptable assets might be—if the Fund should so decide—might be considered as including warehouse receipts. This is what the Committee did on Section 2 ["Conditions under which Any Member May Purchase Currencies of Other Members"], governing purchases.

On Section 6 ["Multilateral International Clearing"], the question was removed from our agenda.

[On] Section 9, "Transferability and Guarantee of the Assets of the Fund," agreement was reached in our Committee, and therefore I don't feel it necessary to speak more about that. I only have to say that the USSR delegation reserved its position.

Now I come to Section 10, referring to "Charges and Commissions," page 13. [p. 34] On this point there was absolutely no agreement, and the question is referred to your Commission. Discussion was on the right of charges and commissions, on the scales, and also on the principle itself. Several delegations said that these charges and commissions have the effect to penalize a country which has been obliged to leave a considerable amount of its national currency in the hands of the Fund, but some delegations said that this was not very fair because it often arises that a country has an unfavorable balance not because it is unwilling to export, but because other countries, creditor countries, are not willing to import, so this question was discussed and is referred back to this Commission.

On Section 12, agreement was reached, "Consideration of Representations of the Fund." You have the text and I shall not read.

Then Article IV was also discussed and agreed upon, with some minor reservations. Article IV, may I remind you, deals with the changes in par value. Then Section 5 of [Article] IV, "Uniform Changes in Par Value," was also removed from our agenda and referred to another ad hoc committee of this Commission.

Finally, we had another question, [on] Article XIII, Section 5 ["Fixing Initial Par Values"], concerning the fixation of initial par values. I have the feeling that this discussion was not entirely completed, and a small committee was expected to offer a report on this question. Since this report has not yet come into my hands, I cannot tell about what are the results of the committee and subcommittee discussion. I can only mention to you what the issue was. As a matter of fact, there were several issues. One was about [p. 35] the question of provisional [par values] or fixing definite initial par values, and another question referred to the position of occupied and then liberated countries. If a country can make use of the resources of the Fund only after the initial value has been fixed, it follows that liberated countries during a certain length of time may not be able to draw from the Fund because the initial par value is not fixed. Therefore, some way should be found to permit, under certain limits, liberated countries to resort to the Fund in this first transitional period, even though the rate of exchange has not been definitely agreed.

Chairman: The first provision for your consideration will be the first paragraph on page 1 of Document 333, taken separately, I guess, and the first paragraph on page 1 reads:

["The Committee accepted the recommendation of the ad hoc subcommittee that Section 2(3) of Alternative A (page 6a) be approved. The Committee also agreed to accept the recommendation of the ad hoc committee to revise the sentences of following paragraph (4) of Section 2 as follows:

'The Fund may in its discretion, and on terms which safeguard its interests, waive any of these conditions, especially in the case of members with a record of avoiding large and continuous use of the Fund's resources. In making such waiver it shall take into consideration periodical or exceptional requirements of members.'"]

United States ([Ned Brown?]): Mr. Chairman, it seems to me that the recommendation of the committee on this point is entirely appropriate. It safeguards the interests of the Fund and gives it discretion. At the same time, it calls to the attention of the Fund the necessity of taking into consideration the basic uses of the Fund by the member, and the special needs of the members for periodic and exceptional requirements. It seems to me that we should send this to the Drafting Committee as entirely satisfactory.

Chairman: Any other views?

Cuba ([Juan Menocal?]): Mr. Chairman, I don't know if it is in order to ask that the Chair and the Commission accept the interpretation given by the Committee on Warehouse Receipts as being full collateral and considered acceptable under "other assets." [p. 36]

Chairman: Would you mind if we postpone that until the second paragraph? We are confining the question to views of the first paragraph.

[William Mackintosh] (Canada, Vice Chairman, Committee 2): Point of order. I think there is some misunderstanding here. The Reporter has correctly reported the various points of discussion, but Committee 2, of which I am acting chairman, has approved of this paragraph, which has not been referred to the Commission. The committee reached agreement on this paragraph.

Chairman: Committee 2 has reached agreement on that paragraph.

[William Mackintosh, Vice Chairman, Committee 2]: The paragraph, with the addition of the Mexican amendment, and all that remains is for the Drafting Committee to deal with the wording. There is no question of principle outstanding, as I understand it, in Committee 2.

Chairman: The delegate from Canada points out that both provisions had been passed by Committee 1 [Committee 2] and were to go to the Drafting Committee. The question raised by the delegate from Cuba [is] as to whether or not the collateral changes indicated in the second paragraph could include the warehouse receipts of staple commodities and international trade. Is that your question, Dr. [Menocal]?

[Cuba (Juan Menocal)?]: Yes, Mr. Chairman. [My question is] if warehouse receipts are considered as good collateral, included in "other acceptable assets," as it was interpreted by the committee.[147]

Czechoslovakia: Mr. Chairman, we should like to reserve our position for the Drafting Committee, but if this [Article III,] Section 2 ["Conditions under Which Any Member May Purchase Currencies of Other Members"] could be decided here, then we should like to say that we think there was no change in substance [p. 37] between our proposals and that accepted by the committee [Committee 2?]. We want to stress, first of all, the principle, to say that it is in the Fund's discretion to waive any of these conditions, and in the second sentence to say that the Fund, in making such waiver, has to take into consideration two things, the need of a member, and its good name.

Chairman: I think further discussion of this point is out of order. The matter has been referred to the Drafting Committee, and will come to this Commission when the Drafting Committee will incorporate it in the draft. Inasmuch as it is incorporated in the draft, further discussion will be delayed until we come across it in the draft.

We then pass to the second point of the committee report, [Article III,] Section 6, the "Multilateral International Clearing" arrangement. That was one of the items reported by an ad hoc committee and [it] has

---

147 It is unclear to us whether "the Committee" means the Committee on Warehouse Receipts or Committee 2.

already been passed on by this Commission. No part of it was referred back to the special [i.e., ad hoc] committee.

Turn then to [Article III,] Section 9(b), ["Transferability and Guarantee of the Assets of the Fund."]

United States ([Ned Brown?]): Committee 2, which considered this question yesterday, was unanimous in agreeing with the principle it provides. I suggest that this be referred to the Drafting Committee, and that when the corresponding sections involving repurchases from the Fund have been approved by the Commission, this can be incorporated with the others in the final draft.

Chairman: The suggestion has been made that this provision be referred back to the Drafting Committee in order for possible incorporation in another draft. Unless there is any objection, this will be referred to [p. 38] the Drafting Committee.

The next item on the agenda is [Article III,] Section 10 ["Charges and Commissions"], on charges, which, with your permission, I am going to pass until we get the rest of this report.

[Article III,] Section 12 ["Consideration of Representations of the Fund"] was reported to Committee 2 and was approved by the committee, and therefore is referred to the Drafting Committee. That has already been dealt with and will come before us in Article IV.

The same thing is true of [Article XIII,] Section 5 ["Fixing Initial Par Values"], as we have already dealt with it in the Ad Hoc Committee [on Article XIII, Section 5] which is not yet completed its report. Article XIII, Section 5—there is a committee considering that, an ad hoc committee, which is to report to the Reporter on this matter.

United States: Mr. Chairman, Committee 2, which considered this question yesterday, was in full agreement on the principles involved, and it seems to me that because of it, we may dispense with the report of the Ad Hoc Committee [on Article VIII, Section 5] and send that report to the Drafting Committee directly.

Chairman: In view of the fact that Committee 2 has considered this provision and was in accord with the principles, the suggestion was made that the matter be referred to the Drafting Committee.

Norway ([Wilhelm Keilhau?]): I do not quite understand, but it is included in this report here. It is on one point a little less than—according to my view [it] was agreed upon, and I have already—I really do not know how matters stand, but I only wish to make the reservation because I was also of the opinion that some proviso should deal with the question of an occupied country which had to adopt a completely new monetary unit. That [p. 39] must be included in the final draft, and I call the attention of the Drafting Committee to the fact.

France ([Pierre Mendès-France]): (The chief of the French delegation spoke in French.)

Chairman: Lest there be somebody who would not be able to fully understand everything the minister has said, I will call upon Mr. Istel or his colleague to translate.

France (André Istel): (Read a translation of the minister's talk.)[148]

Norway ([Wilhelm Keilhau?]): May I just say that I really think the remarks made by the head of the French delegation [verge] on perfect misunderstanding. The fact is that it is not claimed from such countries that they *shall* declare a provisional rate, but if they *wish* to declare a provisional rate in order to obtain some facilities from the Fund, they shall have that right. If France is afraid of such a [thing happening], there is no reason for France to give such a declaration, and in the provision of this drafting as I suggested to the Drafting Committee, there is also an alternative possibility which would be available for France. I should like to suggest that any suggestion on this point be deferred until we see the text, which will make it clear that Committee 2 has not based itself on the opinions expressed by the French delegation.

Chairman: The delegate from Norway suggests that there might be some misunderstanding of the provision and therefore unnecessary discussion until the draft of the provision is before the Commission for consideration. Unless there are objections then, we will refer this matter to the Drafting Committee. [p. 40]

We now turn to [Article III,] Section 10, "Charges and Commissions," in which the Reporter stated there were some differences of opinion on the matter and has placed it before this Commission for consideration. Does anyone wish to comment on the provision?

New Zealand ([Walter Nash]): The report, on page 13a, together with the tables attached to it[149]—it seems to me that if it was given effect, it might be detrimental to the purposes of the Fund, rather than helpful to the purposes of the Fund. The discussion in the committee is very lengthy and very definite. The point of importance in connection with the matter is that the creditor country can have a greater effect of bringing about the results desired than any of the debtor countries. If the country

---

[148] We found no record of the talk. Perhaps one exists in French archives, which we have not consulted.

[149] The table of charges on loans by the IMF in Document 285, pp. 464-465. Page 13a of the loose-leaf conference binder is Document 277, pp. 441-442.

having a majority, or the largest [export] volume of the Fund,[150] is willing at the same time to have a large [[trade deficit?]], we are not likely to have the troubles which were set out here. If there is some procedure that is necessary in this connection, I would suggest that we take pains and give some thought to stopping prices [practices?] of member countries ill-using the Fund. In case that they shouldn't do that, it is quite possible, inside the procedure that you have here, to penalize the countries that do not ill use the Fund, that are placed in difficulties because of certain differences that may arise with the principles set out here in the interchanges.

[[Such penalties?]] are wrong and harmful, and we will be doing more good introducing that country to take steps other than were taken in previous years when the exports went down and they [p. 41] never took any imports to enable them to get—make—the payment; and as this conference is setting out to try to avoid this, I think a large amount of the difficulties that are occasioned by endeavoring, to be prevented by this table here, in this provision, would be avoided if there was some penalty put on the country that didn't take the imports to pay for their exports. There will be quite a number of countries that will be put into a disadvantageous position, having commodities that they can export; [but] the countries competent to import those commodities not doing so puts them into a bad position, and they are penalized, and it seems to me that the proposal here will be detrimental to achieve the purposes of the Fund.

Chairman: Am I correct in assuming that everyone was able to hear clearly what the delegate from New Zealand has stated, and it is not necessary to repeat? Therefore, we can ask for further comment.

United States ([Ned Brown]): This matter came up before Committee 2; it seems to me that the delegate of New Zealand was the only one who strongly expressed that point of view.

Delegates: No, no—I did, and others.

United States (Ned Brown): I apologize. The United States delegation made its position very clear in going into this: the purpose of the Fund was to stabilize currencies, and that unless some deterrence was put on countries which utilized the resources of the Fund so as to create overdrafting—have more of their currency in the Fund than they originally put into it—that the Fund would get out of balance. Certain currencies would become scarce and the Fund could not function; that, in the opinion of [p. 42] the United States delegation, it was absolutely impossible for this Fund to work unless a deterrent charge was put on

150 The United States.

countries which would get out of balance and stay out of balance a long while. The charges made were discussed, with more opinion expressed by the two or three countries which were opposed to the principle of any charge, or that the charge was too high. The position of the United States delegates was that the charges were very moderate, and if countries used the Fund moderately for a short period, for several years, before the rate got as high as 4 percent, there was a provision that when the rates got to 5 percent, they should not go higher; that at 4 percent, the Fund should call the countries in and take steps to have them reduce their excessive use of the Fund. It cannot be a Fund for the stabilizing of the [[fundamental imbalances?]]. If the country cannot bring its position into a balance within several years, it is not acting in a way to permit stability of the currency.

Objections to the proposition that the rates proposed in the table are high are considered relatively low [i.e., few], and it is perfectly clear in this agreement, in the implication of this conference, that the United States did not propose in this conference or in this agreement to give up its rights to adopt such import duties as it saw fit to adopt. I think most of [us] would [agree] that countries do not definitely export more than they import, [except?] eventually to take payment in goods. If [they] can, over a long period of time, correct that situation, [they are] doing it by the receipt of goods, or the export of capital would go on forever.

We regard these charges, which [p. 43] increase both in amount as the amount that is used, [and] as a percentage of the quota, according to the length of time, as absolutely necessary and imperative to give effect to the working of this agreement. I am sorry I minimized the dissent on the question of principle. I think Mr. Nash, the delegate from New Zealand, was the one who spoke more fully on the question of principle—more general criticism of the rates. I think that clearly the great majority of Committee 2 has expressed their opinion, approving the principle of progressive rates, both as to amount and length of time. I want to make the position of the United States clear that I think without accepting the principle [of] a progressive [charge related to the] rate of the use of the Fund, increasing as the amounts in relation to the quotas go up, [and] as to the length of time [[a country has drawn from]] the balance of the Fund, that it would be impossible for the United States delegation to go ahead with this plan.

United Kingdom ([Dennis Robertson?]): I feel that I should repeat before this Commission what I said before Committee 2, namely, that to the United Kingdom delegation, the principle lying behind the scale of charges seems reasonable and necessary, and also that so far as at present can be humanly foreseen, the scale itself appears to be reasonable. Our sole reservation is concerned with the lack of symmetry in the arrangements which are proposed for the possible alteration upwards or downwards of this whole schedule in the light of future events. As we read the text of the document, as it stands, it will be possible to the Fund to shift this whole scale upwards by a bare majority vote, but in [p. 44] order for the scale to be shifted down, an amendment of this whole instrument would be required. To us, it seems that while revision should not be lightly undertaken, whether upward or downward, the conditions for undertaking it should be symmetrical, and we should like to propose an amendment whereby a two-thirds majority would be required for shifting the schedule either upward or downward.

Chairman: In view of the hour and the prior understanding that Commission II will begin at 5:00 p.m., and in view of the further fact that a number of delegates would undoubtedly like a brief recess, the continuation of discussion of this will take place at the beginning of our next meeting. I would like to ask this Commission which of the two alternatives is preferable to them; we can either meet tonight at, let us say, half past eight, or we can meet tomorrow morning at ten o'clock. The time is passing rapidly and we must meet as soon as we can, but we don't want to impose an evening meeting on you unless the majority of the delegates feel inclined to that idea and express an opinion.[151]

[151] The typescript ends here, although it seems to us as though there should be a few more lines, containing the delegates' response to the Chairman's question and his formal adjournment of the meeting.

6

Commission I International Monetary Fund Fifth meeting: transcript July 14, 1944, 10:00 a.m.[152]

Report of Special Committee on Unsettled Problems • Purposes of the IMF • Proposed alternative (amendment) on purposes of the IMF • Membership • Quotas and subscriptions • Net versus gross holdings of gold and convertible foreign currency for subscriptions • Par values of currencies • Uniform changes in par values of currencies • Transactions with the IMF • Capital transfers • Scarce currencies • General obligations of IMF members • Status, immunities, and privileges of the IMF • Relations of IMF members with nonmember countries • Organization and management • Transitional period • Withdrawal from membership • Liquidation of the IMF • Interpretation of the IMF Articles of Agreement • Initial determination of par values

Edward Bernstein of the United States, chairman and reporter of the Special Committee on Unsettled Problems, presents the committee's report, which is the result of staying up through half the night negotiating. This meeting of the Commission is mainly devoted to addressing items on which the Special Committee achieved agreement.

The Commission then proceeds to debate and approve some of the articles of the IMF agreement. (Articles are numbered here as in the intermediate draft, Document 321, not as in the preliminary draft agreement, Document 32.) First is Article I, "Purposes." Sir Shanmukham Chetty of India proposes an alternative that would place more emphasis on the economic development of poor countries as a purpose. Commission chairman Harry Dexter White suggests referring the alternative and the clause it would amend to the Special Committee to save the Commission's time. The Commission approves the rest of Article I. It also approves Article II, "Membership," and part of Article III, "Quotas and Subscriptions." A key point for the later functioning of the Bretton Woods version of the gold standard would be that Article III

---

[152] Summarized in Document 393, pp. 627-629.

was amended to substitute "U.S. dollars" for "gold convertible exchange," on the grounds that no other major currency was then convertible into gold. The privileged status of the dollar in the Bretton Woods system would lead to problems in the 1960s, when American monetary policy changed the dollar from an unquestionably strong currency to a weaker one.

The Commission turns to Article IV, "Par Values of Currencies," and the delegates debate the section on uniform changes in par value, that is, the circumstances under which IMF member countries would act together to change the value of their currencies in terms of gold. Antonio Espinosa de los Monteros, president of Mexico's development bank and a director of Mexico's central bank, opposes the original provisions, under which the three largest shareholders in the IMF could conceivably override the rest in imposing a uniform change. By the time of the meeting, though, the original provisions have been modified, and the Commission approves Article IV with the modification.

Next the Commission considers Article V, "Transactions with the Fund," which includes rules about the interest rates and other fees the IMF may charge to countries that borrow from it. The delegate from New Zealand makes the case that proposed schedule of fees may be so high as to hamper international cooperation. The delegate from China replies that the fees are necessary to prevent a small number of countries from tying up the IMF's resources. A long discussion then follows about loans, called "repurchases" in IMF jargon. The Commission ends by approving the sections of Article V before it for consideration.

The Commission concludes the meeting by quickly approving many articles that had been agreed by its committees or are uncontroversial: Article VI, "Capital Transfers"; VII, "Scarce Currencies"; VIII, "General Obligations of Members"; IX, "Status, Immunities and Privileges of the Fund"; X, "Relations with Other International Organizations"; XI (XII in the final agreement), "Organization and Management," with the exception of a section on Executive Directors; XIV (XV in the final agreement), "Withdrawal from Membership"; XV (Schedule E in the final agreement), "Liquidation of the Fund"; XIX (XX in the final agreement), "Final Provisions"; and XVII (XVIII in the final agreement), "Interpretation."

Chairman (Harry Dexter White, United States): The meeting will please come to order.

May the Chair take this opportunity to express the gratification of the Commission and the thanks of the Commission to the committees that have been working very late. And the fact that they have been doing so is sufficient indication of the recognition that the time is very urgent, and inasmuch as the committees have been working so hard, it would be a little ungenerous of us here to take too much time to consider the various recommendations. Let us take all the time that is necessary, but let's try to keep our remarks down to a bare minimum. We don't want in any way to interfere with careful consideration, but if we avoid unnecessary speeches or repetition, I think we will be able to get through a good deal of the work, but let no member hesitate to raise any question that troubles him, and to speak up when he has anything of any importance to say. We first call upon the Reporter of the Special Committee.

[Edward Bernstein] (United States, Chairman and Reporter, Special Committee): Mr. Chairman, the Special Committee of Commission I commenced work last night at 8:30 and continued its work until 3:30 this morning to consider items of the Fund agreement on which recommendations had not been completed by other committees of the Commission. This Special Committee included United States, Belgium, Canada, China, Cuba, Czechoslovakia, French delegation, Mexico, Netherlands, New Zealand, USSR, and United Kingdom. I must say that the committee had what we all regarded as a very successful meeting, accomplishing the purposes for which it was appointed by the Chair. The spirit of the meeting was of the highest quality, and I hope it will be reflected in the deliberations of this Commission. The full report of the committee has been presented to the Commission in the form of Document 374.[153] [p. 2]

Chairman: That contains a full report which was distributed to you this morning, entitled "Report on Special Committee of Commission I, July 14, 1944."

[Edward Bernstein] (Chairman, Special Committee): May I recommend, however, Mr. Chairman, for your consideration, the taking up of each of these points in the appropriate order in the Drafting Committee's report. In that way it will be easier for the group in this Commission to see the appropriateness of the recommendations of the Special Committee in the body of the document itself.

Chairman: The Reporter suggests that we take up each one of the items in the report of the Special Committee in their appropriate place so that it will facilitate their consideration in relation to other paragraphs which would be included in the same article. Unless there is objection, the Chair will proceed in that manner.

United Kingdom ([Dennis Robertson?]): I should like to add my tribute to the work, if I may do so, accomplished by the committee last night, to the high spirit of accommodation that was shown under the firm guidance of Mr. Bernstein, and say, I hope the great thoroughness with

---

[153] Document 374, pp. 604-608.

which many of these matters were discussed in the small hours may save us time this morning.

Chairman: The Chair proposes to proceed in the following manner unless there is some objection from the members of the Commission. We will take up an article at a time. If any member wishes to consider or reconsider any section, he will, of course, secure the floor and raise the question. But when we come to sections which have been handled by the Special Committee, we will take that part first and then we will take the remainder of the article.[154]

We turn first to Article I, the "Purposes." That includes sections [paragraphs] (a), (b), (c), (d), (e), and (f). I may say that the justification for that procedure lies in the fact that we assume every delegate by this time is thoroughly familiar with the various sections, having participated in discussions at subcommittees and committees and commissions, and that, therefore, taking a matter up as an article in the whole should not interfere with the ability of the delegates to follow exactly what is being done, nor should it make difficult their desire to raise a question on any provision which they have in mind to discuss.

Before the Commission first is Article I, "Purposes." Do I hear any comment?

India ([Sir Shanmukham Chetty]):[155] Mr. Chairman, I must first apologize to the Commission for venturing to take up just a few minutes, but I shall certainly keep in mind, sir, the appeal that you made that we must be as brief as possible. I am referring to Section (b) of Article I, the "Purposes" of the Fund. The Indian delegation would submit a very small amendment to this article which you will find in page 1e, Alternative I of the document.[156] The amendment is very brief and very short. It is to add after the words "to facilitate the expansion," etc. the words "with due regard to the needs of economically backward countries." This section would then read as follows: "To facilitate the expansion and balanced growth of international trade and to contribute thereby to the promotion and maintenance of high levels of employment and to the development

---

[154] The draft of the IMF Articles of Agreement that the delegates discuss in this meeting is Document 321, pp. 518-537, the so-called "New Testament" draft, or as we sometimes call it, the intermediate draft. The numbering for most articles differs from the numbering in the preliminary draft, or "Old Testament," Document 32, pp. 21-60. We note where the numbers of articles and sections in the intermediate draft differ from those in the final agreement, Document 492.

[155] This speech was also published with minor changes as Press Release No. 31, Document 383, pp. 1180-1181.

[156] Document 162, p. 184.

of the sources of productive power in the territories of all members, with due regard to the needs of economically backward countries."

I venture to bring this amendment for the attention of this Commission, sir, because of the very great importance which the Indian delegation attaches to the principle which is involved in my amendment, and the practical consequences of that amendment. I want to make it [p. 4] perfectly clear on behalf of the Indian delegation that is not our object to enforce upon the Fund obligations and responsibilities which the Fund is not expected to carry and for which the Fund is not equipped. The object of my amendment is only to make fuller or more complete the statement of the primary objective of international policy.

We are in full accord with the general text as stated in the document, namely "the expansion and balanced growth of international trade," but the term "balanced growth" has been understood in a narrow sense as meaning an increase in the volume of trade which is more or less equal—imports and exports—so as to avoid disequilibrium in the international balance of payments. This regard is certainly one of the primary aspects of balanced growth of trade. But such [an] interpretation refers in the mechanical sense to the volume of imports and exports. But we contend that about this the balanced growth of international trade must refer therefore, in our judgment, to an expansion of trade which has a more balanced character and composition, not a simple flow of raw materials and foodstuffs from certain countries and the flow of highly finished articles from other countries; and this object, if it is considered [[essential?]], can only be achieved by greater attention to the development of the resources of the economically backward countries.

Sir, it may be objected that this aim cannot be achieved through the Fund, but the same will apply to promotion of high levels of employment, which are referred to in this section. The Fund can only indirectly facilitate and give you the general object as a guiding principle, and it is a matter of great importance to the economically backward countries that the Fund should incorporate this proposal for the operation of the Fund. We are constrained to make this amendment in view of the experience which we have had in the past of the working of [p. 5] various international organizations during the last twenty years and more. It has been our sad experience that in the working of these organizations, the approach to every problem has been from the point of view of economically advanced countries, and it is our answer, sir, that in the new organizations that we are setting up, the need of the less advanced countries must be prominently kept in view, and that is the only consideration which impels us to move this amendment, and I will make one final appeal in commending this amendment for the acceptance of this Commission. I want this Commission to realize the psychological value to the world [[of the words?]] that I have suggested. If these words are there in a charter of the international body that we are setting up, less advanced countries will then have greater hopes of the possibilities of economic development than they were led to believe in the past.

United Kingdom ([Dennis Robertson]): Mr. Chairman, I hope that it is in order for me to allude to what is being done elsewhere. If it is so, Mr. Chairman, I would like to address an appeal to our friends who are moving this amendment, to direct their attention to the draft of the statement of principles which has been prepared to affix to the document relating to the Bank [for Reconstruction and Development]. Mr. Chairman, some of us working at a very late hour the other evening spent a great deal of time drafting a clause which, I venture to suggest, fully covers the aspirations which have been so eloquently expressed by the last speaker. We are all in sympathy with those aspirations. Some of us have them very much at heart, but I would urge our Indian friends to reflect at this late hour whether those aspirations are not better satisfied in the framework of the preambles of the Bank than in the framework of the preambles of the Fund. [p. 6]

Chairman: The delegate from the United Kingdom expresses complete sympathy with the Indian delegate, but feels that the matter is more appropriately taken care of in the statement of purposes of the Bank.

The delegation of the United States.

United States: I wonder, Mr. Chairman, whether in the interests of quick progress we can refer this paragraph with the suggestion of the Indian delegation, and whatever other information which may arise, to the Special Committee.

Chairman: One would hardly want to delegate that to the Special Committee unless there is anyone who desires any further change. The proposal of one amendment would not in my judgment refer that back to the committee. Do you have any other thought in mind?

United States: I would like to suggest the wording: "To facilitate the expansion and balanced growth of international trade, and to contribute thereby to the promotion and maintenance of high levels of employment and to the development of the sources of productive power in the territories of all members as primary objectives of economic policy."

Chairman: You are suggesting a further change. In view of the fact that there have been two changes to be made, the Chair will recommend that the matter be referred to the Special Committee.

Now let us take up Article I without Section (b). If there is no comment on that, I will ask for a vote. All of those in favor of accepting Article I without Section (b), leaving Section (b) to be referred back to the Special Committee, please say "aye."

(Chorus of "ayes.")

So approved.

Article II. Article II, on "Membership." Is there any comment on Article II?

If no delegate wishes to speak on Article II, I will put that to a vote. All those in favor of accepting Article II, please say "aye."

(Chorus of "ayes.")

All those opposed?

(No response.)

The article is approved.

In Article III ["Quotas and Subscriptions"] we have an insert, that is, [p. 7] item 12 of the Special Committee's report ["Subscriptions: Terms of Payment"].[157] It belongs in Article III and we will consider that item first. We are considering merely the item reported by the Special Committee, which is item 12. It refers to the time of payment. That appears on page 4 of the Special Committee's report: item 12. May I call upon the Reporter of the Special Committee to report on that one item?

[Edward Bernstein (Chairman, Special Committee)[158]]: Mr. Chairman, the Committee was unanimous in recommending to the Commission that "In determining the gold subscription to the Fund, official holdings of gold and gold convertible exchange be taken as of the time of the entry into force of this agreement."

Chairman: You have heard the report of the Special Committee, which included the phrase that was read. Is there any comment?

Mexico: I hope that it will be approved as made.

Chairman: A vote that it will be approved has been seconded. Any discussion? I will put it to a vote. All those in favor of accepting item 12 as reported by the Special Committee, say "aye."

---

[157] In Document 374, p. 608.

[158] Listed in the typescript as "Delegate from U.S." It is sometimes hard to tell in this session when Bernstein spoke in his capacity as the chairman and reporter of the Special Committee and when he spoke as a delegate from the United States. He may also have spoken at other times when the typescript indicates that a U.S. delegate spoke without specifying who it was. We list Bernstein as the speaker in a number of places where the typescript only identifies the speaker as being from the United States, but the context makes it likely that it was Bernstein.

(Chorus of "ayes.")

It is approved. Now then, we will take Article III—the remainder of Article III.

United Kingdom ([Dennis Robertson]): Mr. Chairman, may I just be assured that the intended change will now read "ten percent of its net official holdings in gold and [U.S. dollars]."

Chairman: I am sorry, Mr. Robertson, but I don't get the significance of your suggestion.

United Kingdom ([Dennis Robertson]): I want to be assured that the correction suggested last time is being duly embodied in Article III [Section 3, "Subscriptions: Time, Place and Form of Payment"] now. On page 3, in place of the phrase "ten percent of its official holdings [in gold and gold convertible] exchange," read "ten percent of its net official holdings of gold and U.S. dollars." [p. 8] On the following page, it reads "[If, however, on the date when a member approves an increase,] its net official holdings of gold and gold convertible exchange [are less than its new quota, the Fund may reduce the proportion of the increases] to be paid in gold."

[Edward Bernstein (Chairman, Special Committee)]: It has been my intention to refer to this change when the question of definition arises. I think, however, that it is the thought of those who have considered this question that the change "gold convertible exchange" into "U.S. dollars" would be in effect a restatement of the same principle. There are few, if any, currencies other than U.S. dollars which would now meet this definition, and if we may insert it at this point, it would facilitate progress.

Chairman: Would the delegate from [the] United Kingdom accept the definition that will come later without making any alterations here? Is that your question? If it would be defined in the definition in the matter which has been suggested, then I gather there is no need to alter this point.

[Edward Bernstein (Chairman, Special Committee)]: I believe the suggestion is that we alter it here and then we need not make [[an issue of it later?]].

Chairman: I see. Then the alteration is suggesting replacing "gold convertible exchange" with "U.S. dollars."

Any other comments?

United Kingdom ([Dennis Robertson]): And adding the word "net" before "official."

[Edward Bernstein (Chairman, Special Committee)]: And then define the concept of "net official" [holdings] in the definition.

Chairman: Do I understand that the committee accepts the affixing of the word "net" at this point?

[Edward Bernstein (Chairman, Special Committee)]: We may use the word "official holdings" and define it later as needed. We may use the term "net official" and define it in the definition. In either case, the end result is intended to be the same.

Chairman: Any further comment? [p. 9]

Norway (or perhaps United Kingdom): I think it is clearer to have "net" here than in the definition.

[Edward Bernstein (Chairman, Special Committee)]: It would be necessary to define "net."

Chairman: Do I understand that it would be preferable to have a more comprehensive definition applying to the term wherever it is found in the document?

[Edward Bernstein (Chairman, Special Committee)]: That will be done in the definition.

Czechoslovakia: The Czechoslovakian delegation has suggested an addition to the section about time of payment [Article III, Section 3], which is now being dealt with in the Committee [on] Liberated Areas. May I understand that the acceptance of this article, of this section, doesn't preclude us from bringing this addition to the consideration of the Commission?

Chairman: What was the subject matter of this?

Czechoslovakia: It was special arrangements about payments for liberated countries.

Chairman: No, that is not precluded from the discussion this morning.

Are there any other comments on Article III? If there are no other comments, we will call for a vote. All those in favor of accepting Article III with the exclusion of the possible recommendation that the Committee on Liberated Areas, which has not yet been submitted to this Commission; and with the alteration of the phrase "U.S. dollars" in place of "gold convertible exchange"; and with the further understanding that [the] definition which will be submitted to this commission later will take care of and make it "net." With those changes, all those in favor,—

Netherlands: It is to be understood that "net" will be included here.

Chairman: The word "net" will be included here, but will be defined in the definition. All those in favor of accepting the article, say "aye."

(Chorus of "ayes.")

The article is [p. 10] accepted.

We will turn then to Article IV ["Par Values of Currencies"]. Article IV, item 1 of the Special Committee report. Will the Reporter discuss it?

[Edward Bernstein (Chairman, Special Committee)]: Mr. Chairman, the Special Committee considers the language appropriate for [Article IX,] Section 3, "Foreign Exchange Dealings Based on Par Values."[159] It was the unanimous view of the Special Committee that the language on page 1 of this report, under Recommendation 1, should be adopted by the Commission. May I read that? "Section 3(a): The maximum [and minimum rates for exchange transactions in member countries shall not differ in the case of spot transactions by more than one percent, from the official par values, and in the case of other exchange transactions by more than a reasonable spread from the spot rates. The Fund shall be the judge of what constitutes a reasonable spread. No member shall use the resources of the Fund for the purpose of covering forward exchange transactions in the currency of any other member without the permission] of the Fund."

Chairman: Would you wish also to report on item (b) of that same section [paragraph (b) of item 1]?

[Edward Bernstein (Chairman, Special Committee)]: Mr. Chairman, on part (b) the Committee agreed that something should be done to reconcile the differences between this language and that of Alternative A,[160] to indicate that there is no intent to impose criminal penalties. It was the general view although there may have been one or two reservations, that all that can be asked of members is that they bar access to the courts for transactions which are in violation of the exchange regulations of other members.

Chairman: You have heard the report on item 1 of the Special Committee. Is there any discussion?

South Africa (or perhaps Poland): Mr. Chairman, may I ask a question in regard to paragraph (c)?[161] You will see in the report of the Reporting Delegate that article [paragraph] (c) is composed of two sentences. There is some difference of opinion on the first part of article [paragraph] (c), But it seems to me that it is the understanding that the second part of this article [paragraph] (c), reading "each member agrees [to cooperate with other members in their efforts to effectuate exchange

---

[159] In Document 374, p. 604.

[160] In Document 32, pp. 54-55. Alternative A was a proposed change to Article IX, Section 2 of the preliminary draft agreement, "Gold Purchases Based on Parity Prices."

[161] In Document 343, p. 576, referred to in Document 374, p. 605.

regulations prescribed by such members in accord with] this agreement"—I would like to state that this second part is agreed upon.

[Edward Bernstein] (Chairman, Special Committee): I believe that it was the view of the Special Committee last night that the language needed [p. 11] certain further definition to make it perfectly clear that cooperation did not include the necessity for imposing criminal penalties in any country which enforced the regulations of another country. On the other hand, there would be some effort made to express the feeling that we should work out some way of cooperating, but not so as to involve any use of criminal penalty.

United States ([Edward Bernstein again?]): I should add that it was the agreement of the Committee in substance. It was also the opinion of this Committee that the appropriate language for this purpose should be prepared by the Drafting Committee.

Chairman: The statement has been made that the recommendation of the [Special] Committee was one of substance; that there are, I gather, some changes to be made in form and possibly in language, but in no way is there to be any alteration in form of substance, so that a vote on this at this stage would be either approval or disapproval; and if it be approved, that any change we make in the Drafting Committee would not come before this Commission for another vote unless any member felt redrafting further would involve a change of substance. Am I correct in this recommendation?

[Edward Bernstein (Chairman, Special Committee)]: That is the recommendation of the Special Committee, Mr. Chairman.

Chairman: Is there any further discussion on item 1?

United Kingdom ([Dennis Robertson]): We support that, Mr. Chairman.

Chairman: The delegate from the United Kingdom supports the recommendation. Any other comment?

If not, we will put it to a vote. All those in favor, please say "aye."

(Chorus of "ayes.")

The item is approved.

We now come to item 2, which is likewise a part of the same article. Will the Reporter of the Special Committee discuss that—item 2, "Uniform Changes in Par Value." [p. 12]

[Edward Bernstein (Chairman, Special Committee)]: The item 2 of the report of the Special Committee refers to Section 8 of this article on "Uniform Changes in Par Value."

Chairman: Section 8 of Article IV is the reference.

[Edward Bernstein (Chairman, Special Committee)]: The Special Committee has had this problem: after extended discussion in Committee 2—and an ad hoc committee—the problem before the [Special] Committee was whether or not the uniform change in the par value of the member's currency would require a majority of the member countries voting as countries. After extended discussion, it was unanimously agreed in the Special Committee that the language in this recommendation be reported to this Commission as representing the views of the Special Committee. There may be a statement on the principle to be made by one member of that committee. May I read that language that is proposed? "The Committee recommends [the acceptance of Alternative A with an addition that any member not wishing to make a change in its par values may so notify the Fund within 72 hours and be relieved of an obligation to alter its par value. The Mexican delegate as indicated, however, that he will present his views on this item[162]] to the Commission." Alternative A would therefore read somewhat as follows. I'll summarize how Alternative A will read. "A uniform change in par values may be provided a majority of the votes so agree, including the votes of all countries with 10 percent or more of the aggregate quota." However, any member that prefers not to have the par value of its currency changed in accordance with this uniform change would so notify the Fund within 72 hours, and its par value would then remain unchanged.

Belgium ([Camille Gutt]): Mr. Chairman, I move that the suggestion made by the Special Committee be approved. The Special Committee had before it three alternatives on which no agreement was possible. They agreed on a form which was in fact the first one amended, and I move that the Commission accept it.

Chairman: Do I hear a second?

Honduras ([Julián Cáceres]): I second the motion.

Chairman: It's open for discussion. [p. 13]

Mexico ([Antonio Espinosa de los Monteros]):[163] I regret very much to take a few minutes of the Commission's valuable time. Nevertheless, the Mexican delegation wishes to make a clear statement of its views on the point under discussion. It should be evident to all the delegates here that in this case we are dealing with one of the fundamental sovereign rights of nations. We must, therefore, be extremely cautious in relinquishing rights which all our governments have sworn to uphold. It

---

[162] We have filled in the omitted text from Document 374, p. 605.

[163] This speech was also published with minor changes as Press Release No. 29, Document 353, pp. 1178-1180.

is obvious, of course, that international cooperation would be impossible unless we surrender some degree of our sovereign rights, but the question now before this Commission is not whether we shall ask our countries to surrender some measure of its sovereign rights in order to make our cooperation possible and truthful. The question here, gentlemen, is how much of that right need our countries surrender?

Mexico is strongly opposed to the original formula, Alternative 1 [Alternative A],[164] according to which a uniform change it up our values of all currencies can be affected by the decision of the three major powers alone. We are opposed firstly because should it be approved, the smaller nations would thereby surrender a maximum of their monetary sovereignty to the three largest countries. In the mind of the Mexican delegation, this is entirely uncalled for and unjustifiable. What reasons are there to submit small countries to the absolute will of the larger ones? How can we help cooperation by blind submission of small countries?

Secondly, we are opposed to that formula also because we do not believe it can ever be accepted by a community of self-respecting nations, for no one here can seriously believe that small countries would be willing to have the gold parities of their currencies changed at will by the larger nations. Certainly not a single one of the major powers would be willing to relinquish to a foreign agency the right of fixing the value of its currency. This is indeed one of the attributes of the [p. 14] sovereignty which [we] are prone to guard most jealousy. How then can we expect small countries to accept this formula when we submit it to them for ratification? What possible reason would they have for doing so?

Thirdly, the Mexican delegation is against the formula because it is wholly unnecessary. We know, of course, that no country would be ready to submit once more to the rigidity of the gold standard. All of us want a great degree of flexibility, but why should we, in order to obtain such flexibility, set aside the sovereignty of smaller countries that are respecting [the sovereignty of the] the larger ones? We hold this [to be] entirely unnecessary, for in any case the major powers will be able to change the gold parities of their own currencies all at once if they so decide. Inasmuch as they have agreed [[to such a course,]] by doing so, they would naturally change the international price of gold. Almost all small countries would probably follow suit, but they would do so of their own free will. Thus, are we not really sufficiently insured against rigidity? Why should we ask small countries to participate in decisions which probably

[164] Article IV, Section 5, page 38 of the loose-leaf conference binder, in Document 32, p. 54.

will be made as they have always been made in the past, without their consent? Why should they give up in vain such large measure of their sovereignty?

Lastly, the Mexican delegation will vote against the original formula because it shows a great disregard for the problems of the smaller nations. Instead, it assumes that these countries would have no problems at all if the uniform changes were agreed upon by the largest ones. It presupposes that smaller countries will change their laws and perhaps even their constitutions at a minute's notice, regardless of social or economic difficulties. It takes for granted that these countries can brush aside, if they so desire, the gold clause which they might have subscribed in international contracts. But are all these suppositions really valid? Are we not taking too much for granted?

The Mexican [p. 15] delegation wants to thank other delegations for their efforts towards conciliation between their point of view and Alternative A. We regret to say, however, that in the matter of principle, a compromise is hardly possible. The essential difference between Alternatives B and C[165] before the Commission is that whereas under the former, a majority of countries is required to approve a uniform change, under the latter, a vote of only one-third of the member countries would be necessary. I must not tire this Commission with all the enumeration of the reasons on which we base our opposition to the South African proposal. Basically, they are the same which I have said before. Suffice it to say, nevertheless, that while Mexico would agree to submit to the decisions taken in this important matter by a majority of countries, she does not consider it necessary for cooperation to accept the [will] of a small minority, as proposed by South Africa.

Certainly, Mr. Chairman, the implications of this whole question are very serious. It is because Mexico believes sincerely in not doing unto others which she would not wish them to do unto her that we insist that this Commission approve a formula whereby due respect be paid to the sovereign rights of large and smaller countries alike.

Chairman: Notwithstanding the necessity for urgency, I think that we would all recognize that the delegate from Mexico has been brief when one takes into consideration the importance of the subject which he was discussed.

---

[165] Alternative B is Document 108, p. 121; Alternative C is Document 164, p. 184.

Unidentified: Please take a point of order that you referred this matter yesterday not to the Special Committee but to a subcommittee, the report of which has not been presented to you yet.

[André Istel] (France, Chairman, Ad Hoc Committee on Uniform Changes in Par Value): I am not the chairman of the French delegation, but am chairman of the ad hoc committee which was formed to deal with this matter, and I have understood [p. 16] that the matter would not come up before we would come into agreement with the Reporter of the Special Committee, which works tonight, and which came to conclusions which apparently were different to those which we adhere to, and unanimous with the consent of Mexico. Only by our Special Committee do I suggest, Mr. Chairman, that the matter be delayed to the next Commission so that the chairman of the [Ad Hoc] Committee [on Uniform Changes in Par Value] can get into agreement with the chairman of the Special Committee.

Reporting Delegate ([Louis Rasminsky, Canada]): My understanding [of] the report of the Special Committee was in fact that the formula outlined by Mr. Bernstein was in fact acceptable to all who were present at the meeting of the Special Committee. A certain confusion has arisen, but I do think that we could save time if we could agree with the words of the Special Committee.

United States ([Edward Bernstein]): I regret if the Special Committee unwittingly assumed that every unsettled question by definition was referred to that committee. The fault may be ours. We hope, however, the Commission will take the view that the report of the Special Committee be given precedence, because we have unanimous consent of all the countries represented on this Special Committee and a representative of the French National Committee. This Commission will then move forward on the recommendation of the Special Committee. [p. 17]

Chairman: The Chair regrets the misunderstanding that has taken place.

The delegate from France.

France ([Pierre Mendès-France]): (The remarks, given in French, by the delegate were interpreted as follows: "The representative of the French Committee said that he was not present yesterday evening at that meeting—")

Chairman: The Chair will request the view of the Commission—

France ([Pierre Mendès-France]): (Interpreter continued as follows: "— when this question was discussed at the beginning of the meeting.")

Chairman: The Chair will request the view of the Commission whether we should proceed to act on the recommendation of the Special Committee, or whether they would prefer to refer the matter back to the Special Committee in the light of the statement of the delegate from France.

France ([André Istel?]): I move that it be referred back to the Special Committee, Mr. Chairman.

Chairman: You move that it be referred back to the Special Committee.

France ([André Istel?]): Back to the Ad Hoc Committee [on Uniform Changes in Par Value], not to the Special Committee.

Chairman: Well, then, the question before us is whether to defer consideration and refer this matter back to the Special Committee, [which] has already considered the matter and is reporting unanimously. All those in favor of referring it back to the Special Committee, as against voting on the report of the Special Committee, please say "aye."

Is my question clear? All those who favor referring it back to the Special Committee, please say "aye." [p. 18]

Delegates: Aye.

Chairman: All those opposed?

Delegates: No.

Chairman: May I put the question again? Apparently, there is some doubt. All those in favor of referring this matter back to the Special Committee, [which] has already considered this matter and has voted unanimously—I don't want to influence your vote.

(Laughter.)

France: We do not understand whether you mean to refer it back to the Ad Hoc Committee [on Uniform Changes in Par Value] or to the Special Committee.

Chairman: I raised the question whether to refer it back to the Special Committee. If the vote to refer it back to the Special Committee is "no," I will then ask whether it should be referred back to the Ad Hoc Committee, and if it is not, we will put the question before you. All those in favor of referring the matter back to the Special Committee, please say "aye."

Delegates: Aye.

Chairman: Opposed?

Delegates: No.

Chairman: All those in favor of putting it before the Ad Hoc Committee, please say "aye."

Delegates: Aye.

Chairman: All those opposed?

Delegates: No.

Chairman: Let me put now the question of the acceptance of the report by the Special Committee. All those in favor of accepting the report of the Special Committee—is that a point of order? [p. 19]

South Africa: May I speak to that point?

Chairman: The delegate from South Africa.

South Africa: Mr. Chairman, when this matter was before this committee [Commission] yesterday, the statement was made by the chairman of the Ad Hoc Committee [on Uniform Changes in Par Value] that although at the last meeting of the Ad Hoc Committee there was disagreement, he understood that agreement had now been reached as between the members, Mexico dissenting on the proposal originally put by South Africa. That proposal was that for uniform change the following revision should be necessary:

No. 1, that the countries having more than 10 percent of the quota should agree.

No. 2, that there should be a majority vote of all committees.

No. 3, that one-third of the member countries should agree. That, I understood yesterday, to be acceptable to everybody.

There was some question of wording, which you raised yourself, and, fourth, the matter of getting the wording brought into line was referred back by you to the Ad Hoc Committee, not to the Special Committee.

The Ad Hoc Committee has met and changed only one word or, rather, there was discussion there through the chairman and they have changed only one word for clarification, and the Ad Hoc Committee now brings forward the report to which they thought this Commission agreed yesterday. The Special Committee has, however, brought in a new report which differs in substance from what we understood this Commission to agree to yesterday. In other words, may I suggest with respect to the Special Committee, it is on the wrong foot because they have brought in a change of substance. They [p. 20] have not just redrafted what this Commission was in agreement with yesterday.

Chairman: Owing to the misunderstanding, the Chair asks the view of the Commission whether or not the matter should be referred back to the Ad Hoc Committee. The Chair ascertained that the Commission voted against such proposal. It then inquired of the Commission whether it should be returned by it to the Special Committee. The Commission again voted "no." There is, therefore, before the Commission the question of the acceptance or rejection of a report by the Special Committee. Is there any more discussion on that point?

The delegate from Colombia.

Colombia: (The remarks, given in Spanish by the delegate from Colombia, were interpreted as follows: "The chairman of the delegation from Colombia wishes to state the following: it, the delegation from Colombia, heartily approves the statement made by the delegation of Mexico and states that if Alternative A is left as it is now, it would make it extremely difficult for their government to approve the agreement.")

Chairman: The delegate from Belgium.

Belgium (Camille Gutt): I heard another statement made by the South African delegation and I was astonished at that, because yesterday at the Special Committee meeting we discussed for a long time that precise amendment, and although there were a good deal of members who were in favor of it, it was not possible to reach an agreement on that, and that is why we had to amend Alternative A, on which we reached unanimous agreement. Therefore, I support the motion by which we should approve the proposal of the Special Committee.

Chairman: Are there any other comments? [p. 21]

The delegate from South Africa.

South Africa: It seems the Commission has decided to deal with the matter which I proposed as an amendment to the report of the Special Committee, that we accept Alternative C.[166] I will explain that with the addition of these words from the report of the Special Committee: "Any member not wishing to make a change in its par value may so notify the Fund within 72 hours and be relieved of an obligation to alter its par value." The effect of that would then be the change of par value—countries with 10 percent or more of the quota would have to agree, 50 percent of quotas would have to be cast, and one-third of the members would have to vote for it. And if, after that, any particular member does not want to change its currency, then it must notify within 72 hours. I propose that as an amendment to the report of the Special Committee.

Chairman: Then, I understand that the amendment contains this difference: as against the recommendation by the [Special] Committee, that you are adding that the vote by members shall include one-third of the members. Is that the only difference?

---

[166] "Uniform Changes in Par Values," Document 164, p. 184; Article IV, Section 5 in the preliminary draft. It is Article IV, Section 8 in the intermediate draft, and the language is supplied in Alternative C, because Document 321, p. 522, contains only a placeholder for the clause.

South Africa: That is the only difference.

Chairman: The delegate from the United States.

United States (Ansel Luxford): I rise in opposition to the proposed amendment by the Union of South Africa. I would like to emphasize two points here: that I know of no better way to protect the sovereignty of every country present than to give them the full right, in the event that they do not want to go along with the uniform change in par value, to ad hoc take themselves out of it. Therefore, this provision [p. 22] could not hurt any country that wishes to say, "We do not want to go along with it." All they have to do is give the Fund 72 hours' notice and they have that right.

Chairman: When you say "take themselves out of it"—take themselves out of what?

United States (Ansel Luxford): Out of the provision. It expressly states that any country "may so notify the Fund within 72 hours and be relieved of an obligation to alter its par value." No better way could be found to protect the sovereignty of every country.

Chairman: Does it apply to small nations as well as large?

United States (Ansel Luxford): Large and small.

Chairman: Any further comments?

The delegate from France.

[André Istel] (Chairman, Ad Hoc Committee on Uniform Changes in Par Value): Mr. Chairman, as the Ad Hoc Committee had prepared a report on the basis which has been accepted both by the representatives of the United States and of the United Kingdom, and [as] this report is very short, may I read this report?[167]

Chairman: Does the report differ from the amendment by the delegate from South Africa?

[André Istel] (Chairman, Ad Hoc Committee on Uniform Changes in Par Value): It is practically the same.

Chairman: Then, do you think it is necessary to read?

[André Istel] (Chairman, Ad Hoc Committee on Uniform Changes in Par Value): Well, it is in order to make it absolutely clear. I would have much preferred that that discussion had not taken place, but now it has taken place—

Chairman: Is the matter unclear to any members of the Commission? Is there anyone who doesn't understand what the issue is?

---

[167] We have not found the report in the conference documents.

(After a pause.) Would it be all right with the delegate [p. 23] from France, then, if we proceed to a vote?

[André Istel] (Chairman, Ad Hoc Committee on Uniform Changes in Par Value): All right.

Chairman: I call for a vote, first, on the amendment offered by the delegate from South Africa, which added to the 10 percent and the majority vote and the 72-hour withdrawal the requirement that one-third of the member countries approve. Am I correctly stating your amendment, Mr. Delegate?

South Africa: Yes.

Chairman: All those in favor of the amendment, signify by saying "aye."

Delegates: Aye.

Chairman: All those opposed?

Delegates: No.

Chairman: I am afraid I will have to call for hands. All those in favor of the amendment, please raise their hands.

(Show of hands, the number not stated.)

All those opposed?

(Show of hands, the number not stated.)

The amendment is defeated.

We now go back to the [Special] Committee report. All those in favor of accepting the committee report, please raise their hands.

Greece: May I—

Chairman: Do you raise a point of order?

Greece: Yes.

Chairman: The delegate from Greece.

Greece: I should like to ask why this short 72-hour term is accepted here. I think it is too short a time to decide the matter if the Fund decides to [[make a change in par values?]].

Chairman: The delegate from Greece feels that 72 hours is too short a time to permit a country to act properly on the matter.

Greece: Mr. Chairman, I think it would be a very serious [p. 24] decision for the country to declare that it can't accept the decision of the Fund to raise or to reduce the rates, and I think that this country ought to have some much more time. Seventy-two hours is too short.

Chairman: The delegate from Greece feels that the time 72 hours is too short for any foreign country to be required to act on a matter of such importance.

The delegate from the United States.

United States (Edward Bernstein): Mr. Chairman, a change of this character can be undertaken only by the Board of Governors. It is not a matter that can be made by the Executive Directors. Therefore, every member of the Fund would be present, have full notice of the question before the Board, [and] every opportunity for prompt consideration would be available to every member on this question.

It appears to me that this is a question on which delay is not possible. If the uniform change in the par value is voted, a country that withholds its decision for any extended period of time is merely encouraging the greatest disorder and exchange markets for its own currency. The world will remain uncertain for an extended period what action will be taken. I know of no better way of destroying the stability of the exchanges that withhold a decision on such a question. Furthermore,—

Greece: I am completely satisfied.

(Applause.)

Chairman: Is there anything further?

(After a pause.) All those in favor of accepting the report of the [Special] Committee, please say "aye."

Delegates: Aye.

Chairman: Opposed?

(None.) [p. 25]

Chairman: The report of the [Special] Committee is accepted.

We now turn to Article IV ["Par Values of Currencies"]. We are going to vote on the whole of Article IV, including these two sections [Section 3, "Foreign Exchange Dealings Based on Par Values," and Section 8, "Uniform Changes in Par Values"]. These two sections haven't been approved. We are now asking approval on the remainder of the article.

Any discussion? Does anyone want to discuss any one of the provisions?

If not, I am going to ask for a vote on Article IV as a whole. All those in favor of accepting Article IV—does the delegate from the Soviet Union wish to discuss this?

USSR: (Inaudible.)

Chairman: I am sorry, I will have to ask you to speak a little louder.

USSR: The delegation of the Soviet Union wants to make a [[point of order?]]. Yesterday night there [was] tendered a new proposal on this point, not discussed today at the Commission.

Chairman: Is the delegate from the Soviet Union discussing—

USSR: Excuse me.

Chairman: You have reference to the next article.

We are now calling for a vote on Article IV. All those in favor of Article IV, please signify by saying "aye."

Delegates: Aye.

Chairman: Opposed?

(None.)

Article IV is accepted.

We now come to Article V ["Transactions with the Fund"]. The new Article V is the old Article III. There is a little confusion here. We will clear it up in a moment.

The Special Committee had considered two provisions under [p. 26] Article V. They are listed in the report of the Special Committee as item 3 and item 5. We will first call for a report on item 3.[168]

United States (Edward Bernstein): Mr. Chairman, the item "Charges and Commissions," which your Special Committee considered and reports on today, has been the subject of extended discussion in Committee 2 of Commission I, in this Commission itself, and last night and this morning in the Special Committee. It appears to me that there is little need to summarize the views expressed at the Special Committee. I believe ten of the countries represented on the Special Committee agreed to the recommendation of the Committee. Two countries reserved their position on this recommendation.

In substance, what the Committee recommends is the following: that a charge of three-fourths of one percent be levied by the Fund on exchange transactions in member countries, in those cases in which a country initiates a purchase of foreign exchange from the Fund.

The Fund itself may raise this charge to one percent or lower it to one-half percent. That is the first point recommended by the Committee. The second point is to leave to the Fund the levying of reasonable handling charges on gold transactions with members. The Committee, I believe, was unanimous on that one recommendation.

The third recommendation of the Committee is that the table of charges already familiar to you in Alternative B[169] be regarded as standard charges, and that they be progressive in the manner indicated in that Alternative in time and in amount; that there be a consideration of the position of a member country in the Fund whenever the charge levied on that number rises to 4 percent.

---

[168] In Document 374, p. 605. The item refers to Article V, Section 8 ("Charges and Commissions") of the intermediate draft, Document 321, p. 524.

[169] Document 285, pp. 464-465.

And, finally, it was recommended by the Committee that [p. 27] this table of charges be subject to revision downward or upward by a three-quarters vote.

That is the recommendation of the [Special] Committee.

Chairman: You have heard the recommendation of the committee. Did I understand you to say that was the unanimous recommendation of the Special Committee?

Edward Bernstein (Chairman, Special Committee): Two countries reserved to their position on some aspects of the recommendation; one, I believe, on the first part regarding the three-fourths percent charge for exchange transactions; two on the levying of charges on excess holdings of currency by the Fund. It is unanimous on the three-fourths vote if the standard charges are levied.

Chairman: You have heard the report of the committee. Is there some discussion?

The delegate from Bolivia.

Bolivia ([René Ballivián]): When this matter was discussed in the Commission or the committee—

Chairman: Could I ask you to speak a little louder?

Bolivia ([René Ballivián]): Certainly. The Bolivian delegation proposed two changes, which I understand have not been taken into account. One, I understand that the Special Committee has [in] its working paper combined Alternatives A and B on page 13a.[170] Is that right, Mr. Bernstein?

United States (Edward Bernstein): That's right.

Bolivia ([René Ballivián]): On that page there is a paragraph (b), which reads as follows: "The Fund may levy a reasonable handling charge on any member buying gold from the Fund or selling gold to the Fund." The proposal was to eliminate the last words, the words appearing after the word "Fund." That is, for selling gold to the Fund, because I feel that it is in the interest of the Fund that gold be sold to the Fund, and besides that, [p. 28] there are provisions which compel a country to sell to the Fund the excess of their gold holdings. So I don't think it would be reasonable to impose any charge on the sale of gold to the Fund. That is one point.

And the second one was that the period within which a country could purchase foreign currency from the Fund without any charge be extended to six months. That comes under paragraph (c), [subparagraph] (i), "Amounts [up to] 25 percent."

---

[170] Document 277, pp. 441-442.

Those were the two proposals made by the Bolivian delegation, and I don't see that they have been considered or discussed in any document.

United States (Edward Bernstein): Mr. Chairman.

Chairman: The delegate from United States.

United States (Edward Bernstein): The proposal of the delegate from Bolivia on gold was in fact discussed by the Special Committee. Their recommendation is that the statement on the charges as reported be accepted. But may I explain why we did not accept the amendment, or any similar amendment such as that proposed by the delegate from Bolivia. It is quite clear that the Fund is not expected to levy charges where there is a compulsory sale of gold or foreign exchange to the Fund. Where the initiative comes from a member, the Fund levies charges; where the initiative comes from the Fund, it is not intended that charges be levied.

On the question whether the Fund can dispense with the charge when it purchases gold, it appears to me that we cannot bind the Fund on that point. So long as any member has a handling charge when it purchases gold from the Fund, so long as steamship and air companies have charges for transportation and insurance companies for [p. 29] insurance, the Fund may have to charge for its dealings in gold. Otherwise, we may simply be burdening the Fund with the obligation of undertaking every gold transaction in the world, underwriting the costs, and providing the currency that would otherwise be acquired outside the Fund. It would be an impossible burden on the Fund. Nevertheless, there may be occasions when the Fund can dispense entirely with charges, and for that reason it is recommended that the Fund be given complete discretion in levying reasonable handling charges.

Chairman: Any further discussion?

China: Mr. Chairman.

Chairman: The delegate from China.

China: This paragraph was discussed last night at length. It was generally recognized that the principle and the table[171] were to help [[the Fund?]] serve a large number of nations. Otherwise, the Fund may be tied up in long-term borrowings and the benefit of the Fund would be limited to a small number of countries. It was generally agreed that the principle of these charges was sound and the schedule was reasonable. Therefore, Mr. Chairman, I move acceptance of this report.

Chairman: The delegate from China moves acceptance of the report.

---

[171] Again apparently the table of charges on loans by the IMF in Document 285, pp. 464-465.

Mexico: I second the motion, Mr. Chairman.

Chairman: The motion has been seconded by the delegate from Mexico.

The delegate from New Zealand has the floor.

New Zealand: Mr. Chairman, as New Zealand was one of the countries which tabled a reservation about the scale of fees, and as the chairman of the New Zealand delegation is not here, I wish to ask leave to state very briefly New Zealand's attitude about these charges. [p. 30]

We feel very strongly that in principle they are not in the best interests of carrying out the spirit of the Fund as a whole. A country which wishes to cooperate with the spirit of the Fund and to assist in international trade will both export and import to the fullest extent of its ability, having regard to balancing its payments in exchange over the period. To the extent that these charges are designed not for revenue purposes, but to discourage leaning on the Fund within the proper scope of its provisions, they actually do impede a country which desires to cooperate with the Fund to the fullest extent of its ability. Therefore, it is earnestly urged that other means of dealing with those countries who do not cooperate with the spirit of the Fund, or who lean on the resources of the Fund too heavily and for too long, should be found. If it were done, the countries who were delinquent would be dealt with for their delinquencies, and, on the other hand, those countries which do cooperate to the best of their ability and carrying out the spirit of the Fund would not be penalized in any way, but, rather, encouraged.

Chairman: Have any of the delegates not been able to hear the delegate from New Zealand?

(No reply.)

Then it will not be necessary to summarize what the delegate from New Zealand has said.

The delegate from the United Kingdom asked for the floor.

United Kingdom ([Dennis Robertson]): Mr. Chairman, the degree of accommodation which has been reached on this difficult matter, while not complete, is very great, and I feel very gratified and I hope that the Commission will accept this report.

Chairman: Any further discussion?

Canada: Mr. Chairman. [p. 31]

Chairman: The delegate from Canada.

Canada: I think we ought not to leave this discussion without making two points clear. In the first place, it is, as I understand it, not possible to operate this Fund without a scale of charges very much as the one suggested. In the second place, the point raised by the delegate from New Zealand is very effective and, may I say, very generously dealt with on the part of those countries which might conceivably come under it in the section on "scarce currency" much more effectively than it would possibly be dealt with by a scale of charges, such as suggested by the delegate from New Zealand on what we might call "creditor" countries, and I think we should certainly accept the report of the committee.

Chairman: Is there any further comment? If not, the Chair will put the matter to a vote.

(After a pause.) Those in favor of accepting the report and the recommendations of the Special Committee on charges and commissions, please say "aye."

Delegates: Aye.

Chairman: Opposed?

Unidentified: No. (One voice.)

Chairman: The report is accepted.[172]

We will now turn to item 5 ["Other Acquisition of Gold by the Fund," Article V, Section 7 of Document 321], which also is included in this Article. We are skipping item 4 because that belongs to another article. We are now going to report on item 5, page 2 of the Special Committee's report.[173]

Edward Bernstein (Chairman, Special Committee): Mr. Chairman, on this section of Article V there was considerable discussion. It was not possible in this, as in one or two other cases, to provide the Special Committee the final language. It was possible for the Special Committee to discuss the principles involved [p. 32] and to secure a consensus on the question.

I summarize the views of the Committee as follows: so far as regards the rights of the country to repurchase its currency from the Fund with gold, there was unanimous agreement. That is Alternative A, page 10.[174]

So far as regards the principle that a country which uses the resources of the Fund so that the Fund's holdings of its currency rise during the financial year of the Fund, that member should be obligated to repurchase from the Fund enough of the Fund's holdings of its currency to assure that it has drawn upon its independent monetary reserve to the

[172] Became Article V, Section 8 in the final agreement.

[173] In Document 374, pp. 605-606.

[174] Article III, Section 7 ("Acquisition by Members of Currencies of Other Members for Gold") of the preliminary draft agreement, in Document 32, p. 33; Article V, Section 6d of the intermediate draft, Document 321, p. 524.

same extent as it has drawn on the Fund. That is the principle. On that principle I think there was general agreement, with perhaps one reservation. On the matter of implementing it, in the case of countries who keep their monetary reserve in the form not only of gold but of other currencies, it was agreed that some appropriate method of utilizing each type of reserve would have to be worked out. The Committee, showing full confidence in Professor Robertson,[175] turned over the principle to him in the light of the discussion of the Committee, and requested that he draft a provision which would make that principle quite clear. On the principle, except I believe with one reservation, there was no disagreement whatever in the Committee.

The second part of this same provision (a) states that when a member country is increasing its monetary reserve after having made use of them in the manner already described, if there is still an increase in its monetary reserve, it shall thereafter repurchase from the Fund the Fund's holdings of its currency to the extent of one-half of the increase in those monetary reserves during the year, though this provision should not apply to a country [p. 33] whose monetary reserves are less than its quota, nor should the obligation to repurchase be extended if the Fund's holdings of that currency are down to 75 percent of the quota. On this point, too, there was, I believe, general agreement in the Committee, with perhaps one reservation, and it was again suggested and agreed in the Committee that Professor Robertson be entrusted with the preparation of a statement embodying the substance and giving effect to the concept of appropriate—whether gold or other types of monetary reserves should be used for this purpose.

The Committee's report on the same section also involves the obligation of a member country whose currency is not used in international trade to repurchase its currency from the Fund, with the whole of the increment in its convertible currencies in its monetary reserves in the form of foreign exchange which it has built up as a result of transactions with third countries. That is the question that had already been accepted by this Commission yesterday. There was no need for further consideration by the Committee. It was merely embodied at this point because of its logical position. Though the Committee approves of it, I doubt whether it is before this Commission in any sense, having been approved yesterday.

Chairman: The last point only?

---

[175] Dennis Robertson of the United Kingdom.

Edward Bernstein (Chairman, Special Committee): The last point only. One final point: that none of these obligations can be imposed by the Fund on a member where it involves the purchase by the Fund of the member's currency whose holdings the Fund already has in excess of the member's currency which would be repurchased, both being reckoned in terms of proportion of the quota.

And, finally, in the transfer of any currency to the [p. 34] Fund under any of these provisions, the consent of the members whose currencies is being transferred would be required.

That is the recommendation of the [Special] Committee. That will be available in the language drafted by Professor Robertson, which would then be submitted to the Drafting Committee if this Commission approves it.

Chairman: The delegate from France.

France ([Robert Mossé]): Concerning this section about the acquisitions of gold by the Fund, as submitted now by the Special Committee, we are somewhat in doubt about the exact meaning and interpretation, especially when we are comparing [it] with the original text of the Joint Statement,[176] and we have one interpretation which I would like to lay down upon you gentlemen in order to contribute to clarification.

I understand from this new text that now with this new text, practically the yearly drawing power or, if you so prefer, the drawing power for a twelve-month period, will be reduced for the countries having gold reserves and convertible currency in excess of the quota—will be reduced from 25 percent to 12½ percent because in this text, if this interpretation is correct, there is the necessity of paying half in gold. Now, you remember, gentlemen, that the various discussions concerning the purchases of currency in another article lead to a relatively small amount—I mean that particularly the concessions made were very small and were only 25 percent. Now, in the case of such countries having more than an excess of their quota, it is no longer, if this interpretation is correct, 25 percent, but 12½ percent in a twelve-month period. Now, if this interpretation is correct, I want to draw the attention of this assembly to the importance of the question, and if this interpretation is correct we would reserve our right to speak again about it. [p. 35]

Chairman: I understood the question. I doubt whether the interpretation is correct. I call on the Reporting Delegate from the United States to answer.

176 In Document 32, pp. 28-30.

Edward Bernstein (Chairman, Special Committee): Mr. Chairman, I regret to say that the interpretation of Professor Mossé is not correct. There is nothing in this provision which in any way limits the right of a country to proceed with its purchases of exchange from the Fund, all other conditions being complied with, to 25 percent of its quota in any twelve-month period. I doubt whether a lengthy exposition of this fact is needed, but if it is it can be given.

France (Robert Mossé): I am glad to know that my interpretation is not correct.

Chairman: Any further discussion on this point?

The delegate from the Soviet Union.

USSR: Mr. Chairman, the delegation of the USSR wants to make two remarks concerning these principles governing the repurchase of currency from the Fund. [As] concerns the first point, [paragraph] (a),[177] this text was sent to us only yesterday late in the night, and the Soviet delegation had no opportunity to consider this text and to make the [[necessary study]]. Therefore, the Soviet delegation wants to reserve its right to refer to this question we have the opportunity to consider it, and I think it would be better when the Drafting Committee will elaborate the final text.

[As] concerns the second part of this text, tendered to us yesterday night, paragraph (b), we want to point out that when this paragraph was

---

177 The delegate is referring to item 5 in Document 374, p. 606. This item becomes the subject of an involved discussion just below. The text reads:

"(a) If, at the end of the Fund's financial year, a member's monetary reserves exceed its quota, and the Fund's holdings of its currency have increased during the year, the Fund shall require that it use a part of these reserves to repurchase its currency with gold or with convertible currency as appropriate, up to the point when its reserves have fallen by an amount not more than the amount by which, after this adjustment, the Fund's holdings of its currency have increased. Furthermore, if, after this adjustment (if called for) has been made, a member's monetary reserves have increased during the year, the Fund shall require it, whether or not the Fund's holdings of its currency have increased during the year, (p. 3) to use half of this increase for a further re-purchase of its currency with gold or with convertible currency as appropriate; provided, always, that after these adjustments have been made its reserves do not stand below its quota nor the Fund's holdings of the currency below 75 percent of its quota.

"(To replace part (b) of III, 9 and to be shifted to III-8)

"(b) If a member country increases its holdings of another member's currency, or acquires gold from another member otherwise than as a result of transactions with that member, the Fund at the request of the latter member may require the gold or the increase of currency to be offered to the Fund."

discussed in the Special Committee yesterday it raised the question if it is standard (intended) that the countries [that] put definite pieces [i.e., shares?] in a currency of another member country should be obligated to offer this [p. 36] increase to the Fund for repurchase of their currency immediately at every particular transaction, or if it is meant that they will repurchase by this increase their currency at some intervals, at the end of a financial year or something like it.

And the second question which we raised yesterday was, if a country had any such an increase of a currency of a third country, would be entitled to use this increase for payments of a normal amortization of its foreign debts expressed in this currency?

The United States delegation explained to us that it is not meant to require the repurchase of a currency immediately after every transaction, but it is meant to divide it at short periods of time and, secondly, that such countries would be able to use this increase for the payment of normal amortizations of their foreign debt.

We would like to call the attention of this explanation to the Drafting Committee and in the drafting to include this clause: "the Soviet delegation has no objection against this [[clause]]."

Chairman: The delegation from the Soviet Union has indicated that it did not receive a copy of the proposed provision (a) in time to give it adequate study. That is regrettable. However, one must bear in mind that the proposal differs very little in substance from the material which has been under discussion for many months.

Edward Bernstein (Chairman, Special Committee): Mr. Chairman—

Chairman: And the Soviet Union also points out that with regard to [paragraph] (b) there is no difference in principle, but he is calling attention of the Drafting Committee to certain [p. 37] interpretations which, as stated, have been given by the [Special] Committee, and [he] would wish the Drafting Committee to take note of such interpretations and make them a little more explicit.

The delegate from United States.

Edward Bernstein (Chairman, Special Committee): Mr. Chairman, I regret that a copy of the statement was not available to the delegate from the Soviet Union, but I call attention to this important fact, that this provision, word for word, with the exception, I believe, of two words—"as appropriate"—has been in the hands of the Soviet experts for three or four weeks. The preparatory work of the technical men at Atlantic City involved the study of precisely this provision, which has now been changed as a statement of principles to include only two words.

Nevertheless, I do recognize that it would have been desirable to give longer notice, prior to producing it before the Special Committee, that it is the same provision which was being considered.

On the other point, I gather that no further statement is needed. In Committee 2, the point raised by the representative of the Soviet Union on the use of currencies acquired by a country through dealings with third countries was fully covered in the Committee and in a memorandum to the Committee. There is no doubt that it is free to use the resources acquired in that way.

Chairman: In view of the difficulties of language and the fact that this is a very complex clause, the fact that the Soviet Union didn't have adequate time to ascertain how much difference there was in this new draft and others must be taken into consideration. There may be only small changes, but you couldn't tell that unless you had an [p. 38] opportunity to study it, and particularly unless you had an opportunity to translate it into the language with which they were most familiar.

Is there any further discussion?

The delegate from Greece.

Greece (Kyriakos Varvaressos): Mr. Chairman, if I understood from the very clear explanations of the member from the United States and from his report that in connection with the obligations expressed in paragraph (b) on page 3, the member country will not be asked to repurchase [its] initial contribution in local currency through foreign exchange acquired in accordance with paragraph (b). And this refers only to any local currency which the Fund would hold in excess of the original subscription of the country—that is to say, in excess of 75 percent of its quota. That is what I have always understood from the declarations, and I ask if it is the exact interpretation.

Edward Bernstein (Chairman, Special Committee): The interpretation, Mr. Chairman, is not correct when applied to provision (b). Provision (b) covers the case of the country which is asked to finance its favorable balance of payments. In financing its favorable balance of payments, if it dealt directly in its own currency, the Fund would be fully authorized to go below 75 percent of its quota. The accidental fact that a country—for example, Greece—may carry on its foreign trade in sterling or in dollars ought not to limit the Fund's use of the subscription of Greece. To treat Greece, or any other country in the same position, precisely in the same way as the United States and the United Kingdom are treated in the use of the subscription to the Fund, no limit can be placed in that respect.

Chairman: Any further discussion?

The delegate from Greece.

Greece ([Kyriakos Varvaressos]): Mr. Chairman, may I ask, is there any [p. 39] difference between a country which originally has a large amount of holdings and foreign exchange and gold, and a country which afterwards may acquire some foreign exchange and gold by accepting payments in currency and gold by a third country than the countries interested in these accounts? If, for example, a country has large holdings of foreign exchange and gold, this country is not asked to contribute to the Fund by more than 25 percent of its quota in gold and convertible currency. Why, then, will a country which afterwards acquires by any means whatever some foreign exchange be required to repurchase its local currency by this gold or foreign exchange?

Chairman: The delegate from Czechoslovakia.

Czechoslovakia: I should like to draw the attention of the Commission to the fact that if the wording of the first sentence, "the Fund shall require," is not correct, and ought [not?] to be their main requirement, then it is all right. But I am not quite sure, having just heard it last night.

Chairman: The delegate from the United States.

Edward Bernstein (Chairman, Special Committee): Mr. Chairman, on the point of the delegate from Czechoslovakia, it was clear that there was a mixture of "shall" and "may" involved there. In the case of gold, for example, it was clear that the "shall" was intended. In the case of currencies, since the Fund may find it already has adequate amounts of the currency tendered, and particularly in connection with their proportions set forth in the very last paragraph, it should probably be interpreted as "may." I understand the Special Committee turned the problem over to Professor Robertson to prepare the appropriate draft.

Chairman: The delegate from the United Kingdom. [p. 40]

United Kingdom (Dennis Robertson): I am afraid I misunderstood the instruction in that respect. I thought the word "may" was to be substituted for "shall" in both places where it occurred. I would like to be clear upon that before I begin.

Chairman: The Chair is not quite clear which "shall" is being referred to. Will the delegate from Czechoslovakia repeat that?

Czechoslovakia: It is the fifth line of the first sentence.

Chairman: Suggest that it "may" require?

Czechoslovakia: Yes.

Chairman: Might the Chair interpret that as calling for a change of considerable substance in the provision?

The delegate from the United States.

Edward Bernstein (Chairman, Special Committee): Mr. Chairman, there are two stages in this. That is what causes the difficulty. The Fund *shall* require that the member offer the gold and the currency. The Fund, in turn, is in the position where it *may* not wish to take the currency, in which case there can be no compulsion on the Fund. It is that successive "shall" and "may" which leads to the difficulty in finding a single word covering both contingencies.

I should suggest that once the draft has been prepared by Professor Robertson, since it will embody a great deal more of the technique by which the Fund will—or a member will—repurchase from the Fund the currency it holds, it might then be simple to make clear what is the precise point of the "shall" and "may."

United Kingdom (Dennis Robertson): I am very sorry, but I am afraid to leave this matter as it stands. I understand the word "may" will be correct in both cases: [p. 41] "the Fund may require." That is qualified by the fact that there are certain respects in which the Fund shall not make the [[repurchase?]]. That is the last paragraph of all here. But apart from that, the Fund has no discretion, as I understand it, whether it takes or does not take.

Chairman: The Chair sympathizes with the doubt of the delegate from the United Kingdom as regards the change from "shall" to "may," as it is one of substance, and the uncertainties would seem to preclude the delegate from the United Kingdom from drafting the will of the Commission unless that is clarified.

The delegate from New Zealand.

New Zealand: Mr. Chairman, if I can make a small contribution in this respect, as the delegate who raised the question as to whether it should be "shall" or "will"—that is what you said?

Answer: "Shall" or "may."

New Zealand: "Shall" or "may"—as to whether it should be obligated beyond the future, my understanding was that the Special Committee last night left it that it would be altered to "may." In other words, there was no reservation specifically in favor of leaving the "shall."

India: Mr. Chairman.

Chairman: The delegate from India.

India: There is one point which is not quite clear to me in the light of the question raised by the delegate from Greece. The USA delegate tried to explain the position. My difficulty is this: if a member country does not draw on the Fund at all, but as a result of transactions with other member countries acquires gold or convertible exchange, what is the obligation on such member? [p. 42] Will the Fund require such member to hand over its additional holding of gold or convertible exchange against its currency held by the Fund and [[require?]] that a member country will have to hold its currency in the Fund below 75 percent of its quota?

Edward Bernstein (Chairman, Special Committee): Mr. Chairman, that is precisely the intention. Let me explain again what is the purpose of this provision. If all of India's transactions were expressed in rupees, there would be no problem but that the country with an unfavorable balance of payments with India would have access to the Fund to buy rupees and pay for those rupees with its local currency. India would then have financed the favorable balance of payments it has with other countries to the extent that other countries are eligible to use the resources of the Fund and to the extent that the Fund has resources of rupees. That would be the fact if all of India's transactions were in rupees.[178]

If all of India's transactions were in currencies other than rupees, but in each instance in the currency of another member, all the members with whom it is trading, India would then have the option of holding such currency. There is no intention to deny India that option. If India has a favorable balance of payments with the United States dealing with the United States in dollars, it would under this provision be permitted to keep all of the dollars that it acquires in that way. If India has a favorable balance of payments and dollar dealings with other countries, it will have forced on these other countries the use of their monetary reserves or the use of the Fund's resources of dollars to settle an unfavorable [p. 43] balance of payments with India. It would in effect have shifted away from itself any obligation, any responsibility, to help finance adverse balances of payments with other countries.

Does that answer the question?

India: It answers the question, Mr. Chairman, but if Mr. Bernstein's interpretation is correct, pushed to its logical extreme, what will happen in the case of a member country that no part of its quota at a certain time may be had in its own currency?

Edward Bernstein (Chairman, Special Committee): I am afraid I don't understand that statement. If I could have a concrete illustration, it might be easier for me.

---

[178] The typescript says "in currencies other than rupees," which seems to be a mistake by the speaker or the stenographer.

Chairman: I think, Mr. Chairman,[179] that it might be helpful to clear that point up if you look at the last four lines of that last section [paragraph], (a), in which it says, "after these adjustments have been made its reserves do not stand below its quota, nor the Fund's holdings of the currency below 75 percent of its quota." In other words, if the country has purchased enough back so that there is only 75 percent left, or if from the very inception the particular country has bought no foreign exchange with its local currency, it is under no obligation to repurchase any further currency and it can continue to increase its gold holdings.

Edward Bernstein (Chairman, Special Committee): That is correct, Mr. Chairman, so far—

Chairman:—As this provision is concerned.

Edward Bernstein (Chairman, Special Committee):—So far as this part of that provision is concerned. In part (b) there is a limitation, but not in terms of 75 percent. The Fund cannot have to surrender a currency which is less scarce than its own. That is to say, the Fund cannot draw [p. 44] down rupees steadily in order to build up even larger balances of another currency in its own holdings. There is that limitation.

India: It follows the view I expressed, that if the Fund operates in a manner by which it will [[convert?]] rupee holdings, it might well reach a stage where the Fund's holdings of rupees were extremely small—nil or an infinitesimal part of its quota.

Edward Bernstein (Chairman, Special Committee): Mr. Chairman, the percentage could never be nil. It is very unlikely that the percentage could even be so low as to be a scarce currency, for this reason: the Fund may not sell to India rupees and take in exchange dollars or sterling or any other currency whose holdings it has in the larger proportionate amount. It cannot make rupees scarcer than the currency that is being offered. That is point number 1. That is for protection in that sense.

The second point is, putting aside the arithmetic, if India dealt in rupees in its foreign trade, it might be true that the Fund's holdings of rupees would fall until it [the rupee] is a scarce currency. It might happen. It is less likely to happen under this provision—less likely. It is conceivable in an extreme case that it would happen here, too.

Chairman: The Chairman would like the Commission and delegations' [permission] to speak on this point. I should like to turn the Commission over to the Vice President and ask his permission, but the

---

179 Harry Dexter White is referring to Edward Bernstein as Chairman of the Special Committee.

Vice President is not here, and so I shall have to ask the approval of the Commission to speak on this point. Anyone not in favor of permitting me to speak, please say so.

(No response.) [p. 45]

I will not be long. I want to speak because I consider this matter quite important.

The question of whether this shall be "shall" or "may" relates to the vital question of the strength of the Fund. It relates to the question as to whether all members of the Fund shall be in a position to participate in the increasing strength of the Fund. The requirement is that when a country is increasing its gold holdings, it should give to the Fund the possibility of participating in that increase. You thereby assure that the Fund remains strong in the sense that there are always the resources in the Fund to acquire any currency that is becoming scarce. That means that the Fund will be in a position to not only acquire more scarce currencies, but that the Fund will always be in a position to restore its makeup, its structure, to the original position and thereby function as a stabilization fund, which is its primary purpose.

The insertion of the word "may" would subject the Board of Directors, the Executive Committee, to all kinds of pressures on the part of countries who for one reason or another would prefer to increase their own gold holdings at the expense of the rest of the members of the Fund. By the insertion of the word "shall" instead of "may," all that pressure ceases. It merely becomes then a matter of applying the principle. There will no longer be the question as to whether or not the Fund is favoring this country or that country. It will become an instrumentality to increase the strength of the Fund without in any way diminishing the weakest country involved, because the country that is required to repurchase the additional local currency which it has, in the first place has been increasing its gold holdings so that it never has only so much as it had before. [p. 46] Remember, this is only sharing in the increase, and it is sharing in the increase in a manner which increases the strength of the Fund and makes it possible for other members to participate in that strength.

Therefore, I would strongly urge that the wording at that point "shall" shall not be replaced by the word "may," and that the delegate from the United Kingdom be instructed in his drafting to use the word "shall" at that point.

United Kingdom ([Dennis Robertson]): That is the second "shall" two lines from the end of the page? Is that right?

Chairman: I was referring to "shall" in the fifth line of [paragraph] (a).

United Kingdom ([Dennis Robertson]): The word occurs twice.

Chairman: The second one?

United Kingdom ([Dennis Robertson]): First in the fifth line, and secondly in the last line or two at the end of the page. Is it the wish of the Commission that "shall" shall rule in both those places?

Chairman: It would appear to me that the logic of the situation requiring the first "shall" would likewise require the second "shall."

The delegate of the United States.

Edward Bernstein (Chairman, Special Committee): Mr. Chairman, I understand the difficulty to arise from this fact, and when we understand the difficulty I think there is no difference of opinion as to how we proceed. Under this provision, a member must offer to the Fund part of an increment of its monetary reserve. Those monetary reserves consist of gold and certain currency. We want to assure the Fund the opportunity of strengthening its position by acquiring the gold. We want to assure the Fund that it will not diminish its [p. 47] liquidity by acquiring currency of which it has already in ample supply. Therefore, on the first, the acquisition of the gold, the liquidity of the Fund always being strengthened by the transaction, the "shall" part is appropriate. On the part where it is an acquisition of currencies, the Fund must have the option of not taking it.

United Kingdom ([Dennis Robertson]): No. That is not my understanding of what is being said in any of these discussions. My understanding is that I am instructed to draft something which will make the distribution of what is handed over between the different currencies and gold subject to purely automatic test, so that there will be no discretion with the Fund to say it will not have this currency and it will not have that one. It is a fundamental point.

Chairman: It was the understanding of the Chair that it was clearly understood that the discretion of the Fund shall not be whether it shall or shall not take a particular currency, except in instances—and this is the important point which I gather Mr. Bernstein is making, and which it was my understanding was agreed on in the [Special] Committee meetings—except where the purchase or the required sale of that particular currency makes any other currency scarcer than the currency question, those exceptions which would be the great justification for applying any flexible authority on the part of the Fund. Is that your understanding, Mr. Bernstein?

Edward Bernstein (Chairman, Special Committee): Mr. Chairman, I regret the very crude language I used. I should have worded it with mathematical accuracy, in which case it probably would not have been so disturbing. It is simply this: while a member is obligated to offer a certain portion of the increment of its monetary reserve in the form of currency, that requirement will not [p. 48] apply when the currency that is being offered is more abundant than the currency that would be withdrawn, in which case if it is so clearly stated, perhaps the "shall" would be completely satisfactory.

Chairman: That's right. The use of the word "shall" and the proviso, I think, would take care of the uncertainty which prevails.

United Kingdom ([Dennis Robertson]): I am happy to think that there is, after all, no real difference, that this what you call an "exceptional" case is not an exception to the principle that the Fund may not exercise its discretion.

Chairman: The Chair will now ask for a vote on that provision, item 5, as recommended by the Special Committee. All those in favor of accepting item 5, please say "aye."[180]

Delegates: Aye.

Chairman: Those opposed?

(None.)

Chairman: It is approved, and the Chair notes the reservation of the Soviet Union on part [paragraph] (a).

Greece: Mr. Chairman.

Chairman: The delegate from Greece.

Greece: I am compelled to reserve my opinion until I see the actual draft of the [Drafting] Committee, because I am afraid that, if I understand well, the explanations given by the United States representative that any country [that issues a] weak currency which is not accepted in international payments and which country is obliged to ask for other members' currencies for his payments will not be permitted to have a favorable balance of payments unless this country is obligated to repurchase the initial subscription of its currency in the Fund. Therefore, I think this interpretation is not just. [p. 49]

Chairman: When the Drafting Committee reports, the delegate from Greece will have an opportunity to study it carefully and earnestly, [to see]

---

[180] Article III, Section 8 of the preliminary draft agreement, in Document 32, p. 33; Article V, Section 7 of the intermediate draft, in Document 321, p. 524, and in the final agreement. See also Document 374, p. 606.

whether the drafting alters in substance the provision as accepted in principle by the Commission.

Reporting Delegate (Louis Rasminsky): May I say as chairman of the Drafting Committee that nothing has given me greater pleasure than to have the drafting of this committed to the skilled hands of Professor Robertson.

Chairman: The delegate of the United States.

Edward Bernstein (Chairman, Special Committee): I regret I must report on the point which I am informed may have been misunderstood. That is the question of Professor Mossé.

I would like to make clear again what it is I have in mind. As I understood Professor Mossé's point, he believed that, as stated in this last provision we have before us, if a country—France, for example—should buy foreign exchange from the Fund, the very technique that is laid down in this provision just amended would in fact compel a limitation of France's use of the resources of the Fund to 12½ percent a year, since it would buy 25 percent and, assuming that no change had taken place in its monetary reserve, it would repurchase 12½.

In my opinion, that statement is not correct. If France needs 50 percent of its quota in foreign exchange, it can finance this by buying 25 percent from the Fund in gold and by paying for the other 25 percent in its national currency.

Chairman: I think the Commission understood that that was your exposition in the first place.

May we now turn to the next item, Article V ["Transactions with the Fund"], with the inclusion of the two provisions which have just been accepted? [p. 50] The whole of Article V is now before the Commission for acceptance or amendment, with the exception of the two provisions which have just been accepted.

All those in favor—or is there any comment anyone wishes to make on any other provisions in Article V?

(After a pause.) If not, the Chair will ask for a vote of those in favor of Article V completely. Please say "aye."

Delegates: Aye.

Chairman: All those opposed?

(None.)

Chairman: Then Article V is accepted.

We now turn to Article VI, item 4[181] on page 2 of the Special Committee's report. Article VI is ready for your vote. Does anyone wish to discuss Article VI on "Capital Transfers," which has already been discussed in the earlier meeting?

(After a pause.) Then I will put Article VI to a vote of the Commission. All those in favor of Article VI, labeled "Capital Transfers," please say "aye."

Delegates: Aye.

Chairman: Opposed?

(None.)

Then Article VI is accepted by the Commission.

Article VII, dealing with "Scarce Currencies," is the next article before you. That is also complete. Is there anyone who wishes to discuss any one of the provisions in Article VII?

(After a pause.) If not, I shall call for a vote on Article VII. All those in favor of Article VII *in toto,* please say "aye."

Delegates: Aye. [p. 51]

Chairman: Opposed?

(None.)

Article VII is accepted.

In Article VIII ["General Obligations of Members"], we will call on the Special Committee to report on item 4 ["Multilateral International Clearing"], page 2 of its report, which belongs under Article VIII, [Section 3].[182]

Edward Bernstein (Chairman, Special Committee): Mr. Chairman, for easier reference by this Commission, I ask that they turn to page 14, where the last four terms on the page are marked "not yet available."

Chairman: Page 14 of what?

Edward Bernstein (Chairman, Special Committee): Page 14 of the Drafting Committee Annex 2.[183]

May we cross out the part marked "Section 4," which is in fact the (b) clause [i.e., paragraph] which we have just considered?

Chairman: Would you please repeat that?

---

[181] There is no such item in the place the Chairman mentions, and it is unclear to us what he means.

[182] In Document 374, p. 605.

[183] In Document 321, p. 527.

Edward Bernstein (Chairman, Special Committee): Section 4 of Article VIII, "Acceptance of Currency from [Purchased by] the Fund," has been replaced by the (b) clause we have just discussed.

Chairman: Then, that is deleted as having been already discussed.

Edward Bernstein (Chairman, Special Committee): That is correct. Section 2.

Reporting Delegate (Louis Rasminsky): Before we leave that, I don't think there is a relationship between the (b) clause that we have discussed and what was previously covered by Section 4, but I would suggest that the Drafting Committee be instructed to consider whether the old Section 4 remains necessary in view of the (b) clause which has been approved. I am not certain that it still isn't necessary.

Edward Bernstein (Chairman, Special Committee): Mr. Chairman, I see no objection to leaving to the Drafting Committee consideration whether the new text which will be available supersedes completely the old text, or whether some segment of the old text is still necessary. [p. 52]

Chairman: You are now going to discuss provision 4, labeled "Multilateral International Clearing," as reported by your Special Committee.[184]

Edward Bernstein (Chairman, Special Committee): Mr. Chairman, the Special Committee considered at some length the meaning of certain aspects of Article VIII, Section 3, on "Multilateral International Clearing."

Chairman: May I interrupt and ask whether that, likewise, will replace Section 3 on page 14, which you mentioned?[185]

Edward Bernstein (Chairman, Special Committee): That is Section 3, page 14, we are talking about now.

The problem before the Committee was not one of substance, but of interpretation. The Committee was asked to express its views on two points in connection with multilateral international clearing. The first was whether the obligation to repurchase its currency by a member when such currency is in the hands of another member shall extend also to the repurchase of balances which are being transferred as capital or the acquisition of securities or for the holding of balances elsewhere.

After extended discussion, much consideration was given to the fact that in Article V,[186] on "Capital Transfers," there is provision for certain

---

[184] Document 329, pp. 544-546; see also the reference to this document in Document 374, p. 605.

[185] Again, in Document 321, p. 527.

capital transfers to be financed through exchange acquired from the Fund, their general desirability being recognized, despite that it was the opinion of the Committee that the right of a country to control capital transfers is unlimited, precisely as Article V now states. In this provision there is, however, a statement that where a country wishes to transfer funds for the purpose of acquiring goods, for paying for current transactions, the [p. 53] capital transfer aspect would not be regarded as applying. That, I understand, was the sense of our Committee. There may have been one or two reservations, though toward the end it seemed to me that there were few indeed. Those are the points.

Mr. Chairman, might we proceed on that point before going to the second?

Chairman: Any further discussion on that point?

(After a pause.) Would you continue, then, with the remainder?

Edward Bernstein (Chairman, Special Committee): The second point, Mr. Chairman, was—

Chairman: Before proceeding, it may be helpful to call your attention to the fact that what was being discussed at that point was Document 329,[187] for those who wish to refer to it. That had been discussed yesterday and was really referred to the Special Committee for some interpretation, which will continue with the report.

Edward Bernstein (Chairman, Special Committee): The second point placed before the Special Committee was again a matter of interpretation. There was agreement on the language, and inquiry was pressed as to whether the last clause "nor shall apply to a member which has ceased to be entitled to buy currency of other members from the Fund in exchange for its own currency" should be interpreted to mean that this obligation to redeem one's own currency under certain conditions is terminated when the Fund's holdings of the member's currency has reached 200 percent, or whether it may be terminated at certain intervals when it has exhausted its 25 percent for any twelve-month period.

After some discussion, it was agreed in the Committee that any termination for any cause of the right of the member to acquire foreign exchange from the Fund constitutes a termination of this obligation, without prejudicing, however, [p. 54] the other obligations which may be involved in [Articles] IX, [Section] 5 ["Freedom of Assets [of the IMF]

[186] Article V of the preliminary draft, which became Article VI in the intermediate draft and the final agreement.

[187] Document 329, pp. 544-546.

from Restriction"] or IX, 6 ["Immunity of Officers and Employees from Suit"]. On that I think there was almost no difference within the Committee.

Chairman: You have heard the report of the Special Committee on that provision. Is there any discussion?

(After a pause.) If not, the Chair will put the question. All those in favor of accepting the report of the Special Committee on item 4, page 2 ["Multilateral International Clearing"], please say "aye."[188]

Delegates: Aye.

Chairman: Those opposed?

(None.)

We now turn to [Section] No. 5 in the [Special Committee] report, the furnishing of information. It is [Section] No. 5 of Article VIII [of Article VIII, "Furnishing of Information"—item no. 6 in the report].[189]

Edward Bernstein (Chairman, Special Committee): Mr. Chairman, on this point, on the section, the Special Committee considered two points. The first was a rearrangement of the language on page 14(c). No change in words except the dropping of "however" was involved. The shifting of some words was involved. If those who have page 14c of the "bible," Document 182, on "Furnishing Information," [will please turn to it]. It is proposed in the first paragraph, reading, "The Fund may require members to furnish it with such information as it deems necessary for its operations," to delete there after the sentence down to "The minimum amount of information necessary for the effective discharge of the Fund's duties includes the following." In those two sentences, strike out the word "however" on the third line. Then take those two sentences and add them as a new paragraph after no. 12 [i.e., the last item on the list] on page 14b. There is then no change whatever except a rearrangement of form, in which two sentences are removed from the preamble, so to speak, and put in as a summary.

On the question which I place as the second point [p. 55] considered in this connection by the Committee, shall I proceed?

Chairman: Please.

Edward Bernstein (Chairman, Special Committee): In addition to that, the Special Committee had before it Document 345,[190] reading as follows:—

---

[188] Became Article VIII, Section 4 , "Convertibility of Foreign Held Balances," in the final agreement.

[189] Document 182, pp. 224-225; see also the reference to this document in Document 374, pp. 606-607, where it appears as item 6, not item 5.

Chairman: Document 345, page 14(b).

Edward Bernstein (Chairman, Special Committee): The language is simple and brief, and I will read it for the convenience of those members who don't have the document:

"The Fund may arrange to obtain further information by agreement with members. It shall act as a central point for the collection and exchange of information on monetary and financial problems, thus facilitating the preparation of studies designed to assist members in developing policies which further the purposes of the Fund."

The [Special] Committee recommends to the Commission that this be added to [Article VIII,] Section 5, on "Furnishing Information."

Chairman: Any discussion on that provision?

The chair will call for a vote of those in favor of accepting the recommendation of the committee on item 5 [Article VIII, Section 5—item no. 6 of the Special Committee report], the furnishing of information. Please say "aye."

Delegates: Aye.

Chairman: Those opposed, "nay."

(None.)

It is approved by the Commission.

Edward Bernstein (Chairman, Special Committee): Mr. Chairman, for the final clarification of page 14, I call attention to the fact that [Article VIII,] Section 2, entitled "Exchange Controls on Current Payments," was in fact approved by this Commission yesterday. While the Special Committee examined the point perhaps briefly in connection with multilateral clearing, there is no doubt whatever that it has been approved by the Commission. [p. 56]

Chairman: That was before the Commission and was approved yesterday, and I gather there is no need to take it up again. It is the last half of the Document 329[191] that you had before you, and it was before this Commission yesterday and was approved.

Now consider Article VIII ["General Obligations of Members"] as a whole. You have already approved [Sections] 3 ["Multilateral Clearing"] and 5 ["Furnishing of Information"]. We now ask for a discussion on the remainder of the provisions. Is there anyone that wants to raise questions on the remaining provisions?

---

[190] Document 345, p. 577.

[191] Document 329, pp. 544-546.

(After a pause.) If not, the Chair will ask for a vote on Article VIII as a whole. Those in favor of approving Article VIII, please say "aye."

Delegates: Aye.

Chairman: Those opposed?

(None.)

Article VIII is approved as a whole.

We now turn to Article IX ["Status, Immunities and Privileges of the Fund"]. Article IX is complete as it is. It deals with—

Reporting Delegate (Louis Rasminsky): Mr. Chairman, I am obliged to point out that there is a mistake. A very short section was amended from this article in the Document 321.[192]

Chairman: Document 321.

Reporting Delegate (Louis Rasminsky): That is the Annex 2 to the Drafting Committee's report. It becomes [Article IX,] Section 5, and is headed "Immunity of Archives." The section reads: "The archives of the Fund shall be inviolate." There will, of course be changes in succeeding sections.

Chairman: It is to protect the archives of the Fund.

Reporting Delegate (Louis Rasminsky): That's right, sir.

Chairman: Is there any discussion on any provision under Article IX, dealing with immunities? [p. 57]

(After a pause.) If not, the Chair will put the question on the whole article. All those in favor of approving Article IX, please say "aye."

Delegates: Aye.

Chairman: Those opposed?

(None.)

I can see that the delegates are getting tired even of saying "aye."

Article X is before you, "Relation with Other International Organizations." Does anyone wish to raise a question with respect to Article X?

(After a pause.) Then we put the question on the whole of Article X. All those in favor of approving Article X, please say "aye."

Delegates: Aye.

Chairman: All those opposed?

(None.)

The Article X is approved.

We now come to Article XI ["Organization and Management"].

---

[192] In Document 321, pp. 527-529.

Reporting Delegate (Louis Rasminsky): Mr. Chairman, I am afraid I am obliged to point out a mistake made by the Drafting Committee. On page 19 in [Article XI, Section 2, "Board of Governors,] small paragraph (d), we have said, "In order to constitute a quorum for any meeting of the Board of Governors there must be present a majority representing not less than one-half of the voting power of all the Governors."[193] The decision of Committee 3 was that a quorum for the Board shall consist of not less than two-thirds of the total voting power of the Governors, and that will have to be corrected in order to convey correctly the decision of Committee 3. [p. 58] I might also point out that Sections (f) and (g) on pages 20 and 21 of the "New Testament" [Document 321, inserted into the loose-leaf "bible"] are thereby mistaken. These matters are already under consideration by a committee of the Commission, and they should not have appeared in this document.

Chairman: I take it you were referring to the financial "New Testament."

The first item to be considered will be [Article XI], Section 5 ["Voting"], on voting. The [Special] Committee has a report, [item] no. 8 in the committee's report, on voting.[194]

Edward Bernstein (Chairman, Special Committee): Mr. Chairman, the first and last paragraphs of [Article III, Section 3, "Voting," in] Alternative A on page 26 of the basic document[195] have already been approved by other committees. The Special Committee recommends the adoption of the second paragraph of this section, involving increases in votes for countries under certain circumstances and decreases in votes for other countries under similar circumstances, [specifying] that the change in the figure be from 200,000 United States dollars to 400,000 United States dollars. It was the general feeling of the Special Committee that this was a provision that might usefully be included and it is recommended to your Commission.

Chairman: Any discussion on page [Section] 5?

(After a pause.) If not, I shall ask you to vote on the recommendation of the Special Committee on provision [Article XI, Section] 5. All those in favor of approving the recommendation of the Special Committee, please say "aye."

Delegates: Aye.

---

193 In Document 321, p. 531.

194 In Document 374, p. 607.

195 In Document 32, p. 47, the preliminary draft, rather than in the intermediate draft, Document 321.

Chairman: All those opposed?

(None.)

It is approved.

Item [Section] 3 ["Executive Directors"], as I understand, is not yet complete under [Article] XI. I should, therefore, like to raise the question of the [p. 59] remainder of Article XI. Is there anyone that wants to raise any question or discuss any provision in Article XI except that [on] Executive Directors, [in Section] No. 3, which we will postpone for a later discussion?

(After a pause.) If no one wishes to discuss any provision under Article XI, "Organization and Management," I should like to put the question on the whole article with the exception of Section 3, which, as I said, will be reported by back to us at the next meeting. All those in favor of accepting Article XI with the exception of Section 3, please say "aye."

Delegates: Aye.

Chairman: All those opposed?

(None.)

Article XI is accepted.[196]

We would like to clear up as much as possible of the committees' reports rather than continue on, to make sure that we get as much [done] as possible. Might I ask the [Special] Committee to report the next item, "Settlement of Accounts after Withdrawal" [Article XIV], so that we could take that and possibly [Article] XV ["Liquidation of the Fund"] before we adjourn. I would like you to report on item [Section] 3 of Section [Article] XIV under "Withdrawal from Membership," which is the item listed as "Settlement of Accounts after Withdrawal." That is [item] no. 10 on the [Special] Committee's report.[197]

Edward Bernstein (Chairman, Special Committee): Mr. Chairman, the Committee recommends the adoption of Alternative A, pages 36 and 36a,[198] subject to minor drafting changes which are referred to the Drafting Committee.

Chairman: You have heard the report of the [Special] Committee on item [i.e., Section] 3 of Article XIV, bearing in mind that the Drafting Committee report will be before you, and if there is anyone who feels that there has been any change in substance [p. 60] he will, of course, have the privilege of raising a question on the floor. Those in favor of accepting

---

[196] Became Article XII in the final agreement.

[197] In Document 374, p. 607.

[198] In Document 124, pp. 132-134.

the recommendation of the [Special] Committee on item [Section] 3 of Article XIV, please say "aye."

Delegates: Aye.

Chairman: All those opposed?

(None.)

It is approved.

I will now call for a vote on the entire article, Article XIV, which includes the three items listed. Does anyone wish to discuss any of those provisions?

(After a pause.) If not, the Chair will ask for a vote on the whole of Article XIV ["Withdrawal from Membership"]. All those in favor of accepting Article XIV, please indicate by saying "aye."

Delegates: Aye.

Chairman: All those opposed?

(None.)

Article XIV is accepted by the Commission.[199]

The next item is [Article] XV, "Liquidation of the Fund." That is [item] no. 9 in the [Special] Committee's report. I ask the Committee's report on that item.[200]

Edward Bernstein (Chairman, Special Committee): Mr. Chairman, the Committee discussed the question of liquidation and agreed in substance on that provision. We have, fortunately, had enough time since the meeting of the Committee to draft the provision, and since it will be available within an hour or so, we might perhaps more profitably turn to some other provision. It is to some extent technical, and some people would unquestionably prefer to see the manner in which the principles have been applied on which they have agreed.

Chairman: The Reporter suggests that this particular provision can be more intelligently acted on if you [p. 61] have a copy of the draft before you. We shall, therefore, postpone consideration of Article XV.

On Article XIII ["Transitional Period"], does the Reporter for the Commission feel that that, too, should be given an opportunity for study by the Commission, in view of the importance and complexity of the subject?

Edward Bernstein (Chairman, Special Committee): Mr. Chairman, this provision has been in the hands of the Commission for

---

[199] Became Article XV and Schedule D in the final agreement.

[200] In Document 374, p. 607.

some 32 hours. I believe it was available yesterday morning. If I am mistaken, the Secretary will indicate that.

Chairman: If that is correct, then would you proceed with your recommendation on that article? We now discussing Article XIII, "The Transitional Period," which is item—

Edward Bernstein (Chairman, Special Committee): Item 7, Mr. Chairman.[201]

Chairman: Item 7 of the report of the Special Committee, entitled "Transitional Arrangements."

Edward Bernstein (Chairman, Special Committee): The report of the Committee, as stated, recommends the adoption of Alternative A, pages 44a and 44b,[202] with the addition of the following at the end of the section: "Nothing in this agreement shall be [[prejudicial to the?]] interests of members."

The representative of the Netherlands raised an inquiry at the meeting on the first sentence of the transitional provision, which I believe was answered to his satisfaction. The Special Committee was in complete agreement on the desirability of every aspect of the transition provisions, and it recommends that with the very minor changes that may be needed it be sent to the Drafting Committee.

Chairman: The delegate from the United Kingdom. [p. 62]

United Kingdom ([Dennis Robertson?]): Mr. Chairman, I think the only very slight error in the report is the words following at the end of Section 2. I think the sense was that it was left to the Drafting Committee to decide where that reservation should be placed, and that it might have a rather wider application than it would have if it was put immediately following that section.

Chairman: In other words, that the particular order would be determined by the Drafting Committee.

Does the Reporter accept the interpretation?

Edward Bernstein (Chairman, Special Committee): Mr. Chairman, I had thought it would be clear from the reading of this that this is a provision that belongs with "Exchange Controls and Restrictions" in general, and that it would be moved there by the Drafting Committee.

Chairman: Does the Drafting Committee agree to that, or is there any question as to the appropriate order?

---

201 In Document 374, p. 607.

202 Document 323, pp. 537-538.

Reporting Delegate (Louis Rasminsky): I think this is left in quite a satisfactory manner. As I understand it, Mr. Bernstein has said that the place in which this article will be placed is left to the discretion of the Drafting Committee, and he suggests that it may come in the section dealing with obligations of member countries [Article VIII].

Chairman: The next item we would like to take up, which is [in] the report of the [Special] Committee, is item [Section] 4 of the "Final Provisions," [Article] XIX. Will the committee please report on 4, XIX, the title of which is "Initial Determination of Par Values," and which is listed as no. 11 in the special report of the committee, page 4.[203]

Edward Bernstein (Chairman, Special Committee): Mr. Chairman, the Committee discussed this point at length, but it would prefer to have the point raised again at the next meeting of the Commission. [p. 63]

Chairman: Unless there is objection, that point will be deferred until the next meeting.

With regard to the definitions [Article XVIII, "Definitions"], do I understand that the committee is prepared to report on that?

Edward Bernstein (Chairman, Special Committee): Mr. Chairman, the Special Committee, having considered the importance of definitions, agreed to turn the various documents it had before it into the capable hands of Professor Robertson, who will attach to himself such other people as he will require in the preparation of the definitions for this document.

Chairman: May we move up, then, to consideration of Article XVII, called "Interpretation"?

Before you report on it, the Secretariat calls my attention to an oversight. He informs me we did not call for an expression of approval or disapproval on Article XIII, entitled "Transitional Period," which had been discussed here a few minutes ago. I am now going to ask for the opinion of this Commission on Article XIII, on the transitional period, which had been reported on, but on which I overlooked getting the opinion of this Commission. All those in favor of accepting Article XIII *in toto,* please signify by saying "aye."

Delegates: Aye.

Chairman: All those opposed?

(None.)

Article XIII is approved by the Commission.[204]

---

[203] In Document 374, pp. 607-608.

[204] Became Article XIV in the final agreement.

Is the Reporter of the Special Committee—no, that was not a subject for report.

We are now asking for discussion on Article XVII, "Interpretation," and since the time is getting close to dinnertime, I think that that will be the last article that we will ask for an opinion on at this meeting. [p. 64] Is there anyone who wishes to discuss that article?

(After a pause.) All those in favor of Article XVII, called "Interpretation," please signify by saying "aye."

Delegates: Aye.

Chairman: All those opposed?

(None.)

Article XVII is approved.[205]

Before adjourning, just one or two notes. The chairman of the Drafting Committee would like to have the members of the Drafting Committee of this body to meet with him in this room at adjournment.

The next meeting of the Commission will be this afternoon. It will be on the bulletin board, and we will allow you a little more time than we originally planned.

(Whereupon, at 12:45 p.m., the meeting of Commission I was adjourned.)

---

[205] Became Article XVIII in the final agreement.

7

Commission I
International Monetary Fund
Sixth meeting: transcript
July 15, 1944, 12:45 p.m.[206]

Correction of minutes regarding British remark on convertibility of pound sterling • Report of Special Committee on Unsettled Problems on liquidation of the IMF • Article on initial determination of par values • Article on final provisions • Proposed alternative on purposes of the IMF; referral to Special Committee • Subscriptions of liberated countries damaged by war • Gold production in countries damaged by war • Changes in initial par values of currencies leaving international transactions unaffected • Depositories

Dennis Robertson of the British Treasury begins by clarifying that a remark he made at the Commission's meeting of July 13, responding to a point raised by A.D. Shroff of India about the postwar convertibility of India's holdings of pounds sterling. He states that sterling acquired in current-account transactions will become convertible. Robertson, a Cambridge University economist, was second only to Keynes in the British delegation in his contributions to the Bretton Woods conference.

Edward Bernstein of the United States, chairman of the Special Committee on Unsettled Problems, submits up for consideration two matters from the Special Committee's report that the meeting of the Commission the previous day had lacked time to consider. The Commission accepts without debate provisions about liquidation of IMF, and with only a short discussion it also accepts provisions stating how long member countries will have to declare initial par values (exchange rates of their currencies in terms of gold). The Commission also approves Article XIX, "Final Provisions" (Article XX in the final IMF agreement).

Bernstein then turns to new matters, including some the Special Committee had not been able to resolve. A brief but vigorous debate occurs on a clause in Article I, on the purposes of the IMF. Bernstein makes it clear that the United States objects to

---

[206] Summarized in Document 409, pp. 650-652.

language desired by India, which the United States thinks might change the IMF's focus from short-term currency stabilization to long-term economic development. The British delegate plays a mediating role and Commission chairman Harry Dexter White recommits the clause to the Special Committee for resolution. The Commission refers to the Drafting Committee a provision about payment of quotas (capital subscriptions) by countries occupied during the war. The next topic is whether countries devastated by the war should receive a temporary exemption to retain gold mined within their borders in their reserves rather than be required to offer a portion of it to the IMF in their quota subscriptions. After a few statements of support for the measure, the Commission approves a five-year exemption. It likewise approves a provision that member countries may change initial par values without the IMF's consent if they do not affect the international transactions of other members.

Finally, the Commission debates a proposed provision on depositories—the places where the IMF will hold its gold and other assets. The provision requires the IMF to hold at least 50 percent of its gold in a depository designated by the member where the IMF has its principal office (the United States), and at least 40 percent in four other principal depositories (expected to be those selected by the other Big Five World War II allies: the United Kingdom, USSR, France, and China). Wim Beyen of the Netherlands, a former banker and former president of the Bank for International Settlements, criticizes the proposed provision as being unnecessarily specific about a question that he considers best left to the business judgment of the IMF's management. Other delegates join in. Harry Dexter White steps out of his role as chairman for a moment and, as the person most responsible for the draft IMF agreement, explains that he considers the debate to be largely based on a misunderstanding of what the provision means. The Commission approves the proposal on depositories as it stands and breaks for lunch.

Chairman (Harry Dexter White, United States): The meeting of the Commission will please come to order. The Quota Committee will join us when they are through.

The first order of business consists of further reports from the Special Committee, some of which were held over from yesterday's meeting. Will the Reporter from that Special Committee please report the first item on that agenda?

United Kingdom ([Dennis Robertson]): Am I in order to asking leave to raise a point on the minutes of the meeting of July 13? I would like to ask for a small correction to be made in those minutes, though it is of very small importance, in order to avoid misunderstanding.

Chairman: A point of order has been raised to mention a correction to get the approval of the Commission, which I understand is a very small matter, but a correction in the minutes of the last meeting. Is there any objection?

United Kingdom ([Dennis Robertson]): The record deals with the answer which was given by myself to the question by the delegate from India as to whether sterling would be freely convertible after the transition period was over. Exactly what the meaning of that phrase was [I wish to clarify]. My answer, as recorded, is that it was indicated that the provision was applicable to such transactions, and that sterling acquired as a result of current transactions would be freely convertible after the transition period. I wish to ask that that record may be altered to read "and that currently acquired sterling will be freely convertible." Currently acquired sterling is that which is coming into the hands of the exporter day by day as a result of transactions which are [[part of his normal operations?]]. Sterling acquired as a result [p. 2] of current transactions might mean sterling that has piled up as a result of transactions which have consisted in the export of goods, etc. The distinction is one of substance, which I hope and believe has been made sufficiently plain on a number of occasions. The record as altered [should state that] the provision was applicable to such transactions and that currently acquired sterling will be freely convertible after the transition period.

Chairman: The Chair remembers distinctly the discussion that took place in the committee [Commission] on that point, and is of the opinion that the delegate from the United Kingdom is correct in his request that the correction may be made.

India ([A.D. Shroff?]): May I ask Professor Robertson a question? If exporters from India acquired sterling but do not use it immediately, do I understand that [the phrase] "at any time whatever" involves the exclusion of time from the definition of currently acquired assets? (Interruption [apparently by Dennis Robertson, words unrecorded].) No, it is not a time lag of one second or two seconds. You must leave questions of that sort to the common sense of people who are going to run this Fund.

Chairman: Many of the delegates have not had the advantage of being professors of economics, and so possibly [an] interpretation may be necessary from the Chair.[207] The last speaker spoke of it more being a question of seconds; we will all recognize that, however, [as ridiculous]. The delegate from India is asking a question that is a reasonable one and the answer, from prior discussion, in the minds of the British delegation

---

207 Dennis Robertson and Harry Dexter White had been professors of economics; A.D. Shroff had studied at the London School of Economics.

is also a reasonable one. The suggestion of the reasonableness of the answer includes months and even possibly a year or two, depending on the judgment of the Fund. Am I correct? Mr. Robertson, it should be [p. 3] clear that the balances that are held in the country might not be a matter of seconds, as you pointed out, but might be a matter of months or years.

United Kingdom ([Dennis Robertson]): When you say several months, I do not feel any difficulty, but when the year is mentioned, I think we should.

Chairman: In other words, as you go towards years and away from months, the problem becomes more difficult to answer ahead of time. Does that answer meet with the approval of the delegate from India?

India ([A.D. Shroff]): I don't think the position is quite so clear as is sought to be made out by the delegate from the United Kingdom. From the answer he gave me the other day, I took it that after the transitional period had ended, all sterling that we had as a result of current transactions, irrespective of time, would be free [[of exchange controls?]]. [Article IX,] Section 5 [of the preliminary draft, "Avoidance of Restrictions on Current Payments"], on which I raised the question, only referred to the transitional period, and I think it is a matter of new substance which is being sought to be used by the delegate of the United Kingdom, and he is trying to put a time limitation on it.

United Kingdom ([Dennis Robertson]): I am very sorry to take up the time of the Commission on this, but here is the point. The governing provision, as I read it in the case of a country such as India (whose balance is the accrual of those export proceeds piled up in the form of central bank balances), is the first sentence of [Article] IX, Section 4 ["Exchange Controls on Current Payments"], as it used to be, which is in Document 329.[208] That obliges for the transitional period, and over that, obliges a member to deal with [redeem?] a sterling balance. In this case, [it] would be [the] U.K.'s option [to redeem] in gold. If the Indian authorities represent either that the balances in question have been currently acquired, that is, acquired [p. 4] in the space of let us say, the last month or two, or that their conversation is needed for making immediate current payment, those two conditions are alternative. If the balance is one of quite recent acquisition, it can be withdrawn [redeemed] without explanation. If, on the other hand, it has piled up for some period, say several years, to make the point plain, then there would be no obligation to retain it unless evidence is given that its withdrawal is required for the

[208] In Document 329, pp. 545-546.

purpose of buying goods or indulging in other current transactions. There would, for instance, be no obligation to relieve it if it is plainly going to be used in order to transfer this holding from London to some other center.

United States ([Edward Bernstein?]): It seems to me that the explanation of the delegate from the United Kingdom even broadened the privileges that were explained at the last hour. A person or a central bank holding sterling balances may not only convert them if they are currently acquired, but even when the question of "currently acquired" has been passed over, they are still convertible in accordance with the provisions of [Article] IX, [Section] 4 if they are to be used in connection with current transactions. As far as I can see, the only points excluded under this provision are the transfer balances, where they are to be used. And if [you have] idle funds in your acquisition of securities or similar transactions, where they ought to be put into use in accordance with the provisions of the Fund in current transactions, no question whatever arises.

Chairman: Unless there is objection, the Chair will declare the correction in the minutes suggested by the United Kingdom shall be made.[209]

Now I will call on the Reporter of the Special Committee to report on the first item of [p. 5] his agenda.

Edward Bernstein (United States, Chairman and Reporter, Special Committee): Mr. Chairman, the report of yesterday left two items still unsettled: the liquidation provision and the initial determination of par values.[210]

Chairman: Which is the first one you are going to discuss?

Edward Bernstein (Chairman, Special Committee): Document 376.[211]

Chairman: Document 376 is a liquidation provision, and it is to be the first discussed, [on] pages 37d and e in the Joint Document [Joint Statement].

Edward Bernstein (Chairman, Special Committee): Mr. Chairman, this question was given extended discussion by the Special Committee. I am glad to report that there was unanimous agreement that

---

209 Document 370 (Correction), p. 600.

210 Items nos. 9 and 11 in Document 374, pp. 607-608.

211 Document 376, pp. 608-610. The document referred to Article VIII, Section 4 ("Liquidation of the Fund") of the preliminary draft, Document 32, p. 53, and Article XV (also called "Liquidation of the Fund") of the intermediate draft, Document 321, p. 534, both of which had left blank spaces to be filled in later.

the liquidation principles presented in this document are completely fair, that they give every measure of protection to every country [up]on the liquidation of the Fund, if that should ever be necessary. I summarize the principles of this liquidation:[212]

["Alternative D.

"(a) The Fund may not be liquidated except after a decision taken by a majority of the aggregate votes in the Board of Governors. In an emergency, if the Executive Directors decide that liquidation of the Fund may be necessary, they may by a majority vote temporarily suspend all transactions of the Fund, pending an opportunity for further consideration and action by the Board of Governors.

"(b) If a decision to liquidate the Fund is carried, the Fund shall forthwith cease to engage in any activities except those incident to an orderly liquidation of assets and the settlement of its liabilities.

"(c) The liabilities of the Fund, other than the repayment of quotas, shall have priority in the distribution of the assets of the Fund. In meeting each such liability the Fund shall use its holdings of the currency in which the liability is due. If these holdings are insufficient, it shall use its gold. If this is insufficient to complete the payment, it shall draw on the currencies held by the Fund as far as possible in proportion to the quotas of the members.

"(d) The net assets of the Fund available after the discharge of the above liabilities shall be distributed as follows:

"(i) The Fund shall distribute its holdings of gold among the countries whose currencies the Fund holds in amount less than their quotas in proportion to the amounts by which the quotas exceed the Fund's holdings of those currencies.

"(ii) The Fund shall distribute to each member one-half of the Fund's holdings of the currency of that member but not to exceed 50 percent of the quota of the member.

"(iii) The remainder of the Fund's holdings of the currency of each member shall be divided among all the members in proportion to the amount still due to them.

"(e) Each member shall redeem its own currency held by other members as a result of the liquidation of the Fund. Each member shall agree with the Fund upon an orderly procedure for the redemption of its currency, and pending such agreement the Fund may withhold distribution of the member's share of the division of the Fund's holdings

212 The transcript merely says, "(Summarizes and reads Alternative D)." We have reproduced Alternative D from Document 376, pp. 608-610.

of currencies in accordance with (d)(iii) above, and it may apply such share to the redemption of the member's currency on an equitable basis. The Fund shall immediately apply the currencies apportioned to each member whose share is not withheld under the preceding sentence, in redeeming the currency of that number divided among other members.

"(f) Currencies held by members as a result of this division after the redemption undertaken in accordance with (e) above, shall be redeemed in gold or in the currency of the country requesting redemption, or in such other manner as may be agreed by the members. If the members involved do not otherwise agree, redemption shall be made within five years but shall not be effected at a rate in any semiannual period greater than one-tenth of the amount distributed to any other member. If the member fails to redeem its currency in this manner, the currency may be disposed of in any market at the same rate in an orderly manner. Each member who is under an obligation to redeem its currency under this paragraph, unconditionally guarantees at all times the unrestricted use of such currency for the purchase of goods or for the payment of other sums due to it or to its nationals. Further, each member agrees to make good any loss resulting from the exchange depreciation of its currency until it has been used or redeemed."]

Chairman: You have heard the gist of the report of the Special Committee.

Edward Bernstein (Chairman, Special Committee): Beyond that, there are certain obligations in connection with the distribution of assets which I think it would help to summarize. (Here summarizes and enlarges point (e) and (f) of page 37e.) Mr. Chairman, that is as brief a summary as I can give of these principles to all members of the Commission.

Chairman: You have heard the report of the Special Committee on liquidation. Does any delegate wish to comment on that report? [p. 6]

Mexico: Mr. Chairman, I move that it be accepted.

Chairman: It has been moved that the report of the Special Committee on liquidation be accepted.

Belgium ([Camille Gutt]): Seconded.

Chairman: The delegate from Belgium seconds the motion. Is there any delegate who wishes to discuss the recommendations?

Then the Chair will call for a vote. All those in favor of accepting the report of the Special Committee on liquidation, say "aye."

(Chorus of "ayes.")

Contrary minded?

(No response.)

The Commission accepts the report of the Special Committee.[213] The Chair now turns to the second order of business.

Edward Bernstein (Chairman, Special Committee): Mr. Chairman, there is another point which remained from yesterday's Commission meeting. It was the initial determination of par value. I regret that there is no final document that has yet been distributed. Several documents have previously been in the hands of the delegates, and I believe that the recommendations of the Special Committee are entirely familiar to every interested delegate. If I may proceed therefore with an oral presentation of the recommendations. We shall have a document covering these recommendations sometime this afternoon.[214] The document is ready but has not been mimeographed.

The Special Committee considered at great length this important question of the determination of initial par values. In addition, every delegate who is known to have any interest in this question was seen alone or in groups to assure him and others that the Special Committee's recommendations were in thorough accord with their needs in the communication of initial par value. I know of no dissenting voice in the course of all these consultations of the recommendations of the Special Committee. [p. 7] These recommendations are different.

There shall be communicated to the Fund an initial par value based on the de facto exchange rates. This initial par value shall be *the* par value for the purposes of the Fund, unless within some reasonable period of 90 days a member indicates to the Fund that it would find another par value satisfactory and this one unsatisfactory. In cases where countries have been occupied by the enemy, they may communicate an initial par value, which par value would be open to a statement of its satisfactory nature by the country involved for a longer period than the 90 days proposed for other countries. Any par value communicated to the Fund which is satisfactory in the sense that the Fund does not express any view as to its unsatisfactoriness would remain the par value, and would be subject to change in accordance with the procedures that are elsewhere provided.

In the case of an occupied country, it will have a longer period to communicate an expression of its views on whether that par value is

213 Article XV ("Liquidation") of the intermediate draft became Schedule E in the final agreement.

214 Document 414, pp. 696-697. The document referred to Article XIII, Section 5 ("Fixing Initial Par Values") of the preliminary draft, Document 32, p. 60, and Article XIX, Section 4 ("Initial Determination of Par Values") of the intermediate draft, Document 321, p. 537, both of which had left blank spaces to be filled in later.

satisfactory. It may postpone communication of that par value. It may await certain developments without which it cannot communicate par value without having to take into account these considerations. It will communicate that par value, and it will then be the par value for the time being, the Fund continuing operations in agreement with the countries under terms and conditions to be agreed and in amounts to be agreed. The understanding would be that it would be limited. At some stage, a country would agree with the Fund that limited operations are removed, and thereafter any change in exchange rates would be subject to the usual procedure. While all of this may sound complicated, it is, in fact, a fairly simple procedure. It parallels the usual procedure, except that in the case of an occupied country, a little more time was given to communicate par value, and operations [p. 8] are on a limited scale.

There are sufficient overall safeguards in connection with these par values. First, the Fund need not undertake exchange transactions if it feels that the par value [that] has been communicated to it may involve damage to the Fund or to other members. Second, no transactions are to be undertaken in exchange at all until satisfactory par values have been communicated for the currencies of countries with 60 percent of the aggregate quotas. No transactions in exchange would be undertaken until the European phase of the war is over. No transaction would be undertaken in the currency of any member until some satisfactory arrangement with respect to that currency has been made with the Fund, if that is governed by the provisions I mentioned before. Finally, it is understood that no member will undertake transactions with the Fund unless it could undertake those transactions without damaging the Fund's position, its own position in the Fund, and the position of the members in general.

Chairman: You have heard the report of the Special Committee on the initial determination of par values. The question is before you for discussion. Does any delegate wish to comment on the report?

China: I would like to ask whether the Reporter of the Special Committee bases his report on a document typewritten but not mimeographed, in the style of Alternative C.[215]

Chairman: The delegate wishes to know if the Reporting Delegate bases his report on a typewritten document which is not mimeographed. [p. 9]

Edward Bernstein (Chairman, Special Committee): It is based on that document. The oral presentation covered the highlights and not

[215] The delegate is referring to Document 405, pp. 643-645.

every possible point. Any difficulties in the actual wording would still be open and covered by the Drafting Committee, which would get the statement of principles which the delegate of China has referred.

South Africa ([Jack Holloway]): Mr. Bernstein said that there was a substantial agreement on this, and that singly or in group, the dissenting delegates had been consulted by the [Special] Committee. Probably it is just a point that the remarks I made in the committee here were overlooked, and I express great doubts about this method of dealing with the matter in committee. Certainly no discussions would be [possible?] afterward. I don't place that point [of view forward] because of any importance of the views I may forward, or to hold up the progress, and if this is the point [of] view of the committee, I am quite prepared to risk it.

My own view of the matter is that this thing will break down. This is based on the assumption within a reasonable period if the country were to be put in a position to determine what the consequences are or what the par value that can be maintained is; but I don't think within [the] short period [that] seems to be visualized here that the more important countries or less important countries will be able to do it, because they don't have the information. It is the order of the parities. I do not want to go over the reasons which I gave in the committee to show that those parities will reflect realities. I only made the point—it seems to me the provisional period, the period of provisional parities, would be carried on for a period of considerable time, and an attempt should be made at final parities. The effect of the basic thing to my mind is this: in order to be able to deal with the Fund, it [i.e., a country] will have to fix [p. 10] a parity, and the chances on this [going wrong] are very great. If it does that, then, the only further way of getting things straight is to use the safety valve provision, that is, the 10 percent,[216] and then to have arguments with the Fund.

It would be an exceedingly unfortunate thing that in the early stages the Fund would have to start having arguments with a large number of countries, because immediately they would create the impression that there is haggling and bargaining about parities in order to get some little [advantage] from competitive [devaluation]. I think that that could be avoided by having all parities [initially for] a period of two years, possibly

---

216 Article IV, Section 4 of the preliminary draft (in Document 32, p. 33), which became Article 5, Section 5 of the final agreement ("Changes in Par Values"), permitted members to change parities as much as 10 percent from the original par values without consulting the IMF. Parities more than 10 percent distant from the original par values required notifying the IMF and receiving its approval.

a little longer, and then having the general overhaul period for the new economic structure starting after the war—that opportunity of settling down on its obligation.

Edward Bernstein (Chairman, Special Committee): Mr. Chairman, I want to make it clear that what the delegate from the Union of South Africa was referring to was not the Special Committee. When this question first arose in Committee 2, Mr. Holloway expressed his views. A small group was appointed by the Chair in Committee 2 to consider the views expressed. When this question came to the Special Committee, it was considered at very great length, and there was unanimity in that committee on the special point. Every delegate who had expressed the need for some special consideration for his country and the termination of par values was consulted.

I gathered that the delegate from South Africa did not feel that his country was in a position of needing special consideration on that problem for his country. It seems to me that if we start with the concept of provisional exchange rates, we are in fact saying that there is a shadow of doubt on the whole possibility of maintaining a structure of exchange rates that will have order and stability. There are at this conference more than thirty countries whose exchange rates are in better than good shape; [p. 11] whose resources are more than adequate to maintain the stability of those exchange rates; whose entire economic system has been adjusted to those exchange rates. To call those thirty-odd exchange rates provisional is to raise a problem and not to solve it. What are in fact set exchange rates would now be called under this provision, if we adopt the suggestion of the delegate from South Africa, possibly unsatisfactory exchange rates. We must recognize that there are these thirty-odd exchange rates on which the world has been doing a considerable volume of business without any difficulty to those countries, without any difficulty to the world.[217] We must recognize that the resources of those countries are adequate for maintaining those exchange rates. We must then provide for the few rates on which there may be some question. That is precisely what this recommendation has done. It proceeds from the question of general exchange rates to those of the few countries to whom there is a [[question]].

Chairman: Any other delegate wish to make a comment?

United Kingdom: There is one point I wish to mention. It is not at all the point raised by Dr. Holloway or which Mr. Bernstein took up.

Chairman: Is it on the point which is before us for discussion?

---

[217] Most countries other than those under German occupation.

United Kingdom: It does relate to this provisional fixing of par values. I will first refer to the place on the paper where those who have got it will find the point which I am raising which comes at the end of the paper. The paragraph reads:

["(f) The Fund shall begin exchange transactions at such date as it may determine after par values have been established for the currencies of members having sixty percent of the aggregate quotas set forth in Schedule A but in no event until after the Fund shall have found that major hostilities in the present war in its European phase have ceased."][218]

We wish to add "or before 1 August 1945, whichever is the later," the point being that in any event we did not wish the Fund to begin before the [p. 12] 1st of August 1945. That is a question of substance. I want to raise it here.

Chairman: The delegate from the United Kingdom recognizes this is the year 1944, and wishes to put the date "[or before] August 1, 1945, whichever is the later." [p. 1 (13)]

Edward Bernstein (Chairman, Special Committee): Mr. Chairman, I think that it should be reported that that specific proposal was presented to the Special Committee. I do not believe that there was ever a recorded opinion on the matter. There were, however, divergences in point of view. The other view that was suggested by the U.K. delegate is that it may be unfortunate to say that in no event may operations commence until 1 August 1945, from a purely psychological point of view as suggesting that the war will be prolonged to such a period of time that that will be a reasonable date.

Chairman: Are there any further comments?

If not, the Chair will put the question to vote. Those in favor of fixing initial par values, please say "aye."

(Chorus of "ayes.")

Contrary minded?

The Chair declares that the Commission has accepted the report of the Special Committee on the fixing of the par values—that [old] Article XIX[219] has been considered and passed by this Commission.

I therefore begin with [new] Article XIX. Article XIX, entitled "Final Provisions," contained on page 27 of the so-called "New Testament."[220] Does anyone care to discuss any of the sections listed under Article XIX,

---

[218] Document 347 (278), pp. 578-580.

[219] Became Article XX, Section 4 in the final agreement.

[220] In Document 321, pp. 535-537.

Sections 1, 2 and 3, Section 4 having already been accepted by this Commission?

Australia: Mr. Chairman, in Section 2 ["Entry into Force,"] it is provided that this agreement has come into force—

Chairman: Would you mind stating specifically what you are discussing?

Australia: Yes, I am discussing Section 2, signed by 65 percent of the aggregate quotas. We haven't got the quotas yet, but I should think that it would be the agreement of very few countries, very few major countries and we feel that the agreement should not come into force [p. 2 (14)] unless it also has the agreement of some of the smaller countries, and there is, therefore a case, I think, depending, of course, upon the actual quotas, when they are available, for raising that to perhaps 70 percent so that there will have to be agreement by some of the smaller countries as well as by the four or five major countries.

Chairman: Does the delegate propose that as an amendment?

Australia: I propose that as an amendment.

Chairman: The delegate from Australia proposes as amendment that there be required in addition to the 65 percent of the aggregate of the quotas an additional number of countries. Could you specify how many?

Australia: I suggest 70 percent instead of 65 percent.

Chairman: The amendment was to require 70 percent instead of 65 percent.

Norway (Wilhelm Keilhau): In the Committee for Liberated Areas the question of the funds was discussed, but we did not get an opportunity of having a final meeting. There was, however, an absolute agreement that the countries which are original members of the Fund must have the opportunity of remaining as such even if it should happen that for formal reasons requirements are not being able to be rectified before an inaugural meeting is held. I think everyone is in agreement with that principle. I have not been just able this morning to see whether it has been covered by any of these provisions, but I raise the question, and I think that if it is not covered, it should be referred to the Drafting Committee.

Reporting Delegate (Louis Rasminsky, Canada): The point raised by Dr. Keilhau has, I think, been covered in the report of the Drafting Committee [p. 3 (15)] itself. If you will look at page 2 of that report, section [paragraph] (g) has been added [to Article XIX, Section 1], stating: "In the case of [governments whose metropolitan territories have been under enemy occupation, the deposit of the instrument referred to in (d) above may be delayed until _____ months after the date on which these territories have been liberated. If, however, it is not deposited before the expiration of this period by any such government, the signatures affixed in its behalf shall become void and the portion of its subscription paid under (f) above shall be returned to it]."[221]

Chairman: There is a motion before the Commission which has not been seconded. Does anyone wish to second that motion made by the delegate from Australia?

If not, the motion is lost.

Any other discussion?

Edward Bernstein[222] **(Chairman, Special Committee):** I would suggest that the Special Committee be empowered to insert appropriate dates into Section 1(a) and (b) where they are presently blank.

Chairman: The request is made that the Special Committee the empowered to insert the appropriate dates in Section 1(a) and (b) where they are now blank. Unless there is some objection, the Chair will accord that authority to the Drafting Committee.

Does any delegate wish to discuss any one of the other provisions: 1, 2 or 3?

If not, then the Chair will put the question on the whole of Article XIX, having accepted [Section] 4. All those in favor of accepting the entire Article XIX, with final provisions, please say "aye."

(Chorus of "ayes.")

Contrary minded?

The Chair declares that the Commission has accepted the entire Article XIX.[223]

Reporting Delegate (Louis Rasminsky): May I request that Mr. Luxford's motion be extended to the blank dates in section [paragraphs] (f) and (g) of this article as well.

Chairman: A request has been made to extend the authority to extend the appropriate dates in sections (f) and (g) in the Drafting Committee's report. Unless there is objection, the Chair so orders.

The next item on the agenda is the report by the Special Committee. What is your next item? What is the title?

Edward Bernstein (Chairman, Special Committee): Our next points are the new ones we took up today. No written report has been prepared [p. 4 (16)] because our meeting adjourned to come here. We

---

221 In Document 342, p. 573.

222 The typescript identifies Bernstein as the speaker, but a remark below by Louis Rasminsky suggests that it may actually have been Ansel Luxford.

223 Became Article XX, Sections 1-3 in the final agreement.

have six or seven items we would like to put before this Commission: the amendment on purposes; the question of time and payment of subscriptions to liberated countries; some minor changes in wording in [the section on] par values; some provisions for newly mined gold in connection with the repurchase provision; depository of the Fund; the emergency measures; definition. But then we would like to recommend finally to the Commission what has on one point been raised: the problem of delegating to the Special Committee authority to consider any questions that remain unsettled after the commission adjourns.

Chairman: Will you please proceed with item 1.

Edward Bernstein (Chairman, Special Committee): I am afraid that the work of the Special Committee this morning was not quite so successful as that of the night before last. On paragraph (b) of Article I, after considerable debate, there was a disposition to allow the wording of this paragraph.

Chairman: I am not certain that the delegates are understanding the subject matter which you are speaking of at the moment.

Edward Bernstein (Chairman, Special Committee): Article I, Annex 2 of the report of the Drafting Committee—

Chairman: So-called "New Testament."

Edward Bernstein (Chairman, Special Committee): "New Testament," Article I, paragraph (b), second paragraph. Shall I read it?

Chairman: Can you get that? We will proceed here—is it necessary to discuss it first?

Edward Bernstein (Chairman, Special Committee): I will submit a report of the Special Committee.[224] If that is satisfactory we can proceed with the next point.

Chairman: All right. I take it it's a brief matter. [p. 5 (17)]

Edward Bernstein (Chairman, Special Committee): The [Special] Committee recommended that on the fourth line of that paragraph, after the word "employment" add "and real income." The Committee, being in a mood to add words, recommended to add some more words on the sixth line after the word "members": "whatever the stages of their economic development." It was impossible to get any words stricken out. Nobody was in a striking mood. And that is the recommendation.

Chairman: Do I understand that the recommendations of the Special Committee do not include the striking out of "and to the development of the sources of productive power"?

---

[224] Document 414, pp. 696-697. Parts of this document refer to Annex II of the Drafting Committee's report, Document 321, pp. 518-537.

Edward Bernstein (Chairman, Special Committee): I am afraid the Special Committee would not recommend that. It remains in.

Chairman: You have heard the report of the Special Committee on item [i.e., paragraph] (b), Article I, "Purposes." Anyone wish to comment on the report?

United States (Edward Bernstein): I should like to suggest that we do what the Special Committee failed to do, and strike out all of the words that were proposed to be added and leave the text as it now appears in (b).

Chairman: And the text as it now appears in (b) includes "and to the development of the sources of productive power." So were you suggesting to strike that out—

United States (Edward Bernstein): My motion shall also include striking out all of those words.

Chairman: Therefore, the proposal is to amend the recommendations of the Special Committee so that the purposes will read as follows: "to facilitate [the expansion and balanced growth of international trade, and to contribute thereby to the promotion and maintenance of high levels of employment and real income and to the development of the productive resources of all members as primary objectives of economic policy]." Is that your motion?

United States (Edward Bernstein): That is right.

Chairman: The motion is before you. Does anyone second it? [p. 6 (18)]

Brazil: I second the motion.

Chairman: May I say that the subject of purposes has been discussed at very great length at Commission and committee meetings, and the aspects are clear to all members. Unless there is an objection, the Chair will limit the speaking on this amendment to what he regards as a reasonable time.

India: I am not going to say anything on the merits or the demerits of what has been proposed by the U.S. delegates. At this morning's meeting of the Special Committee, I came under the impression that the compromise which was agreed to by the committee, according to which the words added after "all members" were the words "whatever the stages of their economic development," which in my opinion made our [[position better]]. I have only met to state that if the amendment proposed by the United States is accepted, it makes our position much worse.

Chairman: Does the delegate of the United States making that amendment wish to add that phrase, "whatever the stage of economic development"?

United States (Edward Bernstein): No, sir.

United Kingdom: I should like very much to appeal to the United States delegation not to press their objection. I would like to say, Mr. Chairman, that I have very considerable sympathy with the statement which denies that application. I feel, Mr. Chairman, that we are discussing in all the debates which have taken place on this particular paragraph, shop window questions rather than questions of substance. And it is clear that the delegation of the United States and other members of the conference feel that the shop window is being dressed in such a way as to give a false impression of what the Fund is actually intended to do.

Mr. Chairman, I agree entirely with the view that if [p. 7 (19)] the impression is conveyed that the purpose of this Fund is to do things which are proper to the Bank, that would be very unfortunate. I believe further, and I would say, that if any member of the Fund were to entertain the intention to use the resources of this Fund in such a way, that would be a very grave thing. But, Mr. Chairman, I want to suggest to our friends that that position is sufficiently safeguarded by the word "thereby." We say in the first part of this paragraph what the Fund is intended directly to do, and then we say in order to meet the rather difficult position of some of our friends, who say that they will find difficulty in making the Fund acceptable in their own country, we say "thereby." It will achieve all sorts of things which are desirable. [[Hence,]] on that understanding that the word "thereby" is retained, I ventured to suggest that not much harm is done by what follows and if it helps any of our friends, its retention should be allowed.

Chairman: Does the Chair understand that there is a comma at the end of "employment"? The draft I have here is not clear on that point, and it makes a change in substance. Does the delegate from the United Kingdom understand—

United Kingdom: I am not quite sure.

Chairman: The position of the comma would seem to alter the substance.

Reporting Delegate (Louis Rasminsky): There is no comma after "employment."

Edward Bernstein (Chairman, Special Committee): Mr. Chairman, I wonder whether another stretch of wrestling with this in the Special Committee would not give us something that would be satisfactory, and if those who are present would consent, we might send it back to the Special Committee, where they can [p. 8 (20)] again consider the same point and free this Commission to proceed with the important problem that it still has before it.

United Kingdom: I sympathize with the Drafting Committee, [and] all those members of the Commission who feel some impatience at the suggestion that this matter should be considered once more, but I join with Dr. Bernstein in suggesting that we should not sink the ship for hate of the tower. We should send it back and see if reason and persuasion can achieve some satisfaction.

Chairman: Would the delegate of the United States that made the amendment before us withdrawal the amendment?

United States (Edward Bernstein): I withdraw my amendment.

Chairman: Will the delegate from Brazil withdraw his second to the amendment?

Brazil: I withdraw.

Chairman: Unless there is an objection, the Chair recommits this provision (b), Article I to the Special Committee for reports at our next meeting, which will follow the adjournment of this meeting when I announce such adjournment.

The next item on the agenda will be taken up. [p. 9 (21)]

Edward Bernstein (Chairman, Special Committee): The time of payment of subscriptions for liberated countries was raised in the Special Committee, and there will be some slight problem of wording. It is quite possible that the provisions already made for making payment in currency and in gold will not be quite adequate for all of the purposes of the liberated countries. The discussion in the Special Committee indicated it probably would be. Since it is only a matter of wording, I recommend on behalf of the Committee that this question be referred to the Drafting Committee to re-examine the wording. It has to make sure that every liberated country can comply with the present wording.

Chairman: The recommendation has been made that the matter be referred to the Drafting Committee. Unless there are objections, the Chair will so declare it.

The next item to be reported on, newly mined gold. The delegate from the United States.

Edward Bernstein (Chairman, Special Committee): The case was put to the Special Committee this morning that in the case of some members that produce gold, the devastation during the war and urgent need for reconstruction after the war has caused serious interference with the maintenance of gold production and with the holding of adequate gold reserves. On that account, the Committee considered this proposal as an addition to the repurchase provision. In the case of members whose metropolitan territories have been occupied by the enemy or severely damaged by enemy action, the obligation of this section shall not apply for five years after this agreement goes into force to gold newly produced from mines located within the territories of such members. It was the view of the Committee that this should be recommended to the Commission.

A substantial proportion of the members of the Committee reserved their position on that point and opposed the recommendation. Speaking for the majority [p. 10 (22)] of that Committee, I may say that we feel it is completely fair that the provision is necessary to permit a country whose gold production was suspended in order to defend its territory from the enemy to give it an opportunity to resume the production of gold and to build back its normal gold reserve with the new production of its mines. That is the position of the majority.

Chairman: The delegates have heard the report of the Special Committee and the recommendation of the majority of that committee.

The Chair recognizes the delegate from the Soviet Union.

USSR: I want to commend this proposal. It is a proposal instead of two other additions, which refer to Article II, Section 3 of the Joint Statement ["Gold Subscriptions"].[225] We completely consent to the general principle expressed in the provisions of the Joint Statement after [Alternatives] B and C, but there are exceptional cases where the general principle should be temporarily abandoned. I have in mind the special conditions in some countries who suffered during this war particularly great damage from enemy occupation and hostilities. When the hostilities are over, these countries shall be confronted with the difficult problems of rehabilitation…(speech read[226]).

Chairman: You have heard the delegate from the Soviet Union expound of the reasons for supporting the recommendation of the majority of the Special Committee. The delegate from Mexico.

Mexico: The Mexican delegation feels great sympathy for the amendment as proposed by the Special Committee. We believe that the period of five years for the recuperation of invaded and devastated countries is reasonable. Therefore, Mr. Chairman, the Mexican delegation supports the exception regarding newly mined gold.

Chairman: Was that a motion?

---

225 In Document 32, pp. 26-27.

226 The rest of the speech does not seem to exist anywhere in the conference documents.

Mexico: A support, sir. [p. 11 (23)]

Czechoslovakia: Mr. Chairman, the Czechoslovakian delegation supports the amendments suggested by the report of the Special Committee and accepted by the majority of votes of this Commission. The strain put on balance of payments of some devastated countries will be tremendous. When these countries undertake (and they are bound to do it) a timely and effective work of reconstruction, keeping in mind the fact that in particular cases such countries have rather limited export capacity, the gold newly mined there may be one of the crucial items of the overburdened balance of foreign payment[s]. We believe there is a good case for granting an exceptional treatment or temporary basis of five years. It is hoped that these countries will use the period of reconstruction for establishing the type of economic ties with the world and contribute in this fashion to world prosperity. Therefore, I make the motion that the amendment of the Reporter be adopted.

Chairman: The delegate from Czechoslovakia moves that the report of the majority of the Special Committee be adopted. Does anyone second that? The delegate from France.

France ([Pierre Mendès-France]): (Spoke in French.)

Translator: The French representative states that the French delegation supported all proposals made in favor of occupied and devastated countries. He states further that he hoped that fuller measures would have been taken in favor of the occupied and devastated countries. The amendment receive[s] the full approval of the French delegation.

Chairman: The delegate from the United Kingdom.

United Kingdom: We support the amendment. [p. 12 (24)]

Chairman: [Apparently after seeing signs of support from other delegates:] The delegate from the United Kingdom supports the amendment; the delegate from New Zealand supports the amendment; the delegate from Belgium supports the amendment; the delegate from Yugoslavia supports the amendment.

The Chair will call for a vote. All those in favor of the amendment, please signify by saying "aye."

("Ayes" heard.)

Counter minded?

The amendment is accepted.

The next item on the agenda is the depositories of the Fund.

Edward Bernstein (Chairman, Special Committee): We have a typewritten text of the proposal. May we move on to another item for a minute or two as the text is being brought in, which covers the agreement of the [Special] Committee? The Committee considered a suggestion that provision be made for emergency measures that the Fund might find it necessary to take. The Fund already had made provision for emergency measures, but in a Fund so technical in its construction, so carefully drafted to assure passivity, there may be problems which we have overlooked which may arise, and the Committee considered the possibility of giving the Fund authority to take emergency measures on some aspects of its operations. The Committee is not in a position to report in any general sense on this important problem. It would like an opportunity to consider this question again this afternoon or evening.

Chairman: Is the text of the other before you now?

Edward Bernstein (Chairman, Special Committee): The Special Committee considered briefly a suggestion for rewording a part of Article IV ["Par Values of Currencies"] along these lines.

Chairman: What section?

Edward Bernstein (Chairman, Special Committee): Section 5(a).

Chairman: Page 5 of the so-called "New Testament" draft. [p. 13 (25)]

Edward Bernstein (Chairman, Special Committee): Page *6* of the so-called "New Testament" draft.

Chairman: Page *6*.

Edward Bernstein (Chairman, Special Committee): "A member of the Fund may change"—

Chairman: Apparently there is some difference in point of view as to what page you are referring to.

Edward Bernstein (Chairman, Special Committee): Page 6, Section 6, part [paragraph] (b).[227]

Chairman: Page 6 of the so-called "New Testament."

United States (Edward Bernstein): Page 6, Section 6, paragraph (b), to replace that with this slight change in wording. "A member of the Fund may change the par value of its currency without consent of the Fund if the change does not affect international transactions of the members of the Fund." It is recommended by the majority of the [Special] Committee that this be sent to the Drafting Committee for inclusion in the appropriate part of the text.

Chairman: You heard the recommendation of the majority of the Special Committee. Anyone wish to discuss the amendment? Does any delegate wish to discuss that suggestion?

---

[227] In Document 321, pp. 522.

The delegate from the United States.

United States ([*not* Edward Bernstein]): Mr. Chairman, I would just suggest that the place where this provision will appear is not under consideration, but only the text of the provision, and the Drafting Committee would like to have full permission to place it in the appropriate place in the document.

Chairman: Request is being made to authorize the Drafting Committee to place this provision in its appropriate place in the document. Unless there is objection, the Chair will so order. Have you received the text of that next amendment? [p. 14 (26)]

Edward Bernstein (Chairman, Special Committee): Yes, Mr. Chairman. Returning to the problem of depositories, the Committee considered this morning a new provision or a new wording of the provision on depositories and agreed by a close vote to recommend the following text as the view of the majority of the Special Committee. May I read it? The nearest thing to this in the "Old Testament," page 29. If you will follow the text in the old document, SA/1, I will read slowly.[228]

Chairman: Page 29 was the reference.

Edward Bernstein (Chairman, Special Committee): [Article VII,] Section 6, part (b), on page 29: "The Fund may hold other assets, including gold, in depositories in the five members having the largest quotas and in such other depositories as it may select. At least one-half of the holdings of gold of the Fund shall be held in the designated depository in the member in which the Fund has its principal office. At least 40 percent of the holdings shall be held in the four other principal depositories. All transfers of gold by the Fund shall be made with due regard to the costs of transporting and expected requirements of the Fund. In an emergency, the Executive Directors may transfer all or any part of the Fund's holdings of gold to any place where it can be adequately protected."

Chairman: The delegate from Netherlands.

Netherlands ([Wim Beyen]): I won't repeat what I said last time, when we were a little less hungry than today,[229] but I want to make clear that this new proposition is not acceptable to the Dutch delegation. Mr. Chairman, I think we may say that on the whole this conference has been very happy in trying to do justice and give satisfaction to all [p. 15 (27)] present, whether large or small, and in the particular cases where it was

[228] In Document 32, pp. 49-50.

[229] At this meeting, the delegates had not yet eaten lunch despite having started after noon.

not possible to give satisfaction, I think we have tried to spread dissatisfaction equitably; but Mr. Chairman, for that particular reason, I would consider this clause a completely unnecessary and regrettable flaw on what is shown as the spirit of this conference and the document that will come out. I can still not see what is the reason for this clause. I cannot see that [but] it will not be the cause of an enormous [amount] of practical differences, because when you sell gold it will force the Fund to do a lot of re-shifting. It is not at all connected with the realities and necessities of gold in connection with the transactions, and it is in no way whatever connected with the safety of gold, because as I tried to say before, nobody can foresee which place in the world will be safe, or not.

Apart from that, we have two things to consider. First of all, and I am sorry that I repeat myself again, I always hoped it would be assumed that the Executive Directors of this Fund will have some sense and that in matters like this we do not need to legislate, but apart from that, the countries that apparently are concerned where the gold is have a voice, a strong voice, in the directorate. I would urge this meeting not to go in the direction to which the amendment points. I think it would make it difficult to make the world believe that at this conference, rights, claims and interests of countries, large and small, have been considered, and that the spirit of the conference has been one of expediency and justice. [p. 16 (28)]

Chairman: The delegate from the Netherlands has indicated his reasons for urging the Commission not to go in the direction which is inherent in the proposal. May I say I think there was some misunderstanding about the interpretation of the provision as I heard [it]. Could the delegate from the United States correct that misunderstanding?

United States ([*not* Edward Bernstein]): I can reread it, Mr. Chairman, but the text of the statement was as read by Mr. Bernstein. That was the text as voted out by the Special Committee today. I would only want to say that the views which the delegate from the Netherlands has expressed in this meeting have been expressed, as he indicated, on a number of occasions in the past by a number of countries. On the other hand, there were an equal or greater number of countries that felt that it was important to include in this provision some reassurance that the gold holdings of the Fund will be adequately protected. Further than that, they do not conceive the allocation here indicated as economically irrational, since you are taking the five countries with the largest quotas, which also will represent a wide geographical distribution of the depositories. It may be said from purely economic grounds this is still a reasonable allocation of the gold of the Fund. Beyond that, I would call the attention of the conference to the fact that there is an express provision that all transfers of gold by the Fund shall be made with due regard to the cost of transfer or import and export requirements of the Fund, and I would join with the delegate from the Netherlands in assuming that the Fund would use good sense. [p. 17 (29)]

Chairman: Do I understand that the present provision which is being recommended by the majority of the Special Committee in no way discourages or prohibits the economic movement of gold, nor does it require any shifts of gold that are not called for by economic considerations?

United States: As I understand it, that is correct, sir.

Canada: The Canadian delegation would like to associate itself with the protest which the delegate from the Netherlands has made against this. I think this limitation on the margin in the places in which they hold their gold is quite at variance with the general spirit of this document which we hope to issue from this conference.

Chairman: The delegate from Cuba.

Cuba: Mr. Chairman, if this Fund was strictly a business corporation, I would agree with the gentleman from the Netherlands, but this Fund is an international organization in which the nations [are] participating; and nations, before they join this Fund and give up the sovereign rights to keep their gold where they please, would be asking each one of us, "Where is our gold going?" I believe that the formula submitted by the majority of the Special Committee [gives] the Board of Governors, and in turn the Executive Directors, sufficient margin to use their best ability to locate that gold where, in their opinion, it should go, because we say that at least one-half should be in the country where the principal office of the Fund should be established, and it leaves a wide margin for the Board of Governors and Executive Directors to place the [p. 18 (30)] remaining half of the gold in any nations, including at least 40 percent in those nations having the highest quotas. I believe that the small nations, although they have little gold, it seems to me, would like to know where their gold goes.

Belgium ([Camille Gutt]): Gentlemen, I don't want to repeat what has been excellently said by the delegates from the Netherlands and from Canada. I want only to say that the Belgian delegation wholly supports their point of view.

Ethiopia ([Ephrem Tewelde Medhen]): Mr. Chairman, on behalf of the Ethiopian delegation, I wish to express our hearty support of the views expressed by the member from Cuba.

Chairman: The delegate from Ethiopia supports the views of the delegation from Cuba, who supports the majority of the Special Committee.

United Kingdom: Mr. Chairman, I wish to speak of the merits of the proposal before us. I can't help but feel that it might be the case that some of us had very little time to reflect upon the exact wording of the proposal which has been put before us. That lack of opportunity may very well be our problem, but I do wish to urge the Commission to consider that the speeches which have been made by the delegates from the Netherlands, Canada, and elsewhere are speeches which obviously rest upon very deep conviction and upon an accumulated weight of banking experience which I think we should do well to take into full consideration. I therefore suggest, Mr. Chairman, that it would be well if further opportunity would be given for discussion of this particular point, [p. 19 (31)] and I move that it be referred back to the Special Committee.

Chairman: Motion has been made to refer this back to the Special Committee.

Peru: Mr. Chairman, we feel very much like the delegate from the United Kingdom. We feel that we have hardly had time to consider the wording, and if I understand rightly, the Special Subcommittee was going to take this matter up, but then it never met. We feel very strongly as the delegate from the Netherlands does, and therefore we would very much like this matter to be referred back either to the Ad Hoc Committee [on Depositories] or some other committee where the matter may be taken up.

Chairman: May the Chair take the floor, inasmuch as the Vice Chairman is not present?

The Chair would wish to express complete sympathy with the views expressed by the delegate from the Netherlands and Canada, but he fears that it rests upon a misinterpretation and a misunderstanding of the proposal. The proposal in no way requires any uneconomic movements of gold after the Fund has been initiated. On the contrary, it calls for such movements. The gold will remain, in accordance with the proposal in the five largest countries—the five countries with the largest quotas—and some in other countries. From then on, gentlemen, it satisfies all the requirements that you have asked for. From then on, any movement of gold which will be called for will proceed according to economic considerations.

For example, what need would there be for the movements of gold by the Fund? Clearly the most obvious one would be that possibly in time there might be a scarce currency. Then the Fund wishes to use some of its gold. I am not speaking of imports of gold [p. 20 (32)] which will take place in various parts of the world. I am speaking now of outward movements of gold. Those outward movements will not occur until there appears to be a scarcity of currency, and once that scarcity of currency appears, the gold will be shipped from that point which satisfies the various criteria which have been suggested along with the proposal. The accretion of gold will likewise be sent to those places which are most convenient and most economic, and which take into consideration the possibility of future withdrawals.

I therefore cannot see any discrepancy between the views which were expressed by the delegates who were troubled by the amendment and those who supported the amendment. I think it rests on a misunderstanding, and therefore, in view of the fact that the Special Committee is already burdened with work, and in view of the fact also that we wish to complete this session so that we can go on with the [World] Bank, I would urge the members to disapprove of the move to return it to the Special Committee, and accept the majority of the report of the Special Committee.

Czechoslovakia: Mr. Chairman, I second that motion.

Reporting Delegate (Louis Rasminsky): I wonder whether we could have the amendment read again. I think the impression is that the Fund has for free disposal only 10 percent of its gold holdings at all times, and that the other 90 percent had to be located in the member countries with the five largest quotas. [p. 21 (33)]

Chairman: Let us be practical about this, and know that the five centers named are the countries which in any event would have in due time at least 90 percent of the gold.

Netherlands ([Wim Beyen]): Mr. Chairman, may I raise a point of order. I don't think you can have a vote on two things at the same time. You can't have a vote on whether the amendment should be sent back to the Drafting Committee and at the same time on the acceptance of the majority suggestion, because they are entirely different things. I would be against sending it back to the [Drafting] Committee, and I may use two minutes to explain why it seems very difficult for anybody to imagine that anyone who is or has been a businessman is not contented with the limitation on horizon of which he can never free himself.

I want to explain that my objection doesn't go so much against any sort of wording, nor is it only a matter of practicability. It goes to the spirit of this amendment. It brings in a connection between the size of the quota and the purposes for which the Fund will hold gold, which to my mind is entirely wrong, and if someone asked me in my country,

"Where is my gold going?" my answer would be, "The gold is going to the Fund," because I have participated in the Fund, and the Fund will be needed for some time. Therefore, I would be against referring the matter back to the Drafting Committee.

Chairman: The point of order is clear, and a motion was made to send the matter back to the Special Committee. That motion was seconded and amended by the delegate from Czechoslovakia that the majority report be accepted. The [p. 22 (34)] amendment to the amendment is now before the Commission. Did I hear a second to that second amendment?

The delegate from Ecuador seconds the amendment. We have now before you the amendment to the amendment that the report of the majority of the [Special] Committee be accepted.

New Zealand ([Walter Nash]): I would not want to question the ruling, but I have found it tremendously [odd] to take two amendments at the same time, one of which is referring it back to the [Special] Committee, and the other to support the report.

Chairman: There was no motion in the first place to accept the report, Mr. Nash.

New Zealand ([Walter Nash]): When the report comes, might I refer to what the chairman of the Netherlands delegation had to say? He said members of his country, when being asked to put in their gold, would want to know where it is going. I say that the report has submitted by the [Special] Committee does say where it is going. It is going to the Fund—wherever it is, it is going to the Fund. It says nothing else here but the Fund. This conference determines where the Fund shall keep it, but it is going to the Fund. That would answer the point that the chairman of the Netherlands delegation is asking, where the gold is going. It will go to the Fund, he would say.

Netherlands ([Wim Beyen]): I didn't ask the question.

New Zealand ([Walter Nash]): The chairman of the Netherlands delegation said that someone associated with them would ask where the gold is going, and he said he wanted to be able to say it was going to the Fund, and [p. 23 (35)] I say he can, in accordance with the proposal, say it is going to the Fund. And this country [which is one of the depositories] determines where the Fund should keep authorized proportions of its total holdings of gold. If there is an objection to a part going to four countries and not being under the complete control of the Fund, that objection can be made to one of the countries where the principal office of the Fund is. If we are going to designate one country, it seems just as justifiable to me to designate other countries too. If we are going to do any discriminating, it seems a good case to designate 50 percent where the Fund has its principal office, 40 percent in other countries, and 10 percent in smaller countries.

USSR: Mr. Chairman, we completely agree with the view expressed by you that there is some misunderstanding on the question. There is not a real divergence between the proposal made by the majority of the [Special] Committee and the views expressed by the Netherlands delegate. We support this motion to accept the report of the committee, but I should like to make one remark. The last sentence of this proposal is rather too indefinite, and would it not be better to delay this last sentence, because it is in some contradiction with the general principle expressed in this proposal?

United Kingdom: Mr. Chairman, doesn't the course of our discussion illustrate the extreme difficulty of debating the subject of this degree of intricacy without some written material before us? Mr. Bernstein reads very clearly and distinctly, but many of us, I think, have difficulty retaining in our heads all the various aspects of so complicated a provision, and I do seriously suggest that although I am well aware that time is pressing, we shall be making a very important decision in unseemly haste if we proceed to a vote until the paper is before us. [p. 24 (36)]

Chairman: Delegate from United States.

United States ([*not* Edward Bernstein]): Mr. Chairman, as Mr. Bernstein stated at the opening of his remarks regarding this provision, if the delegate of the United Kingdom will refer to page 29 of the "Old Testament" he will find the substance of what we are now discussing, the two modifications which have been made in the text of [Article VII, Section 6](b), on page 29, which is as follows: before the last sentence, add the following: "at least 40 percent of the holdings shall be held in the four other principal depositories. All transfers of gold by the Fund shall be made with due regard to the cost of transfer and expected requirements of the Fund."[230] And the delegate of the USSR has suggested the deletion of the last sentence of 6(b); with that the United States would like to join.

Chairman: May we clear the docket by taking up the various amendments so that the specific problem may be before you? The first amendment for the floor is the amendment to the amendment made by the delegate from Czechoslovakia, that the majority of the report be accepted. In view of the fact that since that there was a suggestion for a

---

[230] In Document 32, p. 49.

deletion of the last phrase, then the Chair suggests [p. 25 (37)] that with the approval of the delegate of Czechoslovakia that we pass the second amendment and come to the first amendment, and we will have the provision before us.

Then, the proposal that is before you for action is the motion by the delegate from the Netherlands that the matter be referred back to the Special Committee for action. I am sorry, then it was not the delegate from the Netherlands; the delegate from the United Kingdom made that statement. Am I correct? If so, that is the motion before you now. Shall this matter be referred back to this Special Committee for action? All those in favor, say "aye."

("Ayes" heard.)

All opposed, "no."

("Noes" heard.)

I am afraid I shall have to call for hands. All those in favor of referring this proposal back to this Special Committee will please raise their right hands. Will the Secretary please count?

All those opposed, please raise their hands.

The motion is lost.

We now have before us the proposal that the majority recommendation of the Special Committee be accepted with the last sentence deleted, so that it shall read, "The Fund may hold other assets, including gold, in depositories in the five members having the largest quotas and in such other depositories as it may [select. At least one-half of the holdings of gold of the Fund shall be held in the designated depository in the member in which the Fund has its principal office. At least 40 percent of the holdings shall be held in the four other principal depositories. All transfers of gold by the Fund shall be made with due regard to the costs of transporting and expected] requirements of the Fund."

Norway: Mr. Chairman, may I suggest that there is a special word about deletion of the last sentence. ["In an emergency, the Executive Directors may transfer all or any part of the Fund's holdings of gold to any place where it can be adequately protected."] I think if we delete the last sentence, we are all blind, blind, blind. [p. 26 (38)]

Chairman: The Chair will put a motion.

The delegate from Belgium.

Belgium ([Camille Gutt]): Mr. Chairman, I would just bear out what Mr. Rasminsky [the Reporting Delegate] said a few minutes ago. We are just confronted now with the text and some explanations. It does not seem to agree with the explanation you gave, because according to the text as we read it, it seems that only 10 percent of the whole gold will remain free, definitely, whereas, according to your explanation, after the beginning the gold will flow freely.

Chairman: In view of the fact that the dining room is about to close, the Chairman will adjourn the meeting, to be opened again. It is now 2:20. This meeting will begin in this room at four o'clock.

8

Commission I
International Monetary Fund
Seventh meeting: transcript
July 15, 1944, 4:15 p.m.[231]

Depositories, continued • Report of Committee on Quotas • Disagreements with proposed quotas • Election of Executive Directors • Gold contributions of countries damaged by war

The Commission resumes the discussion of depositories it started before lunch. An amended draft specifies only that the IMF shall initially hold the bulk of its gold in locations specified by the five largest shareholders, not that it shall hold the gold there permanently, as the previous draft said. Despite objections by some small countries, supporting the criticism made by Wim Beyen of the Netherlands before lunch that the matter was best left to the business judgment of the IMF's management, the Commission approves the amended provision.

Fred Vinson, the vice chairman of the American delegation and the chairman of the Committee on Quotas, presents the committee's report. Vinson had a background as judge and politician; at the time of the Bretton Woods conference, he was the director of the Office of Economic Stabilization, a government agency that administered wartime price controls. He offers a lengthy justification of the committee's recommendation, observing that wartime economic problems and other considerations made it impossible to determine quotas by a simple formula, and that determining the proposed quotas consequently involved a large measure of judgment. He acknowledges that the proposal will leave many delegations unhappy, but pleads with the delegates to act in a spirit of unity.

Despite Vinson's plea, delegates from many countries immediately register their displeasure with the proposed quotas. The common complaint is that the quotas are too small and do not adequately reflect the economic standing the delegates imagine their countries will achieve, or reattain, after the war. That is particularly the case for China, France, and India. Harry Dexter White, temporarily stepping out of his role as chairman of the Commission twice during the debate and speaking as the main

[231] Summarized in Document 410, pp. 652-653, and Document 431 (410), p. 733.

originator of the IMF agreement, says that the emphasis on quotas is exaggerated. He points out that quotas do not measure the assistance that the IMF will be prepared to give to countries experiencing balance of payments problems. He does not sufficiently acknowledge, however, that quotas will be closely related to voting power and that voting power, which will affect the ability of countries to influence the selection of the IMF's Executive Directors, is the real underlying issue. After further debate, the Commission approves the proposed quotas without changes. (They would become Schedule A in the final agreement.)

The Commission then turns to Cuba's proposal that two of the elected Executive Directors be appointed by "American Republics." The IMF agreement as it stands at the start of this meeting provides for the members with the five largest quotas (understood to the five major World War II Allies: China, France, the USSR, United Kingdom, and United States) to appoint Executive Directors representing the exclusively. The remaining Executive Directors will be elected by coalitions of countries with smaller quotas. Cuba defines the "American Republics" as the Western Hemisphere countries other than the United States. The unstated expectation is that in practice the group will be the Latin American countries, because Canada will choose to form coalitions with other countries. Canada proposes that the Executive Directors include representatives of the two largest net creditor countries so that the Executive Directorate does not become a "debtor's club." Egypt proposes that two Executive Directors be from the Middle East. The Commission accepts Canada's proposal.

The USSR proposes to allow countries substantially damaged by the war to reduce their initial gold payments by 75 percent. The Commission rejects the proposal, apparently because too many delegations think it would weaken the IMF's financial position.

The Commission then returns to the section on Executive Directors, as amended, and approves the whole section (Article XI, Section 3 of the intermediate draft; Article XIII, Section 3 of the final agreement).

Chairman (Harry Dexter White, United States): The meeting will please come to order.

We have had mimeographed the provision [on depositories] which we were discussing before lunch.[232] You will notice that the second sentence

[232] Document 403, p. 642. The provision was a substitute for Article VII, Section 6(b) of Alternative A in the preliminary draft. In the intermediate draft it was renumbered Article XII, Section 2 ("Depositories of the Fund"). The text reads:

"(b) The Fund may hold other assets, including gold, in designated depositories in the five members having the largest quotas and in such other depositories as the Fund may select. Initially at least one-half of the holdings of the Fund shall be held in the designated depository in the member in which the Fund has its principal office and at least 40 percent of the holdings shall be held begins with the word "initially," and that the presence of that word and the subsequent sentence were the grounds for the statement of the Chair that the previous provisions seemed to be misunderstood. Is there any discussion on the provision, since you have it before you and have had an opportunity to examine it carefully?

Netherlands ([Wim Beyen?]): Mr. Chairman, I of course appreciate the technical difficulty brought into this clause by the word "initially." The technical difference is [that] with the word "initially" brought into it, the text has lost whatever meeting it ever had. If I base myself on that one word, I argue that as it has no meaning, there could be no objection to it. Still, Mr. Chairman, [we oppose it] not [on] any basis [that] the hard-boiled businessman wanted this or that, but on the basis that he perceived that it is dangerous to have a clause that has no meaning, and that the principle should read [i.e., should be] that the Fund should decide where the gold should be always, considering that the people should have sufficient influence in the Fund. The Netherlands delegation regrets that it has to stick to its opposition against a clause of that kind. We are perfectly willing to accept the fact that the larger quota holders must have in various aspects special rights. But there must be some justification for the special rights in the matter itself. We have not been convinced that there is any justification in this matter for giving the larger quota holders any rights in this respect and therefore we regret we have to stick to our objection. [p. 2]

Belgium ([Camille Gutt]): Gentlemen, I am awfully sorry to prolong the discussion, therefore I will [say only] a very few words in wholehearted support of the position taken by the Netherlands. I would be quite ready as a practical suggestion to accept that the whole of the gold shall be deposited in the principal office of the Fund, and then it would go to and fro according to necessity. I would be quite ready to accept that the gold be deposited in the country where the currency is the most likely to become scarce, because it seems to me the gold would have to be shipped to those countries, [so] then let's do it at once. I am quite ready to [accept] any suggestion. In other words, it takes care of the practical aspect of the thing, but not of the theoretical aspect as set forth in this paper. Therefore, I support the [motion] of the Netherlands delegate.

---

in the other principal four depositories. However, all transfers of gold by the Fund shall be made with due regard to the costs of transport and expected requirements of the Fund. In an emergency, the Executive Directors may transfer all or any part of the Fund's holdings of gold to any place where can be adequately protected."

Peru: Mr. Chairman, apart from the reason given by the Netherlands and Belgium, I want to say that I am very much afraid that if this clause were to remain as it is, there would be a lot of misapprehension in some of the countries like ours, because I assume that the depositories would be located in the capitals of the five countries holding the largest quotas. In our country, where there is no great danger from the war, and although the countries [such as ours] have the greatest trust and confidence in their governments [i.e., those of the countries with the largest quotas]—this is no reflection on the countries themselves, or depositors—the experience of the last five years unfortunately has created this impression.

Chairman: I might call attention to the phrase in the third line to avoid misunderstanding: "and in such other depositories." In other words, the gold is not limited to the five cities, but 10 percent may be in other depositories.

Norway: I should like to say that the new wording is in a sense a great improvement. But from my point of view, [p. 3] the main fault of the previous job [i.e., draft] was that it tied down the Fund too much, made the rules to strict to operate for the Fund. But I understand the introduction of the word "initially" to mean [recognition of] a great reality, namely, that the Fund will not completely be tied [down], and [it can move] away from the [initial] distribution if it finds that practical. And from the point of view of business, I think that all central banks will have [such] great connections with the central banks of the five great depositories that will be quite easy for them. I should like therefore to move, Mr. Chairman, that we accept the amended draft.

Chairman: Was the comment of the Netherlands a motion or merely a comment?

Netherlands(?): I make it into a motion not to accept this clause.

Belgium ([Camille Gutt]): Seconded.

Chairman: The comments of the delegate from Norway—in view of the fact that the motion already made on the floor may either take the form of an amendment, or, if you prefer to express your reasons for not accepting the motion, suppose we interpret your remarks as not in favor of accepting the motion of the Netherlands. Would that be satisfactory to the delegate from Norway? Are you in favor of the draft as presented by the [Special] Committee?

(Chorus of "ayes.")

Chairman: Any other comment?

France ([Pierre Mendès-France]): (interpreted) The chief of the French delegation was very much impressed by the arguments presented by the representative of the Netherlands. The new draft, he says, contains the point of view which indicates great promise. He does not understand the concern about the new text. He says that we are assured by the [p. 4] text that the needs will be met. The French Committee approves [of] the amended draft.

Chairman: Are there any other comments?

Canada: Mr. Chairman, I would agree that the practical effect of this amended draft is not one that we would feel. We do agree, however, with the delegate from the Netherlands that the text as it stands in the wording is not one that we would like to see go into the document, even though our understanding is that after operations began, the management of the Fund is free to move gold as it feels it is necessary to move it.

Chairman: The Canadian delegate was supporting the position of the Netherlands. Is there any further comment on this position?

USSR (Aleksei Smirnov): Mr. Chairman, the Soviet delegation has already expressed its view that it is in consent with this proposal and with the drafting proposed now, with the exception of the last sentence. I think that the last sentence is not necessary in this provision, and that it is perhaps not suitable in a document establishing a Monetary Fund in which the countries who take part in this agreement in advance make doubtful the normal conditions in which the Fund would function. Therefore, the Soviet delegation proposes to delete this last sentence from the draft.

Chairman: Is that in the form of an amendment? Mr. Delegate, I presume the Soviet delegation is amending the motion to delete the last sentence in this paragraph. Does anyone second that amendment?

United States: Have we not for discussion the resolution which has been moved?

Chairman: The resolution has been moved to eliminate this discussion from the motion before the house, unless a new motion [p. 5] is before the floor. I thought we could handle this as merely an amendment. We revert to the original motion. Any second?

If not, the amendment is lost.

Proceed to the original motion. Would it be satisfactory to use the simple form to vote on whether the recommendation of the [Special] Committee in the form now before you is accepted or rejected? All in favor of accepting the provision as stated in the mimeographed sheet which was handed to you this session, please say "aye."

(Chorus of "ayes.")

Contrary minded?

(Some "noes.")

Unless there is objection, the Chair rules that the recommendation has been accepted.

The next item on the agenda is the report from the Quota Committee.

The Chair recognizes the delegate from the USSR.

USSR: Mr. Chairman, the Soviet Union delegation wants to make a reservation in respect of the last sentence of this proposal, in the words "in an emergency," etc. We believe it is not necessary to insert in this document such words, which make doubtful the normal functioning of the Fund, and therefore the USSR expresses the view that this last sentence should be deleted from the draft.

Chairman: The Secretary will note the reservation stated by the USSR. Will the delegate from the United States proceed? [p. 6]

Fred Vinson (United States, Chairman, Committee on Quotas):[233] Mr. Chairman, as chairman of the Committee on Quotas, I present to this Commission the report of its committee,[234] which has been distributed, and I move its adoption.

Prior to action upon the motion, it might be well to review the efforts made and the difficulties encountered in a work of this character. I assure you that it has been a most difficult task, one that has occupied hours of close attention to its purpose. It should be stated that there is some confusion in our midst relative to certain statements, certain figures that came to countries assembled here at one time and another. The government of the United States spent a great deal of the time last year and this year assembling data upon which quotas might be based. In the initial stages, it was thought that the world total for the Fund should be $10 billion, and that the aggregate quota for member countries, excluding neutral and enemy countries, should reach the figure of $8 billion.

A uniform formula was sought, which, if it could be effectuated, would permit the fixing of quotas practically on a slide-rule basis. Much consideration was given to attempting to work out a formula that would fit all the countries assembled here and the other countries of the world. Immediate questions of the period that would be used came up for discussion, and it had to be discarded because a period that would be fair to one country could not be fair to other countries. The question of trade

---

233 The National Archives transcripts contain a typescript of Vinson's remarks separate from the typescript of this meeting of Commission I. They appear to be prepared remarks from which he departed at times to extemporize. We follow the typescript from the Commission meeting, but have used the separate typescript to compare some passages.

234 Document 395, pp. 634-635.

was considered, and particularly trade in which there were excessive fluctuations. The question of gold and gold convertibles [i.e., gold-convertible currencies] was discussed—purely as a measure to show capacity to pay, and need for the Fund. I am told that the information in respect [p. 7] of national income, while for some countries good, for other countries [was] nil, but still the technical experts struggled on, and at different times to different representatives of this group, certain statements were made. Most of those, as I understand it, [were made] last year; some, at least, this year.

It has been determined that we can [stretch], possibly with some danger, the maximum amount of the quota, and your Committee has reached the maximum in the sum of $8.8 billion. Immediately we see that there has been an increase above the $8 billion of $800 million. I want make it clear to the Commission that I think it is needless to state it, but I, with your permission, will make the statement that the determination of quotas is a matter for the delegates, for the Commission, and for the conference. Certainly no nation could be [bound] by tentative statements, tentative figures before we meet here in this conference. I want to say to you candidly that the delegates of the United States here submitted a list of the quotas aggregating $8 billion. There has not been a single reduction from the figures submitted to the American delegates, and [among] the countries who made reservations this morning, five of them, there is only one country whose figure was not increased. Fifteen members constituted the Committee on Quotas. Reservations were made by five of the representatives present.

The agreement, if reached in this country, and if confirmed by the legislators of the countries signatory thereto, will be an agreement of obligation and benefit. Quotas naturally are a considerable part of the benefit. Some members seemed to feel that once a quota is established that no change can be made in it. Anyone having that idea of course is proceeding upon a false premise, because the agreement itself contains unequivocable [p. 8] language in respect to either increasing or decreasing the quota initially fixed. As I recall, it required a four-fifths vote of the governments. Basically, the question of need to use the Fund is the central theme, or should be the central theme, in the amount fixed. At least, that has been the "thread of gold" of those who have been working upon the subject.

We regret that every member is not completely happy with the quota proposed by your Committee. Having been engaged in public life for a few years, I assure you that I have no hope that such a condition would be obtained. But I do ask you to consider the difficulties presented, the different conditions that exist in various countries, the fact that it was impossible, I repeat, impossible, to put a slide rule on the economy of forty-four nations and come up and say that "this is it." Your Committee has performed as well as it could. I think more is involved, gentlemen, in the consideration that will be given to the report of the Committee than the dollars or pride of position that may be in the minds of some of you. I would not take away benefit from any country in dollars, nor would I seek in any sense to depreciate her prestige or her standing.

We are met here in Bretton Woods in an experimental test, probably the first time in the history of the world that forty-four nations have convened seeking to solve difficult economic problems. We fight together on sodden battlefields. We sail together on the majestic blue. We fly together in the ethereal sky. The test of this conference is whether we can walk together, solve our economic problems, down the road to peace as we today march to victory. Sometimes [certain] problems seem to be most important on a particular day. Some folks think that the problems of the world were made to be solved in a day or in one conference. That can't be. We must have cooperation, collaboration; utilize the machinery, the instrumentalities, that [p. 9] have been set up to provide succor to those who are hungry and ill; to set up, establish instrumentalities that will stabilize or tend toward stabilization of economies of our world. Maybe then some of the germs will be attacked either by serum or friendship and destroyed; maybe wars may be deferred or postponed indefinitely. I know it is our hope, our objective, to reach that. The delegation of the United States submits that in respect of certain amounts, they may not be just exactly what the delegates from that particular country desire. If there be any irritation or unhappiness, we certainly regret it, because any error on our part is of the head and not of the heart. [p. 10]

Chairman: You have heard the report of the Quota Committee.

The delegate from Iran.

Iran: In spite of the very eloquent and moving speech of the United States delegate, on behalf of the Iranian delegation I wish to state that the quota proposed for my country is entirely unsatisfactory and unacceptable. I, therefore, wish to make a reservation on that point.

China: Mr. Chairman.

Chairman: The delegate from China.

China: Mr. Chairman, after listening to the moving appeal of the chairman of our Quota Committee, I hesitate greatly to sound a note of discord at this conference. It has been the effort of the Chinese delegation to promote harmony and the success of this great common enterprise. But every delegation has its difficulties. Candor requires me to state simply and briefly the difficulties facing the Chinese delegation.

Before the conference met, we had been told that the total of this Fund would be about $8 billion. And we in China, calculating our needs and our economic position, had hoped that we would be assigned a quota of about $700 million. During these days at Bretton Woods we have found it desirable to increase the total beyond the original $8 billion, and we have also found it necessary and wise to increase substantially the quotas of some countries beyond the figure suggested before the conference. The present quota, as stated by the Quota Committee, for China, when published, would be received with general disappointment by the people of China. The Chinese delegation is compelled to state that the quota is not acceptable and suggests that the Quota Committee [p. 11] reconsider the matter.

Chairman: Any further comments?

The delegate from Greece.

Greece (Kyriakos Varvaressos): Mr. Chairman, I see that the aggregate of quotas has been increased by [$]800 million and I remark that all countries in the position of my country have a slight share in this increase except Greece, and I should like to ask for reconsideration of this fact. All countries in the same position as my country have participated to a small extent in this increase except our country, and I think that there is little doubt that Greece after the war will have to meet some requirements which are recognized as very heavy.[235]

Chairman: The delegate from the Netherlands.

Netherlands (Wim Beyen): Mr. Chairman, I will start by stating that the Netherlands delegation is well aware of the enormous difficulties that the making up of this list involved and it, therefore, agrees with what was said by Judge Vinson about it. As regards the quota for the Netherlands, I am not going to say that we are dissatisfied, but I would like to make three points which I don't think will hold up, as far as we are concerned, the coming to a general agreement. The three points are the following:

First of all, I would like it to be understood that the acceptance of this figure by no means means the acceptance either of the formula or of the application of the formula. I think that it is necessary to state that. It means that this will in no way prejudice any future talk about quotas when the circumstances might arise that the quotas would be revised. I don't mean to say the figures are wrong; I only want to say it should not

[235] The implication is that despite expecting high costs for postwar reconstruction, Greece will still wish to share in the increase in quotas.

[p. 12] prejudice us in any way in any future talks, and we want to have it understood the acceptance of the figure does not mean acceptance of its basis or its statistical form.

The second point is that we have not yet officially accepted the clauses about election of directors. A slight reservation is that respect seems to be necessary. In connection therewith, I want to point out that a quota is not an absolute figure; it is a part of a total figure. And, therefore, acceptance of the quota implies that the total figure should not be changed.

My third reservation is the purely formal one that though I know that signing the final draft does not actually bind governments, I think for my part I am under the obligation to submit the figure of the quota to my government, and I am sure[236] I can give you a definite opinion before the end of the conference.

Chairman: The delegate from Australia.

Australia: Mr. Chairman, the Australian delegation recognized the difficulties that the Quota Committee had to face in drawing up this list of quotas and, within the limitations set, it appreciates that it has done well. Nevertheless, this quota, combined with the limitation of the annual drawings to 25 percent, presents Australia with difficulties, and I feel I must place those difficulties on record very briefly.

We will finish the war with very small reserves of gold or dollars outside of what is in the Fund. We must rely, therefore, almost entirely on the Fund for our needs, and because of the fluctuations in our balance of payments, the quota will not be adequate for that purpose. The task we are faced with, therefore, is one of building up free [p. 13] liquid reserves outside the Fund. That means that unless immediately after the war it so happens that we have very favorable seasons,[237] we will be forced to a restrictive process in trade, which is in conflict with the purposes and policies of this Fund. Therefore, I have to add my reservation on behalf of the Australian delegation to the reservations of other countries.

Chairman: The delegate from India.

India: Mr. Chairman, I feel I must say a few words of explanation of the fact that it has been necessary for me to make a reservation on behalf of India. The delegation from India is fully conscious of the extreme difficulties which have had to be met in handling this complicated matter. At the same time, they are aware of the strong feeling in the countries which they represent that India's importance, India's economic

---

[236] Perhaps the speaker or the typescript should have said "not sure" here.

[237] "Favorable seasons" refers to good weather for harvests, since Australia's exports were mainly agricultural.

importance, should be recognized in international institutions of this character. It is not merely the size of India; it is not merely the population of India—and I may say that one out of every four of the people represented at this conference is an Indian—it is that on purely objective economic criteria, India feels that she is an extremely important part of the world and will probably be an even more important part in the years to come.

Now, sir, India is not disposed to argue about the absolute figure of the quota in the way in which other countries might wish to do. She is more concerned with their relative position among the countries which will subscribe to the setting up of this institution. India feels that in an institution of this character, if due regard is paid to her economic significance, she should be in no danger of failing to secure an adequate place [p. 14] in the councils of the institution. We recognize that other considerations than the economic criteria which underlay the formula applied have to be taken into account, but we feel that the application of such considerations should not result in injustice being done, or in such a distortion of the economic merits of the case as would leave India at a disadvantage. It will be clear, therefore, sir, that I agree with what has been said by the delegate from the Netherlands, and it is not merely the question of the quota, but the question of the combined effect of the quota and the arrangements for the management of the Fund which are India's concern.

Chairman: Is there any further comment?

The delegate from Yugoslavia.

Yugoslavia ([Vladimir Rybar]): Mr. Chairman, I appreciate the appeal of Mr. Vinson and the reason he has given for the cooperation, but on behalf of my government I would like to make some reservations concerning the quota of Yugoslavia in view of the economic disruption and heavy destruction Yugoslavia suffered from the war.

Chairman: The delegate from New Zealand.

New Zealand: Mr. Chairman, I believe that the country I represent is the one out of the fifteen that didn't get a little more. I understand that fifteen made representations that the sum they had originally been proposed [to] be allocated [was too small,] and all had made representations with the exception of one. I want to bring up this point with regard to New Zealand. Because of the various factors that come into its peculiar position, the sum that has been allocated, $50 million, on the list is inadequate, and I am not in any way detracting from all that [p. 15] Judge Vinson had to say. I believe that this Fund is more important than any single quota. The establishment of this Fund is more important than satisfying every individual country, and it would be wrong for any representative to come here and accept something that was likely later to cause disruption and dislocation without saying what he thought of it.

I think it ought to be known that while it is comparatively a small country, very small, only a little bit larger than the United Kingdom in area, and [of] the same potential if we take the years that are to come instead of the years that are passed. Taking those factors into account, and the smallness of its population, it is correct to say that it has got the largest per capita trade of any country in the world, and in the main I think there are only two other countries that export more of their total production than does New Zealand. And the commodities that we do export are those types of commodities that automatically feel the pressure of change in economic circumstances throughout the world. I could give one year when we had a lot of trouble when our exports exceeded our imports by something like £19 million sterling. That would be an unfair figure because it was 1921, and that was when the trouble came to a head after the last war. But I have got one or two figures that I can give, and I am only stressing this on the basis of need, need of facilities to use, need of facilities to use if circumstances become bad. Here are disparities. Within a short period [[we went from a]] £16 million surplus in one year, 1934, [to] £10 million the next, in 1938 it was only £5 millions, and it is worthwhile remembering that we have an overseas commitment that [p. 16] we have always met, and I hope will always meet, of something more than £5½ million sterling, but we have that to meet *and* current transactions on debt. Well, now, those factors are such that when the first figure was suggested to us we said what we thought had to be done, and I am sorry,[238] but we were the one country, we did not go to the United States. I want that to be emphasized, we did not make any representations whatever to the United States or to the chairman of the [Quota] Committee or to anyone else before the committee meeting this morning, and we did discuss it with other people.

Now, if we take the points that are raised and still weigh them, there are two different types of need. If our need is measured alongside those countries that have lost all chance of making exchange during the past four years and may have no chance for some other use, it is very small; we have no need of that kind. We have no need with regard to the ravages of war. We can care for ourselves. It does mean that we can care

---

238 That is, sorry to identify New Zealand as the one country that did not get a higher quota, thereby depriving the chairman of the Committee on Quotas, Fred Vinson, deniability about what particular countries did or did not get.

for ourselves. And we would like, in so far as we are a member of this Fund, to be a contributing party on the basis of capacity to produce to help those that are in need. I am talking about general credits as well as in relieving those needs ourselves.

We think, first of all, that the two types of need ought to be stressed: the one, the war needs—[for these,] we ought to be helpful, rather than receiving [i.e., being a debtor] ourselves. With regard to the other need, though, our country's trade is such that throughout the century that we have been a country subject to such difficulties in connection with falls and rises in prices that we have had two or three crises in [p. 17] the last thirty or forty years. We can't very well have an exporting deficit as against imports and at the same time meet commitments other than trade commits. That is what we have had to do in the past.

The next [point], with regard to ability and capacity: we do not need any help for that. We want to [help], insofar as the Fund is built up into figures which tend to denote the extent to which each country having a quota allocated to it can help in world trade. I think for that reason we ought to have, again, a high quota. We ought to have a high quota because the products of our area are so good in general that there is a fairly large demand for them, and the lower this quota the worse and the greater our difficulty will be—and the potential, which I think also is tremendous. We have got to take those factors into account. I do not know the exact measures that the committee tried to use. I do know that whoever tried to use them had a task that seemed impossible to satisfy everyone.

I happen to be one [delegate] that was not satisfied. I know that they have tried inside the two years, about two years now, since the first inquiry for figures, to find a measure.[239] And now I thought that we would be able to argue a reason [to] show that this wasn't a fair sum, taking into account the country that I represent, its production, its trade, and all other factors. I do not think it is, but I would say this, with all the implications attached it, that even though the committee is not for it—and I hope it will be, unless there are other factors that suggest to me that the Fund will not do what the promoters of it intended it to do—I will go back and advocate the figure that is given, whatever it might be. I don't want it on the basis of charity, of somebody [p. 18] being kind. Don't misunderstand me. I don't want anybody to be kind to us. There are a lot of people that ought to be subject to kindness, not with others feeling that we are kind to them. We don't want that. We have got probably

[239] That is, a satisfactory formula for determining quotas.

comparatively, inside our little country, as good a living standard as there is in any other country in the world—it isn't that. There are difficulties that arise inside the country that it would be impossible for us just for the moment to meet unless we in effect are a factor in world trade. We want to help the expanding side of it. We ought to have more. If we get more,[240] I will still fight for the Fund to go into operation.

Chairman: The Vice Chairman being absent, I should like the permission of the Commission to make a few remarks on this point.

If there is no objection, I shall do so.

The delegate from New Zealand has marshaled some impressive facts and has made a convincing talk, raising the point that the needs of his country, the swings and the balances of payments, justified a larger quota. We recognize the cogency of that. We did recognize the fact that several countries may be in that very same position, and it was in recognition of that fact that [Article III, Section 2, Alternative A,] Section [paragraph] (4)[241] was introduced. And I should like to quote but one sentence from that Section 4. It says that in making such waiver—namely, the waiver of the conditions of the quota—the Fund shall take into consideration periodic or exceptional requirements of the members. I have no doubt that the delegate [p. 19] from New Zealand or the representative of any other country that happens to be a member of the Fund will, if it has a convincing case, be able to present it effectively to the Executive Committee. I have equal confidence in the good judgment of the Executive Committee, and know that if a convincing case is submitted to them, they will utilize this flexible provision, which is designed to take care to precisely such developments.

One word about the attitude toward quotas in general. One gets a little the feeling that the question of quotas and the distribution of the amount of quotas has attained a degree of exaggeration which can be explained only on the grounds of concentration on the particular problem in hand at the moment. The quotas, after all, do not measure the assistance which the Fund is prepared to extend to countries whose balance of payments requires such assistance. One of the important characteristics of the Fund

---

[240] Perhaps the speaker or the typescript should have said "fail to get more" here.

[241] In Document 32, p. 29. In the intermediate draft, Document 321, p. 524, it became Article V, Section 5, and read in part, "The Fund may in its discretion, and on terms which safeguard its interests, waive any of the conditions prescribed in Section 3 above, especially in the case of members with a record of avoiding large or continuous use of the Fund's resources. In making such waiver it shall take into consideration periodic or exceptional requirements of members."

is its flexibility. It has flexibility in its resources; it has flexibility in its power to extend assistance to various countries, and that cardinal principle is an essential requisite for the successful operation of the Fund. There is nothing in any of the provisions which in any way prohibits the Executive Committee from extending such assistance by way of making it possible to purchase foreign exchange by any country to any given amount.

The quota has certain reasons for existence. It measures participation; it measures approximately the economic and financial power of the members; but that measure is not intended to be a precise measure of the amount of assistance which a country might need for the amount of assistance which a country might want. And so, I would urge you to consider, first, the [p. 20] difficulty of arriving at quotas which are satisfactory to all, as Judge Vinson has so well pointed out, and as those who have worked with this problem over months so readily recognize. Secondly, and more important, we would urge you to bear in mind that the quotas are not a measure of the assistance which the Fund can grant; that there are a number of provisions in there that assure to countries who merit the additional assistance which the Fund may provide that such assistance shall be forthcoming.

Any further comments?

The delegate from France.

France ([Pierre Mendès-France]): (The comment of the delegate from France, given in French, was interpreted as follows): The delegation of the provisional government of the French Republic is concerned about the problem of the quota. The delegation listened with great interest to the appeal made by the United States delegation, who at the same time is the chairman of the Quota Committee, and also by the chairman of this Commission. The delegation is fully aware of the great difficulties which exist in order to fix the quotas according to the relative interests of the countries. The delegation, however, has been proud since the very beginning of this conference of the great cooperation and international solidarity, which we feel certain will readily be recognized by the other countries.

It is, therefore, with great disappointment that we have noted that the quota which was just established does not meet our expectations. First of all, it was intended to establish quotas on the basis of mathematical arguments which it was supposed would be readily accepted by public opinion. However, this found difficulties, [p. 21] and it came to negotiations among different nations and bargaining among other nations, and several nations saw their quotas increased while others saw theirs diminished. This has resulted in a great deal of confusion, which the chief of the French delegation objects to. He believes that the influence which should be attributed toward Europe, and especially to Western Europe, and, least but not last, France, does not seem to amount to its just value.

What the American delegation has called "experimental experience" is recognized as being very important by the French delegation to success. However, the French delegation wishes to draw the attention of the Commission to the fact that it should actually not benefit out of the fact that some countries actually do not benefit out of their usual interest which has existed previously, and they believe if no just consideration is being taken toward the influence which those countries will probably occupy again in the postwar world, that the situation might add to the ruin and destruction which will exist after the war is over in these countries.[242] For this reason, the delegation of the provisional government of the French Republic wishes to send back to the Quota Committee the proposed figures for reconsideration, and reserves its right [to do so. It] does very much regret, as a matter of fact, to have to reconsider the entire participation of this delegation at this conference if the question could not be reconsidered.

Chairman: Any further comment?

The delegate from Ethiopia. [p. 22]

Ethiopia ([Ephrem Tewelde Medhen]): Mr. Chairman, I do not wish to make the already difficult question of the quota still more difficult by raising an issue, but we feel compelled by the quota allocated Ethiopia that we must express our views. In view of the needs of Ethiopia, of the size of the population and of its large possibilities, the Ethiopian delegation considers that the quota allocated to Ethiopia is totally inadequate and the delegation, therefore, requests that that be reconsidered.

Chairman: Any further comment?

The delegate from Canada.

Translator [of France's remarks above]: If you please, may I correct the statement?

Chairman: Certainly.

Translator: "If this question of quotas could not be reconsidered"—I believe I interpreted it wrongly, and [should have said that] this matter

[242] The apparent meaning of this sentence is that quotas should take account that despite their current wartime poverty, France and other countries can be expected to experience an economic rebound after the war.

could be reported to the government in Algiers, [and] it might be a fact that the government of Algiers [would then] request the delegation to reconsider its participation [in] the Fund.[243]

Chairman: The delegate from Canada.

Canada: Mr. Chairman, may I say very briefly that in view of all the very difficult circumstances associated with determining of quotas, I think that it should be said that the Quota Committee has performed its job on the whole very well. No one would defend this list as an ideal list. No one would stake his reputation that every quota conformed exactly to all the equitable considerations, but the problem is one of extreme difficulty.

Having recognized the fact that it is possible to change these quotas—there is provision in the Constitution of this Fund when it shall be established that there should be, not in the governing body, changes to [p. 23] represent the members—I feel that this Commission should accept the quota list recommended as one on which, if governments so decide, this Fund can begin its operations, and which can be adjusted far more equitably than in any process at this meeting on the basis of experience.

Chairman: Are there any further comments?

The Chair would beg the indulgence of the Commission again to make a remark that is called forth by the statement of the delegate from the French Committee.

Surely the members here are all cognizant of the objectives of this Fund. Surely the members recognize the breadth and the scope of those objectives. It is a little difficult to understand that one's participation in the attainment, in the attempt to attain those objectives, would be to any significant degree influenced by the question as to whether or not you could buy [i.e., borrow] $10 million or $15 million worth more than a year over a period of four years without any special permission from the Fund. There may be more to it than that. There may be political considerations that seem to some of the delegates to justify the view that unless they get a little more than their neighbor, or a little less than somebody else, or a little more than some combination of states, that it is a matter of permanent importance.

Those of you who have struggled with this proposal for many months, and that includes a very great number not only in the United States but in other countries, find it not only difficult to understand but, I confess, difficult to sympathize with the view that the value of this proposal to the

---

[243] We have done our best to make sense out of the garbled words in the typescript. Algiers at the time was the headquarters of the Free French government, most of France itself still being under German occupation.

future world can be interpreted [p. 24] either in the sense of any slight political, assumed advantage that it may give, any slight political prestige which it may accord, or certainly any advantage with respect to the monetary difference between a larger and smaller quota. I say this because I am wondering whether those delegates who have suggested that their participation or adherence to a matter of such profound importance to the coming generation can be determined by considerations which, shall I say, strike me as being something less than befits the [i.e., their?] nation or any of the nations that are represented here. I hope that the delegates, in evaluating the most difficult work of the Committee on Quotas, in recognizing the provisions which were made in the Fund to take care of adjustments, will put in its proper place the question as to whether or not a particular quota is a little higher or a little lower than expected. Quotas are only a small part of the Fund, and they should be so evaluated. I hope that the countries who have taken any definite position on the quota will give careful evaluation to their statements with respect to the importance of the quota at this time to their own country.

Are there any other comments?

Norway: Mr. Chairman.

Chairman: The delegate from Norway.

Norway: When I have listened to those delegates here who have criticized very much the proposal placed before us, I have sometimes got a certain impression that those delegates in a way misunderstand the position which this Fund shall take in the world tomorrow. Some of those delegates—maybe I misunderstood them, but on me their [p. 25] speeches have made the impression as if they thought that the Fund and the Fund alone was an institution which would provide them with the necessary help in those cases where an adverse balance of payment threatens that country. Mr. Chairman, this is not the role which is assigned to the Fund. The Fund is not going to replace the ordinary short-term credit of the world. It is going to be in addition. It is going to be in addition. When I particularly think of a country like New Zealand and others, those countries must rely upon the continuance of that system of short-term credit. It is a support the Fund shall give. It shall not take the whole thing over. And I think, therefore, that those delegates should look a little to their credit their nation would have.

Take, for instance, France. France will have after this war an excellent credit—no doubt of that, that France will be able to get support all over the world without just going to this Fund. I think on the whole we shall, every one of us, remember the restricted means, the restricted role, of the

Fund, and I think that on that basis, Mr. Chairman, the [Quota] Committee has done very good work.

I will add [that] my own country, Norway, belongs to the occupied countries of Western Europe. If the entire quota were what should be assigned to us on the basis of the questionnaire, we have got a reduction of 25 percent, but we accept that because we think that within the framework as it is now we should not try to claim too much. And I would very much like to appeal to a number of the other delegates to look at that. Here is set up something which may be of great use to the whole world. Let us not make it too difficult at this initial state [stage] by [p. 26] pressing our own national claims too much.

(Applause.)

Chairman: The delegate from the United Kingdom.

United Kingdom: Mr. Chairman, we should just like to add our voice to the voices of those who have appealed to the Commission to take the large and practical view of this question. We are quite sure that this list, in common, I venture to say, with anything which could be drawn up, is incapable of giving complete satisfaction to all the nations here represented. But we think, as has been said by the delegate from Canada, that it does form a practical basis on which the Fund could commence its existence, and we think, as you, Mr. Chairman, have said, that the Fund contains in its Articles adequate provision for elasticity and adjustments as need is shown. And we, therefore, join with what the last speaker has said, in appealing to those who have expressed reservations on this matter to ask themselves in all sincerity whether they wish to press these reservations in a way which may prevent there coming to the world the manifold benefits which all of us expect to come if the Fund is brought into existence.

Chairman: If there is no further comment, the Chair will put the question to a vote. Does anyone wish to make any further comment?

The question before us is the acceptance of the report of the Quota Committee. All those in favor of accepting the report of the Quota Committee, please say "aye."

Delegates: Aye.

Chairman: Contrary minded, "nay."

Delegates: Nay.

Chairman: I don't think it is necessary to have a show of hands, but if any member wishes it, I shall do so. [p. 27] The Chair will declare the report of the Quota Committee accepted.[244]

---

[244] Became Schedule A in the final agreement.

The delegate from Cuba.

Cuba (Luis Machado): Mr. Chairman, at the meeting of this Commission two days ago, the question of the formulation of the Executive Directors was postponed until the matter of the quota was known; and now that we have disposed of the question of the quota, I ask the Chair to bring Alternative J, submitted by the delegation from Cuba, up for discussion.

Chairman: The delegate from Cuba has requested that the alternative provisions on the election of the Executive Directors be brought before the Commission for action. If there is no objection, we will place before this Commission for consideration Alternative J. The page number is 26j, Document 310.[245]

The Secretariat will read the first paragraph. It is not necessary to read the remainder. Alternative B was Schedule B, which deals with the maximum voting. By reading the first paragraph, the Commission will have the opportunity to consider the merits of the whole problem.

Secretary ([Leroy Stinebower, United States]): (reading) "There shall be twelve elected Executive Directors of whom (a) five shall be appointed by the five members having the largest quotas, (b) five shall be elected by the remaining members, other than the American Republics, and (c) two shall be elected by the American Republics, exclusive of any entitled to appoint an Executive Director under (a), above. Elections shall be conducted biennially in accordance with the provisions of Schedule B. Persons chosen as Executive Directors need not be Governors."

Chairman: The provision is before us for discussion. [p. 28]

The delegate from Poland.

Poland: Mr. Chairman, we have submitted a slight modification of [paragraph] (a) [of] Schedule B, which is contained here in Alternative L on [page] 26m. This alternative is only a slight modification of Schedule B, and [is] provided in Alternative L.[246] The main feature is that in the place of the provision that 19 percent [of total quotas] must be obtained for a seat, and [if] one [person] supported will take more than 19 [percent], the votes, so to [speak], "wasted" can be used to a further balance. We suggest that they may be considered as voting for this person. But if the person so elected should dispose in the meeting of

[245] Document 310, pp. 502-504. It refers to Article VII, Sections 2-3 ("Voting") in the preliminary draft, Document 32, p. 47; Article XI, Section 5 ("Executive Directors") of the intermediate draft, Document 321, p. 532, which was left blank; and Document 212, pp. 275-277, a proposal to fill in the blank.

[246] Document 346, p. 578.

directors that the number of votes which is greater, and corresponding to the full amount of votes which is given for them, then more than 19 [percent]—perhaps 23, 25 or more, if with such [[a share]] of votes, the respective person was elected, that is only the slight modification which is, in my opinion, in our opinion, much better than the first because it avoids the bargaining with [these] additional excess votes and gives for all the parts the possibility to obtain a seat, but with the lesser number of votes than the other directors chosen before would have.[247]

Chairman: Any further comment?

The delegate from Canada.

Canada: Mr. Chairman, I would like to bring to the attention of the committee [Commission] that the committee considering the Executive Committee[248] reported that it had had before it Alternative K[249] on page 26m of the document, and that it had considered this sympathetically, but in view of the fact that it did not wish or did not see its way to consider the whole subject of the Executive Committee prior to knowing the quotas, it gave no verdict on it. [p. 29] I would just like to say in explanation that Alternative K would be an amendment to Alternative J or any other similar alternative which the Commission selected. It would not in any way affect the working of Alternative J.

It was the thought of the Canadian delegation that in consideration of this question there was one standard which had been overlooked, namely, that some countries were providing funds, providing resources, for the use of the Fund; other countries at other times or at the same time were drawing on those resources. It seemed to us desirable that at any time on the Executive Committee there should be at least two countries which were at that time providing resources rather than drawing upon them, two creditors at least in a committee on which there might be many debtors. To achieve this, we suggested that at the second [election]—and only [then], not until the second election of the Executive Directors—that if the two countries whose quotas have been used over the past two years on the average in the largest absolute amount did not appear among

247 The meaning of this passage, which seems garbled because of the delegate's imperfect command of English, was to explain the procedure that Alternative L proposed for successive rounds of voting to select the five "at large" Executive Directors. The "at large" Executive Directors were those other than the five representing the countries with the largest quotas and the two reserved for the "American Republics" (Latin America).

248 Apparently Committee 3's Ad Hoc Committee on Article VII, Section 2 ("The Executive Directors") of the preliminary draft.

249 Document 328, p. 544. Alternative K was Canada's proposal.

the five appointed directors, then one or two additional directors as might be required should be appointed to a share that there should at all times on the committee be at least two creditors.

It was our suggestion that those additional directors, if it should at any time prove necessary to appoint them, should be additional to the total number, and not disturbing in terms of Alternative J the five appointed directors on the one hand, or the seven elected directors on the other.

Since the committee reported that this alternative had been before them and drew it to the attention of the Commission, since the Canadian delegation feel that this [p. 30] is a healthy principle to write into the constitution of the Executive Committee, I support it before the Commission.

Chairman: Is it clear that Alternative K on page 26m, which the delegate from Canada is discussing, in no way replaces or interferes or is in opposition to the Alternative J which the delegate from Cuba was discussing—that it is merely added to it?

Canada: That is correct.

Chairman: The delegate from Belgium.

Belgium (Camille Gutt): I think it is very much to the point, [the discussion] made by the Canadian delegate, and therefore, without expanding upon it, because he has discussed it very ably and given all the reasons which militate in favor of it, I would like to support it.

Chairman: The delegate from Norway.

Norway: Mr. Chairman, this question has been discussed for a very long time in committees and subcommittees, and it has been all the time impossible to reach agreement because we haven't known the quota. Now we know the quotas and there are a number of alternatives before the Commission. The matter is extremely complicated, and what makes it even more complicated is that the Bank Commission [Commission II] is wrestling with exactly the same problem and has been unable to reach an agreement. Mr. Chairman, since there are so many alternatives and since this is a very large group to discuss this problem, I wonder whether it would be practicable to refer this question to the Committee on Unsettled Questions [Special Committee on Unsettled Problems]. Now that we know the quotas, we might be able to get one alternative to which everybody would seem to agree to some extent, at least.

Chairman: Does the Commission wish to consider the possibility of returning something to the [Quota] Committee, which, [p. 31] as the speaker has said, has been discussed a long time and without reaching an agreement, and in the light of new quotas which may not have been known even approximately by certain members? The possibility of that makes it easier to come to a decision. Is there any comment on that?

The delegate from Cuba.

Cuba (Luis Machado): Mr. Chairman, I would ask the Chair, in order to facilitate the discussion and the decision of this very important point, that we request that the amendment submitted by the delegate from Poland be deferred until we know what the final setup of the Board of Directors [Governors] or the Executive Directors is. It seems to me that Schedule B, which provides the method of electing the directors, is very important, but it will not come into operation until we know how many directors are to be elected.

And I would request the delegate from Canada to defer consideration of Amendment [Alternative] K, which he has explained does not interfere and is not inconsistent with Amendment [Alternative] J, but would be supplemental to J. In order to simplify the matter, I would ask your permission that we now discuss and put to a vote Amendment [Alternative] J. I would like to tell the delegates here present that for the last hour we have heard the feelings and impressions of each one of the delegates regarding the very delicate subject of the quota. I heard not less than fifteen or sixteen speeches, and not one of them came from the Latin American countries. It doesn't mean to say that the Latin American countries feel that the quotas submitted by the [Quota] Committee and now accepted represent the resources or the financial set-up or the income or any of the economic [p. 32] factors of our share of the world.

We seem to feel that in the matter of a quota, it was not proper for us to enter into a competition with our friends on the other side [of the Atlantic], since it has been clearly stated [that] an increase in the quota was largely sought for the purpose of providing additional foreign exchange. We could have very easily got into that race if we wanted to, because your Latin American countries are so enormous in their resources that a slight change in any of the multiplication factors would have considerably enhanced the quota position. We believe that Latin America, which represents practically one-half of the nations here assembled, has come to this meeting in the fine spirit of cooperation. We have come here to help the world get itself on its feet again and to stabilize the finances of the future world. We have come here, not to get any immediate benefits—we realize that the economic position of our countries, although in a minor degree, is very similar to the position of the United States. We have been lucky at this time to have our financial structure strengthened. We are at this moment more or less in the position of creditor nations.

We, therefore, come here to participate in a world institution to whom we are going to surrender some of our sovereign rights. From now on, the right to determine what the content of the Mexican peso is in terms of gold will no longer be vested in the Mexican government but in an international body where the voting power would be very small according to the quotas. From now on, the Peruvian [sol, i.e., currency unit]—its point of exchange will not be determined by the Peruvian government, but by an international body in which, as I said before, we have very little voice or voting power.

We do feel [p. 33] that twenty nations here assembled, which constitute one-half of all the countries here assembled, are at least entitled to two seats on this Board of Executive Directors. We feel that our contribution would be worth it, that the opinions of two men of experience from our side of the world might be extremely helpful to the directors in making decisions, and we feel that we can go back and explain to our countrymen that we have [been] taxed, but the taxation goes with representation.[250] We feel we are not asking very much, and we have tried to meet all the points of view of the delegates, and I hope that this assembly unanimously approves the [Alternative] J, which will give us what we consider is adequate representation on the Executive Directorate.

Chairman: The delegate from Egypt.

Egypt: Mr. Chairman, I would like to bring the attention of this committee [Commission] to the Alternative E, page 25h, Document 315.[251] This alternative, as a matter of fact, supports Alternative J as submitted by the Cuban delegation. But we demand that the Middle East countries—once you have adopted the original basis for this representation, we believe that the Middle East countries as one economic unit should be represented by one seat. I need not urge you for the small countries to be well represented; the Middle East countries have their own economic situation more or less the same. And it would not be inconsistent if we adopt the same principle.

Chairman: The delegate from France.

---

250 A reference to the slogan, "No taxation without representation," a rallying cry in what became the United States in the years before the American Revolution of 1776.

251 Document 315, pp. 506-507. Alternative E provided for five Executive Directors representing the five countries with the largest quotas; three representing the British Empire; three representing the American Republics; one representing the Middle East; and three representing other countries.

France: I would like to raise a question for clarification. If Amendment—Alternative—J is accepted together with Alternative K concerning two representatives of the creditor nations, is there a possibility in that [p. 34] case that there should be fourteen—that there might be fourteen Executive Directors instead of twelve?

Chairman: Will the delegate from Canada respond to that question?

Canada: The answer is that theoretically there might be fourteen. The probability of that coming about is extremely small. I would say it was impossible. There is a possibility that there might be thirteen directors.

France: Thank you.

Chairman: In view of the fact that the time is getting very late and the day of the final end of the conference is approaching,[252] and in view of the further fact that I am informed that this matter has been discussed in great detail at committees and subcommittees, I wonder whether it might not be appropriate to put the question to the vote, and that any additional expression of opinion would in the main merely repeat what has already been said on the subject. In order to not shut out discussion completely, I suggest that any delegate who wishes to speak on this matter from now on shall be limited to what, in the opinion of the Chair, is a reasonable time. In the light of all the circumstances at the moment, it seems to me to be three minutes.

The delegate from Iran.

Iran: I support the amendment proposed by the Egyptian delegate.

United States (Ansel Luxford): Mr. Chairman.

Chairman: The delegate from the United States.

United States (Ansel Luxford): I do believe that, as the delegate from Cuba has said, it will facilitate consideration of these issues if we can narrow and consider them and their order. For that reason, [p. 35] I would like to see us focus on Alternative J, which was the first issue before this committee [Commission], and I would like to express the support of the United States for such alternative.

Chairman: The delegate from India.

India: Mr. Chairman, the delegation from India wishes to draw attention to Schedule [Alternative] D,[253] the main feature of which is the proposal that there shall be twelve Executive Directors, of whom six shall be appointed by the six members having the largest quota. I need not enlarge on the reasons why the delegation from India has put forward this

[252] At the time, the conference was scheduled to end on July 19, 1944. It was later extended to July 22.

[253] Document 179, p. 222.

amendment.[254] I would only say, Mr. Chairman, that we would be quite prepared to see this combined with Alternative J.

Chairman: The delegate from Iraq.

Iraq: Mr. Chairman, I wish to support the proposal made by the delegate from Egypt. In the opinion of the Iraq delegation, the proportionate representation as shown by Schedule B[255] shows quite well representation and protects the interests of small countries, but that if it is decided that regional representation should be admitted by the conference, then the Middle East, as an independent economic unit, should have its own representation.

Chairman: The delegate from Iraq supports the proposal of the delegate from Egypt and feels that that will give the small countries adequate representation.

The delegate from Mexico.

Mexico (Antonio Espinosa de los Monteros): I think the question has been sufficiently discussed. Therefore, I move that Alternative J be put to a vote.

Chairman: The motion has already been made.

Mexico (Antonio Espinosa de los Monteros): [Then,] I second that motion. [p. 36]

Chairman: The motion has been made and seconded that Alternative J be placed before the Commission for a vote.

The delegate from Belgium.

Belgium (Camille Gutt): I would just like to put a question. We began by discussing the first paragraph of part No. 2 [Section 2] of Alternative J. I want to know whether the vote we will take is on that, or on the whole of the Alternative J. In the latter case, I have two remarks to make, not very important, but I should like to make them before the vote.

Chairman: Is there any objection to taking up the first paragraph? Does the delegate from Cuba have any reluctance to have it done that way?

Cuba: No.

Chairman: Then, we will confine the question to the first paragraph of Section 2 of Alternative J.

The delegate from Czechoslovakia.

---

[254] India had the sixth largest proposed quota, so Alternative D would have given it its own appointed director. When the IMF began operations in 1946, India got its own appointed director because the USSR, which had been assigned the third largest proposed quota, had decided not to join.

[255] In Document 310, pp. 504-505.

Czechoslovakia: May I ask a question, please? Does it mean that the first directors stated here in Alternative J are only for the present number of members, or for the future members accepted in the Fund?

Chairman: The Chair will suggest that it is for the present and the future, unless altered under the provisions which will permit it. However, I will refer that question to the delegate from Cuba, since it is his proposal.

Cuba (Luis Machado): Our duty is to solve the problems of today having in view the problems of tomorrow. We believe for the present twelve directors will do. We may want to change our opinion on the subject when other nations not participating at this conference at the proper time are invited to participate in an International Monetary [p. 37] Fund, but we would not want at this time to go into a discussion of what shall be the future when we can heartily agree on the present.

May I again appeal to all of you, that if we did not have so many reasons of an economic, social, and political order to support Alternative J, the fact that at least one-half of the members of this conference can agree on one thing should have enough merit to have it voted favorably.

Chairman: The delegate from Norway.

Norway: Mr. Chairman, may I ask if the original proposals [Alternatives] A and B as amended have been dropped, or whether that is still before the Commission? The reason I ask is that the Norwegian delegation, although it understands the reason for the Alternative J, does not feel that it is to join in a regional representation the way it has been proposed, yet I can well understand that Latin America should have two seats, but I think it would be much better and much more rational if that representation could be brought about through that proportional representation which has been outlined in the original proposals A and B. There is as much reason for singling out other regions as for singling out one region in that way. Then we should either have complete regional representation or not regional representation, but not a mixture like this. I would like to ask whether A and B as amended[256] is still before the commission. In that case, we will vote for that proposal.

Chairman: My understanding is that all the alternatives are before the Commission, and that if the [p. 38] Commission sees fit to turn down Alternative J, which is before the Commission for our first vote, we will take other alternatives in such order as may appear to the Chair.

---

[256] In Document 280, pp. 454-455. The original Alternatives A and B, in Document 32, pp. 44-47, had been combined into a single proposal, Document 152, pp. 162-164.

The delegate from the Netherlands. [p. 1 (39)]

Netherlands: I want to ask a question about the order. If we vote about J, does that does that mean Alternative K is out of order? I am not quite sure about that if we accept Alternative J.

Chairman: The ruling of the Chair on that is that J is not an alternative to K. K is not an alternative to J; it is, rather, in the form of an amendment.

Netherlands: It is an addition which will be put to the voting officials.

Chairman: Voting commission, so it seems.

India: On a question of procedure: Alternative J is the main proposition before the Commission, and the Indian delegation has the amendment to Alternative J; and the usual procedure with which we are familiar is that the amendment is first put to the vote. If the amendment is carried, it is incorporated.

Chairman: I thought that was what we were to do. We are now putting before the house the vote on the question of the amendment of the motion, which is J.

India: That is one independent portion. Am I to understand that you are putting that to the vote now, or the whole of Amendment J?

Chairman: We thought that it might facilitate discussion if we broke the proposal up into two parts, permitting the Commission to vote first on part (a) and secondly on part (b). That was merely for convenience. It is the paragraph within the schedule.[257]

India: Yes. Amendment J says that five [Executive Directors] shall be appointed by members. The Indian amendment is that it shall be six. Therefore, the house must be given an opportunity of either accepting or rejecting.

Chairman: The Chair will question the appropriateness of the amendment, which merely substitutes another alternative [p. 2 (40)] for one which was raised in the first place. The provision which is before the Commission now is Alternative J. If it is the desire of the Commission to pass J, it will be passed. The alternatives which are in fact alternatives would no longer be necessary to serve as a basis for discussion. If, however, the Commission prefers another alternative which they are familiar with, they will not accept J, and we will give the alternative from

---

[257] Alternative J consists of a proposed section in the main text of the IMF agreement and a proposed Schedule B ancillary to the main text; the paragraphs (a) and (b) to which the Indian delegate is referring are in Schedule B. In Document 310, p. 503.

the delegation from India the next place, in as much as they have raised the question first.

Is there any further discussion on Alternative J, Section 2?

If not, the Chair will put the matter to a vote. All those in favor of Alternative J, first paragraph, please signify by saying "aye."

("Ayes" heard.)

Contrary minded, "no."

("Noes" heard.)

The Chair declares the Commission has approved Section 2 of the first paragraph.[258] We now turn to the schedule [i.e., descriptive table], which is the implementation of the principles stated in [Section] 2. Is there any question? The delegate from Belgium had a question about the implementation.

Belgium ([Camille Gutt]): Mr. Chairman, I just want for the sake of clarity, to stress the remarks made by the Czechoslovakian and Cuban delegates [[that the provision just adopted applies only to the original members of the Fund, not to countries that may join later]].

Chairman: The delegate from Belgium endorses the view of the delegate from Czechoslovakia that the provision just adopted applies only to [original] members of the Monetary Fund and not to those who may become members in the future.

Poland: I may say that the same remarks may be made as the Polish suggestion. I support it.

Chairman: Then if there is no further discussion, I propose we turn to the rest of the schedule of Section 2. All those in favor of adopting the schedule, please [p. 3 (41)] signify by saying "aye."

("Ayes" heard.)

All those contrary minded, "no."

("Noes" heard.)

It is the ruling of the Chair that any other alternatives that conflict with Alternative J are no longer before the Commission. However, Alternative K, which does not conflict with Alternative J, is an appropriate alternative to set before the Commission for action now. Does anyone care to discuss Alternative K?

Delegate from Netherlands.

Netherlands: The Netherlands delegation supports Alternative K.

Chairman: The delegate from the Netherlands supports Alternative K.

---

[258] Became Article XII, Section 3(b) in the final agreement.

[Apparently the Belgian delegate made a brief comment that is not in the typescript.] The delegate from Belgium likewise supports Alternative K.

United States.

United States: We would like to support Alternative K.

Chairman: Delegate from United States supports Alternative K.

[Apparently the Mexican delegate made a brief comment that is not in the typescript.]

Delegate from Mexico supports Alternative K.

I think we shall call for a vote. All those in favor of adopting Alternative K in addition to Alternative J, which has already been adopted, please signify by saying "aye."

("Ayes" heard.)

Contrary minded, "no."

("Noes" heard.)

Commission has accepted Alternative K.[259]

The Chair will now call on the delegate from Soviet Union.

USSR: The Soviet delegation has proposed that [an] addition to Article III [Article II], Section 3(b) ["Gold Subscriptions"] be proposed as Alternative B on page 4a.[260]

Chairman: Page 4a and Alternative B on top of the page.

USSR: This addition concerns the gold contribution to the Fund by countries who suffered during the present war from enemy occupation and hostilities. We suggest that this amendment to reduce the gold contribution of these countries to between 75 and 50 percent of the amount they [p. 4 (42)] [would] otherwise have to pay, depending on the extent of the damage to each country by enemy occupation and hostilities.

A discussion of this proposal in the committees and at the Ad Hoc Committee on Liberated Countries had shown that there is considerable doubt in the minds of some delegations whether this provision could be applied in practice. It was emphasized that the determination of which countries suffered more or less damage from the enemy action would meet with considerable difficulties and would lead to divergences of opinion among the member countries. At the same time, there were no objections in this committee [the Ad Hoc Committee] that these

---

[259] Became Article XII, Section 3(c) and part of Section 3(d) in the final agreement.

[260] In Document 32, p. 27.

countries should be authorized to reduce their initial gold payment to a uniform percentage of the amount they would otherwise have to pay.

In order to come to an agreement of this question, the delegation of the USSR is prepared to withdraw its previous amendment under Alternative B, provided that in Article III, Section 3(b) there shall be restored a provision already included in the text of the Joint Statement on establishing an International Monetary Fund (published in Moscow on the 23rd of April in the newspaper [*Izvestia*?]). I have in my hands a copy of this newspaper, and this provision reads as follows: [["The obligatory gold subscription of a member country shall be fixed at 25 percent of its subscription (quota) or 10 percent of its holdings of gold and gold-convertible exchange, whichever is the smaller."]][261]]

We know that some delegations raised objections against including in the agreement of the Fund this provision. The delegation of the Soviet Union cannot withdraw this amendment, because it has been already published in the Soviet Union and it is widely known to the people of our country. The people of the Soviet Union could not be able to understand why this provision included in the Joint Statement of the Fund, which was accepted by technical experts of many countries, could be omitted in [p. 5 (43)] the agreement of the Monetary Fund. We presume, therefore, that this provision accepted by the technical experts of most of the United Nations will be approved by the members of this Commission.

Chairman: Does the delegate of the Soviet Union have in mind putting before this Commission Alternative B as suggested, or as amended? If the delegate from the Soviet Union has that written out, I wonder whether you would get the particular provision, because it is not quite clear which provision you are putting before the Commission for consideration. I gather that the essence of the provision is a reduction of the gold contribution. I will read it when it comes here. In the meantime, if anyone wants to discuss it, it will save time.

The delegate from France.

France: I understand that what the delegate from Russia had in mind was Alternative C, which appears in [page] 4a of the old document. ["Any country represented at the United Nations Monetary and Financial Conference whose home areas have suffered substantial damage from enemy action or occupation during the present war, may reduce its initial

---

[261] We think the delegate is quoting Article II, Section 3 of the Joint Statement, Appendix IV, part 7, which we have inserted in double brackets.

gold payments to _____ percent of the amount it would otherwise have to pay."][262]

Chairman: That is not that figure.

France: Reduce to 75 percent of the amount which would otherwise have to pay—

Chairman: And the 50 percent is deleted?

France: There is no 50 percent; only one figure [is] mentioned in Alternative C.

Chairman: I will read the exact provision when I get it, but the essence of the proposal is that the gold participation of countries who have suffered substantial damage from enemy action or occupation during the war shall reduce the initial gold payment by 25 percent.

Belgium ([Camille Gutt]): That is not the Russian proposal. [p. 6 (44)]

Chairman: We shall wait until we have it before us to read. Delegate from Russia, would you mind designating specifically the provision that you are putting before us? Is it Alternative C?

USSR: These proposals which we made—it is the proposal written on page 4a of the document, Alternative C.

Chairman: And what is the figure?

USSR: The amount is not set in. That is the reduction we propose, by 25 percent.

France: It is to 75 percent.

Chairman: The reduction of 25 percent, to 75 percent. The question is before you for consideration.

Delegate from United States.

United States: The United States is opposed to this amendment.

Chairman: Any other comment? The delegate from Canada.

Canada: No person would in any way limit consideration given to countries that have been occupied and invaded by the enemy, but this provision offers very little, if anything, to such countries. Their drawing power is not in any way increased. The amount involved will not in any way affect the position of those countries, and to set out this reduction in the gold contribution as being an adjustment made on account of enemy action and occupation seems to me to be wholly inconsistent with the whole tenure of this document. The Canadian delegation, therefore, do not feel that this amendment should be made, while at the same time

[262] In Document 32, p. 27.

having every consideration for those countries which find themselves in this position. [p. 7 (45)]

Chairman: Any further comment? If not, the delegate from Belgium.

Belgium ([Camille Gutt]): The Belgian delegation supports Alternative C.

Chairman: The delegate from Belgium supports Alternative C, which was proposed by the delegate from the Soviet Union.

The delegate from Cuba.

Cuba: Mr. Chairman, I think we have taken this afternoon very constructive action toward making a strong international monetary organization. I am afraid that the proposal of the delegate of the Soviet Union would tend to weaken the financial position of the Fund. If there were not simultaneous with the consideration of the International Monetary Fund for consideration of this meeting of nations, a plan for the Bank for Reconstruction and Development, I believe that the delegate of the Soviet [Union] might have a case before this assembly. We have parallel with this consideration: the establishment, by the same nations and on similar lines, [of] a Bank for Reconstruction and Development, which would take care of the needs, as far as humanly possible, of the countries which have been invaded by the enemy. We certainly want to see a strong Monetary Fund, and we do not see how the position of the Fund would be helped by this proposal. We feel that it would be weakened, and as far as we are concerned, we would like to register our position against the motion. [p. 8 (46)]

Chairman: The delegate from France.

France: I would like to answer the argument of the delegate from Canada saying that the [f]act of devastation is not sufficient reason for having to pay less than others in gold. It is not the fact of devastation. Is the fact that our gold is mortgaged for purposes of reconstruction; and as this gold is going for capital transactions, it is not being advanced for current transactions; and therefore I second the proposition of the delegate of the Soviet Union.

Chairman: Any further comment? The delegate from Yugoslavia.

Yugoslavia ([Vladimir Rybar]): I support the proposition of the Soviet Union.

Chairman: The delegate from the Netherlands.

Netherlands: The delegation of the Netherlands wants to support the proposal of the Soviet Union.

[Apparently there are further brief statements of support by other delegations not in the typescript.]

Chairman: The delegate from the Netherlands supports the proposal; the delegate from Luxembourg supports the proposal; the delegate from Norway supports the proposal of the Soviet Union; the delegate from Greece supports the proposal. If there is no further comment, the Chair will call for a vote. Those in favor of accepting the proposal of the delegate from the Soviet Union that the initial gold payment be reduced to 75 percent in those cases where a country has suffered substantial damage from enemy occupation, please signify by saying "aye."

("Ayes" heard.)

Opposed?

("Noes" heard.) [p. 9 (47)]

I think we shall call for hands. Those in favor of accepting the proposal of the Soviet Union, please signify by raising their hands.

Those contrary minded, please signify by raising their hands.

The proposal is defeated by 22 to 12.

The delegate from Egypt.

Egypt: Before proceeding further, if I understand rightly, the Chair said, before voting on Alternative J [on Executive Directors], presented by the Cuban delegation, that any other alternatives not in conflict with Alternative J would be put to the vote after putting Alternative J to the vote. Now, the principle of grouping together countries for the purpose of allocating status has been admitted. I would like to see its extension by adopting Alternative E, page 25h, presented by the Egyptian delegation, granting one seat to Middle East countries.[263] This was seconded by Iraq, and as this is not in conflict with what the Chair said, I move that it be put to a vote.

Chairman: The Chair would like to make certain that this is not in conflict. It is my opinion that that is not so. Is anyone of a different opinion? If not,—

Unidentified: What is the alternative?

Chairman: Alternative B, page 25b.[264] Part of it would seem to be in conflict. Does the delegate from the United States feel that this is in conflict?

United States ([Edward Bernstein?]):[265] I do not believe that it is in conflict.

---

[263] Document 315, pp. 506-507.

[264] In Document 32, pp. 45-47.

[265] We think the Chairman is asking Bernstein here, because Bernstein was the most knowledgeable person about the details of the IMF agreement.

Chairman: The proposal before you is that the Executive Committee shall consist of fifteen Executive Directors. Might it be supposed that fifteen Executive Directors is in conflict with twelve? They mean two different things? [p. 10 (48)]

United States: You are right, Mr. Chairman, it is in conflict.

Chairman: Is there anyone who disagrees that the appointment of fifteen directors is not in conflict with the appointment of twelve? Since no one disagrees with the ruling of the Chair, I will have to hold that it is in conflict with [Alternative] J, and therefore out of order to be brought before this Commission at this time.

Yesterday we adopted Article XI ["Organization and Management"] of the new document [Document 321, the intermediate draft], except Section 3, on "Executive Directors." We have now filled in Section 3, the blank section on voting. There remains only to vote on all of Section 3, Article XI.

The delegate from Belgium.

Belgium ([Camille Gutt]): Mr. Chairman, just coming back, for one second only, to the question of wording which we have just accepted. Now, I mean the election of the directors, biennial election, providing for—I quite understand from all the discussion which took place that that means every two years. I only move the question. That definitely means twice a year? I wonder whether that was a misunderstanding.

Chairman: It is my understanding that the intention of the provision is to have them elected every two years. Is there anyone who has a different definition? The English will be the definitive text, and in English, "biennial" means once in every two years. "Biannual" means twice a year. Will the Secretary note that it is two years, and if "biennial" does not mean that, we will put in whatever is necessary to get that meaning for all countries.

The question before you is the adoption of the entire Section 3, all of which you approved yesterday [p. 11 (49)] except this provision on Executive Directors. All those in favor of accepting Section 3 of Article XI, please signify by saying "aye."[266]

("Ayes" heard.)

Contrary minded?

It is noted the only matters remaining before this Commission are questions of definition and some other matters. The hour is getting late, so that the Chair will adjourn the meeting until the next opportunity to

266 Became Article XII, Section 3 in the final agreement.

hold it, at which time we will be able to complete the matters before us in short order.[267]

Reporting Delegate [and Chairman, Drafting Committee] (Louis Rasminsky, Canada): May I ask that the members of the Drafting Committee remain behind?

Chairman: The Chairman of the Drafting Committee requests that the members of the Drafting Committee remain behind.

(Adjourned 6:30 p.m.)

[267] Actually, the Committee would hold two more meetings, not just one.

9

Commission I
International Monetary Fund
Eighth meeting: transcript
July 18, 1944, 11:30 a.m.[268]

Report of Special Committee on Unsettled Problems • Alternative on purposes of the IMF • Location of offices • Article on offices and depositories • Definitions • Remittances and exchange controls • Emergencies • Amendments • Scarce currencies • Managing Director not to chair Board of Governors

This meeting is devoted to considering a number of items that the Special Committee on Unsettled Problems has proposed. The Commission approves the committee's proposed changes to Article I ("Purposes"), which are important to the poorer countries because they give the IMF more of an orientation toward economic development than originally proposed.

Next, the Commission considers the location of the IMF's headquarters offices. The Special Committee does not report in favor of any particular proposal. The British delegation withdraws a proposal that the first meeting of the IMF's Board of Governors decide the location. The Commission adopts the only other proposal, which is that the location be in the country that is the largest shareholder, which will be the United States. The Commission accepts as a whole Article XII, "Offices and Depositories" (Article XIII in the final agreement).

The Special Committee recommends certain definitions of terms (Article XVIII; Article XIX in the final agreement). Debate ensues whether remittances by immigrants to their country of origin are current (current-account) transactions, therefore subject to fewer restrictions than capital transactions. Delegates from Greece and China, whose countries received substantial remittances before the war and expected to do so afterwards, propose to classify them as current transactions. Pierre Mendès-France, a Free French commissioner of finance, asks whether the classifications of transactions might change over time. In light of the divergent opinions delegates express, Commission chairman Harry Dexter White proposes to accept the principles the Special Committee

---

268 Summarized in Document 455, pp. 824-826.

has recommended but to have the Drafting Committee craft suitable language for the Commission to consider later. The delegates agree.

Next, the Commission considers the recommendations of the Special Committee about empowering the Executive Directors to take extraordinary measures in an emergency, subject to approval by the Board of Directors if the emergency period persists beyond 120 days. The United Kingdom had originally proposed such a provision. Ansel Luxford, the chief legal adviser at the U.S. Treasury and on the American delegation at Bretton Woods, explains how the Special Committee has modified the British proposal, and a British delegate expresses the support of the United Kingdom for the modifications. The Commission accepts the modified provision, which will become part of Article XVI in the final agreement.

The Commission adopts without debate Article XVI ("Amendments"; Article XVII in the final agreement). It then briefly debates the recommendation of the Special Committee on the obligation to sell currency for gold, accepting it with a recommendation that the Drafting Committee make minor changes to bring the provision into harmony with others.

The last item of business the Commission approves is a provision to prevent the IMF's Managing Director, its top managerial official, from also being the chairman of the Board of Governors. The rationale of the provision is to prevent too much concentration of power in the hands of a single person.

Chairman (Harry Dexter White, United States): The Commission meeting will please come to order.

We will first have the report of the Special Committee of this Commission,[269] which has just completed its session this morning. We first have the report on Article I ["Purposes"].

Edward Bernstein (United States, Chairman and Reporter, Special Committee): Mr. Chairman, the Special Committee considered this morning a proposed change in wording in Article I, sub-item (i).

Chairman: Article 1, Section (a).

Edward Bernstein (Chairman, Special Committee): Sub-item (i).

Chairman: I think the document you are referring to unfortunately is not the correct one. The delegates have before them Document 321.

Edward Bernstein (Chairman, Special Committee): That is the one I had in mind.

Chairman: Paragraph (a), Article I, page 1, Document 321.[270]

---

[269] Document 447, p. 765, which, however, contains no details, merely a remark that the report was delivered orally to Commission I and that the Commission adopted its recommendations.

[270] Document 321, p. 518.

Edward Bernstein (Chairman, Special Committee): (reading) "To promote international monetary cooperation through a permanent institution which provides the machinery for consultation on international monetary problems."

Chairman: The change is the insertion of the words "and collaboration."

Edward Bernstein (Chairman, Special Committee): That is right, Mr. Chairman.

Chairman: The recommendation of the [Special] Committee is to insert the two words "and collaboration" after the word "consultation" in the paragraph (a) of Article I. Anyone wish to comment on that recommended change?

The delegate from Colombia. [p. 2]

Colombia ([Carlos Lleras]): (Speaks in native tongue.) (In English) I think, Mr. Chairman, that paragraph (b)—

Chairman: This is paragraph *(a)* of Article I. Your comments referred to the whole article.

Colombia ([Carlos Lleras]): Paragraph (b).

Chairman: Paragraph (b). Anyone wish to comment on the recommended change of the Special Committee?

If not, the Chair will call for a vote. All those in favor of accepting the recommendation of the Special Committee of the insertion of the words "and collaboration" after "consultation," please signify by saying "aye."

("Ayes" heard.)

Contrary minded?

The Commission accepts the recommendation.

Any further recommendations on Article I?

Edward Bernstein (Chairman, Special Committee): Yes, Mr. Chairman, I believe that we have not yet had an opportunity to report a change in provision (b) of the same article. It is now proposed by the unanimous vote of the Special Committee to reword this article as follows: "To facilitate the expansion and balanced growth of international trade, and to contribute thereby to the promotion and maintenance of high levels of employment and real income," and the bigger change comes now, "and to the development of the productive resources of all members as primary objectives of economic policy." The Committee was unanimous in agreeing that this was an improvement on the previous language, and wholeheartedly recommends the adoption of the new wording.

Chairman: Shall I read that change once more? It is the insertion of the words "and real income" after the phrase "levels of employment," and then followed by [p. 3] "and to the development of the productive resources of all members as primary objectives of economic policy."

The delegate from Colombia.

Colombia ([Carlos Lleras]): (Spoken in native tongue.)

Chairman: May we have a translation?

Translator:[271] [The formula proposed by the Special Committee for paragraph (b), Article I, of the Monetary Plan [i.e., IMF Articles of Agreement] is in my opinion a wise solution to the problem that has arisen regarding the purposes of the International Stabilization Fund.[272] The formula harmonizes the technical orientation of the Fund, the resources are which to be used solely to provide foreign exchange for current transactions, with the desire of the delegation from India to include among the ultimate purposes of the new facilities for the growth of international trade the development of the means of production of the member countries. An agreement having been reached on this question, one of the few questions still pending with regard to the Fund has been settled, after a discussion which certainly has not been futile since it has brought to light the economic problems of the future, as a whole, and the function that for their solution correspond to the various instrumentalities for international cooperation which the United and Association Nations are creating or must create in the future.

Moreover, it seems to me that the very wording of this formula implies the recognition of the characteristics that the future economic policy must have, if we take for granted that it must not be opposed to the right of new nations whose resources are not sufficiently developed to move forward on the road which they have already started to travel toward a more complex economy, toward growing industrialization which may alter, and probably will alter, the volume of international trade in many commodities, but which at the same time will open markets with a greater purchasing power for the more advanced forms of the manufacturing industries. The balanced expansion and growth of international trade, which is set forth by this formula as one of the purposes of the Fund, to my mind implies also the fact that consideration must be given in future agreements on commercial policy to the need for

---

271 The transcript merely says, "(Speech read, inaudible)." The speech was published as Press Release No. 35, Document 451, pp. 1185-1187, and we have reproduced it here, inserting additional paragraph breaks.

272 The earlier name for the IMF.

enlarging the consuming markets for foodstuffs and raw materials, the prices of which, before the war, were notoriously out of proportion to the prices of manufactured articles that countries such as mine are obliged to buy from the great industrial countries.

With reference to those future agreements on commercial policy, mention must be made of the fact that they must not be conceived in such a way that they will become obstacles to the necessary protection which must be given in the new countries to their infant industries, as was given at one time by today's industrial countries to their own industries during their first steps industrial development. It is necessary that the conference understand that our assent to a policy greater of greater trade and greater freedom of exchange for current transactions is given in a spirit of [a] broad concept of international cooperation, which could never be based on the idea that this broadening process count be contrary to the development of our own domestic production and to the integration of our economy through a steady access to new industrial techniques.

In requesting that the Commission give its affirmative vote to the formula presented by the Special Committee, I also wish to state a few ideas connected with a spirit of our collaboration in the organization of the Fund, and in general with the whole policy of regulating postwar economy within systems of international organization.

We do not believe that Colombia, and the Latin American countries in general, may have to appeal in the very near future to the Fund for Monetary Stabilization [i.e., IMF] in order to meet their needs for foreign exchange. Nor does the expectation to appeal to the Fund constitute the reason for our action. In fact, we realize that no matter what the amount of the direct aid given by the Fund to a country may be, it is less than the general benefits that may revert to all from the introduction of this new and broad factor of cooperation into the international economic life, in the face of strong forces of competition. We understand further that out of the international economic solidarity there also arise certain duties, and that therefore cooperation becomes not only a solution imposed by general convenience, but also a higher principle of conduct which must be acknowledged before we can hope for a rise to higher and richer levels of universal progress.

In addition, if this cooperative effort happens to be associated, as is the case now, with the solution of overwhelming economic problems in the countries that have suffered the most in the defense of justice, peace, and liberty in the world, our conviction on the desirability of the policy of international cooperation is of course strengthened by the cordial admiration that we feel for those countries and their heroic effort. In the degree that its resources permit, Colombia is taking a part in the coming task of economic rehabilitation, doing so without any feeling of selfishness, but with the sincere conviction that she is doing her international duty within the principles of cooperation which have found in our continent the deepest and most widespread acceptance.]

Chairman: The delegate from Colombia has made a splendid statement in support of the recommendation of the Special Committee and in support of the entire Article I. Is there any other comment?

If not, the Chair will ask for a vote in the recommendation of the Special Committee with respect to the modification of the phraseology in paragraph (b). The Special Committee has recommended that the words "and real income" be inserted and that it read "and to the development of the productive resources." Those in favor of accepting the report of the Special Committee, please signify by saying "aye."

("Ayes" heard.)

Contrary minded, "no."

The report of the Special Committee on the modification of paragraph (b) is accepted by the Commission.

The next item on the agenda report of the Special Committee is on the location of offices. That is in Article XII, [Section 1].[273]

Edward Bernstein (Chairman, Special Committee): Mr. Chairman, on page 31 of the "Old Testament," Document 32,[274] there are two alternatives. The Special Committee recommends merely the consideration of the two alternatives by the Commission. The first reads as follows: "The principal office of the Fund shall be located in the member having the largest quota. An agency or branch office may be established in any member or members." The second alternative [reads]: "The location [p. 4] of the principal office of the Fund shall be decided by the Fund at the first meeting of the Board of Governors, which shall take place in the territory of the member having the largest quota." That is the meeting place. The selection of the principal offices is left to the Board of Governors at the meeting.

Chairman: The Special Committee reports that the choice of Alternatives A and B shall be left to the Commission, and the Special Committee makes no report in favor of either of the alternatives.

---

273 In Document 321, p. 533. The section is a placeholder without text.

274 Document 32, p. 51. In the preliminary draft, the section was Article VII, Section 9 ("Location of Offices").

Edward Bernstein (Chairman, Special Committee): That is right, Mr. Chairman.

Chairman: Then the alternatives are before you. Is there any comment on Alternative A?

The delegate from the United Kingdom.

United Kingdom: Mr. Chairman, on behalf of the United Kingdom delegation, I am withdrawing Alternative B standing in our name, and I wish at the same time to make it clear that in the opinion of the British government the location of the headquarters of the Fund ought not to be considered without reference to the location of other international bodies which will be established. In our view, therefore, it is premature to take any final decision on this matter until more is known concerning the general framework within which these other bodies will work. The same observations apply equally to the location of the projected Bank for Reconstruction and Development. His Majesty's Government, the United Kingdom, may therefore find it necessary at some later date to ask that all such interrelated questions should be considered as a matter for decision between governments rather than [by] the technical conference, and it is subject to that reservation [p. 5] that we accept Alternative A, and withdraw our own amendment.

Chairman: The delegate from the United Kingdom has withdrawn Alternative B, and has accompanied it with the statement which you have heard with respect to the reservation of his government. Any further discussion?

The delegate from Cuba.

Cuba: The Cuban delegation moves the adoption of Alternative A. We believe that the location of the principal office of the Fund is of primary importance to all nations participating in the Fund. We believe that not only because [this?] country [i.e., the United States] had the original idea of the Fund, but because of the fact that geographically it is the center of most of the nations participating at this meeting and finally it is today the center of transactions of international trade, that the officers should be located here. We also feel that since the amounts to be kept in depositories—at least in the initial stage of the Fund, the gold [is] to be, at least 50 percent, in the country where the principal office is located. Most of our governments would like to know, in joining the Fund, exactly where that gold is to be initially located, and therefore we move the approval of the Alternative A submitted now to the Commission.

Chairman: A motion has been made to accept Alternative A.

Ecuador: I second that motion.

Chairman: The motion has been seconded by the delegate from Ecuador. Any further discussion of that motion?

Since there is no delegate that wishes to discuss that motion, the Chair will put the question to a vote. All those in favor of accepting Alternative A, Section 9, [p. 6] which reads: "The principal offices of the Fund shall be located in the member having the largest quota. Any agency with branch officials may be established in any member or members." All those in favor of accepting that provision, signify by saying "aye."

("Ayes" heard.)

Contrary minded, "no."

The Commission has accepted provision [Section] 9, Alternative A.[275]

The next item on the agenda is to act on the whole of Article XII ["Offices and Depositories"]. That one provision was excluded from previous discussion. Now that each one of the provisions have been acted upon and accepted, I want to put to a vote the question of the adoption of the whole of Article XII. Does anyone wish to comment on Article XII before I put the matter to a vote?

Unidentified: What page is that?

Chairman: Pages 23 and 24 of the document before you, Document 321.[276] All those in favor of adopting Article XII, signify by saying "aye."

("Ayes" heard.)

Contrary minded?

Apparently some of you have difficulty finding the particular article referred to. It is Article XII in the so-called "New Testament," pages 23 and 24. I shall put the vote again. All those in favor of accepting Article XII, please signify by saying "aye."

("Ayes" heard.)

Contrary minded, "no."

The Commission has accepted the whole of Article XII.[277]

The next item is a report by the Special Committee on "Definitions."

Edward Bernstein (Chairman, Special Committee): Mr. Chairman, this is Article XVIII in the "New Testament."

Chairman: Article XVIII, Document 417,[278] which has been distributed and should be before you, entitled "Definitions, Alternative A," is a three-page document. [p. 7]

---

275 Became Article XIII, Section 1 in the final agreement.
276 In Document 321, pp. 533-534.
277 Became Article XIII in the final agreement.
278 Document 417, pp. 699-700.

Edward Bernstein (Chairman, Special Committee): The Committee is unanimous in recommending certain definitions to the Commission. These are definitions of monetary reserves, definitions of initial holdings, definitions of convertible currencies, definitions of deductions from gross monetary reserves to get the official holdings, the inclusion of special securities under Article III[279] in the Fund's holdings, the question of taking certain convertible currency holdings—

Chairman: May I suggest that you delay that for a moment.

New Zealand (Walter Nash): Mr. Chairman, while you are doing that, may I call attention to the fact you passed Article XII, and I think the correct number is Article XIII. Article XIII refers to the location of offices. Article XII is [still] to be amended.

Chairman: The delegate from New Zealand calls attention to the possible error. The Secretariat will explain the apparent difference.

Secretary ([Leroy Stinebower, United States]): We have the difficulty of having two documents before some members of this conference and only one document before the conference as a whole. The Drafting Committee in its labors has turned out the document before some of you and [it] has a very limited distribution. The revised draft[280] has no standing because the [Drafting] Committee has not yet finished with it. In that document there [is] some renumbering of articles. The document which is formally before this conference is still [Document] 321, in which the location of offices and depositories is labeled Article XII. [p. 8]

Chairman: Do I understand that the reason that was not distributed more widely [was] because it was necessary only in the Drafting Committee and would have confused the members to have it distributed?

You were correct, Mr. Nash. In the other draft, it was Article XIII.

United Kingdom: For the convenience of the members of the Drafting Committee who only have the one document with them, would the Secretary be kind enough to give the correct number of the document?

Chairman: There are extra copies of [Document] 321 on the table, and if anyone wants them—those that do not have 321 before you, would you just keep your hands raised until they can quickly give them to you?

(Document distributed.)

---

[279] In Document 321, p. 520, Article III, Section 5, "Substitution of Securities for Currency."

[280] Document 413, "Working Draft—Fund Agreement"; Article XIII is on pp. 681-682.

I think we may now proceed. Mr. Bernstein, would you continue? We are now referring to Document 417.

Edward Bernstein (Chairman, Special Committee): I refer to Document 417, which is not included in Document 321. The Special Committee recommends unanimously the adoption of the definitions that are before you in Document 417, although they have been working on some slight modification in words which do not affect the principle of these definitions.

Chairman: Document 417, containing definitions, is before you. The pages [of the loose-leaf binder, based on Document 32] are 47, 47a, and 47b, but it has been distributed as a separate three-page document. Anyone wish to discuss it?

Delegate [from] USSR.

USSR: The Soviet delegation was not yet able to consider the changes made in this provision by the Special Committee, and therefore would be unable to express its final consent to it, [p. 9] and therefore, as [there are also] some other members who have not seen the draft, we should postpone this question for another meeting of the Commission.

Chairman: Would the Reporter of the Special Committee indicate which sections were changed or, rather, were any sections changed?

Edward Bernstein (Chairman, Special Committee): There have been before the Special Committee for its consideration some verbal changes in these definitions. Apparently I was in error in reporting that the Special Committee was unanimously in favor of the principles embodied in these definitions as they are reworded by the Special Committee. I had been under the impression after the discussion this morning that everyone was agreed on the definitions. We have discussed it there, but I don't press the point. If the delegate from Soviet Union wishes to reserve any of these definitions until a final draft from the Drafting Committee has come forward, I suppose it ought to be done that way.

Unidentified: Would it be possible? Have changes been made in all sections, or only two or three of them?

Edward Bernstein (Chairman, Special Committee): There have been slight verbal changes in one or two of them, but if this Commission would agree to the principle of these definitions, it would then be possible for the delegate of the Soviet Union to place his reservation, which would be withdrawn, I presume, when the Drafting Committee report [has] revised definitions to which he might then give his approval. [p. 10]

Chairman: Delegate [from the] USSR.

USSR: I accept this proposal.

Chairman: Delegate from USSR accepts the proposal. [p. 1 (11)]

Chairman: What is before the Commission now is the acceptance of the principles as stated in Document 417,with the possibility that any delegate will have the opportunity of raising a question if the draft—if they do not find the draft in accord with the principle.

Poland: May I refer to point [i.e., paragraph] 7—

Chairman: Point 7 on page 2 of the document.

Poland: May I refer to point 7 on page 2 of the document.[281] On page 2 of the document of [binder page] 47a, reference is made at this point to other documents, to the American proposal and proposal of Professor Robertson. May I ask, have these been published?

[Edward Bernstein[282] (Chairman, Special Committee)]: Mr. Chairman, the very next number is the document which is referred to above. The Special Committee had agreed substantially [on paragraph] no. 8 with some minor restrictions which will make it a little simpler. The principle under 8 [is] following what is referred to in no. 7, and it [was agreed to] unanimously in the Special Committee [with] some slight rewording, but [that] does not change the principles involved.

Chairman: Is the Commission to understand that the reference matter in [paragraph] 7 is merely preparatory to the decision which is embodied in 8?

[Edward Bernstein (Chairman, Special Committee)]: That is right.

Chairman: That in order to understand what the committee is recommending, it is possible to ignore 7 and concentrate on 8.

United Kingdom ([Dennis Robertson?]): Paragraph 7 appears to be a piece of narrative [[summary]]. I originally submitted a much briefer definition of "current transactions," but after full discussion it has been decided to have a rather more extended one, although not quite as [extended as] the one you see before you. But the final form [p. 2 (12)] of [paragraph] 8 adopted by the [Special] Committee is likely to be somewhat briefer than what you see before you, though longer than what is alluded to in my suggestion. It is interesting, but I think not very relevant.

---

[281] This point (paragraph) and the next one in the document discuss how to define current account transactions.

[282] Identified in the text only as "United States" from here to the end of the session, rather than by name as previously, but it is clear from the context that it continues to be Edward Bernstein.

Chairman: Then paragraph 7 may be ignored for the purpose of examining the report of the [Special] Committee. The statement has been made that the Drafting Committee will reword paragraph 8 and will introduce some minor modifications which will shorten somewhat the list.

China: At the meeting of the Special Committee, I had suggested that this list of "current transactions" should include immigrants' remittances. I find it excluded, but I think the Committee may have a good reason for excluding that item, in that [a] further part of immigrant remittances are covered by other [categories], such as income from business, such as payment for personal services and income from business that really constitutes the major part of remittances [by immigrants]. If the Committee omitted that item of immigrant remittance only understanding that they are covered by various other items, [as] they are submitted before us—then I would accept this addition.

Chairman: The Chair will venture the opinion that the term "immigrant remittances" already has a very definite meeting in the literature of the subject, and I would doubt very much that could be included in those two items. What is the view of the Special Committee?

[Edward Bernstein (Chairman, Special Committee)]: It is the view of the Special Committee that a remittance by an immigrant from a country to his home [p. 3 (13)] country—the home of his origin—was a "current transaction" if that remittance was not for the purpose of transferring capital in the evasion of any regulations of the country from which the remittance is made—if not for the purpose of [evading] regulations on capital transfers.

Chairman: Then the Chair will submit that if that be the interpretation of the Special Committee and the recommendation of it, that will be the will of the Commission. It would be quite unfortunate to leave that out, because immigrant remittances mean something definite—[which] would give rise to difficulties later.

[Edward Bernstein (Chairman, Special Committee)]: The definition that has been adopted—the one before you—allows for the fact that it is impossible to cover every transaction in a list. It is intended to cover transactions of which violation in the form of capital transfers hidden as "current transactions" cannot easily take place. No one doubted for a moment that immigrant remittances as defined by the Chair are current transactions. Everybody agreed that it is possible to abuse such an item and use it for capital transfers. Without including [it] in the list, it is nevertheless covered by the concept of other transactions which the Fund would regard as "current."

India: Mr. Chairman, I would like to have one point clarified by Mr. Bernstein. I am referring to the last page of Document 417, the last item—item no. (viii): "other payments, such as reasonable amortization and depreciation, which the Fund may from time to time regard as to on transactions on current account." If a member country raises a loan [from] the bank and has got [an] amortization provision for the repayment of the loan in a period of 20 years, we would say that the amount of amortization in a particular year becomes a "current transaction" for that year. [p. 4 (14)]

[Edward Bernstein (Chairman, Special Committee)]: It was the intention of the Committee to regard a payment of one-twentieth of an obligation due in twenty years as reasonable amortization and be regarded as a "current transaction." The rest of that sentence—"other payments," etc.—is intended to cover just such cases as immigrant remittances.

India: A further point is that if the loan is to be repaid after ten years, the payment of that sum on the due date—will that be considered a "current transaction" for that year?

[Edward Bernstein (Chairman, Special Committee)]: I should make it clear that this list is not restrictive of a country's right to make any type of transfer of capital repayment of the debt out of their own resources if it wishes. This list is supposed to be a list which will govern, but without limitation, those transactions which are of a current-account nature, and in which the restriction of payments (other than during the transition) without the approval of the Fund cannot be undertaken unilaterally by a country. A payment of a very large sum in one lump—an obligation due on a twenty-year bond—would be regarded, I presume, as a capital transfer. Whether it should be regarded in that single case as reasonable amortization is more than I can say. My personal opinion is that it doesn't fall within the concept of amortization, which is a series of payments.

Chairman: For purposes of further clarification, as the Chair understands that in the last clause—(viii) on page 47b—the statement "other payments, such as reasonable amortization and depreciation, which the Fund may from time to time regard as due on transactions on current account"—it is under that clause that you include immigrant and emigrant remittances, provided the Fund decide they are not transactions which are cloaking capital movements. [p. 5 (15)]

[Edward Bernstein (Chairman, Special Committee)]: It is that definition which is without limitation, as you will read in the first line of the first sentence of [paragraph] 8: "International transactions on current account" (or better still, "current international transactions") "shall be deemed to include, but without limitation:…." Therefore, they can be deemed to include, if they would, immigrant remittances. [p. 6 (16)]

Chairman: In other words, the Fund would have determination of inclusion or exclusion [[of remittances]].

Greece: As immigrant remittances have great importance with regard to [some] countries, I would like to have the interpretation that an income which is the result of business in a country will not be treated in a different way if this income belongs to an immigrant or to any other persons. We provide here that payments due as interest on loans, dividends on securities, [or] income from other property or business ought to be considered as current account [transactions]. Now, if this business belongs to an immigrant, there is no reason why the income of the immigrant will be treated in another way as if the business belongs to any other national. On the other hand, in paragraph 2, we say that payments due for personal services [are current account transactions]. If a remittance is derived from [a] personal service of an immigrant, I don't see how this remittance would be dealt with in another manner [just] because this remittance comes from an immigrant. I think that personal services—payment for personal services, or from business, whether they belong to other persons or immigrants, must be treated the same way.

Chairman: I think this refers only to nonresidents. Therefore, I do not see the relevance, unless I misunderstood what your point is. It applies only to nonresidents.

Greece: I am afraid in the interests of the clarification of the subject, we must have some clear definition about the immigrant remittances.

Chairman: I presume the immigrant remittances means either that a family at home is sending money to a son in a foreign country, or the son in the foreign country is sending money home.

Greece: Either way.

Chairman: With the explanation that has been offered by the Special Committee, that that would be included in "current transactions," unless they are of a character or magnitude which, in the opinion of the Fund, become capital movements, and the jurisdiction with respect to the interpretation of the movement would rest with the Fund. Is that the correct statement of the [view of the] Special Committee?

[Edward Bernstein (Chairman, Special Committee)]: I think that is the view of the Special Committee.

United Kingdom: I have been informed by our representative of the Special Committee that this page is being reconsidered. In that case, is it useful for us to discuss it?

Chairman: The Chair might state that the difference between the redrafting [is] no change of substance, just [a] change in the wording, so if the delegate wishes to raise the question "Is it a change in substance?" it would be in order for the guidance of the Drafting Committee.

[Edward Bernstein (Chairman, Special Committee)]: The reconsideration that the Special Committee is giving is not whether something "A" or something "B" is a current transaction. There is no difference, no real difference of opinion on that at all. All that the Special Committee is seeking to do is to find a way of saying in fewer words what we are all agreed on. I think it is inevitable that the delegate from China or Greece will want to ask whether certain types of transactions are intended to be covered by the definition. It is impossible to answer whether a transaction is or is not covered. There may be a good deal about some transactions that must be considered [p. 7 (17)] first, but so far as an immigrant remittance is concerned, if it is not merely so-called and is intended as a transfer of capital, if it is not merely a remittance in the way of a one-sided gift of nominal amount, but in fact a hidden capital transfer, it cannot fall under "current transactions." If it is one-sided, not intended as a capital transfer, it would be a current transaction. We leave to the Fund the question of the very narrow point.

France (Pierre Mendès-France): (Speech by Mendès-France in French.)

[Translator]: The Minister of Finance of the Provisional Government of the French Republic said the following: He thinks that it is necessary to send the question back to the Special Committee and not to the Drafting Committee, because there are problems beyond mere problems of wording and drafting. There is an important question of substance which is involved.

The French delegation, when the question will be referred to the Special Committee, is planning to present a new proposal. The problem may be stated as follows: in this question of defining "current transactions" we are facing two contradictory risks. On the one hand, we might have a definition—too short a definition, too restrictive—and in that case, that would put an obstacle to the development of transactions. On the other hand, if we have a [definition] which is too extensive, we have another risk, namely, that this would be against the interests of the requirement of certain countries which have to take some protective measures in order to maintain the equilibrium of the balance of the payments. Now, the question is a question of time. We can solve this contradiction by introducing a sort of time element. In the first period, it would probably be better to have a narrower definition of current transactions, because in that period [p. 8 (18)] it is not possible to draw much from the Fund, and because in that period it is natural that some controls, or possibly many controls, will be kept. But later on, we can envisage the possibility of widening or broadening this definition of "current transactions" because it would be possible than when the first needs of the reconstruction have been satisfied—[it] will be then possible to have more things included in the conception of "current transactions," and on the other hand, it would be possible to loosen somewhat or much the exchange controls. So, this is the way in which the French delegation thinks that the problem might be solved. And Mr. Mendès-France thinks that this conception should be embodied in the text. If and when the question is referred to the Special Committee, the French delegation will offer a text along these lines.

Chairman: The Chairman sees that there are two questions before the Commission.

France ([Translator]): Mr. Mendès-France wants to state that what has been said refers to the period following the transitional period.

Chairman: Apparently there are two questions before the Commission. One has been raised by the delegate of the French Comité, namely, that the definition be modified in order to make them more restrictive during the earlier period. The other question before you is whether to accept the general principles and framework of the definitions and referred them to a Drafting Committee for possible modification along the lines which have been originally suggested, so that it would come back to the commission after it has been modified by the Drafting Committee. The question raised by the French is a more serious one, and one which would not lend itself [p. 9 (19)] to sufficient clarity of direction to the Drafting Committee so that they would know how to proceed. I think that question has to be settled by the Commission before the matter is turned over to the Drafting Committee.

[Edward Bernstein (Chairman, Special Committee)]: I submit that the suggestion of the delegate from the Provisional Government of France does not cover the point before us. The reason is this: there is no measure of need by a government which can reflect whether a transaction is or is not current. That is a matter of fact. What the delegate is proposing is that during certain periods, governments shall have the right to restrict certain transactions. There is no difference of opinion between us on that at all. A procedure is already available by which every transaction covered in this definition may nevertheless be subjected to the control of a member government. Those provisions are first, during the transition, and second, at any time with the approval of the Fund. I can see nothing gained by setting up a definition of "current transactions" which shall apply during the first three years of the Fund, another definition to apply during the next three years, and finally, another definition to be applied thereafter. We shall never settle the problem of dealing with these restrictions by attempting to do it through a definition of "current transactions."

Colombia: (Speech given in Spanish.)

[Translator]: The chairman of the delegation from Colombia states that it is in agreement with the position taken by the delegation from the United States with regard to the definition of some transactions. The delegate from Colombia would be opposed to a definition which would serve for one period and another definition for another period. In their view, the definition should be permanent. As stated by the delegation of the United States, the Fund provides [p. 10 (20)] for machinery to take care of the transition period. Should the proposal presented by the French delegation be accepted, the delegation of Colombia would have to also present some reservation asking for provision for a special definition should the conditions in Colombia and other similar countries change, not in the period immediately following the war, but in the years after.

United Kingdom: I should like to add my voice to those that have been raised in objection, attempting to handle this problem along the lines suggested by the French delegation. What I think the point of substance was that the delegation from France was making was this: that in the first few years after the transition period, those countries which are still administering exchange control over capital movements may agree to administer them very strictly, while possibly at a later date they may find it possible not to administer them so strictly, not to require them meticulously as to whether it does or does not contain elements of [a] capital nature. That is true and may be all to [the] good, but you cannot handle that in a way in which controls are administered by attempting to define in advance that in one period certain things shall be regarded as being of a capital nature and being [not in the next] period. It is hopeless to deal with this problem by having two different lists for two different periods. It is a problem of administration of controls, not a problem of defining what is or is not a capital movement.

France ([Translator]): Mr. Mendès-France states he has the feeling that he was not clear enough and there has been some misapprehension of his position. He thinks that it would be bad financial administration to have several definitions. In no way did he mean that there should be two or many definitions. The question is not that. What Mr. Mendès-France suggests is that we should [p. 11 (21)] have a flexible system for the definition of "current transactions," and this flexibility should be timed with the evolution of needs and requirements of countries. The needs will be, at first, such that they will require a limitation of capital exports, but gradually it will be possible to facilitate international movements of capital and to give more elbow room to operations. Therefore, he suggests not several definitions—and he insists on this point—but he would accept that there be a list which has to be revised in the Special Committee, but the Fund should be given the power to revise the notion in the daily routine of its work—the notion of current transactions—and would gradually enlarge the number and type of operations which he regards as "current transactions." Now, Mr. Mendès-France has noted the reference made by Mr. Bernstein to Article VIII, Section 2 ["Restrictions on Current Payments"], on page 18,[283] concerning restrictions on current payments. This article says, "Subject to the provisions of Article VII and [Article] XIII, no member shall, without the approval of the Fund, impose restrictions on the making of payments [and transfers for currency international transactions]." Mr. Mendès-France thinks that this article is probably too strict and does not give enough room to the countries, and that is why he would not have the type of presage at least.[284]

Chairman: In light of the interpretation which the delegate from France has offered, it would seem that his point is already fully met in the provisions which are here. In Section [paragraph] 8[285] [of the definitions] it says, "International transactions [on current account, unless the Fund determines otherwise, shall be deemed to include]," etc. In other words, the Fund is given degrees of flexibility, which would seem to me to meet the point of the French delegation.

United Kingdom: We are under a great disadvantage in the fact that we are attempting to discuss the text which is not likely to be the text that shall ultimately be put forward. I hope those words giving the Fund power to declare what everyone has always known to be a capital transaction, or vice versa, will not appear in the text which is ultimately [p. 12 (22)] submitted for the approval of this conference. I repeat again that the right way of dealing with the problem raised by France seems to me not to give the Fund power to redefine from time to time what is [a]

---

[283] In Document 413, p. 671.

[284] The last phrase is reproduced as in the typescript. "Presage" is apparently a mistaken transcription of a word we have been unable to determine. The underlying meaning is clear: Mendès-France did not want the list of current transactions to be too specific.

[285] In Document 417, p. 700.

capital movement and what is not [a] capital movement, but for international exchange control [authorities], when they are able to do so, to interpret more liberally their own national regulations, which they are entitled under the statutes to impose upon movements of capital. If they choose to relax those regulations in the course of time, that is all to the good, but there is no reason, it seems, for the Fund to redefine what is a capital transaction and what is a current transaction, and it would be most dangerous to allow any such power.

Chairman: In view of the ample discussion on this point which has taken place, the Chair will attempt to obtain the will of the Commission. Apparently it is suggested that the matter be referred back to the Special Committee—that the Special Committee make such modifications for the Drafting Committee—or rather, the Drafting Committee make such modifications for the Special Committee—and that it would come before this Commission in drafted form and that the members would be in a position to consider the matters more intelligently. I am therefore going to ask the will of the Commission, whether that is the proper procedure. All those in favor of referring it to the Drafting Committee,—

United Kingdom: One more point. It is not easy to hear exactly the question you are putting to us.

Chairman: The question which is being put before you is whether or not to refer the recommendation to the Drafting Committee.

Unidentified: Not to the Special Committee?

Chairman: No. [p. 13 (23)]

[Edward Bernstein (Chairman, Special Committee)]: Would it be possible to rephrase the point put to the Commission in this form: that the Commission approves the principles in the definition, and that the draft will then be submitted by the Special Committee to the Drafting Committee based on these principles? The final text of this will be included in the document which will ultimately come before them anyway. His point is to approve the principles recommended by the Special Committee, which will send its document to the Drafting Committee.

Chairman: That the Commission accept the principles as enunciated in the recommendation, and that the matter be sent to the Drafting Committee for such modification as the Commission has indicated would be satisfactory. All those in favor of—

United Kingdom: I still don't understand what you propose. Will it come before the Commission in any form or not?

Chairman: It will come before the Commission in its final drafted form.

France: What committee does it go before?

Chairman: We are now going to accept the general principle—whether the general principle as stated in the recommendation of the Special Committee is acceptable to the Commission. If they so vote, it will then be referred to the Drafting Committee for such modification as they deem to be desirable. It will then come before this Commission.

Unidentified: I understand Mr. Bernstein's proposal to be a slight modification of what you are suggesting. The Commission is now invited to accept the principles, and then the document goes to the Special Committee which may make other modifications; and then to the Drafting Committee; and then the Drafting Committee will send it to the Commission in final form.

France: I second the motion.

United States [Edward Bernstein, Chairman, Special Committee?]: I submit that what Mr. White said—[p. 15 (24)[286]] precisely, does this Commission approve the principles?

Unidentified: That the document will go to the Special Committee.

Unidentified [Edward Bernstein, Chairman, Special Committee?]: No, the Special Committee will send a document involving these principles to the Drafting Committee. The Drafting Committee will embody the text and will bring it before this Commission.

Chairman: Does it go back from here to the Special Committee, for the Drafting Committee?

[Edward Bernstein (Chairman, Special Committee)]: It doesn't go back to the Special Committee at all for drafting of the points. It is not any longer, after this Commission votes, concerned with such questions of principles as the delegate of France raised. It is now concerned exclusively with sending a document to the Drafting Committee with the principles embodied here.

Chairman: Are there any other delegates in doubt of what the question is? Now we are going to call on the vote of the Commission to determine whether or not they accept the principles as recommended by the Special Committee, and that a document be referred to the Drafting Committee for modification.

France ([Pierre Mendès-France?]): I wanted to know, however, how should I vote when I support the general principle of this text, but if I want to have substantial change in the form? That is why I hoped it would be possible to accept the principle, but to send it back to the

---

[286] The typescript numbering skips from page 13 to page 15, and it seems that no page 14 ever existed.

Special Committee to get a change in the form before going into the Drafting Committee.

Chairman: If the delegate from France has reference to the alteration of form and not substance, I should say vote "yes" on the question before the Commission. If, however, the views of the delegate are that there is a change of substance that he wishes to introduce, then he would vote "no" on this question. There is a further question that for purposes of clarification that the Drafting Committee will in its modification [p. 16 (25)] take cognizance of the desires of the French Comité and make as much progress towards their objective as is possible without introducing any great change in substance.

New Zealand: The idea is that we approve the principles as they have been enunciated by the [Special] Committee this morning, and in the report, but there are points which have already been discussed by the Special Committee that want slight clarification. Might it not be possible for us to approve the principles and instruct the Special Committee to clarify the points, then send it to the Drafting Committee? The Special Committee would not then have to report again.

Chairman: All those in favor of that procedure, signify by saying "aye."

All agree. Then that will be the procedure.

The next item on the agenda is the emergency provision. Will the Special Committee please report.

[Edward Bernstein (Chairman, Special Committee)]: Mr. Chairman, the Special Committee considers the problem of measures that might be needed to take care of emergency situations. May we request Mr. Luxford, who sat with our committee, to go over this point, and explained to the Commission what is involved.

United States (Ansel Luxford): Mr. Chairman, I believe that everyone present at the Special Committee had a great deal of sympathy for the original proposal of the United Kingdom, that an emergency of one character or another that might arise, which would require action on the part of the Executive Directors to meet it, even though that action might go beyond the narrow text of the document before us for consideration at this time. However, the problem presented was how to meet that emergency and still not delegate to any Executive Directorate the authority to rewrite this document, which everyone agreed would be highly objectionable in many respects.

From the discussion, there emerged another proposal. I will give it to you in principle [p. 17 (26)] rather than in precise terms. In the event of an emergency which threatens the operation of the Fund in whole or in substantial part, the Executive Directors by unanimous vote may suspend for a period of not more than 120 days any of the following specific provisions. At this point would be listed the specific operating provisions which might possibly be involved. Such suspension may be continued by [a] four-fifths vote of the Board of Governors for a period of 365 days, but may not be further extended except by an amendment to this Agreement. The Executive Directors, or the Board of Governors, as the case might be, may lift the suspension. The theory being that it might not be desirable to give the Executive Directors the right to rewrite this provision, and still it might be perfectly all right for the Executive Directors by unanimous vote to agree to suspend a specific operating provision. And using that word in a narrow sense to distinguish voting quotas, on which the Executive Director would have no such right, but on precise operating provisions, such as the repurchase provision and the right of access to the Fund, those would be the type of provisions which the Executive Directors might by unanimous consent suspend temporarily.

Chairman: You have heard the recommendation of the Special Committee on this emergency provision. Is there any comment?

United Kingdom: I should like to advise the Commission to accept the report of the chairman of the Special Committee with the explanation of Mr. Luxford. Late on Sunday night, we had some doubt as to whether it was quite certain that in the future what we are doing would be sensible and practical. We thought it was wise not only for that reason but because of the very complicated character of the technical operating clause that the document which contained [[these provisions should give]] to the Executive Directors if they found that the clause was unworkable, [p. 18 (27)] if it was to give effect to the workings of the Fund to modify the Fund. That obviously created the objection that the Executive Directors might have power to alter substantially what the document intended, and the suggestion has come forward from Mr. Luxford that we will arrive at the same thing in a slightly different way. That if an emergency is created, (inaudible). I agree with them thoroughly. (Inaudible) and the proposal of Mr. Luxford is going to work out exactly as we had in mind.

Chairman: The United Kingdom urges that we adopt the recommendation of the Special Committee without further reservation with respect to the special provision. Is there any further discussion?

New Zealand: I suggest Mr. Luxford and those working very carefully watch the effect of Article VII [XVI], or whatever the number is now, on amendments, because there may be some provisions in that article which would be affected by what they are proposing to do now.

Chairman: Do I understand that the Drafting Committee will exercise care to see that there isn't modification of any other provision?

New Zealand: There is a provision in the agreement for its provisions to be amended under certain conditions, and we want to watch that the amendment proposed and carried out by the directors may be all in order and may not be tending to override the general provisions that are already being provided for.

[Edward Bernstein (Chairman, Special Committee)]: He has thoroughly covered the question. That is specifically what is stated. There would be no question of any informal method of amendment.

Chairman: The Chair is going to call for a vote. Those in favor of accepting the recommendation of the Special Committee on emergency amendments, please signify by saying "aye."

(Chorus of "ayes.")

Contrary minded?

The Commission accepts the [p. 19 (28)] recommendation of the Special Committee on emergency amendments.[287]

Gentlemen, we have asked for the dinner to be postponed slightly, and I think we can get through in about ten minutes, but we shall not carry you beyond. It is now 1:25. We shall not carry you beyond 1:40, whether we finish or not, but I think we can.

The next item is the adoption of Article XVI, which is the article relating to amendments, which the delegate from New Zealand has just referred to. Document 321, page 25 and page 26.[288] Any discussion of that amendment?

If not, the Chair will put the question to the Commission. All those in favor of adopting Article XVI, dealing with amendments, signify by saying "aye."

(Chorus of "ayes.")

Contrary minded, please say "no."

The Commission accepts the report on Article XVI.[289]

The next item deals with the obligation to sell currency for gold [Article VII, Section 2, "Measures to Maintain Fund's Holdings of Scarce Currencies"]. Will the Special Committee please report on that? Page 13 of Document 321.[290]

---

[287] Apparently became Article XVI in the final agreement.

[288] In Document 321, pp. 534-535.

[289] Became Article XVII in the final agreement.

[290] In Document 321, p. 526.

[Edward Bernstein (Chairman, Special Committee)]: Mr. Chairman, this provision deals with the method by which the Fund may replenish its holdings of the scarce currency. It is quite clear that it was the intention of this Commission that when such a contingency arises, the Fund sells gold to a member and the member would be obligated to buy that gold with the currency that is scarce. It has occurred to many that the statement that we have, while clearly understood by the delegates that have been working with it, is not clear enough, so that it may not be understood by those who will have to deal with it later. It is impossible to ask the future managers of the Fund to be bound by the oral statements of this conference, and, therefore, the Special Committee recommends that subsection 2 of Section 2 read as follows: "The Fund may, [if it deems such action to be appropriate to maintain necessary balances of any currency, take either or both of the following steps: (i) Propose to the member that on terms and conditions agreed between the Fund and the member, the latter lend such currency to the Fund or, with the approval of the member, that the Fund borrow such currency from some other source either within or outside the territory of the member, but no member shall be under any obligation to make such loans to the Fund or to approve the borrowing of its currency by the Fund from any other source. (ii) Buy that currency from that member with gold.]"

Chairman: You have heard the report of the Special Committee to substitute the phrase "the Fund," etc., and that comes under this Section 2 of measures to maintain the Fund's holdings of scarce currency. Is there any discussion on that [p. 20 (29)] point?

France: For clarification in the sentence "Buy that currency from the member with gold": has the country the right to decline that?

Chairman: If I understand that, this calls for a change in substance—that it was the understanding of all the delegates that the member was required to purchase the currency with gold, and that is being made implicit in this statement, in view of the difficulty of future persons to know what the general understanding was, so that the statement would now read that the Fund may require the country to purchase its currency with gold—I mean, *for* gold. The Chair will put the question to vote.

New Zealand: There is one other point, and I'm sorry I can't find the reference—there is a reference in the Agreement which gives the members the right to buy gold from the Fund, but if you exercise the two [[rights, suppose there's a country and]] he's got to sell [[gold to the Fund,]] and now he turns around and says "now I'm going to buy," [[it could create a problem. Since]] there is a power under certain circumstances that a member can exercise by using gold to buy currency from the Fund, I am wondering whether the Fund will be required to buy the currency from him with gold. Then he says, "I'm going to buy some currency with the gold." That point it would be difficult to work.

United Kingdom: The reference he is talking about is Article V, Section 7(a), which entitles the member to repurchase from the Fund for gold any part of the Fund's holdings of its currency.[291]

[Edward Bernstein (Chairman, Special Committee)]: It is quite true that Section 7, Article V, states, "A member may repurchase from the Fund with gold [any part of the Fund's holdings of its currency]." It should be made clear that the intention of this section is to make it possible for a country to avoid charges by repurchasing the currency holdings of the Fund with gold. It is obviously not intended as a device by which a country can [p. 21 (30)] make a scarce currency in the Fund somewhat scarcer. I don't think there is any real problem there at all. The problem we have is the overriding problem that the Fund must be in a position to replenish holdings of scarce currency. To do that it must be able to buy the currency from a member with gold and the member must sell the currency for gold.

New Zealand: I accept that under the wording desired that the member is desired to sell the currency of its country for gold, but there is this other provision, and this positively states "the member must repurchase from the Fund for gold any part of the Fund's holdings for currency." You can't have those two transactions and expect it to be properly administered. I am only suggesting that what is desired can't possibly be carried out.

[Edward Bernstein (Chairman, Special Committee)]: That can be taken care of very simply. A member may repurchase from the Fund for gold any part of the Fund's holdings of its currency in excess of three-fourths of its quota, or, if you wish, it can be done by saying a member may repurchase from the Fund for gold any part of the Fund's holdings of currency, provided it had not been declared scarce.

United States (Ansel Luxford): I think what you may need is "provided that such purchase does not reduce the Fund's balances of such currency below the necessary working balances." That is the language you have used now or have contemplated using in Section 2 in order to replenish the Fund's balances when they are below working balances. Now you have given [a country a] right to purchase back its

[291] In Document 413, p. 665. The numbering is the same as in Document 321, p. 524, the intermediate draft, where the section is blank.

gold providing it does not reduce the Fund's balances of such currency below the necessary working balances.

Chairman: That is clearly the intent of the Commission. Couldn't that part of it be referred to the Drafting Committee, namely, that this recommendation of the Special Committee [p. 22 (31)] be accepted and that the Drafting Committee be instructed that the other clause be brought into harmony with this one?

The Chair will call for a vote on this provision. All those in favor of accepting the report of the Special Committee [on Section 2(ii)], please signify by saying "aye."[292]

(Chorus of "ayes.")

Contrary minded?

Then the Drafting Committee will please have in mind the modification of that statement in order to bring it into harmony with the other provisions.

The final item of business is item 9. Please turn to page 18 of Document 321 [Article XI, Section 2, "Board of Governors"].[293] This is the final item, and you have five minutes to get to dinner.

[Edward Bernstein (Chairman, Special Committee)?]: The Special Committee has recommended that we refer back to the Commission this important problem. The last sentence of Section 2 of this article reads, "The Board shall select [a Governor or the Managing Director as Chairman]." A number of delegates have felt this provision would make possible the concentration in one person of the three important executive offices of the Fund: that is to say, the Managing Director, the Chairman of the Executive Directorate, and the chairman of the Board of Governors. Such a concentration of power might be unwise. If we could delete the words "the Managing Director," it would then follow that the Managing Director could not be the Chairman of the Board of Governors since the Board should select a Governor as a chairman, and the Managing Director is not a member of the Board. Then the Managing Director would be with the Executive Director, but he won't be the Chairman of the Board of Governors.

Chairman: Is there any comment with respect to the recommendation?

No, it [the Special Committee] has not made a recommendation.

Does any delegate wish to comment on that? Does any delegate wish to make a motion on that?

---

292 Became Article VII, Section 2 in the final agreement.

293 In Document 321, p. 530.

United States: Mr. Chairman, I move that we delete the [p. 23 (32)] words "or the Managing Director" from the sentence "Board shall select," etc.

Chairman: The motion has been made to delete the words. The motion has been seconded. Is there any discussion?

The Chair will put the motion to a vote. All of those in favor of deleting those three words, which would exclude the Executive Manager [from] being Chairman of the Board of Governors, please signify by saying "aye."[294]

(Chorus of "ayes.")

Contrary minded?

Then the meeting will be adjourned.

---

[294] Became part of Article XII, Section 2(a) in the final agreement.

10

Commission I
International Monetary Fund
Ninth (final) meeting: transcript
July 19, 1944, 9:00 p.m.[295]

Report of Drafting Committee • Report of Special Committee on Unsettled Problems • Repurchases • Executive Directors • Initial deposits for subscriptions • Explanation of terms regarding immigrant remittances • Wording regarding financial systems of centrally planned economies • Election of Executive Directors • Payment of subscriptions in gold • Communication of views to members • Depositories • Number of Executive Directors • Remarks of Commission's Reporting Delegate • Chairman's closing remarks

At the concluding meeting of Commission I, Louis Rasminsky of Canada, chairman of the Drafting Committee, offers its final report to the Commission, which contains the near final draft of the IMF agreement. The Commission has approved in principle all the material in the report, but the some of the committee's formulations are new, and Rasminsky calls them to the delegates' attention. Remember that Rasminsky was also the Reporting Delegate of Commission I to the plenary session of the conference.

Edward Bernstein of the United States, chairman of the Special Committee on Unsettled Problems, delivers its report, highlighting substantive changes the committee has made to matters the Commission had agreed upon in principle. The first concerns "repurchases" (IMF jargon for repayments of loans): the committee recommends making a rather technical change to relieve borrowers of the obligation to repay in currencies whose supply might be small.

Next, Bernstein presents the Special Committee's attempt at a final settlement on the number and nature of Executive Directors, which proposes that there be twelve to

---

[295] Summarized in Document 473, pp. 913-915, and Document 519 (473), pp. 1085-1091. The typescript has a notation, "Take 1 ARB," apparently indicating that the stenographer was Augusta R. Brown, who is listed in the unpublished conference telephone directory (Document 114, p. 2).

fourteen directors: five appointed by the five members having the largest quotas (expected to be the United States, United Kingdom, USSR, France, and China); two elected by the "American Republics" (Latin America); the two largest net creditors, if not already represented; and five elected by other members. Egypt again proposes that the Middle East be accorded a director, but the Commission rejects the proposal.

The Special Committee further recommends reducing the initial deposit due when countries accede to the final IMF agreement from 0.05 percent to 0.01 percent of their quota. Accession will occur after governments debate and approve the final agreement and send representatives to sign it later in Washington, not when their delegates sign it at Bretton Woods, which signifies only that the delegations involved have participated in the negotiation and will try to gain approval from their governments. The Commission approves the reduction in the initial deposit.

Having dispensed with the report of the Special Committee, the Commission returns to the discussion from the previous meeting on whether current (current-account) transactions should include remittances of immigrants to their countries of origin. Such a classification would mean that remittances would face fewer restrictions than if they were classified as capital transactions. The USSR favors omitting mention of remittances, apparently because it is concerned that mentioning them might reduce its ability to impose the strict exchange controls that support its centrally planned economy. France, also concerned to allow its government considerable latitude with exchange controls after the war, supports the USSR. China, Greece, and India, all of which are or expect to become again recipients of remittances, favor including mention of them. The Soviet motion to delete mention of remittances fails, but the word "immigrant" is deleted. The Commission charges the Drafting Committee with crafting final language.

On another point raised by the USSR, a delegate from the United Kingdom points out that language has been added to the draft agreement so that the foreign assets of government-owned banks are not calculated as monetary reserves and therefore are exempt from certain provisions of the agreement about calculating reserves to be contributed to the IMF.

Edward Bernstein, now acting as a delegate from the United States rather than as chairman of the Special Committee, proposes a technical change the Special Committee has suggested concerning voting for elected directors. The Commission accepts the change.

The Commission rejects three proposals by the USSR. One would have the effect of reducing the gold that member countries contribute in their initial quotas. Another would prevent the IMF from making public any report on a country that the country did not wish to have released. Yet another would result in the countries with the four largest quotas initially keeping the gold they had contributed in their national depositories rather than shipping it to the United States.

After a small change proposed by Cuba about the election of Executive Directors, the Commission approves the report of the Drafting Committee in its entirety, that is, it approves a final draft of the IMF articles to send to the plenary session of the conference for final approval. Louis Rasminsky summarizes the reservations that various delegations have entered against certain clauses of the agreement, especially with regard to the assignment of quotas.

Commission chairman Harry Dexter White concludes the meeting by expressing his thanks to the delegates for their work, and an American delegate in turn calls for the delegates to pay tribute to White for his chairmanship. Having completed its work, the Commission adjourns.

Chairman (Harry Dexter White, United States): The meeting of the Commission will please come to order.

The first item on our agenda is the report of the Drafting Committee. The chairman is Mr. Rasminsky of Canada.

Louis Rasminsky (Canada, Chairman, Drafting Committee): Mr. Chairman, I have the honor to submit here with the second and final report of your Drafting Committee. The report consists of the Articles of Agreement of the International Monetary Fund and has been circulated as Document No. 448.[296]

[All the material contained in this report has been approved in principle by the commission at various sessions. The present report contains, however, a new formulation of certain provisions to which I should specifically draw the attention of the Commission.

These are:

1. Section 7 of Article V on pages 11 and 12 of Document No. 448, "Repurchase by a member of its currency from the Fund."

2. Paragraph (b) of Section 2 ["Avoidance of Restrictions on Current Payments"] of Article VIII on pages 17 and 18 dealing with the enforceability of exchange contracts contrary to the exchange control regulations of members and measures of cooperation to enforce exchange control regulations.

3. Paragraph (b) and (c) of Section 5 of Article XII on page 30 of Document No. 448, dealing with special voting provisions.

4. Section 1 of Article XVI on page 36 dealing with temporary suspension of certain provisions of the Agreement in the event of an emergency.

---

[296] Document 448, pp. 765-810. The report is on pp. 808-810. The portion of the transcripts after this paragraph merely says, "(Mr. Rasminsky read his report, concluding with a statement of certain changes in Document 448)." We have reproduced the relevant part of Document 448. The page numbers mentioned are those of Document 448. Article and section numbers are identical to those in the final agreement.

5. Article XIX on pages 39 to 41 dealing with explanation of terms, and

6. Article XX on pages 41 to 47, containing final provisions.

As a result of the dates which, under the authority of the Commission, the Special Committee decided to have inserted in Article XX on "Final Provisions," there has been a consequential change in Article XX on "Final Provisions," there has also been a consequential change in paragraph (b)(ii) of Section 3 ["Adjustment of Quotas"] of Article II on page 3 of the document.

I should also draw to the attention of the Commission the fact that certain material which previously appeared in the body of the document has been incorporated in schedules at the end of the document, namely, Schedule B, "Provisions with Respect to the Purchase by a Member of Its Currency Held by the Fund" (page 49); Schedule D, "Settlement of Accounts with Members Withdrawing" (pages 51 to 52); and Schedule E, "Administration of Liquidation" (pages 53 to 54).]

I must also ask the members of the Commission to correct certain typographical errors which have been found in Document No. 448.] I should not ask the Commission to make these changes if they were merely typographic errors, but in practically every case if there is a mistake and reference it involves substantial meeting, and it is for that reason that I have felt it necessary to ask the Commission to make these changes. There are other typographical errors which I am not asking you to correct.[297]

[On page (i) of the Table of Contents, Article V, Section 7, please add the words "from the Fund" to "Repurchase by a member of its currency." On the same page under Article VII, Section 2 ["Measures to Maintain the Fund's Holdings of Scarce Currencies"], please change "maintain" to "replenish."

On page 3, Section 3(b) ["Subscriptions: Time, Place and Form of Payment"], please change the word "notified" to "notifies."

On page 7, Section 7 ["Uniform Changes in Par Values"], first line, please change "Section 5(a)" to "Section 5(b)."

[297] We have made a guess about the placement of this section of the transcript within Rasminsky's report. After this section, the transcript says, "Mr. Rasminsky read further changes in Document 448, and concluded with request that the Commission permit the Secretariat to correct other typographical errors." We have reproduced the relevant part of Document 448, namely pp. 808-810.

On page 11, Section 7, please change the heading, "Repurchases by a Member of Its Currencies" to "Repurchase by a Member of Its Currency Held by the Fund."

On page 34, third line, please change "intention" to "retention." Again on page 34, at the end of Section 4 ["Action of the Fund Relating to Restrictions"], please change "Section 2" to "Section 2(a)."

On page 37, section [paragraph] (b) of Article XVI ["Amendments"], please change "Schedule E" to "Schedule D" in the last line but one.

On page 40, fourth line under paragraph (e) [of Article XIX, "Explanation of Terms"], please change "other fiscal similar agencies" to "similar fiscal agencies," and on the same line, after the phrase "of other members," add the words "or nonmembers specified under (d) above. On page 40, paragraph (h), first line, you eliminate the word "initial."

On page 41, fourth line of Section 1 ["Entry into Force"] of Article XX ["Final Provisions"], please change "investments" to "instruments."

There will no doubt be other typographical errors or mistaken cross-references discovered when Document No. 448 is re-examined at greater leisure. I would therefore request that the Commission give the Secretariat authority to correct any formal mistakes of this type which may be found after the Commission has finished its work.]

Norway (Wilhelm Keilhau): Mr. Chairman, may I draw the attention of the Commission to one more error, on page 47? It states that this is done at Washington instead of Bretton Woods.

Louis Rasminsky (Chairman, Drafting Committee): I believe that the position is that, though no one would deny that this was done at Bretton Woods, the agreement itself will be open for signature and will be signed at Washington, and not at Bretton Woods. [p. 2]

Vice Chairman (Rodolfo Rojas, Venezuela): Is that satisfactory?

(After a pause.) The Chair will ask for the approval of the proposal made by the Drafting Committee to the effect that the Secretariat be empowered to make due and formal corrections of typographical errors and any erroneous cross-references. Any comment on that?

Nicaragua: Mr. Chairman, I think that the Reporting Delegate at the very moment is pointing to a few omissions and typographical errors which seem to have crept into the documents. I have been able to see some of the work of the Drafting Committee and I know this: that for many nights we have been working to the early hours of the morning, and [it is remarkable] that all the effect [of their mistakes] would just amount to a few typographical errors. I think we must compliment them on their work, and I think that this meeting should be very, very grateful to Mr. Rasminsky and his collaborators and doing all this for us.

(Cries of "hear, hear" and applause.)

Vice Chairman: I understand that the opinion of the full Commission is that the request made by the Secretariat be granted.

(Cries of "yes" and "hear, hear.")

Vice Chairman: The report of the Special Committee. Mr. Bernstein.

Edward Bernstein (United States, Chairman and Reporter, Special Committee): Mr. Chairman, I am not sure which of the points that the Drafting Committee has brought forth in its report as changes of greater or lesser degree in substance should again be brought before the Commission. Nearly all the new material that you find in this draft was approved in principle by this Commission before the Special Committee undertook the further consideration of the subject in greater detail. There are a few points, however, that the Special [p. 3] Committee has taken the liberty to modify in some degree, which the Committee would like to bring before this Commission for its approval.

In Article V, Section 7, on page 7, on the repurchase of its currency by a member from the Fund.[298]

Vice Chairman: What page?

Edward Bernstein (Chairman, Special Committee): Page 7. In paragraph (c) of that section on page 12,[299] the Special Committee has made a change. Previously, when brought before this Commission, the repurchase obligation was not terminated when the currency repurchased under one of the repurchase provisions had fallen to 75 percent of [a member's] quota. There was another provision requiring the consent of the country whose currency was being sold to the Fund or, rather, was being used to repurchase the member's currency. In the opinion of the Special Committee, it was desirable to drop the requirement of consent and to place the further limitation that the repurchases should not extend beyond the point where the Fund's holdings of the currency have fallen to 75 percent of the quota. The Special Committee recommends to the Commission the approval of this change.

Vice Chairman: Any comments on that?

(None.)

If no comments are made, the Chair assumes that the matter is approved.

(After a pause.) It is approved.[300]

---

[298] In Document 321, p. 522.

[299] In Document 448, pp. 775-776.

[300] Became Article V, Section 7(c)(iii) in the final agreement.

Edward Bernstein (Chairman, Special Committee): Mr. Chairman, at the meeting of the Special Committee last night, the delegates of several countries suggested that some modification in Article XII, Section 3 on "Executive Directors" would be desirable to meet future contingencies. [p. 4] It is proposed on page 26 [27][301] to amend paragraph (b) to read as follows:

"There shall be not less than twelve directors, who need be governors, and of whom five shall be appointed by the five members having the largest quotas."

I am sorry. [[I should have said]] the twelve directors "need *not* be governors."

"(i) five shall be appointed by the five members having the largest quotas;

"(ii) not more than two shall be appointed when the provisions of (c) below apply;[302]

"(iii) five shall be elected by the members not entitled to appoint directors, other than the American Republics; and

"(iv) two shall be elected by the American Republics not entitled to appoint directors."

"For the purposes of this paragraph"—and this, I believe, is the addition—"'members' means governments of countries whose names are set forth in Schedule A, whether they became members in accordance with Article XX or in accordance with Article II, Section 2. When governments of other countries become members, the Board of Governors may by a four-fifths majority of the total voting power increase the number of directors to be elected under (iii) above by adding one director for each of the members having quotas equivalent to 500 million of United States dollars of the weight and fineness and effect on July 1, 1944; provided that [a director] may be added [when the members in any such group] have more than one-half of the necessary [quotas]."

---

[301] In Document 448, p. 787. The proposed amendment is Document 466, pp. 832-834.

[302] Paragraph (c) ensured that the Executive Directors would include representatives of the two largest net creditor countries. It said, "If, at the second regular election of directors and thereafter, the members entitled to appoint directors under (b) (i) do not include the two members, the holdings of whose currencies by the Fund have been, on the average over the preceding two years, reduced below their quotas in the largest absolute amounts in terms of gold as a common denominator, such member or members, as the case may be, shall also be entitled to appoint directors." In Document 448, p. 787.

Now, in order that this change shall be in harmony with certain other provisions of the Agreement, so that the quota strength necessary for increasing the unit of Executive [p. 5] Directors shall not be varied by [a] uniform change in par value, Article [[IV]] should be amended, and the computation under Article XII, Section 3 ["Executive Directors"], paragraph (iii) should be amended by adding the following sentence:

"Whenever the Board of Governors increases the number of directors to be elected under (b) (iii) above, it shall issue regulations making appropriate changes in the proportion of votes required to elect directors under the provisions of Schedule C."

The substance of this provision, Mr. Chairman, was considered by the Special Committee, and there was unanimous agreement within the Committee to recommend to the Commission the adoption of this article to provide for future contingencies on the basis of a four-fifths vote of the Board of Governors.

Egypt: On a point of order, there was an amendment by the Egyptian delegation which was not taken into account on account of a technical misunderstanding. We had brought an amendment asking or requesting for the Middle East to be represented by one seat, and this was turned down on account of a supposed difference or conflict with the Cuban delegation's amendment, but this, as we explained subsequently, was not the case, and we were quite in accord with the Cuban delegation's amendment.

I now beg to recognize Mr. Falaky to explain the situation.

Egypt (Mahmoud Saleh el Falaky): Mr. Chairman, in the last meeting of Commission I, when the Egyptian amendment providing for the allotment of one seat on the Board of Executive Directors to Middle East countries was brought forward with the object of putting it to a vote, it was passed [p. 6] over and not put to a vote on the ground that it was in conflict with Amendment [Alternative] J of the Cuban delegation. The conflict was that the number of Executive Directors suggested in J was twelve, whereas the original Egyptian amendment had provided for fifteen. The facts, however, are that in the [meeting of the] Ad Hoc Committee [on Voting Arrangements and Executive Directors?] which was held before the last meeting of this Commission, the Egyptian delegate modified his amendment by reducing the number of directors to twelve instead of fifteen, in compliance with the suggestion made by one of the delegates of the United States.

The Egyptian proposal, after modification, stands for the allocation of a number of seats on the Executive Directorate to *ex officio* members, the remainder to be allotted equitably between economic and geographical areas. By this we meant two seats for Latin America, which we supported last time and which was passed, [and] one seat for the Middle East countries. I need not, Mr. Chairman, repeat what I have stated on previous occasions in justification for granting one seat to all Middle East countries, beyond stating that this would be the only means of consistently applying a principle already admitted by this Commission.

Gentlemen, I would urge you to consider the proposal, which has already been seconded by Iran and Iraq. Mr. Chairman, if this is not out of order, may I ask you to put it to a vote?

Vice Chairman: I think that the suggestion made by the—or the report by the Special Committee is under discussion, and I think the discussion should go on regarding that Special Committees report. So, is there any other comment on that report? [p. 7]

South Africa: Will the Egyptian delegate tell us where the Middle East starts and where it ends?

Egypt: The Middle East countries were represented in a financial conference in Cairo last April[303] and are absolutely definable.

South Africa: It would be helpful if he would be able to tell us exactly which those countries were.

Egypt: They certainly include Egypt and the Sudan area, Lebanon, Ethiopia, Tripoli, Iran, Iraq, and Cyprus even is included. India was included then, but I would like to exclude India now because it may have to have a seat by itself, it is such a huge country.

India: Do you include India among the central countries?

South Africa: May I ask another question, just as a matter of elucidation? I take it that the proposal of the Egyptian delegation refers to what is referred to in this document as "original members," and I think, therefore, if a proposal of that kind went through the whole of this clause would have to be reconsidered when other members came in to consider whether, for example, a country like Turkey is or is not in the Middle East.

Egypt: A point of order.

Chairman: There is a point of order before us, I understand, and in order to obtain the view of the Commission as to whether or not it wishes to sustain the point of order which was given at the last meeting with respect to the matter raised by the delegate from Egypt, I will ask the opinion of the Commission. The question is, does the Commission support the point of order which was made at the last meeting with

303 The Middle East Financial Conference, held at the American University, Cairo, April 24-29, 1944.

respect to the motion made by the delegate from Egypt? Is the question clear?

(After a pause.) If the question is clear, I am going to put the question. [p. 8] Those in favor of supporting the decision of the Chair at the last meeting with respect to the motion made by the delegate from Egypt, please signify by saying "aye."

Delegates: Aye.

Chairman: Contrary minded?

(None.)

Chairman: Then, the Commission supports the decision of the Chair and the point of order is sustained.

The next item of business is the report by the Special Committee. Mr. Bernstein. [p. 9]

Edward Bernstein (Chairman, Special Committee): The recommendation of the Special Committee on Article XII, Section 3 ["Executive Directors"], is before the Commission at this stage.

Chairman: Article XII, Section 3. It is now being distributed to you, contain[ed in] Document 466.[304] Will the Reporter indicate what is the specific paragraph which is before the Commission? (Whispers to Reporter.)

He has done that already. Any comment on the report of the Special Committee on this item? Does any delegate wish to comment on this report that is before us?

Delegate from South Africa.

South Africa: Gentlemen, on a point of order. The voting of your ruling at a previous meeting which the Commission has just given was, I think, based on the fact that at that meeting you ruled that there was a difference in substance between the [Executive] Committee consisting of twelve members and a Committee consisting of fifteen members.

Chairman: That is my recollection of the ruling.

South Africa: In that case, I would like to ask your ruling on the question of whether this proposal is in order. This proposal is to increase the number from twelve to fourteen, and I would submit, if I may, [that] if this would be in order, the proposal of the Egyptian delegation would also be in order.

Chairman: This report comes out of the Special Committee, which was ordered by this Commission to prepare a report on the subject.

---

[304] Document 466, pp. 832-834.

Therefore the report of the Special Commission [Committee] is very much in order.

Gentleman from Luxembourg.

Luxembourg ([Hugues Le Gallais]): I presume the Egyptian delegate can move this proposal as an amendment to the proposal now before us. [p. 10]

Chairman: I am very sorry sir, there was so much noise. I am sorry, I did not hear you. Would you mind repeating your remarks?

Luxembourg ([Hugues Le Gallais]): Mr. Chairman, we have in the draft before us submitted by the Drafting Committee a section which is based on the substance of what we agreed to previously. We are now having put before us an amendment to this proposal, suggesting some alterations in this article. I presume the Egyptian delegation can put forward another proposal also amending this article.

Chairman: Point of order is well taken. The delegate from Egypt or any other delegate may now propose an amendment to this report of the Special Committee.

Delegate from Egypt.

Egypt: The only amendment I should submit would be that the Middle East be allotted one seat on the regional basis after the Big Five or Big Three or whatever. The official members would select two for Latin America and one for the Middle East.

Chairman: Without adding to the total?

Egypt: Without adding to the total.

Chairman: The delegate from Egypt proposes an amendment that there shall be included in this provision the statement that one delegate from the Middle East shall be added—

Egypt: Middle East, by election.

Chairman: Shall be included among the delegates indicated here. The motion is before the house. Any delegate second the motion?

Delegate from Iraq.

Iraq: I second the amendment. [p. 11]

Chairman: The delegate from Iraq seconds the amendment. It is before you for discussion. Anyone care to [comment on[305]] the amendment?

Since no delegate wishes to comment on the amendment, the Chair will put the matter to a vote. The amendment is before you for voting. All

305 The typescript says "second," which we think is an error because the amendment had already been seconded.

those in favor of approving the amendment raised by the delegate from Egypt, signify by saying "aye."

("Ayes" heard.)

Those contrary minded, signify by saying "no."

("Noes" heard.)

The amendment is disapproved.

We will then return to the report of the Special Committee.

Edward Bernstein (Chairman, Special Committee): I notice on the mimeograph sheet, four lines from the bottom, that "under (iii) above" is included as a limiting provision.[306] "Under (iii) above" is no part of this provision. May we strike it? Four lines from the bottom.

Chairman: Fourth line, beginning with the word "under (iii) above": that phrase shall be stricken as not being part of the report?

Edward Bernstein (Chairman, Special Committee): That is right.

Chairman: [It] is stricken as being a typographical error. Any further discussion on this report by the Special Committee?

If not, the Chair will put the report of the Special Committee to a vote. All those in favor of accepting the report of the Special Committee indicated on Document 466, please signify by saying "aye."

("Ayes" heard.)

Contrary minded, "no."

The Commission has accepted the report of the Special Committee, Document 466.[307]

Are there any other further items to be reported by the Special Committee? [p. 12]

United States (Edward Bernstein): There was one item I proposed for change in Article XX ["Final Provisions"], Section 2(d) ["Signature"].[308]

Chairman: Article XX, Section 2(d), page 42.

United States (Edward Bernstein): That is 2(d), at the bottom of the page.

Chairman: 2(d), at the bottom of the page.

United States (Edward Bernstein): We propose to change the word in the third line of the paragraph, "At the time this agreement is signed on its behalf, each government shall transmit to the government of the

---

306 In Document 466, p. 833.

307 Became Article XII, Section 2(b), part of Article XII, Section 3(d), and part of Schedule C in the final agreement.

308 In Document 448, p. 798.

United States" from "one-twentieth of one percent," change that to "one-hundredth of one percent" of its total subscription.

Chairman: The report is to change from "one-twentieth" to "one-hundredth." That would reduce the amount to one-fifth of the present provision.

United States (Edward Bernstein): This is not a report by the Special Committee, but a proposal by the delegate from the United States.

Chairman: This is a proposal by the United States delegate. Any discussion of that amendment?

If not, the Chair will call for a vote. All those in favor of substituting "one-hundredth" for "one-twentieth," please signify by saying "aye."

("Ayes" heard.)

Contrary minded?

The Commission accepts the change from one-twentieth to one-hundredth.

The next item on the agenda—any further report by the Special Committee?

Edward Bernstein (Chairman, Special Committee): The Special Committee has no further material to report.

Chairman: Delegate from USSR.

USSR: The USSR delegation wants to present its remarks concerning Article XIX ["Explanation of Terms"] on page 40 and 41.

Chairman: Article XIX, page 40 and 41.

USSR: "Explanation of Terms."[309] The Soviet delegation is in consent with this Article with the exception of point (i), which provides that the term "current transactions" should include the item [p. 13] "Moderate immigrant remittances for family living expenses." This item was included by the Special Committee yesterday in the night. The Soviet delegation is of the opinion that in some cases it would be difficult to distinguish those remittances from capital export transactions, which under the provision of the Fund can be restricted by the export regulations of the members. Therefore, the Soviet delegation suggests that immigrant remittances should not be especially mentioned among the current transactions. In our opinion, the last sentence of Article XIX authorizes the Fund to determine in any particular case whether transactions connected with immigrant remittances should be considered current transactions or capital transactions. Therefore, we propose to omit this item from the enumeration of the current transactions.

---

[309] The title of Article XIX. In Document 448, pp. 796-797.

Another point to which the Soviet delegation would like to draw the attention of the Commission is the fact of applying the provisions regarding the term "monetary reserves."

Chairman: Would the delegate from the Soviet Union feel that it would be desirable to act on the first suggestion before taking [up] another one?

USSR: It is only [our] wish to express—the Soviet delegation—that the Fund in its future operations will pay due attention to the fact that in the Soviet Union, the monetary reserves and banking activities are strongly centralized, and this fact must be taken into consideration in applying the terms "Fund's monetary reserves."

Chairman: The delegate from the Soviet Union has raised two points. The first refers to the reference to immigrant remittances, which is on page 41, last sentence, and the delegate from the Soviet Union suggests or moves—Mr. Delegate, do you wish to move that this last sentence be deleted?—moves that [p. 14] the last sentence be deleted from the section, the sentence beginning with "The Fund may, after consultation with the members concerned, determine whether certain specific transactions are to be considered current transactions or capital transactions." Does your proposal also include [paragraph (i)](4) above that?

USSR: Only (4).

Chairman: Will the delegate from [the] Soviet [Union] inform me whether you refer only to (4), or to the last sentence, or both?

USSR: Only to (i)(4).

Chairman: Only to point (4)—"Moderate immigrant remittances for family living expenses"—leaving to the Fund's determination, as expressed in the last sentence, whether it is one or the other.

The question before you is whether or not to delete the sentence "Moderate immigrant remittances for family living expenses" under paragraph (4). Anyone wish to discuss that motion? I might say that this matter has been discussed at great length, and I hope that the members will confine their discussion at this point to some brief remarks.

Delegate from France.

France ([Pierre Mendès-France]): (Spoke in French.)

Chairman: The delegate from France supports the proposal of the delegate from Russia, advocating the deletion of section [paragraph] (4). Does the delegate from France wish to have that translated?

France ([Pierre Mendès-France]): I think it is useful.

Chairman: Will the translator please translate? [p. 15]

Translator: The chief from the French delegation supports the Russian proposal. He states that paragraph (4) modifies profoundly the definition of current transactions. Paragraphs (1), (2), and (3) refer to obligations to pay which are contractual in nature. Paragraph (4) refers to voluntary payments. Nobody here, in his opinion, thinks that it is necessary to attribute to [i.e., include?] funds sent by immigrants to their families. The French delegation believes the same equilibrium must be maintained.

China: This article (4)—paragraph (4)—was discussed at length at last night's meeting of the Special Committee. It is generally recognized that immigrant remittances are current transactions. On the question of theory—principle—there is no reason why that item should be excluded. There is the fear that immigrant remittances might conceal capital transfers. That difficulty, if it exists at all, exists in all the three categories mentioned in paragraphs (1), (2) and (3). If we are going to exclude paragraph (4) on that ground then we have to exclude all the [previous] three paragraphs. Then the point is advanced that the three categories involved are of [a] contractual nature, whereas the fourth one is voluntary. I would submit to this Commission that obligations to one's family are more binding than contractual. They are contractual and they are more than contractual. If a member—if a man—refuses, fails to support his family, he is failing in more than a contractual duty. So, Mr. Chairman, I hope that this Commission, both on grounds of sound economy and sound morals, that this paragraph (4) be retained. [p. 16]

Chairman: Delegate from Greece.

Greece: Mr. Chairman, I want to support without reserve the proposal of the member from China. I think we have here to discuss a problem. The object of this proposal [paragraph] no. (4) is to meet a real necessity. We know that some countries, they have to export labor, and I think that the guarantees provided in this section are quite sufficient to prohibit any export of capital. In the first paragraph, we say that payments for current transactions means payments which are not for the purpose of transferring capital, and in paragraph (4), I think it is very moderate what we say here: "Moderate immigrant remittances for family living expenses." I don't think that anyone, under this clause, can suspect that the question is of a capital transfer, but if [[so, adequate provisions exist to limit such a transfer]]. The supposition is that these remittances are in no case to be considered as capital transfers, otherwise every member has a right to prohibit it.

Chairman: The delegate from Greece supports the comments of the delegate from China.

Delegate from Cuba.

Cuba ([Luis Machado]): Mr. Chairman, I sympathize with the moral position and the human point of view which this amendment represents, but the word "immigrant" in this section brings up a constitutional question of disparity among our own population. It would establish, in fact, a discrimination in favor of the foreigners in our own land. Where a Cuban would not be allowed perhaps by national law to make remittances to his family for his living expenses, a foreigner, just because he is a foreigner, would be allowed. If this provision is retained, that would be contrary to the constitution of our country, which prevents discrimination against foreigners, and if we cannot establish a discriminatory measure against a foreigner, we cannot establish a discriminatory [p. 17] measure against a national. I don't want to put obstacles in the way of this amendment, but I must draw our constitutional difficulty to the attention of this assembly, because we could not very well accept here something that would be contrary to the principles of our political Constitution.

Chairman: Delegate from India.

India: Mr. Chairman, the Indian delegation desires to associate itself with the remarks of the delegates of China and Greece. It is notorious that certain countries are in the position of having a substantial proportion of [their] adult labor population seeking a living in other countries, and their families at home are in the habit of subsisting on a portion or the whole of their earnings, which these immigrants or emigrants earn; and it would be a serious embarrassment to a large number of these governments if remittances were not included, as this draft rightly includes them, among current transactions. The Indian delegation supports the remarks of previous speakers.

Chairman: Delegate from India supports the remarks of previous speakers.

Delegate from Netherlands.

Netherlands: Mr. Chairman, I would like to strongly support the standpoint of the Chinese delegate. I think that while I quite agree with the French delegate that the first three points have a bearing on the legal obligations, the fourth point is certainly related to other obligations, the obligations which arise from family ties and other ethical bases. I think that the remittances for family living expenses are so essential and are so widely common in history for a great many people that I think it would be very wrong to exclude them from this item. I think that the point of Mr. Machado might be met by leaving out the word "immigrant." I think it is [p. 18] not necessary, and I don't know whether the delegate from China would be in agreement with that, but anyway, whether it is in or not, I would strongly support the Chinese standpoint. I am not talking here of the financial interest of my own country, as we are in the habit of making these remittances.[310]

Chairman: The delegate from Netherlands supports the view of China.

If the Commission approves, I should like to limit the debate on the subject [to] another ten minutes. Is there any objection?

Delegate from Bolivia.

Bolivia ([René Ballivián]): I wish to submit, Mr. Chairman, [a] consideration in connection with this provision. From the very beginning I was not very keen about it, but I did not want to raise the point. However, I submit that in a country poor and undeveloped, such as Bolivia, to which large numbers of immigrants have been going in the last years, these remittances would cause serious embarrassment in our economy because, as everyone understands, our supply of foreign exchange is very limited, and in a small country 30,000 or 40,000 immigrants sending money abroad might really cause serious financial economic embarrassment. I wish to submit this [for] the consideration of the Commission, and I know that there are quite a few countries in Latin America in the same position as Bolivia.

Chairman: The delegate from Bolivia supports the position of the delegate of the Soviet Union and Cuba.

Delegate from Canada.

Canada: I would not add to the discussion, but I would simply say that the Canadian delegation strongly supports the Chinese position.

Chairman: Delegate from Canada strongly supports the Chinese delegate.

Delegate from Egypt. [p. 19]

Egypt: The Egyptian delegation strongly supports the proposal as put by China.

[Chairman]: The delegate from El Salvador.

El Salvador: The El Salvador delegation supports the view of China.

Chairman: The discussion is before the Commission.

Cuba ([Luis Machado]): I would like to move as an amendment that the word "immigrant" be eliminated.

China: Mr. Chairman, I accept that amendment.

---

310 That is, the Netherlands is a net payer rather than a net recipient of remittances.

Chairman: The amendment that the word "immigrant" be eliminated is accepted by China. The question before you is that the phrase, "Moderate remittances for family living expenses," shall be deleted from the report. All those in favor of eliminating the phrase, "Moderate immigrant remittances for family living expenses," as sponsored by the delegate from the Soviet Union, please signify by saying "aye."

("Ayes" heard.)

Those contrary minded, "no."

("Noes" heard.)

The motion is lost.

The delegate from the French Committee.

France: I wish to make a reservation.

Chairman: You wish to make a reservation?

France: Yes.

Cuba ([Luis Machado]): I was wondering what we were just voting on. Were we voting on the amendment or the substance?

Chairman: I thought we were voting on the whole phrase, but the Secretariat informs me that there was some misunderstanding. You are now going to be asked to [p. 20] vote on the amendment, on the elimination of the word "immigrant." That is the sole question before us. We will then vote on the rest of the phrase. All those in favor of eliminating the word "immigrant" from paragraph (4), so that the phrase will read, "Moderate remittances for family living expenses," please signify by saying "aye."

("Ayes" heard.)

Contrary minded, "no."

Then, the motion of the Commission is to eliminate the word "immigrant" from the phrase. Then I am now going to put the original motion.

The delegate from Czechoslovakia.

Czechoslovakia: It is necessary to add something "for family living expenses abroad"; otherwise it has no sense.

Chairman: The word "remittances" is usually foreign remittances. May we have unanimous consent to add that word [phrase], "for the living expenses of families abroad"? This refers to families living abroad. The Drafting Committee will figure it out if you pass it.

Now I am going to put the question before the Commission. The question before the Commission is the proposal of the Soviet delegate that the phrase "Moderate remittances for family living expenses" be deleted from the section. All those in favor of deletion, please signify by saying "aye."

Contrary minded, "no."

The Commission accepts the decision that the phrase be permitted in there with the deletion of the word "immigrant." Will the chairman of the Drafting Committee see that "abroad" is put in the proper place?

(He [chairman of the Drafting Committee] shakes his head [in agreement].)

The Chair will ask the will of the Commission in delegating this task to the Drafting Committee. All those in favor of turning this task over to the Drafting Committee, signify by saying [p. 21] "aye."

("Ayes" heard.)

The next item: we will now turn to the second point raised by the delegate from the Soviet Union. If I understand correctly, he wishes to call the attention of the Commission to the fact that the Soviet Union, by virtue of its state trading, has some of its balances held by some of the state institutions which correspond to the balances of private banks in other countries, and that the Fund should take that matter into consideration in estimating what are the initial holdings. Is that a correct interpretation?

USSR ([Aleksei Smirnov]): Yes.

Chairman: Delegate from the United Kingdom.

United Kingdom: The difficulty to which Dr. Smirnov has called attention was very much in the minds of the Special Committee and their numerous attempts to find a satisfactory solution of the drafting problem. I do hope that it has become met in a way which does justice to the point which he has raised. It attempted to do so, because Section (c) of Article XIX ["Explanation of Terms"], page 39,[311] does place "other official institutions," that is, official institutions other than [the] Treasury, stabilization fund, etc., on a level with private banking concerns. With regard to the extent to which it is expected that whoever is entrusted with the task of computing monetary reserves takes into account foreign holdings in respect of such other official institutions, which I imagine would include the Soviet trading institution, as in respect of private banks, it is suggested that in computing the monetary reserves of a country, that [i.e., the foreign reserves of state banks] should only be taken into account in so far as there is reason to suppose that their foreign holdings exceed their reasonable [p. 22] working balances. This paragraph then is an attempt to make allowance for the particular situation of the Soviet

[311] In Document 448, p. 796.

Union by assimilating the treatment of its trading institutions through private banks in other countries.

Chairman: Does the delegate from the Soviet Union feel that the explanation made by a member of the Special Committee as to the interpretation of paragraph (c) clears up the doubts which may have been in his mind as to the understanding of the committee and of the Commission, for accepting the committee's report?

USSR ([Aleksei Smirnov]): Yes, Mr. Chairman, I should like that this be left to the [Special] Committee.

Chairman: Those remarks will appear in the minutes of the meeting. Any further point to be raised?

The delegate from the United States.

United States (Edward Bernstein): That means that the motion of the delegate of the Soviet Union is withdrawn.

Chairman: For your information, it was not a motion. It was merely a suggestion; am I correct? It was a request for a clarification.

Any further business?

Delegate from United States.

United States ([Edward Bernstein)]: Mr. Chairman, the delegation of the United States would like to propose some very minor modifications in Schedule C ["Election of Executive Directors"], on page 50.

Chairman: Schedule C, what page?

United States ([Edward Bernstein)]: It is on page 50. These changes that we proposed are on page 2 of Document 466, which has just been distributed. The changes are as follows, Mr. Chairman:—

Chairman: Now, what document are you referring to? [p. 23]

United States ([Edward Bernstein)]: Report of the Drafting Committee.

Chairman: Document 466?

United States ([Edward Bernstein)]: Document 448, page 50; but Document 466 contains the explanation and is before this Commission.[312]

Chairman: Document 466 contains an explanation of the change on page 50 to which you will presently refer.

United States ([Edward Bernstein)]: That is right. The changes are as follows: page 50, paragraph 3, the fourth line from the bottom of that

---

[312] The passages being discussed are in Document 448, p. 804, and Document 466, pp. 833-834.

paragraph reading, "elected, and (b) those governors"—cross out the next four words, "all or part of."

Chairman: "All or part of" to be deleted from Section 3 on page 50. Could you indicate the significance of the deletion of that phrase?

United States ([Edward Bernstein]): I shall, as soon as I make one or two consequential changes in paragraph 4. In the first line, [which begins] "In determining whether," delete the next three words, "any portion of." For paragraph 5, substitute [the] paragraph at the bottom of page 2 of Document 466. That is a very brief paragraph of four or five lines, so that it would now read, "Any governor[,] part of whose votes must be counted in order to raise the total of any persons above 19 percent[,] shall be considered as casting all of his votes for such person even if the total votes for such person thereby exceeds 20 percent."

These changes, Mr. Chairman, have for their purpose the elimination of the provision which permits the division of the votes of a country when cast for a member of the Executive [p. 24] Directors. Hitherto, under this schedule, if a country cast a certain number of votes, part of which were necessary to elect a director, and the rest were excess, the excess could be transferred. When a considerable number of directors are to be elected in this form and when a considerable number of countries are to vote, this division of votes for a country may be exceedingly important, but as we have now restricted the number of directors to be elected in any one body by having five elected from one group [i.e., the five largest quota holders], [and] two elected from the American Republics, there is a great danger that this division of votes for a country may lead to some difficulty. It is not a significant change in substance, but merely for the purpose of adjusting Schedule C to a smaller number of directors now elected.

Chairman: You have heard the explanation of the Reporter for the Special Committee in the discussion of those changes. The Chair will put the question to the Commission. All those in favor of accepting the report of the Special Committee as changed, signify by saying "aye."

("Ayes" heard.)

Contrary minded, "no."

The Commission accepts the report of the Special Committee on the election of Executive Directors.[313]

United States ([Edward Bernstein]): I will suspend until you finish.

---

313 Became part of Schedule C in the final agreement.

Chairman: I was about to say that the Reporter informs me that was a report from the delegate of the United States and not a report from the Special Committee.

Delegate from United States. [p. 25]

United States ([Edward Bernstein]): It gives me pleasure on behalf of the United States to move the adoption of the whole document.

Chairman: The delegate from the United States moves for the adoption of the whole document.

Czechoslovakia: I second that motion.

Chairman: The delegate from Czechoslovakia seconds the motion. The motion is before you to accept the whole document, 448, as corrected and amended and as accepted in tonight's proceedings. Any discussion on the motion?

Delegate from the Soviet Union.

USSR: Mr. Chairman, the Soviet delegation should like to refer to some questions already discussed on this document. May I proceed with this explanation?

Chairman: You are in order to raise any question on the document you wish.

USSR: The first one is concerning Article V, Section 8(f) ["Charges"], at page 14, paragraph (f): "All charges shall be paid in gold. If, however, the member's monetary reserves are less than one-half of its quota, it shall pay in gold only that proportion of the charges due which such reserves there to one-half of its quota, and shall pay the balance in its own currency."[314] The monetary reserves and gold reserves don't represent a factor relative to the prosperity of the country. Therefore, we propose a uniform order to pay these charges, [such] that all countries would be allowed to pay a certain part of the charge in gold and the remaining part in [their] own currency. [p. 26]

Chairman: The delegate from the Soviet Union, referring to paragraph (f), page 14, proposes that all countries be treated alike and that the requirement that each country pay a specified portion of the charges in gold and currency be indicated in that provision to replace the provision that all charges shall be paid in gold with the exception which follows. Any discussion of that proposal?

The Chair will then put the matter to a vote by the delegates. All those who wish to accept the proposal by the Soviet delegation that section [paragraph] (f) be altered in the matter which he has indicated, please signify by saying "aye."

[314] In Document 448, p. 777.

Contrary minded, "no."

("Noes" heard.)

The Commission does not accept the proposal, and the paragraph (f) remains as proposed by the Drafting Committee.

The delegate from the Soviet Union.

USSR: The delegate from the Soviet Union would like to reflect the proposal of the Soviet delegation in the records.

Chairman: The Secretariat will see that the proposal of the Soviet delegation is contained in the records.

USSR: The second point to which we should like to return is the Article XII, Section 8, "Communication of Views to Members."[315]

Chairman: What page may that be?

USSR: Page 31, Section 8. This concerns the second sentence in this section: "The Fund may, by a two-thirds majority of the total voting power, decide to publish a report made to a member regarding its monetary or economic conditions and developments which directly tend to produce a serious disequilibrium [p. 27] in the international balance of payments of members." In our opinion, these reports presented to the members, as well as other communications made by the Fund to the members,[316] should not be published. We propose to omit the words "to publish the report" and to say, "to present a report."

Chairman: The Soviet delegation wishes to replace the words in the fourth line, starting "to publish a report," with the words "to present a report." Is that correct?

USSR: Yes.

Chairman: Mr. Rasminsky.

Louis Rasminsky (Chairman, Drafting Committee): May I ask whether that proposal also involves the elimination of the word "may," because the sentence requires a two-thirds vote to publish a report, which has been made. Is the proposal of the Soviet delegation to require a two-thirds majority vote to make a report?

Chairman: Did the Soviet delegate have in mind that the change should affect the making of the report, or merely the publishing of the report?

USSR: Our opinion is that [the] report, as well as the communications of the Fund to members, should not be published.

---

[315] In Document 448, p. 790.

[316] The typescript has here the additional words "should be published reports," which seems to be either a mistake by the delegate, the stenographer, or the typist.

Chairman: It refers then to the making *public* of the report and not the *making* of the report. Any discussion on that proposal?

You have heard the proposal of the delegate of the Soviet Union. Since there is no discussion, I will put the matter to a vote. Those in favor of accepting the proposal of the delegate of the Soviet Union, please signify by saying "aye."

("Ayes" heard.)

Contrary minded, "no."

("Noes" heard.) [p. 28]

Chairman: The Chair will ask for a show of hands. Those in favor of accepting the proposal of the delegate from the Soviet Union, signify by raising hands.

(Hands raised.)

Contrary minded, please raise their hands.

(Hands raised.)

Chairman: The Commission votes not to accept the proposal of the delegate from the Soviet Union on this matter.

USSR: Mr. Chairman.

Chairman: The delegate from the Soviet Union.

USSR: We propose to change this amendment in this way, that this report should be published only with the consent of the respective member.

Chairman: The delegate from the Soviet Union proposes that the provision be altered to read that the report shall be published only with the agreement of the member to whom the report is directed. Is that correct?

USSR: Yes, sir.

Chairman: Is there any discussion of that proposal?

The Chair will put the matter to a vote. Those in favor of accepting the proposal of the delegate from the Soviet Union that the report be published only with the consent of the member, please signify by raising their hands.

(Hands raised.)

Those in favor of not accepting the proposal of the delegate from the Soviet Union, please raise their hands.

(Hands raised.)

Chairman: The Commission does not accept the proposal of the delegate from the Soviet Union.

The delegate from the Soviet Union.

USSR: We propose to amend the proposal contained in Article XIII, Section 2 ["Depositories"].[317]

Chairman: Article XIII, Section 2.

USSR: Page 32. [p. 29]

Chairman: Page 32.

USSR: The provision in paragraph (b).[318] We are in accord with this provision in principle, but we want to add after the second sentence before the words "however, all transfers of gold," to include after the words "at least one-half of the holdings of the Fund shall be held in the depository designated by the member and whose territories the Fund has its principal office and at least 40 percent shall be held in the depositories designated by the remaining four members referred to above," to add "in each of the four other countries with the largest quotas the Fund shall hold gold in an amount not less than the amount of their contribution of gold."

Chairman: Would the delegate from the Soviet Union, if he has the proposal written out, send it up to the Secretary? If that is written out, will the delegate from the Soviet Union please send it up to the Secretary? In the meantime, I will put the question. The delegate from the Soviet Union states that he is in accord with paragraph (b) of Section 2, but proposes that there shall be added to the sentence ending with "four members referred to above," which is on the sixth line from the bottom of the paragraph, a phrase indicating that in each of the four other countries with the largest quotas that at least the gold which is contributed by that country shall be held there. I am not certain that is precisely what it is. When the Secretary receives the written document you will correct it, if necessary. In the meantime, does anyone want to

---

[317] In Document 448, pp. 791.

[318] The paragraph reads:

"(b) The Fund may hold other assets, including gold, in the depositories designated by the five members having your largest quotas and in such other designated depositories as the Fund may select. Initially, at least one-half of the holdings of the Fund shall be held in the depository designated by the member in whose territory the Fund has its principal office and at least forty percent shall be held in the depositories designated by the remaining four members referred to above. However, all transfers of gold by the Fund shall be made with due regard to the costs of transport and anticipated requirements of the Fund. In an emergency, the Executive Directors may transfer all or any part of the Fund's gold holdings to any place where they can adequately can be adequately protected."

discuss the proposal? Is the proposal clear to the members, or would they like to have it read over again?

Unidentified: Will you have it reread, sir?

Chairman: Will the delegate from the Soviet Union mind reading just the sentence he wishes added? [p. 30]

USSR: To insert in this article, paragraph (b), after the words "initially, at least one-half"—

Chairman: I think they know that paragraph. If you don't mind reading just the phrase you would like inserted?

USSR: To insert the following words: "in each of the four other countries with the largest quotas the Fund shall hold gold in an amount not less than the amount of their contribution of gold."

Chairman: I understand that that phrase is part of the sentence. It is not a separate sentence. It is part of the sentence following the word "above," and therefore is modified by the word "initially." Is that correct?

USSR: Yes.

Chairman: The Chair wants to make that clear, that the statement is that initially each of the four largest countries shall have the gold which they contribute. I don't very well see how it is possible to be otherwise. You have heard the proposal. Does anyone wish to discuss it?

If not, the Chair will put the matter to a vote. Those in favor of accepting the proposal of the Soviet delegation that the phrase which you have heard be added to the sentence beginning with "initially," signify by saying "aye."

("Ayes.")

Contrary minded, "no."

("Noes.")

The Chair will ask for the raising of hands. All those in favor of the proposal of the Soviet delegation, please raise your hands.

(Hands raised.)

Contrary minded, please raise your hands.

(Hands raised.)

The proposal is lost.

If there are no further matters to come before the Commission at this time, we will return to the original motion which is before you. The delegate from the United States moved, [p. 31] and the delegate from Czechoslovakia seconded the motion, that the Commission accept the report [Document] 448 in its entirety.

The delegate from Cuba.

Cuba: Before the adoption of that motion I would like to have a clearly understood that in accepting the Report No. 6 of the Special Committee on the election of Executive Directors, everything after the word "election" in the last paragraph of Section 1 has been deleted.

Chairman: Has it been documented?

Cuba: Document 466, Report No. 6 of the Special Committee of Commission I, the first page.[319]

Chairman: On the first page of Document 466, and would you mind repeating your proposal?

Cuba: My understanding is that in voting for this proposal, everything was deleted after the words "number of directors to be elected."[320]

Chairman: No, just three words: "under," the "(iii)" in parentheses, and the "above"—these are the only three words.

Cuba: I am afraid we voted on a misunderstanding, and I move that everything after that be deleted.

Chairman: The point of order has been raised that there was a misunderstanding in the voting with respect to the Report No. 6 of the Special Committee, and the delegate from Cuba now proposes that all the words following "elected" shall be stricken from the paragraph. The Chair will call upon the Reporter of the Special Committee to indicate whether or not that was intended, or is that a change of substance?

United States (Edward Bernstein): It was intended, Mr. Chairman, but I see no objection to it. It leaves just that much more flexibility for the Board of Governors, which must act by four-fifths majority. I can see no objection to it. It is not from the Special Committee, but the American delegation reports that change. [p. 32]

Chairman: In view of the fact that [the] vote of accord arose as a result of misunderstanding, the Chair will put the proposal of the delegate from Cuba to a vote. The proposal is that all words after "elected" be stricken from the paragraph. That is the last four lines.

Cuba: And three on the next page.

Chairman: Would you mind indicating what on the next page you would have stricken out?

Cuba: May I read the paragraph?

Chairman: Would you please?

Cuba: "For the purposes of this paragraph, "members" means governments of countries whose names are set forth in Schedule A

---

319 In Document 466, p. 833.

320 See several paragraphs below for the sentences to be struck.

["Quotas"], whether they become members in accordance with Article XX ["Final Provisions"] or in accordance with Article II, Section 2 ["Other Members"]. When governments of other countries become members, the Board of Governors may, by a four-fifths majority of the total voting power, increase the number of directors to be elected." That is all.

Chairman: And the rest of the paragraph on page 1 and the part on page 2 are deleted?

Cuba: That is right.

Chairman: You have the proposal before you. Does any delegate wish to discuss the proposal?

Ecuador: I support the proposal.

Chairman: The delegate from Ecuador supports the proposal of the delegate from Cuba.

If there is no discussion on the proposal, the Chair will put the proposal to a vote. All those in favor of accepting the proposal of the delegate from Cuba that all words be stricken out after "elected" in Document 466, signify by saying "aye."

("Ayes.")

Contrary minded?

The Commission accepts the proposal of the delegate from Cuba. The Secretary will designate [that] this replaces the vote taken already on the basis of misunderstanding.

Now we will [p. 33] return to the motion [made] by the delegate from the United States and seconded by the delegate from Czechoslovakia, to accept the Report [of the Drafting Committee, Document] 448 in its entirety, which now includes the proposal, Document 466, as corrected. Is there any discussion of that motion?

If not, the Chair will put the motion to a vote. All those in favor of accepting the drafted report of Commission I in its entirety, please signify by saying "aye.'

("Ayes.")

Contrary minded?

The Commission accepts in its entirety the Report of the Drafting Committee, Commission I.[321]

Mr. Rasminsky.

---

[321] Document 466, pp. 765-810. By approving the report, with the additions specified, Commission I approved the whole of what would become the final agreement on the IMF.

Louis Rasminsky (Chairman, Drafting Committee, and Reporting Delegate): I would like to request the assistance of the members of the Commission to report accurately to the plenary session the formal reservations which delegations have entered with regard to particular sections of the Fund agreement. I have examined the records of the Commission, and the only reservations I have knowledge of and which it is my duty to report to the conference are the following:

First, the reservation of the Soviet delegation with respect to the last sentence of Article XIII, Section 2 on page 32 of Document 448, which reads, "In an emergency the Executive Directors may transfer all or any part of the Fund's gold holdings to any place where they can be adequately protected."[322]

Second, the reservation of the following delegations regarding the size of their quotas: Australia, China, Egypt, Ethiopia, French delegation, Greece, India, Iran, New Zealand, and Yugoslavia.

Third, the statement of the United Kingdom delegation that in the opinion of their government, the location of the headquarters of the Fund ought not to be discussed without reference to the location of other international bodies which will be established, and [that] the United Kingdom's government may therefore find it necessary at some later date to ask that all such interrelated questions be regarded as a matter for decisions among governments rather than at the technical conferences.

And fourth, the formal reservation which I understand was entered tonight by the French delegation, objecting to the inclusion in item 4, "Moderate [p. 34] remittances for family living expenses," on page 41 of the interpretations of terms in this agreement.

If any delegation wishes to remind me of any formal reservation which they have made at meetings of the Commission which have escaped my attention or which they wish reported to the conference, and if any delegation wishes to withdraw any formal reservation now standing in its name, I would ask that I be informed immediately after this meeting. If I am not so informed, I shall report in plenary session the reservations to which I have just referred.

Chairman: I have been asked to make this announcement. The Special Committee of Commission II has been appointed, and there will be a short meeting of the committee immediately after this meeting in Room W-1. The countries represented on the committee are Belgium, Brazil, Canada, China, Czechoslovakia France, India, Mexico, the

[322] In Document 448, p. 791.

Netherlands, Union of Soviet Socialist Republics, United Kingdom and the United States.

We cannot close this meeting without expressing our gratitude, appreciation, and commendation for the splendid work which the committees have done. They have worked long hours, way into the early mornings. Those of you who may have passed through the halls and committee rooms at 2:00 or 2:30 or even 3:00 in the morning will have seen large groups of men working over the problems which they have been assigned. I haven't been to many conferences, but certainly I have never seen anything like the extent to which these committees have taken their responsibilities seriously and their keen desire to perform their tasks well. That they have performed their tasks well is apparent to all of you who have examined the document. I should like to give heartfelt thanks of the Commission to the committees who have labored so long and well, and I hope that posterity will indicate its appreciation [p. 35] through an adherence to the peace and prosperity which we hope will be one of the results of the work of this Commission. The final meeting of this Commission—

The delegate from United States.

United States: Before we adjourn—I speak on behalf of the delegation from the United States, but I doubt not [that] what I shall say will be joined in by many delegations present—I rise to pay tribute to the earnestness, ability, and good nature of the presiding officer of this Commission, Mr. White.

(Rising to feet and loud clapping.)

Chairman: I sincerely thank you, gentlemen. The meeting is adjourned.

(11:00 p.m.)

PART II

COMMITTEES OF COMMISSION I

Committee 1:
Purposes, Policies, and Quotas of the Fund

Committee 2:
Operations of the Fund

Committee 3:
Organization and Management of the Fund

Committee 4:
Form and Status of the Fund

11

Commission I, Committee 1
Purposes, Policies, and Quotas of the Fund
First meeting: summary
July 4, 1944, 10:00 a.m.[323]

Chairman's opening remarks • Committee procedures • Purposes of the IMF

The subject of Committee 1 was the "Purposes, Policies, and Quotas of the Fund" (IMF). The committee chairman, Tingfu Tsiang, was an experienced Chinese diplomat and bureaucrat who had obtained his good knowledge of English when he earned a Ph.D. in history at Columbia University two decades earlier.

After being introduced by Harry Dexter White, the chairman of Commission I, Tsiang outlines procedures the Committee will follow. Delegates briefly discuss procedures before beginning debate on Article I of the preliminary draft IMF agreement ("Purposes"). They immediately become bogged down in a question of wording in the first section of the article, whether a phrase characterizing the IMF as "a permanent institution" should appear in the clause. The Committee rejects the phrase.

Lionel Robbins of the United Kingdom, an internationally renowned economist, then points out the difficulties of drafting language in a large group, and suggests that the Committee appoint a small drafting subcommittee, which would report its recommendations to the full Committee. The Committee approves. As the Committee begins consideration of the second section of Article I, Harry Dexter White expresses his view that the Committee should not vote on each question, because that would slow down its work. Tsiang replies that on secondary matters, he does not intend to hold votes, but on important matters he thinks the Committee should freely express its views. Tsiang envisions playing a less muscular role as chairman of Committee 1 than White does as chairman of Commission I.

The Committee then returns to consideration of the second section of Article I. Sir Jeremy Raisman, a British colonial administrator who as India's minister of finance took India's interests strongly to heart, proposes an alternative that adds a phrase emphasizing the economic development of poor countries as among the purposes of the

[323] Summarized in Document 102, pp. 117-118.

IMF. Throughout the conference, India would press for more emphasis on the economic development of poor countries as a purpose of the IMF, while the biggest rich countries (the United States, United Kingdom, and France) and some others argued that such goals more properly belonged to the World Bank. An Indian delegate claims that language from a U.S. Treasury publication, Questions and Answers on the International Monetary Fund, *supports his view. The South African delegate suggests that the matter be referred to the Committee's Drafting Committee. Chairman Tsiang agrees, provided that the alternative not enlarge the purposes of the IMF as listed in the Joint Statement. It is agreed that an Indian delegate will be present when the Drafting Committee discusses India's proposed alternative. In commenting on the Indian alternative, Emanuel Goldenweiser makes his first appearance in the transcripts. Goldenweiser was the director of research and statistics for the Board of Governors of the U.S. Federal Reserve System, and as such the top economist at the Federal Reserve. The Committee then adjourns.*

Dr. [Tingfu] Tsiang [China] took the chair upon introduction by **Dr. [Harry Dexter] White [United States]**, chairman of Commission I of the conference. He outlined briefly the procedure to be followed by the Committee, indicating that the Committee would follow the topics assigned to it in Document No. 51 distributed by the Secretariat, entitled "Assignments."[324] He indicated that the Committee would follow these assignments within each article and proceed section by section. Where there was only one alternative, embodying no substantial change, the Committee would endeavor to reach agreement. Where there was more than one substantial change, the Committee would take up the alternative involving substantial change first.

The representative of **Ecuador [Esteban Carbo?]** moved that where an alternative does not make a substantial change, it should be referred by the Chair to the subcommittee of three or five members in order that that [sub]committee might agree on the changes it thinks advisable.

Mr. [Wilhelm] Keilhau of [the] Norwegian delegation made the following suggestion on procedure. He indicated that of the topics assigned to this Committee all were important, but only the question of quotas was difficult, on account of the great interest of governments in the matter, and because neither the Joint Statement nor the Committee Document F-1[325] made definite provision with respect to it. Mr. Keilhau therefore suggested that for quotas, there be a small expert committee of three, including lawyers and bankers among its members. He suggested

[324] Document 51, pp. 88-91.

[325] The preliminary draft IMF agreement, Document 32, pp. 21-60.

that the Committee discuss provisionally the proposed formula for quotas and thereafter refer the matter to the subcommittee, who would ascertain the views of various delegations and make a report.

The **Chairman** then put the motion of the representative of Ecuador for a small Drafting Committee involving no substantial change, but this motion was lost for a lack of a second.

The **Chairman** replied to Mr. Keilhau that shortly a paper on the subject of quotas would be presented to the Committee, and that it would be best to defer discussion on the subject until then.

Mr. [Wilhelm] Keilhau [Norway] agreed to postpone it until that time.

The **Chairman** then read Section 1 of Alternative A to Article I: ["The purposes of the International Monetary Fund are: 1. To promote international monetary co-operation by providing permanent machinery for consultation on international monetary problems."][326]

Judge [Fred] Vinson of the United States delegation moved that it be adopted on the ground that involved no change in substance.

There was discussion in which **Mr. [Walter] Nash of New Zealand** [and] the **Egyptian delegation** stressed the omission [in] Alternative A, Section 1 of the words "a permanent institution," and suggested this was a serious omission, since "machinery" might be understood to read mere consultative arrangements. **Mr. Nash** therefore moved that it would be better to return to the original wording of the Joint Statement and was supported by **Mr. [Kyriakos] Varvaressos of Greece** and **Mr. [Ts-Liang] Soong of China**. [p. 2]

The **Canada** representative defended the language of Alternative A, Section 1 in preference to that of the Joint Statement on the grounds that the whole instrument set up an institution in its other provisions, and that the reference to "machinery" was appropriate for a Statement of Purposes.

The **Chairman** put the motion, indicating that the only important point was whether to retain the words "a permanent institution" or not,

---

[326] The following discussion concerns passages in Document 32, pp. 22-23. The delegates often call the subdivisions of Article I "sections," and we follow this usage, but unlike the case for other articles, at no stage does the IMF agreement ever term them "sections" in the document itself. The original language of the Joint Statement for Section 1 reads, "To promote international monetary cooperation through a permanent institution which provides the machinery for consultation on international monetary problems."

and the motion was lost. (The United States and United Kingdom voted for the motion).

Professor [Lionel] Robbins of the United Kingdom referred to the difficulties of drafting in a large group and pointed out that since the conference was to complete its duties by July 19,[327] it was essential that we focus attention to completing the committee assignments. He therefore suggested a small Drafting Committee as proposed by Mr. Keilhau, but suggested that it be a permanent subcommittee of this Committee, and suggested that sections marked with an asterisk (indicating substantial change) be referred to the subcommittee by the Chairman with the approval of the full Committee.

Mr. Jeremy Raisman of India seconded the motion.

Mr. [Jan] Mládek of Czechoslovakia asked whether the right of the Committee to decide whether the change was one of substance should be fully safeguarded.

[Professor Lionel] Robbins [United Kingdom] replied that this was implicit in the Constitution of the conference as a paramount principle, and that the motion would have needed no amendment in this respect.

The representative of **Iran** asked whether the Committee would have an opportunity to review the findings of the [sub]committee.

The **Chairman** replied that the subcommittee would report to the full Committee.

Professor [Robert] Mossé of [the] French delegation seconded the motion, which was then put by the Chairman and carried. ([The] United States supported the motion.)

Judge [Fred] Vinson [United States] then said that though he did not address himself to the results of this vote, [he did] wish to raise a question of procedure. It was, he said, his understanding that differences of opinion in the Committee would be reported fully to the Commission.

The **Chairman** replied that the Committee was not under obligation to report on all purposes of the differences, since in that case it would not fulfill its purpose of saving time for the Commission.

The **Chairman** then submitted the alternatives to Section 2, Article I of the Joint Statement, indicating that there were two without substantial change and one with substantial change, and that he proposed the Committee consider the latter.[328] [p. 3]

---

[327] The original end date of the conference, later extended to July 22.

[328] In the Joint Statement, the section reads, "2. To facilitate the expansion and balanced growth of international trade and to contribute in this way to the

Judge [Fred] Vinson of the United States delegation then requested that Dr. White, Chairman of the Commission, be given the floor.

Dr. [Harry Dexter] White [United States, Chairman, Commission I] said that it was his feeling that a vote on each question would be undesirable and would slow down the Committee's progress, and asked whether in cases where the Chair recognized the differences of opinion, the Chair would not refer the matter to the Commission, and if there is general agreement on this procedure, pass on to the next point. Dr. White suggested that the Chairman thus not attempt to obtain a vote on each provision.

The **Chairman** replied that it had been and was his intention to dispose of secondary matters in this manner. On matters of importance, it was his intention that the Committee should have free expression of its views, and that all shades of opinion should be reported fully. He said that the question raised in regard to Section 1 of Alternative A was a matter more of language that of form.

Dr. [Harry Dexter] White [Chairman, Commission I] then asked whether, when the matter is not brought to vote, the Chairman could not pass to other points, because there might be a difference of opinion as to what might be important and what not important, and that it might be unfortunate to oblige the Committee to make this distinction in a formal way when the Committee decided whether or not to take a vote.

The **Chairman** said that motions like the one to constitute a subcommittee to facilitate the work of the Committee would have to be put to a vote. With regard to other matters, it would probably be satisfactory if the Chair would consult the Committee on whether or not there should be a vote.

The **Chairman** then proposed that Alternative C to Section 2 should be considered and read the alternative, which is as follows: ["2. To facilitate the expansion and balanced growth of international trade, *to assist in the fuller utilization of the resources of economically underdeveloped countries* and to contribute thereby to the maintenance in the world as a whole of a high level of employment and real income, which must be a primary objective of economic policy."]

Sir Jeremy Raisman of the Indian delegation then explained to the Committee the reasons in the mind of the Indian delegation proposing

---

maintenance of a high level of employment and real income, which must be a primary objective of economic policy." Alternative C, the alternative with substantial changes, is discussed below in the main text. See Document 32, pp. 22-23.

this alternative. These reasons were, in the first instance, that the wording of Section 2 of Article I of the Joint Statement gives undue emphasis to the high level of income and of employment in already highly industrial countries. It cannot, he said, be the object of the Fund to restrict its activities in this respect to highly industrialized countries. The Fund should have as its objective also to bring low-income countries up to a high level quite as much as to maintain the high level in other countries Sir Jeremy said that the [word] "maintenance" implies that such a high level of employment of real income already exists. Therefore, the Indian amendment is intended to give explicit expression of what is really meant by this section of the Joint Statement by implication. [p. 4]

Mr. [Pedro] Beltrán of Peru suggested that the intent could be made clear by adding the words "promote and maintain" to the section, so that it would read that the objective of the Fund was "to promote and maintain high levels of full employment and real income."

Mr. [Wilhelm] Keilhau of Norway observed that if any of the alternatives were adopted, it would be necessary to have the word "promote" in this section.

The view of the Indian delegation was supported by the delegate from **Ecuador [Esteban Carbo?].**

Mr. [Jack] Holloway of South Africa suggested that the Indian motion goes beyond the main objectives of the Fund, and that in all of the Committee's discussions, the danger of going beyond the proper purpose should be guarded against. He said that as the Indian alternative is worded, the purpose is really the purpose of the Bank rather than a purpose of the Fund. He referred to Alternative F of Article I, in which cooperation with other agencies is suggested as an objective, and indicated that the point was really covered there.

In the further debate on this issue, the **Australian** delegate supported the Indian alternative, stressing in particular that a conflict might arise between objectives such as exchange stability and the basic economic objectives such as stressed by the Indian alternative, and [stressing that it] should be clear that the Fund in determining its actions should have in mind these major economic issues, which should be governing in its policy decisions. He suggested, however, that the word "thereby" in the Indian alternative be dropped.

This was agreed to by the Committee, including the **Indian** delegation.

The **Chairman** said that further consideration of the Indian alternative would be without the inclusion of this word.

Judge [Fred] Vinson [United States] asked for permission to have Dr. Goldenweiser address the Committee.

Dr. [Emanuel] Goldenweiser [United States] said that it would be helpful, in [the] view of the United States delegation, if the Committee should agree that the word "maintain" includes the idea[s] of "attain" and "promote." He said that if the Committee agreed to refer this alternative to the Drafting Committee,[329] the United States delegation would be quite ready to see the word "thereby" dropped. He said, however, that it would, in the United States delegation's view, be unfortunate to include the words about the fuller utilization of the resources of undeveloped countries suggested by the Indian delegation. This view was taken on the same grounds put forward by the South African delegation. [p. 5]

The **Brazilian** delegation agreed with the thought of the Indian alternative, but felt that as worded it included an objective of the Bank among the objectives of the Fund.

Mr. [Daniël Crena] de Iongh of the Netherlands delegation said that he was very much opposed to the Indian suggestion for reasons which had been expressed in the debate, and thought the original text of Section 2 was excellent.

Mr. [Walter] Nash of the New Zealand delegation said that the [expansion] of trade, which is already in the language of the Joint Statement, carries by necessary implication the idea of fuller utilization of resources and higher real income. He emphasized the dependence of the Fund for its success upon a national policy of the member countries. He suggested the following revised words for the Indian alternative: [typescript is blank here, and we have found no other record of the proposed change].

Prof. [Robert] Mossé of the French delegation also proposed new wording for Section 2, as follows: [typescript is blank here, and we have found no other record of the proposed change].

At the request of the delegate from **Cuba,** there was discussion of the meaning of the word "balance" as it appears in Article I.

It was brought out by **Dr. [Emanuel] Goldenweiser [United States]** that unless so qualified, the other expression might be taken to mean a growth of imports without a corresponding growth in exports.

The **Indian** representative said that the additional words proposed by the India delegate did not enlarge the purpose of the Fund, but merely made it more complete. He quoted from the *Questions and Answers [on the*

[329] The reference here is to the Drafting Committee of Committee 1 that would be chaired by Emanuel Goldenweiser of the United States, not the Drafting Committee of Commission I chaired by Louis Rasminsky of Canada.

International Monetary Fund][330] to show that the purpose he mentioned was already in the Fund.

The **South African** representative suggested that Alternative C be referred to the Drafting Committee.

The **Chairman** agreed to so refer the question if the Committee agreed that the alternative does not enlarge the meeting of the purposes of the Fund as stated in the Joint Statement.

The representative from **Ecuador [Esteban Carbo?]** asked the question of whether all the alternatives on this article should not be referred to the Drafting Committee.

He was overruled by the **Chair,** with the support of the Committee.

It was agreed that when the Drafting Committee reaches this alternative, a member of the Indian delegation should be present.

The meeting was adjourned.

---

[330] A booklet issued by the U.S. Treasury on June 10, 1944. It is reproduced in Margaret G. de Vries and J. Keith Horsefield, *The International Monetary Fund 1945-1965: Twenty Years of International Monetary Cooperation; Volume III: Documents* (Washington, D.C.: International Monetary Fund, 1969), pp. 136-182. The Indian delegate is apparently referring to Question 3 ("Is the Fund intended to provide for international expansion of production and exchange which is one of the objectives stated in Article VIII of the Mutual Aid Agreement? Is it intended to introduce measures for controlling the trade cycle?")

12

Commission I, Committee 1
Purposes, Policies, and Quotas of the Fund
Second meeting: transcript
July 4, 1944, 4:00 p.m.[331]

Purposes of the IMF, continued

Meeting later the day of its first meeting, Committee 1 continues its discussion of Article I, on the purposes of the IMF. It considers further proposed amendments to the second section of Article I, which concerns trade and employment. Because the changes are merely verbal, the Commission approves chairman Tingfu Tsiang's suggestion to refer them to the Drafting Committee.

On the third section of Article I, concerning the balance of payments, on making the IMF's resources available to member countries to correct maladjustments in their balance of payments, the committee has a brief discussion on phrases about confidence and maladjustment. The committee refers the section to the Drafting Committee.

The fourth section of Article I concerns exchange rate stability. The delegates debate how much emphasis the statement of purposes should place on exchange rate stability. Is it an end, at least as far as the IMF itself is concerned, or a means to a broader end of economic stabilization? If it is a means, changes in exchange rates become more expected. The chairman suggests referring the matter to the Drafting Committee for a report at a later stage of the committee's deliberations, and the Committee agrees.

The committee accepts without debate an alternative to the fifth section of Article I, on multilateral payments. On the sixth section, about lessening disequilibrium in the balance of payments of member countries, one proposed alternative is referred to the Drafting Committee and another is postponed for consideration until a related clause is discussed.

India proposes to add a section to Article I stating that one of the IMF's purposes shall be to promote settlement of abnormal indebtedness arising from World War II. India has in mind the payments it has received in pounds sterling from the United Kingdom for war supplies, which because of exchange controls it can only use to buy goods within the "sterling area"—the countries that use the pound sterling as their

[331] Summarized in Document 111, pp. 122-124.

anchor currency—and not from outside countries, such as the United States. The United Kingdom, United States, and France oppose including the section on the grounds that it would overburden the IMF with problems better settled between nations. Wilhelm Keilhau of Norway suggests referring India's proposal to Commission III, which addresses "Other Means of International Financial Cooperation." The chairman states that he will recommend the matter to Commission I without any recommendation on what the Commission should do about it. This is an admission that Committee 1 is unable to resolve the matter.

The chairman then names the members of the Drafting Committee and Committee 1 adjourns.

Chairman ([Tingfu Tsiang, China]): The second meeting of Committee 1, Commission I has come to order.

This morning we ended by considering Alternative C to Article [I, Section] 2.[332] You remember in that Alternative, [Section] No. 4 consisted of certain verbal changes, and there were certain explanations, and that article was referred to a Drafting Committee with materially the changes suggested by the member [delegate] of New Zealand. Now this afternoon we have to consider Alternatives A and B to the same section, Section 2. We will consider first of all Alternative A [as it concerns] Section 2. The alternative reads, ["2. To facilitate the expansion and balanced growth of international trade and to contribute thereby to the maintenance of high levels of employment and real income, as a primary objective of economic policy."]

You will notice that there are changes proposed in this alternative which are purely verbal. Instead of "here" you have this word "hereby." In the Joint Statement it was "in this way." They changed from "in this way" to "thereby." In the Joint Statement, the last clause has three more words: "which must be a primary objective of economic policy." The alternative drops those words "which must be" and states, "as a primary objective of economic policy."

In view of the fact that the changes suggested in Alternative A are purely verbal and, in fact, minor verbal, I would suggest that this alternative be referred to the Drafting Committee without discussion. Is that agreeable to you?

Agreed. Alternative A, Section 2 is referred to the [p. 2] Drafting Committee.

Now we will look at Alternative B, Section 2 again. Here the change is even less than in Alternative A. This alternative simply suggests the

---

[332] The discussion that follows concerns passages in Document 32, pp. 22-24.

omission of this word "thereby" or "in this way." There is no other change. So, I will also suggest that Alternative B, Section 2 be referred to the Drafting Committee. Is that agreeable to you?

Unidentified: Mr. Chairman, does that mean that these alternatives are going to be referred back to the Committee after the Drafting Committee modifies the three of them?

Chairman: The Drafting Committee may suggest a reconciliation or a new wording—that we cannot tell—but whatever the conclusions the Drafting Committee arrive at will be reported to this Committee.

Is that agreeable to you, that Alternative B, Section 2 be referred to the Drafting Committee?

I hear no objections. It is so ordered.

Now we will consider Section 3. In Section 3 we have two alternatives: Alternative A and Alternative B. [p. 3] Alternative A is very simple. I will read Alternative A: ["3. To give confidence to member countries by making the Fund's resources available to them under adequate safeguards, thus giving them time to correct maladjustments in their balance of payments without resort to measures destructive of national or international prosperity."]

This word "them" in the original draft is "members"—a change in a single word, "thus giving them time to correct maladjustments in their balance of payments [without resort to measures destructive of national] or international measures."

Alternative B. We will look at Alternative B: ["3. To make the Fund's resources available to members under adequate safeguards and to assist them to correct maladjustments in their balance of payments without resort to measures destructive of national or international prosperity."]

This alternative differs from the Joint Statement in that the Joint Statement starts by an additional phrase, "To give confidence to member countries by making the Fund's resources available."

Do you wish to have a discussion on Alternative B?

Delegate from Australia.

Australia ([Leslie Melville?]): Mr. Chairman, may I suggest the adoption of B. The language is that the Fund shall inspire the confidence of member countries as well as the public; therefore to mention confidence here looks very strange, in my view.

Chairman: Any further discussion?

Unidentified: Mr. Chairman, are we taking the whole clause 3? [p. 4]

Chairman: Yes, Section 3.

Unidentified: I will agree with Dr. Keilhau in his comment on the phrase "giving confidence," and that was the reason for the alternative suggested in B. But there is another alternative, which I do not think makes any substantial change in the meaning intended in the original draft but may in fact give some difference in meaning. The original draft [says] "thus giving them"—that [is,] members—"time to correct maladjustments in the balance of payments." The alternative says "and to assist them in correcting maladjustments in the balance of payments." There is just a possibility that the original draft might be interpreted to mean that if members did not make adjustments, then they would be expected to resort to measures destructive to national and international prosperity. That, of course, was not intended. We think it better to remove that possible ambiguity by the alteration of the wording.

United States ([Emanuel Goldenweiser?]): Mr. Chairman, it does not seem as though these were only verbal changes, but I think they have some significance, and it may be worth the Committee's while to have me explain them as best I can, because they have a bearing on other sections that come up later.

The word "confidence" may not have been very aptly chosen, but it had a very definite intent, which I am afraid it does not carry out. The idea of the word "confidence" was to make it possible for countries to make plans with assurance that if untold circumstances should develop, and it [i.e., a country] would temporarily find itself unable to proceed, it had recourse to the Fund. It gave them the [p. 5] same sort of assurance as the central bank [i.e., as the central bank does for commercial banks?], making it possible for them to lend with the understanding that should there be a temporary decline in the deposits, the members could resort to the central fund for assistance. This is the same sort of thing in an international way. A country can plan its international financing and feel that if it should fall short, there is an international organization to come to its assistance, and that's what is intended.

I think the other point brought out by the representative of Australia is a little more important, because while the words are very close in Alternative B, as they were in Alternative A, they too change the impact of the sentence because they give the impression that it is the Fund's business to assist in the correction of maladjustments. This Fund will not be equipped to do this. This Fund's function is to make it possible to delay the consequences of maladjustments and to give the country an opportunity to take such measures as are necessary to correct the maladjustments. This Fund will not be large enough to correct any substantial maladjustments in this war-torn world, and if you should start out with the intention of having the Fund correct maladjustments, the Fund will not be able to live up to its purpose.

Australia ([Leslie Melville?]): This should also be referred to the Drafting Committee, but I would like to say that the first point about "confidence" might be made perhaps somewhere else. On the second point, I still feel that giving members time is also assisting them to correct maladjustments, and the alternative words suggested are appropriate. However, that whole thing might be thrashed out elsewhere than this Committee. [p. 6]

Chairman: Shall we refer this to the Drafting Committee with the understanding that opinions expressed here shall be taken into consideration by the Drafting Committee? Is that agreeable to you?

[Australia? (Leslie Melville?)]: Agreed.

Chairman: I hear no objection, it is so ordered.

Now we consider [Article I,] Section 4. In Section 4, Alternative A—really, as I can see, there is not a single word of change—there is no alternative at all. It was put there because the whole page was suggested as one alternative. It was not because that alternative had anything particular to suggest with regard to Section 4. I think I'm correct in that reading. If so, we will drop Alternative A from our discussion. Then we have Alternatives B, D, and E.

We have three drafts to consider. I will read first Alternative B: ["4. To secure orderly changes in exchange rates among member countries where necessary to correct exchange disequilibrium, thus promoting exchange stability and avoiding competitive exchange depreciation."]

Alternative D reads as follows: ["4. To promote exchange stability and avoid exchange depreciation by securing, where necessary to correct exchange disequilibrium, orderly changes in exchange rates among member countries."]

Alternative E reads:

["4. To promote exchange stability.

"5. To avoid competitive exchange depreciation by securing, where necessary to correct fundamental disequilibrium, changes in par values of member currencies."].

Discussion now open on these alternatives.

Belgium ([René Boël]): Mr. Chairman, I suggested Alternative D, but in view of Alternative B, I would suggest that Alternative D should not be discussed here, and I am willing to drop it and support E.

Chairman: The original proposer of D is willing to drop it, so consider only Alternatives B and E.

Norway ([Wilhelm Keilhau?]): As Alternative G was suggested by Norway, I wish in a few words to draw attention to the reason why this change is suggested. Among all the purposes, the purpose [p. 7] to promote exchange stability is the one which has been all the time the center of discussion, and I think it would be wise to let that purpose stand out by itself and direct [attract?] attention. To a great extent, that is a matter of policy—that is one thing—and another thing is that what here is stressed as point [Section] 5 is in a way a quite different thing, because if we completely succeeded in promoting exchange stability, there would be no use in making the orderly alterations in a member currency. That is the reason we propose to drop that. May I also say that where [whereas?] in the new proposed [Section] 5, the intention has been to bring the rule here in conformity with the expression concerning alterations in five ways that I used in later articles of the draft.

Australia ([Leslie Melville?]): Australia proposed the amendment contained in Alternative B because, while we are entirely in sympathy with it being an objective of the Fund to promote exchange stability, we think that exchange stability should be of a certain kind. It should not be exchange stability pursued for its own self. The danger that we see both in the original draft and also in Alternative E is precisely that the Fund may under this feel that it has a directive to aim at exchange stability, irrespective of whether that is desirable or not. Now, it is perfectly true that in a later portion of the text, provision is made for orderly changes in exchange rates, but there seems to us to be some conflict in the interpretation as to what is done later in the text and what is here made one of the purposes and policies of the Fund. We think that it would be undesirable, for example, if a country were inflating internally [p. 8] that the Fund should seek under those circumstances to promote stability in the case of that particular country. It would be obviously undesirable to try to tie down exchange rates while the country was pursuing a domestic policy of inflation. Such a policy would be undesirable, but the harm that it might do would be aggravated by any attempt to aim at stability of exchange rates under the circumstances.

If it is only a matter of the public attitude towards this document, then it seems to me that the point is met sufficiently by Alternative D, which was proposed for withdrawal. And [in] that alternative, the proposal to promote exchange stability was put first in order in the section, and that may perhaps meet the point of view of those who fear the possible public reception to any weakening of the references to the exchange stability in this document, but we do feel that promotion of exchange stability in itself as an objective should not be one of the policies and purposes of this Fund.

United States: It seems to me the statements of the delegate from Norway, particularly the alternative suggested by him, come forward at this time because of other provisions that appear in the Joint Statement of Principles. It seems to me that if there are to be changes in the latter language, that then the Committee might return to the purposes of the Fund. Certainly there is injected into this discussion in the alternative that we amend the provision agreed upon by the content in the Joint Statement of Principles, a very important matter that must be met and resolved upon a later occasion. I trust that the gentleman may await the resolving of those provisions before amending or seeking to amend the purposes of the Fund. [p. 9]

Ecuador ([Esteban Carbo]): I wish to move that article [Section] No. 4 remain as it is written in the project [Spanish *proyecto,* i.e., draft], that is, "To promote exchange stability, [to maintain orderly exchange arrangements among member countries, and to avoid competitive exchange depreciation]." I make a motion that it remain as it is, without any changes.

[Australia (Leslie Melville)?]: I second the motion of the delegate from Ecuador because [of] the amendment of the words "promote and secure stability." It would be easier, for the Bank [i.e., Fund] should not secure exchange stability. For this reason I second the motion.

Chairman: What is your pleasure? Shall we proceed to vote, or shall we report the opinion here to the Commission?

[Australia (Leslie Melville)?]: I should prefer to vote on this matter. I think this is a matter of purpose, and I think that unless you hear the opinion of everyone present here the only way to get a good idea of the prevailing opinion is to vote. I think this is a matter to which we must attach the highest importance.

Reporter (Kyriakos Varvaressos, Greece): I think we must consider Article [I, Section] 4 of the Joint Statement. In this article [Section] 4, all clauses with regard to the stability of exchange or the possibility of changing the rates are stated. I think that it would be wise for our Committee, in agreement with the proposals of the member of the United States, to wait and see how this article would be definitely formulated. If in this article some provisions will be passed providing for [the] rate of exchange, then we shall come back to the purposes of the Fund and include the purposes of the Fund in this matter, but I think we all agree that [p. 10] the principal purpose of the Fund is to promote and secure stability. If we shall agree to compromise in this scope [then the agreement will include] something which will indicate that the Fund will facilitate changes which will prevent the countries to have recourse to avoid competitive discriminations [devaluations], and I think we must come back to this.

I should like then to propose we accept the postponement of Alternative D: ["4. To promote exchange stability and avoid exchange depreciation by securing, where necessary to correct exchange disequilibrium, orderly changes in exchange rates among member countries."] I prefer this to E, because in paragraph [Alternative] E we give the impression we consider both the establishing of the promotion of the exchange stability and changes as the main objects of the Fund, while the main object is the stability of the countries. So, I should like to come back to proposal D, and not E.

Brazil: Mr. Chairman, I beg to second the suggestion made by the Reporting Delegate, because the spirit in which article 4 or chapter 4 [i.e., Section 4] is drawn up is the spirit of promoting stability, and only considers changes in special cases, so the whole idea in paragraph 4, which is intimately connected with what we are now discussing, seems to be the promotion of stability as the governing principle. However, as the American delegation pointed out, perhaps we might consider this point now of the preamble after having considered the question of par values of member countries, to see whether the Committee will approve the general principles laid down in chapter 4 is that of promoting stability. Generally speaking, the Brazilians had rather favored among all the amendments that which has been withdrawn by the Belgian delegation, which seems to be, among the members who wanted it, more in accordance with the spirit of the Fund. But the suggestion made by the Reporting Delegate to postpone any change in this article of the preamble until such time as we discussed the whole matter in more detail seems to me the best one. [p. 11]

United Kingdom ([Lionel Robbins?]): I should like to support what has been said here. I hope very much that we shall not proceed at this juncture to put this matter to a vote. It seems to me, Mr. Chairman, that it would be highly undesirable if at this stage we would proceed to vote on matters which, to some members at any rate, seem to engulf fundamental points of principle. By all means let us proceed. Let us not linger on unimportant points; there are other points. But where these points are involved, surely for us to be taking sides before we have a preliminary run through would be a mistake. I therefore support what has been said by the delegate of the United States and the other speakers who spoke in that sense.

France: I wish to support the preceding speakers. I think it is premature to vote at the present time on a matter of principle.

Chairman: I think we have devoted enough time to the discussion of this section. We had a variety of opinions discussed. We have one very important point which we shall bear in mind. This principle affects the nature of the whole Fund, and what we are to adopt here should be harmonious with the total which we will build. So, if it should be agreeable to the Committee here, I would suggest that we temporarily ask the Drafting Committee to take this section in hand, with due consideration of opinions expressed here and with consideration of [the] proceedings of this Committee as a whole, not only at the present stage but in later stages. In other words, the Drafting Committee should report somewhat later, and not together with other articles. [p. 12]

Norway ([Wilhelm Keilhau?]): It was necessary for us to bring this question up at this time for this Committee, because as far as I remember, the problem which it involves [has] realities [that] should be treated by another committee.

Chairman: Do I hear any objection to my suggestion?

If not, so ordered.

Now we shall proceed to consider Section 5. Section 5 is only [in] Alternative A. The alternative reads, ["5. To assist in the establishment of a multilateral system of payments in respect of current transactions between members and in the elimination of foreign trade restrictions which hamper the growth of world trade."]

The change is in the first part of the section, the second part remaining the same. In the first part we substitute—the alternative substitutes—this phrase "multilateral system of payments" instead of "multilateral payment facilities." Then [in] the second part, on current transactions of member countries, there is a word in respect to "current," and so forth.

What is your pleasure with regard to Alternative A, Section 5?

United Kingdom ([Lionel Robbins?]): Might we agree to accept that, Mr. Chairman?

Chairman: It seems to be a happy improvement on the wording. Shall we adopt Alternative A, Section 5? Is that agreeable to all?

I hear no objection, so ordered. Alternative A, Section 5 is adopted.

Now we proceed to Section 6. Section 6 has two alternatives. Alternative A: ["6. To shorten the periods and lessen the degree of disequilibrium in the international balance of payments by members."] There is no change, but Alternative B [says, "6. *In accordance with the above principles,* to shorten the periods and lessen the degree of disequilibrium in the international balance of payments by members"]—[it contains the] addition of this phrase "in accordance with [the] above principles," and the word "countries" instead of "members."

What is your pleasure in regard to Alternative B? Shall we add or shall we not that phrase "in accordance with the above principles"? [p. 13]

Australia ([Leslie Melville?]): This amendment is also put forward by Australia. It seemed to us that the statement of purposes and policies of the Fund as set out in [Section] 6 gave to the Fund altogether too wide a discretion. It must be remembered that the Fund has the power to refuse member countries access to their purposes [resources?] if any member is not complying with the policies and purposes of the Fund. In addition to that, the Fund must take into account the purposes and policies of the Fund. [Section] 6 says quite bluntly, ["To shorten the periods and lessen the degree of disequilibrium in the international balance of payments by members."] One way of doing that would be, in the case of any disequilibrium, to lessen the degree of equilibrium of balance of payments—for a country to follow a rigid policy of deflation, such as wage cutting and other policies of deflation which have to be met in such circumstances. Now, we doubt if in the present state of knowledge on monetary methods whether this is an amendment which should be adopted. We think there are other ways of correcting disequilibrium of that kind, and those other ways are preferable. Our proposal is intended to restrict the discretion of the Fund to the principles which were set out under [Sections] 1 to 5, and to eliminate what seems to us a possibly objectionable method of correction.

Chairman: Any further discussion?

United States: Mr. Chairman, if there are no objections as far as the delegates from the United States are concerned, we think it means the same thing with the language in as it does with the language out.

Unidentified: Will we put that in every clause: "in accordance with the above purposes"? [p. 14]

Chairman: No, the suggestion is only to insert that clause in Section 6.

Unidentified: Then the remainder will not be in accordance with the purposes?

Chairman: That, of course, is not intended.

Unidentified: Mr. Chairman, what occurs to me is whether it is really necessary to [include] that [phrase] "in accordance with the above purposes."

Mexico: The change of alternatives is contradictory with another phrase in article [Section] 3, which says to give [members] "time to correct maladjustments," since it is the purpose of the Fund to provide short-term credit. But what the Fund can do is to maintain this disequilibrium without having to take restrictive measures; and we feel that the wording of that phrase of this article is unfortunate, and we should like to propose that it be referred to the Drafting Committee.

Chairman: I wonder if you all got the point of the suggestion made by the member from Mexico. He finds that the phrase "to shorten the period" [[is problematic]]. That might be contradictory to something we said about giving the members time to correct maladjustments, so that it may well be referred to the Drafting Committee to find out whether the words are contradictory and, if so, to find a better expression.

Unidentified: May I ask how the Fund would shorten the period of [a country's adjustment to equilibrium?]?

Chairman: Is someone in a position to answer that question? [p. 15]

United States (Emanuel Goldenweiser): I shall attempt to answer it. I think the idea of this section is that it would shorten the period by relieving the country temporarily from the pressure of its exchange [rate] while it is undertaking adjustments, and therefore make it easier for them to bring about the adjustment and bring them about in a shorter time. The help [is] extended to [assist] the members, rather than [to] shorten the [adjustment to] equilibrium—because we seem to be expanding the Fund beyond its real scope if the idea is to actually shorten the [adjustment to] equilibrium. I thought the Fund's scope was to lend help to the members who are in need of such help, but not in holding [i.e., delaying?] adjustment of its equilibrium.

Chairman: I thank you, Dr. Goldenweiser. I understand how by so doing, it would help the country while it effects its own equilibrium. The country itself is adjusting its own position to lessen [[the period of disequilibrium]], so the Fund itself will not shorten. The Fund will lessen the *effect* of [adjustment to] equilibrium while it [the country] is effecting its readjustment.

United States (Emanuel Goldenweiser): Mr. Chairman, may I say that the intention of the language is not to indicate that the Fund in itself will do anything to bring about corrections in maladjustments merely because it will relieve the country of the exchange pressure during the period; but in view of the fact that the language is subject to misunderstanding, I think it would be best to refer it to the Drafting Committee, which will have heard the comments and will attempt to correct any misleading impression that it may give.

Chairman: With respect to the first part, "in accordance with the above principles," there are two opinions. [p. 16] One limits the Fund's possibilities with member countries. The other opinion is that everything the Fund does must be in accordance with the principles. There is nothing the Fund can do without being in accordance with the Fund's principles. [In] the second part, "to shorten the period," the language is not clear. It is subject to misunderstanding. Therefore, it seems to me to be proper to leave this matter to our Drafting Committee. Let them work on this section and bring to us something better, clearer; then we will spend time to consider this. Any objection?

I hear no objections, so ordered.

Now we have to consider certain matters that were added to the original Joint Statement. We have Alternative F, which is an addition. It is intended to be a new section of this article. Alternative F: ["To correlate procedures for exchange stability with policy for the promotion of international investment by the international financial agencies and to evolve a working relationship with such agencies."]

Discussion is open on Alternative F.

Brazil: Mr. Chairman, this was the suggestion made by the Brazilian delegation. The idea was to indicate the advisability of establishing connection between the actions of the Fund and those of the Bank. It is somewhat connected with the point I had the opportunity to raise this morning, in respect of a discussion of an amendment suggested by the Indian delegate. It is not, we think, the purpose of the Fund to deal with investments. It seems to me, and [in] as far as we have understood it, the general principle is that the Fund will deal with short-term or even perhaps at the most medium-term credit. The long-term credit will be dealt with by the Bank. The two policies, however, should, it seems to us either [be] connected or, in some cases, the equilibrium, the balance of payments of a certain country which might be absorbed by the governing period of the Fund may be due to lack of investment. In this case, the Fund may get in touch with the Bank, and call attention to the advisability of directing [p. 17] investments to that country in order to give them the means of re-establishing the balance of payments. It seems to us that this should be inscribed as one of the purposes of the Fund, to establish a connection with the Bank's purposes. That was the idea of this amendment.

Chairman: Any further discussion?

Poland: The statement made by the chairman of the delegation of Brazil—I think that we all understand very well [that] to correct maladjustments in the balance of payments of many countries, some other means are necessary, as we have found—as they are in their own resources. So, we see here that also we should consider the proposal of the Bank of Reconstruction and Development and it should be very advisable to put into the status of the Fund the proposal of the delegate from Brazil, which points to the necessity of collaboration of these two international institutions.

United States (Emanuel Goldenweiser): When you read Alternative F, it seems on the face of it to be innocent, and in general it is clear that the functioning of this Fund would have to be correlated with the functioning of other international machinery, but we have no real assurance at this stage that both the Fund and the Bank machinery would be established, and it seems somewhat outside the scope of the purposes of the Fund to indicate that it is one of the purposes to cooperate with something else which may or may not exist. There is a proposal which will come up in due time about cooperation between the Fund and other international agencies, and it seems to me that it would be very much better to pass this up at this time, and consider that section as one of the substantive matters rather than one of the purposes of the Fund. [p. 18]

Chairman: Any further discussion?

Brazil: Of course, the proposal made of establishing correlations between two institutions presupposes the existence of both. If one of them does not materialize, of course there is no possibility of establishing relation between two things, one of which does not exist. I quite agree that in view of Dr. Goldenweiser's announcing to us that there will be certain proposals in connection with the subject to be further discussed, that the matter should be postponed until such time as the other proposal in connection with it could be taken up by the Committee.

Chairman: The member proposing this alternative agrees to the postponement of this alternative until we consider the proposal of other international agencies. So, the consideration of Alternative F is postponed.[333] [p. 1 (19)]

[[We turn now to consideration of Alternative G, proposed by India, which would add as a purpose of the Fund, "To promote and facilitate the settlement of abnormal indebtedness arising out of the war."]]

India ([Sir Shanmukham Chetty?]): This proposal found [a] place in earlier drafts of the scheme of [an] international monetary plan,[334] and

---

333 At this point in the U.S. Treasury Library copy of the typescripts, one typescript ends and we continue from another, which appears in a later section of the same bound volume, under the heading "Discussion in Committee 1 of Abnormal War Balances."

334 See Margaret G. de Vries and J. Keith Horsefield, *The International Monetary Fund 1945-1965: Twenty Years of International Monetary Cooperation; Volume III:*

it was a feature to which the utmost importance was attached by certain countries. The future has now been omitted from the Joint Statement, and as far as I am aware, there has been no explicit indication of the reasons for omitting it. I have no doubts that those reasons were important. At the same time, it is impossible to exaggerate the importance which is attached to this problem by the countries directly affected. Indeed, it may be said that it is difficult to conceive how a monetary plan for postwar international relations can be drawn up without any attention whatever being paid to this extremely large and urgent problem. We recognize that the problem may have attained such dimensions that it would not be susceptible of complete handling through the medium of an international monetary plan of this kind. At the same time, it is difficult to accept a complete exclusion from the scope of the plan of any provision whatever for facilitating the treatment of this problem. It is conceivable that arrangements may be made—arrangements of a bilateral nature which would impinge on the operations of the Fund—and it may be urged that the Fund should include provisions which would recognize arrangements of that kind and enable some advantage to be taken of the existence of the Fund by the participants in such arrangements. I do not think, Mr. Chairman, that the subject could be completely disposed of in the course of discussion in this Committee, as it is a matter of great substantive importance to the countries concerned, and therefore I merely confine myself to stating the nature of the proposal and the reasons for it. [p. 2 (20)]

Egypt: The Egyptian delegation has presented an amendment similar to the one presented by the Indian delegation, but it was not presented in good time. It reads as follows: ["To promote multilateral settlement of foreign credit balances accumulated during the war."][335] It is similar to the Indian proposal, but is more acceptable because the term "multilateral" would permit the countries concerned to deal in foreign currencies, and it seems to me that it is more acceptable. A similar resolution was adopted by the monetary conference held in Cairo last April and was supported by the Indian delegation.

Chairman: I am informed that the amendment of the Egyptian delegation is being printed and will be circulated among members of the Committee as soon as printed. Any further discussion on Alternative G?

Documents (Washington, D.C.: International Monetary Fund, 1969), pp. 19-118, for the British (Keynes) plan, the U.S. (White) plan, and the Canadian plan.

[335] Alternative H, Document 109, p. 122.

[United States] (Emanuel Goldenweiser): Mr. Chairman, I am afraid I am taking too much of the Committee's time, but it behooves me to some extent to explain the origin of the various proposals and of the changes. In the first place, I should like to say that I agree that the matter is so fundamentally important that it is not likely to be disposed of in the brief session of this Committee today. The delegate from Egypt referred to the fact that in an earlier draft published last year there was some reference about it. I am not at the moment in a position to say why it was included in the [earlier] draft, but I am in a position to say why it was excluded from the following draft. As the study of the subject proceeded, it became perfectly clear that a machinery that was charged with the duty of facilitating exchanges based on current rates in the [p. 3 (21)] postwar world would have as much a load to carry as any human institution would be expected to carry, and if that new experimental machinery which we hope to fashion here were to be loaded with the duty of helping to pay off previously accumulated indebtedness, it would certainly have a much less prospect of success and survival. As Sir [[Shanmukham Chetty?]] indicated, the amounts involved are so great that they far exceed the entire operation of the Fund. The Fund could only make very small inroads on that problem, and might very easily in the process be robbed of its ability to serve those purposes. Prewar indebtedness and indebtedness during the war present problems which need entirely different treatment of adjustment of arrangement, and [are] not a question of current exchanges which arise out of current rates, which is the purpose of the Fund. I join with Sir [[Shanmukham?]], the gentleman from India, that with the voicing of two views on it, it would best to have this section remain unacted upon, even tentatively, because it would be best to consider whether or not it would fit into such plan as will evolve out of the other sections of the Fund [agreement], and particularly out of the work of Committee 2, which it has with [i.e., which is discussing] "operations of the Fund."

Norway ([Wilhelm Keilhau?]): I think that this rather serious stage [statement?] by Dr. Goldenweiser made a certain impression on us all. There will not be any one of us who wish to add too heavy a burden to the Fund. But when the idea originally had its origin to give certain references in this draft to all the blocked balances and to war indebtedness, it was because those are facts which are found when the Fund begins to work, and in certain ways there might be important arrangements which at the same [p. 4 (22)] time would be agreeable to the Fund and to the countries involved. Now, I think it might be a way out of this dilemma to refer this question to Commission III, which has to do with recommendations, because that might [result in] a resolution concerning this question taken by the conference without it being necessary to include it in this chapter. And there is one reason more for this: when we now formulate the policies and purposes of the Fund, we give a fundamental law which may be in effect for hundreds of years, while these blocked balances in normal war indebtedness, I hope, will not be with us too long. I will therefore suggest that this question be referred to Commission III [with] the recommendation that this be considered in a most serious way.

Chairman: In connection with the suggestion by the member from Norway, I would like to call attention to the fact that Committee 1 is a constituent part of Commission I. The proper procedure would be to report to Commission I with the suggestion that this section might be referred to Commission III. Whether Commission I will be willing or not to refer to this matter to Commission III is up to Commission I. That is a matter of procedure. The main suggestion is that this Alternative G might be referred first to Commission III.

France: Mr. Chairman, it is my impression that any suggestion mentioned to facilitate the settlement of abnormal indebtedness, whether arising out of the war or other purposes, is not the purpose of the Fund. The Fund is established for current business and will have sufficient opportunity if it gets stuck with its loans to have abnormal indebtedness to deal with, but it should not start with abnormal indebtedness. Therefore I agree with the suggestion [p. 5 (23)] [that it] be proposed to Commission I to refer it to another organization.

United Kingdom ([Lionel Robbins?]): Perhaps I should say one or two words making clear the United Kingdom's position. We agree with the view which was taken by the delegate from India in his very temperate remarks that this is a most important problem. We are anxious to find a solution to this problem, but we are not able to agree with you that this is a problem which it would be right to refer to the Fund. We agree with the admirable remarks made by Dr. Goldenweiser that it would be an unfortunate thing if the Fund, which is created to facilitate current business, were to start on its career waterlogged with the stupendous heritage of the past. We believe that this is a problem which can best be settled by discussions between creditors and debtors, and for that reason we should not ourselves be ready to support its reference to any part of this conference.

Brazil(?): If we do take into account the present purposes of this Fund and the Fund is largely based upon facilities for payment between countries for goods, will it not be inevitable that countries meet[ing their] war commitments would have to lean further on the Fund and use the Fund more, so it is inevitably tied up with war debts? Although I am in accord with Dr. Goldenweiser that we might jeopardize the good works that could be done in this field by adding another purpose, yet it is inevitable that countries having war indebtedness will have all their transactions with this Fund affected by the extent of their indebtedness and having to meet its needs. And yet, I agree that it would be unfair [p. 5 (23)] to the Fund to include the load of war.

Chairman: Is there any further discussion? In view of the opinions expressed at this point, it seems to me to be proper to suggest that this Committee refer this matter to Commission I without any suggestion as to its future dealings. Will that be acceptable to all?

Guatemala ([Manuel Noriega Morales]): It is my belief that it would be necessary to take the matter of this important question in some of the commissions of the conference and it seems to that if this Committee only referred to its own Commission the matter without any comment, it probably would not be treated fairly. As very well stated by Dr. Goldenweiser and the other gentlemen who have spoken before me, the war indebtedness is a problem really connected with the matter we are dealing [with], too; but it is entirely agreed, it seems to me, that inclusion of this matter in the purposes of the Fund will really be a danger for the correct functioning of the Fund. For this reason, it seems to be advisable that the conference will deal with the matter, but entirely outside of the Fund, and perhaps in this connection it would be advisable that the Committee refer [the matter] to the Commission as Mr. Chairman suggested, but suggesting at the time that this question be turned to Commission III, which is supposed to take into consideration all the other financial measures which would be necessary for the postwar arrangements.

United States: I move that the Committee adjourn.

Chairman: A motion is made that we adjourn, but before we adjourn [p. 6 (24)] I want to announce—this morning you remember it was moved and passed that we have a Drafting Committee. I appoint—I ask—the following delegations to furnish members for the Drafting Committee: Australia, Brazil, Czechoslovakia, United Kingdom, and the United States of America. The Reporting Member [Reporter] and the Secretary have the right to appear with other members of the Committee. Any delegation whose proposal is referred to the Drafting Committee may send somebody to appear before the committee to explain this proposal. This committee will meet tonight at nine o'clock in Room A, and the member from the United States will be the chairman of the committee.

I wish also to call attention to this fact, that we have almost finished Article I and the six sections. But will you please notice Alternative A; there is a slight modification in language.

"The purposes of the International Monetary Fund are:

["1. To promote international monetary co-operation by providing permanent machinery for consultation on international monetary problems.

"2. To facilitate the expansion and balanced growth of international trade and to contribute thereby to the maintenance of high levels of employment and real income, as a primary objective of economic policy.

"3. To give confidence to member countries by making the Fund's resources available to them under adequate safeguards, thus giving them time to correct maladjustments in their balance of payments without resort to measures destructive of national or international prosperity.

"4. To promote exchange stability, to maintain orderly exchange arrangements among member countries, and to avoid competitive exchange depreciation.

"5. To assist in the establishment of a multilateral system of payments in respect of current transactions between members and in the elimination of foreign exchange restrictions which hamper the growth of world trade.

"6. To shorten the periods and lessen the degree of disequilibrium in the international balance of payments of members.]

"[7.] The Fund shall be guided in all its decisions by the purposes set forth above."

Now, if the Committee has no objection, I will ask the Drafting Committee to consider the sentence.

India: I understand the Drafting Committee is considering Alternative C on page 1b. Is India's delegation to send one representative?

Chairman: I have already discussed this—yes.

(Adjourned.)

13

Commission I, Committee 1
Purposes, Policies, and Quotas of the Fund
Third meeting: transcript
July 5, 1944, 4:00 p.m.[336]

Purposes of the IMF, continued • Membership and subscriptions • Payment of quotas • Revision of quotas • Minimum gold subscription

Committee 1 continues its consideration of Article I, on the purposes of the IMF. Emanuel Goldenweiser of the United States, the chairman of the Drafting Committee that chairman Tingfu Tsiang had appointed, delivers its report. Goldenweiser reports that the Drafting Committee tried to craft language that would satisfy the desire of the Australian and Indian delegations for more emphasis on employment, and development, as opposed to what they considered an overly strong emphasis on addressing balance of payments problems. Committee 1 defers consideration of the Drafting Committee's recommendations because not enough copies of the report have been printed for all delegates.

The next item on the agenda is Article II, "Subscription to the Fund." The committee does not discuss the proposed amounts of quota subscriptions, which would be determined by a separate ad hoc committee of Commission I, the Committee on Quotas. Instead, it begins by discussing whether there will be any distinction of privileges between countries that join the IMF immediately and those that join later. Given that the delegates agree that countries that join later should have equal privileges once they join, the chairman refers the matter to the Drafting Committee to hone the language.

Concerning the time and place that subscriptions are to be paid, August Maffry, who represents the Department of Commerce in the U.S. delegation, explains that the American conception is that the IMF will not begin operations until member countries holding a certain percentage of total quotas have accepted membership. The delegates, led by Jan Mládek of Czechoslovakia and other delegates of German-occupied countries, then discuss what special consideration to give to occupied countries. It is

[336] Summarized in Document 138, pp. 150-151.

apparent that the committee is sympathetic to allowing them special consideration in making their subscriptions, and the chairman states that he will convey the sentiment to Commission I.

Next, the committee briefly debates periodic reviews to consider adjusting quotas. It decides that reviews shall occur every five years, but may occur more often if the need arises. The committee then considers what minimum share of quotas must be paid in gold. It sets the share at the smaller of 25 percent of a member country's quota or 10 percent of its official holdings of gold and gold convertible currency, on a date to be specified later. In response to a question from Iraq, whose holdings of foreign exchange are all in pounds sterling, which is not considered a gold convertible currency, an American delegate points out that 10 percent of nothing is nothing, so Iraq would not have to pay any gold as part of its initial quota; it would be able to pay the quota in pounds sterling and Iraqi dinars.

Chairman ([Tingfu Tsiang, China]): The Committee will come to order.

You have before you the report of the Drafting Committee of Committee 1 on matters referred to it yesterday. I will now ask the chairman of that committee to make the report.

Emanuel Goldenweiser (United States, Chairman, Drafting Committee):[337] [The Drafting Subcommittee met on July 5 to consider the matters referred to it by the full Committee.

The following members were present: Mr. [Emanuel] Goldenweiser [United States] (Chairman); Dr. [Tingfu] Tsiang [China], Dr. [Eugênio] Gudin [Brazil], Mr. [Jan] Mládek [Czechoslovakia], Mr. [Leslie] Melville [Australia], Professor [Lionel] Robbins [United Kingdom], and Mr. [Kyriakos] Varvaressos [Greece].

The [Drafting] Committee considered Alternatives A, B, and C relating to Section 2 of Article I ["Purposes"] in the preliminary draft Articles of Agreement (Document F-1)[338] and also considered alternative language submitted by the Colombian, New Zealand, and French delegations bearing on this Section. The Drafting Committee recommends for the consideration of the full Committee the following language:

Article I, Section 2: "To facilitate the expansion and balanced growth

---

[337] The transcript merely says, "(Mr. Goldenweiser read the report of the Drafting Committee of Committee 1 of Commission I on matters referred to it at the meeting of Committee 1 on July 4)." We have reproduced the report from Document 122, pp. 130-132.

[338] In Document 32, pp. 22-23.

of international trade and to contribute there by to be promotion and maintenance of high levels of employment and to the development of the sources of productive power in all member countries as primary objectives of economic policy."

In recommending this new formulation, the Drafting Committee wishes to report that the representatives of the Indian delegation who were present during the discussion expressed themselves as regarding the language as an improvement from their point of view, but not completely meeting their wishes on the point.

The representative of the Australian delegation also agreed that the new language was an improvement, but stated that its suitability from the point of view of his delegation was partly dependent upon the language to be adopted under Article III, paragraph [Section] 2, sections [paragraphs] (a) and (d) of the Joint Statement, which deal with the conditions under which a member is entitled to buy another member's currency from the Fund in exchange for its own currency.

The Drafting Committee therefore recommends that if the new wording it suggests is adopted by the [full] Committee, the attention of Committee 2 shall be drawn to the position of the Australian delegation on this matter.

The Drafting Committee wishes also to report that the suggestion was made in its discussions that many of the difficulties encountered in the drafting of the language of Article I, Section 2 might be overcome if there were a suitable general preamble to the final document of the conference, in which the basic objectives of all its work, both Fund and Bank, were clearly stated. The Drafting Committee recommends the following language for Article I, Section 3:

"To give confidence to member countries by making the Fund's resources available to them under adequate safeguards, thus providing them with opportunity to correct maladjustments in their balance of payments without resorting to measures destructive of national or international prosperity."

In accordance with its instructions, the Drafting Committee deferred consideration of Article 1, Section 4 [on promoting exchange rate stability as a purpose of the IMF].

The Drafting Committee considered Alternatives A and B of Article I, Section 6 and recommends to the Committee the following language:

"In accordance with the above objectives, to shorten the periods and lessen the degree of disequilibrium in the international balances of payments of member countries."

The Drafting Committee calls the attention of the [full] Committee to the words at the end of Article I, Alternative A, which read:

"The Fund shall be guided in all its decisions by the purposes set forth above."

The Drafting Committee recommends that the whole Committee approve the inclusion of this language at the end of Article I.]

Chairman: We will now proceed to consider the recommendations of the Drafting Committee. First we will take up Article I, Section 2, which reads, "To facilitate the expansion and balanced growth of international trade and to contribute thereby to the promotion and maintenance of high levels of employment and to the development of the sources of productive power in all member countries as primary objectives of economic policy."

South Africa: Point of order. There are not enough copies to go around. Some delegations haven't a copy. In the file room they say they haven't enough copies yet.

Secretary ([William Brown, Jr., United States]): I just received a note that says additional copies will be available in a few minutes.

Peru: In accordance with what the President [i.e., Commission Chairman] said this morning with regard to the reports of the Committee to the Commission, shall we take it that we will receive the printed report of the Drafting Committee one day and the Committee will take it up the next, giving the delegates time to read and study? In other words, we would take up this report tomorrow. [p. 2]

Chairman: I think the suggestion is well made. Since we do not have enough copies, we will defer consideration of this report until tomorrow morning's meeting of this Committee.

I wish to draw your attention to another fact: that the delegate of Egypt has submitted Alternative H.[339] That has been circulated. Has everybody a copy? That is available, and since that is new material and since some members have even up to this moment not received a copy of that alternative, I will also defer consideration of that alternative until the tomorrow morning meeting.

Now we will take up our regular agenda. Today we consider the second big topic of our Committee agenda, namely, "Subscription to the Fund." That is on page 2 of that big document—Document F-1.[340] It is Article II of the Joint Statement—Article II, Section 1. The original of the Joint Statement reads, "Member countries shall subscribe in gold and in their local funds amounts (quotas) to be agreed, which will amount

339 Document 122, p. 122.

340 The discussion that follows concerns passages in Document 32, pp. 24-27.

altogether to about $8 billion if all the United and Associated Nations subscribe to the Fund (corresponding to about $10 billion for the world as a whole)."

Alternative A, "Section 1. Countries Eligible for Membership. The members of the Fund shall be those of the countries represented at the United Nations Monetary and Financial Conference whose governments accept membership in the Fund.

"Membership in the Fund shall be open to other countries at such times and in accordance with such terms as may be prescribed by the Fund."

This is additional material, and there is no other alternative, so we will consider this section now. Any discussion on Section 1, "Countries Eligible for Membership"?

Norway ([Wilhelm Keilhau?]): As one of those tedious lawyers mentioned by Professor Tsiang, I wish to draw your [p. 3] attention to one little thing in the language. The first paragraph says that "The members of the Fund shall be those of the countries represented," etc., but the second paragraph says that "Membership in the Fund shall be open to other countries." Accordingly, I think Article II, at the beginning of the first paragraph, is wrong. There should be substituted either "founder members" or "original members" or any other phrase signifying their real position.

Chairman: Any other discussion?

Netherlands: Mr. Chairman, the Netherlands delegation thinks that an important improvement in paragraph [Alternative] A would be that no mention should be made of 8 billion or 10 billion [dollars], and particularly that the implication no longer exist that this conference should mean to imply that the neutral countries and the now enemy countries should be entitled to a share in this Fund to an aggregate quota of 2 billion, which would be 20 percent of the total and which would be far more than according to present understandings would be assigned to many of the United Nations here present. If it were possible, Mr. Chairman, to have some clarification as to whether or not the views of the Netherlands delegation are correct, we would appreciate it.

Chairman: I am sorry; I did not understand clearly your point. Will you state it again?

Netherlands: The Netherlands delegation considers it a great improvement to say that Alternative A no longer mentions the figures of 8 billion for United [and] Associated Nations subscriptions to the Fund and the figure of 10 billion as corresponding to the subscription if all countries of the world were members. The Netherlands delegation thinks that it would be wrong to imply that a total quota of 2 billion, which [p. 4] is 20 percent of the total, should be left aside by implication to the countries with which we are now at war and to the few remaining countries, because this would present such a quota for those countries as is much in excess of the quotas certain of the nations now united would probably receive under the present consideration for the Fund.

Chairman: Is there any delegate who wishes to make a remark or explanation on the point raised by the delegate of the Netherlands?

Emanuel Goldenweiser (Chairman, Drafting Committee): Mr. Chairman, I don't want to take up time, but I would say to the delegate of the Netherlands that his interpretation of the object of the change is entirely correct, that paragraph [Section] 1 of [Article II in] the Joint Statement was more an indication of the general figures that were being contemplated so it wouldn't be too wrong or too fantastic—too low a Fund or too big a Fund. But now that we have come much closer to reality, the figures are no longer appropriate, and [the] amounts involved will be the results of what would be done under [Article II,] Section 2, "Quotas."

Chairman: Any further opinion on Section 1? There has been expressed already one more opinion, that is, in the first paragraph there seems to be the need of adding a word. A member from Norway has suggested that the word "original" members of the Fund—the word "original" be inserted there. Is that agreeable to all, the addition of the word "original?"

I hear no objection. I take it that the addition of that word is agreeable to us all.

Emanuel Goldenweiser (Chairman, Drafting Committee): I am sorry to be a little late, but I think the word "original" is not a good selection, because an "original" member means that everyone joins right then and [p. 5] there. As a matter of fact, the joining might take some time in some instances, and you wouldn't want to deprive any of those members of the privilege of belonging to the original group. I think that some more neutral word would be preferable, but at the moment, it doesn't occur to me.

Norway ([Wilhelm Keilhau?]): Mr. Chairman, "founder members."

Emanuel Goldenweiser (Chairman, Drafting Committee): Couldn't that be referred to the Drafting Committee?

France: It seems to me that the word "original" or some similar word would have the drawback of implying that there are two classes of members. If such is the meaning it ought to be stated. I assumed that it is not the meaning. That is why I would propose another slight change which I believe would meet the objection of the delegate of Norway. This is my proposal: "The members of the Fund should be at first those of the countries." Later on, "Membership in the Fund," etc.

Chairman: I think if there is no discussion on some substance we had better not take the time to discuss the words yet. Is there any opinion on the substance of this section?

If not, I take it that the substance of this section is agreed to by this Committee and that the language there be referred to our Drafting Committee. If there is no objection, it is so ordered.

Now we have the extra copies of the report of the Drafting Committee, and will a Boy Scout distribute them to those who have not received copies. [341]

Now we will proceed with our regular agenda. Section 2 is on quotas. You will see that in this section there is a blank, and Schedule A can be added later. Since that paper is still under preparation, I suggest that we pass by this section and proceed to discuss [Article II], Section 3.

"Section 3. Time [p. 6] and Place of Payment. Each member shall provide the Fund at the appropriate depository with the full amount of its quota on or before the date fixed for exchange transactions in its currency to begin. Any member whose quota is increased shall provide the full amount of the increase within thirty days of the date on which the member approves the increase in its quota."

Discussion is open on Section 3, "Time and Place of Payment."

Venezuela: I should like to have an explanation of the expression "for exchange transactions in its currency to begin," at the beginning of the paragraph where it says "on or before the date fixed for exchange transactions in its currency to begin."

Emanuel Goldenweiser (Chairman, Drafting Committee): The meaning of those words is that before a country can draw on funds by the use of its quota, it must have made its deposit of its quota with the proper department. Does that answer the question of the member for Venezuela?

---

[341] Local Boy Scouts, or more precisely Cub Scouts, helped distribute documents and move microphones from speaker to speaker at the conference. See Shirley Boskey, "Bretton Woods Recalled," *International Bank Notes* (World Bank), July 1957; World Bank Archives, "Bretton Woods Conference," <http://web.worldbank.org/WBSITE/EXTERNAL/EXTABOUTUS/EXTARCHIVES/0,,contentMDK:64054691~menuPK:64319211~pagePK:36726~piPK:36092~theSitePK:29506,00.html>, viewed April 5, 2013.

Chairman: That is a very important explanation. I think that phrase puzzled more than one member of this Committee. We are more than grateful to Mr. Goldenweiser for it. It simply means before a member can draw upon the Fund for exchange, a member must pay his quota.

South Africa: The country may wish to associate itself with the Fund, but may not for a long period want to have any exchange transactions with the Fund because it does not require them. The Fund will not have the advantage of the quota of that country if the text stands as it is. I think if we are going into a club, the membership subscription should generally be paid to the club before we are admitted, and this money should be paid before you become a member; and once you are a member, other things follow. [p. 7]

Chairman: Any other opinion?

India: For example, you stated that until the subscription is paid up the country will not start operations. Similarly, can we state that unless so many members join the Fund or so much quota is paid, the Fund will not really come into existence and operate?

Emanuel Goldenweiser (Chairman, Drafting Committee): Mr. Chairman, I believe there is another clause that covers the point made by the gentleman from India. I would suggest that Mr. Maffry of the American advisers have an opportunity to throw some light on the language of the section.

United States (August Maffry): If the Committee will refer to page 49 of Document F-1, it will find listed a Section 4 of an additional Article XIII, entitled "Fixing Initial Par Values."[342] The difficulties that have been pointed out in the discussion of the last two minutes are dealt with or will be dealt with in Section 5, in this Section 5 of the additional Article XIII. Without going into the details of the proposed provision, it is contemplated that the Fund will come into operation when member countries holding a given percentage of the aggregate quotas have accepted membership. It is contemplated further that on or before a date agreed upon for the beginning of exchange operations, countries which have accepted membership will be required to pay their quotas into the Fund. In other words, it is contemplated that the Fund will come into operation in two stages: first, the acceptance of membership, and second, the payment of quotas and the beginning of exchange operations. [p. 8]

Czechoslovakia ([Jan Mládek?]): Mr. Chairman, I would strongly support the American concept of dividing operations of the Fund and the effectuation of the membership into two stages. It applies very much to

---

[342] In Document 32, p. 60.

occupied countries which participate in establishing this Fund. However, we will be unable to join the Fund if we are compelled to pay into the Fund at once. So the American concept appears very much to us.

Norway ([Wilhelm Keilhau?]): Inasmuch as this is a problem of the Fourth Commission [Committee 4] I would suggest that we do not discuss this matter anymore before it has been treated by the Fourth Commission [Committee 4]. I wish to draw attention to the fact that here we are only dealing with time and place of payment, while in those other sections we are dealing with initiation of member rights. I would say that the substance of the draft is all right.

Chairman: In connection with this section, I think we better continue with Alternative B, because the two are really closely related. I will read Alternative B, which is in substance Alternative A—it is in addition to Alternative A. Alternative B reads, "Notwithstanding the fundamental principles on payment of quotas particular arrangements may be made with countries whose currency system has been disrupted as a result of enemy occupation. Such arrangements may not extend over more than nine months i.e., after nine months, at the latest, the obligations of the country will be the same as they would have been if such an exception had not been granted. The government of the respective country has to guarantee by a specific act that the Fund will not suffer any loss because of that particular arrangement."

Is there any discussion of this paragraph? [p. 9]

Czechoslovakia ([Jan Mládek]): Mr. Chairman, this amendment has been suggested—I mean the amendment, as pointed out, is the supplement to Alternative A. It has been suggested by our delegation and we have been guided by the following reasons. We believe that although we fully agree with Alternative A, it may prove to be too rigid for the countries liberated from occupation. There will be certain irregularities present in the monetary systems. It would be of no use, I think, to try making a full list of the difficulties which may arise. Just for the purpose of elucidation I may perhaps give an instance. You know that the gold holdings of several occupied countries went into enemy hands and they are still in their hands. It is hoped that this gold will be restored to the local owners, but there is no doubt that it will take some time before the redistribution of the gold will be effected, and we feel that it would be wise not to prevent the Fund from entering into dealings with such countries because of such more or less formulation difficulties. It would be wise, I think, for two reasons. The strain put in the monetary systems in these countries will be tremendous, and of no period will it be so true as of the early transitional period after the war. Assistance delivered promptly helps best; that the money used today may be worth more than shillings thrown in tomorrow and although the countries will definitely have to find most remedies for the distorted currency situations in our own countries, it is nevertheless equally true that the common knowledge that a powerful international organization is backing up such restoration processes in a country would help greatly to restore the very shaken confidence in [p. 10] currency in this area.

There are other reasons. We are very particular about the language we are using, and we would appreciate any amendment of language, but I would like to call the attention of the Committee to two principles used in our proposal. The first one is that it is left fully to the discretion of the Fund to judge whether any such exceptional arrangement should be used, and [during] what time it should be used, and under what conditions. And secondly—the second principle is that these exceptional arrangements should be limited in time. The third one, but [a] no less important one, is that the Fund, and implicitly the other members of the Fund, should be safeguarded against any losses which would arise out of this arrangement.

Mr. Chairman, we recommend this provision to the Committee in the belief that it can't harm anybody and it can provide for a lot of help.

Netherlands: Mr. Chairman, I would like to ask a question to the member [delegate] for Czechoslovakia, who proposes the amendment. Access to the Fund is not possible for any member who has not fixed with the Fund the value of its currency. I think the situation in Prague, as described by the delegate from Czechoslovakia, allows for the succession [accession?] of her currency during the period in which it may be [most] difficult, and I understand that very well. [Tasks to be accomplished during the period will include] to fix the amounts of assets, gold available, and to arrange transactions necessary to opening relations with the Fund. I do think that in that situation it will be very difficult to fix a par value, which anyway is necessary to start relations with the Fund. Thank you very much for suggesting that point. [p. 11]

Czechoslovakia ([Jan Mládek]): It was not in my mind just to use this arrangement for somehow supplementing the existing system. I might agree with the Dutch delegation. It would be very difficult, and I think we are encroaching upon a field which exceeds the scope of our work, because it is a matter belonging to the Second Committee [Committee 2] and there have been provisions suggested by various delegates for coverage.

Poland: Mr. Chairman, I second the motion of the delegate from Czechoslovakia. I would like to say that in many countries which are now occupied by the enemy, the currency is still very much disrupted. Here is a motion put to us by the Czechoslovakian delegate, with respect to exceptional arrangements. We see it there a term of nine months, not more than nine months. For my country, I think this term will be quite sufficient, but may be for other countries it will be more advisable—it may also be for Poland—maybe I am too optimistic in that. [I propose?] to give to the Fund the facility to make arrangements for a certain period as the Fund will think necessary for the particular country, taking into account all the circumstances of this country, all the currencies which are now there in force and which must be unified and supplemented by a new currency system.

South Africa ([Jack Holloway?]): Mr. Chairman, the delegate from Czechoslovakia has brought in a very important issue here, an issue which to my mind goes a good deal beyond the particular article on which it has been raised. I think it will be generally agreed that it will be exceedingly difficult for any conference to lay down beforehand in any detail what is to be done in the case[s that] are going to be. We do not know what the conditions [p. 12] are going to be. We do not know the kind of liberation the period of nine months may mean to a particular country. It seems to me that if we tried to go ahead and lay down the details as to what is to be done to aid liberated countries, we shall simply be trying to do the impossible task. It seems to me that there will have to be somewhat general overriding clause, not a proviso to one section only, but a general overriding clause to enable the Fund to come into being before these countries are liberated, to make such arrangements and give such extensions of time to the liberated countries as may be necessary in [each] particular case.

I think perhaps it should be examined by a special subcommittee which you might appoint for that purpose, to give such latitude to such countries as is consistent with the general principles of the Fund. It will enable them to get over the difficulties with which they are faced. One thing which we do not want is when the Fund starts, it should look at this document for whatever the lawyers will make of this conference afterwards—[we do not want that] if a comma is in the wrong place, we must technically rule out the country. There must be some latitude in that way, and I think the instruction should go out from this Committee to a subcommittee to consider that problem, which is not to my mind being considered, and to bring it up for consideration to the Committee.

Iran: My remarks, Mr. Chairman, referred to Alternative A, if I may proceed now. In the Joint Statement the mode of payment of the local funds was not stated. In Alternative A it is said that the full amount must be paid. In a document which was circulated, I think, [p. 13] under the title of *Answers and Questions,*[343] this reference was made to this question, which it seems to me is very important perhaps to a number of countries represented here. It may not be necessary to require the payment of the local currency to be made in full immediately after the Fund is instituted; and if that is the case, it seems to me that it would create unnecessary difficulty for certain countries, such as mine, for instance, which have to find deposits by putting up 100 percent cover for their currency; and I would, therefore, suggest that unless it is absolutely essential that the local currency should be provided in full and immediately after the Fund comes into being, that special consideration should be given to those cases; and I would like to ask, Mr. Chairman, that if there is any particular reason why this change has been made, that it should be stated.

Norway ([Wilhelm Keilhau?]): Mr. Chairman, I should like to make a short comment on the suggestion from the delegate from South Africa. He suggested that there should be appointed a subcommittee for making a draft for special arrangements in all fields concerning the occupied countries. I will draw his attention to the fact that this can't be done by this Committee because a number of those provisions, and the most important of them, come under the heading of other committees, and that must be deferred by resolution by the Commission. But there is another thing: the representative for South Africa—maybe I [mis?]understood him—seemed to think that it would be satisfactory for the new occupied countries if it was left to the Fund to make such decisions as might be found expedient to make. From the point of the occupied [p. 14] countries, that will not be satisfactory. We must have our rights, and [they] must be given as our rights, and that I should really think that if we understand that is easier nevertheless to accept the proposal suggested by Czechoslovakia that the rights are laid down wherever we meet the programs, and I wish to add to what Mr. Mládek has said: that in this big document there are a sufficient number of alternatives which will take care of these cases. I would therefore like to support Dr. Mládek.

Poland: I think the procedure that Norway puts out in regard to the rights—I feel [that] in conformity with the principles, any rights given her will be given to them. My thought is to make such concessions as the

[343] *Questions and Answers on the International Monetary Fund,* a booklet issued by the U.S. Treasury on June 10, 1944. It is reproduced in Margaret G. de Vries and J. Keith Horsefield, *The International Monetary Fund 1945-1965: Twenty Years of International Monetary Cooperation; Volume III: Documents* (Washington, D.C.: International Monetary Fund, 1969), pp. 136-182.

circumstances may make essential in order to enable them to use those rights.

United Kingdom ([Lionel Robbins?]): I don't think it is necessary for me to say much, Mr. Chairman, because the delegate of Norway has said with his characteristic force much of what I intended to say myself: namely, it seems to me that the very important points which have been raised by various speakers do in fact far transcend the context of this particular section and it would, therefore—I submit it would be unfortunate if we were to reach a conclusion on this matter here now, or if we were to appoint a committee to deal with this specific point only. Therefore it seems appropriate—I suggest, Mr. Chairman, that we should report to the Commission that this point has been raised, and we should add that in our judgment it is a point which is best considered in conjunction with a number of other asterisks of the draft of the Joint Statement by a Special Committee of the whole Commission. [p. 15]

Reporter (Kyriakos Varvaressos, Greece): I wish to report as to the proposal of the member [delegate] from Czechoslovakia, and in connection with the proposal of the delegates from South Africa and the United Kingdom, I think the best procedure would be to apply to the Commission and ask for the appointment of another, smaller committee which will consider this matter in connection with other similar matters relating to the liberated countries.

Egypt: I wish to raise two points. One, simply to mention that the question of payment of quotas has been raised this afternoon. That, of course, will raise the whole question of the denomination in which payment has to be made. I only mention that now because I have given notice to the Secretary General of a suggestion that will raise the whole question of the common denominator in which the funds of the Fund are to be kept.[344] I leave that point then for future consideration, but the second point is different.

Occupied countries have said that they must have time before their currencies get settled down to a certain extent. In the Middle East we must make the same claim for a totally different reason. I take Egypt, for example, which I know best. At the present moment, Egyptian currency—the purchasing power of it internally has depreciated to 30 percent of its prewar value. The external purchasing power is on an exact par with sterling, but as regards to internal purchasing power, to judge by what happened in the last war, the purchasing power of our currency may be expected after the armistice to double in value inside of a year. There

[344] Document 153, pp. 164-165.

would be a very large movement in its external value, so we also in the Middle East will have a certain lapse [p. 16] of time before our currency gets settled down, but I have not the slightest doubt that it will settle down.

Chairman: It seems to me we have discussed this point long enough.[345] [p. 1 (17)]

In regard to Alternative B, I would like to summarize our discussion as follows:

1. Special consideration should be given to the countries which have been occupied. That matter concerns [not only the] matter of initial payment but a number of other matters also. This Committee suggests to the Commission that a special committee be created to consider the matter of special treatment of countries which have been occupied. Is there any objection to this summary up to the present time?

Canada: Special consideration should be given to the problem of these countries rather than to the particular country—that is to say, the problems of the countries that have been occupied.

Chairman: [2.] Special consideration too shall be given to the problem of initial payment and other related matters of the countries which have been occupied, and the Commission should make a special committee to consider the related matters.

Alternative A deals in fact simply with the matter of time and place of payment. Shall we say that so far as that section goes we see no objection, but since it is related to matters on page 49, [Article XIII,] Section 5, ["Fixing Initial Par Values," it] will be deferred until the Committee has considered that section? Is that agreed to?

Iran: Kindly repeat.

Chairman: (Summarized as above.)

Chairman: Now let us consider [Article II,] Section 2.[346] "The quotas may be revised from time to time but changes shall require a four-fifths vote and no members quota may be changed without its assent."

"[Alternative A. Section 4. Adjustment of Quotas.] The Fund may, at intervals of five years, adjust the quotas of the members. It may also, [p. 2 (18)] if it thinks fit, consider at any other time the adjustment of any particular quota at the request of the member concerned. A four-fifths

---

[345] At this point in the U.S. Treasury Library copy of the typescripts, one typescript ends and we pick up from another, which appears near the end of the volume for the full Commission I, instead of in the volume with the rest of the typescripts for Committee 1.

[346] In Document 32, pp. 25-26.

majority vote shall be required for any change in quotas and no quota shall be changed without the consent of the member concerned."

Australia ([Leslie Melville?]): I think it would be preferable to leave the Fund free to revise the quotas at any time, as it was in the original statement. I see no reason for "[The Fund may,] at intervals of five years" or "The Fund may from time to time adjust the quotas of members."

United States (Emanuel Goldenweiser): The idea in this section was that the Fund would be expected to review the whole matter every five years, but it could at the request of the member or members take it up at any time that it saw fit. I think that, anyway, meets the suggestion made by the member from Australia, but if it does not, there would be no objection on the part of the United States delegation to having the words "at intervals of five years" changed to "from time to time."

Norway ([Wilhelm Keilhau?]): I should like to speak in favor of retaining the clause as it is. "In uncertain times" means "no time," and I think any expression "from time to time" wherever it is used means it is never considered. It will be necessary in my mind to fix a definite time. That is one side of the picture. But there is also another side. I think that it will be of certain importance to governments, I should say, a very great importance, that these quotas which they have now got should not be revised for five years. That gives them better ground to stand on. I am very much in favor of the proposal as it is being made now. I think it is very wise. [p. 3 (19)]

Brazil ([Eugênio Gudin?]): I wonder whether the matter would not easily be reconciled. "The Fund will at intervals of five years consider the advisability of adjusting the quotas." That means that every five years the Fund will study the matter and consider the advisability or otherwise of adjusting the quotas, and then if it sees fit at any other time, the Fund will at intervals of five years consider the advisability of adjusting the quotas. I wonder if that is of any help.

Chairman: Change the first sentence to read, "The Fund will, at intervals of five years, consider the advisability of adjusting the quotas of the members." The rest will remain as before.

Australia: That still does not suffice. If something was added at "any other time" to make it clear that it was not limited [to once every five years]...

United States (Emanuel Goldenweiser): This section becomes clarified to the point where it is reasonably clear there is no substantial difference. We have the sentiment of those who have spoken, and it seems to me that it would be desirable to have the language deferred to the Language Committee.

India: I should like the word "review" instead of "adjust." "Adjust" carries implication that the only function of this assembly is to change the quotas of different countries. And another drafting point: substitute the word "shall" for the word "may."

Chairman: We have discussed long enough on this matter. It is the sense that we should have a definite opportunity at intervals of five years to reconsider the quotas. We also wish that even before [p. 4] (20) the five-year period [the Fund should have] the freedom to consider quotas. The language of this paragraph should cover both those needs. If agreeable to this Committee, we will refer this section to our Subcommittee on Language as to cover both those needs expressed in this discussion. Is that agreeable?

So order.

We shall proceed to Section 3: "The obligatory gold subscription of a member country shall be fixed at 25 percent of its subscription (quota) or 10 percent of its holdings of gold and gold convertible exchange, whichever is the smaller."[347]

"Alternative A. Section 5. Initial Payments. Each member shall pay in gold the smaller of (a) 25 percent of its quota or (b) 10 percent of its official holdings of gold and gold convertible exchange [on __(date)__]. In the case of any member occupied by the enemy whose holdings are not ascertainable as of __(date)__, the Fund shall fix an appropriate alternative date." Any discussion on this section, Section 5, Alternative A?

Haiti ([Pierre Chauvet]): I would like to ask the United States why the following phraseology was dropped: "A member country may include in the legal reserves and the published statement of the reserves of its gold and foreign exchange an amount not to exceed its gold contribution to the Fund."[348]

United States (Emilio "Peter" Collado): The phrasing in that document was rather a broad suggestion regarding the way the Fund might be handled in connection with individual payments, etc. Whether or not a country decides whether it is desirable to include any reference to its membership [p. 5 (21)] in the Fund in its legislation in connection with its reserves requirements is purely a matter of domestic legislation. I do not believe it would be proper for an international agreement on the subject to dictate the form of the reserves of international central banks.

---

347 In Document 32, p. 26.

348 We are unsure when the phraseology was considered. It does not appear in the Joint Statement or any of the alternatives.

Iraq: Concerning the position of any of those countries which hold no gold or no convertible exchange: in the case of the Iraq, we have no gold holding. As to whether we have any gold convertible exchange would appear to depend upon the definition which is given to that expression. Are we right in assuming that the country holding no gold and no convertible exchange contributes nothing under this?

United States: That is a purely mathematical question: 10 percent of nothing is nothing.

Iran: Alternative A to Section 2 may apply equally to this alternative. "Each member shall pay the balance of its quota in its own currency."

Chairman: That point is covered in the Joint Statement, page 29.[349] Any further discussion?

Poland: Two of the points raised in Alternative A are points that we have just referred back for further consideration after certain other things have happened. Is not the only point for consideration whether these proportions of 10 and 25 percent are checkable?

Norway ([Wilhelm Keilhau?]): In the Joint Statement [Article] II, [Section] 3, ["Time and Place of Payment," it says],"The obligatory gold subscription of a member country shall be fixed at 25 percent [of its subscription (quota) or 10 percent of its holdings of gold and gold convertible exchange, whichever is the smaller]. [p. 6 (22)] It is written in Alternative A, "Each member shall pay the gold the smaller of 25 percent of its quota or 10 percent of its official holdings of gold [on __(date)__]" and "Each member shall pay the balance of its quota in its own currency." Here is made a substitution which I should like to ask about. According to the Joint Statement, any country which thinks that it has enough of gold, or which might be very fond of gold, could pay up to 100 percent of its quota in gold. It is written that it shall pay as a maximum 25 percent and the rest in its national currency. I think I prefer the more flexible system of the Joint Statement, and I should like to ask about this point and I will come back to it in time.

United States (Emanuel Goldenweiser): It isn't intended to insist that the country pay not more than 25 percent, so that those taken care of in [Article III,] Section 7 ["Repurchase by a Member of Its Currency Held by the Fund,"] on page 11[350]—the intent of the matter is to indicate in [Article III,] Section 5 ["Convertibility of Foreign Held Balances"] the minimum that is required in gold, and not the maximum.

---

[349] Article VII, Section 7 ("Form of Holdings of Currency"), in Document 32, pp. 49-50.

[350] In Document 32, p. 33.

Norway ([Wilhelm Keilhau?]): I think it should be put in here, at least.

United States (Emanuel Goldenweiser): The language should be changed but the intent is clear.

Norway ([Wilhelm Keilhau?]): Insert "the minimum of" or "at least."

Chairman: The Committee accepted the meeting of the sense of this section and decided that the language be left to the Language [Drafting] Committee. It is so ordered. We will take up at this point tomorrow morning.

14

Commission I, Committee 1
Purposes, Policies, and Quotas of the Fund
Fourth meeting: summary
July 6, 1944, 10:00 a.m.[351]

Purposes of the IMF • Credit balances accumulated during the war • Payments when quotas are changed • Gold subscriptions by countries damaged by war • Prices of gold purchases and sales by members • Maximum and minimum rates of exchange • Compliance with gold parities • Violation of exchange regulations of other members • Restrictions on current (current-account) transactions

Committee 1 begins by considering the report of its Drafting Committee, deferred from the previous meeting. After debate in which delegates from New Zealand, India, and Australia advocate that Article I, on the purposes of the IMF, contain a more explicit emphasis on economic development in one of its clauses, the committee accepts the Drafting Committee's recommendations on that and some other clauses of the article, with an added clause emphasizing that the IMF should be guided by the purposes in Article I and with the proviso that India may bring up its reservation for consideration by Commission I if it wishes.

Egypt proposes to add to Article I a clause adding as a purpose of the IMF the promotion of multilateral settlement of blocked wartime balances. India, which like Egypt has accumulated large credits in pounds sterling from British payments for war supplies—credits that it cannot use except with other countries that use sterling as their anchor currency—supports Egypt's proposed alternative. Poland, the United Kingdom, the United States, France, and China oppose the alternative, arguing that asking the IMF to resolve the problem of blocked balances would overburden it, chairman Tingfu Tsiang suggests reporting Egypt's proposed alternative and a summary of the committee's discussion to Commission I.

The committee accepts without discussion a proposal dealing with Article II, Alternative A, Section 6 ("Payments when Quotas Are Changed"). It then turns to

[351] Summarized in Document 172, pp. 216-217.

Article II, Section 3, Alternative B, which proposes to reduce by 50 to 75 percent the gold subscriptions of countries that have suffered from enemy occupation. After the USSR and Belgium express their support, the chairman suggests referring the matter to Commission I.

The committee then takes up Article IX ("Obligations of Member Countries"). After discussion, the chairman refers Sections 1 and 2, and parts of Section 3, to the Drafting Committee. Section 1 deals with the obligation of member countries not to buy and sell gold at a price that departs from parity (the central rate of exchange) by more than a prescribed margin. Section 2 deals with maximum and minimum rates for exchange transactions. The committee agreeing on the substantive point that exchange rates should remain within specified margins. The parts of Section 3 the committee touches on are those about compliance with gold parities and violation of the exchange regulations of other members.

Finally, the committee considers the obligation not to impose restrictions on current transactions, that is, transactions connected with payment for goods and services as opposed to capital transactions involving financial assets or investments. It is obvious from the discussion that there are differing ideas of how to define current transactions, though Emanuel Goldenweiser of the United States remarks that there is an understanding that the control of capital transactions remains with each country, and that the IMF agreement will not commit members to remove capital controls. The chairman refers the matter to Commission I.

The fourth meeting of the Committee began with a discussion of the report of the Drafting Committee. The revised wording of Article I, Section 2, Alternative C (page 1b)[352] was considered. This alternative was sponsored by the Indian delegation, and proposes that there be included in the purposes of the Fund [the phrase] "To assist in the fuller utilization of the resources of economically underdeveloped countries."

Professor [Lionel] Robbins of the United Kingdom said that he believed the ideas of India could be adequately met in a preamble covering the whole work of the conference.

Mr. [Walter] Nash of New Zealand said that there were three objectives that should be kept in mind if the Fund were to be successful. These are (1) the expansion of trade; (2) a fuller utilization of resources; (3) a better distribution of real income. These objectives should be fully stated, but Mr. Nash agreed that he would be satisfied if they were covered in the Preamble [i.e., Article I, "Purposes"].

Mr. [Leslie]Melville of Australia agreed with Mr. Nash.

---

[352] In Document 32, p. 23.

Mr. [Tingfu] Tsiang [of China], the Chairman,[353] said that while the wording was not perfect it was as good as could be agreed upon. He, therefore, suggested that the wording of the Drafting Committee be accepted.

[Sir Shanmukham] Chetty of India desired to suggest a new wording.

[Professor Lionel] Robbins ([United Kingdom]) proposed that India reserve the right to raise the question again if their views were not met in the Preamble, but that in the meantime they accept tentatively the present wording of the Drafting Committee.

[Sir Shanmukham] Chetty ([India]) agreed to this. [p. 2]

Mr. [Walter] Nash ([New Zealand]) then suggested the words "unused resources" instead of "productive power" and asked the meaning of "productive power."

The **Chairman** replied that the words of Mr. Nash were considered and rejected by the Committee, since they implied capitalistic development.

Mr. Eugênio Gudin of Brazil said that it was intended that the Fund confine its operations to current transactions and that there should be a distinction between the purposes of the Fund and those of the Bank. The words "unused resources" implied investment and were more appropriate for the Bank.

Mr. [Kyriakos] Varvaressos of Greece said that he believed the present wording as proposed by the Drafting Committee was more comprehensive than that suggested by Mr. Nash.

The **Chairman** then said that the subject had been discussed to the limit of fruitfulness and suggested that the Committee accept the report of Article I, Section 2, with the understanding that if any delegation was dissatisfied it could raise the question subsequently.

The report of the Drafting Committee on Article I, Sections 3 and 6 was accepted. The Committee also accepted the recommendation of the Drafting Committee that the addition at the end of Article I, Alternative A, page 1a, which says, "The Fund shall be guided in all its decisions by the purposes set forward above," be included at the end of Article I.

The Committee then considered [adding to Article I] Alternative H, submitted by Egypt, which reads, "To promote the multilateral settlement of foreign credit balances accumulated during the war."[354]

---

[353] For uniformity, we have changed most subsequent references to "Mr. Tsiang" to "the Chairman."

[354] Document 122, p. 122.

The representative of **Egypt** discussed at length the relation of the balances to Egypt's economic position. He outlined the United States proposal regarding blocked balances contained in the July 10, 1943 draft of the Fund.[355] [p. 3]

Mr. [A.D.] Shroff of India supported what the Egyptian representative had said and made a vigorous presentation of India's economic problems. He read from the earlier United Kingdom plan for a clearing union.[356] He said that it was his desire that the Fund provide at least some machinery for converting a portion of the blocked balances into liquid form.

The **Polish** representative took exception to Mr. Shroff's position and pointed out that Poland had debts due from Germany, but did not consider it appropriate that the Fund be burdened with these balances.

Professor [Lionel] Robbins of the United Kingdom replied to the representatives of India and Egypt, saying that his government recognized the seriousness of the problem and was not unaware of the cost of the war to these countries, both in blood as well as in material resources. Nonetheless, he said, the Fund should not be asked to settle this stupendous problem, and the United Kingdom had a fixed objective to burdening the Fund with it.

Mr. [Emanuel] Goldenweiser ([United States]) supported Professor Robbins, saying that the United States was fully aware of the difficulties of the countries owning [owing?] the balances. We were slightly embarrassed, he said, by an earlier attempt to solve the problem before we had given it really mature consideration. He called attention to Article V, Section 1, page 21, on "Capital Transactions,"[357] which

---

[355] "Preliminary Draft Outline of a Proposal for an International Stabilization Fund of the United and Associated Nations," whose main author was Harry Dexter White, published by the U.S. government on July 10, 1943. It can be found in "Postwar International Monetary Stabilization," *Federal Reserve Bulletin,* June 1943, pp. 501-506.

[356] "Proposals for an International Clearing Union," whose main author was John Maynard Keynes, published by the British government in April 1943 (White Paper Cmd. 6437). It can be found in "Postwar International Monetary Stabilization," *Federal Reserve Bulletin,* June 1943, pp. 506-521.

[357] In Document 32, p. 40. The version of this section in the Joint Statement says in part, "A member country may not use the Fund's resources to meet a large or sustained outflow of capital, and the Fund may require a member to exercise controls to prevent such use of the resources of the Fund. This provision is not intended to prevent the use of the Fund's resources for capital transaction of reasonable amount required for the expansion of exports or in the ordinary

provides that while the Fund's resources are not to meet a large outflow of capital, it is not intended to prevent the use of the Fund's resources for capital transactions of a reasonable amount. To go beyond this, however, he said, would be unwise. Therefore, to refer to war balances and to imply that the Fund might facilitate a solution of the problem would be misleading. [p. 4]

Mr. [André] Istel of France agreed with what had been said by Professor Robbins, Mr. Goldenweiser, and the Polish representative. He said that France, like Poland, had debts due from Germany but was not asking the Fund to help in their liquidation.

Mr. [Tingfu] Tsiang, [speaking in his capacity as a delegate from China,] said that China was also in this position.

The **Chairman** then suggested that with reference to Alternative H, the Committee report this alternative, together with the sense of the discussion, to Commission I.

He then turned to the agenda on Document F-1 and referred to Article II, Alternative A, Section 6 (page 4), dealing with "Payments When Quotas Are Changed."[358] This was accepted without discussion.

The discussion then turned to Alternative B (page 4a), which has to do with the reduction in gold payments by countries which have suffered from enemy occupation and hostilities.

The **Chairman** also read Alternative C, which is a variation of Alternative B.

The representative from [the] **USSR, Mr. [A.P.] Morozov,** read a statement of the Russian position on this proposal.[359]

Baron [René] Boël of Belgium agreed with the proposal, but disapproved of the feature that the reduction should vary according to the amount of damage. He said this would require the Fund to evaluate the damage for each country. All countries damaged by enemy occupation, he said, should be treated alike and should have their gold payments under this alternative reduced by 25 percent, namely, [to] 75 percent of the amount that they would otherwise pay.

The **Chairman** said that this question was related to that raised by Czechoslovakia regarding the date of payment, and which had been

---

course of trade, banking, or other business." The language in Alternative A, added for the preliminary draft, is similar, although it says "request" instead of "require."

358 The text discussed in the next several paragraphs is in Document 32, pp. 26-27.

359 We have found no record of the statement.

referred to the Ad Hoc Committee [on Special Problems of Liberated Areas]. The present problem, he said, has to do with the [p. 5] amount of payment. He said that this should also be referred to Commission I. There was no dissent.

The **Chairman** then took up Article IX, Section 1 (["Gold Purchases Based on Par Value"], page 38), which has to do with the obligation of member countries not to buy and sell gold at a price which departs from parity by more than a prescribed margin.[360]

Professor [Lionel] Robbins ([United Kingdom]) said that Committee 2 had questioned whether Article IX ["Obligations of Member Countries"] should not be considered by them. He suggested a joint session with Committee 2.

The **Chairman** said that he had talked with Mr. [Harry Dexter] White, chairman of Commission I, and informed him that Committee 1 did not object to a discussion of this subject by Committee 2. Mr. White informed [the Chairman] that a joint committee might be appointed on this question and that Committee 1 should proceed with its assignment. [The Chairman] said that Committee 1 was, therefore, required to continue with its assignment.

In response to an inquiry as to the meaning of Section 2, which was missing and to be inserted later, **Mr. [Emanuel] Goldenweiser ([United States])**[361] replied that he had no information.

The Committee then considered Alternative A, Section 2 [of Article IX, "Foreign Exchange Dealings Based on Parity"]. The representative from **Czechoslovakia** inquired as to the meaning of the words, "from or to the monetary authorities" in the sentence which reads, "No member country shall buy or sell gold from or to the monetary authorities of another member at prices [which vary from the agreed parity of its currency by more than the prescribed margin]." [p. 6]

Mr. [Emanuel] Goldenweiser ([United States]) replied that it was intended to deal only with governments, and that since monetary authorities vary from country to country, the language was in general terms.

The **Netherlands** representative asked whether the language was intended to exclude transaction with nonmember countries.

---

[360] In Document 32, pp. 54-55.

[361] From here until the end of meeting, Goldenweiser seems to be speaking in his capacity as the chairman of the Drafting Committee of Committee 1, not as a delegate of the United States.

Mr. [Emanuel] Goldenweiser ([United States]) replied that the intention was merely to require countries to stay within the specified margin in the transaction.

The **Chairman** referred the question to the Drafting Committee and turned to Section 2 on page 39, paragraph (a), which deals with maximum and minimum rates for exchange transactions.[362]

Mr. [Walter] Nash of New Zealand questioned this phraseology and feared that the wording implied the Fund had the right to fix rates, as distinct from specifying the range.

Mr. [Emanuel] Goldenweiser ([United States]) said that the intention was that the Fund merely fixed maximum and minimum points from parity; parity being determined in accordance with other provisions.

Mr. [Walter] Nash ([New Zealand]) suggested this be referred to the Drafting Committee since the wording was ambiguous. He agreed, he said, with the substance as explained by Mr. Goldenweiser.

Mr. [Esteban] Carbo of Ecuador inquired whether it was possible to fix identical percentages for all countries. He believed that the prescribed variation should vary.

The **Netherlands** representative referred to the place in this section regarding the percentage of variation. He believed the amount of variation should be discussed. [p. 7]

Mr. [Emanuel] Goldenweiser ([United States]) said that the spread should take into consideration such things as cost of transportation and other items which were included in the familiar gold points under the old gold standard. He said that the range would be determined for each rate within the prescribed range.

The **Chairman** referred the question to the Drafting Committee.

He then took up Article IX, Alternative A, Section 3, paragraph (b), page 39 ["Foreign Exchange Dealings Based on Par Values"]. The discussion turned to the last sentence of this paragraph, which says, "A member whose monetary authorities in fact freely buy and sell gold within the prescribed range, [to settle international transactions,] shall be deemed to be fulfilling this undertaking."

Mr. [Emanuel] Goldenweiser ([United States]) explained that the country was under obligation to see that its rates did not vary beyond the

---

362 In Document 32, p. 54. In the Joint Statement, the section read, "(a) The Fund shall prescribe maximum and minimum rates for exchange transactions in the currencies of member, which shall not differ by more than _____ percent from parity."

allowed amount, and that buying and selling gold would be the more usual method of accomplishing this.

The **Peruvian** representative said that some countries could not sell gold, but could merely sell foreign exchange.

The **Chairman** referred this question to the Drafting Committee.

The Committee then considered [Article IX, Alternative A, Section 3,] paragraph (c), which deals with the obligation of a member to prevent violation of exchange regulations of other members.

Mr. [Emanuel] Goldenweiser ([United States]) said that the intention was that a country would agree to attempt to cooperate and not to tolerate violations of other members' authorized regulations. Legal technicalities, he said, were involved, and suggested that this be referred to the Drafting Committee.

This was done, and the Committee was asked to postpone its consideration of this paragraph until Committee 2 had completed its consideration of matters relating to this question. [p. 8]

The Committee then considered Article IX, Alternative A, Section 4 (["Exchange Controls on Current Payments"], page 40[363]), which refers to the obligation not to impose restrictions on current transactions [unless authorized by the Articles of Agreement or approved by the IMF].

The **Czechoslovak** representative asked if there was any attempt to define the meaning of "current international transactions."

Mr. [Emanuel] Goldenweiser ([United States]) replied that this was being done along with the preparation of definitions of other subjects. Considerable discussion took place as to the precise nature of the exchange control which member countries obligate themselves to eliminate under this section.

Mr. [Kyriakos] Varvaressos of Greece said that this section did not prevent exchange control for purposes other than current transactions.

Professor [Lionel] Robbins ([United Kingdom]) said that there was confusion between the institution [of] exchange control and policies of exchange control.

Mr. [Walter] Nash of New Zealand desired that it be clearly stated that control of exchange was not vested in the hands of an outside body. New Zealand desires, he said, to be able to control all types of exchange transactions.

Professor [Lionel] Robbins ([United Kingdom]) said that there was nothing in the agreement which asked for the abandonment of the

---

[363] In Document 32, p. 55.

institution [of] exchange control and that control of capital transactions was permitted.

Mr. [Zygmunt] Karpinski of Poland referred to the absence in the present draft of earlier provisions on this question.

Mr. [Emanuel] Goldenweiser ([United States]) said that Committee 2 is discussing the question of the rights to control capital movements and that there is an understanding that control of capital movements remains with each individual country. He suggested that this question be referred to Commission I with the request that there be elucidation of the extent to which control may [p. 9] be exercised. The question would then be referred back to this Committee or to Committee 2.

Mr. [Leslie] Melville of Australia said that he felt it was clear that the intention is to prevent restrictions on exchange transactions which interfere with imports or with the payment of interest and dividends.

The **Chairman** referred this to Commission I.

The meeting adjourned.

15

Commission I, Committee 1
Purposes, Policies, and Quotas of the Fund
Fifth meeting: draft minutes
July 8, 1944, 9:30 a.m.[364]

Report of Drafting Committee • Acceptance of Drafting Committee recommendations on sections of article on subscription to the IMF • Obligations of member countries • Gold purchases based on parity prices • Foreign exchange dealings based on par values • Obligations with respect to gold and gold-convertible exchange • Illegal exchange transactions • Deferral of certain proposals

Because the minutes are brief, we omit narrative summaries for this and the next meeting of Committee 1.

The Chairman announced that the procedures of the Committee would be governed by the document on procedures issued by the Steering Committee.

Document No. 202, "Status of Committee Assignments,"[365] was circulated and the Chairman requested members to note what action was taken on the various items to be considered so as to keep their records up to date.

The second report of the Drafting Committee[366] was presented by its Chairman, Dr. Goldenweiser.

The Committee accepted the language of the Drafting Committee for Article II, Section 1 (page 2), "Countries Eligible for Membership," and for Article II, Section 4 (page 3), "Adjustment of Quotas," with a slight change in wording. The Committee also accepted the recommendation of

---

[364] Published almost unchanged as Document 224, pp. 286-288.

[365] Document 192, pp. 230-233.

[366] Document 202, pp. 259-267.

the Drafting Committee to retain the language of Article II, Section 3, Alternative A (page 2), "Time and Place of Payment."[367]

The Committee approved the language of the Drafting Committee for Article II, Section 5 (page 4), "Initial Payments," with a minor change.

The Committee debated the language of the Drafting Committee on Article IX, Section 2, "Gold Purchases Based on Parity Prices" (page 38). Various members felt that the language was too rigid since it excluded certain gold purchases at prices beyond the prescribed margin which might be perfectly consistent with the purposes of the Fund. A request was made not to exclude payments involving no international transactions made as bonuses to the gold-mining industry in gold-producing countries, and other legitimate variations, such as sales to meet a hoarding demand, were also suggested. The close relationship of this clause to the work of Committee 2 was emphasized and the provision was referred back to the Drafting Committee with instructions to consult with Committee 2 and report again on the matter.

The Committee considered the language of the drafting committee for Article IX, Section 3, paragraph (a), "Foreign Exchange Dealings Based on Par Values" (page 39). The discussion of the Committee revealed two questions of substance: (1) whether the margin to be prescribed should be for spot and for futures and other types of contract, or whether there should be only one maximum range for spot transactions, and (2) whether it was intended that there should be only a general maximum range applicable to all countries, or whether the Fund should prescribe, within this overall maximum, a range for each member country. This section was referred again to the Drafting Committee with the same instructions as were given with respect to Section 2.

The Committee considered the language recommended by the Drafting Committee for Article IX, Section 3, paragraph (b) (page 39). The Committee discussed the [p. 2] necessity and exact force of the last sentence, which states that a member freely buying gold and gold-convertible exchange has fulfilled its obligation under this paragraph. The Chairman referred this section back to the Drafting Committee.

The Chairman read to the Committee Alternative B of Article IX, Section 3, paragraph (c) (page 39), which deals with illegal exchange transactions carried on in a member country in the currencies of other members. Since the provision is still in the Drafting Committee, the amendment was referred to the Drafting Committee.

---

[367] Page numbers from this paragraph through the next to last paragraph of the minutes refer to the conference version of Document 32, pp. 21-60.

The time of the Committee had run out before it was able to consider the following proposals which have been circulated as alternatives to the articles assigned to it: Alternatives C and D under Article II, which provide for the inclusion of silver in the subscriptions of the member countries and which appear on pages 2b and 4b of SA/1 [Document 32]; and Article IX, Section 8, Alternative A (page 43b),[368] which adds to the obligations assumed by members that of cooperating with other members in rendering permissible and approved exchange restrictions effective.

The meeting adjourned at 11 a.m.

[368] Document 145, p. 157; Document 146, p. 157; and Document 191, p. 230.

16

Commission I, Committee 1
Purposes, Policies, and Quotas of the Fund
Sixth (final) meeting: draft minutes
July 12, 1944, 2:30 p.m.[369]

Recommendations of Drafting Committee • Date for initial payment of quota subscriptions • Purposes of the IMF • Partial payment of quota subscriptions in silver • Cooperation in controlling capital movements • Margins for gold parities • Exchange transactions exceeding margins

At the request of the Drafting Committee of Commission I, the Chairman resubmitted to the Committee that portion of the language of Article II, Section 5 ["Initial Payments"], which reads as follows:

"Each member shall pay in gold as a minimum either (a) twenty-five percent of its quota or (b) ten percent of its official holdings of gold and gold convertible exchange[370] as at _____, whichever is smaller. If the holdings of any member are not ascertainable as at such date because its territories have been occupied by the enemy the Fund shall fix an appropriate alternative date."

The Committee was requested to fill in the date in this provision. After some discussion the Committee agreed to refer this question directly to Commission I on the ground that the various delegations had not had time to consider the problems involved.

The Committee, after consideration, agreed to drop Alternative F of Article I (page 1c of SA/1), relating to the purposes of the Fund.[371] It also considered Alternatives C [page 2b][372] and D [page 4b][373] under Article II,

---

[369] Published almost unchanged as Document 326, pp. 541-543.

[370] The draft minutes have a footnote here that says, "The phrase 'gold and gold convertible exchange' is subject to definition and to such change in terminology as may be agreed upon."

[371] In Document 32, p. 24.

[372] Document 145, p. 157.

which provide for a payment of a portion of a member's subscription in silver, and referred them to Commission III. The Committee then considered Article IX, Section 8, Alternative A [page 43b],[374] which makes it an obligation of member countries to cooperate with other members in the control of international movements of capital. Since it appeared to the Committee that this objective was covered under new language to be proposed for Article IX, Section 3, paragraph (c) [page 39],[375] this Alternative was not pressed.

The Committee then received the third report of its Drafting, or Language, Committee.[376] It agreed to the recommendation to accept Section 4, Article I,[377] which deals with the promotion of exchange stability, and Section 2 ["Gold Purchases Based on Parity Prices"], Article IX (page 38 of SA/1), which reads as follows:

"The Fund shall prescribe for transactions in gold by member countries a permissible margin above and below the agreed parity. No member country shall buy gold at a price above the prescribed range, nor sell gold at a price below that range."

In accepting this language, the Committee felt that member countries were not excluded thereby from giving special encouragement to their gold-mining industries for purely domestic reasons by means other than paying a higher price for gold. [p. 2]

The Committee received the recommendation of its Drafting Committee of the following language for Article IX, Section 3 ["Foreign Exchange Dealings Based on Par Value"], paragraph (a):

" (a) The Fund shall prescribe a uniform maximum margin not exceeding _____% by which rates for transactions in the currencies of members may differ from parity. In exceptional circumstances the Fund may authorize a member country to establish a wider margin for transactions in its currency."

Since in the Committee's view this matter clearly related to problems in Committee 2, it referred the suggestion to Commission I for consideration by the appropriate *ad hoc* committee. It was pointed out in the discussion that the proposed language does not clearly provide that the margin fixed could not be changed from time to time by the Fund but was to be a maximum determined at this conference. The points of

---

373 Document 146, p. 157.

374 Document 191, p. 230.

375 The original language is in Document 32, pp. 54-55.

376 Document 307, pp. 501-502.

377 In Document 32, p. 22.

substance referred to Commission I were the determination of the figure to be inserted and the question of whether the margin should apply to spot transactions only or also to futures.

The Committee considered Alternatives A and B of Article IX, Section 3, paragraph (c), pages 39 and 39a, Document SA/1,[378] and, in addition, new language proposed by the Drafting Committee reading as follows:

"(c) Exchange transactions in the territory of one member involving the currency of any other member which are outside the prescribed variation from parity set forth in (a) above shall not be enforceable in the territory of any member country.

"Each member agrees to cooperate with other members in their efforts to effectuate exchange regulations prescribed by such members in accordance with this Agreement."

The delegation of the United Kingdom expressed willingness to recede from Alternative B, providing Alternative A were accepted; and the United States delegate, expressing a preference for the Drafting Committee language, requested more time for consideration. The Committee referred all three alternatives to Commission I with the recommendation that they be worded in a manner similar to that proposed for paragraph (a).

This action completed the work of the Committee on all the matters assigned to it for which material had been provided.

[378] In Document 32, pp. 54-55, and Document 236, p. 334.

17

Commission I, Committee 2
Operations of the Fund
First meeting: transcript
July 4, 1944, 11:30 a.m.[379]

Channels for financial dealings between the IMF and members • Limitations governing the use of IMF resources • Purchases (borrowings) of foreign exchange and balance of payments cycles

The subject of Committee 2 was "Operations of the Fund." Those operations included the all-important matters of declaring and changing par values (exchange rates) with gold, and outlining the terms on which the IMF would lend. The committee chairman was Pavel Maletin, Deputy People's Commissar (deputy minister) of Finance of the USSR. In practice, he did not run its meetings because he was not comfortable in English, the working language of the conference. William Mackintosh of Canada, the vice chairman, therefore assumed those duties.[380] *Mackintosh was a professor of economics at Queen's University in Kingston, Ontario, who had been recruited into Canada's Ministry of Finance after World War II began. At the time of the conference he was a special assistant to the deputy minister of finance, a high-level position.*

The committee begins its work with consideration of Article III ("Transactions with the Fund"). It first disposes of a change in wording in a section specifying through what government agencies the IMF shall conduct its financial dealings with member countries.

Next, it takes up the more controversial matter of limitations governing the use of the IMF's resources. Several alternatives are discussed. Ned Brown, a U.S. delegate

---

379 Summarized in Document 104, pp. 119-120. The typescript contains a handwritten date of July 3, but the conference minutes and other documents indicate that the session occurred on July 4. The transcripts also contain minutes of this session, which we have not reproduced because they are almost the same as Document 104.

380 A.F.W. Plumptre, *Three Decades of Decision: Canada and the World Monetary System, 1944-75* (Toronto: McClelland and Stewart, 1977), p. 42.

who was president of a large Chicago bank and president of an advisory council to the Federal Reserve Board of Governors, explains that the American alternative is intended to clarify the extent to which members may gain access to IMF resources by right versus the extent to which access is a privilege granted by the IMF. He explains that in the American view, a certain amount of access is a right. At the suggestion of an unidentified delegate, the vice chairman defers discussion of the U.S alternative until a later discussion of scarce currencies.

Australia and France then explain their alternatives. Australia is represented by Leslie Melville, an economic adviser to the Commonwealth Bank of Australia, a government-owned bank that exercised some central banking functions. Australia proposes to loosen the conditions under which a country may purchase (IMF jargon for "borrow") the currency of another member through the IMF. Melville argues that looser conditions are necessary to meet the needs of countries that have large swings in their balance of payments. Australia falls into that category because commodities, which fluctuate more in price than manufactured goods, are a large share of its exports. France proposes to allow a carryover of borrowing capacity from year to year to fix a clause that could offer perverse incentives to borrow. The United States and United Kingdom oppose the alternatives, on the grounds that existing provisions are flexible enough to accommodate larger borrowings if countries really need them. Mexico and South Africa also express skepticism about the alternatives. Brazil and New Zealand, which like Australia are dependent on commodities for export revenue, support the Australian and French alternatives. The meeting ends with the major participants having expressed their views, but without a resolution of the issue.

Edward Bernstein, Assistant Director of Monetary Research at the U.S. Treasury and executive secretary of the American delegation, appears here, as in later meetings of Committee 2, to explain the thinking behind certain provisions of the draft agreement on the IMF. He was the American delegate most deeply involved with the details of drafting the agreement, and had an unmatched understanding of its technical details.

Delegate [and Committee Chairman Pavel] Maletin of [the] Union of Soviet Socialist Republics presided until appointment of [the] Vice Chairman, delegate [William] Mackintosh of Canada.

Vice Chairman (William Mackintosh, Canada): As the Chairman said, the assignment of this Committee is concerned with [Article III, "Transactions with the Fund"], Section 3 ["Limitation on the Fund's Operations"] and the following sections of the Joint Statement and the Committee Document 1.[381]

381 To be precise, the Committee was assigned Articles III ("Transactions with the Fund"), IV ("Par Values of Member Currencies"), V ("Capital

The first question to be considered by the Committee is the sale of exchange. You will find material has been prepared by the Secretariat on pages 5 to 7 of Document F-1.[382] This material covers Section 3, provisions 1, 2 and 3 [i.e., Article III, Sections 1-3] of the Joint Statement of Principles. If it is agreeable to the Committee, I would propose that we proceed with the discussion of Document F-1 section by section. [Concerning] the first section of the document [Section 1, "Agencies Dealing with the Fund"], for the first section of the Joint Statement there is an Alternative A suggestion. The original statement, "Member countries shall deal with the Fund [only through their Treasury, Central Bank, Stabilization Fund, or other fiscal agencies. The Fund's account in a member's currency shall be kept by the Central Bank of the member country]," is replaced by a slightly revised statement, "[Each member country shall deal with the Fund only through its Treasury, Central Bank, Stabilization Fund, or other similar agency *and the Fund shall deal only through the same agencies.*"] The second sentence of the Joint Statement, we are told, is to be dealt with elsewhere in the document.

Is there any discussion of that pure and formal change in wording? Would you propose an alternative wording?

Cuba ([Felipe Pazos]): I do suggest that at the beginning of the paragraph, the phrase "except as otherwise provided" should be introduced, so that made the other way, [the] "for further discussion" Alternative A, page 8 [phrase] "borrow such currency within that country from some other source," and the phrase "except as otherwise provided," would permit the discussion of this alternative without modifying substantially the clause which has been proposed. [p. 2]

Vice Chairman: I would suggest it would probably be better in dealing with Alternative A on page 8. Having dealt with it, we might then come back to this clause, if there is any consequential amendment that would have to be made. Is there any other discussion, or is it your wish we should pass on to Section 2 ["Conditions Governing Use of the Fund's Resources"]? Under Section 2 you have very substantial amendments in Alternative A and additional amendments in Alternatives C and B. The meeting is open for discussion of proposals on Section 2.[383]

Transactions"), VI ("Apportionment of Scarce Currencies"), and X ("Transitional Arrangements").

[382] In Document 32, pp. 27-31.

[383] The discussion below is about the terms on which member countries may borrow from the IMF. Alterative A, proposed by the United States, is a long proposal that adds detail to the provisions agreed in the Joint Statement. Australia's Alternative B and France's Alternative D propose to loosen the terms

United States (Ned Brown): Alternative A, which has been proposed by the United States after some discussion, is designed to clarify and state the position of the United States of America in regard to the sections of the Joint Statement [Article III, Sections] 2(a), (b), (c) and (d). I think everybody here realizes that this is one of the most important sections of the Joint Statement. The statement as it appears in the Joint Statement of Principles by itself is not sufficient, and the statement in the Joint [Statement of] Principles represents the compromise between two points of view, a compromise which I think everybody here realizes is necessary and desirable. On the one hand, everybody agrees that the countries must have access to the Fund. The question is how far that right of access is an absolute right—how far, perhaps I should say, a privilege. The delegation of the United States of America recognizes very clearly the difficulties of the problem. They feel the right of access to the Fund must be subject to conditions. The Fund must in extreme cases [p. 3] and under certain circumstances have a right to point out the conditions that are violated and have some discretion in refusing. The right of access to deal [with the Fund] is primarily a right, and not a privilege. Regarding this section, we provided this provision in order to give us all the aid in attempting to state the conditions under which that right should be exercised. I do not know how the Chairman will go on with the discussion. I think the discussion will, however, begin with the very first clause and it will probably continue, and the separate clauses will be taken up one by one.

Vice Chairman: This is a highly technical section of the document. I refer to the statement of the representative of the United States. Alternative A represents to some degree a compromise, which when used—I note that in condition [Section] 2 of Alternative A—shall I state it this way—I note that we have Alternative A, which has some conditions and some rewording of the Joint Statement. You have also [Alternatives] B, C, and D. B and D are conditions to alter funds, particularly clause (c) of the section. Is that agreeable to the Committee that we should proceed to discuss this clause by clause, or it is it better to discuss Section 2 as a whole?

If there is no objection, I suggest we proceed with a discussion of clause by clause. I know that with respect to [Article III, Section] 2(a) of the Joint Statement, which is rewritten as [Section] 2, [paragraph] (1) of

---

for borrowing. The Vice Chairman inadvertently skips consideration of Czechoslovakia's Alternative C, which concerns generalities rather than specific terms of borrowing. He returns to it in the next meeting of Committee 2.

Alternative A, that there is no alternative offered to that particular clause. Is there any further discussion or explanation which any delegate cares to offer on Section 2(1) as an alternative?

Section 2, [paragraph] (2), then; there are Alternatives B, C, and D. I suggest we discuss 2(2) taking any alternatives in the order in which they appear in the document.[384] [p. 4]

Unidentified: May I suggest that Section 2(2) of the American proposal be reserved until we come to the discussion of scarce currency, and then come back to it and proceed to [Section] 2, [paragraph] (3), which is the same as [Section] 2(c) in the original document?

Vice Chairman: I take that to be agreeable to the Committee. I am sorry I misstated the situation before. The clause to which there are a number of alternatives is clause 2(c) of the Joint Statement, of which there is Alternative A as [Section] No. 2(3); Alternative B; Alternative C; and [Alternative] D. We are open for discussion on clause 2(c) and the various alternatives proposed to it.

France ([Jean de Largentaye?]): Mr. Chairman, is it better to discuss now amendment [Alternative] D, or first to discuss the other amendments?

Vice Chairman: I suggest we might discuss them in order: A, B, C, and D.

Australia ([Leslie Melville]): Mr. Chairman, Alternative B was proposed by Australia because we felt the limitations on the use of the Fund as contained in the Joint Statement and as retained in [Section] 2(3) do not provide sufficient elasticity in the case of many countries. Certainly, [not] in the case of agricultural countries or countries producing a narrow range of raw material and foodstuffs. Their balances of payments are subjected from time to time to very great disturbances. The prices of raw materials are notoriously subject to variations, and when they fall temporarily, the countries affected cannot avoid heavy deficits in their balance of payments. We appreciate, of course, that [p. 5] this Fund is intended to provide countries with working balances that they draw out in some years. They are expected to pay back in other years of others. Of course, if the proposal we put forward is adopted, or Alternative D is adopted, it would be perfectly satisfactory as far as we are concerned.

We know, of course, that if there is a great deal of liberty permitted the country, then to that extent, it will be pledged subsequently to pay back to the Fund a larger amount, but we feel that for a number of countries this greater degree of elasticity is essential. It is difficult to

[384] In Document 32, pp. 28-30.

discuss this with the absence of a figure for quotas, but whatever the quotas will be, some greater degree of elasticity will be needed. Of course, it is true that the Fund can anytime waive the restrictions, but the lender's use of the resources of the Fund—but that would mean, certainly in the case of Australia, that every few years we should have to apply to the Fund for permission to make further use of its resources than was automatically provided by the Fund under the Constitution of the Fund and that, I suggest, would not be a satisfactory position for any government or any [central] bank to find itself in. It would continually be uncertain whether resources needed to meet a temporary disturbance in its balance of payments would be available to [through?] the Fund. It would have to apply to the Fund for permission to use money and comply [with] the conditions laid down by the Fund. Now, we suggest that some greater degree of elasticity is essential to the covenant as provided in [Alternatives] B and D's wording [on] the Fund. [p. 6]

Vice Chairman: I think it would assist in the discussion at this point if the delegate of the French Committee would explain Alternative D, which is directed to the same point which, as I understand it, it is a slightly different method from that proposed by the Australian delegate.

France ([Jean de Largentaye?]): I wish to state that the purpose of Amendment [Alternative] D is as much [in] the interest of the Fund as in the interest of the countries which wish to make use of the resources of the Fund. In the present draft of clause [Section] 2(c), a country has inducement to use the resources of the Fund in a regular way even though it has not met the specific requirements. The reason is that if a country does not use [resources] during the first period of 12 months, then during the second and third years, the country may not be able to retain the total resources which the country thus doing should be entitled to [borrow], so that the lack of possible carryover will have the probable effect [of increasing] the amount of currencies which the Fund will hold.

The reply to this argument may, of course, be that countries are not entitled to appeal to the resources of the Fund except for current[-account] purposes. But there are a number of cases where a country might think that if it would have a possibility of obtaining the resources which it would require in the future, that it would not for the present time appeal to the Fund, so that a provision of carryover is something which is very important. In the amendment which has been suggested, Amendment [Alternative] D, there are two points. There is a point of principle: whether a carryover [p. 7] would be acceptable to others. The second point of the issue is the specific figures which have been mentioned. On the matter of the specific figures, if those figures are considered to be not quite appropriate, the French delegation would be pleased to revise those figures if the majority of the delegates would think those figures inappropriate. But on the question of the principle, I think it is in the interest of the Fund of accepting that principle.

I would just like to mention a very small point which I have already mentioned in Atlantic City, that we do not need any more [[wording]] which either complicates the wording or confuses the meaning. Thank you.

Vice Chairman: Is there any further discussion?

Norway: I beg to state that the proposal of the French delegate—I think that the principle laid down in Alternative D is much better reading. The French delegate has already forwarded the arguments which I think [apply]. The word[ing] of the Joint Statement perhaps might be unjust [[to countries that do not immediately use the resources of the Fund?]].

USSR: I believe that the suggestion proposed as Supplement [Alternative] D by the French delegation is a practical proposal which improves the using of the resources of the Fund. I think this proposal meets practically all the needs of such countries, [which,] as we heard from the delegate from Australia, are made for the reason of considerable deviations in their balance of payments and credits. From the other side, I think the suggestion shows that the countries will borrow more [p. 8] freely, will more liberally use the resources of the Fund when they actually need it. The proposal in the Joint Statement is of such character that it can induce the countries to use their maximum possibilities in the Fund and also in these cases when they don't actually need larger resources to assure them against the future needs. Therefore, I think that it would be appropriate to support the suggestion made by the French delegation.

Vice Chairman: I am of the opinion that the clause on page 3 of the Joint Statement by which the Fund can use its discretion to waive conditions provides sufficient elasticity, and would take care of the needs of agricultural countries, as the delegate from Australia suggested—

Brazil: Mr. Chairman, there are two questions, it seems to me, in the suggestion made by the French delegation, one which is less important and which refers to the figures, and the other which is more important which refers to the principle, which is the carryover principle. The Brazilian delegation considers it an open question to examine the question of the figures, but wishes to give its support to the principle of the carryover in the type of manner that it be applied in the best interest of the Fund.

United States ([Ned Brown?]): I shall speak only on the point that was raised by the Australian delegate. I believe that point has really been answered by others who have called attention to the waiver provisions. The 25 percent a year limitation is[385] [p. 9] merely a standard provision—one that applies to all countries irrespective of the peculiarities of their papers. Where exceptions are necessary, where particular countries require additional support from the Fund, that can be given at the Fund's discretion to any extent that the Fund deems such support necessary. Now, the conception of the Australian delegate seems to be that countries with a wide seasonal movement in the balance of payments would eventually meet that seasonal trend by drawing on the Fund. This is not our conception of the use of the Fund. Most countries will have substantially independent gold reserves, gold and foreign exchange reserves of their own, even if they are meeting a large seasonal movement. Many countries will be able to meet that movement entirely by utilizing their own resources. They may come to the Fund only for rather small marginal amounts. We cannot make the standard provision cover the extreme cases of countries that have both large seasonal moves [movements] and no independent reserves of their own. What we have put in, therefore, is the standard provision that applies to all countries like that, with allowance [for] the cases that are not—in the form of power to waive that provision if the Fund deems it necessary.[386]

United States (Edward Bernstein): Mr. Chairman, we all recognize that there is considerable merit to the proposal of the delegate from France. There may, no doubt, be instances in which a country would be permitted to use the resources of the Fund when, while at other times, the full rights under the conditions of the provisions would not be used. The question [p. 10] is whether the merits of this proposal are not offset by important difficulties. In the first instance, it should be noted that the concept of this provision, Alternative A, is that in effect countries do not make use of the Fund's resources when they are not needed. When the resources are needed, in accordance with the provisions of the Fund, they are available. A country is not entitled to acquire the resources of the Fund to purchase foreign exchange of the Fund merely to build up vital balances to await future use because their current needs are not fully up to the provisions in [Article III, Section] 3. The difficulties I have in mind, and they are, I believe, important difficulties, are these:

---

385 In the U.S. Treasury Library copy of the typescripts, the transcript of this session ends abruptly here with page 8. Pages 9 to 18 of the typescript were mistakenly placed after page 8 of the first set of typed pages transcribing the Committee's third meeting, on July 5. We have restored the contents to their proper place.

386 We have omitted some words in the typescript to make the sentence clearer.

Just as countries need certainty—some degree of assurance that the needs that they will have in the near future will be met by the Fund—so the Fund needs assurance that it will be in a position to provide the resources that will be needed by member countries in accordance with the provisions of the Fund. If after four years the Fund in fact may be faced by a request for the unlimited purchase of exchange for any [parity] rate, limited only by the maximum barter provisions, it may find itself in a position where it will be pressed—a condition of uncertainty in which it cannot make its own balance. We must find, of course, some balance between certainty needed by member countries and certainty needed by member funds [i.e., by the Fund?]. We believe that the provision of Alternative A, calling for use of resources as needed but limited to 25 percent a year, provides that necessary balance. [p. 11]

The second difficulty, in some respects, holds up the first. We all know that Alternative A represents a common view of many of the technical experts who have been studying this question. It would be a mistake to conceive of this [Section] 3 as the provision of the United States technical experts. It has, in a sense, the full force of the opinion of all experts whose discussion is found in the Joint Statement. That is not to say that every technical expert agreed with that particular provision, but it is more than one country and more than two countries.[387] In the course of finding a common view, it was clear from the beginning that if the Fund is to avoid the continuous exercise of authority on the sale of exchange, it must somehow have what we may call "rule of thumb"—a reasonable basis for proceeding with the assumption that the use of the Fund's resources is being limited to the purposes and the provisions of the Fund.

If this quantitative limitation of 25 percent of the quota in a twelve-month period is modified or withdrawn, it seems to be unavoidable at we will have to restore to the Fund a balancing provision which will give the Fund an opportunity of examining from time to time whether the use of the Fund's resources are not excessive and are at a rate which will cause disequilibrium. The disturbance of the balance of payments leads only to the taking of further steps which are undesirable to others and which should be avoided as far as possible. If the Fund is to depend on the concept that some quantitative use is a measure of reasonable access to the resources of the Fund, it would not be possible to modify [the] provision [p. 12] in such a way as to open up after a stated period the

387 "More than two countries" means the provision had support from countries besides the United States and United Kingdom.

purchase of as much exchange as the country is prepared to use without submitting that to the discretion of the Fund somehow, and for these reasons I feel it would be a mistake to relax [Section] 3 to take account of the very reasonable point that the delegate from France has made. That can fully be taken care of in the waiver provision of this alternative.

[France (Jean de Largentaye)?]: Mr. Chairman, as far as I can hear them, the arguments which are given by Mr. Bernstein—there is one thing which I must say does not answer our purpose. It is the idea of a waiver. I do not see how the possibility of waiver by the Fund does protect the country which does not know any difficulties—whether they will receive that waivers and, in the absence of knowledge, will take the protection each year to draw what is reasonable in order to be assured of its requirements of the future—in order to be assured of the possibility of having [access to] the Fund. I quite agree with the idea that the resources of the Fund should be used exclusively as temporary [in] nature, and that therefore provisions must be made and should be made if the principle of carryover is accepted, whereby a country which would use for more than two years up to the extent of 150 percent [of its quota] as an average, whose currency [drawings exceed] more than 50 percent of its quota for more than two years. I think it would be quite normal, whereby [besides charging a] penalty interest [rate], the Fund can request the country to take such measures as to reduce the amount of currency [drawn]. I must confess I have been unable to find satisfactory wording. I suppose the wording [could be] similar to [that] suggested in [Alternative] A, concerning ineligibility to [use] the resources of the Fund. [p. 13] Of course, an amendment of that kind has [requirements?] that bind after a period of four years. I think it is also proper to afford us something whereby a country cannot at any time ask 200 percent if that country has had 200 percent previously.

United Kingdom: My delegation is by no means lacking in sympathy with the condition of those countries which, whether because of their dependence on particular crops or for other reasons, find that their end is particularly heavy in particular years, but we do feel that their difficulties ought to be sufficiently looked after by the discretionary powers vested in the Fund under section [paragraph] (4) in [Article III, Section 2 of] Alternative A, and by the practice which we hope [for] of continuous consultation between members and Fund about the prospective troubles and difficulties; and we do feel, therefore, that the limitations which are set out in Section 3 of Alternative A are desirable, and indeed necessary, if the Fund is to be assured of being always in the position to fulfill the heavy obligations which are going to be laid upon them.

Vice Chairman: Unless the Committee feels otherwise, I think that the views of this clause have been fully expressed, except I would ask Mr. Melville of Australia if he wishes to add any further statement.

Australia (Leslie Melville): I should like to refer to some points made an objection to Alternative B and D. The first point is in Mr. [Largentaye's?] comment there was implicit suggestion that the countries would have reserves outside the Fund on which they can draw. That is by no means certain. [p. 14] It is by no means certain that [at] the end of the war the countries I have in mind will have reserves outside the Fund on which they can draw. If they have not, and if this Fund implies that it will not work unless they have reserves outside the Fund, then the creation of the Fund inevitably imposes on those countries the duty of building up large reserves outside the Fund's. We cannot discuss this satisfactorily until we know more about quotas. I think this Committee should consider very carefully what the implications are of forcing countries to build up large reserves outside the Fund. It seems to me that would, to some extent, be inconsistent with the purposes of the Fund. The purpose is to provide countries with working balances. If Mr. [Largentaye's?] impression of the Fund is right, member countries must get their working balances outside the Fund and look to the Fund to provide them with resources only in exceptional circumstances.

Second point: whether the power of the Fund to waive conditions is really satisfactory. If, of course, the need for waiving conditions of the Fund is only required in exceptional circumstances occasionally, then I would agree that this provision would be satisfactory. It can deal with that type of case quite satisfactorily. But, as I see the operation of the Fund in its application to some countries, it will not be at all exceptional for a country to request the Fund for a waiving of those conditions. I think it is most unsatisfactory for a country to be placed in that uncertain position to have to ask that the limit of 25 percent be waived. That does not [p. 15] seem to be a very satisfactory method of procedure or a condition [in] which governments would feel at all happy to place themselves. I want to make this point: I was referring not only to ordinary seasonal fluctuations, not merely to the trend of events during one portion of the year. Agricultural funds are affected far more by fluctuations in prices which are constantly going on, more so through the business cycle than other times. Fluctuations in prices are quite customary, and these fluctuations do affect their balance of payments during the course of the year or [over a] few years, and it is that sort of movement that would make requests for waiver of conditions, which I think is unsatisfactory.

Mexico: Mexico, as a producer of raw materials, should be in favor of Alternative B presented by France, but there are considerations which have made us modify that apparently obvious attitude. On the matter of principle, we believe that each country has to consider itself both as a debtor and creditor of the Fund. As a debtor, of course, Alternative D is favorable to Mexico, but are we sure that Alternative D covers sufficiently all the risks which all of us are undertaking as creditors and as shareholders of the Fund? A situation might arise if we are too liberal, that a country normally a debtor country would become a creditor, but when the time comes for that same country to ask the assistance of the Fund, if the Fund has been too liberal, it might be possible that its resources of vital or important currencies would have been exhausted.

Also, there is another argument which we would like [p. 16] to underline. If the Fund carries its transactions with a conservative spirit, then its reputation in world capital markets would certainly be better. Conservative handling of the Fund's resources may be in the long run much more favorable to the countries which are normally debtor countries.

New Zealand: As a delegate from a country which is very largely dependent upon the export of primary production, I should like to associate my delegation with the Brazilian and the French delegation and Australian delegation. New Zealand as a country is first liable to fluctuations from time to time in great amounts in prices—the points raised as to the provision for flexibility and waiving of clause [Section] 1—but on the other hand, that does not seem to cover sufficiently the point which is one of the objects of the Fund: the confidence to make use of the Fund—whereas I recognize the point that is made that clause [Alternative] D, that if clause [Alternative] D replaces the clause which is already in the Joint Statement, it places the Fund in the position of not having quite the same protection. On the other hand, I think we can rely on the caution of the Fund just as much as we can rely on the generosity of the Fund in order that countries dependent on the export of primary products can use the Fund in the ordinary course. I feel in any event it will be helpful to have the clause inserted in considering the waiving of these restrictions. Due regard would be had to special conditions of those countries which are dependent very largely on external trade. [p. 17]

South Africa: I find myself unable to support either of these alternatives. I would draw the attention of the Committee to this point: it is a big thing indeed which is proposed here that a country can go to the Fund and have a certain overdraft without too much investigation as to its proper financial position. That is a big advantage. That advantage you can only maintain if you establish what would be in the opinion of the countries which have funds—that figure of 25 percent is under—33 percent would be just as good figure—but I should say it does suggest that we do not put any unnecessary strain on this machinery we are trying to build. Increasing strain may put the Fund into the difficult position of increasing obligations. From 25 to 33-1/3 percent is a wrong move.

As far as the proposal of the French delegation is concerned for the carryover, I would like to draw attention to a fact which we must foresee. Let us hope, at least for the first few years of the Fund, there will be a number of countries who will not require the help of the Fund. But we cannot hope that there will not come the time of increasing the number of countries. Let us say that this period of four years takes us up to the maximum. For every country which has not used any of its resources in the past, you will have a country that can immediately come to the Fund for 100 percent quota. You are going to have a rush on the Fund. I repeat my point that we want to start, but on a very conservative basis. Provision made in the original draft for a waiver provision will have to be exercised very carefully in a period such as the one which I have just reviewed, when a large number [p. 18] of countries will have to come to the Fund for assistance. It may not be possible at that time to help all the countries.

(Adjourned at 1:00 p.m.)

18

Commission I, Committee 2
Operations of the Fund
Second meeting: transcript
July 4, 1944, 5:30 p.m.[388]

Committee procedures • Appointment of Asterisk Committee approved • Purchases (borrowings) from the IMF, continued • Purchases of currencies by net lenders • Conditions under which members become ineligible to use IMF resources • Limitations on the operations of the IMF • Scarce currencies and purchase of scarce currencies with gold

Vice chairman William Mackintosh makes some suggestions for improving the working of the committee. In particular, he suggests appointing a drafting committee, which the delegates approve under the name of Asterisk Committee.

Returning to the subject of purchases (borrowings) from the IMF that was discussed in the committee's previous meeting, that morning, the vice chairman states that the arguments were fully presented without any agreement being reached, so the committee will send the matter to Commission I for resolution. The committee then proceeds to new business, still concerning Article III ["Transactions with the Fund"]. It agrees, without debate, to some minor changes in wording. A more substantial proposal is an alternative by Canada to allow countries that are net lenders to the IMF to buy foreign exchange from the IMF for any purpose, including capital transactions. Canada expects to be a net lender. The Canadian delegate who explains the proposal is Louis Rasminsky, an economist specializing in money and banking who was an official of Canada's central bank and alternate chairman of Canada's Foreign Exchange Control Board. The United States, which also expects to be a net lender, supports the alternative, and after Rasminsky offers some clarifications there seems to be no sentiment against it, so the committee approves it.

Next, the committee agrees on a clause allowing the IMF to declare members

388 Summarized in Document 112, pp. 124-125. The transcripts also contain minutes of this session, which we have not reproduced because they are almost the same as Document 112.

ineligible to use its resources if they are doing so in a manner contrary to the IMF's purposes. It then agrees that, except as otherwise provided in the agreement, the IMF's operations shall be limited to lending the currency of one member to another member in exchange for the other member's currency or for gold.

After consideration of some points of language, the committee considers a provision that the IMF may use gold to buy a currency that has become scarce from the member country that issues the currency. New Zealand asks whether the IMF may offer to buy a scarce currency at the official gold parity, or whether it has a right to buy it from the member country at the official parity. Ned Brown of the United States replies that the American view is that the IMF has a right to buy, that is, the country must sell its currency to the IMF. He proposes, though, to leave further consideration of the matter for the next meeting, and the committee adjourns.

[Vice] Chairman [William Mackintosh, Canada]:[389] The Committee will come to order. The Secretary will call roll.

Secretary ([Karl Bopp, United States]): Australia; Belgium; Bolivia (absent); Brazil (absent); Canada; Chile; China; Colombia; Costa Rica; Cuba; Czechoslovakia; Dominican Republic; Ecuador; Egypt (absent); El Salvador; Ethiopia; French Committee of National Liberation; Greece; Guatemala (absent); Haiti (absent); Honduras (absent); Iceland; India; Iran; Iraq; Liberia (absent); Luxembourg (absent); Mexico; Netherlands; New Zealand; Nicaragua; Norway (absent); Panama; Paraguay (absent); Peru; Philippine Commonwealth; Poland; Union of South Africa; USSR; United Kingdom; United States; Uruguay; Venezuela; Yugoslavia.

Vice Chairman: Before turning to the agenda, there are one or two matters on which I would like to say a word. In the first place, the acting Vice Chairman was at more than one disadvantage this morning in not knowing what is any effect this microphone had on his voice, and I would be very glad if the members of the Committee would inform me if at any time I cannot be heard.

In the second place, there were certain questions of procedure raised at the end of this morning's session on which I think we should have some discussion and a meeting of minds. It has been understood [p. 2] through earlier conferences, [by] the heads of delegations, that committees would not proceed to formal voting, but that they should use every means to try and reach agreement to clear as many of the problems as possible before reporting differences to the Commission. I take it is the

[389] Identified in the typescript in this and subsequent meetings of Committee 2 only as "Chair," but the identity is apparent, so we identify him as the Vice Chairman.

wish of the Committee to follow procedures which will achieve that, as far as possible. One practice which has been developed in other committees, which I think might be considered by this Committee, is to authorize the Chair to appoint a small Drafting Committee to which might be referred proposed changes which do not involve changes in substance and, secondly, points on which it is the view of the Chair with the concurrence or at the suggestion of the Committee, points on which it is thought that the real differences can be adjusted and an accommodation reached and a rewording of the alternative. It would not be part of such a proposal, I would think, that we would burden a Drafting Committee with questions on which there were real and firmly held differences of opinion.

Further in the matter of procedure, I think that we might proceed by having the Chair take alternative steps following a discussion, or in the divert [i.e., absence] of discussion, the Chair might well state that there seems to be [p. 3] a consensus of opinion and divert [absence] of any objection [and] the Reporting Delegate would so report. If there are objections which are not held by many representatives, but only a few, it would be open to the Chair to say that if so desired those objections would be recorded by the Reporting Delegate. Where, on the evidence of the discussion or on the stated objectives [objections] of members of the Committee, it is apparent that there are real and substantial differences of opinion which have not been reconciled, the Chair should state in its view there are such differences and the Reporting Delegate should so report them to the Commission, unless there is any suggestion from the Committee as to means by which the differences might be reconciled, either by consultation among delegations, by appointment of special subcommittee, or by any other device which members of the Committee care to suggest. The Chair will always be open to suggestions for any step which will avoid stating differences unnecessarily.

Though I make these suggestions from the Chair, I would welcome any brief discussion of them if there is any accord for them. I would entertain a motion for the Drafting Committee.

Netherlands: Mr. Chairman, the meeting this morning was especially to make sure that procedures should be followed. (The member stated also that discussions should be postponed [where disagreement existed] and [that] the procedure presented by the Chair was practical.)[390] [p. 4]

South Africa: I have only one comment to make on your excellent suggestion, and that is the name of the body to which you propose that

[390] This sentence is a summary by the stenographer rather than a transcription.

these verbal questions should be referred. Looking ahead, I think there is some slight danger of misunderstanding if we think of this small body as a Drafting Committee. It seems likely, sooner or later, if things go well with us, [that] all these conclusions which these committees and commissions arrive at will have to be looked over by lawyers to see that they make sense and are consistent. These things have already been through a Drafting Committee[391] and therefore [are] sacred. The sort of committee I believe you have in mind is a committee on language; call it an Asterisk Committee because it is the asterisk paragraph referred to.[392]

Vice Chairman: Is there any motion for the appointment of an Asterisk Committee?

South Africa: I propose—

Netherlands: Second.

Vice Chairman: It has been proposed by the representative of South Africa and seconded by the representative of Netherlands that a committee be appointed. I take it [to be] a committee named by the Chair to deal with the changes in wordings of the various proposals, particularly those [p. 5] paragraph proposals which are marked by an asterisk. We can call it, if you wish, a Wording Committee, or we can call it simply a Drafting Committee.

Unidentified: Language Committee.

Unidentified: Grammatical Committee.

Vice Chairman: Is there any discussion of the proposals?

If there is no objection, I take it that it is agreed that the Chairman should appoint such a small committee for this purpose. It is so ordered.

Is there any further discussion? Is there any discussion on the remarks which the Chairman made with respect to procedure?

If not, we might turn to the agenda. May I say just a word on the discussion this morning? I am afraid that I did not make clear that it was in respect to the alternatives proposed by the Australian delegation and the delegation of the French Committee that it appeared clear to the Chair that there were wide differences of opinion firmly held, and that it was not possible in the discussion in this Committee to reach any reconciliation of them. I did not wish to close off the discussion, but the view seemed to me on both sides to have been fully stated, and at the

---

391 The Drafting Committee of Commission I.

392 In the preliminary draft agreement for the IMF, comprising the Joint Statement plus alternatives proposed before the conference began (Document 32, pp. 21-60), an asterisk indicated that a proposed alternative contained no substantial change from the corresponding provision of the Joint Statement.

time of the adjournment no progress was being made in any reconciliation of those views, so that I could have taken it as a result of this morning's discussion that the differences in view would be fully recommended by the Reporting Delegate.

The next item on the document which we have before us [p. 6] [is] paragraph (4) of [Article III,] Section 2 [Alternative A, "Conditions upon Which Any Member May Purchase Currencies of Other Members"], to replace in part paragraph (d) of Section 2 of the Joint Statement.[393]

New Zealand: Mr. Chairman, may I raise a question arising out of [Section] 2 before we pass away from it? This question was not discussed this morning. In the Joint Statement the change is contained then also in the Alternative [A] paragraph 2(a): ["The member represents that the currency demanded is presently needed for making payments in that currency which are consistent with the purposes of the Fund"]. The words "member represents that,"—I am not sure whether those words are set there for a fell purpose, or whether it is in the drafting. Is it intended that it should be an open(?) Fund, or is the Fund to have any say in the question whether that currency is, as a matter of fact, required as the member represents it?[394]

Vice Chairman: My own understanding is that the words are of substance, but if any member of the Committee wishes to explain the words further, I would be glad.

United States (Ned Brown): Mr. Chairman, the [Joint] Statement of Principles used the words "the member represents that the currency demanded is presently needed to make payments [in that currency which are consistent with the purposes of the Fund]." The same language is continued without any change, except to add the words "of currency" and the insertion of the words "provisions of this Agreement," as I tried to explain [earlier] today. We all realize that a country has a right of access to this Fund, and if the Fund isn't inclined to go broke in short order, that right has got to be conditional. The representation is made that unless it is obvious that the currency is demanded [p. 6] for some other purpose, it would be necessary that the Fund accept a representation.

---

393 In Document 32, pp. 28-29. Recall that in the jargon of the IMF, to "purchase" means to borrow from the IMF.

394 By an "open" IMF, if the stenographer transcribed the word correctly (a question mark in the typescript indicates some doubt), the speaker apparently means that a member country may borrow a certain amount from the IMF without being required to offer reasons.

I should imagine, although I should hope it would never arise in the civilized nations, [that] sometimes under a government, not in effect,[395] a representation would be made which would be so flagrant and false the Fund, on its face, would see that it was false, and in such case I should say that the Fund would either have to say that the representation was false. I can scarcely imagine such a case arising. If, however, a nation made false representation regarding money, it might be the ground for the Fund, the next time the nation came to the Fund, to make a very careful investigation. We are faced with the fundamental difficulties of reconciling the extreme idea of absolute and complete right without restriction and the other idea of coming to this Fund as the privilege similar to a broker going to a private bank. It is possible to accept either of those theories, and we think this language is the right subject and condition to represent the best compromise possible between the two. I tried to explain that.

Vice Chairman: Does that answer?

[South Africa]: [I wish to point out] the contrast between this particular draft, which puts the judgment on what are the purposes of the Fund in the hands of the members, and other portions of the texts, where [there] are such words as "other expressions in the opinion of the Fund." This is neglect(?) of the moment, the only case where the judge of the purpose is not the Fund, but the member. And that is why it struck me that possibly it may [p. 7] not be the intention to make an exception in this particular case. What is the general rule? I myself would feel that the text would be a very much more closely shorn one and a more direct one if (the wording here suggests that he read the passage beginning with "currency demand[ed is presently needed for making payments in that currency which are consistent with the purpose of the Fund]").

Netherlands: I think, if I may say so, we have good reason in this particular case for emphasizing the discretion of the member. If these rights are to be of real help and comfort to the nations concerned, it is surely necessary that on occasion they should be exercised very quickly, and that a central bank which is going to use these rights should be able to present its demand on the Fund and expect them to be honored at very short notice, [or] immediately. It mustn't be left in doubt as to whether it is going to be kept days, weeks, or months waiting for its money while an argument takes place and they're wondering whether the money is really needed or not. I think that is in itself sufficient reason for the slight difference in emphasis which the delegate from South Africa

---

395 This phrase may have been mistranscribed.

has pointed out. There are, of course, elsewhere in this document provisions for the Fund to get its loan back by a [[repayment?]] if a member is caught in the act of behaving improperly, flagrantly or dishonestly. I think it would be better to leave it at that, and place the emphasis here on the ability of the member in this case to get the money quickly on his own representation that he is entitled to it. [p. 9]

Vice Chairman: I think that as we are here to answer a question, and not reopen a discussion on a clause which is been accepted this morning, that that probably meets the question of the representative of South Africa.

South Africa: I will not question the matter anymore, sir.

Vice Chairman: With reference to Alternative A, Section 2, paragraph (4), you will notice a change that is been made from the Joint Statement is that the referred-to suspension has been transferred to a later section—a new Section 3—and that what is set forth in Section 4, Alternative A, adds nothing of substance. On that basis, the Committee may be willing to agree to Section 4, discussing [instead] the proposed new Section 3, which contains the substance of the changes. Is the Committee agreed to that suggestion?

I take it that it is agreed.

There is then also in Alternative A a sentence added following the numbered paragraphs—the first sentence, which is changed in only very slight detail: "The Fund may, in its discretion, and on terms which safeguard its interests, waive any of these conditions." Added, "In special circumstances, where the Fund considers it necessary, it may require collateral security as a condition of such waiver." Is there any discussion of that proposal?

If there is no discussion, may we take it as agreed that the sentences of Alternative A are acceptable to the Committee?

Agreed. [p. 10]

The next proposal is under Alternative A and is for the addition of a wholly new paragraph, numbered here Section 2(a), "Conditions Governing Purchases for Capital Transfers." It reads that ["If the Fund's holdings of the currency of a member have remained below 75 percent of its quota for a period of not less than six months such member shall be entitled, notwithstanding the provisions of Article V, Section 1, to buy the currency of another member from the Fund for its own currency for any purpose, including capital transfers, provided, however, that purchase for capital transfers may not have the effect of raising the Fund's holdings of the currency of such holdings of the currency purchased below 75[396] percent of the quota of the member whose currency is purchased."] I take it the footnote indicates some uncertainty as to the correct percentage to insert in the last place and some willingness to adjust. I would ask the delegation responsible for the proposal to explain it further.

Canada ([Louis Rasminsky]): Mr. Chairman, this proposal is designed to enable the countries which have not been net purchasers of exchange from the Fund, those countries which have not used the Fund's resources, to buy exchange from the Fund for any purpose, including a capital transfer. I take it there is general agreement that the primary purpose of the resources of the Fund is to facilitate current-account transactions. This is stated by implication at several points in the Joint Statement, and it is stated explicitly in [Article] V, paragraph [Section] 1 of the printed text ["Use of the Fund's Resources for Capital Transfers"], which reads, "A member country may not use the Fund's resources to meet a large or sustained outflow of capital, and the Fund may require a member country to exercise controls to prevent such use of the resources of the Fund." I think that it could also be argued that it is stated by implication in [Article] III, [Section] 2(a) of the printed booklet,[397] which reads, ["2. A member shall be entitled to buy another member's currency from the Fund in exchange for its own currency on the following conditions: (a) The member represents that the currency demanded is presently needed for making payments in that currency that are consistent with the purposes of the Fund."] Since the purpose most relevant in this connection is purpose 5 [p. 11] on page 2, ["To assist in the establishment of multilateral payment facilities on current transactions among member countries and in the elimination of foreign exchange restrictions which hamper the growth of world trade,"] I think that it is beyond dispute, Mr. Chairman, that the main purpose of the resources in the Fund is to facilitate current transactions.

But it has appeared to some of us who have studied this problem, the problem of the restrictions that should be placed on the access of creditor countries to the Fund, that so long as a country is not making net use of the Fund's resources—that is to say in terms of this document, so long as the Fund's holdings of the currency of a member are not less than 75 percent of their quota of that member—there is no disadvantage, and on the contrary, [there is] an advantage in allowing such a member to

[396] Alternative A contains a footnote here asking, "Should this figure be 60, 75 or 100 percent?" (Document 32, p. 29n).
[397] That is, Document 32, p. 28.

purchase exchange from the Fund for any purpose, including capital transfers, on certain conditions and subject to certain safeguards. If a country's currency is held by the Fund in amounts under 75 percent of its quota, that country—I think we can take by hypothesis—is a creditor country with a favorable balance of payments on current account.[398] Anything that that country can do to increase the world supply of its currency is to the general advantage of the community. There therefore appears to be no reason, subject to qualification which I shall introduce later, why that country should not buy exchange from the Fund for capital purposes. If it does, in other words, why it should not be able to use [the] mechanism of the Fund to lend abroad? If it lends abroad, outside the mechanism of the Fund, there is no positive assurance that the domestic currency which it places at [p. 12] the disposal of the rest of the world will find his way in whole or even in part into the coffers of the Fund. That will depend on the situation of the countries to whom the loan is being made.

Therefore, the underlying thought in this proposal is that the countries which have not used the resources of the Fund should not [let their quotas?] be used for capital purposes. Obviously, it would be against the general interest if countries, as a result of purchasing exchange from the Fund for capital purposes, precipitated in any degree a scarcity in the Fund's holdings of the currency which [was] being required. That would be contrary to the interests of the community as a whole, as well as contrary to the interests of the country whose currency is being required under the circumstances. That explains the proviso at the end that this procedure must not reduce the Fund's currency purchases below 75 percent of the quota of the member whose currency is purchased.

The Chairman has referred to the three figures mentioned in the footnote at the bottom of the paragraph, and they do indicate, indeed, a certain flexibility of mind as to the precise figure to be inserted. My own view, the figure should be [something?] like 60 percent. What one wants to avoid is a country which is initiating [purchase of?] a currency scarcer than its own in the Fund. This provides, however, that the Fund's holding of such a currency must remain below [p. 13] 75 percent over a six-months' average on the level, so that by the time the country could utilize that right, the Fund's holdings would be something like 60 percent. On the other hand, I understand that from private conversations with some delegations, there are some delegations who are approving the general

[398] That is, the IMF has lent 25 percent or more of the quota subscription because other countries have wanted to borrow in the currency of that country.

principle of this taking the view that the figure should be 75 percent, which would necessarily produce a situation under which currency which the Fund was getting was less scarce than currency the Fund was giving up. It would seem to us, Mr. Chairman, in using the Fund for capital purposes, one must avoid any suspicion or any thought of acting in any way that could be injurious to the Fund itself or to the rest of the community, and notwithstanding our original desire to have the figure of 60 [percent] inserted, we are quite prepared to agree to a form of words which would leave the same figure of 75 percent in both cases.

Vice Chairman: Any discussion?

United States (Ned Brown): Mr. Chairman, I would like to state that on behalf of the U.S. delegation, we think this section proposed by Canada is an excellent section, one which helps the Fund to work more efficiently. We believe 75 percent of the currency purchased should be retained and [that the level should not be] not reduced to 60 percent. One other comment: we feel that when the happy day comes when the agreement on every disputed principle is in the hands of the lawyers, [as Professor Robertson mentioned], we think this particular section of [Section] 2(a) might more appropriately fit into some other article of the Agreement. [p. 14]

Vice Chairman: Any further discussion?

New Zealand: In view of the fact that this provision now under discussion is contained in a separate clause, I am inclined to doubt whether it is sufficiently clear whether the facilities provided by that clause cannot be undertaken if the currency question has been declared scarce. In the previous clause it is provided that a country may obtain another currency for its own currency provided its own currency hasn't been declared scarce. Should that provision also be included in this clause?

Vice Chairman: Any comment on that?

Canada ([Louis Rasminsky]): I think that point raised by the delegate of New Zealand is in fact covered by the reference to the fact that purchases for this purpose must not reduce the Fund's holdings required below 75 percent. It would be only [in] inconceivable [contingencies] that the Fund would declare the currency scarce at a time when the Fund's holdings of that currency amounted to 75 percent of the quota of that country that the situation raised by the delegate of New Zealand would arise.

Vice Chairman: Any further discussions?

Czechoslovakia ([Antonin Basch]): In the section, it is stated that as long as [the Fund's holdings of] a currency [have] remained below 75 percent [of its quota] for not less than six months, then the second part states, ["such member shall be entitled, notwithstanding he provision of Article V, Section 1, to buy the] currency of [another] member [from the Fund for its own currency for any purpose]." But [the clause] does [p. 15] not state whether [the clause] applies also [to the other country's quota of] 75 percent, [which it] should, it seems to me, for reasons of safety. [There] should be a set period during which [the Fund's holdings of the] currency would remain at least 75 percent [of quota].[399]

Another [point]: I wonder whether this provision, [though it] is certainly very good, should be introduced immediately, or whether we should not wait and see how the whole Fund will operate.

My third remark is whether in such a case when a member country buys [the] currency of another country, should the [other] country be asked to give its consent?

Vice Chairman: Any comment?

Greece ([Kyriakos Varvaressos]): May I ask, Mr. Chairman, if in case that the country has controls on capital transactions, does this paragraph here affect the control[s] of [such] a country? Is a country which has imposed a control to determine the capital transaction? Is this country affected by this clause?

Vice Chairman: I would welcome assistance.

Canada ([Louis Rasminsky]): I don't see why it should be, Mr. Chairman. If a country has controls on capital transactions, that control is not necessarily a complete prohibition of all capital transactions, and it may be that through the facilities provided in this way, such a country would permit capital transactions to take place which you would otherwise prohibit.

I wonder whether I might refer to points by the delegate of Czechoslovakia, while I am up. [p. 16] The first suggestion that he made was that not only should the currency of the country which is purchasing exchange for capital purposes have remained below the level of 75 percent over a period of six months, but also that the currency of the country which is being purchased should have remained above a 75 percent level for six months. That does appear to me, Mr. Chairman, to be going an unnecessarily long distance to undo the effects that we are seeking to obtain in this clause. If a currency has remained above 75 percent level for six months, then by definition that country has been a consistent net purchaser of the exchange from the Fund, because the

399 We have revised this paragraph extensively from the original to make its meaning clearer.

Fund begins by holding—forgetting for the moment the complications that may arise by the fact that some of the initial subscriptions may not be 75 percent, but a higher figure—the Fund begins by holding 75 percent of currency of each country. Now the Fund, having held 75 percent of the currency of each country over a period of six months, has plenty of the currency of that country. There is no danger involved to the Fund in getting back to the position in which it originally started. [As] I pointed out in introducing this proposal, the practical working of it, under the present formulation, would necessarily be that the currency that is being supplied to the Fund is scarcer than that obtained from the Fund, and why should [one] set up restrictions [p. 17] making it impossible for others to come to assistance of the Fund in supplying it with their currency? [We] don't see why those restrictions should be necessary.

The same comments apply to [the] transitional period. If in the course of the transitional period the Fund supply of any particular currency does become scarce—not in a technical sense, under which provisions of placement would come into operation—but then this clause would not come into operation of all, either during the transition period or at any time.

The third point [raised by the Czechoslovak delegate], on the consent of the country required, I think, is unnecessary, and from some point of view objectionable. What one is seeking to establish here is definite provisions that countries will be able to count on, barring misbehavior, and on which they will be able to base their plans. The introduction of the consent of the country whose currency is being acquired does mean that no country will be able to count on the operation of this provision, and I should have thought that interests of the country whose currency is being acquired is adequately safeguarded.

Greece ([Kyriakos Varvaressos]): I am sorry that I must repeat my original question. I agree that this provision is very useful and might be helpful both to the country and to the Fund. I am afraid that the unlimited right of the member country to purchase local currency from [the central] bank of another country over and above 75 percent of the holdings of a country might [p. 18] be against the interest of the country and the purposes of the Fund. What is the real object of the Fund? It is, in my opinion, to collect the different subscriptions and to accord facilities in order to promote the best growth of trade. If a country, over and above the original contribution, has made use of facilities of the Fund, has paid to the Fund its local currency in a prior foreign exchange [transaction], this country has a right to expect that this local currency would be used by other countries on current account for the purchase of goods for payment of services which will be considered as capital account. If this country, without its consent, must accept that this currency will be utilized by other countries for investments, it is not quite in agreement with the Fund. It is the general feeling that this clause is a useful one. I should think that the limit should be set somewhat above the 75 percent, and then to come to the other [alternative], that the holdings of this council [i.e., the IMF] are not below 100 percent.

Czechoslovakia ([Antonin Basch]): I propose the following problem. According to the Fund, a country is supposed to accept its local currency for all payments on current account. It is not obliged to accept them on payments for capital income, as Mr. Varvaressos stated, and ask whether capital incorporations will not be transferred by this clause. I understood by the answers that he gave [that] he agrees with this interpretation. [p. 19] Then we can see that the local currency held by the Fund, which could be freely used for all kinds of payments and transactions, would not be beyond import capital control if used for the import of capital.

Canada ([Louis Rasminsky]): It is obvious that I misunderstood Mr. Varvaressos's questions. I had in mind the country which was exporting capital, and not the country which was importing capital. Dr. Basch referred to imported capital. There was nothing in this proposal which would, in any sense, make it necessary for countries to change such regulations which they may have respecting imported currency. If any country wishes to take the position, though, I can't think of a single example of a country that has taken this position—that it requires to get foreign exchange—willing to accept local currency for its exports of goods by foreign exchange of its exports of capital. If any country wishes to take that position, then I would concede, Mr. Chairman, it is open to that country to take that position, and in that case, local currency acquired under this provision would not be available for capital purposes, and therefore it would not be required by the purchasing country.

Vice Chairman: May I ask how far that meets the question asked by the representative of Greece?

Greece: Yes [it does].

Vice Chairman: I take it from this discussion that there is general agreement that this is a desirable clause. There is [p. 20] also the suggestion of the representative of the United States that when the stage of ultimate drafting comes, that it not be included as [Article III], clause

[Section] 2, [paragraph] (a)[400] here, but might be placed in some more suitable location. Is it the wish of the Committee to adopt this clause and recommend it to the Commission, or are there modifications which are proposed? Does the Chair take it that it is agreed that the clause is approved?

So agreed.

The next proposal is the additional Section 3 in Alternative A, additional to the Joint Statement.[401] As I said before, it takes the part of the wording [of Section] 2(d) of the Joint Statement and binds it into a new section, "Declaring Members Ineligible to Use the Resources of the Fund." ["Whenever the Fund is of the opinion that any member is using the resources of the Fund in a manner contrary to the purposes and policies of the Fund, it shall present to the member a report setting forth the views of the Fund and stating a suitable time for reply. After presenting such a report to a member the Fund may limit the use of its resources by the member. If no reply to the report is received from the member within the stated time, of the reply received is unsatisfactory, the Fund may continue to limit the member's use of the Fund's resources or, after giving reasonable notice the member, declare it ineligible to use the resources of the Fund."]

Any discussion of that proposal?

There being no objections, may I take it that that proposal is agreed?

Cuba ([Felipe Pazos]): Mr. Chairman, may I ask whether the differences which are contemplated between the article of the declaring members ineligible to use the sources of the Fund and the provision announced on page 35 of this draft, [Article VIII, Section 2,] "Preliminary Articles on Suspension of Membership or Compulsory Withdrawal"—may I ask what is the difference between the ineligibility and suspension of membership, because I couldn't get quite clear from the discussions in Atlantic City which was exactly the difference between those two provisions.[402] [p. 21]

---

400 This could also be a reference to Article III, Section 2a, proposed in the preliminary draft, p. 29, instead of to Joint Statement Article III, Section 2, paragraph (a).

401 In Document 32, pp. 29-30.

402 In the preliminary draft agreement on the IMF, there was only a placeholder for a section on suspension of membership (Document 32, p. 53). The Atlantic City conference to which the delegate refers was held on June 15-30, 1944 in Atlantic City, New Jersey as a preliminary meeting to facilitate the work of the Bretton Woods conference.

United States (Ned Brown): Mr. Chairman, in the first place the United States, which proposes this, would like to strike out the words "and policies" in the second line, subsequently to leaving it "in a manner contrary to the purposes." I do not think any country here would care to bind itself to the probable degradation of the use of the Fund, and suspension, by disobeying policies, which might mean policies adopted by the Board of the Fund at some later date. The original section of the Joint Statement of the Experts provided [for] nothing except suspension. It is the view of the U.S. delegation that something less than suspension was highly desirable, and that it would be much less contrary to the dignity of a nation to limit its resources to the Fund temporarily than to suspend or throw it out of the Fund. Consequently, the proviso was changed from the experts' statement declaring its ineligibility to use resources of the Fund or limiting its use.

The other substantial change is that after the Fund is presented a report and therefore a reply is received, it has, in special circumstances, the right to limit or to propose conditions on access to the Fund. This was designed to take care of the case of the country which would not reply immediately, or the reply might be unsatisfactory when it did come in, and the maximum amount which was still drawable. Again, I think it is a case which is very unlikely to arise, but it is possible. I think the alternative section is much better for all countries, in that it does not involve the indignity of suspension. [p. 22] In case of disagreement, it does allow much lesser punishment of limitation, which might be instead of drawing 25 percent at one time, rather 5 percent a month for five months, but not all in a day. This section will be rarely used, but it seems to me the main effect would affect the dignity and honor of various countries which joined the Fund.

Vice Chairman: I am not sure the representative of the United States was entirely heard. I shall state briefly the point which was raised. The explanation was that it was desired in these circumstances to have a restriction on countries which fell short of suspension, or anything which would involve the dignity of a country, where it was contemplated that the Fund might withdraw the use of its resources entirely, but limit the use of its resources for a period of time; and that for the remainder, [the proposal] is mainly spelling out in fuller language the brief statement which appeared in the Joint Agreed Statement of Experts. Is there any further discussion?

Cuba ([Felipe Pazos]): Mr. Chairman, might we postpone the consideration of this article, particularly in its last line on declaration of ineligibility, [until] the time that we know what the final draft or the draft of suspension of membership—

Vice Chairman: May I ask the representative of the United States whether it is considered [that] to declare a country ineligible to use resources of Fund is equivalent to [a] discussion, or is there additional [[action to be taken]]? [p. 23]

United States (Ned Brown): I should say that the difference was a real difference, that if a country is suspended, I can scarcely conceive of any country risking its own national honor which wouldn't immediately withdraw from the Fund and tell it politely to go to the Devil, whether it could meet its obligations to the Fund or not. If it is declared to be ineligible to use resources of the Fund, it means there is every opportunity for conciliation and clearing up misunderstandings which might arise between sovereign nations as between individuals, and that the country will come back into the fold of the Fund without any hard feelings. I think it is a very important difference from the point of both national honor and also of keeping this Fund permanently going as an organization which we hope all the civilized nations of the world will ultimately join.

Vice Chairman: There is some difficulty in accepting the suggestion made that this should be left open, and that the section referred to on page 35 [Article VIII, Section 2, "Suspension of Membership or Compulsory Withdrawal"] should not come before this Committee but before another committee. In view of the fact that it is open to any delegation to raise this question in this Commission, where both points may be raised, would be satisfactory if we left it there, that any delegation could discuss it in the [Commission], as we are not able at this Committee to answer questions in respect to suspension?

Cuba ([Felipe Pazos]): It is satisfactory.

Vice Chairman: Is there any further discussion of this section? [p. 24]

If there are no objections, accept this section as agreed.

So agreed.

The next item is Alternative C.[403] We passed over it this morning inadvertently. Alternative C relates to [Article III,] Section 2 ["Conditions Governing Use of the Fund's Resources"], paragraph (a) of the Joint Statement, and refers to Section 2, paragraph 1, of Alternative A, which we have already accepted. You will note there have been certain changes in the Joint Statement. The final phrase reads "which are consistent with the purposes of the Fund." In Alternative A, that has been changed [to]

---

[403] In Document 32, p. 30.

"which are consistent with the provisions of this Agreement." Alternative C proposes the wording "consistent with the purposes and provisions of the Fund."

Czechoslovakia ([Antonin Basch?]): This alternative [was introduced] before Alternative A was known.

Vice Chairman: Alternative C is withdrawn. That completes the discussion of Section 2.

We turn to Section 3 of [Article] III, Joint Statement ["Limitation on the Fund's Operations"].[404] The original section reads, ["The operations on the Fund's account will be limited to transactions for the purpose of supplying a member country on the member's initiative with another member's currency in exchange for its own currency or for gold. Transactions provided for under 4 and 7, below, are not subject to this limitation."]

The proposal would be [i.e., would add] a new Section 4 ["Limitation on the Operations of the Fund"] to the section, in view of the fact that a new Section 3 has been proposed. It would read, ["Except as otherwise provided in this Agreement, operations for the account of the Fund shall be limited to transactions for the purpose of supplying a member, on the initiative of such member, the currency of another member in exchange for the currency of the member initiating the transactions or for gold."]

The changes seem to be minor changes in wording. Is there any discussion?

If there is no objection, may I take it that Alternative A, Section 3 of the Joint Statement is agreed?

[Old Article III,] Section 4 ["Measures to Replenish the Fund's Holdings of Scarce Currencies"]. Read in the Joint Statement, ["The Fund will be entitled at its option, with a view to preventing a particular member's currency from becoming scarce: (a) To borrow its currency from a member country; (b) To offer gold to a member country in exchange for its currency."] That has been reworded in Alternative A to read, ["The Fund may, if it deems such action appropriate to prevent the currency of any member from becoming scarce, take either or both of the following steps: (1) Propose to the member that it lend such currency to the Fund or, with the approval of the member, borrow such currency within that country from some other source, but no member shall be under any obligation to lend its currency to the Fund or to approve the Fund's borrowing its currency from any other source. (2) Offer to buy the currency of that member with gold."] [p. 25]

---

[404] In Document 32, pp. 30-31.

Any discussion of this proposal?

If there is no objection, may we take it [as agreed]?

Ecuador: This morning the proposal was that the Fund would not operate [i.e., deal with a member] except through a [member's] central [bank] and stabilization fund. Is it here authorized to make transactions outside? Wouldn't that be in contradiction to what was proposed this morning? I assumed that it was a borrowing operation and would be handled through the approved institutions.

United States (Ned Brown): The member from Cuba raised the same point this morning, when he stated that except as otherwise provided in this Agreement, all transactions should be central banks or the other fiscal agencies, and called attention to the fact that this indicated that the Fund might borrow from private chartered banks with the approval of the country in which they were located and whose currency was being borrowed. I think the member from Cuba's point was entirely correct this morning. I think it may be left to Mr. Robertson's friends, the lawyers, for the day when we are all agreed on principles.

Vice Chairman: Does the explanation cover the point?

Unidentified [Ecuador?]: I have no objection whatever, but since it was emphasized "only," that had not been in the original proposal, but here emphasis has been placed on it. I have no objection.

Vice Chairman: That is a point to be looked after by the drafting people.

Canada ([Louis Rasminsky]): The points I have to raise are also drafting points. [p. 26] There is a typographical error on this page (page 8) in the section that reads "borrow such currency within that country [from some other source]." I believe that the word "or" has been omitted: "*or* from some other source." My understanding of the meaning of this paragraph was that if the currency was becoming scarce, the Fund might attempt to borrow that currency either from the country concerned or from some other country which had adequate holdings of the currency which was becoming scarce. That is the first point. I stand to be corrected.

The second point is perhaps more a point of substance, "but no member shall be under obligation to lend its currency to the Fund were to approve the funds borrowing its currency from any other source." I raise the question whether there is not in that form of words an implied obligation on the part of the third countries holding the currency which is becoming scarce to make loans to the Fund. Say [instead], "but no member shall be under any obligation to make such loans to the Fund or to approve the Fund's borrowing its currency from any other source."

United States (Ned Brown): May I ask Mr. Bernstein of the United States [to comment].

United States (Edward Bernstein): First, if I may revert to the point that Mr. Pazos raised, there is the problem of drafting in connection with [Article III,] Section 1 ["Agencies Dealing with the Fund"] and this section, but I should call attention to the fact that Section 1 reads that ["Each member country shall deal with the Fund only through its Treasury, Central Bank, Stabilization Fund or other similar fiscal agency and the Fund shall deal only through the same agencies."] It is not intended that the Fund shall necessarily limit its transactions to dealing *with* those agencies, provided it deals [p. 27] *through* such agencies. That may clarify Mr. Pazos's point somewhat. I gather this is entirely correct.

I have a few more words. Perhaps the best thing is to turn it over to the Asterisk Committee. In the second line of [Article III, Section 4, Alternative A, Section 5 ("Limitation on the Operations of the Fund"), paragraph] (1), "Propose to the member that it lend such currency to the Fund or with the approval of the member," I think these words are omitted: "that the Fund borrow such currency within that country."[405] [The paragraph] may be a little equivocal; maybe it needs another word. I think it is intended that the loan should be made either by the central bank or another fiscal agency within that country. It could also be from some other source than the central bank, or it would be through the fiscal agency in such a case. I think if so interpreted it might be clear. If not, the Asterisk Committee is the proper committee for it.

Vice Chairman: Would it be the sense of the Committee that we would refer this clause to the committee to be named to deal with these problems of wording?

Netherlands: Mr. Chairman, I would like to be sure that I got the substance there. The proposal is that the Fund may, with the consent of a member government, borrow either from that government *or* from private persons under the jurisdiction of that government *or* from any other source. Is that right? Three alternatives. I must confess that the word had been omitted from the sentence.

United States (Edward Bernstein): I am not certain, Mr. Chairman, whether that might be so. I would have to think [at] more leisure [whether] to agree. [p. 28]

Vice Chairman: I take it as agreed to refer this to the subcommittee, who will consult with Mr. Bernstein and others as to the original intention of this proposal.

---

405 In Document 32, p. 31.

Section 5 ["Limitation on the Operations of the Fund," paragraph] (2). The change is only a change in wording: "offered by the currency of that member with gold." Is there any discussion?

Netherlands: Perhaps you are right. It is just a matter wording. We wanted to make sure by putting in that no country have the right to refuse gold for its currency.

Vice Chairman: Any further discussion? I take it it would be appropriate to link with this discussion Alternative B, which is "To sell gold to a member country [in exchange for its currency."] I was referring to Alternative A, or the alternative to sell gold to a member country in exchange for its currency.

New Zealand: I think in order to protect the interests of the country concerned, it is desirable to offer [to sell gold]. Otherwise, it is not sufficiently clear that the country would have the option of refusing, and if compared with the clause of the previous draft, it says "offer to buy currency of that country with gold." It doesn't make it clear there that the country's permission must be had, because the country's consent must be had before the Fund must borrow its currency. Just a question as to whether the same provision should apply. It is a question as to whether the Fund must *offer* to buy, or whether it has the *right* to buy.

Netherlands: That is just the point. We are wondering [p. 29] whether any country would be in a position to refuse to sell its currency for gold, and we are of the opinion that the gold should always be accepted. It may not work, but in other words, that is the essence of the proposal.

Vice Chairman: Is there any further comment that will make clearer the difference between these alternatives?

Netherlands: I think I see the difference, and the language of Alternative B sufficiently expresses the difference. But even so, Alternative B seems to me very unacceptable. I think the option must remain with the country whether or not it furnishes its currency to the Fund in exchange for gold.

Vice Chairman: Any further discussion?

Unidentified: Might I ask the professor how he reconciles the remarks just made with the provisions of [Article] IX, [Section] 1 ["Gold Purchases Based on Par Values"] of the Joint Statement?[406]

---

[406] "IX. Obligations of Member Countries. 1. Not to buy gold at a price which exceed[s] the agreed parity of its currency by more than a prescribed margin and not to sell gold at a price which falls below the agreed parity by more than a prescribed margin." In Document 32, p. 54.

Netherlands: It has nothing to do with any obligation on any part of a member country to take gold, whether from the Fund or from anybody else.

Unidentified: Provisions of the Joint Statement—there is nowhere any provision which covers an obligation on the part of any country other to sell gold—

United States (Ned Brown): Mr. Chairman, I think it is the view of the American delegation [that it is] implicit in the whole argument: the country must sell its currency for gold, or else the Fund won't work. It is a very large question. I think it is such an important question that it would be desirable to start the discussion tomorrow with that question.

Vice Chairman: Adjourned.

19

Commission I, Committee 2
Operations of the Fund
Third meeting: transcript
July 5, 1944, 5:30 p.m.[407]

Commission referral back to Committee 2 of section on purchase of currencies • Clarification by Canadian delegate of remarks on capital transfers • Convertibility of foreign held balances • Acquisition by members of the currency of other members for gold • Transfer and guarantee of assets of the IMF • Silver

In its first and second meetings, Committee 2 had been unable to resolve a disagreement about purchases (borrowing) from the IMF. It referred the matter to Commission I for resolution, but the Commission referred it back to the committee. Vice chairman William Mackintosh defers consideration of the matter, to allow a specially appointed subcommittee time to reach an agreement. Louis Rasminsky of Canada clarifies for the record some remarks he made at the previous meeting about capital controls.

The committee then discusses an alternative to Article III, Section 5 ("Convertibility of Foreign Held Balances"). Edward Bernstein of the United States and a French delegate, perhaps André Istel, clarify that under the alternative, IMF member countries holding the currencies of other members will have the right to sell those currencies for their own currencies or for gold if the currencies of other members are needed for current payments (current-account transactions). Members therefore commit themselves to a certain level of currency convertibility, although what will become Article XIV of the final IMF agreement will allow those that do not have full current-account convertibility when they join the IMF to delay it indefinitely in practice if they wish. After some debate, the committee defers a decision on the section until it considers related material currently assigned to Committee 1.

The committee approves without discussion a section stating that members shall sell gold to the IMF in exchange for the currencies of other members if it is no less

---

[407] Summarized in Document 140, pp. 152-153. The transcripts also contain minutes of this session, which we have not reproduced because they are almost the same as Document 140.

advantageous than making the exchange through other channels. The committee passes over until later a section on the IMF's acquisition of gold from member countries because one proposed alternative is not yet ready.

Next, the committee considers the transfer and guarantee of the assets of the IMF. Ned Brown of the United States explains an American alternative, which provides that assets of the IMF shall be free from exchange controls; that members must accept their currencies purchased (borrowed) from the IMF by other members in payment of current transactions; and that members guarantee the IMF against losses resulting from the failure of their central banks or other agencies that act as depositories for the IMF. Some discussion makes it clear that there are matters in the alternative that need to be clarified, and it is referred to the Asterisk Committee.

Last, the committee hears a Mexican proposal that would allow "silver-hoarding countries"—those where silver coins are a large share of the currency—to purchase (borrow) another member's currency in exchange for silver, up to a value of 80 percent of their silver hoardings. The Mexican delegate making the proposal is Antonio Espinosa de los Monteros, president of Mexico's development bank and a director of Mexico's central bank. Because the hour is late, the committee adjourns without rendering a decision on the proposal.

[Vice] Chairman [William Mackintosh, Canada]: Committee 2 will come to order.

As the first order of business, I will report that our Reporting Delegate reported to the Commission this morning, and as a result of that report, Section 2 ["Conditions Governing Use of the Fund's Resources"] under [Article] III, paragraph (c), the Alternatives A, B and D,[408] on which we had not been able to agree, were referred back to this Committee. We have already had a discussion on those points. I do not know that the participants in that discussion have either changed their minds in the meantime or that there is additional information or additional argument to place before the Committee. Immediately it appears, however, the wish of the Commission that we should address ourselves to the subject and try and present a definite recommendation. I am therefore open to suggestions as to any procedure which we might adopt by means of a committee or otherwise by which we might follow up the wishes of the Commission.

France: In order to save time, I move that the Chair appoint and have the committee for dealing with this problem.

Vice Chairman: It has been moved by the French representative—

---

[408] In Document 32, pp. 28-30.

United States: I would like to second the motion of the French Committee.

Vice Chairman: It has been moved and seconded that the Chair should appoint a committee to consider the problem which has been referred back to it and referred back to this Committee. May I take it that in the sense of this meeting, the motion is carried?

Canada ([Louis Rasminsky]): Mr. Chairman, I would like to ask permission to make a short statement in connection with some observations I made as to [Article III,] Section 2(a) regarding the "Conditions Governing Purchases for Capital Transfers," on page 6a. It is [p. 2] evident that I didn't express my meaning clearly in connection with one observation, since the Reporter in his admirable report to the Commission this morning reported that I had made a certain statement which it was certainly not my intention to make. The question relates to the condition of the country which is imposing import control on capital movements. The matter was raised by the representatives of Greece and Australia as to whether such countries would be obliged to permit the sale of exchange for the purchase of their exchange for capital inflows. I said at that time that if there were general restrictions of capital inflows, they would equally apply to capital inflows to the Fund, but if there were no such restrictions, currency purchased through the Fund would be good payment for capital inflows. In no case would the specific consent of the country into which capital was moving be required. I think that this inadvertence arises purely out of my own lack of clarity yesterday, and I would ask the Reporter whether he would be good enough to correct his report to the Commission in this respect.

Vice Chairman: The matter which is been raised by the delegate from Canada seemed to me entirely a matter of the recording of what he said, and not of any action of the Committee, and I would suggest that the Reporter might amend is report in the sense of Mr. Rasminsky's remark, and I know Mr. Rasminsky would be willing to assist in making the report accurate.

At the end of the last meeting we were engaged in a discussion of [Article III,] Section 4 of the Joint Statement, Alternative A of the Code [agreement] ["Operations for the Purpose of Preventing Currencies from Becoming Scarce"], particularly section [paragraph] (2) of that alternative, page 8.[409] I have been informed [that] a number of countries, including those participating in that discussion, would like to discuss the matter informally before going on with further discussion in the Committee. The

[409] In Document 32, p. 31.

matter will be taken up later in the Committee, and if I have the concurrence of the Committee we will [p. 3] pass over it now to permit those informal discussions, and take up this section again at a later date. Is there any objection?

It is so ordered.

We then pass to Section 5 of the Joint Statement, which has been extensively rewritten in the proposal, Alternative A ["Multilateral International Clearing"].[410] The alternative reads:

"Each member shall buy balances of its currency held by another member with currency of that member or, at the option of the member buying, with gold, if the member selling represents either that the balances in question have been currently acquired or that their conversion is needed for making currency payments which are consistent with the provisions of the Fund."

May I at that point ask someone more fully informed that I whether "currency payments" is a misprint for "current payments," or is it as written?

Philippines ([Andrés Soriano]): I take it to be a misprint.

Vice Chairman: "Currency" in the fifth line should read "current." [Continuing to read:] "This obligation shall not relate to transactions involving: (a) capital transfers, except those transactions referred to in the second and third sentences of V, 1, below;"—those exceptions are on page 21 of the document—"(b) holdings of currency which have accumulated as a result of transactions affected before the removal by a member of restrictions on multilateral clearing maintained or imposed under X, 2, below; or (c) the provision of a currency which is been declared scarce under VI, above; or (d) holdings of currency acquired as a result of dealings of illegal under the exchange regulations of the member which is asked to buy such currency; nor shall it apply to a member which has ceased to be entitled to buy currencies of other members from the Fund in exchange for its own currency. Nothing in this section shall be deemed to modify or affect the obligation of a member under IX, 2 and 3, below." [p. 4]

This proposal is open for discussion.

Are there no comments or discussion, since this is the opening proposal?

Philippines ([Andrés Soriano]): Probably this section will ultimately find a place under Article IX ["Obligations of Member Countries"] rather than Article III ["Transactions with the Fund"], in that it seems to me it

[410] In Document 32, pp. 32.

might be well if the last sentence of this were deferred until we have considered Article IX. I don't know if anyone will feel any objection to that, but it is a little difficult to see at present. This may ultimately [[need to be delayed?]] until we have cleared up Article IX.

United States (Ned Brown): There is a section [of Alternative A, paragraph] (d): "holdings of currency acquired as a result of dealings illegal under the exchange regulations of the member which is asked to buy such currency." The United States would like to suggest that in place of the words "as a result of dealings" the words "contrary to" be inserted. I think it is a matter of drafting, and I think it might be well if that particular section of [paragraph] (d) be referred to the Asterisk Committee. I don't want [the Asterisk Committee] to get too many jobs, but the question which arises in the minds of the American delegation is that the language as it is phrased might be held to mean that a transaction comes through with a [words not recorded]. The country might refuse to recognize the obligation as to that currency. I want to make [clear] the United States's position that the balance passed by a country, the currency control as between the United States and the United Kingdom—that the third country, say Czechoslovakia, couldn't say that the transaction some year, or England couldn't say that some [y]early transaction of Czechoslovakia violated the provision, and I think the words "contrary to" in place of the words "as a result of dealings under" will clarify the situation.

Vice Chairman: As I understand the proposal of the delegate of the United States, it was that [paragraph] (d) under this section should be [p. 5] referred to the Asterisk Committee with the suggestion that "contrary to" be substituted for "as a result of dealings illegal under."

United States (Ned Brown): So that it would then read "holdings of currency acquired contrary to the exchange regulations."

France: I would like to support the suggestion made by Officer [[Soriano]] concerning the deferment. I would mention an additional reasons for deferring. I think there is a de facto [problem in?] the former text of [Article] IX, [Section] 2 ["Foreign Exchange Dealings Based on Parity"], because I do not see if section (c) is applied [[how that other text harmonizes with it?]].

Canada ([Louis Rasminsky?]): I should like to support the suggestion that this be deferred until the consideration of line 3. I should like to extend that as a whole to the preceding two lines: "nor shall it apply to a member which has ceased to be entitled to buy currencies of other members from the Fund in exchange for its own currency." It seems to me that there is some contradiction between that exemption in this new Section 6, covering multilateral international clearing, and old [Article] IX, [Section] 3 ["Avoidance of Restrictions on Current Payments"], not to impose restrictions on payments for current international transactions. The latter does not contain a qualification that the obligation "not to impose such restrictions" is not to apply in the case of members which have ceased to be entitled to buy currencies of other countries in exchange for their own. I would, therefore, suggest that those two lines as a whole be deferred for later consideration.

Reporter ([Robert Mossé, France]): The Reporting Delegate would like to ask for some clarification concerning the word "balances" in the first line of this section, if it is in order. Which balances are those? In what cases may a country ask payment in gold for the balances it holds from another money? I mean, are the balances left from transactions with the Fund, are they balances held from other [p. 6] transactions, or both? Now if it were balances held as a result of transactions with the Fund, that would be, it seems to me, in conflict with another text, on page 12, Sections 9 and 8 [of Article III; "Transferability and Guarantee of the Assets of the Fund," and "Other Acquisitions of Gold by the Fund," on page 11[411]]. From this article I understand that when a country has some currency left from the Fund or has bought rather currency from the Fund, currency from Country B, Country B must accept its own currency in payment of current transactions, but Country B is not to pay in gold for that currency. If we take Section 6, the first line, as meaning balances coming from the Fund,[412] that means that Country B would have to rebate in gold, and you can see the great difficulty which might arise. Let me take one illustration. Suppose that, say, Brazil would have bought from the Fund some French francs. Now, it might happen that the actual operation might not be exactly as forecast; there might be a balance left. Would in that case France be obligated to make payment in gold?

France ([André Istel?]): It is optional.

Reporter ([Robert Mossé]): Well, anyway I would like to have a clarification.

Vice Chairman: Will some members of the Committee clarify this point? I hesitate to do it myself.

[411] In Document 32, pp. 33-35.

[412] Apparently a reference to Alternative A to Joint Statement Article III, Section 5: "Each member shall buy balances of its currency held by another member with currency of that member,…." In Document 32, p. 32.

Honduras ([Julián R. Cáceres]): As far as I can ascertain, it is the obligation of the buyer to pay in gold. Where the option rests, the option is not with the seller, but the buyer.

Poland ([Zygmunt Karpinski]): It seems to me that the wording as it stands here may certainly have the effect which the delegate from France has put forth. That is, the member shall buy the balances, may buy them for the currency of another country or, [at] its option, for gold, but it is still committed to buy the balances, so that if it has no currency of another country, it is obligatory to pay in gold—which is in conflict with the whole program.

United States (Ned Brown): I would like to introduce Mr. Bernstein, who will speak. [p. 7]

United States (Edward Bernstein): Mr. Chairman, the provision of Section 6 must be read with all its qualifications. In the first instance, it states that a member country holding the balances of currency of another currency may sell such balances under certain conditions specified in that first country, and in return for such balances it will be paid its own currency, or if the buying country prefers, it will be paid in gold. What Dr. [Karpinski] states would be true, that a country holding no currency of the selling country would have to pay in gold if it were compelled at that stage to continue to buy that currency and had no other source of getting the other member's currency. Presumably it has access to the Fund and can get the currency in that way. If it has no access to the Fund, if the buying country does not have access to the Fund, the obligation in this form terminates. That is the intention, it seems to me, of the paragraph [in Article III, Section 5, Alternative A] following (a), (b), (c), [and] (d), which states, "nor shall it apply to a member which has ceased to be entitled to buy currencies of other members from the Fund in exchange for its own currency." That is the way the obligation with regard to the balances specified in the first paragraph with the other members currency may lapse, if the country that is doing the buying cannot secure the needed currency from the Fund.

France ([André Istel?]): I just want to mention that my understanding is exactly the same as Mr. Bernstein's, and as some have not understood it correctly and as you have not understood it, it may be better if the country has the right to sell [foreign] exchange to that country from the [foreign] exchange from the third country—[I mean,] from the second country. The reason why it has not the right to buy from that country is because several countries object to our currency. So if it was not possible to put a clause stating that the Fund is to buy the currency of the third country but the second country, it is necessary to devise a clause which looks rather complicated, explaining the conditions by which the transactions can take place.[413] [p. 1 (8)]

Vice Chairman: Is there further discussion of the viewpoints?

Canada ([Louis Rasminsky]): I should like to ask a question of qualification. Is it the intention that the application of multilateral convertibility of currency has a general application—is one which lapses when the country has used up its quota?

Vice Chairman: Can Mr. Bernstein answer that question?

United States (Edward Bernstein): I gather that Mr. Rasminsky is not inquiring as to what I like, but as to what the provision states. The provision states that the application in this form lapses. Mr. Robertson[414] has asked us to postpone the discussion of the section reading "nothing in this section shall be deemed to modify or affect the obligation of a member under [Article] IX, [Sections] 2 and 3 of the Joint Statement." I think the question that Mr. Rasminsky has asked is the reconciliation of this provision with other obligations of member countries as stated in that article of the Joint Statement. As the document reads, it is intended in effect to terminate the obligations of a country to sell—to buy, I mean—its own currency from other countries in the form stated here. I can see no great advantage in going into a long and detailed discussion of that point. If a country's access to the Fund has ceased—if it has inadequate resources in the judgment to maintain this type of repurchase—that is, until we have had some opportunity to discuss [Article] IX, [Sections] 2 and 3 of the Joint Statement in the later provisions of this document. [p. 2 (9)]

Vice Chairman: May I state what I gather from this discussion, namely, that Alternative A ["Multilateral International Clearing"] is acceptable to the Committee down to and including [paragraph] (a). With respect to [paragraph] (d), it is suggested that it be referred to our Asterisk Committee, with the suggestion that the words "as a result of dealings [illegal]" be replaced by the words "contrary to," and that the last clause of that paragraph following the paragraph no. (d); and that our consideration of that [paragraph] should be deferred until consideration has been given to the later paragraph dealing with the later section, dealing with the multilateral application; and consideration of the final

413 Here the U.S. Treasury Library copy of the typescripts contains some misplaced pages, which we have moved to their proper place at the end of the Committee's first meeting, on July 4. We resume with the first page of what the typescript identifies as part 2 of the transcript for this session.

414 Dennis Robertson of the United Kingdom, who was involved with writing a revised draft, and who is the likely speaker below.

sentence should be deferred until consideration has been given to [Article] IX, [Sections] 2 and 3.

[United Kingdom (Dennis Robertson)]: I do feel that it might be a very queer situation that the Committee were to approve down to the end of [paragraph] (b) and to defer the two following lines, because they really covered the whole of the sentence. They are an integral part of which many people would not be willing to accept the rest of the section and then be quite clear that the last two lines, the two lines after [paragraph] (d), were an integral part of the whole story, where my suggestion for deferment was a tightening up that relation was to be made between this section and Article IX. I think this further suggestion of deferring these two lines is a dangerous one, because it means a complete gap of the whole provision and makes nonsense of the whole section. I hope the delegation would not press these lines to be deferred. [p. 3 (10)]

Canada ([Louis Rasminsky]): I agree there is a great deal of substance in what Mr. [Robertson] has said. On the other hand, this is the coming decision of this whole plan and [[we would benefit?]] by deferring consideration of this entire article until [Article] IX, [Sections] 2 and 3 have been considered.

Vice Chairman: That would seem to be the logical outcome of this discussion.

Unidentified: Mr. Chairman, I want to emphasize the point raised by Mr. [Robertson]. I think many members of this Committee would not be inclined to agree to [paragraph] (a), (b), and (c) unless the other provisions of this section would also be agreed to.

Unidentified: A question of order: is it intended that this point—this last sentence—should be left to another committee?

Vice Chairman: No, I understood the suggestion to be merely that we should defer our discussion until it would be discussed in connection with this latter clause.

Unidentified: This Committee would discuss then Article IX ["Obligations of Member Countries"]?

Vice Chairman: There perhaps the difficulty has arisen. There are Articles IX, [Section] 2 ["Gold Purchases Based on Parity Prices"] and IX, 3 ["Foreign Exchange Dealings Based on Par Values"], which do not come under this Committee. They come under Committee 1. However, in two or three instances, these cross-references, which are difficult to deal with—is it the wish of the Committee that we defer consideration of the whole section to Committee 1 and Committee 1 deal with it, or shall we draw attention [concerning it] to the Commission? My [p. 4 (11)] understanding of the difficulty with respect to the last clause we have referred to is that it could not be fully discussed without discussing the substance of these later sections.

Mr. [Ned] Brown, delegate of the United States, introduces Mr. Bernstein.

United States (Edward Bernstein): Mr. Chairman, I regret that in the process of dividing the work with the hope of equalizing somewhat the tasks before the different committees, the Secretariat thought it might be helpful to give the committee that deals with purposes [of the IMF—Committee 1] at the same time the provisions on obligations of member countries. In my opinion, it is of the utmost importance that this provision, "Multilateral International Clearing," be retained in this Committee. In many respects, the whole of the operations section of this document depends upon the proper understanding of this section, and my suggestion would be that the Secretary of this Committee arrange with the Secretary of the Commission some proper assignment of the sections of Article IX that are concerned with multilateral clearing, perhaps arranging to have them transferred for consideration by this Committee.

Vice Chairman: Is that suggestion acceptable to the Committee?

Hearing no objections, I take it that it is. Is it then further acceptable to the Committee we defer any further discussion of Section 6 until it can be discussed in the light of the later sections which we hope can be brought before you? [p. 5 (12)]

Unidentified: An alternative possibility that a joint session of this Committee and [the] No. 1 Committee, which I understand has an overwhelming amount of material at the moment, would take place tomorrow morning.

Vice Chairman: Is there any support to that suggestion?

May I take it then that the other suggestion, [that] we try to arrange for the transfer of this consideration for the consideration of this Committee, should be—we should try and arrange the transfer of this clause in [Article] IX, which should be considered here, and that we defer discussion until we can take them both together?

There being no objection, I take that to be the view of the Committee.

As to [Article III,] Section 6 of the Joint Statement ["Purchases of Currencies from the Fund for Gold"]: "A member country desiring to obtain directly or indirectly currency of a member country for gold, is expected, provided it can do so with equal advantage, to acquire the currency by sale of gold to the Fund." It is proposed to replace that by Section 7 [in Alternative A], headed "Acquisition by Members of the Currency of Other Members for Gold." ["Any member desiring to obtain, directly or indirectly, the currency of another member for gold shall, provided that it can do so with equal advantage, acquire the currency by the sale of gold to the Fund. Nothing in this Section shall be deemed to preclude any member from selling in any market the new production of gold from mines located within territory subject to its jurisdiction."][415] Section is marked as one in which there are changes of words rather than substance. Are there any comments?

There is no comment. May I take it the Committee is agreed in approving [Alternative] A?

I take that is [as?] the view of the Committee.

[Article III,] Section 7 of the Joint Statement ["Repurchase by a Member of Its Currency Held by the Fund"]:[416] I note there have been Alternatives B, C, and D proposed to certain clauses. Alternative A is to be submitted later. Is it the wish of the Committee to discuss these other alternatives in the absence of Alternative A, or defer discussion relating to this part?

United States ([Ned Brown?]): Mr. Chairman, I suggest that discussion of Alternatives [p. 6 (13)] B, C, and D be postponed until Alternative A is submitted, which the United States expects to do shortly. It has been the subject of some discussion among the experts. It is absolutely impossible to understand B, C, or D except in connection with Alternative A, which I regret is not here, but which is thought of great service to this discussion.

Vice Chairman: That would seem to me to be the procedure which we should adopt. Is there any objection?

If not, we will pass on [to] page 12 of the document, in which there is a suggestion for an additional section to Article III, Alternative A, Section 9, "Transferability [and Guarantee of the Assets of the Fund." "(a) All assets of the Fund shall, to the extent necessary to carry out the operation prescribed by this Agreement, be free from restrictions, regulations and controls of any nature imposed by members. (b) The currency of a member country purchased from the Fund shall always be accepted by that member in payment of current-account obligations due to that member. (c) All assets of the Fund shall be guaranteed by each member against loss resulting from failure of default on the part of the depository designated by such member."][417] Is there any discussion of this proposal?

[United States (Ned Brown)]: I would like to explain it, Mr. Chairman.

---

[415] In Document 32, pp. 32-33.

[416] In Document 32, pp. 33-34.

[417] In Document 32, pp. 34-35.

Chairman: Do you volunteer to explain the proposal, Mr. Brown?

United States (Ned Brown): [Paragraph] (a): "All assets of the Fund shall, to the extent [necessary to carry out the operation prescribed by this Agreement, be free from restrictions, regulations and controls of any nature imposed by members]"—seems to me to go with the general article [Article III, "Transactions with the Fund"], which deals with the operation of the Fund. It might be contended that it is covered by later sections regarding immunities of the Fund. Obviously, if the currency required by the Fund cannot be used to carry out current transactions—to carry out the operations prescribed by this agreement, which altogether relate to current payments—unless that currency is free from any special restrictions or regulations or controlled by any members, the Fund won't work. That is the reason for the insertion of [paragraph] (c). [p. 7 (14)]

[Paragraph] (b) is to the same general effect. As restated, current-account obligations can be settled in currency purchased from the Fund, and it is intended to apply either before or after suspension or withdrawal. Otherwise, members of the Fund who would have a credit balance would be unable to use the currency of the nations having an overdraft on the Fund in the event of any trouble.

[Paragraph] (c) reads, ["All assets of the Fund shall be guaranteed by each member against loss resulting from failure of default on the part of the depository designated by such member."] The earlier section of the article provides that the funds shall actually—to keep the currency of each member in the central bank of that country, if it has one, or with the treasury or some similar financial institution designated by the member country. It was explained that some nations fortunately or unfortunately have no central bank, the United States being one of them.[418] In many cases the central banks or other depositories are not under government control, but a nation designates a corporation within its limits as a depository, a bank. If no option to keep this money in such bank so designated, it seems to me obvious that the nation guaranteeing the bank should guarantee the solvency in which the funds of that country are held.

[418] This statement is puzzling given that the U.S. Federal Reserve System had been in operation for thirty years. Perhaps Brown had in mind that, unlike almost all other central banks, the Federal Reserve does not hold funds and make payments from its headquarters in Washington; rather, the regional Federal Reserve banks, especially the Federal Reserve Bank of New York, act as its agents.

France ([André Istel]): May I ask clarification of a vital point? Does section (d) [paragraph (b)[419]] apply also during the transition period [[or only afterwards?]]?

Vice Chairman: [Can] any member answer the French delegate's question, which is, as I understand, whether [paragraph] (b) as proposed here would apply during the transition period when a member has established a closer exchange control?

United States (Ned Brown): Obviously, Mr. Chairman, if the currency is purchased from the Fund and it is put in by the member nation, then the restrictions dealing with Article X ["Transitional Arrangements"], [p. 8 (15)] dealing with the transition period, [apply,] that any currency [has] got to be used during the transition period. I don't know that I quite understand Mr. Istel's question.

France ([André Istel]): My question was whether if a country has established the full exchange control during the transition period, whether it is bound to satisfy the needs of any country which has purchased its currency from the Fund [for] requirements of a current nature.

United States (Ned Brown): It would seem to me obvious that the answer is "yes."

France (André Istel): All right. I just wanted to understand it fully.

Norway: It seems to me that there is a difference between [paragraph] (a) on the one hand and (b) and (c) on the other hand. [Paragraph] (a) seems to me to refer to the extraterritorial right of the Fund, and that amendment [in] (a) is that a member government in signing the convention for establishing and entering into membership of the Fund will undertake to secure by proper national legislation or by examination of existing legislation within the degree of the extraterritorial assets provided for in (a). If that is really the case, I think the wording of (a) should be altered.

Poland ([Zygmunt Karpinski]): I think the same thing in regard to (a). I don't think I have the same position with (b) or (c), but with regard to (a) the wording seems to be unfortunate. The accredited representative of one country, for example, to another, may be said to be free from restrictions. That is to say, he may move about. He has certain rights, but he is still subject to one restriction, [p. 9 (16)] that is, he has to carry a document to show who he is. The same thing is true in a country maintaining exchange control. It makes exchange control impossible. Anyone can come along and say, "This is currency belonging to the Fund,

419 Alternative A has no paragraph (d), and the Vice Chairman's remark immediately below makes it clear that this was a stenographer's mistranscription.

and I am free from restrictions." That obviously is not the intent I think the draft wants put out. It naturally has to confirm whatever regulations there are to show intent, but having done that, that money should then be free to leave the country. I think that is all that is intended. I think that section [paragraph] (a), as the gentleman from Norway stated, should be referred to the Asterisk Committee for improvement in drafting.

Vice Chairman: Is there any further comment?

France ([André Istel]): A further question, Mr. Chairman. I suppose [paragraph] (b) reads [i.e., intends to read] "expressed in this currency." For instance, if the currency was expressed in gold, I suppose it applies [[to the currency itself as well as to gold?]].

Vice Chairman: May I ask Mr. Brown to answer Mr. Istel? Mr. Brown, we are perfectly willing that it be referred to the Asterisk Committee, [but] as long as there is a question of difference of meaning it should be discussed.

United States (Edward Bernstein): I think it was intended when Section 9(b) was provided that it should be referred to the Asterisk Committee. That was really the intention in the drafting of 9(b). The reason is that the drafters of this provision had great difficulty in making clear their purpose. They also had great difficulty in finding the technique for achieving the purpose. Provision [paragraph] [p. 10 (17)] (b) is intended to cover cases of this sort. In the first instance, in some countries it is quite conceivable that all international transactions will take place in a currency other than their own. This may be true of state-trading countries.[420] It may be true of countries whose own currencies have very limited use in international transaction. If in those instances a country should have a favorable balance of payments on current account, it would be difficult, if not impossible, that a "passive" Fund should utilize the subscription of that country for the purposes of the Fund, that is, in financing a favorable current balance with that country.

The answer, therefore, to Mr. Istel's question is this: this provision is intended to assure the Fund that the resources subscribed by member countries are still usable for the purposes of the Fund in practice. Exchange regulations need not be in any way involved, though they may be. These resources are to be useful in practice, and consequently, as stated, an obligation to, say, France, the government of France, by the government of another country—however that obligation is expressed—would be dischargeable if it were a current-account obligation by

---

[420] That is, centrally planned economies, where foreign trade is a government monopoly.

tendering of [French] francs which were sold by the Fund for that purpose. It is not intended, of course, to cover non-current-account transactions, since the Fund is not designed for this other purpose. [p. 11 (18)]

Canada ([Louis Rasminsky]): On the very last point mentioned by Mr. Bernstein, to the extent that the Fund does sell foreign exchange for current-account transactions, I would take it that currency purchased by the Fund would also be good, and I suggest that question, which is related to [Article III,] Section 2(a) ["Conditions Governing Purchases for Capital Transfers"], which was discussed yesterday, should also be considered by the Asterisk Committee.

United States (Edward Bernstein): That was a slip on my part. We have corrected that since the broadening of that concept.

Vice Chairman: We are told that it was the intention of Alternative A that it be resubmitted to another committee on the matter of wording. I take it the Committee is willing to do that. Before we do so, are there any other views on matters of substance, if any?

We will commit this section to our Asterisk Committee. What is needed there is not merely verbal change, but clarification of the real substance of the section.

Before passing on to the next page, there are two matters which I might properly take up. They are in the agenda, but they escaped my attention. Since yesterday there have been two alternatives proposed to earlier clauses in this document. The first was circulated in this morning's distribution. [It] is Alternative E to [Article III,] Section 2 of the Joint [Statement, "Conditions Governing Use of the Fund's Resources"], or rather an addition to that section, which I believe was put forward by the delegation from Mexico. Is it the wish of the Committee to discuss this now, or do they wish further time for consideration of it? In other words, have they had ample time to read the alternative? [p. 12 (19)]

Brazil ([Francisco Alves dos Santos Filho]): I would like to inform the Committee that the Brazilian delegation has submitted an alternative draft of [Article] III, [Sections] 5, 6, and 7, which however is consequential to an earlier change to the second part of the draft of the Joint Statement.[421]

Vice Chairman: That proposal I take it will be circulated?

Brazil: I believe so, tomorrow.

---

[421] Apparently Document 284, p. 463.

Vice Chairman: Is there any objection to discussion now of this Alternative [E], page 6d, which was circulated this morning?[422] My only reason for asking is in case members did not come prepared.

Unidentified [Sir Shanmukham Chetty, India?]: Sir, before you invite discussion, may I ask whether the work of this proposed addition is in order. It talks about a "silver hoarding"; does that mean the silver-hoarding country?

Mexico ([Antonio Espinosa de los Monteros]): In reply to the [question] by Sir [Shanmukham?], we mean by "silver-hoarding country" a country which has more silver [currency[423]] in circulation—more silver [currency] than token [currency]—and which would be used for reporting purposes in that particular country.

Vice Chairman: If there is no objection, I take it we may discuss this Alternative E, as proposed by the delegate from Mexico.

Unidentified [Sir Shanmukham Chetty, India?]: I would like to have this reported: what is meant by "silver-hoarding country"? [p. 13 (20)]

Mexico ([Antonio Espinosa de los Monteros]): Mr. Chairman, we mean—the delegation means by that—it is often [termed] "silver-using nation." In other words, [a] nation that uses silver for its normal trade purposes. Now, we want to make a distinction [between a] country which normally uses silver as token money and [a] country which uses silver also for saving or hoarding. I don't know whether I've made myself clear.

France ([André Istel?]): I understand that the question of silver used for monetary purposes would be dealt with by Commission III. Would it be proper to refer it to Commission III?

Mexico ([Antonio Espinosa de los Monteros]): This is a subject that the Mexican delegation deems it proper to deal with the [Commission dealing with the] Fund. It is credit for silver [coins].

Vice Chairman: I would see no objection to the proposal that facilities of the Fund be provided for countries which use silver in a certain way. It is related to the operations of the Fund. It may be a proper proposal or it may be an undesirable proposal, but it seems to me that it refers to the Fund and its operation before this Committee. I am open for a discussion of this proposal.

---

[422] Document 107, p. 121.

[423] The typescript says "accounts" or "counts," which the speaker is using as the English equivalent of the Spanish *cuentas*.

Mexico ([Antonio Espinosa de los Monteros]): Mr. Chairman, on behalf of the Mexican delegation, I want to explain why we make this proposal.[424]

It is easy to misunderstand our position. Mexico produces 40 percent of all the silver. Therefore, one might think, Mexico is interested, above all, in furthering the interests of her mining industry.

However, we do not come before this Committee as the largest [p. 14 (21)] producers of silver. Certainly no one can believe that the gold-producing nations represented are here to further their own interests. Rather, we are all here to present our common monetary problems and to seek an agreement on how to meet them in the brotherly spirit of cooperation.

We wish to emphasize, therefore, that Mexico wants to present for your consideration a strictly monetary problem. We believe that this problem has international implications, undoubtedly small in economic significance for the world as a whole, but certainly large and vital for some members of the community of nations. Furthermore, we are certain that this problem has never received the unprejudiced consideration it deserves by the nations which do not have to face same conditions.

Mexico's problem arises from the fact that her people continue to hoard large amounts of silver coins. They, of course, have been doing that for centuries. They know not as yet any of the great advantages of savings banks and fiduciary currencies. Nor do they seem to be very anxious to learn about them. What they know is to hoard silver and nothing else, probably because all their ancestors have done so and certainly because the personal income does not permit them to hoard gold.

Because of this fact, Mexicans absorb large quantities of silver coins when their income is increasing and return them to the central bank when they have to draw on their holdings. This means our central bank has to invest heavily in silver coins during the upward trend of a cycle. On the other hand, the bank is compelled to get silver in foreign markets during the downward swing, when silver is cheaper. Thus, [our] [p. 15 (22)] central bank loses not only the difference between [the] buying and selling prices, but also the cost of melting.

Therefore, because of the hoarding requirements of our people, Mexico has to invest in silver a large part of her international gold and

[424] This speech was published with minor changes as Document 157, pp. 182-183, and we have used the published version to make some corrections to the typescript.

gold-convertible currencies [when her balance of payments is favorable. But when the situation is reversed, she has to sell that silver in order to support the parity of the peso. In the bargain she is always the loser,] since there is no manner in which she can go ahead against the fluctuation of silver.

This is the essence of Mexico's plea. Is it not true that many other nations partake of the same risk? Is it too much to expect that the Fund extend credit facilities especially adapted to meet this special need? It might be said that the Fund, under the proposed revisions, is already authorized to waive all specific conditions set forth under Article 3, Section 2 of the draft proposal in order to meet exceptional cases. But Mexico's case is not exceptional. Her problem is, we believe, common to several countries and it is recurrent in character. Should not the Fund, which is essentially an instrument for international cooperation, be authorized specifically to extend credit to the silver-hoarding countries of the world?

Specifically, Mexico is proposing that the Fund shall extend credit to those nations for [their] silver over and above the normal credit extended by the Fund to all other nations. Mexico therefore proposes the silver hoarded by her nationals as an adequate collateral security.

Should the conference accept this proposal, henceforth Mexico and any country in her position would not be required to buy and re-coin silver only to melt and sell it again. Instead of that wasteful and unnecessary process, whenever a silver-hoarding country is running [short of foreign exchange] with which to [p. 16 (23)] maintain the parity of its monetary unit, the Fund would provide that exchange as a credit, with the understanding that all the risks due to the fluctuation in the price of silver will remain with the borrowing country.

The Mexican delegation feels certain that this proposal will be supported by many delegates, inasmuch as the amount of the Fund's resources needed for the purpose will be relatively small and adequately safeguarded, and above all because the approval of Mexico's proposal will be an act of elemental international justice.

Vice Chairman: Is there any further comment?

Peru: I second the motion of the delegate from Mexico.

Vice Chairman: Is there a discussion on this proposal?

India: Might ask, Mr. Chairman, exactly how the hoardings of a country are to be determined? We in India of course have silver hoarders, but we would never be in a position to determine the exact size of those hoards at any time, and I don't quite understand how one could offer them as collateral for any purpose.

Mexico ([Antonio Espinosa de los Monteros]): It is, of course, understood that under another article of the draft that the Fund shall deal only through the central bank. Therefore, what is meant by the phrase the delegate from India is referring to—we mean, naturally, that the silver funds offered by the [central] bank to the Fund [are the] collateral guarantee.

Vice Chairman: We have now reached the hour to adjourn. As the proposal has not been before the Committee with a great deal of notice, we perhaps might defer the remainder of the discussion until our next meeting.

I would like to draw attention of the [p. 17 (24)] Committee to another proposal, which was circulated at the beginning of this meeting and which I did not refer to at the outset. It is circulated on the small sheet by the Netherlands delegation and is marked Alternative E, which we will place on our agenda for the next meeting. It is a substitute of Alternative A, Article III, Section 2, paragraph (3).[425]

France ([André Istel?]): I suggest that these amendments be [referred] for discussion [to] the appropriate committee which the Chairman designates for discussing them.

Vice Chairman: Is that an acceptable proposal, that this new draft be referred to the ad hoc committee, which has been referred back by the Commission?

We shall do that.

(Meeting adjourned at 7:00 p.m.)

---

425 Alternative E is Document 107, p. 121; Alternative A is in Document 32, pp. 28-30.

20

Commission I, Committee 2
Operations of the Fund
Fourth meeting: draft minutes
July 6, 1944, 2:30 p.m.[426]

Language Committee • Ad Hoc Committee • Transactions with the IMF

Because the draft minutes are brief, we omit narrative summaries for this and subsequent meetings of Committee 2.

The Chairman asked the delegations of the following countries to name a member to serve on the Language Committee: United States, Chairman; China; Ecuador; France; South Africa; Union of Soviet Socialist Republics. The Chairman asked the delegations of the following countries to name a member to serve on the Ad Hoc Committee to Consider Article III, Section 2 ["Conditions Governing Use of the Fund's Resources"], [Alternative A, paragraph] (3), Alternatives A, B, D, and F (Document SA/1, pages 6a, 6b, 6c, 6e):[427] France, Chairman; Australia; Brazil; Canada; China; Mexico; Netherlands; United Kingdom; Union of Soviet Socialist Republics; United States.

The Committee continued its discussion of Article III, "Transactions with the Fund."

On [Article III, addition to Section 2,] Alternative E [on silver-hoarding countries] (page 6d),[428] it was decided to defer action pending informal discussions among certain members of the Committee looking toward the submission of a compromise proposal.

On Alternative A, [Article III], Section 5 ["Operations for the Purpose of Preventing Currencies from Becoming Scarce,"], [paragraph] (2) (page

426 Published almost unchanged as Document 171, pp. 215-216.

427 Alternatives A, B, and D are in Document 32, pp. 28-30; Alternative F is Document 147, p. 158.

428 Document 107, p. 121.

8), and Alternative B (page 8), the Committee agreed to revise Alternative A, Section 5, [paragraph] (2) to read "buy that currency from that member with gold." Alternative B was withdrawn.[429]

On [Article III, Section 10, "Charges and Commissions"], Alternatives A and B (page 13), the Committee agreed to defer discussion until the material to be inserted in Alternative A is available.[430]

The Committee deferred discussion of [Article III, Section 11, "Furnishing Information"], Alternatives A and B (pages 14, 14a, 14b) until all members have had a chance to study them.[431]

The Committee agreed to refer [Article III, Section 12, "Consideration of Representations of the Fund,"] Alternatives A and B (page 15) to the Language Committee.[432]

The Committee agreed to approve [Article IV, Section I,] Alternative A (["Par Values of Currencies of Members,"] page 16).[433]

The Committee discussed [Article IV, Section 5, "Uniform Changes in Par Value,"] Alternatives A and B (pages 18, 18a) at some length.[434] A third alternative was presented informally and will be circulated. The Committee will continue its discussion of these alternatives at its next meeting.

---

[429] Both alternatives are in Document 32, p. 31.

[430] Both alternatives are in Document 32, p. 35.

[431] In Document 32, p. 36.

[432] In Document 32, pp. 36-37.

[433] In Document 32, p. 37.

[434] Alternative A is in Document 32, p. 38; Alternative B is Document 108, p. 121.

21

Commission I, Committee 2
Operations of the Fund
Fifth meeting: draft minutes
July 7, 1944, 2:30 p.m.[435]

Par values of currencies • Capital transactions

The Chairman read the procedural decisions of the Steering Committee (Document 175)[436] and urged the necessity of handling all items with dispatch.

The Committee continued its discussion of Article IV, "Par Values of Member Currencies."

On [Article IV,] Section 5 ["Uniform Changes in Par Value"], it was decided to report to the Commission the differences of view indicated in Alternatives A (page 18, document SA/1), B (page 18a), and C (page 18b).[437]

On [Article IV,] Section 6 (["Protection of the Assets of the Fund,"] page 19), the Chairman announced that the last paragraph of Document 166[438] had been misplaced and was intended to be an addition to Section 6. The Committee approved Section 6 as thus amended.

On [Article IV,] Section 7, Alternative A (["Separate Currencies within a Member's Jurisdiction,"] page 20) was approved with the suggestion that the word "however" in line 5 be deleted.[439]

The Committee discussed Article V, "Capital Transactions."

On [Article V,] Section 1, Alternative A (["Use of the Resources of the Fund for Transfers of Capital,"] page 21) was approved with the amendment that the words "make net" be inserted between the words

---

435 Published almost unchanged as Document 205, pp. 268-269.

436 Document 175, p. 220.

437 Alternative A is in Document 32, p. 33; Alternative B is Document 108, p. 121; and Alternative C is Document 164, p. 184.

438 In Document 166, p. 185.

439 In Document 32, p. 39.

"not" and "use" in line 1 and that the word "of" be inserted between the words "use" and "the" in line 1. In Section 2, Alternative A (["Limitation on Controls of Capital Movements,"] page 22) was approved with the amendment that the words underscored and line 1 be replaced by the following: "members may exercise such controls as are necessary to regulate international capital movements."[440]

The Committee deferred discussion of Article VI, "Apportionment of Scarce Currencies" (page 23a).

At its next meeting the Committee will receive reports from the Ad Hoc and the Asterisk subcommittees and will reconsider items that were deferred at earlier meetings.

---

[440] In Document 32, pp. 40-41.

22

Commission I, Committee 2
Operations of the Fund
Sixth meeting: draft minutes
July 7, 1944, 11:30 a.m.; continued 3:00 p.m.[441]

Report of Language Committee • Deferral of certain sections for later consideration • Transferability and guarantee of IMF assets • Par values of currencies • Scarce currencies

The sixth meeting of Committee 2 of Commission I was held on July 8 at 11:30 a.m. The Committee agreed to reconsider all material submitted to it on which action was pending in the order of its appearance in the basic document, SA/1 [Document 32].

The Committee accepted the report of the Language Committee that Article III, Section 1, Alternative A (["Agencies Dealing with the Fund,"] page 5) be approved with the addition of the words "with or" after "only" in the third line.[442]

The Committee accepted the report of the Language Committee that in [Article III,] Section 5, Alternative A (["Operations for the Purpose of Preventing Currencies from Becoming Scarce,"] page 8),[443] paragraph (1) be amended as follows:

"Propose to the member that, on terms and conditions agreed between them, it lend such currency to the Fund or, with the approval of the member, that the Fund borrow such currency from some other source either within or outside the territory of the member; but no member shall be under any obligation to make such loans to the Fund or to approve the funds borrowing its currency from any other source."

With respect to Article III, Section 6, "Multilateral International Clearing"; Section 7, "Acquisition by Members of the Currencies of Other Members for Gold"; [and] Section 8, "Other Acquisitions of Gold

---

[441] Published almost unchanged as Document 225, pp. 288-289.

[442] In Document 32, pp. 27-28.

[443] In Document 32, p. 31.

by the Fund," the Committee agreed that Alternative B (page 9a), Alternative B (page 10a) and Alternative F (page 11c) be deferred for later consideration pending the report of Committee 1 of Commission I on a proposal to which these alternatives are consequential.[444]

On Section 9 ["Transferability and Guarantee of the Assets of the Fund"], Alternative A (page 12), subsections (a) and (c) were approved.[445] The United States delegation agreed to distribute a memorandum explaining the purpose is to be achieved in subsection (b) and an appropriate phrasing of that subsection.

The Committee discussed Article IV, "Par Values of Member Currencies."

With respect to Section 1, "Par Values of the Currencies of Members," it was decided that Alternative B (page 16a) should be transferred to Article XIII, Section 5 ["Fixing Initial Par Values"] (page 49).[446]

On [Article IV,] Alternative A, Sections 2, 3, 4, ["Changes in Par Values," pages] 4a, 4b, and 4c (pages 17a and 17aa),[447] the Chairman noted that the Committee was near agreement but that specific reservations should be reported to the Commission if delegations so indicate, and that final approval should be deferred until alternatives that have not yet been circulated can be considered.

The Committee discussed Article VI, "Apportionment of Scarce Currencies."

The Committee approved substitute Alternative A, Sections 1 ["General Scarcity"] and 2 ["Scarcity of the Fund's Holdings"] (page 23b) and Sections 3 ["Administration of Restrictions on Scarce Currencies"] and 4 ["Effect of Other International Agreements on Restrictions on Scarce Currencies"] (page 23c).[448]

---

[444] Alternative B, page 9a is Document 144, pp. 156-157; Alternative B, page 10a is Document 149, p. 159; and Alternative F is Document 148, pp. 158-159.

[445] In Document 32, pp. 34-35.

[446] Alternative B is Document 177, pp. 220-221; Article XIII, Section 5 is in Document 32, p. 60. In the preliminary draft it was a blank placeholder for additional sections on putting the IMF into operation.

[447] Document 208, pp. 270-271.

[448] Document 207, pp. 269-270.

23

Commission I, Committee 2 Operations of the Fund Seventh meeting: draft minutes July 11, 1944, 2:30 p.m.[449]

Items removed from agenda • Par values of currencies • Deferral of action on changes and initial par values of currencies • Conditions for purchasing currencies

The seventh meeting of Committee 2 of Commission I was held on July 11 at 2:30 p.m.

The Chairman announced that Article IV, Section 5 ["Uniform Changes in Par Value"], Alternatives A, B, and C (pages 18, 18a, and 18 b of Document SA/1) were referred by Commission I to an ad hoc committee of Commission I, and that Article III, Section 6 ["Multilateral International Clearing"], Alternatives A and B (pages 9 and 9a) and Article IX, Section 4 ["Exchange Controls on Current Payments"], Alternatives A, B, C, and D (pages 40, 40a, and 40b) were also referred by Commission I to an ad hoc committee of Commission I, and that all of these items are therefore removed from the agenda of Committee 2.[450]

The Committee then continued its discussion of Article IV, "Par Values of Member Currencies." The Committee agreed to approve Article IV, Sections 2, 3, and 4 [on exchange rates and par values] of Alternative A (page 17a)[451] and Article IV, Sections 5 and 6 of Alternative

---

449 Published almost unchanged as Document 302, pp. 497-498.

450 Article IV, Section, 5, Alternative A is in Document 32, p. 38; Alternative B is Document 108, p. 121; and Alternative C is Document 164, p. 134. Article III, Section 6, Alternative A is in Document 32, pp. 31-32; Alternative B is Document 144, pp. 156-157. Article IX, Section 4, Alternatives A and B are in Document 32, p. 55; Alternative C is Document 196, pp. 234-235; and Alternative D is Document 219, pp. 279-280.

451 Document 208, pp. 270-271.

D (["Changes in Par Values,"] circulated as [page] 18c).[452] The Committee, however, reserves the right to reopen discussion of Section 5(b) [on the Fund's concurrence in changes in par values] (page 18c) after it has discussed Article III, Alternative A, Section 9(b), (["Transferability and Guarantee of the Assets of the Fund,"] page 12).[453] The Australian delegate asked that his reservation on Alternative C ([on changes to par values,] page 17c)[454] be noted in the report to Commission I. The delegates of New Zealand, Czechoslovakia, and the Netherlands withdrew the reservations they had sent to the Reporter after the discussion of Alternative A at the last meeting. The Chairman said that the observation of the Canadian delegate was not withdrawn.

The Committee deferred action on Alternative III, Section 10, "Charges and Commissions" (page 13),[455] to allow the Committee members more time to study the material. The Committee also deferred discussion of Article XIII, Section 5, "Fixing of Initial Par Values" (page 50).[456]

The Committee began discussion of the report of the ad hoc subcommittee of Committee 2[457] appointed to consider Article III, Section 2, [paragraph] (3) [conditions for purchasing currencies], Alternatives A, B, D, and F (pages 6a, 6b, 6c, and 6e),[458] and will continue discussing this report at its next meeting at 10 a.m. on July 12.

---

452 Document 284, p. 463.

453 In Document 32, p. 35.

454 Document 217, pp. 278-279.

455 In Document 32, p. 35.

456 Document 278, pp. 442-44.

457 Document 284, p. 463

458 Alternatives A, B, and D are in Document 32, pp. 28-30; Alternative F is Document 147, p. 158.

24

Commission I, Committee 2
Operations of the Fund
Eighth (final) meeting: draft minutes
July 12, 1944, 10 a.m.; continued 2:00 p.m.[459]

Conditions for purchasing currencies, continued • Charges and commissions • Representations by the IMF • Transferability and guarantee of IMF assets • Use of currencies held by the IMF • Changes in par values of currencies • Initial par values of currencies

The Committee continued its discussion of the report of the Ad Hoc Subcommittee on Article III, Section 2, "Conditions under Which Any Member May Purchase Currencies of Other Members," paragraph (3), Alternative A (page 6a), Alternative B (page 6b), Alternative D (page 6c), and Alternative F (page 6e).[460] The Committee approved the report of the subcommittee as amended by the Mexican delegation. Section 2, [paragraph] (3) of Alternative A (page 6a) is thereby accepted as it stands and the sentences following paragraph (4) are revised to read as follows:

"The Fund may in its discretion and on terms which safeguard its interests, waive any of these conditions, especially in the case of members with a record of avoiding large or continuous use of the Fund's resources. In making such waiver it shall take into consideration periodic or exceptional requirements of members. The Fund shall also take into account a member's willingness to pledge as collateral cold, silver, securities, or other acceptable assets having a value sufficient in the opinion of the Fund to protect its interests and may require as a condition of such waiver the pledge of such collateral."

---

459 Published almost unchanged as Document 325, pp. 539-540. The National Archives also have a second version of the draft minutes, whose page numbering differs from the version we refer to here.

460 Alternatives A, B, and D are in Document 32, pp. 28-30; Alternative F is Document 147, p. 158.

The Committee then considered Article III, Section 10, "Charges and Commissions," combined Alternatives A and B (pages 13a, 13b), Alternative C (page 13b),[461] and Document 285,[462] containing two tables in explanation of the combined alternatives. The Committee agreed to report substantial agreement on the principles involved but considerable divergence of views as to the nature and amount of the charges contemplated in the combined alternatives. Alternative C (page 13b) received substantial support.

The Committee then discussed Article III, Section 12, "Representations by the Fund," Alternatives A and B (page 15).[463] The Language Committee recommended that the section read as follows:

"The Fund shall have at all times the right to communicate its views informally to any member on any matter arising under this Agreement. The Fund may, by a two-thirds majority, publish a report to that member with regard to its monetary or economic conditions and developments which directly tend to produce a serious disequilibrium in the international balance of payments of members. If the member has not among the Executive Directors a Director appointed by it, the provisions of Article VII, Section _____ apply. The Fund shall not publish a report which would involve changes in the fundamental structure of the economic organization of members." [p. 2]

The Committee accepted the recommendation of the Language Committee after considerable discussion.

The Committee then discussed Article III, Section 9, "Transferability and Guarantee of the Assets of the Fund," paragraph (b) (page 12).[464]

The "Memorandum to Committee 2 on Use of Currencies Held by the Fund," Document 281,[465] was explained, and the wording suggested on page 4 of that document was discussed at length. The Committee agreed that paragraph (b) of Section 9 (page 12) should be eliminated entirely from the document, and that a provision embodying the substance of the provision suggested on page 4 of Document 281 as revised in the light of the committee discussion should be worked out by a small subcommittee and presented to the Reporter, to be in turn presented by him to Commission I as recommended by Committee 2. The Committee agreed that this provision should be made part of Article III, Section 8, "Other

---

[461] All in Document 277, pp. 441-442. The document lists all alternatives as being on page 13a, and shows no page 13b.

[462] Document 285, pp. 464-465.

[463] In Document 32, pp. 36-37.

[464] In Document 32, pp. 34-35.

[465] Document 281, pp. 461-463.

Acquisitions of Gold by the Fund" (page 11).[466] The delegate of the Union of Soviet Socialist Republics asked that his reservation be reported to the commission.

The Committee then turned to the discussion of Article IV, Section 5, "Changes in Par Values," Alternative D, paragraph (b) (page 18c),[467] since consideration of this provision had been deferred pending discussion of Article III, Section 9, paragraph (b). The Committee approved Section 5, paragraph (b) (page 18c).

The Committee then discussed Article XIII, Section 5, "Fixing of Initial Par Values," Document 278 (page 50), Alternative A (page 50b), Alternative B (presented orally), and Alternative B (page 16a) originally presented as an alternative to Article IV, Section 1, "Par Values of the Currencies of Members."[468] The Committee agreed to report that there was general agreement on paragraphs (a), (b), (c), and (d) of Document 278 (pages 50 and 50a), and also on the Alternative B presented orally at the meeting, which revises paragraph (e) of Document 278 and adds a new paragraph (b). The Committee also agreed to report that paragraph (b) be expanded to meet in part the proposals made in Alternative B (page 16a) and Alternative A (page 50b).

A small subcommittee was appointed to work out the revision on the basis of the committee discussion and communicate directly to the Reporter, who in turn will report the recommendations of that subcommittee to the Commission.

The Chairman then pointed out that the only other items on the agenda of Committee 2 were Article III, Section 8, "Other Acquisitions of Gold by the Fund" (pages 11, 11a, 11b, 11c),[469] and Article X, "Transitional Arrangements" (page 44).[470] In both cases material was not available, and it was agreed that those items would be taken up directly in Commission I.

The United States delegation said that it would prepare an explanatory memorandum on Article III, Section 8 ["Other Acquisitions of Gold by

---

[466] In Document 32, pp. 33-34.

[467] Document 284, p. 463.

[468] Document 278, pp. 442-444; Alternative A is Document 294, pp. 486; Alternative B presented orally does not seem to be in the conference documents; Alternative B, p. 16a, is Document 177, pp. 220-221.

[469] Pages 11 and 11a are in Document 32, pp. 33-34; page 11b is Document 110, p. 122; and page 11c is Document 148, p. 158.

[470] In Document 32, pp. 56-57.

the Fund"] and on Article III, Section 6 ["Purchases of Currencies from the Fund for Gold"].[471]

[471] We have not found the memorandum.

25

Commission I, Committee 3
Organization and Management of the Fund
First meeting: transcript
July 4, 1944, 10 a.m.[472]

Introduction of officers • Management of the IMF • Board of Governors • Quorum to convene Board of Governors

The subject of Committee 3 was "Organization and Management of the Fund." The committee chairman was Artur de Sousa Costa, Brazil's minister of finance.

Harry Dexter White, the chairman of Commission I, introduces de Sousa Costa and the other officers of the committee. The committee begins with a consideration of sections from Article VII, "Management of the Fund." It considers first a proposed alternative on the Board of Governors, the highest authority of the IMF, composed of representatives of all member countries. The reporter, Ervin Hexner of Czechoslovakia, helps the chairman keep the committee on track by clarifying the issues involved. Before World War II, Hexner had been a lawyer, university lecturer, and specialist on cartels. He immigrated to the United States in 1939, eventually becoming a professor of economics and political science at the University of North Carolina. An involved discussion occurs about how large a quorum should be necessary to compel the Board of Governors to meet. The underlying issue is how to protect the rights of member countries that may be numerous but only hold a small portion of the quotas (capital subscriptions), hence have few votes in the weighted voting scheme envisioned for the IMF. The solution the delegates arrive at is to allow either countries with at least 25 percent of the votes or a group of at least five countries to call a meeting of the Board of Governors. The 25 percent threshold implies that the United States would be able to call a meeting by itself, since it is expected to have more than 25 percent of the votes initially.

---

472 Summarized in Document 103, pp. 118-119. The typescript says "AR Brown, reporter"; apparently this is Augusta Brown. The transcripts also contain minutes of this session, which we have not reproduced because they are almost the same as Document 103.

After this long discussion, the delegates vote to strip a clause requiring that annual meetings shall not be held in the same country more than once every five years. As of 2012, the practice of the IMF and the World Bank is to hold their joint annual meetings at their Washington, D.C. headquarters two years out of three, and at rotating locations outside the United States every third year.

Harry Dexter White ([United States, Chairman, Commission I]): The meeting will please come to order. This is the first meeting of Committee 3, Commission I.

I should like to introduce to you your permanent chairman, Dr. de Souza Costa, of Brazil.

Chairman ([Artur de Souza Costa, Brazil]): I thank Dr. White for his kind words. I have the pleasure to introduce to you the Reporter of this Committee, Dr. Hexner from Czechoslovakia.

(Applause.)

I have the pleasure to introduce to you the Secretary, Mr. Malcolm Bryan, first vice president, Federal Reserve Bank of Atlanta.

(Applause.)

And the Assistant Secretary, Dr. J.H. [H.J.] Bittermann, United States Treasury.

(Applause.)

Now I call upon the Secretary to make the announcements.

Secretary (Malcolm Bryan, United States): Chairman and gentlemen: The temporary office of the Secretariat is in the Mount Washington Hotel, Room 162. I said temporary. We may have to shift that later today, but if so, we will post a notice as to the location of the permanent office of the Secretariat.

As the Secretariat understands, unless there is objection, the minutes of the meetings will not generally attribute points of view to a particular delegation or individual unless specifically so requested.

By agreement, the press is excluded from the meetings, [p. 2] and members of the press, persons not delegates, advisers, observers, or members of the Secretariat will retire.

The minutes will not be verbatim unless desired on a specific point and notification given.

Each delegation is requested to list the names of their representatives and give them to the Committee's Secretariat and to send an official copy to the Secretary General of the conference, Dr. Kelchner.

Speakers are requested to announce their names and countries. Members wishing to propose amendments or additions to the draft are requested to submit them in writing, as alternatives to be considered with the original or with other alternatives. The Secretariat of the Committee will gladly assist in the drafting of proposals, if so requested.

A supply of extra documents will be available here on this table for the members of the Committee and others attending. We have also available extra copies of the committee assignments for those who do not now have them and desire copies.

Chairman: Initiating the discussion of the matter contained in the agenda, I call upon the Secretary to read the first point about the Board of Governors.

Secretary (Malcolm Bryan): The Joint Statement reads as follows. I am reading from page 24 of the document, now SA/1.[473] ["Article VII, 'Management of the Fund,' Section 1, 'Structure of the Fund.'] The Fund shall be governed by a board on which each member shall be represented and by an executive committee. The executive committee shall consist of at least nine members including the representatives of the five countries with the largest quotas."

"Alternative A. Section 1. Board of Governors.

"(a) The administration of the Fund shall be vested in a Board of Governors consisting of one governor and one alternate appointed by each member in such manner as it may determine. Governors and alternates shall serve for five years, subject to the pleasure of their respective governments, and may be reappointed. No alternate may vote except in the absence of the governor. The Board shall select a chairman from its members.

"(b) The Board of Governors may delegate to the Executive Directors authority to exercise any powers of the Board, except:

"(1) Determining what new members may be admitted and the conditions of their admission;

"(2) Approving a revision of quotas;

"(3) Approving an agreed uniform change in the par value of the currencies of all member countries;

"(4) Requiring a member to withdraw;

"(5) Deciding appeals against interpretations of the Agreement by the Executive Directors given on the application by a member country;

"(6) Making agreements to cooperate with other international organizations;

"(7) Deciding to liquidate the Fund.

---

473 In Document 32, pp. 42-43.

"(c) The Board of Governors shall hold an annual meeting and such other meetings as may be provided for by the Board or convened by the Executive Directors. Meetings of the Board shall be convened by the Executive Directors whenever requested by one quarter of the members or by members having one quarter of the aggregate votes.

"(d) The Board may by regulation establish a procedure whereby the Executive Directors, when they deem such action may be in the best interest of the Fund, may obtain a vote of the governors on a specific question in lieu of calling a meeting of the Board.

"(e) Governors and alternates shall serve as such without compensation from the Fund, but the Fund shall pay such reasonable expenses as are incurred by the governors and alternates in attending any meetings."]

That completes the reading of Alternative A.

Chairman: Read Alternative B.

Secretary (Malcolm Bryan): By direction of the Chairman, I will now read Alternative B. ["[Substitute paragraph] (c) The Board of Governors shall hold an annual meeting and such other meetings as may be provided for by the Board or convened by the Executive Directors. Meetings of the Board shall be convened by the Executive Directors whenever requested by five member countries. Annual meetings shall not be held in the same country more than once in five years."] [p. 3]

Chairman: Now, the first point of our agenda is Alternative A, and so the discussion is open. And if any delegate may wish to make any comment on the record, I [shall] recognize him.

Cuba (Luis Machado): I would like to ask as a matter of information—the matter covered by our Committee is "organization and management"—if the question of when shall the Fund be considered organized is [within] the scope of this Committee, or goes under any other committee? In other words, when shall the Fund be considered as organized? Assuming that there are a number of nations that are decided to go into the Fund, some number of nations would be required to consider the Fund as organized. I am purely raising the question for my information whether that is the object of this Committee or not.

United States (Ansel Luxford): Mr. Chairman, I think that if I read the agenda that was furnished to us this morning,[474] that about the question of setting up the Fund, which I believe is what you meant by "organization"—

Cuba (Luis Machado): Exactly.

---

[474] Apparently Document 51, pp. 88-91.

United States (Ansel Luxford): —is under Committee 4, "Form and Status of the Fund." It being contemplated that the word "organization," as I understand it, relating to this committee [Committee 4], was in the same sense as "management"—what kind of an organization will run the Fund—rather than in the sense of the creation of the Fund.

Unidentified: As I understood the comment of the delegate from Cuba, what he really meant was, when will this be a going concern and begin to operate?

Cuba (Luis Machado): That's right.

Unidentified: In other words, how many assents and supporters are required to put it into operation? Is [p. 4] that correct?

Cuba (Luis Machado): Correct.

United States (Ansel Luxford): Mr. Chairman, I think the answer to that is that that is one of the questions that must be discussed by Committee 4. I think I can answer the question for the gentleman—that is, just as I see the text here, it is contemplated that some 60 percent of the countries when you calculate it on the basis of quotas must agree before the Fund would start. But I believe that is one of the subjects that will be discussed more fully and developed in Committee 4, and that this Committee [Committee 3], as I conceive it, would be, accepting the fact that the Fund had been set up, [addressing,] How would you run it?

Ethiopia (George Blowers): I imagine that the form our discussion is going to take here is that we will decide whether we want the paragraph [in Article] VII or not, [Section] 1 of [Article] VII of the original Joint Statement, to stand, or whether we want to make amendments to the alternatives as proposed. Is that the way we are going to approach the subjects under discussion?

Reporter (Ervin Hexner, Czechoslovakia): I suppose in order to introduce this discussion we have to break it down into one or two principles, this Article VII, [Section] 1. And there are two main principles involved, obviously. The first is whether the main organ of the Fund should be a Board of Governors; what should be the skeleton of the basic organization or the legislative body of the Fund; whether you wish to have a Fund that each country designates a man who is a governor and this is going to be the basic legislative body of the Fund. This is the first principal question.

The second principal question included into this alternative is whether there should be a delegation [p. 5] of powers at all to a smaller organ called the executive body; whether the delegation of powers could be absolute—that means whether all powers could be delegated; whether no powers could be delegated; whether the delegation of powers should be expressed as expressed here in this Alternative A; whether [the] general delegation excepts certain points, 1 to 7;[475] or whether the opposite procedure should be accepted to delegate certain powers: what isn't delegated is prohibited to do for the executive body. It means to accept the enumerated powers as we have it in the United States between the federal government and the Constitution.[476]

I suppose these two points are the two principles involved in this Article VII, [Section] 1.

United States (Ansel Luxford): I feel, in answer to Mr. Blowers's inquiry regarding procedure and whether we would assume that the Joint Statement provision, which is about four lines, should be adopted into the final document, or whether one of the alternatives should be adopted, that we should keep in mind that the Joint Statement was merely a statement of principles. It did not in any sense attempt to spell out the machinery for achieving that principle. I think that Alternative A is an attempt to implement that principle to carry its purposes out in a manner that might be inserted into the final agreement, so that you will have specified in this final agreement the machinery by which the Fund will operate. And I do not believe that it would be adequate to simply specify a principle in the final agreement, and we must arrive at some agreement on the precise machinery that will be employed in carrying out our agreement.

Chairman: I think we may carry on the discussion and reach the second point of our agenda. [p. 6]

United Kingdom (Sir Wilfrid Eady): I don't want to appear to challenge your ruling, but should we not have a discussion on Alternative A? I think the Reporting Delegate put the two questions that are involved very clearly. In the first part, paragraph (a) of Alternative A, we have the suggestion of the method of electing the Board of Governors, the duration of their appointment at the pleasure of their governments, the conception of an alternate who has no voting rights except in the absence of his governor, and the provision that the Board from among its members shall select its own chairman.

Now, if I may say so, those seem to be sensible machinery principles. But, of course, they do contain certain questions which it might be

[475] These are paragraph numbers in Article VII, Section 1, Alternative A, Section 1(b), in Document 32, pp. 43-43.

[476] Hexner, a Czech exile, speaks as if we was an American because he was at the time a professor at the University of North Carolina at Chapel Hill. He may have held dual citizenship.

convenient to take now. They are not difficult questions. I think it is clear that each member country is entitled to, and indeed must, appoint its representative onto the Board of Governors, and it must be free to choose whom it wants by what manner it wants, which is the first point.

The second point, of course, begins to raise a question. I don't think, myself, it is unreasonable, but it is a question whether the governors shall serve for five years, subject of course to the government which has appointed them being satisfied with their general conduct and that they may be reappointed. That contains the idea that there is some continuity of personal [personnel?] knowledge, subject to your satisfying the government, but that this continuity is restricted to five years. That is an important principle. That is a very important second [point] in the statement of principles. However wise and however good and however full the articles as a whole are, it will be upon [p. 7] the success and wisdom of the machinery that we here create that the working of the Fund will depend, and therefore, even at the risk of underlining some of these things, I think they ought to be considered. I am not suggesting they need to be debated if we are in general agreement, but I think we must not overlook what we are doing.

Now, [paragraph] (b) raises a set of different principles. Are we to contemplate that the day-to-day business of the Fund shall be conducted by Executive Directors, a small number, not all the member countries, but a smaller number to whom the member countries entrust these wide and important tasks? It is difficult to conceive of any other practicable arrangement, seeing the highly technical, highly urgent matters that may come up for decision. But, as I understand the intention of Alternative A, it is felt that while the Executive Directors can only derive their specific powers from the General Assembly, the Board of Governors represents all the member countries and, while they must have such powers as are required to be delegated so that the business of the Fund can be convened, if they can do it, there are certain things where the Fund stands in a different relationship to the member countries who elect the governors—where the judgment of the whole of the member countries or by the appropriate voting procedures should be required before action is taken.

Now, [paragraph] (b) contains a question of principle and a question of detail. The question of principle is whether it is right, and indeed necessary, that a large body of governors to start with, perhaps 50 or 55 in the end, shall attempt to do the business of the Fund by an assembly or shall delegate it. I personally have no doubt that the answer is it must delegate if it wants the business done, and I don't [p. 8] think that there will be much hesitation in accepting that principle. But I think, if I may suggest the problem, we should look very briefly in detail on each of these seven nondelegable powers and see whether we are satisfied that it is right that these shall not be delegated. I venture to suggest that, although this looks very straightforward and very sensible and, therefore, has not obtained much criticism, we are doing something rather important. So, without any wish to stop your ruling that we proceed to the next item, I do suggest that the representatives might have a minute or two more to raise questions on [paragraphs] (a) and (b) on page 24.

United States (Ansel Luxford): I think we would like to join with the gentleman of the United Kingdom in emphasizing the importance of Section 1, including paragraphs (a) and (b) thereunder. To illustrate: item (b): "The Board of Governors may delegate to the Executive Directors authority to exercise any of the powers of the Board itself." And then it lists the powers.

I think it might be worthwhile to examine the specific powers that are regarded under this document as not being desirable to delegate to an Executive Committee or some smaller operating group. The first of those is determining what new members may be admitted and the conditions of their admission. As I understand this document, it is contemplated that the admission of a new member to the Fund is one of the broad problems which all the members have an interest in, and that every country should participate in the decision as to whether a new member should be invited to join the Fund and the terms upon which they should join the Fund. That is particularly important. If we conceive the Fund as an organization that at some point or another may want to invite some of the present enemy countries into its organization—assuming [p. 9] that they have been fully defeated, unconditionally surrendered, and there is then the question of whether they should be brought back into the fold of civilized countries—by all means, that should be a question on which all the countries should vote, and all the countries should have a voice in deciding whether (a) to invite them back into the fold, and (b) the terms upon which they will be invited back into the fold.

Turning, then, to the second provision under [paragraph] (b), the provision is that only the Board of Governors should decide whether there should be a revision in the quotas under the Fund. Again, keep in mind that one of the principal considerations on the part of every country is the question of what is its quota, since it decides, first, the accession of a country to the Fund and, secondly, its voting power. Therefore, that is one of the considerations which only the Board of Governors should decide. That is a question which no subcommittee should decide—

whether a country's quota is going to be changed, whether its voting power is going to be changed—but every country around a table should have a full voice in what happens to its quota. Accordingly, under this provision, the major body, the Board of Governors, must make those decisions, and cannot delegate it to an operating body.

Turning, then, to [item] (3) under [paragraph] (b), "Approving an agreed uniform change in the par value of the currencies of all member countries," again you are raising at this point one of the fundamental decisions of the whole Fund: are you going to change the gold value of every country's currency? And under this draft it would be, as interpreted by me at least, one of the problems which only all the countries sitting in plenary session could decide. [p. 10]

[Item] (4), "Requiring a member to withdraw." I think that there would be little doubt but [that] on a momentous issue of that character, compelling some member to leave the Fund, in a sense to step out of the fold of the whole organization, [it] is not just an economic problem but also a political question and, being so, it is a question which should only be decided when all the countries are present in giving the country a full opportunity to be heard by all on whether or not its conduct has been such as to warrant the Fund in ousting it.

Item (5), "Deciding appeals against interpretation of the agreement by the Executive Directors given on application by a member country." As I understand that provision, it only means that, assuming that it may be necessary in the operation of the Fund for the operating group, the Executive Directors, to make day-to-day decisions on what are the meanings of the provisions of this Fund in their relationship to countries; nevertheless, if a country feels that the operating group's decision is wrong that it will have a right to raise that question when all the countries are present in plenary session, and there discuss whether the decision of the Executive Committee was correct. When I say "Executive Committee," I am referring to the managing group, to the Executive Directors as distinct from the overall body.

[Item] (6), "Making agreements to cooperate with other international organizations." Again, you are running into one of the political or major policy decisions of the Fund: should they enter into certain agreements [p. 11] with some other international body? And I think we would all feel that this is something that every country should have a voice in and [it should] not be decided by any small group.

Finally, [item (7)], "[Deciding] to liquidate the Fund." That really means whether or not the Fund should cease to operate, and just as it takes all countries to vote and decide whether you should create this

Fund, the meaning of this provision is that all countries shall be present by their own representatives in any decision to close down the Fund.

Australia (Jim Brigden): Mr. Chairman, it occurs to me that we can only make a provisional recommendation on this proposal until we know more about the operations of the Fund. For example, it may become part of the system to suspend a country from the facilities of the Fund, from the use of its resources or for other purposes, and therefore we would under this text be giving power to delegate to the Executive Committee this right of suspension—with which I do not disagree. I think it may be a necessary function of the Board [of Governors]. Nevertheless, I think we shall need to come back to these principles when we know more about the operation of the Fund as recommended by the Commission or by Committee 2. Meanwhile, this appears to be a very good starting point, although I am not clear what item 5 [is] or why item 5 is necessary at all. Can you, in fact, appeal against the decisions of the Executive Committee to the Executive Committee? Is it not automatic that you must appeal to the full body? I should have thought that 5 was not necessary at all—not necessary to specify 5.

United States (Ansel Luxford): My interpretation of [item] 5 is—others may differ with me on it—I think the point is that [p. 12] the decision was that the operating group should not be final, that there should be a right of appeal to the Board of Governors. That is all that was contemplated by 5.

Does that answer your question?

Australia (Jim Brigden): It seems a little awkward to say that the Board of [Governors] may not delegate the right of appeal to themselves.

Mr. Luxford: That's right, and they do not delegate the right of appeal to anyone else. It is not just the Executive Committee; they cannot delegate the right of appeal to anyone else.

Reporter (Ervin Hexner): I should like to indicate one or two issues. The first idea, which is emphasized by Sir Wilfrid Eady, is the problem whether we should delegate members for five years and to the Board of Governors. However, there is no doubt that everybody could be recalled by his government whenever the government wanted to recall him. There may be an issue if you by any chance selected to the Executive Committee [a governor] representing several countries how this is going to operate. But there is no doubt that the Board of Governors is going to consist of gentlemen, or ladies, who may be recalled whenever the governments want to recall them. The five-year period means that they have to be reappointed after five years. Otherwise, there is no significance in the five years.

Now, the second point is that the Board of Governors obviously has all the rights which are not enumerated or which are not delegated to other bodies. It plays a role like the British government—it [has the] rights which are [p. 13] not given to any other body.[477] The problem whether any single governor not sitting in session has any right of interpolation or a right to ask questions in the meantime is not solved. I suppose it is going to be solved in other regulations. The problem whether one-quarter of the votes should be necessary to call the board meeting is something touching on the rights of smaller countries, and perhaps they may discuss it or put it under discussion.

Canada (Joseph Blanchette): I think that all of us will agree that from the comments we have just heard [that] this section is one of the very important ones which will be used in the management of the administration of this act. If I may be permitted to make a suggestion in order that we may proceed with the order, would it not be advisable, Mr. Chairman, to go from section to section and from subsection to subsection in our discussions? In other words, it might be for example, subsection of [Article] VII (a), and then another member will refer to subsection (a) of [Section] 1…I feel it would be orderly procedure if we could take one section and then each individual subsection afterwards for commenting consideration.

Cuba (Luis Machado): I second the suggestion made by the delegate from Canada. I understand it is more or less the consensus of opinion that we should try to go as far as we can on Alternative A as a working medium to accomplish what the Joint Statement intended to imply. If we adopt the procedure, I would like at the right time to bring in discussion of Alternative B.

Chairman: Do I hear objection?

(None.) [p. 14]

(An affirmative vote was taken.)

Accordingly, the proposal has been approved.

I think we may initiate the discussion of subsection 1(a).

Mexico (Antonio Espinosa de los Monteros): It appears clear that the main question to be discussed is whether one-quarter of the member countries should be required to call a meeting, or whether, as Alternative

---

477 The reference is unclear to us. Perhaps Hexner is thinking of the relationship between the British imperial government and the colonial governments, under which the imperial government had decision-making power on issues not within the scope of the colonial governments.

B suggests, only five countries could [i.e., would be necessary to] call a meeting of the Board [of Governors].

United Kingdom (Sir Wilfrid Eady): We have no objection if Alternative B is going to be taken at the same time—and I haven't heard you say it.

Mexico (Antonio Espinosa de los Monteros): I just wanted to see whether we were discussing [paragraph] (a) under Section 1 ["Structure of the Fund"]. Therefore, there appears to be an alternative [paragraph] (b).

Cuba (Luis Machado): It refers to [paragraph] (c).

Mexico (Antonio Espinosa de los Monteros): I beg your pardon.

Chairman: As we have no remarks to the (a) [paragraph] first, I think we may pass to the (b) [paragraph].

Cuba (Luis Machado): Mr. Chairman. I don't want to control [monopolize] the attention of the assembly, but the word "administration" in the English language has a broader meaning than the word "administration" in the Spanish language, particularly from a legal point of view, and I was wondering if the word might be broadened so that it conveys exactly what I presume it intends. In other words, the Board of Governors would be able to do practically everything and exercise all the powers of the Fund. As I translate it into legal language in Spanish, I suppose some Latin American countries would be of the opinion it would not convey that meaning, so [p. 15] may I suggest in the final draft of this proposal, and recommend to the Drafting Committee, that the proper word be used so that the thought be conveyed that all the powers of the Fund shall be vested in the Board of Governors, who shall be in charge of administration of the Fund. Perhaps by reducing the wording more or less of that type we can cover both the English point of view and the Latin American point of view. We have to present this to our legislatures, and they would not be construing exactly the meeting unless we have some phraseology that will cover both cases.

Assistant Secretary (Henry Bittermann, United States): Mr. Chairman, to make it entirely clear, Dr. Machado suggests that in the first sentence of [Section] 1(a), in place of the words "the administration of the Fund" there should be substituted in the final draft the words "all powers of the Fund," so as to make it clear that this is an all-inclusive thing, because in Spanish "administration" has a more limited significance that in English. While I assume that English is to be the final language, it might be cleared, in Dr. Machado's view, so that we will know what we are doing.

United States (Ansel Luxford): Mr. Chairman, I think that is a decided improvement in the clarity of the language.

Reporter (Ervin Hexner): If I understand well, the proposal is that all powers except those enumerated or assigned in this draft or in this treaty to other agencies or delegated belong to the Board of Governors.

Chairman: So we may pass on to the letter [paragraph] (b) of Section 1. [p. 16]

Mexico (Antonio Espinosa de los Monteros): Mr. Chairman, on [paragraph] (b) I might add to the comments that have been expressed before you that it seems to me that the Fund can operate with efficiency even if these powers are not delegated in the managing group, in as much as all these matters that are not nondelegable do not require an immediate decision, so that all of them, in my opinion, can be postponed when they arise until there is a meeting of the Board of Governors. In other words, the element of time is not here as one of the principal considerations. The Board may meet when it is willing to consider these questions without hampering the functioning of the Fund as a day-to-day matter in its day-to-day operations.

[Czechoslovakia][478] **(Josef Hanč):** Regarding the clarification of this Section 1(b), in reading these two lines, "The Board of Governors may delegate to the Executive Directors authority to [exercise all powers of the Board, except:]"—does it mean that assuming that these exemptions are approved, that the Executive Directors would be in authority to exercise all the powers? That is, except those exempted ones.

Reporter (Ervin Hexner): Yes.

Secretary (Malcolm Bryan): Yes.

United States (Ansel Luxford): That is my interpretation.

I think there is one further point. The power to delegate is in the Board of Governors. In other words, the Board of Governors could say, "We are going to delegate certain powers, but we have some other powers we don't intend to delegate besides the seven of this document." First, they would not delegate the seven enumerated powers, but they might say that "We see five other powers that we do not choose to delegate." They have the right to limit further, but they cannot go this far. [p. 17]

Reporter (Ervin Hexner): I would suggest to discuss or to approve the idea whether there is [the] necessity of a quorum to delegate these powers. This is one of the most important decisions in the Board of Directors' [Governors'] power, and perhaps it would be worthwhile to consider in defense of the rights of smaller countries whether the

[478] The typescript mistakenly identifies Hanč as a delegate from Yugoslavia. We assume that Hanč rather than the Yugoslav delegate is in fact speaking here.

delegation of powers [should be discussed] here, or whether there should be a discussion about that even if it is discussed later in separate sessions. But it is rather important to know whether this delegation of powers can be done by an ordinary majority vote of the Board of Directors [Governors], or by a particular quorum.

United Kingdom (Sir Wilfrid Eady): Mr. Chairman, there is in effect a proposal which comes before the Committee later, on page 26a of the mimeographed document, which makes a proposal for the quorum of the Board of Governors.

Reporter (Ervin Hexner): B.

United Kingdom (Sir Wilfrid Eady): Alternative B [to Article VII, Sections 2-3, on voting] on 26a makes a proposal so that it will be ensured that this article, when finished, does contain an appropriate provision for a quorum.[479]

Chairman: Are there any new remarks about the letter [paragraph] (b)?

Australia (Jim Brigden): Just one minor point, if I may. I am assuming that the rules of the Board of Governors when they are established will safeguard their rights to vary their delegations at any time at any meeting; that once established, it wouldn't be a permanent delegation.

Chairman: We may pass on to the letter [paragraph] (c).

Cuba (Luis Machado): In connection with (c), I raised the question of whether it is appropriate to discuss Alternative B, which is an amendment to [paragraph] (c).

Reporter (Ervin Hexner): Yes. [p. 18]

Cuba (Luis Machado): I am not familiar with parliamentary rules applicable to the case, but perhaps the approval of (c) would exclude (b) and, vice versa, the approval of (b) would exclude (c). If it is in order, I would like to speak about your Alternative B, in which we are interested. We recommend that the right to call a special meeting of the Board of Directors [Governors] be given at the request of five member countries. The original proposal of (c) provides that one-quarter of the members shall be required to call a special meeting. At the present moment, one-quarter of the members would be 11 nations, but when the Fund grows—and we hope that it will grow—it may include as many as 55 or perhaps 60, and the question might be raised where the whole of Latin America in the Fund might not be able to call a meeting. And it is our intention with this suggested amendment that if there is any important

[479] In Document 32, p. 48.

problem on which five countries feel that a meeting of the Board of Governors should be called, that they should be given the right to do so.

United States (Ansel Luxford): Mr. Chairman, I do not think there is any difference in principle anywhere around this table on that question. Everyone agrees in principle, as I should say, that some group less than a majority should be entitled to assemble the whole group for a plenary session. The only question might be whether five countries is adequate. There may be a question as to whether if you did have fifty countries in this organization, the forty-four in assembly here, whether it might be right to assemble the whole Board on a vote of five, on the decision of five, and whether there might be great inconvenience. I am not sure. I think it should be discussed, though, whether that [p. 19] might mean that you would be having meetings very frequently, so instead of the Board meeting a few times a year on major issues that they will be meeting most of the time, and I should think that if an issue was important enough that it would be possible to get a larger bloc of countries to support assembling a meeting. But I just throw that on the table for discussion, and not in any sense to evaluate whether five is the right figure or whether it ought to be 10 or 25 percent. I think it should be explained in [paragraph] (c) in Alternative A that the language there is either one-fourth of the countries or one-fourth of the aggregate votes, so that it would be very clear that at all times the American Republics, which are around twenty, could clearly assemble a meeting, since it would only require approximately ten countries, under Alternative A, to assemble a meeting.

Cuba (Luis Machado): Mr. President [Chairman], I would like to explain further. Among the powers the Board will have will be the power to decide on an appeal from a member nation who may consider it is injured by some decision of the Board, and if a nation has to wait until an annual meeting takes place to decide an appeal, that decision may be so injurious to the national economy and the national safety of that nation that we would create a worse situation by not holding a meeting than we would by holding it. It isn't easy to get all nations to agree to hold a meeting. We have nations in Latin America who do not always agree on a question of policy, so when a matter is important enough to call five member countries to call a meeting, it must have some merit. I believe this would facilitate and give some small nations the right to be heard. It is worthwhile preserving that amendment. [p. 20]

Reporter (Ervin Hexner): I would like to clarify this point. There is no general right to appeal against the declaration of the executive body. This refers to one single point and the interpretations of the agreement according to [paragraph] (b), [item] (5). However, in order to deal with this point, perhaps this point (b)(5) could be clarified by the statement of what should happen between the interpretation of the Executive Committee and the final decision of the Board of Directors [Governors]. But there is no general appeal, so that this problem of five countries wouldn't have to be discussed from this one aspect. I don't want to discuss myself the question whether it should be given to five countries, the right to call a Board of Directors [Governors] meeting.

Mexico (Antonio Espinosa de los Monteros): Before, I was going to speak of this point, which to me is very important principle. It appears in Alternative A—I mean in point (c) of Alternative A—that it is either 25 percent of the member countries' vote, voting as countries, and they [can] call a meeting, or that 25 percent of the quota vote can call a meeting. Therefore, it appears to me a matter of principle that whereas one or two larger quota members would call a meeting, I see no reason why we should not support the Cuban proposition, if I may say so—

Cuba (Luis Machado): Right.

Mexico (Antonio Espinosa de los Monteros): —in making it a little larger even than the one or two larger countries, if they feel that there is a matter of substance to be discussed by the Board. I feel maybe the difference that Cuba has pointed out is most important for small countries, not only in the matter of appeal but in many other matters that might come up for discussion. [p. 21]

United Kingdom (Eric Beckett): The speaker just now referred particularly to the reference in subparagraph (b) about appeals on interpretations. I suggest, Mr. Chairman, that one cannot go into that in detail until another committee, which is in fact Committee 4, has dealt with the proposals about interpretations. If this Committee would look for a minute on page 46, they will see there are on that page two separate proposals about interpretations [Article XII, "Interpretation of the Agreement," Alternatives A and B].[480] When another committee has discussed that and come to some conclusion, the reference to interpretations in (b) of what is before us will become more clear. Until those have been discussed and elucidated, the exact meaning of [item] (5) here must remain slightly in the vague.

My second point was with regard to the calling of meetings—and I think it applies to an observation which was made over here, under little (c) at the top of page 24a—you have this: first of all, a meeting of the Board of Governors can be called whenever the Executive Directors

[480] In Document 32, pp. 58-59.

think it necessary. There is no limit on that. What you have got is a compulsory provision that the Executive Directors must call a meeting even if they otherwise didn't want to under certain conditions.

Well, then there is the question of the exact conditions which shall be compulsory when the Executive Directors do call a meeting, and there we have a point which, after all, reduces itself to somewhat small dimensions, as to whether it should be a quarter of the members—which, if the total was forty or forty-five, would be about ten, as Mr. Luxford said—or whether it should be five. But it is a problem which reduces itself to fairly small dimensions. [p. 22]

Brazil ([Francisco Alves dos Santos Filho]):[481] It seems that the principle of preserving the rights of minorities to ensure that meetings of the Board [of Governors] shall be held is an important one. It is simply the question of the judgment one might make as to the exact number of members who by getting together shall be able to exercise that right. I think our feeling would be that the proposal the Cuban representative that the board would have to be summoned if five member countries so desired might lead to an unnecessary number of meetings—that is, five is rather a small figure. But, on the other hand, assuming that all the countries were represented joining the Fund, it would be necessary to have eleven and, as the Cuban representative pointed out, in the course of time that number might be increased to fifteen. There is rather a substantial difference between five and fifteen. I would think the figure eight, or something of that nature, would be a reasonable compromise.

Ethiopia (George Blowers): Mr. Chairman, the delegate from Cuba referred to the one-fourth figure because of the possibility of the Board increasing the number to possibly sixty. Why don't we compromise and name a number of eleven, which is one-quarter of the present countries? So I suggest the number of eleven instead of five.

Greece (Alexander Argyropoulos): I would suggest that the proposal of the representative of New Zealand to take an intermediate number [of] eleven—I think that eleven would be rather a large number. We could fix a definite number between the two—for instance, eight members.

Cuba (Luis Machado): Mr. Chairman, may I again call [i.e., have] the attention of the assembly. Five, I know, may look like a rather small number of nations to call a special meeting. As I explained before, I don't believe that there will be [p. 23] many special meetings except for very special occasions, but take the whole of Central America: we have five

[481] Identified in the typescript as "Mr. F___."

nations there; a decision would be taken by the Board of [Executive] Directors or some question of policy may be raised in between interim of meetings that may decide the fate and the future of the stability of Central America. Well, if the purpose of this Fund is to precisely create a stable condition around the world, I don't believe that nations will be calling meetings continuously just for the pleasure of calling meetings. They would have to call meetings for very unusual circumstances, and I asked if we are going to create a situation where the future of the entire Central American section of the world might be in a situation of chaos by not giving them an opportunity to call [a] special meeting of the Board of Governors. I agree that it might be a very small point to some of those countries that because of their accumulated votes or by some other reason have the opportunity to call a meeting at any time, but I believe that if a big nation like the United States or United Kingdom can at its pleasure call a special meeting of the Board of Governors for some problem fundamental to their safety and to their economy, why shouldn't we give a Central American nation the same right?

Chairman: Well, we aren't making a general discussion of the matter, and so I think in order not to lose time it would be good if every representative could present a point to the Secretariat and we shall have another discussion about the same points, and so we may have a good knowledge of the matter and we can discuss it better. I propose this to you. [p. 24]

United States (Ansel Luxford): Mr. Chairman, on behalf of the American delegation, I would like to say that we are greatly impressed by the arguments that have been made on the part of Cuba and the other countries here that the original proposal, one-quarter of the countries, is too large, and that we are greatly impressed with their argument, and we feel that perhaps it should be five countries *or* 25 percent of the votes. That is, there is no reason why you shouldn't vote two of them and put them both into the document. I think that that would probably satisfy everyone around this table.

(Many assents.)

Then five countries can call a meeting, *or* 25 percent of the votes.

United Kingdom (Sir Wilfrid Eady): I should like to associate myself, on behalf of the United Kingdom, with Mr. Luxford's proposition. We felt the situation was protected by the power of the directors to call a meeting in connection with one country's difficulties, with the one country's dispute; for we also are impressed with the argument of the Cuban delegate and, if I may, on behalf of the United Kingdom, I should like to associate myself with Mr. Luxford's statement.

China (Te-Mou Hsi): Mr. Chairman, on the question of calling meetings by minority support, the view expressed by Mr. Luxford—that is, with five member countries or one-quarter of the aggregate vote—

Canada (Joseph Blanchette): Mr. Chairman, we from Canada feel, also, that the argument of the delegate from Cuba is sound and we would be acceptable to the proposition made that either 25 percent of the votes or five countries could call for a special meeting. [p. 25]

Colombia ([Carlos Lleras]): I also would like to support the suggestion made by the American delegation. I think it meets the spirit in which the conference should operate in the future. The Colombian delegation believes that, after all, there is a Constitution of the Fund and that [in] the spirit of the Fund, a plan could be incorporated, a principle in which countries could be individually representative and maybe each country ought to have to a certain extent an equal voice or vote. That is limited, of course, with the proposal with respect to the capital subscriptions of each of the various countries. I think as a point of principle the adoption of the alternative suggestion of the American delegation is very important, because it proves that the smaller countries are not going to be overrun on the principle of proportion to capital, and they will feel that they are sharing on a basis of equality to a further extent than they would otherwise.

Unidentified:[482] Mr. Chairman, as one of the delegates, I have been very much impressed with the action of the Conference Committee on the question initiated by the distinguished delegate from Cuba, Dr. Machado. It brings to my mind because of the unity and the meeting of minds the words of the psalmist David, some thousands of years ago, when he said, "How blessed is for brethren to dwell together in unity."[483] And that has been marked all through this conference.

Chairman: And so we may have the proposal of the American delegation. The gentlemen who are in favor of the proposal of the American delegation may say "aye."

Delegates: Aye.

Chairman: Approved. [p. 26]

Cuba (Luis Machado): May I thank the assembly for the splendid spirit of cooperation that has been demonstrated at this meeting, and I feel that the small countries are perfectly happy.

---

[482] Most likely from one of the English-speaking countries.

[483] Psalms 133:1.

United States (Senator Charles Tobey): I was just going to say we recognize what an important country is involved and we are very glad to cooperate with you on this proposal.

Chairman: We may pass on to the letter [paragraph] (d).

United Kingdom (Sir Wilfrid Eady): May I have your attention about the last sentence in Alternative B about annual meetings of the Board [of Governors], whether you would wish to discuss it separately at the end of [paragraph] (c), or as part of [paragraph] (a) once Alternative B has been put in an amendment to (c)?

Cuba (Luis Machado): May I say that we have really no interest in the last sentence of [paragraph] (c), and it was purely trying to adapt our amendment to the original draft.

Haiti (André Liautaud): I believe, Mr. Chairman, that if we are going from (c) to (d) we should underline the last sentence of Alternative B [that] annual meetings shall not be held in the same country more than once in five years. Personally, I don't see the necessity for such a statement, because if I think of the difficulties that might arise for the Board of Directors [Governors] to move around from one country to another, I personally don't agree with the last sentence of Alternative B, so I would recommend that this sentence be not taken into consideration.

Chairman: Is there any discussion?

Cuba (Luis Machado): I suggest that it be deleted from Alternative B—the last sentence.

Chairman: The delegation of Cuba has proposed that the last sentence of the letter [paragraph] (c) in Alternative B be eliminated. [p. 27]

Netherlands (Wim Beyen): I only want to support the protocol.

Chairman: Members in favor, say "aye."

Delegates: Aye.

Chairman: Approved.

Now, we must adjourn our discussion to four o'clock this afternoon, because we haven't time to go to another point. The session is adjourned.

(Whereupon, at 11:25, the meeting was adjourned.)

26

Commission I, Committee 3
Organization and Management of the Fund
Second meeting: transcript
July 4, 1944, 4 p.m.[484]

No compensation for governors • Executive Directors • Who may serve as Executive Directors

Committee chairman Artur de Souza Costa being detained, his fellow Brazilian Valentin Bouças, a wealthy businessman and sometime financial adviser to the president of Brazil, presides as temporary chairman. De Souza Costa apparently enters later in the meeting and takes over the chairmanship.

The committee briefly resumes its discussion of the functions of the Board of Governors, agreeing that governors and alternates shall serve without compensation by the IMF other than expenses for attending meetings. It then moves on to consideration of the Executive Board, a small group to which the Board of Governors will delegate supervisory responsibility of the IMF's day-to-day affairs. The preliminary draft IMF agreement proposes an Executive Board composed of twelve Executive Directors. Five directors are to be chosen by each of the five member countries with the largest number of votes, envisioned to be the five major World War II Allies: the United States, United Kingdom, USSR, France, and China. The other seven directors are to be elected by coalitions of countries. Henry Bittermann of the United States, the assistant secretary of the committee, explains at length the rationale of having Executive Directors and how voting for elected directors is envisioned to work. Bittermann, a U.S. Treasury official, had been secretary of the informal drafting committee at the Atlantic City conference preceding Bretton Woods, hence his familiarity with the details of the subject.

Wim Beyen of the Netherlands argues that the Executive Directors should not be a body in permanent session because then they will become cut off from the life and ideas

---

484 Summarized in Document 113, pp. 125-126. The typescript says, "Stenographic report by: Mary E. Fitchett." The transcripts also contain partial minutes of this session, which we have not reproduced because they are almost the same as Document 113 for the portion of the meeting they cover.

of their countries of origin, becoming too tied to the IMF. Beyen has in mind as a model the Bank for International Settlements, of which he was the president shortly before World War II began. Its directors were top officials of the central banks of its member countries, who spent their time mainly in their home countries and only met periodically to discuss the affairs of the Bank for International Settlements. It would turn out that the IMF's Executive Directors would become a board in permanent session. The United Kingdom suggests that at an appropriate time, it will propose that Executive Directors can but need not be governors of the IMF. After further debate, the committee adjourns without making any decisions about Executive Directors.

Secretary (Malcolm Bryan, United States): Dr. Bouças will preside. The Chairman is temporarily detained. We are going to continue our work of this morning.

Chairman ([Valentin Bouças, Brazil]):[485] The Secretary understands that we have completed [Article VII,] Section 1 ["Structure of the Fund"] through [paragraph] (c), and that in accordance with the rule of proceeding subsection by subsection, we are now on Section 1(d), found on page 24a of the draft document that you have read.[486] Subsection (d) reads, "The Board may by regulation establish a procedure whereby the Executive Directors, when they deem such action to be in the best interests of the Fund, may obtain a vote of the governors on a specific question in lieu of calling a meeting of the Board."

Discussion is open.

Cuba (Luis Machado): I would like to ask just what is meant by this section. What would be considered a suitable procedure? Would that be construed as far as to eliminate the annual report?

Reporter ([Ervin Hexner, Czechoslovakia]): There is a 100 percent probability that the Board wouldn't give such a regulation, but I don't think the Board would be entitled to give such a regulation. There may be secondary rules and regulations to indicate whether the Executive Committee may do that. [p. 2]

Cuba (Luis Machado): How about the occasion of a special meeting called at the request of one-fourth of the members or of five nations; would that procedure substitute [for] the holding of such meeting, or—

United States (Ansel Luxford): As I would read the provision as a whole, it would be my understanding that by no means might a meeting requested by five of the members be supplanted by any polling of the

485 The typescript minutes imply that at some point, Artur de Souza Costa entered the room and took over as Chairman, but do not specify when.

486 In Document 32, p. 43.

Board of Governors. There may be minor issues on which the Executive Directors would like to get the advice of the Board, and rather than calling them from all over the world, they might do it by cable, for instance.

Chairman: Do any other delegates want to present any suggestion?

If not, we will pass immediately to [paragraph] (e). Will the Secretary be kind enough to read (e)?

Secretary: "Governors and alternates shall serve as such without compensation from the Fund, but the Fund shall pay such reasonable expenses as are incurred by the governors and alternates in attending any meetings."

Chairman: Discussion is open.

No objection?

Then we go to the following. The Secretary will read Joint Statement [Article] VII, [Section] 1, [Alternative A].

Secretary ([Malcolm Bryan]):[487] ["Section 2. The Executive Directors.

"(a) There shall be twelve Executive Directors, namely, the General Manager, the governors representing the five member countries having the largest quotas, and six other governors elected biennially by the governors who were not automatically Executive Directors. The General Manager shall be chairman of the Executive Directors. The Executive Directors shall exercise all authority delegated to them by the Board of Governors and shall be in continuous session at the principal office of the Fund for at least the first three years of operations. In the absence of any Executive Director, his alternate on the Board of Governors make certain his place. Executive Directors shall be compensated by the Fund in an amount fixed by the Board of Governors.

"Whenever a member country not having a governor among the Executive Directors has requested action or will be directly affected by a decision of the Executive Directors, the governor representing such country shall be entitled to be present at the meeting of the Executive Directors considering such request or decision, but he shall not be entitled to vote.

---

[487] The transcript merely says, "(The Secretary read Joint Statement [Article] VII, [Section] 1, Alternative A, Section 2, "The Executive Directors)." We have reproduced the section from Document 32, pp. 44-45. Document 32 contains two sections labeled "Joint Statement VII, 1," the first on the Board of Governors, the second on Executive Directors.

"(b) In balloting for the elected Executive Directors, each governor eligible to vote shall cast for one governor all of the votes to which he is entitled under the first paragraph of Section 3 of this article (J.S. [Joint Statement, Article] VII, [Section] 2). The six persons receiving the greatest number of votes shall be Executive Directors, except that no person who receives less than sixteen percent of the aggregate eligible votes shall be considered elected. When six persons are not elected on the initial balloting, a second balloting shall be held in which the person receiving the lowest number of votes shall be ineligible for election and in which there shall vote only those governors who vote for a person not elected and those governors all or part of whose votes for a person elected are deemed to have raised the votes cast for such person above seventeen percent of the aggregate eligible votes. In determining whether any part of the votes cast by the governor raises the total of any person above seventeen percent, there shall be considered as not forming part of the excess the votes of any governor casting the largest number of votes for such person, than the votes of the governor casting the next largest number, and so on until the total reaches seventeen percent. Any governor whose votes are partly not in excess and partly in excess shall be eligible to vote in the second balloting only to the extent of the votes in excess. If enough additional persons are not elected on the second balloting to bring to six the total number each of whom has received at least sixteen percent of the aggregate eligible votes, further ballots shall be taken on the same principles until six such persons have been elected, provided that after five persons are elected the sixth may be elected by a simple majority of the remaining votes and shall be deemed to have been elected by all such votes.

"(c) Each governor who is automatically an Executive Director shall be eligible to cast the number of votes allotted under Section 3 of this article (J.S. [Joint Statement, Article] VII, [Section] 2) to the country which he represents. Each elected Executive Director shall be entitled to cast the number of votes to which the governors who elected him would be entitled. A member whose election is due in part to his having received a portion of the votes of a particular governor shall be entitled to vote only those votes of such governor which contributed to his election. When the provisions of the second paragraph of Section 2 of this Article are applicable to a vote on any question the votes to which an Executive Director would otherwise be entitled shall be increased or decreased proportionately. The General Manager shall have no vote.

"(d) the Executive Directors may appoint such committees as they deem advisable. Membership of such committees need not be limited to governors and alternates."]

Chairman(?):[488] I want to report here. I see we have Alternatives A and B, and they are very long ones, and I think it will be best for us to read A now.

[Canada]: We find it rather difficult to consider the significance of the suggestions here in Alternative A [p. 3] regarding the number of permanent seats on the Executive Committee without knowledge of what the quota structure is going to be. Similarly, it is difficult also with respect to what follows, to consider the significance of the method of electing the remaining delegates without knowing what the structure of the quotas will be. Therefore, I would like to suggest to the Chairman that we postpone the consideration of those two points until we have more knowledge of what the structure of the quotas will be. That will be undertaken by another committee. It is only with respect to those two points. I think the remaining material on these suggestions [is] not affected.

Chairman: What are the two points?

[Canada]: The number of permanent seats on the Executive Committee, and the method of electing the remaining members of the Executive Committee.

Belgium ([Camille Gutt]): I second the motion made for the very reasons expressed by the member from [[Canada?]].

Chairman: Well, we will suggest the motion by the delegate from [[Canada?]], seconded by [[Belgium]]. Any suggestions will be welcome, because we are making some important work for the benefit of our countries, so I want everything to be free.

Cuba ([Luis Machado]): Mr. Chairman, perhaps I do not understand exactly what was said by the distinguished gentleman who preceded me. It seems to me that it might be very helpful to read through these [p. 4] two proposals, because they approach the question of the number of directors and the Executive Committee and the method of election from two different angles, and regardless of what the position of our quotas may be, I think there is a [[question of?]] principle involved in the two separate sections. It would be very helpful, I think, and would save time to read the two proposals.

[Canada?]: I agree. They are quite complicated, particularly on the matter of election, and we are prepared to offer some written

---

[488] The typescript has a question mark here. It could be that the Reporter was speaking.

amendment, certain suggestions that perhaps might be considered by a subcommittee and might help in bringing the general Committee a direction that might help us to get on quicker. I would therefore request the Chair, if it is proper, to have the two alternatives read.

Chairman: So I understand the delegate from Cuba would propose to read all of them.

Cuba ([Luis Machado]): Both, and have a discussion as to the principles involved.

United Kingdom: These are very long discussions. I am not sure that we will be any nearer the discussion of the principles merely by having them read. I think the delegate from Cuba has raised a very important point. I think that we might discuss this without having the formality of having this read.

Assistant Secretary ([Henry Bittermann, United States]): Mr. Chairman, I understood the delegate from the United Kingdom to propose that we dispense with the reading and discuss the provisions. I didn't know whether any action had been taken on that. [p. 5]

United Kingdom: That was what I suggested, and I thought that the delegate from Cuba accepted that amendment to the discussion.

Chairman: We have been discussing the letter (a) of Section 2.

Cuba ([Luis Machado]): Mr. Chairman, at this point I would like to suggest, [concerning] Alternatives A and B, in regard to the Executive Directors, that they [i.e., the number of directors] be increased from twelve to fifteen, in order to enable the smaller nations to have a larger representation, and I would also suggest that the principle of distribution of geographic arrangements be adopted and be referred to a subcommittee to report with proper legal phraseology to cover that point. It seems to me that in order to have this further work properly, all geographical areas should be represented in that Fund, and the method of election of directors should be adopted that would assure such geographic distribution. It seems to me that the big monetary powers would retain the right to veto, safeguard, but we do feel that the benefit of advice of Executive Directors from wide parts of the world would be effective in carrying out [work] more efficiently—and refer [it] to the subcommittee in order to bring a complete proposal to the Commission at the next meeting.

Assistant Secretary ([Henry Bittermann]): I would like to discuss the provisions of Alternative A before we focus on a proposal to commit any part of this to some special amending process. I think that it would be in order to outline in general what was intended by Alternative A, so that all here will agree on what was the purpose of this [p. 6] alternative. As we turn to Section 2, and keeping in mind this morning that we discussed in great detail the fact that the Board of Governors is, so to speak, the plenary session, or the plenary body, holding all powers under the Fund, and that in turn they may delegate certain round [i.e., general] powers to an operating group. In other words, as was stated this morning by a number of the delegates, it is not possible for a group of forty-five or fifty countries represented by members to operate and manage a fund. They by all means should decide and form the policies, but if you must have a smaller operating group, that is designated in Alternative A, the Executive Directors. Now, the thought of paragraph (a) under Section 2 is that there should be around twelve Executive Directors. No one is arguing at this point whether there be eight or thirteen or something like that. It is the principle of a smaller number of directors who shall be responsible for the day-to-day operations of the Fund, operating, of course, under the authority vested in them by the Board of Delegates.

The question then comes up, assuming that you are going to have a small board who are going to handle the day-to-day operations, of who should comprise the group. Alternative A proposes, again for purposes of discussion, that you should first take the General Manager; that is, the man who is going to be responsible for the actual administration in a technical sense, to [[run?]] the operations of the Fund. [p. 7] The General Manager should, of course, be on the Executive Directorate, but he is going to be the man with the fullest knowledge of the day-to-day problems. Then it is suggested that the five member countries having the largest quotas should have seats on the Executive Directorate group. Finally, it is proposed that there be approximately six other seats on that Executive Directorate, and that those seats should be chosen from the governors who do not have a position on the Executive Director as a matter of right.

To illustrate concretely, you will have the countries with the five largest quotas naming specific men to the members of [the] Executive Directors. Then the balance of the countries, without any information or power to vote on the part of [those] who name a specific man, shall themselves decide who the other six members will be. Again I say, six is only being used as an example, and without any effort to argue [whether the number should be] six or seven or five.

This proposal also contemplates that perhaps the business of the Fund during the first three years, at least, will be so heavy as to make it wise that the Executive Directors remain at the head office at all times for the first three years. Again, that is for everyone here to decide, whether that is a good idea, the only thought being that in the transition period, in particular when we all realize the difficulties that will confront the world, and the contest in the monetary field, that it would be very fortunate if you would have the Fund in a position to act and act at once on the measures that are bound to be raised by the [p. 8] respective members. If someone else wants to say we can achieve the same result by having them available on 24 hours' notice, fine. We won't try to argue whether they constantly remain in one place, but we do want them there to handle the business when it comes up, and not have to wait weeks. When, for instance, some country wants a change in [exchange] rate, they should be available to act.

Then there is following that a provision that each Executive Director may have his alternate, who will be his alternate on the Board of Governors. Now, that again is to give us flexibility. I think we all realize the physical impossibility for a director to be constantly out of his own country and in attendance at a meeting, so we provided that his alternate might serve in his absence, so that you may always have available at the head office of the Fund the necessary members to handle the decisions that will come up.

Now, in recognition of the fact that you will have, whether you call it fifteen members on the Board of Governors or five or ten or twelve, you never are going to have all the countries represented on that Board of Governors.[489] That being so, the second paragraph of (a) attempts to remedy that problem, so that at least each country shall have the right to be present when the Board of Governors is considering business directly affecting that country. To illustrate: suppose one of the countries not having a representative on the Executive Directorate wants to have a change in [exchange] rate. [p. 9] This paragraph would permit the director or some other representative of that country to be present and to argue fully the case of his country before the Executive Directors when that matter is being considered by the Executive Directorate. That would also apply in any other case in which a problem of serious and vital concern to a particular country is before the Executive Directors. At that point they should have an opportunity to present their position to the Executive Directorate.

I believe that that covers all [of paragraph] (a). Now, I gathered from the discussion by the delegate from Cuba that some of the problems that he would like to raise go beyond part (a). For that reason, I would like the Chair's permission to develop the whole of part (a). I will attempt to

[489] That is, most countries will have to share an Executive Director with other countries.

avoid getting into the niceties of how many seats there will be on this directorate, any precise method of voting. It is the principles that I would like to develop.

Part (b) spells out a technique for the voting. I could spend a great deal of this time indicating the technique suggested, but I think that there is a principle involved that can be spelled out much more quickly. I have already indicated that five members of the Executive Directorate would represent the countries with the five largest quotas. I have also indicated that one other man, the General Manager, would have an *ex officio* position on the Executive Directorate. You then have the question of how do you name from the balance of the countries those persons who are to represent them on the Executive Directorate. [p. 10]

Now, the proposal here, in short, is that every country will have the opportunity to name or cooperate in naming a specific man a specific Executive Director, who will be answerable in a broad sense to that country or group of countries. If I might turn to the suggestion of the [delegate] from Cuba that there should be geographical representation, I would like to suggest that this will permit the achievement of that very end, namely, that any group of countries who can control 12 or 15 percent of the votes, after you have cut off the five countries who name a man by virtue of their possession of the highest quotas—the balance, any country or group of countries that can work together, will say, "We would like to have a man represent our interests," [and] will have complete power to name a man on this Executive Directorate. Now, as to whether that should be always geographical, I do not know whether that will always be the best committee. I suggest that in many cases they will be, and this technique will allow that. On the other hand, countries which may not be geographically associated together may have economic interests that may be associated. They may be on two sides of the world, and rather than put me side-by-side of a country that just happens to be beside me, I would rather pool my votes with a country that may have the same economic interests that I do. This would permit those two countries to pool together and name a member to the Executive Directorate. [p. 11]

I would like to touch on the remaining problem of voting on the Executive Directorate as contemplated in Alternative A, and again, I will give you principles, rather than details. What is contemplated is strictly in accordance with the provision of the Joint Statement, that if I may refer back now to Joint Statement, [Article] VII, [Section] 1—I believe that I am confused—I can call your attention, though, to the provision that I have in mind, namely, that voting on the Executive Committee shall be closely related to your quota, and it was with that end in view that we attempted to write language that would produce that result. I am informed that that is [Article] VII, [Section] 2 of the Joint Statement, which reads, ["The distribution of voting power on the board and the executive committee shall be closely related to the quotas."]

Therefore, the problem is one of seeing that each Executive Director represents or has the power to vote the votes to which the countries which named him are entitled under the quota system. This document contemplates that that would be done in the following way. The five countries which are *ex officio,* so to speak, represented on the Executive Directorate, namely the five who by virtue of having the highest quotas have automatic representation on the Executive Directorate, would be entitled to vote their quotas plus [[any additional votes?]] for [a] country vote. For instance, if the country was entitled to vote 500 votes on the Board of Governors, that country would also be entitled to vote 500 votes on the Executive Directorate. That takes care, then, of the first five members of the Executive Directorate. [p. 12] The problem remaining is what shall be the vote of the six members that are elected, and the answer there is the same, namely, that after countries agree on who they want—the group of countries wants—to designate as the representative on Executive Directorate, the Executive Directors shall then be entitled to cast the votes of that group of countries. Finally, the General Manager has an *ex officio* position on the Executive Directorate and it would [not][490] be his position to vote. He is simply the presiding member of the Executive Directorate.

The last provision, (d), simply provides that the Executive Directorate may appoint such further committees as they may deem desirable, and that they need not be comprised entirely of governors and alternates. In other words, the Executive Directorate may want to appoint technicians to consider problems of [exchange?] rate and similar problems.

Chairman: I thank you very much.

Netherlands (Wim Beyen): Mr. Chairman, I understand that you decided, and I think wisely decided, that we should discuss Alternatives A and B at the same time. I say this is a wise decision because it is quite impossible to have any opinion on any sort of rules about Executive Directors unless one tries to visualize what sort of an institution this Fund will be. Now, when I listen to many people discussing the importance of voting rights, I fear that many people have a conception of

490 Both the context and the text of the proposed section (Article VII, Section 2, Alternative A, in Document 32, p. 45) make it clear that the word "not" should appear here.

this Fund which in practice would not work, or would be, to say the least, disastrous. This Fund is meant [p. 13] to create and maintain in the world healthy and, as far as possible, stable financial and monetary conditions. Now, if we imagine that this Fund would succeed in doing that, when we assume that there would be a continuous number of cases brought up to it about which there would be voting, I think we would be sadly mistaken. If, in the future of this Fund, voting would play an enormous part, the Fund would be a complete failure. We would be in the same position as parents who are so afraid of the health of their children that they have the doctor living on the premises, with the consequence that healthy children would become crippled and diseased persons for the rest of their lives.

What can this Fund do? This Fund must try to be, first of all, a center of concentration amongst the monetary authorities of the world, because only if it is [[possible?]] that the countries of the world cooperate in the monetary [sphere, is] there any chance that it can maintain a healthy monetary condition. Let us not forget, gentlemen, that evaluation is not anything that comes on the surface from one day or another. Now, if we imagine that this principle of evaluation can be solved just by voting, and that it will depend on our voting, I think that we will just fool ourselves. If anyone knows anything about the history of finance, if there is a case where evaluations is the only way out, then we will just have to accept it.[491] If there is a case where the vote is not accepted, the member will just quit. If this Fund is going to have any meaning, and it is important that it have a meaning [p. 14] for the benefit of the world, then it should be a center of concentration. It depends entirely on the sort of people who will be the Executive Board, and secondarily the way these people can deal with those who are not continuously present.

We cannot do any good by having on that Board people who will devote their lives sitting in the country where it happens to be the seat of the Fund, who will not play any part in the financial life of their [own] country. It is not any good for the purposes of this Fund to have a board of high officials. What we want on this board is to have on this Fund the highest monetary officials of the countries, and they could be in residence in their own countries, and be not continuous residents in the city of the central bank, because it is no good saying these people will sit here and study economics. I have the greatest admiration for economists, but their work is in a way so frightfully dull. What is the good of people sitting

[491] The intended meaning of this passage seems to be that evaluating and resolving international financial problems requires continuous engagement with them in a setting where the emphasis is on achieving consensus rather than simply on voting to approve or reject loans for countries with problems.

there and studying statistics? We want people who live the actual monetary life of their countries. If the world were very small, we could meet once a month, but that is quite impossible. We have to make a choice. It is essential that there should not be only people who only know the monetary values of Western Europe, but these people know nothing about the monetary values of China, India, or South America. It should be people who know intimately the problems in the monetary life of their country, and should be people who represent all these various monetary [[tendencies?]]. It is not necessary that they should be there in permanent residence. [p. 15]

I happen to have a certain experience of an institution of that kind, an institution that has not been frightfully successful.[492] It had the bad lot [i.e., bad luck] of starting its work when any international cooperation was crumbling in the world. It did one thing. It created a center of concentration among the banks of Central Europe. There was always [[a place for]] banks to come and discuss without the thing becoming a stunt in the press. And the situation is not such that we can just go up to the place where the Fund will be, because [[it is far away from many members?]]. Now, the question arises whether the Fund can be run by these people meeting only once a month. I don't see why it couldn't be run that way, because apart from the votes on various questions, which if the Fund is successful at all, which will happen [[infrequently?]]. If there is no practical work to do that could not be done by high officials sitting there, [then] you couldn't possibly ask nine, twelve, or fifteen of that high standing that we want them to have [just] sit around the place and have practically no daily work to do. It means that these people will either be bored, or they will poke their nose in business where it doesn't belong. It may be a little bit worthwhile in the first few years to come there. Again, it should be a binding principle that these people should not be in continuous residence, but not be bound to leave the countries,[493] [rather] than to have extremely difficult problems of the postwar world settled by people who just are in that place, and have no contact with the actual life of their countries. [p. 16]

I am much less interested in whether I can vote or have a majority or minority than that the Fund will be a meeting[-place] where we will have to learn, gentlemen, what financial cooperation means, but we still have to learn. I would rather see the thing in a shape that can develop

[492] The Bank for International Settlements, of which the speaker had been alternative president from 1935 to 1937 and president from 1937 to 1939.

[493] Apparently the speaker means that Executive Directors will remain in the country of the IMF's headquarters.

something with the goodwill and interest of everybody, whether I have one vote more or ten votes less, and there is certainly every hope that it could develop. With war hanging around, I have seen cooperation which went so far that, except for the position of Germany, it would have been possible to re-establish in Europe, Eastern Europe, something very much more like free exchange without control than anything we will see in the world in a very short time. We are afraid, first of all, that the big [countries] will outvote us, and the big ones are afraid that the small ones will not cooperate. From what I have seen, I don't think there is any sense in being too much concerned. First of all, let us not forget that the world consists of human beings, and we are going to run something that, if you want to compare it, we can compare it with a horse and a motorcar, and if we spent days and days discussing votes we will never achieve anything at all.

Assistant Secretary ([Henry Bittermann]): Mr. Chairman, I would like to say there is very much that Mr. Beyen has said that I would like to agree with, for instance, that we should not overemphasize the vote aspects of the Fund. In my explanation I only attempted to make it very clear what this provision does provide. I would much rather say that on most issues there will be unanimity or there will be no need to vote since everyone will agree on the course to be taken. I am afraid, though, that the choices will not [p. 17] always be that clear, that it will not be possible to find every one of the [Executive Directorate] of the same mind, and in that contingency it becomes important to call out this vote, and in that contingency, Alternative A does provide a special form of voting.

I would also like to comment on certain other aspects of this problem. I would also like to see the postwar world through the same glasses as Mr. Beyen, namely that the Fund will not have too much to do. You will have cases when you will have to meet, but I do not see how you can talk in terms of an Executive Directorate that will meet once a month unless that Executive Directorate is prepared to turn over to some person the responsibilities which I would concede to be its and no other. To give you some concrete example, the provisions of the Fund state explicitly that if a country wishes to make a change up to 10 percent in [its] exchange rate, the Fund shall give it an answer within 24, 48, or 72 hours. What are you going to do with an Executive Directorate which meets once a month? Who is going to decide this question? I do not believe that there is any Managing Director who is going to decide this question. I do not contemplate that this group attended to and trust to an appoint officer who is going to pass on the question of whether a country is entitled to have resources of the Fund made available to it, and Article III specifically.

Now, that would be fine if no country ran into an emergency, but I don't see that that will be the world into which we are entering at the termination of the war. We should all recognize that there will be a constant emergency, and countries should be free to come to the Fund and ask for [p. 18] a change, and ask for it immediately. [Words not recorded.] But I do feel that there should be men there at all times to answer those questions [if] a country feels that it must [re]impose exchange controls after it has left [i.e., removed] them.

A further question, that of borrowing: the Fund may find it necessary to borrow one or more currencies in the postwar period, and again, those are decisions which I believe should clearly be by the Executive Directorate and not any appointed officer. I did not understand the gentleman from the Netherlands to indicate that the management should handle all those questions. I just want to make it very clear that I do not think one [person only] should handle them, and there will be many questions of that kind, and that they [the Executive Directors] should be available at all times to handle the matter. The Fund is entitled to as much of their time as is necessary to discharge their duties.

United Kingdom: I don't know whether I have your permission or the permission of the group....[494] Just for the purpose of explaining certain differences, the point of view that Alternatives A and B represent, I think it will help the group to see just what are the questions on which we should focus our minds. I want to clear other things out of the way. Alternative B does not provide in terms for the method by which the voting to choose the Executive Directorate is fixed. It is silent on that, because there is a question where [Article] VII, [Section] 2 ["The Executive Directors," is concerned,] and Alternative A has made elaborate proposals for that. We are dealing with one of the most important parts of the whole matter referred to this Committee. I hope I am not lacking in respect to Committees 1, 2, and 4 if I say that I regard our work here as not the least important. [p. 19]

Now, the delegate from the Netherlands has explained from his experience, which is rather unique in this respect, from the doubts he has, about the consequences of Alternative A; and I would like to say, as can be seen from Alternative B, we share a number of those doubts. If I may, I will take Alternative A and just illustrate the difference. We are trying to

---

[494] It is unclear in the typescript whether ellipsis points here indicate a pause by the speaker or words not transcribed by the stenographer.

contribute from our own knowledge and experience into the pool of this meeting so that something may come out of it. We are not interested in the voting. First of all, the proposal [that] the General Manager shall be a governor. Now, that looks very sensible, but it disfranchises the country to which that man belongs. If he is one of the twelve governors [Executive Directors] and is not allowed to vote, insofar as voting is important, he is disfranchised. Now, I attach no particular importance to that, so that you have an outside man, one country having to give up a seat, or having two seats.

But more serious [is], I think, this question of the Executive Directors being chosen from among the governors and [the idea that] nobody else should be considered. There are two possibilities: that the governments will prefer on matters of the [[most]] immense importance to send to the governing board a member representing the government directly in the government of the country, [[or that it will rely on its Executive Director?]]. Now, it is quite clear that [for] a number of countries, that that [i.e., the Executive Director] is the rightful man to choose. It is quite difficult to contemplate that he shall be in permanent residence because he can't fulfill the duties in the country. He may take with him all the knowledge of the government, but he can no longer represent the government in that sense. However, on the other hand, there is a wish on the part of the countries to bring the central monetary authority to the [p. 20] Fund; then again, I think it is impracticable to believe that that will be possible. Mr. Beyen pointed out that that means that he [i.e., the Executive Director] must choose.

I have, at the appropriate stage, a suggestion to make which would enable the principle that directors can be governors, but will enable any country which does not want the man it wants as governor [to be an Executive Director?]. I venture to put to the meeting that there is rather a difficult problem of working in the field for which you may choose the Executive Directors if you narrow it to the Board of Governors. I think you may lose the help of people who will be invaluable in the difficult times ahead of the Fund.

The next point is on the question of continuous session. There are enormously important subjects which the Executive Directors have got to decide, and I share the view of the spokesman of the United States that those can[not[495]] be decided by one man, however important he may be. Alternative B provides that they could delegate some things but could not

[495] The typescript says "can," which is obviously a mistake by the speaker or the stenographer.

delegate others, so in Alternative B there is a suggestion that some things must be done by the Board of Executive Directors elected. And if there are important judgments, I think are likely to be very frequent at the beginning and sometimes may arise rather urgently. I don't think I see these continuous crises, if there are going to be continuous crises, for the first three years after the war, which will require your Executive Directorate to be in continuous session, but I hope that is not what is going to happen. I think they have a series of immensely important decisions to make, largely in the beginning, and then, from time to time as they may rise. But there are technical operations perfectly under the competency of a good [p. 21] staff and the direction of [[the General Manager?]], and it seems to me that the position could be met by not [[requiring Executive Directors to be selected from among the governors?]] I want to lay down that first of all you limit your selection of the Executive Directorate to those [words not recorded]. And requiring that they be in continuous session for three years is putting an unwise limitation on your choice which it is undesirable to make.

The article might provide words to the effect that the Executive Directorate shall meet not less frequently than, say once a month, and as much more often and for such periods as in the opinion of the General Manager is required to conduct the business of the Fund properly. That puts the man who is in charge of the officials who are following the economic and financial trends in countries, who are watching the developments that are going to lead to a situation—that puts him in a position to know that he must have a meeting of many directors. [He will think,] "There is something coming here on which I should like to inform them, and on which I would like to have their counsel; and their counsel and advice will have been all the more valuable to me because they will have been in the stream of life." There is some risk [of the Executive Directorate] being detached and living in a world of its own and not seeing the living life in the countries. Delegate powers of certain limited functions, delegates chosen in the widest possible way; then, knowing that if they are chosen, they are required [words not recorded].

There are one or two other consequences that might arise. I thought it might help the meeting to see these two balanced points of views. There may be a middle course. Our view is that it is at least as important [p. 22]—more important than the Articles of the Fund will be—the way it looks, the kind of people it will attract to itself, the kind of relations they will establish. This Fund must grow in strength and not have its strength [only?] in the beginning. You ought to give yourselves the widest possible choice, and you ought to have no conditions which limit, especially in the beginning, the field of your choice.

Unidentified: I find myself in agreement with what has been said by the delegate of the United Kingdom. It seems to me that this is an excellent suggestion, which will take into account the equally splendid suggestion made by the delegate from the Netherlands that we should amend it, having the top man in the field, and the equally good suggestion of the United States delegate that the delegates should be on hand at all times. If we have executive secretaries who are not necessarily governors, such men could be in close contact with the top man. It has been expressed as undesirable to have the Executive Directorate delegate to an individual or a group of individual powers which have been delegated to it by the Board of Governors. It seems to me that there is a slight mechanical detail that we can handle when we discuss the wording of the project either under Alternative A, subsection (d), where the Executive Directors are permitted to appoint subcommittees or committees. It can be stated there that in appointing such committees. those committees have to report back to the Executive Directorate, and that action will be taken by the directors and not by the committee. Or, if we discuss Alternative B, subsection (d), which reads, ["The Executive Directors shall conduct all of the business of the Fund delegated to them by the Board of Governors,"][496] it could be added there that they are not allowed to delegate such power to a subcommittee or to any division. [p. 23]

Reporter ([Ervin Hexner]): Mr. Chairman, both [Alternatives] A and B propose a two-year term for the Executive Committee, but there is an interesting deviation from the term of the Board of Governors, and the deviation is that where[as] the [members of the] Board of Governors serve at the pleasure of their governments, this isn't the case with [the Executive Committee in] either of the proposals. Now, this would matter with those members of the Executive Committee who represent countries which have the right to be represented, but there arise many complications with those members of the Executive Committee who are supposed to represent several countries. If we imagine that such a country would recall the member in the Executive Committee, especially according to [Alternative] A, where he is bound to be a member of the Board of Governors, there would arise some complications, so that I

[496] In the conference proceedings, there is a misprint: the item "Executive Directors," is listed as (b) instead of (d), and subsequent paragraphs in the alternative are also mislabeled (Document 32, p. 46).

think we should discuss this point. [Alternative] A doesn't have the extra chairman for the Executive Committee, but the Managing Director is *ex officio* the chairman of the Executive Board. This is proposal [Alternative] A.

[Alternative] B elects an extra chairman, so that there would be in the article two chairmen, one of the Board of Governors and the second of the Executive Committee. Proposal A provides for a continuous session of three years; proposal B no continuous session. Proposal A: persons elected [[are]] not elected again. There would arise a slight [[problem]] with those countries who elected a certain person by trust. So that now there is a very important difference between proposals A and B. According to B, if I understand the proposal, countries are elected, which eliminates this difficulty and eliminates the difficulty. If I understand proposal B, countries are elected and not persons. According to A, only members of the Board [of Governors] are eligible to be elected into their executive body, whereas according to proposal B, either [an Executive Director] may be [a governor] or he may not be. According to A, an election process is indicated. According to A, the votes are related to a certain extent to quotas. [p. 24] According to B, there are rigid quotas. According to A, the country may be present which is directly touched by the question. I do not know how this can be made possible if there is an urgent thing to be decided.

Now, the last one I would like to mention: proposal A mentions special committees, where Proposal B doesn't mention it in this connection, [but] probably doesn't exclude it.[497] [p. 1 (25)]

India: I feel some doubt if I would be able to participate in the scheme where the directors are not essentially [[resident?]] on account of the difficulty of distance. I think it can be particularly difficult, as mentioned by Mr. L[uxford?], namely the consideration within two days [of] the application of the member countries who vary the rate of exchange by 10 percent. I find it difficult to see how the General Manager can anticipate this and get the information in time to the Executive Director representing India at the headquarters of the Fund. It is true that

[497] Here one typescript in the copy at the U.S. Treasury Library ends and we pick up from another, placed near the middle of the bound volume on Committees 1 and 2 rather than in the volume for Committee 3. The tab for the typescript says "Discussion on abnormal war balances." On the top of the first page there is a handwritten note describing the pages as "Discussion in Committee 1 of abnormal war balances," but the context indicates that the discussion actually belongs here, as does the copy in the National Archives, which contains no reference to abnormal war balances.

the scheme of alternates may mean a difficulty, but I think it would be preferable to have the Executive Directors in residence at the headquarters of the Fund, and that it could be said for the suggestion that these Executive Directors need not necessarily be either the governors or their alternates. As the representative from the United Kingdom said, that it would give us a wider field of experience on which to draw.

[Chairman]: Delegate from [[United Kingdom?]] is recognized.

[United Kingdom?]: May I ask you for a few minutes to explain the matter of permanent residence. Generally, I think that even in the earlier stages the urgent decision should be an exception, for the following reason. Whether it applies to the 10 percent [exchange rate parity] consideration or the 25 percent [quota] excess, or the difficulty of exchange control over borrowing, I cannot very well conceive that if the Fund's business is run in the way it should be run that these things would happen overnight. I cannot very well conceive that a country that is running its business well would overnight find itself faced with the necessity of getting more than [[25?]] percent of its quota. Exceptional cases might arise, but especially when both the Fund and the country are running their [p. 2 (26)] business well, they should generally see a little ahead, and everybody knows, who has seen all these sort of developments, and it is exactly when you have people who are taking part in the monetary life of the countries that they see them coming.

Now, one can mention that in the earlier stages there would be so much to be discussed that a monthly meeting would not be enough. Now, what I think important here is that a continuous residence should not be forced upon the Fund, because if you talk about continuous residence it is quite impossible that the man who is a director should have some sort of function in his own country. What would be a much more sensible solution, and welcome to anybody participating, is that many of the people who were directors of the Fund were people who had all their time available for the Fund, but would at the same time be in responsible position in their own country. The major central [banks] would have, during the early periods after the war, one of the directors [who] could be a deputy governor who would give most of his time to the business, and I don't see any objection to this man being at headquarters all the time; but I would not force the Fund into a situation where the man having to be in residence there could not possibly be a special deputy general of his [central] bank. I don't see any use in putting so strictly into the statutes that even when times become more normal—it would not be more necessary—that is the only explanation, because it seems to be the impression that if you do not have the forced residence, it would be impossible to give important decisions. Continuous residence is not always a guarantee for big decisions. [p. 3 (27)]

Chairman: The delegate from Belgium, Mr. Gutt, has the floor.

Belgium (Camille Gutt): We are going to adjourn in a few minutes, but before that I think it would be necessary for us to know exactly where we stand. We have been lately discussing the statutes [French *statut,* i.e., status?] of Executive Directors. We have been discussing their [legal] personality and whether they would have to have a permanent residence. I am leaning in that regard on the side of the delegate for the Netherlands and for the United Kingdom, but this was part of the discussion of the beginning of Alternative A and Alternative B. And in [that] regard, I want to refer to that motion of the delegate for Canada. Those two beginnings on A and B include several questions, raise several issues amongst them for preliminary [[consideration:]] that is, so that number of delegates, the number of permanent delegates—the way in which the number of permanent delegates are to be elected and possibly the way in which they are going to vote. In that regard there have been two motions, as far as I understand, one which I supported, coming from the delegate from Canada, asking that this matter be postponed until the questions are reported. The second [was] coming from the [[United Kingdom?]] delegate, proposing that this question be referred to a subcommittee which would have to get in touch with the committee for quotas[498] and report when we are better posted about the work. But I would like to know which of these ways is chosen.

Secretary: Gentlemen, not all delegations have given the names of their principal delegate and country to the Secretariat. As I understand it, the Commission [Commission I] will probably meet tomorrow morning, and there will therefore not be a meeting of this Committee. Will you want a meeting at four o'clock tomorrow afternoon?

Therefore the Committee will meet at four o'clock tomorrow afternoon in continuation.

Chairman: The session is adjourned.

---

[498] The Committee on Quotas of Commission I.

27

Commission I, Committee 3
Organization and Management of the Fund
Third meeting: transcript
July 5, 1944, 4 p.m.[499]

Board of Governors • Voting in the Board of Governors • Weighted voting • Minimum number of votes per country • Reduction in voting power for debtor countries • Quorum of Board of Governors

Committee chairman Artur de Souza Costa suggests discussing the voting procedure for the IMF Board of Governors, leaving questions relating to the Executive Directors until the next meeting because countries are negotiating about them. There are two proposals for voting power in the Board of Governors. The British proposal (Alternative B) is that voting power be strictly proportional to quotas (the capital subscriptions of members). The American proposal (Alternative A) is that every country receive a minimum number of votes, say 250, and that further voting power should be distributed proportionally to quotas paid in, with countries that borrow from the IMF suffering some reduction of voting power. Giving each country a minimum number of votes would give small countries more voting power than the scheme of strict proportionality. The chief explainer of the minimum-vote proposal is Ansel Luxford of the United States, the chief legal advisor at the U.S. Treasury and on the American delegation at Bretton Woods. The United States could afford to be generous because its economy was a greater share of the world economy than before or since, so under any realistic voting scheme the United States would have a far larger vote than any other country. The British participants in the discussion are Eric Beckett, a lawyer with the Foreign Office (ministry of foreign affairs), and Sir Wilfrid Eady, a British Treasury official. The British delegation withdraws its proposal after seeing a strong consensus emerge in favor of the American proposal. The United Kingdom would have the second-largest number of votes under any realistic voting scheme.

---

[499] Summarized in Document 141, pp. 153-154. The typescript says "AR Brown, reporter"; apparently this is Augusta R. Brown. The transcripts also contain minutes of this session, which we have not reproduced because they are almost the same as Document 141.

Allan Fisher of New Zealand, a prominent economist, speaks against a voting penalty for countries that borrow from the IMF, because he argues that it will be complicated to implement in practice and because, given that the United States is unlikely to borrow, its voting power would increase from its already large share, converting the IMF from an American-influenced to an American-controlled institution.

The other question at issue with regard to voting power is what share of total votes should be necessary to constitute a quorum of the Board of Governors. To protect small countries from the possibility that the a small group of large countries would establish a quorum and pass decisions unacceptable to the more numerous but less powerful small countries, Ecuador and Mexico propose that a quorum include a minimum number of countries. Antonio Espinosa de los Monteros president of Mexico's development bank and a director of Mexico's central bank, proposes that the minimum requirement for a quorum be two-thirds of votes and one-half of the member countries. The committee approves the proposal and adjourns.

Chairman ([Artur de Souza Costa, Brazil]): The session is open.

I suggest that we will begin our discussion today on page 26 of the Joint Statement of [Article VII, Sections] No. 2 and 3 [on voting procedures],[500] leaving all the questions relating to the Executive Directors postponed for tomorrow morning because certain groups are making certain arrangements in order to arrive at any [i.e., a] conclusion and present a new statement to the Committee. And so, the matter is now in discussion. We may receive the objections or the remarks about this question.

Unidentified: On the question itself, Mr. Chairman, or on the fact of taking up that question first?

Chairman: Of that question, of No. 2 and 3.

Unidentified: Yes, but I mean on substance?

Chairman: On substance, yes, regarding to the matter of Board of Governors but not of the Executive Committee.

Belgium (Camille Gutt): Gentlemen, I am sorry to take up your time again, but yesterday it had been proposed that some matters not regarding the Board of Governors but regarding the Executive Committee should be postponed or sent to a special subcommittee because they are very closely linked to the questions of quotas. Now we have this question of voting power with the Board of Governors, which is again very closely

[500] In Document 32, pp. 47-48. The conference proceedings number this section "Joint Statement III, 2, 3" instead of "Joint Statement VII, 2, 3," which is a printer's error not present in the original.

linked to the question of quotas, and I wonder how we can make quotas if we do not adopt the same system for that as the system which was proposed yesterday. [p. 2]

United States (Ansel Luxford): Mr. Chairman, I merely wish to state that there is much in what the gentleman from Belgium says. On the other hand, I believe that in Section 3, page 26, we are talking about an overall problem that is not closely related to the question of management or the details of management. Rather, it deals with the question of what will be the voting power of each country in the Board of Governors, which we have already discussed and more or less agreed on yesterday morning. That is, [on] page 24, we talked about the Board of Governors, we agreed that there would be a Board of Governors, more or less, and now we are talking about how a Board of Governors will vote. This has nothing to do with an Executive Director, who may be elected some other time.

Belgium (Camille Gutt): I said so. But it is linked, nevertheless, with the quotas.

United States (Ansel Luxford): Both are linked to quotas. Any question about it?

[Reporter] (Ervin Hexner, Czechoslovakia): Gentlemen, I think this Alternative A and B—it is true it is linked to quotas, but in an abstract sense it means whatever the quotas will be, these two proposals apply to it. I could imagine a quota system which would make these provisions inapplicable, but according to those quota systems which are discussed—I would underscore "quota systems"—what is discussed now, according to my knowledge, will be probably the size of the quotas. I do believe that we can attempt to discuss this [p. 3] voting with reference to the Executive Board, and if we hit a further point which makes it impossible to go further, we could probably postpone the discussion of that point until we know the quotas. But we could at least attempt to read it and to discuss it with reference to the Board of Governors in order to make some progress.

Belgium (Camille Gutt): I agree.

United Kingdom (Eric Beckett): Mr. Chairman, perhaps it would help the Committee if I pointed out this: it is rather an accident of the arrangement of the papers in the loose-leaf that you have Alternative A on page 26 and Alternative B on page 26a together. They really have no relation to each other at all, because Alternative B is talking about the Board of Governors and the vote that can be cast there, etc. When you come to Alternative A on page 26, it is talking about a particular matter which probably would be delegated to the Executive Directors, and, therefore, there is no connection between Alternatives A and B at all, and it would be a mistake to try and discuss those two alternatives together.

United States (Ansel Luxford): Mr. Chairman, I think that what Mr. Beckett has said is absolutely true with regard to the second and third paragraphs of Section 3, namely, there you are talking about a special fact situation. I do believe, on the other hand, that paragraph 1 is speaking of a general proposition, namely, how you shall vote on the Board of Governors, and for that reason there is perhaps a reasonable overlapping between the two. I think [p. 4] it might be helpful, since there seems to be a little confusion on the matter, to set forth at least [what is] intended to be covered by Alternative A.

The first paragraph provides that each member shall have 250 votes, plus one additional vote for each part of its equity equivalent to $100,000. Now, that voting you are talking about at that point is, what are the rights of a country on the Board of Governors? What are the votes that each governor on the Board of Governors votes? What votes will he have? So that there we are talking of the highest body, and we are discussing what each country's votes will be on that highest body.

Now, the formula that has been suggested here, in the first sentence, it contemplates the necessity for combining two different factors. There are obvious reasons, which all of you know, why it would be desirable to have each country with an equal number of votes. There has been a technique that has been used before many times by international bodies. On the other hand, there are perhaps equally persuasive reasons why you should not have your voting tied to the amount that each contributes in the sense of a business corporation. What this particular paragraph attempts to do is to equate, to bring together and balance, the rights of each country as a country and its investment, so that both factors are represented in your end product, namely, the votes of a particular country. [p. 5]

Now, the formula suggested here contemplates that each country, by virtue of accepting membership, will be entitled to 250 votes, regardless of what its quota may be. In addition to the 250 votes to which each country is entitled by virtue of membership, it is also entitled to votes depending upon the amount that it contributes. The particular formula which has been suggested here contemplates that for each $100,000 that a country contributes they will receive one additional vote. Therefore, if one country should contribute, let us say $1 million its total votes would be 250 plus 10 votes, which means that it would have a total vote of 260.

Now, this particular formula was intended in particular to give the smaller countries, the countries with the smaller quotas, voting strength by virtue of their acceptance of membership, recognizing that if you were to tie it entirely to their quota, their votes might not represent their true interests in this organization.

Turning from the first paragraph to the second paragraph, there you are dealing with a very particular situation specifically under Article III, Section 2 ["Conditions Governing Use of the Fund's Resources"]. You have a provision that the Fund may waive conditions regarding the access of a particular country to the Fund. To illustrate: under Article III, Section 2, a country is entitled to 25 percent of its quota during any twelve-month period in the event that conditions within that country require in any particular twelve-month period a sum greater than 25 percent of its quota. [p. 6] The country has a right under this document to apply to the Fund for a waiver of this 25 percent provision so that it is possible to give it a much greater amount.

Now, on the question of waivers, you have a vote. The Fund will vote on that question, and at that point this particular provision comes into play. On the date that the Fund is established, each country will have its quota in the Fund and the vote will be in the ordinary way. On the other hand, it is perfectly conceivable that over a period of time you will find that certain countries have drawn heavily on the Fund and other countries have not drawn on the Fund. This formula attempts to adjust for that contingency and the procedure contemplated would be that on this narrow question of waiver each member shall be entitled to a number of votes modified from its normal as follows: (a) by the addition of one vote for the equivalent of each $200,000 of net sales of its currency by the Fund. That is, as the currency is withdrawn from the Fund by other countries, the country whose currency is being taken from the Fund will have an increase in its votes on the basis of one vote for every $200,000 of a country's net purchases of the currency of a member country. Thus, if there were only two countries in the Fund and one country were to take the currency of another country—let us say $100,000—out of the Fund, the net result would be—my example should be $200,000. If Country A [p. 7] took $200,000 out of the Fund or the equivalent, which would only be the currency of the other country (since there are only two countries in the Fund [in this example]), the net result would be that the country taking the $200,000 would lose one vote. The country whose currency was taken would gain one vote.

Now, that provision only applies on the question of waiver plus one other case, and that is in Section 3 ["Voting"] under Article VII, which deals with voting on whether a country is using the resources of the Fund contrary to its purposes. Those are only two occasions on which there is any adjustment on the voting technique.

Now, as Mr. Beckett did point out, probably these votes that we are talking about now would be votes on the Executive Committee, but the point that is attempted to be established here, regardless of when that vote takes place, [is that] you will make adjustment on these two issues depending upon whether a country is either a net—if I may use the term—"borrower" from the Fund or a net "creditor" to the Fund.

Now, the last paragraph again is general. It states that, except as otherwise specifically provided, all matters before the Fund shall be decided by a majority of the aggregate votes cast. That will probably be more clear to you in terms of some of the earlier drafts, where you had sprinkled throughout the document "four-fifths votes." Most of those provisions have been eliminated from the draft. [p. 8] There is one case that I can think of where it still limits, namely, in the case of changing quotas a four-fifths vote is still required. There is one other exception, possibly, to this provision. Probably when you get to the question of suspension, voting on the forcible withdrawal of a country from the Fund will probably be on a country basis rather than on any basis of quotas.

Norway (Ole Colbjørnsen[501]): Mr. Chairman, I should think that this second point is rather closely related to what we are going to do about [the] Executive Committee. At any rate, it is very closely related to the spirit in which we are going to solve the functions of the Executive Committee. And in connection therewith, I should like to remark that it has not been decided, and I hope it will not be presumed to be decided, that the executive will be voted according to quotas. I hope that we will reach a place where we can decide that Executive Directors will vote individually, with the only proviso [being] that in order to avoid that, we will have to give very big members more than one director, two or three to a very large one. It does not do away with the principle of voting as individuals rather than voting as representatives of countries. I do not want to go into that matter any further now, since it will come up for discussion when we discuss the whole question of executive committees. Therefore, we are not quite able to discuss it at all.

The only thing I want to say is of a general nature. I am rather horrified by the spirit that is behind these questions. It makes the

[501] The typescript here and in some other places in this session says that the speaker is Ole Colbjørnsen, but his name is crossed out and a handwritten note says the speaker is Arne Skaug. Ervin Hexner, however, refers to Colbjørnsen by name, and we assume that he was the sole speaker for Norway in this meeting.

impression [p. 9] that we are going to make a distinction here between the virtuous and the sinful, the virtuous being those who do not use the Fund and the sinful being those who use the Fund. The consequence will be that the virtuous will have more votes than the sinful. Mr. Chairman, I think that would be most unhappy if we couldn't get ourselves rid of that conception. It should not be considered a bad thing to use the Fund. If someone abuses the Fund, let us assume if we start in this business that the greatest majority of us sitting around here will work this Fund in good faith. If we don't assume that, what is the good of starting a Fund that is meant to be a Fund of collaboration? But if somebody doesn't do that, there are various means for the Fund to intervene: it can even [impose] sanctions, it can [make] reports. In the exceptional case that somebody tries to make wrong use of the Fund, doesn't take the steps provided, there should be no distinction between Class 1, virtuous, who do not use the Fund, and Class 2, sinful, who do use the Fund. And apart from the fact we can't discuss the details of it, I want to warn all people here against such a conception, as it would wreck the possibility of this Fund ever being useful at all.

[Reporter] (Ervin Hexner): May I assume, Mr. Colbjørnsen, that your objection is only against this exception of provision?

Norway (Ole Colbjørnsen): Yes. Two things: first of all, I don't agree that the direct objective of [p. 10] the directors should [be] vote by quota. Secondly, I am against the conception that you should pursue [i.e., punish] people who use the Fund.

United States (Ansel Luxford): Mr. Chairman, I think that in many of these cases that we are going to run into in the Fund, you are really running into a basic problem of, what kind of animal is the Fund? And I don't know whether it is going to help any of us to talk morals about it. I think when you start gauging these matters as being "sinful" or perfect that it is not going to contribute too much to an evaluation of a concrete proposal. Although I can understand the analogy might perhaps clarify the issues in certain cases, I do not believe that it helps here. No one here is talking in terms of sin.

You have a question here, too, of an international body that has both political and economic phases. In other words, this document is an attempt to marry, to mingle and to blend the political aspects of this agency with the practical business aspects of the agency, the economic aspects. Institutions in the past have been established on more or less completely commercial lines. Others have been established on completely political lines. This whole document is an attempt to blend those two concepts. Neither of them has been perfect. You are dealing with an international problem. The spirit of this document is to bring together political considerations and economic. If you will approach this paragraph in that frame of reference, as a question of being one of economic or business aspects of this problem, it is fairly easy to understand [p. 11] this particular provision.

Specifically, I think all [of us have?] had experience in the past that with credit institutions, and the more that any business borrows from a credit institution, the more the credit institution wants to have a voice in what they are saying. Now, the analogy is by no means perfect. It is probably just as bad as the "sinful" analogy, but somewhere in between is the mean we are seeking here, and the provision contemplated here is that as a country continues to [receive] access to the Fund, the Fund is interested in restoring and in bringing back the [borrowed] funds into the Fund so that it will be able to handle the next emergency. And this is just one of the ways in which you can say that the Fund as a whole is attempting to restore the liquid assets of the Fund so that it can meet the next emergency.

Poland (Leon Baránski): May I ask whether you don't consider it as possible such example as I shall give you here? If my country uses 25 percent of the quota in the first year—it may be also 30 millions of dollars—then according to the formula, Poland may lose completely their voting power in this question in the first year, because that will be more than the voting power of Poland at all. I think that the idea to penalize the country which is using the Fund for the purposes approved and established in the Fund has no justification at all. But even in that time [i.e., case], you might say that the penalization may be too big.

United States (Ansel Luxford): Mr. Chairman, I would just as a point [p. 12] of explanation say that if Poland were to use 25 percent of its quota during the first year—is that your question? Did I understand you correctly?

Poland (Leon Baránski): Yes.

United States (Ansel Luxford): Twenty-five percent of the quota. The reduction in its quota would only be 12½ percent of its votes. Let us take the extreme case. Suppose that Poland used 100 percent of its quota. In that case, Poland would lose 50 percent of its votes and not 100 percent.

Australia (Jim Brigden): I regret to interrupt this interesting discussion, but I want to suggest that the Committee might deal with Section 2 ["The Executive Directors"] and the first of the part of the suggested part of Section 3, Alternative A ["Voting"], and leave this other matter because it is quite definitely a separate principle. I would like to discuss Section 2 and Alternative B, which relates chiefly to Section 2. We have nothing to do with sponsoring Alternative B, but we prefer the text to the original Section 2, and for this reason, that we feel that you cannot actually relate the distribution of voting power to the quotas at all closely in practice. We are departing from it already in this proposal that there shall be votes irrespective of the quota. If you recall the difficulty about the three objectives of participation—first of all, a criterion for contribution; a criterion for participation in the Fund; and then a criterion for voting—you get an impossible combination, so that you cannot use any formula probably for all countries for all three purposes. The capacity of the country to contribute to the Fund may be, and often is, very different from its needs of participation in the Fund. [p. 13]

We in Australia feel we must have a large enough quota for participation. We will contribute what is necessary for that. But we feel that if we seek an adequate quota we did not at the same time want to lay claim for a proportionate amount of voting power, and it is for that reason that, while it may be proper to base voting power upon the quotas and to vary from that base as may seem sensible, I don't think that we can really in practice have it closely related to the quota. I do not wish to make any suggestion of my own. I support Alternative A and Alternative B in that connection, and would suggest that we discuss that and then the first part of Alternative A, distinguishing that from this proposal that we have just been discussing for reasons of simplification.

[Reporter] (Ervin Hexner): Mr. Chairman, may I indicate the points which are at issue, perhaps, in order to have an idea of how to break down the discussion. I suppose that we may best discuss Alternatives A and B together.

The first question is whether the votes in the governing board, unless otherwise provided for—I mean election of the executive—unless otherwise provided for, whether they shall relate directly to quotas, as in Alternative B, or whether it should relate to quotas, in addition [to a base of] 250 votes. This is the first question.

The second question is whether there should be a change in voting power with reference to certain questions, as provided for in A and B. I would ask your consideration whether this point has so very much significance for those who propose it. I suppose there will be a group with very strong voting power which any way could vote down [p. 14] the creditor countries, but I don't want to go further into this question. It would perhaps be wise to consider whether it is really very significant, whether it is worthwhile to make it as a point of issue.

The third point, which is very important, is that [Alternative A proposes that] "Except as otherwise specifically provided for, the votes should be taken by a majority of the aggregate votes cast." Now, this can be understood only with reference to a certain core. There is no quorum in Alternative A—at least, not in this point—so we may take the quorum from [Alternative] B, and this quorum provides for two-thirds of the total voting power.

The next point we could discuss is whether this two-thirds of the total voting power is an adequate quorum. However, I would call your attention to the fact that it would be good to consider what is going to happen if there is no quorum, because there may be urgent matters which have to be decided, [though] there is no quorum. So, there should be an answer given whether there should be a quorum which should decide with [i.e., require a specified share of] members present, or whether that should be regarded as dropped. I suppose there is no doubt that this quorum probably doesn't relate to voting according to [Article] VII, [Section] 1 ["Board of Governors," paragraph] (d)—that means when a vote is taken by cable. It means that in that case if there is no—I don't know how the proponents met this quorum problem in the case of voting taken according to VII, 1(d), by cable. It is an easy thing to answer in one way or the other.

I suppose these are the issues which could be discussed.

United Kingdom (Sir Wilfrid Eady): I think this Committee owes a great debt to our Reporting Delegate for the way in which he regularly brings us back to what we really are talking [p. 15] about. With the permission of the Committee, I would like to comment on Alternative B. First of all, in the agreed [Joint] Statement of Principles which was published, it is clear it says the distribution of the voting power on the Board shall be closely related to the quotas. And that is published as the first item of our agenda. Alternative B, I think, can be criticized as being a rather lazy alternative. It says the number of votes each governor can cast shall be related to the quota of the member appoint[ing the] governor. All that that has done at that stage is to make explicit that votes on the Board of Governors shall be related to quotas. But I am afraid it has not gone on [far enough], and possibly it should have [gone on] to discuss how to calculate the quotas' strength on the Board of Governors. It accepted the principle that voting on the Board of Governors should be by quota strength, but it did not go on to discuss how to calculate it.

Now, the United States delegate, in explaining the first paragraph of Alternative A, said that it was an attempt to weigh two things, to put two things over the calculation of voting strength: first, the universal equality of all member countries because they had become members; and secondly, in accordance with the principle that is in the agreed [Joint] Statement of Principles, weighting by additional votes related—and in the first paragraph, related very exactly—to the quotas.

I think that the quorum part of Alternative B I should like to get out of the way. I think the Reporting Delegate was right, it doesn't really arise now, and what Alternative B was doing was making plain that you did not require all the Board of Governors [p. 16] to be present physically—or [their alternates]—in order to give a valid decision by the Board of Governors. You cannot contemplate that that will always be possible. But the Articles must provide that there shall be a minimum number of governors or their alternates present in order that their decision shall have validity. All the second part of [Alternative] B was doing was to make a suggestion about the minimum voting strength represented on the Board of Governors which would give validity to the decisions of the Board of Governors. It is quite true that it did not provide for the complications of what you would do with a quorum when you could cable to people. I am afraid we were thinking all the time about physical discussions around a table, and not this helpful consequence of the enormous quantity of inventions of American inventors.[502]

May I ask that this quorum question for the moment be outside of the discussion? What we are asked to consider and to discuss now is, do we agree with the Statement of Principles [Joint Statement] that voting on the Board shall reflect fairly accurately what one might call the economic interest of the participating countries and their contribution to the Fund? I suggest that we must accept that principle. It seems the only possible one that will be a working principle.

The second question we are asked is when you are translating that is this combination of the unit value for all members as members, plus a weighted addition equal to their contribution to the Fund. Is that a reasonable way of trying to link the political equality [p. 17] of the members and the Fund to the inevitable economic differences in contribution they are able to make? Is 250 votes plus this additional vote for each $100,000 of the quota a reasonable way of doing it?

I think it would help very much if we kept also quite separate the other part of Alternative A, which the delegate from the Netherlands has criticized, because there is a certain corollary. It is a qualification of the first principle. But I venture to put to the Committee that what we are

[502] The most widely used version of the telegraph was invented by the American Samuel Morse.

asked to decide is, do we accept the principle that on the Board of Governors, voting power shall reflect the contribution that each country has made to the finances of the Fund? Secondly, is this a reasonable way of giving effect to that principle?

Poland (Leon Baránski): I made really a mistake in my calculations, for which I apologize most humbly.

[Reporter] (Ervin Hexner): I think that is the problem at issue, this 250 votes. There is no doubt that what the British delegate explained corresponds verbally to the Joint Statement. I suppose everybody who read the statements—I mean the drafts as they followed each other—knows the story of these 250 votes. In the first draft there were 1,000 votes, or they were 100 related to 1 million votes. So that in this relation there were 1,000 votes. Later on, they were boiled down [reduced] to 500 votes. The idea is to give a certain voting power to small countries. I suppose from the point of view of justice, it is very difficult to state something to the right or to the left [i.e., to give a larger or smaller base quota]. It is a problem of protecting small countries—or, not protecting, that is nothing why they should be protected [i.e., "protecting" is the wrong term]—perhaps "supporting" small countries, something like that, [with] these [p. 18] 250 votes. The question is a question of substance, the question of volition, which can be argued with great difficulties.

Ecuador (Sixto Durán): Mr. Chairman, I have no intention of appearing "virtuous" by what I am going to say. Although I realize that my primary duty is to defend the interest of the country which has honored me with representation, I believe that I have—and I hope that many feel as I do in that case—an even higher duty, and that is to defend the Fund, to aim at making it a success, because in that manner I am not only looking after the interest of Ecuador but of all the nations associated with it in the Fund; and, because of that, I believe we should keep the Fund sound and safeguard it against error or abuse. For that reason, I am wholly in sympathy with the necessity of preserving the principle appearing in the Joint Statement about relating the voting power to the quota.

Furthermore, since the second paragraph on page 26 relates only to Article III, [Section] 3, as has been pointed out by one of the speakers (I believe the United States delegation), I do not take that as a punishment; I take that as one of those safeguarding measures to which I referred. If a country is in the position shown in Article III, [Section 2,] paragraph (c), on page 6, that country's position has been weakened, and it has a tendency to weaken the Fund if no measure is taken to correct that measure. To my mind, the second paragraph on page 26, decreasing the voting power of countries in the Fund, is such a corrective measure, and as such I would be prepared to support it.

United Kingdom (Sir Wilfrid Eady): May I ask the Chairman to give a [p. 19] ruling? I am not sure we have disposed of the first paragraph. May I ask as a point of order that you rule as to whether we have disposed of it or that we will go on to the next question, so that we will not lose ourselves again?

(No action taken.)

China (Te-Mou Hsi): On behalf of the Chinese delegation, I beg to support the case made by the Ecuadorian delegation. The Chinese delegation considers it very important that voting power shall be closely related to the principle as agreed upon in the Joint Statement.

With regard to 250 votes as a basis, this I think is normal. What is important is the [paragraph about] the several hundred thousand dollars. And, turning to [paragraphs] (a) and (b) under Alternative A, the Chinese delegation is prepared to agree in principle, but would like to suggest that the $200,000 for every vote shall be changed into $2 million in order to lighten the penalty.

Norway ([Ole Colbjørnsen]): I must admit, Mr. Chairman, that I am getting a little confused regarding what are the issues here. Now, we all seem to agree that the voting power can be related to the quotas, and it seems to me the question before the Committee is how, and how strictly should they be related to the quotas. As I understand [it], Alternative B proposes voting power which is proportionate to the quotas, while [Alternative] A inserts a 250 basic unit vote. After what has been said from Ecuador and China, it may seem difficult to get up and defend Alternative A, because I understand both Ecuador and China want Alternative B. I was a member of the Norwegian delegation last summer which had the pleasure to discuss this problem with the [U.S.] Treasury representatives, and they took part in the gradual decrease from 1,000 [votes per country] to 500, and sometime it disappeared [p. 20] altogether, and now we have 250. Now, we don't want to give the impression that we are so terribly anxious to get voting power or all these sorts of things, but we do feel that also from the small countries there are good people in these fields, people who understand things and might be able to make a contribution to discussions and to the decisions which are going to be made by the Fund, and for that reason, we think is justified and that we should have a basic vote. I should not object to 500, but I'm not going to raise that question; let [it be] the 250 which is proposed in the alternative. On behalf of the Norwegian delegation, I should like very strongly to support Alternative A.

Mexico (Antonio Espinosa de los Monteros): I want to point out to this Committee that the Mexican delegation is also strongly in favor of that first paragraph that is under discussion, but I must point out that 250 votes have to be taken in relation to the total of votes. In other words, that I would suggest that the question of how many votes of a country should be postponed until, as the delegate from Canada proposed yesterday, we know the scheme, the total schedule, of votes. In other words, I favor the principle of assigning to each country as a member country a number of votes. How many votes, I would leave for discussion which will take place after we know that schedule.

[Reporter] (Ervin Hexner): But, Mr. Chairman, may I suggest that we finish our discussion on the first part of this point by recording that there was a disagreement in the Committee whether voting in the Board of Governors should be related directly or rigidly to the quotas, or whether a certain [p. 21] amount of votes should be added to that vote.

Mexico (Antonio Espinosa de los Monteros): Mr. Chairman, a point of order. I would suggest that we first decide whether this Committee accepts the principle that each country should have a number of votes independent of its quota votes.

[Reporter] (Ervin Hexner): Well, I suppose that the Committee isn't supposed to make majority voting. It means to outvote each other. We are going to put into the record there was a disagreement. It is obvious that the representative of the United Kingdom opposed the adding of a rigid number of votes to the quotas, and this in itself is sufficient to register disagreement.

United Kingdom (Sir Wilfrid Eady): Would it help if the United Kingdom withdrew Alternative B? It was never meant to suggest that the relation of the votes on the Board of Governors should be rigidly related to the quotas. We have no objection in principle to the suggestion in Alternative A and, in order to avoid any implication that there is disagreement on the principle that each country shall have a given number of votes as a country, we are content to withdrawal Alternative B.

[Reporter] (Ervin Hexner): Would the delegate of Mexico oppose this number, 250?

Mexico (Antonio Espinosa de los Monteros): I would not oppose it until we know the relation between 250 and the total aggregate quota votes.

[Reporter] (Ervin Hexner): We could perhaps register the following decision, if you agree, gentlemen: that there is an agreement on the first paragraph of [Article] VII, [Sections] 2 [and] 3, according to Alternative

A, with the remark that the number 250 has to be reconsidered after knowing the quota participations. [p. 22]

United States (Ansel Luxford): Mr. Chairman, I think it might be helpful if the Reporting Delegate could now summarize paragraph 2 and 3 for us. He has done so well on the first paragraph.

[Reporter] (Ervin Hexner): I would not want to compete with Mr. Luxford. I suppose you did an excellent job on that.

United States (Ansel Luxford): I only mean to summarize the sense of the matter. I think we have discussed, and I think in the same way that you have reported, on [Section] 1 to us. Maybe you can tell us there seems to be disagreement on [Section] 2 and we can leave it at that.

United Kingdom (Sir Wilfrid Eady): May I ask, first of all—I understood from the United States delegate that this will be amended to read Article III, [Section] 2(d) and Article III, [Section] 3. It is not the whole of Article III, but Articles III, 2(d), which is giving notice of suspension and the waiver, and Article III, 3—[I mean,] Article III, [Section] 2—on loose-leaf [page?] (a) of the folder.

The second question is rather more technical: what is the meaning to be attached to adjust the votes in the transactions in gold? There are one or two possible meanings, and I would like to know what is involved in this. I don't know whether it would be convenient to the United States delegate when he is replying, with your permission, if I also raised to other things which are not questions of interpretation.

The other is this: I would like to know whether more consideration will be given to the suggestion which was raised by the delegate from China that halving the voting power of the countries in the circumstances may be an [p. 23] unreasonably strict treatment of the situation. It appears to attach more significance to the restriction of voting than one would hope would apply to a situation arising under III, 2(d). It is certainly arising on the waiver. But if the United States delegation feels that something must be done to the country which is in credit to the Fund to weaken its voting position, [I ask] whether it is not simpler and better to say that the country involved does not have a vote.

United States (Ansel Luxford): On the answer to Sir Wilfrid's first question, I think we are in agreement in principle with his proposal to spell out in Article III the specific provisions involved. The difficulty is that while it is very easy to say III, 2, 3—that is, subdivision or Section 3—declaring members ineligible to use the resources of the Fund, and that can be done very simply, it is a little difficult to do that in Section 2, where the only waiver provision is at the end of the section and does not have a letter after it. I think it is a drafting detail, and in the next draft I hope the Secretariat would fix it up so that we can put it in there that way.

Now, as to what adjusted votes [are made] in net transactions in gold, I believe that that provision was intended to take care of the situation so that a country would not be getting votes simply because the gold in the Fund which had been part of its original contribution was being counted. I think that what that really means is that you would deduct the gold part of its quota in calculating the votes that it would gain. I believe the Canadians made that proposal [at] some time, and we accept it as being a reasonable interpretation of what we were driving at. [p. 24]

On the third question, as to whether the figure of [$]200,000 is the right figure, I would only say that that is certainly something that the Committee should consider, and that I do not believe it is something that anybody has any real fixed views on. It was put in there as being a simple way of throwing this matter open for discussion.

On the fourth proposal, that a country involved does not have a right to vote, I would be a little concerned about that as being a fair alternative to what has been proposed. And I would be concerned from the point of view of the country involved. I do not think that because that country may be using the access to the Fund or using the Fund's resources that it should be denied its full vote. At the outside, the proposal that we have suggested would only deprive them of a little less than half of their vote. If they would use all of their quota, they would still be entitled to half of their vote, and I think it might be regarded as a little severe to deprive them of their whole vote. But that is a question for the whole Committee to consider. But it does have the merit that Sir Wilfrid has suggested: it is a little simpler; and to say whether that statement makes up for a possible hardship would be something for this group to determine.

United Kingdom (Sir Wilfrid Eady): May I ask the delegate from the United States about the explanation for Article III on net transactions in gold. I think there is a need in final drafting for simplification. If the amount of currency exceeds 75 percent or 100 percent, then it has the meaning—

United States (Ansel Luxford): I am agreed, fully.

United Kingdom (Sir Wilfrid Eady): I am content that the last suggestion, that the country shouldn't vote, should be left to the [p. 25] Committee. I don't question that.

China (Te-Mou Hsi): The reason I mentioned [$]2 million is because I thought that while the Chinese delegation agrees that there shall be some penalty for a member country to draw on the Fund and, on the other hand, to give the equivalent number of votes to the creditor nation,

I mentioned that in order to say that we agree in principle that the penalty to the member countries should be as light as possible, so instead of 50 percent I [propose] 5 percent.

[Reporter] (Ervin Hexner): May I ask the delegate of the United States whether in practice this provision may be in reality applied, in the sense that it will really influence the voting. I don't want to go into the merits of the question, but I have the feeling that there will be a strong majority in the Fund who are going to defend certain interests. I don't think that this point is going in reality to influence one of the decisions of the Executive Committee or of the Board. And it is a somewhat complicated provision. I suppose the intention is that the bylaws of the Fund—we are discussing first the Constitution of the Fund—that this Constitution should be rather simple. If [it] may not be expected that this is going to influence real situations in practice, I would like the United States delegation to consider whether we should drop this provision from the bylaws.

Mexico (Antonio Espinosa de los Monteros): Mr. Chairman, Mexico has to voice, also, her strong approval of this principle. It may appear inconsistent with her normal position as a debtor [p. 26] country, but has it not always been true that creditors have more to say about lending money than borrowers? Is it not obvious that when the Fund has lent more money to a single country, that country should have less to say about how the Fund's resources will be used. To us, it is one of those principles which are basic in the Constitution of this Fund. Not that it should [necessarily] be so. We question from a higher point of view this principle established in international finance, but we take it as something fundamental that when we undersigned the Joint Statement, we all thought that that was a basic principle, that the creditor nations should have proportionately more voting power than the debtor nations. The matter that my distinguished colleague from China has brought up to us, how to measure this difference in penalty (although it is a word I don't like to use), is to me more important than the matter of principle and, therefore, I would ask also whether there is general agreement in principle and not [about the] quantity. Isn't that, after all, the general feeling [i.e., sentiment] of this meeting [Committee]?

Greece (Athanase Sbarounis): I should like to add to the discussion that I do consider that this principle is in accordance with the aims of the Fund, because the Fund aims to bring in aid to help the small countries that need the help of the Fund. So I don't see why they should be penalized when they use the facility that is afforded them. That is why in the name of the Greek delegation, I ask to be allowed to oppose that principle.

Ethiopia (George Blowers): Mr. Chairman, the Ethiopian delegation wishes to support this Alternative A. I think we are all taking this entirely too personally. I don't believe it is aimed at any one country. As I understand the provision, it was put in to safeguard against the possibility of a combination of debtor nations concerning the lending power of the Fund. I think [p. 27] it is a reasonable safeguard and one that we should keep in the proposal.

New Zealand (Allan Fisher): There are just two points I want to make. It seems probable in practice the adjustment of voting power in accordance with the proposals of the paragraphs here would be likely to be a very complicated matter, and it might turn on the chance whether a vote were taken one day or the following day whether the country had a certain voting power or not. Of course, it seems that these things will [i.e., may] be decided by close votes, which, as the representative of the Netherlands has already suggested, would be pretty clear indication that the Fund was on the verge of foundering. But if the matters are not to be determined by very close votes, then it certainly doesn't seem to be worthwhile making the elaborate adjustments of what for the majority of countries here would be very small voting power in the Fund. In the case of New Zealand, our voting power wouldn't be as much as 1 percent of the whole anyway, and it doesn't matter to us very much whether that is increased by 1,000 [votes] or diminished by 1,000. That won't affect anything of importance at all.

But—and this is my second point—it may be a matter of very great importance if the provisions of these two subsections were applied in the case of one of the really big contributors to the Fund, which might very well, to use the inaccurate phrase, be in credit to the extent of increasing its [p. 28] voting power by, as has been said, practically 50 percent. And that is a matter about which I think we might legitimately be a little concerned. To take the extreme, we don't know exactly what the figures will be, but if we can take as an illustration the figures in the *New York Times* today,[503] the rather paradoxical situation might arise that just at the moment when the biggest contributor to the Fund was on the verge of

[503] Perhaps John H. Crider, "Delay Is Proposed on Exchange Rates; Leaders of United States Group Stress Move to Avoid Controversy," *New York Times,* July 5, 1944, p. 25; but if the speaker is mistaken about the date, an article of the previous day seems more apposite: John H. Crider, "10 Billion Total Seen for Exports; Americans at Bretton Woods Picture Possible Gain From Monetary Fund and Bank," *New York Times,* July 4, 1944, p. 15.

being declared a country whose currency was technically scarce from the point of view of the operations of the Fund, [[its voting power would increase]]. Its voting powers for these purposes would be just a little bit less than 50 percent of the total votes, and it seems to me that an arrangement which would create a situation of that sort is not a very desirable one.

I would suggest quite provisionally as a possible compromise which would meet the arguments that have been put forward about not allowing people who are borrowing to have the same power to deal with the situation as the people who are lending, that we may delete [Alternative A, paragraph] (a) altogether, and be satisfied with the diminution of the voting power by the net purchases from other countries.

United States (Ansel Luxford): Just on the point of issue, [in reply to] the gentleman from New Zealand: in understanding the provision, it was never contemplated that this vote provision in the second paragraph would have general application. It would by no means have any application on the question of whether a currency should be decided to be scarce. It would only have application into narrow cases—I mentioned that—and I think Sir Wilfrid's suggestion [p. 29] of pinning it to those provisions would be most helpful in making it clear. It was not intended to apply to a vote as to whether currency of the country would be made scarce.

New Zealand (Allan Fisher): I understand that perfectly. What I had in mind was when the Fund's supplies of the currencies of the larger contributors to the Fund were being reduced to zero, at that moment for other purposes and the representative of the United States mentioned the voting power of that country would be at its maximum.

United States (Ansel Luxford): That's right. It would be, approximately. I think you are using the United States as an illustration, and as I recall its then voting position might be between 20 and 25 percent. Now, at the outside, this might increase it to about 35 percent, probably not quite that much.

Chairman: I think the matter is already being clarified, but nevertheless we cannot decide at once. And so it seems we must proceed with the second part and carry on the discussion in the meeting this morning, and we can come back and discuss and decide this question [later].

Cuba (Luis Machado): Mr. Chairman, in withdrawing Alternative B, the gentleman from the United Kingdom [did so] in order to help us come to an agreement on Alternative A. There is an important matter at the end of Alternative B that I think has no bearing on the subject [of

Alternative A], namely, establishing a quorum for a meeting of the Board of Directors [Governors]. I think our Reporting Delegate raised that point. And I was wondering if we would like to register in agreement on [p. 30] whether or not the quorum should be established.

[Reporter] (Ervin Hexner): We are going to discuss that in a few minutes.

Chairman: We must discuss this question [in Alternative A], that "Except as otherwise specifically provided all matters before the Fund shall be decided by a majority of the aggregate votes cast."

Unidentified: Mr. Chairman, I am sorry to go back to paragraph (a) and (b), or rather, the first part of Alternative A, but I would like to have some clarification on one point. I believe everyone here agrees on the principle that the distribution of voting power should be related to the quotas, and I can well see how the system of voting is going to function as far as the Board of Directors [Governors] is concerned when every member country is reached [to express its views]. But the Joint Statement speaks also of the Executive Committee, and I would like to have some explanation on how the system of voting is going to function for the Executive Committee, because there we are going to have five members of the Executive Committee that will be appointed by the five largest contributing countries and some other members who will represent the other countries. Now, how are they going to calculate the voting power of those other members of the Executive Committee? That is a clarification that I would like.

Chairman: At the beginning of the meeting I have already explained that all the questions in relation to [the] Executive Committee will be discussed after[wards], when we will receive the new statement being prepared by some groups.

And so we have this part. I think that Cuba wants [p. 31] to discuss this. The exception is made at the end of [the seventh paragraph on page 26], "Except as otherwise [specifically provided all matters before the Fund shall be decided by a majority of the aggregate votes cast,]" and so we may discuss the problem of a quorum as it is proposed in Alternative B, a quorum which must consist of not less than two-thirds of the total voting power. That is the question under discussion.

United Kingdom (Sir Wilfrid Eady): I am grateful to the delegate from Cuba for reminding me that I withdrew or that I intended to withdraw. I did not intend to withdraw this provision for a quorum. I venture also to suggest to our Reporting Delegate that we are really not considering the question of how you get a decision from the Board of Directors [Governors], including cabling. We are considering now when there is a meeting of the Board of Governors, what is the minimum number present who constitute a valid vote? That is all. And we have suggested here that a valid vote requires not less than two-thirds of the total voting power of the governors on the Board.

Mexico (Antonio Espinosa de los Monteros): Mr. Chairman, I believe, sir, that this minimum quorum is really dangerous to the small countries. In other words, that a two-thirds quorum might be easily formed by the largest board members. Therefore, it seems to me that two-thirds quorum is too low in this particular mechanism for validity, especially if regarding certain matters of concern and of great concern to all the countries. Therefore, I would suggest the division of the quorum. I would propose two different [p. 32] kinds of a quorum should be had, some larger quorum for more important issues that the Board will decide, and a small quorum for the less important issues.

Mr. Chairman, just as a suggestion, and the figures I am going to mention are not intended to be specific, perhaps a combination of a quorum of voting power and a quorum of member countries would "do the trick," as they say. Perhaps if we had, and I repeat these figures, the two-thirds voting power *and* one-half of the member countries, or any other figures that might be agreed upon.

United States (Ansel Luxford): Mr. Chairman, I would suggest that by all means we do need a quorum provision in this document. I think that the suggestions that have been made are very good, both by Mexico and by Ecuador, and I am quite certain something along that line should be worked out so that we will give due regard to both the number of countries and the quotas.

United Kingdom ([Sir Wilfrid Eady?]): I would be prepared to accept an amendment in that sense in any form drafted by the Committee. I entirely agree in the suggestion of the delegate.

China (Te-Mou Hsi): All that I want to say is to support the suggestion made by the Mexican delegation.

[Chairman?]: May I suggest we have a small committee to draft that last sentence of Alternative B, incorporating the suggestions that have been proposed here?

[Reporter] (Ervin Hexner): Could we clarify the point made by Ecuador and Mexico? Would it be convenient to the Mexican delegate if we should state a quorum of two-thirds [of voting power], [p. 33] with the minimum [being] half of the member countries present? That would settle one part of the issue.

Now, the second point would be if no quorum is present and business should be performed, would it be agreeable to state that the Chairman should call another meeting within the month, at the latest, and this meeting could decide without regard to a quorum present? Would this be [an] agreeable proposal?

United Kingdom (Sir Wilfrid Eady): Is not that which [i.e., what] happens automatically—that if there is not that quorum present, no business can be transacted at that meeting, and that the Executive Committee has to set another meeting?

[Reporter] (Ervin Hexner): What I assume, Mr. Chairman, is that to suppose such business has to be performed which cannot be delegated to the Executive Committee, that just that happens: that in the second meeting, again there is no quorum. Now, we could decide—I admit that it is [only] a possible solution—that we should state rigidly that if no quorum is present, no business can be performed. It is an alternative, too.

Chairman: I have understood the last part of Alternative B must be read like this: "A quorum for the vote shall consist of not less than two-thirds of the total voting power of the governors and one-half of the countries." That, I think is the proposal of Mexico and of Ecuador. All the gentleman who are agreed to such a proposal, say "aye."

Delegates: Aye.

Chairman: Approved.

I was so happy because we have approved something.

[Reporter] (Ervin Hexner): I assume that the agreement of the [p. 34] Committee is that there should be a quorum always present, two-thirds [of the voting power] and half of the members.

Mexico (Antonio Espinosa de los Monteros): That is right.

[Reporter] (Ervin Hexner): That if there is no such [quorum] present, there cannot be a decision made.

Chairman: All right.

Tomorrow at ten o'clock [we meet again].

Cuba (Luis Machado): Before we adjourn, I would like with your permission to present—I have given it to the Secretariat—Alternative C[504] as to the organization of the Executive Committee, and I would like your permission to hand it to my colleagues, the delegates from various countries here, pending their receipt of formal mimeographed copies, so that they may study it and be ready for discussion.

Chairman: All right.

The meeting is adjourned.

---

[504] Document 150, pp. 159-160.

28

Commission I, Committee 3
Organization and Management of the Fund
Fourth meeting: draft minutes
July 6, 1944, 10 a.m.[505]

Publication of reports • Depositories • Executive Directors • Matters postponed • Miscellaneous powers of the IMF

Because the draft minutes are brief, we omit narrative summaries for this and subsequent meetings of Committee 3.

At the fourth meeting of the Committee on July 6, at 10 a.m., the text of Article VII, Section 5 (["Publication of Reports,"] page 28) was accepted without change.[506] Article VII, Section 6 on depositories was then given extended consideration. Paragraph (a) in Alternative A was agreed without change. Agreement was not reached on paragraph (b), Alternatives A and B, and the question was referred to Commission I for decision. Alternative C was dropped by general consent. Section 7 ["Form of Holdings of Currency"] was agreed upon as proposed in Alternative A (page 29).[507]

The committee resumed consideration of the question of management of the Fund, Article VII, Section 2 ["The Executive Directors"]. New drafts for the relevant sections were submitted. The original Alternatives A and B were combined into a new draft (SA/1/17, Document 152). Alternative C (SA/1/16, Document 151) and Alternative D (SA/1/15, Document 150) were introduced at this meeting.[508] After discussion, it was apparent that no complete agreement was possible in view of the differences of these drafts. Additional amendments to these drafts are to

---

505 Published almost unchanged as Document 173, pp. 217-218.

506 In Document 32, p. 49.

507 In Document 32, pp. 49-50.

508 Document 150, p. 159; Document 151, pp. 159-162; and Document 152, pp. 162-164.

be submitted by several of the members. The Chairman was authorized to appoint a special committee to reconsider the reconciliation of these drafts and to present a new document to the committee as soon as possible. The following countries were named to this committee: the United States, the United Kingdom, the Netherlands, Cuba, and Belgium.

Article VII, Section 8 ["Relationship to Other International Organizations"] and Article VIII, Section 1 ["Withdrawal from the Fund"][509] were not discussed pending clarification of their possible assignment to Committee 4. The Committee recommended that the first three clauses of Article VII, Section 11[510] ["Miscellaneous Powers"] be transferred to Committee 4. Since an amendment is proposed [p. 2] to the fourth clause, action was postponed on this clause, while the fifth clause was adopted as presented.

Adjournment at 1 p.m.

(In the minutes of July 4, 4 p.m., in the third paragraph, lines 6 and 7, the words "Board of Governors" should read "the Executive Directors.")

[509] In Document 32, pp. 50-52.
[510] In Document 32, p. 52.

29

Commission I, Committee 3
Organization and Management of the Fund
Fifth meeting: draft minutes
July 7, 1944, 10 a.m.[511]

Distribution of net income • Furnishing information • Executive Directors • Discussion postponed on withdrawal from the IMF

The Committee amended Article VII (additional Section 10, page 32 ["Distribution of Net Income of the Fund"]) by substituting "the Board of Governors" for "the Fund."[512] With this amendment, the section was adopted. Article III, Section 11[513] (["Furnishing Information,"] page 14) was explained, but discussion was deferred on the request of some of the members. Alternative C to Article VII, Sections 1, 2 and 3 ([on Executive Directors,] Document 178)[514] was presented to the Committee, and was referred to the subcommittee already dealing with the question of the Executive Directors and methods of election. The Committee took no action on Article VII, Sections 1, 2 and 3 [on management of the IMF] pending a report of its special subcommittee. Discussion of Article VIII, Section 3 ["Settlement of Accounts with Countries Ceasing to be Members"] was postponed until the next meeting to allow time for the consideration of a proposed Alternative B.

---

511 Published almost unchanged as Document 200, p. 242.

512 In Document 32, p. 51.

513 In Document 32, p. 36.

514 Document 178, p. 221.

30

Commission I, Committee 3
Organization and Management of the Fund
Sixth meeting: draft minutes
July 8, 1944, 9:30 a.m.[515]

IMF gold holdings • Information to be supplied by members • Withdrawal from the IMF • Liquidation of the IMF • Executive Directors

The Committee considered Alternative D to Article VII, Section 6(b) (page 29b), relating to the deposit of the Fund's gold holdings.[516] After discussion, this was referred to Commission I to be considered along with the other alternatives to this section. The Committee then considered Article III, Section 11 (page 14c), Alternative C ["Furnishing Information"],[517] relating to information to be supplied to the Fund by the member countries, which replaced Alternative A.[518] A new Alternative D, Document 203 [also on furnishing information],[519] was also discussed. Alternatives C and D were referred to the Commission.

The Committee discussed Article VIII, Section 3 (page 36), "Settlement of Accounts of Withdrawn Members."[520] A new alternative was submitted and will be circulated. An amendment to Article VIII, Section 4, "Liquidation of the Fund," was submitted and will be circulated. After discussion it was decided to refer these matters to a special subcommittee, consisting of representatives of Belgium, the United Kingdom, the United States, Australia and Mexico.

The subcommittee on the Executive Directors reported a "final alternative submitted by the special subcommittee appointed to consider

---

515 Published almost unchanged as Document 226, pp. 289-290.

516 Document 181, p. 223.

517 Document 182, pp. 224-225.

518 In Document 32, p. 36.

519 Document 203, p. 267.

520 In Document 32, p. 53.

all proposals relative to the Executive Directors" to replace the combined Alternatives A and B, C, and D with the amendments submitted by various countries.[521] The subcommittee reported that it had been able to reach agreement on all questions before it except the total number of the Executive Directors. After discussion, the whole Committee approved paragraphs 1, 4, 5, 6, 6(a), 7, 8, 9, 10, 11, 12, and 13. Paragraph 3 was referred to Commission I after consideration of an amendment, [p. 2] Document 178, paragraph 3 (page 26d).[522] Paragraph 2 was discussed, but no agreement had been reached at the time of adjournment. An alternative to paragraph 2 and an amendment to Schedule B of the combined Alternatives A and B has been submitted and will be circulated.

Adjournment at 11:35 [a.m.]

[521] Document 212, pp. 275-277.
[522] Document 178, p. 221.

31

Commission I, Committee 3
Organization and Management of the Fund
Seventh (final) meeting: draft minutes
July 11, 1944, 10:00 a.m.[523]

Suspension and withdrawal from the IMF • Liquidation of the IMF • Location of offices

The Committee considered Article VIII, Section 2, Alternative A (Document 210).[524] dealing with suspension and compulsory withdrawal from the Fund. A number of questions about the interpretation of this article were raised in the meeting. After the discussion, the Committee decided to approve the Alternative, Sections 2, 2(a) and 2(b), with suggestion to the Drafting Committee of the Commission to state clearly under what conditions a country would be suspended from using the Fund's resources or be compelled to withdraw from membership and the fair procedure therefore. It was the consensus of the Committee that these sanctions should be applied only when the country's action directly affects the operation of the Fund.

The Committee received the report of its Subcommittee on Liquidation and Withdrawal (Document 243).[525] The Committee agreed to eliminate from further consideration Alternative B, Article VIII, Section 4 (Document 241[526] ["Liquidation of the Fund"]). It was unable to reach agreement on Alternatives A and C for this section and referred the matter to Commission I. Article VIII, Section 3 (page 36), "Settlement of Accounts with Governments Ceasing to be Members,"

---

[523] Published almost unchanged as Document 303, pp. 498-499.
[524] Document 210, pp. 272-273.
[525] Document 243, pp. 363-364.
[526] Document 241, p. 360.

was also referred to the Commission for action.[527] No action taken on Article VII, Section 7, "Location of Offices."[528]

(Document 243 should be corrected in the third paragraph, line 7, to read "Alternative B" in place of "Alternative D." In the fourth paragraph, line 9, to read "Alternative C" instead of "Alternative B.")

---

[527] In Document 32, p. 53.

[528] Actually, the section is called "Form of Holdings of Currency," in Document 32, p. 51.

32

Commission I, Committee 4 Form and Status of the Fund First meeting: draft minutes July 4, 1944, 11:30 a.m.[529]

Introduction of officers • Scope of Committee's work

The subject of Committee 4 was "Form and Status of the Fund." In other words, its subject was mainly how the piece of paper that was the IMF agreement would work, rather than how the IMF as an organization would work. The committee chairman was Manuel Llosa, second vice president in Peru's Chamber of Deputies, the lower legislative house. Llosa had been the commissioner general of Peru to the 1939-1940 World's Fair in New York, and acquired a good command of English then if not before. Because the draft minutes are brief, we omit narrative summaries for this and subsequent meetings of Committee 4.

The first meeting of Commission I, Committee 4 was held on July 4 at 11:30 a.m. The Chairman of Commission I, Mr. [Harry Dexter] White (USA) introduced the Chairman of the Committee, Mr. [Manuel] Llosa of Peru, who in turn introduced the Committee Reporter, Mr. [Wilhelm] Keilhau (Norway), and the secretaries of the Committee.

After expressing appreciation on behalf of his country, the Chairman explained that a document indicating the parts of the preliminary draft of the agreement within the scope of the Committee[530] had just been distributed in the morning and suggested that it would be advisable to delay discussion of the substance until the next meeting. He also suggested that the next meeting be held the following morning. The Chairman stated that it appeared that the following sections of the preliminary draft fall within the scope of the Committee's activities: Article IX ["'"Obligations of Member Countries"], Sections 5 ["Immunity of Assets of the Fund"], 6 ["Immunity from Suit"], and 7 ["Restrictions

---

[529] Published almost unchanged as Document 105, pp. 120-121.
[530] Probably Document 51, pp. 88-91.

on Taxation of the Fund, Its Employees and Obligations"]; Article XI ["Amendments"]; Article XII ["Interpretation of the Agreement"]; Article XIII ["Final Provisions"], Sections 1 ["Entry into Effect"], 2 ["Effective Date of the Agreement"], 3 ["Calling the Initial Meeting of the Fund"], and 4 ["Agenda of the Initial Meeting"]; Article XIV ["Execution of the Agreement"].[531]

As there was no response to the Chairman's inquiry regarding discussion, the meeting was adjourned.

---

[531] All in Document 32, pp. 54-60, except Article XIV, which was still to come.

33

Commission I, Committee 4 Form and Status of the Fund Second meeting: draft minutes July 5, 1944, 5:30 p.m.[532]

Appointment of Asterisk Committee authorized • Status, immunities, and privileges of the IMF • Subcommittee appointed • Assignment of certain matters

The second meeting of Committee 4 of Commission I was held on July 5 at 5:30 p.m. The Chairman announced that the chairmen of all of the delegations had agreed that there would be no formal voting in the committees. The Chair was authorized to appoint a small Asterisk Committee to which minor questions of wording and coordination may be referred.[533] In the case of a lack of agreement on important issues, the lack of agreement will be reported to the Commission. Approval was obtained permitting the technical personnel accompanying the delegations to be allowed, at the request of the representatives, to express the point of view of their delegations without arguing with the delegates.

The Committee proceeded with the discussion of Article IX ["Obligations of Member Countries"], Sections 5 ["Immunity of Assets of the Fund"], 6 ["Immunity from Suit"], and 7 ["Restrictions on Taxation of the Fund, Its Employees and Obligations"], as amended.[534] After considerable discussion and comments by various delegates, Section 5 of Article IX ["Immunity of Assets of the Fund"] was approved without amendment. In the case of Section 7 ["Restrictions on Taxation of the Fund, Its Employees and Obligations"], considerable discussion

---

[532] Published almost unchanged as Document 142, pp. 154-155.

[533] In the preliminary draft agreement for the IMF, comprising the Joint Statement plus alternatives proposed before the conference began (Document 32, pp. 21-60), an asterisk indicated that a proposed alternative contained no substantial change from the corresponding provision of the Joint Statement.

[534] In Document 32, pp. 55-56.

took place between the delegates. From this discussion, the Chair summarized the consensus of opinion by appointing a subcommittee to further review Article IX, Section 7 (Document 121[535]) before final approval. The subcommittee appointed by the Chair consists of one delegate from Cuba, Norway, United Kingdom, United States, and Union of Soviet Socialist Republics. The delegate from the United States was designated as chairman. The assignment of the subcommittee is the review of Section 7 and presentation of the consensus of opinion of the subcommittee.

In addition to the articles and sections assigned to this Committee in Document 51,[536] the following matters were also assigned:[537] [p. 2]

Article VII—Management of the Fund
Section 8—Relationship to other international organizations
Article VII—Withdrawal from the Fund
Section 1—Right of members to withdraw
Section 2—Suspension of membership or compulsory withdrawal

These sections are to be discussed at the meeting of July 6. The above articles and sections were previously assigned to Committee 3 of Commission I.

---

535 Document 121, pp. 129-130.

536 Document 51, pp. 88-91.

537 In the U.S. Treasury Library copy of the typescripts, the material from here to the end of the meeting is mistakenly placed at the end of the minutes of the Committee's next meeting. We have restored it to its proper place.

34

Commission I, Committee 4
Form and Status of the Fund
Third meeting: draft minutes
July 6, 1944, 2:30 p.m.[538]

Asterisk Committee appointed • Progress of subcommittee on taxation of the IMF • Relationship to other international organizations • Miscellaneous powers of the IMF • Right of members to withdraw • Amendments • Interpretation of the Articles of Agreement

The third meeting of Committee 4, Commission I, was held on July 6, at 2:30 p.m. The Chair appointed the delegates from China, Cuba, Ecuador, Poland, United Kingdom, Union of Soviet Socialist Republics, and the United States as the members of the Asterisk Committee, with the delegate from Cuba serving as Chairman. Also serving as *ex officio* members of this committee are the Chairman, Reporter, and Secretary of Committee 4.

The chairman of the Subcommittee to Review Article [IX][539], Section 7 ["Restrictions on Taxation of the Fund, Its Employees and Obligations"] reported that the members, at the meeting held today, were substantially in agreement. It was indicated by the chairman that the revised Article [IX], Section 7 would be submitted to the four committees at the next scheduled meeting.

Article VII, Section 8 ["Relationship to Other International Organizations"][540] was discussed extensively and the consensus of opinion recommended approval without change. At the suggestion of one of the delegates, the Committee approved the discussion at this meeting

---

538 Published almost unchanged as Document 174, pp. 218-219.

539 The typescript and the conference proceedings here and in the next sentence say "Article XI," a mistake.

540 In Document 32, pp. 50-51.

of Article VII, Section 11 ["Miscellaneous Powers"],[541] items 1, 2 and 3, which were previously assigned to Committee 3. After considerable discussion by the various delegates of the interpretation of the proposed wording of the first phrase under the heading (Document 32, page 33) of Section 11 of Article VII, it was agreed that the present wording would be revised and stated as follows: "In order to carry out its purposes, the Fund shall have full legal personality and, in particular, to...." With this amendment and wording, the Committee approved Article VII, Section 11.

Following an extended discussion of Article VIII, Section 1, Alternative A ["Right of Members to Withdraw"],[542] the Chair stated that a consensus of opinion of the delegates indicated approval. During this discussion the delegate of the country proposing Alternative B[543] stated his reasons for recommending changes in Alternative B.

Article VII, Section 2 ["The Executive Directors"] was not available for discussion.

At a joint meeting of the chairmen of Committees 3 and 4, it was agreed that Article VIII, Section 2 ["Suspension of Membership or Compulsory Withdrawal"][544] would be discussed upon its completion in Committee 3 instead of Committee 4, as previously announced in the minutes of July 5, 1944.

In the case of Article XI, "Amendments,"[545] there was a consensus of opinion by the Committee that certain modifications be made to cover the proposals made by the delegates or two of the countries. This article was referred to the Asterisk Committee for their consideration.

Article XII, Section 1 ["Interpretation"][546] was discussed at length. At the conclusion of the discussion, the Chairman stated that the consensus of opinion approved Alternative A, but because Alternative B was an explanation of a part of Alternative A, recommended that the Asterisk Committee meet and prepare one document for presentation to the Committee.

---

541 In Document 32, pp. 52.

542 In Document 32, p. 52.

543 Australia, according to the index to the conference proceedings, p. 1682. (Article VIII, Section 1 in the preliminary draft became Article XV, Section 1 in the final agreement.)

544 In Document 32, p. 53.

545 In Document 32, pp. 57-58.

546 In Document 32, pp. 58-59.

35

Commission I, Committee 4
Form and Status of the Fund
Fourth meeting: draft minutes
July 7, 1944, 2:30 p.m.[547]

Report of subcommittee on taxation of the IMF

The fourth meeting of Committee 4, Commission I was held on July 7 at 2:30 p.m. The chairman of the subcommittee to review Article IX, Section 7 ["Restrictions on Taxation of the Fund, Its Employees and Obligations"] read the document agreed upon by the members of the [sub]committee.[548] He stated that one of the delegates reserved decision on a part of the document read to the full Committee.

As of the remaining material assigned to this Committee had been referred to subcommittee or was not available for distribution, the meeting was adjourned.

---

547 Published almost unchanged as Document 204, p. 268.

548 Document 198, pp. 235-237.

36

Commission I, Committee 4
Form and Status of the Fund
Fifth (final) meeting: draft minutes
July 8, 1944, 11:30 a.m.[549]

Taxation of the IMF • Miscellaneous powers of the IMF • Amendments • Interpretation of the Articles of Agreement • Suspension of membership or compulsory withdrawal • Pre-existing international commitments on exchange restrictions • Matters not ready for presentation

The fifth meeting of Committee 4, Commission I, was held on July 8 at 11:30 a.m.

Article IX, Section 7, Alternative B, Document 194[550] (["Restrictions on Taxation of the Fund, Its Employees and Obligations,"] page 43a), was adopted in the form as presented by the subcommittee.

Considerable discussion was held upon the document presented by the subcommittee relating to Article VII, Section 11, Alternative B, Document 198[551] (["Miscellaneous Powers,"] page 33a). The first three numbered subparagraphs were accepted as presented, subparagraphs 4 and 5 having been referred to another committee previously.

Article XI, Alternative C, Document 198 (["Amendments,"] page 45a): after considerable discussion, it was decided to insert in the second line between the words "from" and "of," the words "the government of"; and in the ninth line, between the words "three-fifths" and "of," the words "of the governments," to make the meaning clear with that indicated in the seventh line and the last line of the first paragraph.

Article XII, Section 1, Alternative C, Document 198 (["Interpretation"] page 46a): discussion on this document was

---

549 Published almost unchanged as Document 227, pp. 290-291.

550 Document 194, pp. 233-234.

551 Document 198, pp. 235-237.

prolonged. It was finally decided to accept the text as presented in Alternative C.

Article XII, Section 3, Alternative A, Document 209[552] (["Suspension of Membership or Compulsory Withdrawal,"] page 48): after the delegate from the United States explained the purpose of the wording which was presented, the text was adopted without change.

The Committee was advised that Article XII, Section 2 ["Definitions"] and Article XIII ["Final Provisions"], Sections 1 ["Entry into Effect"], 2 ["Effective Date of the Agreement"], 3 ["Calling the Initial Meeting of the Fund"], and 4 ["Agenda of the Initial Meeting"] were not yet ready for presentation to the Committee or its subcommittees. With this exception, the Committee has completed the work assigned to it by Commission I.

---

[552] Document 209, p. 272.

PART III

COMMISSIONS II AND III:

WORLD BANK

OTHER MEANS OF COOPERATION

37

Commission II
International Bank for Reconstruction and Development
(World Bank)
Second meeting: transcript
July 11, 1944, 4:00 p.m.[553]

Committee assignments and officers • Committee procedures to speed progress • Matters referred to Drafting Committee • Name of Bank • Purposes • Use of Bank's resources

The subject of Commission II was the Bank for Reconstruction and Development, which by the end of the conference had the prefix "International" added to its name and later became known less formally as the World Bank. The chairman of the commission was John Maynard Keynes of the United Kingdom. Keynes was the most famous and influential economist of the twentieth century. His unassuming title of economic adviser to the Chancellor of the Exchequer (minister of finance) gave little hint that he was at the center of Britain's war finance efforts, and as part of those duties was the chief British negotiator at Bretton Woods.

The first meeting of the Commission, held on July 3, is not in the transcripts, perhaps because it consisted mainly of a prepared speech by Keynes.[554] *In this meeting, Keynes first introduces the committees of Commission II and their officers. To speed progress on the World Bank agreement, he proposes to make the Agenda Committee and the Drafting Committee the same, and to empower committee chairmen to appoint subcommittees immediately as they see fit.*

With those changes agreed, Keynes goes on to suggest dividing the clauses of the draft World Bank agreement into three categories: those that give major difficulty, which should be referred to committee; those that give intermediate difficulty, which the Commission might discuss without referring them to committee; and those that give no

---

553 Summarized in Document 300, pp. 495-497.

554 The minutes of the first meeting are Document 60, pp. 98-99; Keynes's speech is Document 47, pp. 84-88.

difficulty, which the Commission can immediately refer to the Drafting Committee for polishing the language. After the delegates agree to that procedure, Keynes proceeds quickly through the preliminary draft World Bank agreement. He goes so fast that few delegates, especially those who are not native speakers of English, can keep up.

After having made a first run-through of the whole draft agreement, Keynes takes the Commission back to provisions in the beginning of the document that specify the Bank's name and purposes and the use of its resources. The delegates hold a preliminary debate on the name of the Bank, then agree to defer further debate until a subsequent meeting. Concerning the purposes of the Bank, the Commission agrees to refer a clause about countries affected by enemy action to the Drafting Committee. Finally, the Commission accepts a Mexican proposal that a clause on the use of the Bank's resources give equal emphasis to reconstruction and development. Mexico desired the emphasis so that the Bank would not focus only on the postwar reconstruction of Europe, but would offer resources for economic development to poor countries that had not suffered war damage, such as Mexico. As it turned out, the Bank would play only a small role in postwar reconstruction lending because it was still developing its organization in the late 1940s. American aid offered through the European Recovery Program, better known as the Marshall Plan, greatly exceeded World Bank lending for reconstruction.

Other than Keynes, the most active participant in the meeting is Dean Acheson, Assistant Secretary of the U.S. Department of State, who was also the chairman of the Drafting Committee of Commission II.

The transcripts contain no records of the remaining meetings of Commission II or of any meetings of its committees, although the conference proceedings contain minutes for them.

[Chairman] (John Maynard Keynes, United Kingdom): (After calling the meeting to order.)

Gentlemen, there are, first of all, certain matters to report. The Agenda Committee met and approved the circulation of the document you have in front of you with all the amendments that have been received up to a certain hour, without wishing to take the right of any delegation to have second thoughts. They also decided that we would begin with this meeting of the Commission and decide in the course of proceedings precisely what we throw back to the committees. So, now I think it would be convenient for you to know the committee assignments—to be reminded of the committee assignments and to know the committee officers.

Subcommittee[555] [Committee] 1 ["Purposes, Policies, and Capital of the Bank"] will deal with Article I ["Purposes of the Bank"], Article II ["Membership in and Capital of the Bank"], and Article VI, [Section] 4 ["Cessation of Membership in International Monetary Fund"].[556] Committee 2 ["Operations of the Bank"] will deal with Article III ["General Provisions Relating to Loans"] and Article IV ["Operations"]. Committee 3 ["Organization and Management"] will deal with Article V ["Management"] and Article VI ["Withdrawal and Suspension of Membership and Liquidations"], apart from the particular section remitted to Committee 1. Committee 4 ["Form and Status of the Bank"] will deal with Articles VII ["Additional Undertakings on the Part of Member Countries"], IX ["Interpretation of the Agreement"], X ["Approval Deemed Given"], and XI ["Final Provisions"].[557]

Now, the officers of the committees in question are as follows:—

Unidentified: Where is Article VIII ["Amendments"]?

Chairman: Article VIII is in Committee 4.

The chairman of Committee 1 is the delegate of the Netherlands, Mr. [Wim] Beyen. The reporting delegate of that committee is the representative of Costa Rica, Mr. [José Rafaël] Oreamuno. The chairman of Committee 2 represents Cuba and is Mr. [Eduardo] Montoulieu. The reporting delegate represents Australia and is Mr. [Frederick] Wheeler. [p. 2] In Committee 3, the chairman represents Colombia and is Mr. Miguel Pumarejo. The reporting delegate of that committee represents South Africa and is Mr. [Michiel] de Kock. The chairman of Committee 4 is the delegate of India, Sir Chintaman D. Deshmukh, and the reporting delegate is of the Polish delegation and is Mr. [Leon] Baránski.

Now, as regards our procedure today, I think you will all be of the mind that we want to make as rapid progress as we can. Time is running short. Many of the countries here represented attach, I know, primary importance to the Bank, and we cannot afford to spend as much time as has been spent on the Fund, particularly as the Fund committees have not yet finished, so that at least for the next two days or three days we shall not have all the time of the conference at our disposal. Some

---

555 Keynes often calls Committees 1-4 "subcommittees." To spare readers tedium, we change all such references and omit corrective brackets hereafter.

556 References to articles and page numbers are to the "Preliminary Draft of Proposals for the Establishment of a Bank for Reconstruction and Development," Document 245, pp. 365-402.

557 Apparently there had already been some changes to the document, because Document 245 contains no Article XI. We have given Articles X and XI the titles they had later.

important measure of time must still be reserved for the Fund. And I am hopeful, therefore, that the procedure may commend itself to you which will cause the maximum rate of progress.

My first proposal is that the Drafting Committee should be the same as the Agenda Committee with, of course, power to the Agenda Committee to appoint subcommittees. The Agenda Committee consists of delegates of the United Kingdom, Brazil, Canada, China, Cuba, Czechoslovakia, the French Committee, India, the USSR, and the United States. We think that will be a serviceable Drafting Committee, and it would be loss of time to try and find a different one, and if you only have one committee for both purposes, clearly time is saved.

Is there any delegate who disagrees with that procedure?

(After a pause.) May I say that is agreed? [p. 3]

My next suggestion is that we give this document to begin with a quick run-through with a view to discovering the articles, of which there are fortunately a great many, where there appeared to be from the start a consensus of opinion, so that we can remit those articles immediately—those clauses and articles immediately—to the Drafting Committee, and they can get busy on tidying up the language and the legal phraseology. Therefore, at the first stage, I should only pass over those clauses where no one has any observations to make. Anyone will have to pull me up who has remarks.

Then, having done that, we should give another run-through in the opposite direction, picking out those major issues which clearly require further discussion, either because they are very important and have not been fully thrashed out, or because they appear to rouse differences of opinion, selecting those major subjects for preliminary discussion outside this Commission.

Well, now, at this point I have a suggestion to make that you may or may not think suitable. If we remitted all these questions to the full committees—which are, after all, this Commission all over again—we should either have to have the committees meeting simultaneously if we would get through our work, which would be very inconvenient to some delegations, I think, who would have to find representatives for all of them as well as for any work on the Fund that was going on. Or, alternatively, we should have to have them all at separate hours, which we fancy here cannot be fitted into the timetable, along with the hours of your engagements.

Therefore, my suggestion is that when matters are referred to a committee, that the chairman and reporting [p. 4] delegate of the committee should have a certain discretion either to remit to their whole committee if they think that that is the right course, or else to appoint in consultation with the chairman of this Commission forthwith an ad hoc committee of smaller numbers from their own committee, selecting those countries that seem to be particularly interested in the issues in question. In that way, the ad hoc committees might start work first thing tomorrow without having to have it all over, either in this Commission, or in the committee before you reach the ad hoc stage. It will be entirely at the discretion of the chairman and the reporting delegate of each committee whether it [goes] to the committee as a whole or whether in consultation with me they decide to appoint a small ad hoc committee at once. You see how much time this might save.

Well, now, gentlemen, I should be grateful if you would tell me how that proposal strikes you. Is there any opposition to that procedure?

(None.)

Then I may say that is agreed.

After we have selected those questions giving no difficulty and those questions that give major difficulty, there will perhaps remain over an intermediate class, and I suggest that we should then tackle those immediately at this meeting, if we have time, and save time. If they are quickly resolved, then they can fall into the first category and go to the Drafting Committee. If, on others, a few minutes' discussion indicates they cannot be quickly resolved, then they will join the second category and [p. 5] be dealt with according to that procedure.

Dean Acheson (United States, Chairman, Drafting Committee):[558] Mr. Chairman, may I make an inquiry? There may be some sections which will give no difficulty or, at most, a difficulty which can be resolved by the Drafting Committee in the form in which they are in the document at the present time. However, there may be amendments offered from time to time which may raise a more serious question. Could it be understood that the Drafting Committee could take those amendments and go to work on them without remitting it back and sending it to some other committee?

Chairman: That would be a very helpful effort if the Commission is agreeable.

United States (Dean Acheson): Rather than have it referred back and forth between committees.

558 It is often unclear when Acheson is speaking as the chairman of the Drafting Committee and when he is speaking as a delegate from the United States. Hereafter we cease to note that he is the chairman of the Drafting Committee, but readers should keep it in mind.

Chairman: Is there any objection to Mr. Acheson's proposal? It seems to be a very helpful one.

(No objection voiced.)

May we accept that? No doubt, the Drafting Committee would refer back to the committee if there was a serious difference of opinion between them.

United States (Dean Acheson): Unquestionably, but if the Drafting Committee then came to an amendment and the question is, is it substance or is it form, and we will waste time.

Chairman: I think that would be helpful.

Now may we proceed to give our first run-through on this basis? The first question is the title of the Bank. That, I think, comes in the third category, and [in] Article I, on the purposes of the Bank, there are a number of alternatives there. They are either in the second or the third category.

Therefore, I think we might pass [p. 6] immediately to Article II, Section 1, page 3 ["Countries Eligible for Membership"].[559] What I propose now is that every article I now name will go to the Drafting Committee unless some delegate raises his hand to the contrary. If I am going too fast, interrupt me, but they will, broadly speaking, be only those articles where there is at present [only] one alternative in front of us. I shan't be quite strict on that, because I think there are certain important questions, particularly management, where there is only one alternative in front of us at present, but which has not as yet been fully thrashed out and ought to go to a committee first. But, apart from one or two important matters like this, I shall read only those cases where we only have one alternative before us.

Article II, Section 1, page 3. Drafting Committee.

I pass Section 2 ["Authorized Capital"].

[Australia (Leslie Melville)]: Mr. Chairman.

Chairman: Yes?

Australia (Leslie Melville): I am sorry, I didn't raise my hand. We don't like that principle. Could that be discussed?

Chairman: I beg your pardon. There is an amendment relating to this which has got to go into a different part of the draft. You are quite correct. I think this ought to be taken with a letter amendment. I cannot

---

[559] Readers may wish to refer to Appendix E, which lists the page numbers and section names of the draft articles of the World Bank as they existed at the time of this meeting. Few changes occurred in the numbering of articles and sections between the draft and the final agreement.

put my finger on it at the moment; where it is connected with other international organizations, it comes in. Have you the reference, Mr. Melville?

Australia (Leslie Melville): No. I am afraid I haven't it.

Chairman: It is right at hand, isn't it? At any rate, I think that Mr. Melville is right that this should be taken with the amendment, which we shall find further on. [p. 7]

It is at page 45 [Article VI, Section 4, "Cessation of Membership in International Monetary Fund"]. We will take Section 1 here with page 45 and we will come back to that.

Article II: I pass Section 2 ["Authorized Capital"].

Article II, Section 3 ["Subscription for Stock"], Drafting Committee.

Article II, Section 4 ["Availability of Subscribed Capital"] is important. We must pass that. And the same applies to [Sections] 5 ["Payments of Subscription"] and 6 ["Issue Price of Shares"].

Section 7 ["Limitation on Liability"].

United States (Dean Acheson): Mr. Chairman, I think you've gotten a little ahead of us here. May I ask a question about page 5? Was that to be sent to the Drafting Committee, including the preparation of the schedule?

Chairman: Oh, no. I think that the schedule, we must remit—I think that the schedule must be brought up later. We have nothing to bite on yet. I meant Section 3 ["Subscription for Stock"] without Schedule A ["Quotas"].

United States (Dean Acheson): There may be some question raised in connection with the second paragraph of that. But I suppose that could be dealt with by the Drafting Committee.

Chairman: I think they might try it first, mightn't they? But certainly I didn't mean the Schedule.

Now I am passing several pages where there are important matters.

Page 9 [Article II, Section 7, "Limitation on Liability"], Drafting Committee.

Section 8, page 10 [Article II, Section 8, "Disposal of Shares Limited"], Drafting Committee.

Section 9, page 11 [Article II, Section 9, "Return of Subscriptions"]: I think we must take this at the third run-over unless we can talk that over now.

Alternative B [to Article II, Section 9] is making a very sensible addition, I suggest. Would you be prepared to pass Alternative A with

Alternative B added to it to the Drafting Committee? Any objection to that?

United States (Dean Acheson): There is a question on agreeing to Alternative B. [p. 8]

Chairman: Yes. Pass that to the Drafting Committee with Alternative B added.

United States (Dean Acheson): We have doubts.

Chairman: I see. We now pass that.

Page 12 [Article III, Section 1, "Use of Resources Restricted"]. I now pass to page 13 [Article III, Section 2, "Agencies Dealing with the Bank"]. Well, now, here there is a small draft amendment. Does anybody object to Alternative B being passed to the Drafting Committee?

United States (Dean Acheson): Yes.

Chairman: You do?

United States (Dean Acheson): Yes.

Chairman: We pass that.

Page 14 [Article III, Section 3, "Limitations on Loans and Guarantees"]. I would call your attention to the fact that when we come to this, it should be taken with the proposal on page 21 [Article IV, Section 3, "Loans from Borrowed Funds and Guarantees"], which seriously overlaps it.

Then, [Article III,] Section 4 ["Conditions on which Bank may Guarantee or Make Loans"] is very important and clearly has to be preserved; and Section 5 ["Provision of Currencies for Loans"].

Well, now, when we get to Sections 5 ["Provision of Currencies for Loans"] and 6 ["Use of Loans Guaranteed, Participated in or Made by the Bank"], could I ask the proposer of Alternative B of those two whether there is a misprint? We think that these proposals may have got in on the wrong page. They don't appear to make any sense. Pages 17 and 18. Would the proposer of Alternative B put us wise to this?

Norway (Ole Colbjørnsen): The sense of this proposal from the Norwegian delegation is that the Bank shall have the opportunity to give an ordinary loan to a member government, not only for a specific project, and paying out the whole on it once, not in portions, and under supervision.

Chairman: I am afraid the thing as drafted wouldn't have that effect. Perhaps we could take the sense of that, because that tears up the major part of the document, doesn't it? I suppose we could discuss the substance of it in this place. If it was carried over to make it [p. 9] effective, it would be quite different to this.[560] If this amendment was carried out it would mean that no government could ever get any money.

Norway (Ole Colbjørnsen): Mr. Chairman, I am afraid I mistook it for another thing. It comes later. I think the meaning of this is to make it possible for a government to have a loan of foreign currency not only for the purchase of commodities in that country, but for general currency purposes in order to strengthen the currency reserves of the country. And the argumentation is that a project may need currency not only to buy that which is quickly needed for the project, but also to buy consumer articles, like sugar and coffee, which is a consequence of a general expansion in the interior economy, which in its turn again—

Chairman: If I may interrupt you, I don't think we want to talk the substance. This is in the wrong place. It ought to be in Amendment 7 [Alternative B], Article III, on page 15a, where it is provided that "loans made [or guaranteed by the Bank, shall be for the purpose of specific projects]." What you are wanting to do is to dissent from the proposal on 15a. Perhaps we might remove your alternative and redraft it to that place.

Norway (Ole Colbjørnsen): Mr. Chairman, I think it is very difficult to discuss these matters if we cannot go into the substance of it. The general sense of the Norwegian proposal is to make the loans free.

Chairman: Yes, I understand the substance, but I rule it out of order in this section. You must bring it in in another section where it is relevant. It makes no sense here, because, while I quite understand the substance of it, it relates to another clause. [p. 10]

Norway (Ole Colbjørnsen): Well, it may be an error of the Secretariat, and we haven't run through all this matter, but I'm sure in our proposal as we gave it to the Secretariat it made sense. But it must be included not in the right place.

Chairman: It is the place where we were told to put it. Would you object to its being removed to page 15a?

Norway (Ole Colbjørnsen): No. I did not object.

Chairman: Well, if we could remove that to 15a, where I think the substance can be very fully discussed, then perhaps we could pass Section 5 ["Provision of Currencies for Loans"] to the Drafting Committee. But I would call the attention of the Drafting Committee to the fact that [paragraph] (c), which is a drafting point, is redundant. It reoccurs on page 20. May I pass Section 5 to the Drafting Committee? I think the Norwegian delegate may have the same point on the next page, 18.

---

[560] In British usage, "different to" is equivalent to the American "different from."

United States (Dean Acheson): I regret to say we couldn't hear what action you are proposing.

Chairman: I was proposing to transfer Alternative B on page 17 [Article III, Section 5, "Provision of Currencies for Loans"] to a previous page, the previous section, and then to pass [Section] 5 to the Drafting Committee. That's right, isn't it?

United States (Dean Acheson): Yes.

Chairman: Well, now, page 18 [Article III, Section 6, "Use of Loans Guaranteed, Participated in or Made by the Bank"]. I think the same page [i.e., issue?] arises.

Norway (Ole Colbjørnsen): Yes. My first remark really refers to Alternative B on page 18. That is, that when a borrower is a government, it could have the whole amount at once and dispose of it all under its own control, without disapportionment and examination and control, which is provided for specific projects.

Chairman: Yes. I think this is in order in this place. It is proposed as an amendment to [Article III, Section] 6(b) that where [p. 11] it isn't a government [receiving the loan], the Bank may [[take measures?]] to assure that the proceeds of the loan shall be used only for the purposes for which the loan is granted, [and] that where a government is involved, it is proposed that there shall not be that limitation. Therefore, I think we must pass that.

Now, Section 1, Article IV, page 19 ["Methods of Facilitating Provision of Loans"]. Can that go to the Drafting Committee?

Netherlands (Wim Beyen): Why, I shouldn't think so. Mr. Chairman. [[This section merits a?]] discussion on principle. (Inaudible)

Chairman: Well, I think if there is any objection, we better not pass it to the Drafting Committee.

I think that the amendment on page 21 [Article IV, Section 3, "Loans from Borrowed Funds and Guarantees"] ought to be taken with the amendment on page 14 [Article III, Section 3, "Limitations on Loans and Guarantees"], which is the same subject. I think that Alternative B is not really in order here; it is in order on page 14. Does the author of Alternative B [to Article IV, Section 3] accept that?

Norway (Ole Colbjørnsen): Yes. It is accepted.

Chairman: The author of Alternative B on page 21 agrees that the more appropriate place for that is on page 14, so that we transfer it. And I think we can then pass Alternative A to the Drafting Committee.

Article IV ["Operations"] is a major matter which clearly requires further discussion.

That carries us to page 23 [Article IV, Section 5, "Participations"]. Perhaps that can go to the Drafting Committee.

Then we turn to page 24 [Article IV, Section 6, "Guarantees"]. That clearly goes with whatever committee consider Section 4 ["Payment Provisions for Direct Loans"].

[Article IV,] Section 7 ["Order of Meeting Obligations," page 25]. May that go to the Drafting Committee?

(After a pause.) Page 25 goes to the Drafting Committee.

United States (Dean Acheson): I think it better go to the committee. [p. 12]

Chairman: What is the point there?

United States (Dean Acheson): I think there will be questions of substance there.

Chairman: I see. All right.

[Article IV,] Section 8, page 26 ["Miscellaneous Operations"]. Any objection to that going to the Drafting Committee?

Netherlands (Wim Beyen): Mr. Chairman, is Section 6 ["Guarantees"] going to the Drafting Committee?

Chairman: No.

Netherlands (Wim Beyen): Thank you.

Chairman: Section 8? Any objection on that?

(None was voiced.)

Drafting Committee.

[Article IV,] Section 9, page 27 ["Warning to Be Placed on Securities"]. Drafting Committee?

(After a pause.) [Article IV,] Section 10, page 28 ["Political Activity Prohibited"]. Drafting Committee? [p. 13]

Now we come to Article V (pages 29 to 36) ["Management"]. I think the first eight sections should all be considered together by Committee 3 ["Organization and Management"]. Perhaps I anticipate what we are coming to later to be up to the chairman and reporting delegate to decide whether they want it discussed in the whole committee or ad hoc. Although there are no alternatives before us. I don't think any of us feel that those sections are being thrown out—Article V, Sections 1 to 8.

United States (Dean Acheson): May I make a suggestion that there is a general rule of policy. The Commission indicated that wherever comparable paragraphs of Bank and Fund go along, the language agreed upon for the Fund should be incorporated in the Bank.

Chairman: Any objection to that general rule: where the substance is the same, the language should be the same?

Netherlands (Wim Beyen): As a general rule, it is only applicable where the substance *is* the same.

Chairman: Yes.

United States (Dean Acheson): Mr. Chairman, what we are attempting to avoid is the result which comes by saying the same thing differently.

Chairman: It is most important.

Now page 37 [Article V, Section 9, "Form of Holdings of Currency"]. We are now reaching smaller matters. I suggest page 37 might go to the Drafting Committee.

Mexico (Rodrigo Gómez): The last sentence of Section 9, saying that further obligations is "[a credit to the] currency [account] of the Fund."

Chairman: That is a misprint of "the Bank." May we have a correction of that misprint? Put it to the Drafting Committee.

[Article V,] Section 10 ["Protection of the Assets of the Bank"], Drafting Committee. Page 39, Section 11 ["Publication of Reports"], Drafting Committee. Section 12 ["Allocation of Income"] is a little more significant. May that go to the Drafting Committee? [p. 14]

United States (Dean Acheson): We prefer to have that go to the committee [Committee 3, "Organization and Management"].

Chairman: May we add [Article V,] Section 12 to the Third Committee [Committee 3] and the first eight sections and Section 12 to the [same] committee?

Section 13 ["Miscellaneous Powers"], Drafting Committee.

Netherlands (Wim Beyen): Mr. Chairman, may I be excused for objecting? I rather think that Section 10 ["Protection of the Assets of the Bank"] should be discussed. I think that is a very important subject, and it may influence the attitude that people anticipate very much. I think it would be a good thing to have it discussed.

Chairman: I hope it won't be discussed too much. I think it very well wants to go. But have Section 10 ["Protection of the Assets of the Bank"], also Sections 8 ["Depositories"], 10, and 12 ["Allocation of Income"], referred to the committee [Committee 3].

United States (Dean Acheson): Mr. Chairman, that is identical with the provision in the Fund.

Chairman: I know. That is what I thought. Do you really want to discuss it?

Netherlands (Wim Beyen): Yes. The fact that it is identical with the Fund does not mean that it has the same importance in the Fund as in the Bank.

Chairman: We will put that to the committee [Committee 3]. The other goes to the Drafting Committee.

Article VI ["Withdrawal and Suspension of Membership and Liquidation"] is very much a Drafting Committee matter. It follows very closely the lines of the Fund and I think it is more for lawyers. In case any member wants to interrupt, I will take the sections one by one. May Section 1 of Article VI ["Right of Members to Withdraw"] go to the Drafting Committee?

Unidentified: Page?

Chairman: Page 42. [Article VI,] Section 2, page 43 ["Suspension of Membership"], Drafting Committee.

Section 3, page 44 ["Financial Assistance to Be Withheld"], Drafting Committee.

And now, Section 4. This is one Mr. Melville called your attention to, and that must clearly go to committee together [p. 15] with the matter at the very beginning which we associated with it. Here it is a question of which committee it goes to. Insofar as we consider this Article VI, it would go to Committee 1, or 3.

United States (Dean Acheson): Mr. Chairman, have you passed Article VI, Section 3?

Chairman: I was about to pass it.

United States (Dean Acheson): Are you going to send that to Drafting?

Chairman: Yes.

United States (Dean Acheson): That is a pretty important section.

Chairman: It is very important, but I heard no opposition to it.

Now, [Article VI,] Section 4 ["Cessation of Membership in International Monetary Fund," page 45]: we agreed earlier in the afternoon should be taken with page 3 [Article I, Section I, "Countries Eligible for Membership"]. I think we might now refer page 3 and page 45 to the chairman of Committee 1 ["Purposes, Policies, and Capital of the Bank"]. I should think he would very likely want to have a small ad hoc [committee] on those two together, but that is in his discretion. May we add that—page 3 and 45 together [to] be referred to the chairman of Committee 1.

Section 5 ["Settlement of Accounts with Countries Ceasing to Be Members"]: may that go to the Drafting Committee? There is considerable question of drafting and a large question of substance.

Page 47, Section 6 ["Assessments to Meet Losses"]: may that go to the Drafting Committee?

Section 7 ["Liquidation"]: very much the same language as the Fund—Drafting Committee.

United States (Dean Acheson): We don't object to pages 45, 44 and 47 as going to the committee [Committee 1] rather than [to the] Drafting Committee.

Chairman: Page 45?

Mr. Acheson: Page 44 ["Financial Assistance to Be Withheld"].

Chairman: 44 and 47: take those together. May we agree that [pages] 44 and 47 are referred to the chairman of Committee 3 ["Organization and Management"]? Make a note of that: pages 44 and 47 go to Committee 3. [Page] 45 goes to a different committee. [p. 16]

Now we have reached page 48 [Article VI, Section 7, "Liquidation"]. What about that? Do you think that can go to the Drafting Committee?

United States (Dean Acheson): I think that also should be referred to Committee 3 for questions in drafting.

Chairman: We don't want to invent questions, do we? Are there any other questions that the members want to raise? You see, this is very much simpler than in the case of the Fund. Do you think we want to encourage amendments on it?

United States (Dean Acheson): No, we don't want to encourage amendments, but there are different questions here than there are in connection with a liquidation of the Fund.

Chairman: Do you think this then can go to the same committee as we have given [pages] 44 and 47 to? Add this to the same committee as 44 and 47.

Belgium (Camille Gutt): Pages 42 [Article VI, Section 1, "Right of Members to Withdraw"] and 43 [Section 2,"Suspension of Membership," the] original amendment, would go to the suspension of the membership [[and therefore?]] have some connection with this—[they should be] examined in the same lot.

Chairman: 42 and 43 go to that same committee [Committee 3]. Secretary, do you have a note of this? These are different sections of Article VI.

Now, [page] 49 [Article VII, "Additional Undertakings on the Part of Member Countries," Section 1, "Purposes and Scope of Undertakings"], would that go to the Drafting Committee? [Page] 49, Article VII. We have now gotten to Article VII, Section 1. Any objection?

Article VII, Section 2 ["Immunities of the Bank"]: that also seems ready for Drafting Committee.

Now, Article VII—we haven't got any amendment here, but I have heard in conversation some question raised as to whether Section 3 on page 51 ["Suits against the Bank"] doesn't go rather far. I think probably this ought to be referred to a committee. Is that not so? [p. 17]

Netherlands (Wim Beyen): Yes, very definitely.

Chairman: This is under Committee 4 ["Form and Status of the Bank"]. So may we refer page 51 to the chairman of Committee 4 and possibly, I am not sure, but does not the same apply to page 52 [Article VII, Section 4, "Restrictions on Taxation of the Bank, Its Employees and Obligations"]?

Unidentified: Yes.

Chairman: It would have to go to the same committee as page 51.

Now page 53 [Article VIII, "Amendments"], I think, is the same as in the Fund. What is felt about that? How right is that? Mr. Acheson, do you think page 53 is ready for Drafting Committee?

United States (Dean Acheson): Yes, Mr. Chairman, I think that is ready for Drafting Committee. I would raise one question about the Fund [Bank]. On page 49 [Article VII, Section 1, "Purposes and Scope of Undertakings"] there is a question where the Drafting Committee differs from the Bank. At the end of the section ["all of which shall remain binding during suspension"], that may involve obligations which would go on for fifty years, and there would have to be consideration of that question.

Chairman: I think it would be better for the Drafting Committee to pass first on it, with respect to lasting guarantees—yes.

Now there is Article IX ["Interpretation of the Agreement," Section 1, "Interpretation"]; I think that is ready. That is, again, very similar to the Fund and I think this has been lifted from the Fund. The text will be the same. Page 54. So this really has had a good deal of discussion, if not by our Commission. May that go to the Drafting Committee?

Mr. Secretary, page 55 [Article IX, Section 2, "Definitions," to be supplied later]: whom do you expect to supply these definitions? I am told that a volunteer group has offered to work with the definitions. Perhaps we might pass that until we hear from them.

Page 56 [Article IX, Section 3, "Approval Deemed Given"]: does that go to the Drafting Committee?

Page 57 [Article X, "Final Provisions," to be supplied later]: we have to wait until it arrives. I think page 57 is essentially a legal matter which the Drafting Committee will provide us with after everything [p. 18] else is finished. Is that right, Mr. Acheson?

United States (Dean Acheson): Yes.

Chairman: Perhaps, then, we might refer it to them. I don't think we can do any work on that. Page 57 goes to the Drafting Committee.

I have to admit we mixed up stages 1 and 2 to a certain extent. We can now go through and make some references to committees that are apparently going to be necessary, and I should like to pass over one or two points in case we have time to discuss them here after we have done that.

One of the major questions—there are certain miscellaneous questions in Article II which might perhaps be connected together—so far as page 3 [Article II, Section 1, "Countries Eligible for Membership"] is concerned, that we have already referred to the committee. I think we might refer it to [the] chairman of Committee 1 ["Purposes, Policies, and Capital of the Bank"], pages 4 [Article II, Section 2, "Authorized Capital"], pages 6 with its a's [pages 6a, 6aa; Article II, Section 4, "Availability of Subscribed Capital"], and page 7 [Article II, Section 5, "Payment of Subscription"] and page 8 [Article II, Section 6, "Issue Price of Shares"].

Pages 4 to 9 [sections of Article II, "Membership in and Capital of the Bank"] all rather hang together. They might go to the chairman of Committee 1, who will decide whether it should go to the whole committee or to [an] ad hoc [committee]. Now, I think we might also refer to that same committee pages 11 and 11a [Article II, Section 9, "Return of Subscriptions"]—to that same committee. Is that all right? No, there is an alternative. I think 11 has to go to the same committee as 4 to 9.

Now, [page] 12 [Article III, Section 1, "Use of Resources Restricted"]: perhaps we might see if we can discuss that later. We might reserve that for a moment.

Now, [page] 13 [Article III, Section 2, "Agencies Dealing with the Bank"] raises an issue which I think comes sporadically. That is the relationship of this institution to other international institutions, and I think we want a committee which deals with that whole issue. We have had some communications from observers now present from other international bodies, and I think it would be helpful to have a committee to take up all matters so arising. I am not quite [p. 19] sure what the rules and regulations propose, but I think we might wish the observers who are here present to be free to speak before that committee.

Unidentified: That is an ad hoc committee?

Chairman: That is an ad hoc committee which will be appointed by the chairman of Committee 2 ["Operations of the Bank"]. I hope several of those will be ad hoc committees. That is for the chairman to decide. I think there are some proposals about this which are not, as yet, in this paper. Perhaps the Secretariat might send the committee any other matter which reads as it which deals with the relationship of this institution to other international bodies. It is the chairman of Committee 2 who will attend to that.

Now we come to an important matter which I think might usefully be referred to a committee, either separately or in conjunction with the following explanations. I should care for an opinion of this, [Article III,] Section 3 ["Limitation on Loans and Guarantees"]. Now [what] we have incorporated in this page 21 [Article IV, Section 3, "Loans from Borrowed Funds and Guarantees"] is a matter which we have discussed a few moments ago, and on which varying opinions are held. Would it be better to have a separate committee on that, or refer it to the same committee as [Article IV], Section 4 ["Payment Provisions for Direct Loans"], which is also important? I think perhaps they might go together. Subcommittee on 3 and 4 [to] be appointed by chairman of Committee 2, that will cover pages 14, 15 with its [supplementary pages] a, b, c, d, and e. I think we might throw in 16 with that. Yes, pages 14 to 16 [sections of Article III, "General Provisions Related to Loans"] to that committee. It is a separate subject.

Unidentified: Committee 2?

Chairman: I think possibly the Norwegian amendment on page 18 [Alternative B to Article IV, Section 6, "Use of Loans Guaranteed, Participated in or Made by the Bank"] might also go to that committee. Would that be convenient for the Norwegian delegation?

Norway (Ole Colbjørnsen): Yes. [p. 20]

Chairman: Pages 14, 16 and 18. Now we come to a series of very important pages. Page 17 [Article III, Section 5, "Provision of Currencies for Loans"] is now in Drafting Committee. The Norwegian amendment will be transferred, you see, from an earlier page.

Unidentified: It should be given to the Drafting Committee.

Chairman: It is suggested that page 17, instead of going to the Drafting Committee, should go to the same committee which deals with pages 14 to 18, inclusive. I think that is wise.

Article IV ["Operations"] needs to be one committee—pages 19 to 22. Pages 19 to 22 [are] referred to the chairman of Committee 2. I'm sure it will save time if, when a committee has a number of matters referred to it, it could break up into groups to deal with these separate blocks.

Now I think we have dealt with everything except some things at the beginning.

Unidentified: What about page 24 [Article IV, Section 4, "Guarantees"]?

Chairman: Page 22, 23 has gone to the Drafting Committee, and 24 has gone to the same committee, which is dealing with—yes, 24—pages 19 to 22 and page 24 go to that committee, and 23 has nothing at all; that is going to the Drafting Committee.

Now, unless I am mistaken, we have dealt with everything except pages 1 ["Title"] and 2 [Article I, "Purposes of the Bank"] and 12 [Article III, Section 1, "Source of Resources Restricted"].

United States (Dean Acheson): Page 25 [Article IV, Section 7, "Order of Meeting Obligations"], Mr. Chairman?

Chairman: Page 25 has gone to the Drafting Committee. There are some drafting points there which we have got, but I think that is absolutely drafting points.

United States (Dean Acheson): I think that would go to the same committee—Committee 2.

Chairman: Yes. We might put pages 19 to 22, 24, and 25 [sections of Article IV, "Operations"] to that committee.

Now we have got left pages—"Title of Bank," "Purposes of Bank," and [a] question which has been [p. 21] raised on page 12 [Article III, Section 1, "Use of Resources Restricted"] which goes rather deep in the root of everything, and it is your pleasure [words not recorded].

[Unidentified]: Mr. Chairman, I am afraid that there are several persons in this room who are not fair-minded [i.e., quick-witted] enough, so may I suggest that we may have by tomorrow morning a printed list in which it is stated which articles are referred to the Drafting Committee and two other committees.

Chairman: Certainly; that is the intention.

Is it your pleasure that we should proceed for a little longer—it now five o'clock—to discuss one or two matters of a very general character that I think are better discussed in the Commission than anywhere else? Is that all right? Now, the first is on page 1 and 1a ["Title"]. Some of us think that almost any name is better for this than "Bank" because it is not a bank and leads to false associations in the public mind, but when we come to suggest that alternative, perhaps we are not so happily inspired, and I think it would be helpful if we could have an expression of opinion. There were three alternatives on the paper—"Bank," "Corporation," and "Guaranty and Investment Association"—but many other suggestions might be made. Might we hear views on this?

France (André Istel): Mr. Chairman, the reason I suggest "International Guaranty and Investment Association" [is that] it was thought that it was preferable that the name should express the [permanent] function of the Bank rather than the temporary functions such as reconstruction and development. The function of the Bank is either primarily to guarantee or primarily to invest, so I think that those two functions by properly be expressed in the name. Personally I would prefer "Guaranty and Investment" rather than "Investment [p. 22] and Guaranty," because I think the guarantee function of the Association is more important than the investment function, inasmuch as less capital will be available for investment.

Unidentified: "Association" in English is a very weak word.

France (André Istel): I would be perfectly willing to say "Institute" or any other name.

United Kingdom (Robert Brand): I support your view. "Association" is a weak word. It reminds us in England of Young Men's Christian Association. I have no objection to it at all. I think it is a weak word, that is, I personally prefer very much the word "Corporation" and I think it ought to be acceptable in the United States because they have a highly successful institution, the RFC [Reconstruction Finance Corporation], which bears the word "corporation." "Corporation," so far as [the] United Kingdom is concerned, is a word which I think expresses well what this body would carry out, and I think the combination "International Guaranty and Investment Corporation" would be the best solution.

Norway (Ole Colbjørnsen): Mr. Chairman, would it not be proper to defer the question of name until we have decided on the matter of substance, especially under Article IV ["Operations"]? After all, we must decide the general character of the Bank. There is in the new proposals that we have received now another big change from what we have previously [[seen?]]. One is that the role of the Bank as a guarantee bank is more stressed in the later proposal. There may be governments—my government—which are interested more in the role of the Bank [as] an institution as really a bank which may give loans to governments, and not only guarantee specific projects.

This question is also related to that introduced by the Chairman in his remarks during our first [p. 23] session of this Commission, where it was proposed, as we have done now in the latest draft, a flat rate of guarantee commission. That is a complete novelty, because previously, up to at least the question of the United States Treasury which was perceived a month ago, we thought that there ought to be a differentiation between guarantees, as is usual in banking and investment practice. I refer, for instance, to the Question 21,[561] where the American answer is that the rate of interest of loan through the bank will vary with the financial markets with the credit condition of the borrower. That is what we have tried to incorporate in our amendments on the specific point. I think we could profitably defer that question of naming this baby until we have decided the general character of the institution, which will only be decided after having finished more or less with the operative provisions of this institution.

Mexico: I quite agree with the delegate from the United Kingdom as to the weakness of the word "Association," but in Spanish the word "Corporation" has no appropriate translation.

Unidentified: Mr. Chairman, it seems to me that it is of great importance that the purposes of this body should be expressed in the name and therefore it seems to me that the words "Reconstruction and Development" should not be omitted in the name, because it is of importance that the popular opinion of the United Nations may know what is the purpose of the bank which we are creating.

Cuba (Luis Machado): Mr. Chairman, some of us are not prepared to go into details of this discussion, because we have just received this afternoon—or this morning—the complete copy of the final draft, and we would like to have an opportunity to discuss among the members of our own delegation [p. 24] some of the provisions of the final draft. Perhaps some of the details of the name might be left to the proper committee. In the meantime, will we have an opportunity to go over some of the matters referred to the Drafting Committee. For instance, in connection with the management of the Bank, we have some amendments in connection with the management of the Fund, and I noticed that in the final draft submitted here that the language and technique of the management of the Fund is closely followed. I was

---

[561] *Questions and Answers on the Bank for Reconstruction and Development,* issued by the U.S. Treasury on February 24, 1944; reprinted, perhaps with revisions, on June 10, 1944, and apparently also known as "Questions at Issue on the Bank."

wondering if we could save time perhaps if we might not refer it to the committee, by having the delegates express views on this subject.

Chairman: I think the object is to save time, but not preclude any delegation which has studied the matter in having certain thoughts. If we put off until everyone has time to complete the discussion, we would have no Bank. Wouldn't it be better to have a Bank rather than not to have a Bank at all? Aren't you sufficiently protected if nothing is finally settled at this stage so that you can come back, whether it has gone to the Drafting Committee or not, with any suggestion on any point? You have only a few days altogether.

Unidentified: Would we be at liberty to ask what matters be taken from the Drafting Committee to the respective committees?

Chairman: It would depend on that, sure. Any point you want to raise, it would be sent into the secretaries.

Unidentified: I move that the question be referred to Committee 3 ["Organization and Management"].

Chairman: It has been referred.

Unidentified: To Committee 3?

Chairman: I think so. Are there any other remarks on the name of the Bank? [p. 25]

Ecuador ([Sixto Durán]): It seems to me that the name is secondary. I would say a few words that we were invited to discuss the establishment of the Bank. As far as I know, there is going to be a Bank and the Bank is to be dedicated to reconstruction and development, and I think that the object to which the Bank is going to be put, reconstruction and development, is preferable to investment, as the means to be employed in order to reconstruct and develop.

Chairman: Any other remarks?

United States (Dean Acheson): Mr. Chairman, may I make three points in regard to the Bank. First, it seems to us it would be desirable to have the idea of development and reconstruction in the name. Second, that it would be desirable to have a name which indicated that this organization would not itself undertake development and reconstruction. In other words, this is not an operating organization which would go out and build dams, but it is financing that operation. The third point is that the word "Corporation" would raise difficulties in the United States, because if there is one thing about this organization, it is *not* a corporation. In other words, it is not incorporated either by all nations together or one nation, and it is not, according to our conception, a corporation. It seems to me roughly the word "Bank" comes nearest to what it was, but if it is not, let us get some other name.

USSR: This bank is not a corporation or association, therefore the Soviet delegation does not see any reason for substituting "bank" for any other word, and we wish to suggest that the proposal as in the American draft, "Bank of Reconstruction and Development," [[is suitable?]]. [p. 26]

Chairman: I don't know what may be the case in other languages. This performs none of the functions of an English bank, none whatever, and therefore it is terribly misleading.

If I may sum up so far, I think there has been the consensus of opinion to keep "Reconstruction and Development" in it rather than "Reconstruction and Investment." Therefore I think we might draft Alternative C, and I think we should all agree with Mr. Acheson that there must be no suggestion that this is an operative body. Therefore it is a matter of either calling it "International Bank" or "Corporation" or some other third word, and I think we might now have second and third and fourth and fifth thoughts on this, and if anyone has a bright idea he would do a great service if he would send it into the Secretary. I think this is rather a matter of the Commission rather than [of a] committee. I think this is the right body to discuss it. May we pass on, with the suggestion that the bright ideas should be sent in by the delegate.

Now, the next matter is one which we may have to put off, but I think we might have a little useful discussion here, because while it is allocated to Committee 1 ["Purposes, Policies, and Capital of the Bank"], it really overlaps every committee and therefore is really a Commission matter. It has no special connection with the other functions of Committee 1, and I will call attention to the various alternatives. If you look at Alternative A, page 2 [Article I, "Purposes of the Bank"], we have got four suggestions for the first clause. First suggestion is on the first page. Second suggestion is first clause of Alternative C: we amend that one. Third is first alternative of Alternative D: we amend that one. And Alternative F: we amend that one. First paragraph of these four suggestions are very similar to one another in much more than differences of language.[562] [p. 27]

---

562 These alternatives are all in Document 245, pp. 367-369. The clauses are as follows, with the main differences in italics: Alternative A: "To assist in the reconstruction and development of member countries by facilitating provision of long-term investment capital for productive purposes through private financial agencies, by means of guaranteeing and participating in the loans made by private investors." Alternative C: "To assist in the reconstruction and the restoration of the economy destroyed by the hostilities, and in the development of member countries by facilitating provision of long-term investment capital for productive purposes through private financial agencies, by means of guaranteeing and participating in the loans made by private investors." Alternative D: "To assist in

I think the issue here is we might first of all compare Alternative C with A. Alternative C is a little more elaborate in that it adds the words "and the restoration of economies destroyed by hostilities." The question is, does anyone really object to the addition of those words? Is there anyone who feels—I am suggesting possibly that the deciding of Alternative C—to agree on Alternative C by adding these words.

Unidentified: "Affected by enemy action?"

[Chairman]: I think that is our [favored wording?:] "where affected by enemy action."

United States (Dean Acheson): We have attempted to go through with these three alternatives and bring together henceforth all the ideas. I think that there was no objection whatever to restoration, reconstruction, and development [being mentioned] in the particular draft which I have and am willing to propose after I have had a chance to edit it—it is not quite ready to propose. I wonder if this is not a matter where everybody is really agreed and [on] which the Drafting Committee can very speedily get out a draft.

Chairman: I think that is a good suggestion. I think there is a point here except properly descriptive language.

Netherlands (Wim Beyen): I think that it is not destroyed by enemy action, but friendly action. The feeling may be different, but the effect is very much the same.

Chairman: Might we refer it to Committee 1? Perhaps [Committee] 2; we have four alternatives. Alternative A, Alternative B—we might take that first as an amendment to bring Alternative A in conformity with Alternative B. I think that is suggested later—that is to say, it is not strictly commercial in its criteria. Then Alternative C is [p. 28] enlarging the description very much as in the first. Alternative E is only a verbal change, I think, and that is all. That also should be referred to the Drafting Committee. Mr. Acheson, is this also suitable for the Drafting Committee?

---

the reconstruction and development of the productive resources of member countries, more especially those whose economy has been disrupted by the war or has been inadequately developed, by providing or facilitating the provision of long-term investment capital." Alternative F: "To assist in the reconstruction and development of member countries by facilitating provision of capital for sound and constructive international investment through private financial agencies, by means of guaranteeing and participating in the loans made by private investors." Alternatives B and E contain no language for the first paragraph.

United States (Dean Acheson): I think that the same thing can be done with all these, Mr. Chairman, and I think it would take a few hours of the Drafting Committee to bring back a whole statement of purposes.

Chairman: I think that would be very good. May we refer this? I have not discovered in reading this any point of controversy. It is a matter of getting the right descriptive language. May we refer the whole of Article I to the Drafting Committee?

Now I should like to pass to page 12 [Article III, Section 1, "Use of Resources Restricted"], which raises a matter which strikes so deep, that I think it is not appropriate for any single committee. Perhaps the delegation responsible for Alternative B will speak for it?[563]

Mexico: In the first place, I should like to point out that the word "restricted" [should] be deleted from the title. When we submitted the alternative, we put Section 1, "Use of Resources," and we deleted the word "restricted." And, Mr. Chairman, I would further like to ask you, if it pleases the Commission, the Mexican delegation would like to make a brief statement, and explain this alternative proposal.[564]

It may appear to some of you that our proposal would rather hamper the Bank's reconstruction operations during the first years, but we wish to assure you that is very far from our purpose to place obstacles in the way of reconstruction. We are fully aware of the damage that the war has done to the productive capacity [p. 29] of our allies in Europe and Asia, and we realize also that once liberated, the territories now occupied by our enemies would require a great deal of capital in order to be set afoot again, and we are no less aware of the direct sacrifices undergone by those nations. Therefore, it is not with a spirit of denying them a substantial measure of the Bank's resources that we have introduced this. To our mind, our reasons for asking to provide that reconstruction and development be put on the same footing are threefold.

First, we believe that the agreement we are to reach here is to be imposed in a permanent and not in a provisional international instrument. Therefore, it seems to us inappropriate that the document should not contain an equal emphasis on the two great purposes of the Bank, namely, to facilitate reconstruction and development. In the very short

---

563 Alternative B reads, "The resources and the facilities of the Bank shall be used exclusively for the benefit if members. ¶The Bank shall give equal consideration to projects for development and to projects for reconstruction, and its resources and facilities shall always be made available to the same extent for either kind of project." Document 245, pp. 373-374.

564 The speech that follows was published with minor changes as Press Release No. 29, Document 306, pp. 1175-1177.

run, perhaps reconstruction would be more urgent for the world as a whole, but in the long run, Mr. Chairman, before we are all too dead,[565] if I may say so, development must prevail, if we are to sustain and increase real income everywhere. Without denying the initial importance of reconstruction, we ask you not to relegate or postpone development.

Secondly, we believe that we and other nations not actually need of funds for reconstruction can greatly assist in the reconstruction of those who do need it, providing our economies be developed more fully at the same time as rehabilitation of the war-torn nations takes place. We have resources which are still untapped. A large part of our population has not yet attained an adequate standard of living, and yet we have not hesitated to throw in our lot with our allies, disregarding temporarily all our wide domestic problems. If we tackle these, and for that require sums of capital which we do not dispose of at home, we will undoubtedly benefit not only ourselves, but the world as a whole, and particularly the industrial nations, in that we shall provide better markets and better goods. We submit, therefore, Mr. Chairman, that capital for development purposes in our country is as important for the world as is capital for reconstruction purposes.

Third and last, and we again [p. 30] wish to emphasize that it is with no unfriendly spirit that we make this reference, we should like to call your attention to an important provision of the draft. I refer to Article II, Section 5(a) ["Payment of Subscription"],[566] which states that payments in gold shall be graduated according to a schedule that shall take into account the adequacy of the gold and free foreign exchange holdings of every member country. We believe that, having in mind the position in which the war devastated countries are, this is only fair that we have no intention whatever of grudging one ounce of our contribution in gold, but since we happen to have unprecedented holdings of gold and foreign exchange—and we speak, I believe, for the majority of Latin American nations,—and since we feel that we have an opportunity of devoting part of our holdings to the importing of capital goods for our development, it is our considered opinion that in contributing part of them ungrudgingly to the Bank for the benefit of all the nations constituting it, we should desire at least the assurance that our request for capital for development purposes shall, in the words of our amendment, be given equal

565 A reference to Keynes's dictum that "In the long run we are all dead," which appears in his 1923 *Tract on Monetary Reform* as a criticism of economic analysis that focuses on long-run steady states and neglects possibly tumultuous short-run fluctuations along the way.

566 In Document 245, p. 371.

consideration as is given to reconstruction projects; and further, the assurance that the resources and facilities of the Bank shall always be made available to the same extent for either kind of project.

We do wish to make it perfectly clear, Mr. Chairman, that we do not desire to impose on the Bank a rigid 50-50 rule. We believe some discretion on the Bank's part should be provided for. Furthermore, what we ask is only that the Bank's resources and facilities be made available to us in the event these countries requesting loans for development purposes do not use up the resources and facilities made available to them. Countries requiring loans for reconstruction purposes would have a claim on the unused resources. In conclusion, may we emphasize that we do not contemplate a rigid interpretation of the phrase "to the same extent," but that we do think it is a principle which should be embodied in the instrument we are endeavoring to draw up. We are [p. 31] perfectly willing, Mr. Chairman, to accept a better wording of our proposed amendment so long as the same principle is preserved in it.

Cuba: The Cuban delegation desires to state [[its support for the amendment?]].

Netherlands (Wim Beyen): On the part of the Dutch delegation there would not be any obligation against the spirit of this amendment, but I would like to suggest with all due respect to the Mexican delegation that the wording is not very happy. It seems to me a bit strict, and without wanting to be facetious, I want to draw your attention to the fact that if the period of reconstruction is over, this word would mean that we would first have to do a little amount of devastation in order to keep both amounts equal. That can't be the intention of the Mexican delegation, and it is not necessary. What we want is some sort of general indication that projects for development are equally as important as projects for reconstruction, but I don't think we can usefully go any further.

Chairman: Might I suggest something to the Mexican delegation which seems to be in the spirit of their proposal and Mr. Beyen's remarks for it might run, "The resources and facilities of the bank should be used exclusively with equal, equitable consideration, [on] projects for development and projects for reconstruction alike."

Mexico: I think that would be acceptable to us.

Chairman: Would that be generally acceptable to the members of the Commission?

Delegates: Yes.

Chairman: May we adopt those words and refer it to the Drafting Committee as amended?

Agreed.

Now it is after five o'clock, and perhaps the most convenient thing now would be if I would ask the members of the appropriate committees and chairman and reporting delegates of the committees to stay behind that we might clear up some things. One point the Secretary has called my attention to: page 13 [Article III, Section 2, "Agencies Dealing with the Bank"] talks of international bodies. We referred this to Committee 2. The Secretariat pointed out that a similar matter is going to Committee 3, and that Committee 3 is the appropriate body. [p. 32] Is there any objection to that—Committee 3 instead of Committee 2?

I think our idea would be that the ad hoc committees and the committees should start as soon as possible, as soon as their chairmen can get them going, and report to this body not later than Thursday [July 13], I hope earlier in the day. That would give the whole of tomorrow for committees. This is not suggesting that the committees will finish all their work tomorrow, but if we could pass on some to the Drafting Committee, it would help, and we could also receive from the Drafting Committee by Thursday their draft of Article I. And then I suppose we would have to meet on Thursday afternoon. I think it looks as if we might begin to catch up, but it does mean that the committees must meet rather actively tomorrow, and I believe that if the chairmen can work in smaller groups than the whole and then take it to the committee as a whole, we shall go on more rapidly. If every delegate present today wants to be present in the discussion of all these issues, clearly they will have to stay up all night, and that is perhaps something to be avoided.

May we adjourn on that understanding?

Mexico: Mr. Chairman, may I make a suggestion that the Drafting Committee take into account the wording of the clause in the article to which we referred a while ago in our amendment, taking into account that alteration in the wording of our articles and sections of the draft.

Chairman: No doubt they will seek to harmonize, give equal emphasis, to reconstruction and development. No doubt they will attend to that. If you think they haven't attended to it enough to get results, you can raise again. If there is no other question, may I ask the members of the Agenda Committee and chairmen and reporters to remain behind.

No other transcripts are available for meetings of Commission II or its committees. The subsequent meetings of Commission II, and their minutes in the conference proceedings, are as follows: third meeting, July 13 (Document 381, pp. 613-615); fourth meeting, July 16 (Document 423, pp. 705-708); fifth and sixth meetings, July 19, morning and afternoon (Document 469, pp. 858-860); seventh meeting; July 20 (Document 507, pp. 1078-1079); eighth and ninth (final) meetings, July 21, morning and afternoon (Document 525, pp. 1098-1099). The committee meetings are so numerous that we do not list them here, but their minutes are likewise in the conference proceedings.

38

Commission III
Other Means of International Financial Cooperation
First meeting: transcript
July 3, 1944, 5:00 p.m.[567]

Introduction of officers • Chairman's opening speech • Appointment of Agenda Committee

The subject of Commission III was "other means of international financial cooperation" apart from the IMF and World Bank. Commission III was a forum for ideas that did not fit in the other two commissions. Its chairman was Eduardo Suárez, Mexico's minister of finance. Suárez was by training a lawyer, and had participated in drafting a number of Mexican laws on money and banking. He had also been Mexico's representative to the League of Nations. After Warren Kelchner, the Secretary General of the conference, introduces Suárez and the other officers of Commission III, Suárez gives a brief speech suggesting that the Commission confine itself to problems primarily monetary and financial in nature. He then proposes to appoint an Agenda Committee to receive suggestions about what topics the Commission should discussed. The delegates accept the proposal, and the meeting adjourns.

Secretary General (Warren Kelchner, United States): Commission III of the United Nations Monetary and Financial Conference is hereby convened.

As you know, the plenary session of the conference approved the regulations this morning, and those regulations provided for the establishment of Commission III to consider "other means of international financial cooperation." The plenary session also elected the officers of this Commission, namely, the representative of Mexico as chairman, the representative of the Egypt as vice chairman, and the

567 Summarized in Document 61, pp. 99-100. The typescript has two transcriptions, which have some differences. We have taken whichever one reported a particular speech more fully. One of the typescripts says, "Stenographic Report by Mary E. Fitchett."

representative of New Zealand as reporting delegate. I have been informed that the representative of Mexico, who will serve as chairman of this Commission, is Mr. Eduardo Suárez; the representative of Egypt, who will serve as vice chairman, Mr. Sany Lackany Bey; and the representative of New Zealand, who will serve as the reporting delegate, Mr. Allan Fisher.

I am now turning the chair over to the chairman of the Commission, Mr. Suárez.

Chairman ([Eduardo Suárez, Mexico]): This meeting will now come to order.

Before proceeding with the formal business of the day, I would like to introduce Mr. Orvis A. Schmidt, who will serve as Technical Secretary. Mr. Schmidt is a member of the United States Treasury Department, where he serves on the capacity of Acting Director of the Bureau of Foreign Funds Control.

Fellow delegates and members of Commission III:[568]

As I call this meeting to order, I feel that I should take this opportunity to say a few words about the importance and scope of our work.

As we know, we have come together at this conference to consider to definite proposals for dealing with some of our most fundamental problems. The first is the proposal for the establishment of an International Monetary Fund, which has as one of its primary objectives the assurance of a pattern of stable and orderly exchange rates that will make possible the expansion of international trade and the maintenance of a high level of employment and business activity. The second is the proposal for the Bank for Reconstruction and Development for the purpose of encouraging sound international investment, thus contributing to economic reconstruction and development. Commissions I and II, respectively, have been established for dealing with these two specific proposals. This Commission will consider and make recommendations relative to "other means of international monetary and financial cooperation."

I assume that is not necessary for me to stress to the members of this group the importance of the cooperative and united approval to the important international financial problems with which we are confronted. As members of the United Nations, we accept as a basic proviso the desirability of working together to solve our problems.

---

[568] The speech that follows was issued with minor changes as Document 49, Press Release No. 14, pp. 1152-1154.

Unlike the other commissions, Commission III is not deciding the specific proposals which have been the subject of extended joint consultations and study by the technical representations of various nations. Although at this early stage we cannot foresee the character and disposition of our recommendations, it is not impossible that some of them may influence the recommendations approved by the other conditions.

Without seeming to place undue limitations upon the range of subjects to be considered, I feel that our time will be most profitably employed if we restrict ourselves to problems predominantly financial and monetary, and international in scope. For instance, it has been suggested that there be some international agreement with respect to the status of earmarked gold. Some delegations have previously expressed their concern over the fluctuations in international price levels to the extent that they are important to international exchange stability. Some concern has also been expressed about the international monetary functions of silver, for it is felt that the habits and needs of the peoples who continue to use it have not been thoroughly considered and appraised.

I am not sure that there has been ample opportunity for members to bring before this group their suggestions as to problems which might profitably be considered. It may hence be desirable, before appointing committees, to consider any specific problems that make arrangements for the purpose of receiving suggestions which may be appropriately considered in the Commission.

I recognize the delegate from Poland.

Poland: Mr. Chairman, I move that the Chairman appoint a committee for the purpose of receiving the suggestions and making recommendations as to the specific problems which should be dealt with in this Commission. [p. 2]

Chairman: I recognize the delegate from Uruguay.

Uruguay: Mr. Chairman, I second the motion.

Chairman: All in favor, say "aye."

("Ayes" heard.)

Those opposed, "no."

The motion is carried in accordance with the will of the Commission. I hereby appoint the following committee:

Agenda Committee for Commission III: Poland, Chairman; Netherlands, Reporter; Uruguay, Reporter; Chile; Ethiopia.

Suggestions as to specific problems to be considered in this Commission may be made to the committee during the next three days and should be delivered to the Technical Secretary in Room 151.

May [i.e., do] I hear some comments before adjourning?

The meeting is adjourned until further notice, when we will reconvene to receive the report of the Agenda Committee.

(5.30 p.m.)

39

Commission III
Other Means of International Financial Cooperation
Second meeting: transcript
July 10, 1944, 5:00 p.m.[569]

Report of Agenda Committee listing proposals submitted • Proposals referred to committee • Ad hoc committees appointed

The reporter of the Agenda Committee, Wim Beyen of the Netherlands, reads all the proposals that have been submitted to it. Beyen, the chairman of the Dutch delegation, was a financial adviser to the Dutch government in exile, and had been president of the Bank for International Settlements just before World War II. After Beyen reads his report, the French delegate proposes that the Commission accept it and empower the chairman, Eduardo Suárez of Mexico, to appoint three ad hoc committees, on use of silver for international and monetary purposes; enemy assets, looted property and related matters; and exchange of information and other means of financial cooperation. The delegates agree and Suárez names the members of the committees.

Chairman ([Eduardo Suárez, Mexico]): The meeting will come to order.

The Secretary has noted the absentees and advises that there is a quorum.

Mr. Mahmoud el Falaky of the Egyptian delegation is Vice Chairman instead of Mr. Sany Lackany Bey.

Before calling upon the Reporting Delegate of the Agenda Committee to make the report, I want to call attention to the fact that a copy of the report was distributed this morning and additional copies are available. Any delegation wishing extra copies, please raise their hands. I was told that extra copies of the report are available, and any delegations that want an extra copy will raise their hand. I would also like to ask that any person speaking from the floor first give his name and the name of the

[569] Summarized in Document 279, pp. 444-445.

delegation he represents in order to facilitate making a record of this proceedings.

I now call upon Mr. Beyen of the Netherlands delegation, Reporter of the Agenda Committee.

Wim Beyen (Netherlands, Reporter, Agenda Committee): Mr. Chairman, at the first meeting of Commission III, held at 5:00 p.m. on July 3, 1944, an Agenda Committee was appointed to receive and consider topics submitted as appropriate for consideration in Commission III. During the week ten proposals were received by the Agenda Committee.[570]

[1. Proposal on Silver submitted by Mexican delegation:

"Whereas it is undeniable that about half of the world's population prefers silver coins to any other kind of currency for everyday use and trade as well as for hoarding;

"Whereas the economically weaker silver nations silver-using nations of the world, upon becoming members of the proposed International Monetary Fund, would in fact agree, among other things, to collaborate with the stronger nations in the establishment of a world-wide free market for gold, and in the maintenance of a stable and fair price for that metal;

"Whereas it is just and fair that, in due correspondence, economically stronger countries should agree to extend their cooperation to be economically weaker ones, in order that silver may also have an ample market and a relatively stable and fair international price;

"Whereas, to comply fully with the proposed agreement, the silver-using peoples would need proportionately larger, and therefore more burdensome, monetary reserves, since besides their normally heavy investments in silver coins, they would also have to maintain a gold reserve proportionately as large as that of any gold-using nation;

"Whereas it is not fair that the economically weaker peoples should carry the whole weight of their silver stocks, as well as the heavy losses caused by the wide fluctuations of their international value, and carry besides their proportionate share of the gold stocks;

"Whereas it has been fully demonstrated by the far-sighted policy of the United States during the past decade, that it is not only possible but equally feasible, without the slightest danger to the monetary equilibrium

[570] The report of the Agenda Committee, containing all the proposals, is Document 235, pp. 326-333. Where the transcript merely notes that a proposal was read, without giving further details, we have filled in the proposal from the report of the Agenda Committee.

even of a single nation, to maintain stable the relative international prices of gold and silver, and to stabilize both prices in terms of a single currency;

"Whereas it should be relatively easier and less costly for the United and Associated Nations to establish a fair and reasonable international price for silver than to fix one for gold, inasmuch as the present value of the visible stocks of gold is around thirty billion dollars, whereas that of silver is only a fifth or sixth of that amount;

"Whereas one of the main purposes of this conference should evidently be, not to select gold or anything else as a metallic standard which would lead the world back into the rigidity of an arbitrary yardstick for national and international values, but rather to lay the foundations of a well-integrated world monetary system, where in certain important currencies generally accepted in international trade, as well as gold and silver itself, can and should be used to great advantage, each to fulfill a different international function;

"Whereas in the proposed agreement it is foreseen that the Monetary Fund may be forced to change the price of gold in terms of all the member countries' currencies, in order to provide additional means of international payments;

"Whereas silver, because of its traditional monetary use by approximately half of the inhabitants of the world, can and should be used as a collateral monetary metal for meeting such increases and credit requirements of member countries;

"Whereas in principle there can be no better grounds for picking the price of gold in terms of the United Nations' currencies, than those for preventing the wide fluctuations of the international price of silver, in relation to the same currencies;

"Whereas the wide fluctuations in the international value of silver besides placing a heavy risk on the shoulders of those countries least able to carry it, are the direct source of recurrent dislocation of the monetary systems of silver-using countries; and

"Whereas it is technically possible to achieve a minimum price of gold and a maximum price for silver in terms of all the currencies of member countries;

"The Mexican delegation presents for the consideration of this conference the following tentative plan to link silver and gold for international monetary purposes:

"I. That the Monetary Fund should buy and sell from and to member countries gold and silver *together and jointly,* at the fixed rate in terms of member currencies and in a ratio of, say, one ounce of pure gold to ten ounces of fine silver.

"II. That member countries would agree to buy and sell from and to the Fund, and from and to one another, gold and silver *together and jointly*, at the same rate and in the same ratio as above.

"III. That the Fund should have power:

"a. To alter permanently, by a four-fifths majority vote, the proportions of gold and silver set forth above in I and II, only when a permanent and fundamental change in the average yearly rate of production and consumption of both metals has taken place; and

"b. To eliminate silver entirely but temporarily from its joint purchases and sales of gold and silver, and to permit member countries to do likewise, only when and just as long as, due to an increase in the price of silver, over and above an agreed ceiling, the price of one ounce of pure gold in the basic composite unit as defined under I and II above, should be less than the agreed minimum price of thirty-five U.S. dollars per ounce.

"The Mexican delegation submits to this conference the following resolution:

"A. That the Fund shall determine the feasibility of linking silver with gold for international monetary purposes, in accordance with the formula preinserted or any other formula;

"B. That the Fund shall be authorized to carry out whatever policy it deems appropriate as regards the proper role and function of silver within the international monetary structure."

The Agenda Committee recommends that this proposal be referred to Committee 1 on the "Use of Silver for International Monetary Purposes."]

Chairman: Is there any comment on this decision?

United Kingdom ([Robert Brand?][571]): May I ask a clarification of this point? Is it the intention of this Commission at this afternoon's session in submitting these various proposals [p. 2] of the committees to give to these committees various directions as to how they are to handle them at their committees?

Chairman: I think this discussion will give opportunity to all delegates to present their views in support of the motion as recommended and

571 Identified in the typescript only as "Mr. R." The speaker is probably Robert Brand, because he is identified by name just below, but it might also be Dennis Robertson, Lionel Robbins, or Nigel Bruce Ronald.

make comments against them. We will present the reports to the Commission and a full discussion will take place afterwards.

Mexico: Mr. Chairman, I move that this proposal be submitted to the committee proposed by the Agenda Committee for discussion afterwards.

Chairman: No other comments on this proposition?

United Kingdom (Robert Brand): I would like to make a few remarks before this is referred to the committee. They will be very brief. The U.K. delegation has read with interest, and I hope with understanding, the Mexican proposal. On the other hand, we must all realize that introduced [introducing?] bimetallism into the Fund is a proposal of fundamental importance, of fundamental change. You have, no doubt, heard—all of us for many years, perhaps all our lives—controversies with regard to bimetallism, and it seems to me perhaps that it is a late date and a late hour to suggest to this conference that the managers of the Fund should be authorized to introduce a bimetallic principle into the working of the Fund. I feel it is necessary to express that view on behalf of [the] U.K. delegation. I would add one further word, which is, that [the] U.K. delegation has, perhaps like other delegations, no instructions [p. 3] on this matter.

Chairman: Any further comments on this proposition?

Peru: On behalf of the Peruvian delegation, I second the proposal made by the delegate from Mexico, in order that this proposal be referred to a special ad hoc committee.

Chairman: I would suggest that we continue discussing here the report of the Reporting Delegate of the Agenda Committee, and then a decision will be taken by the Commission.

India (Sir Jeremy Raisman): I should like to state that gold and silver has been a matter of very great interest to the country I represent. This [Indian] delegation also would be unable to participate usefully in any discussions for the purpose of attempting to give the metal a special status in relation either to national or international monetary weights [i.e., parities?]. We also have no instructions on this matter. I may say that in India the policy in recent years has been directed towards divesting silver of any special significance in the currency arrangements, and at the present moment the silver currency of India is of a token character, so that if the resolution, when it refers to "silver using countries," has in mind such countries as India, which undoubtedly do use silver on a large scale but nevertheless have not allotted to it a function of importance in the monetary system—if, I say, the resolution includes countries such as India, then we should require considerable time in order to study the matter in all its bearings before we could express views on a scale of this kind. [p. 4]

Chairman: Any further comments?

May I suggest that the Reporter of the Agenda Committee continues the reading of his report. If the delegation approves the suggestion, say "aye."

I call upon the Reporter of the Agenda Committee to continue reading his report.

[Wim Beyen] (Reporter, Agenda Committee): [2. Proposal on enemy assets, submitted by the Polish delegation:

"I. That the members of the United Nations Monetary Fund approach at the earliest possible time the neutral countries with a view to securing their cooperation in blocking all the assets of Axis governments and nationals located in neutral territory;

"II. That the blocked assets referred to above be liquidated by an appropriate United Nations agency and the proceeds be used in settling the claims of the countries which are victims of Axis aggression;

"III. That the neutral countries which will collaborate in the above-mentioned measures become eligible for membership in the Fund and in the Bank."

The Agenda Committee recommends that this proposal be referred to Committee 2 on "Enemy Assets, Looted Property, and Related Matters."]

Chairman: May hear some comments?

There are no comments. I call upon the Reporting Delegate of the Commission.

[Wim Beyen] (Reporter, Agenda Committee): [3. Proposal on enemy assets and looted property submitted by the French delegation:

"That Commission III consider and make recommendations concerning steps to be taken to prevent the enemy from successfully secreting funds in neutral territories or in United Nations territories under assumed names.

"The measures to be recommended should apply to beneficiaries of property looted by the enemy, whether such beneficiaries be enemy nationals, or their associates of whatever nationality. They should be directed in particular against Axis leaders and their collaborators in occupied countries, who might attempt, by retaining control of such funds, to perpetuate their influence, power and ability to plan future aggrandizement and domination in the post-war period."

The Agenda Committee recommends that this proposal be referred to Committee 2 on "Enemy Assets, Looted Property, and Related Matters."]

Chairman: Is there any discussion of this point?

United Kingdom (Robert Brand): When we speak of the Polish resolution and the French resolution, I merely wish to suggest that in remitting these two resolutions, this Commission directs the [Agenda] Committee to whom these things are remitted that it should, in considering the matter remitted to it, find out first of all what has already been done in this matter. I personally would find it rather difficult, as I have not either instructions or information, to say exactly what has been done, in the context covered by the Polish resolution, but it is up to the committee to find out what has been done—what they have been asked to refrain from doing, equally. I think the British [delegation] would be asked to ascertain insofar as we can how these matters are now being dealt with elsewhere and by whom. It could be wasting the committee's time and [p. 5] the Commission's time to deal [with] on imperfect data the same subject which is being dealt with on a more adequate scale by some other party. I think the committee should find out who is doing what, and where.

I would suggest further that the committee satisfy itself that whatever it remits to this Commission should be within the terms of reference to this conference. I think that the Agenda Committee will find themselves in the same position as [the] United Kingdom delegation, which has not instructions or up-to-the-minute information as to who is doing what. Both these things should be done by this committee before they consider the resolutions. For instance, in London there is a committee which is seeking to find out where property which is looted is now located. These subjects are covered by the Peruvian and French resolutions. The committee who are considering this subject must find out who is doing what in other fields already. May I suggest therefore that in remitting these two resolutions of the committees, this Commission should give them on the lines and purposes. Let us at least satisfy ourselves that we do know the present position and let us satisfy ourselves that proposal similar in content to those proposals of Peru and French delegation are not being considered by someone else, somewhere else.

Chairman: Any further comment?

May I call upon the Reporting Delegate.

[Wim Beyen] (Reporter, Agenda Committee): [4. Proposal concerning the liquidation of the Bank for International Settlements, submitted by the Norwegian delegation:

"Be it resolved that the United National Monetary and Financial Conference recommends the liquidation of the Bank for International Settlements at Basel. It is suggested that the liquidation shall begin at the earliest possible date, and that the governments of the United Nations now at war with Germany appoint a Commission of Investigation, in order to examine the management and transaction of the bank during the present war."

The Agenda Committee recommends that this proposal be referred to Committee 2 on "Enemy Assets, Looted Property, and Related Matters."] [p. 6]

Chairman: Any comments on this proposal?

Norway ([Wilhelm Keilhau]): On behalf of the Norwegian delegation, I should like to say some few words concerning this proposal, and I do it for the very special reason that I have been told today by a certain person here that this is a concessionary proposal. There has never been forwarded any *less* concessionary proposal, because it really is what you could call it in the language of Ludwick, "a proposal of the Dutch,"[572] and as I tried to explain that in a few words—the Bank for International Settlements was founded in 1930 in connection with the so-called Young Plan which, as you know, belonged to the history of human failures. To begin with, the main purposes of this bank [were] to receive the German annuities each month in acceptable currencies and distribute the payments, but already after the Lausanne Conference of 1932,[573] that was terminated, and then—this concerns us—there was assigned to this bank another purpose, namely to serve as a central instrument of the banks [in international settlements] in assisting to coordinate the functioning of the gold standard. It is clear that this purpose does come within the scope of the International Monetary Fund which we are now setting up, and it should go without saying that it would be quite a luxury to have two international bodies dealing in that same field. At the moment when the United and Associated Nations is setting up a Monetary Fund for this purpose, it is clear that it would [p. 7] have to be liquidating that other institution which has to deal with the same things. But there is one reason more for the necessity of liquidation. The Bank for International Settlements had seven original members, and out of those seven original members were two chief enemies [of the Allies in the current war], Germany and Japan. It is quite clear that under present circumstances it is

---

572 Perhaps this is an idiomatic Norwegian term. It seems similar to such derogatory English terms as "Dutch courage" or "Dutch uncle."

573 A conference held in Lausanne, Switzerland from June 16 to July 9, 1932, at which representatives of Germany, France, and the United Kingdom agreed to suspend reparations payments for World War I that the 1919 Treaty of Versailles had imposed on Germany.

impossible to have working in the same field an institution while those two main enemy powers partake.

So much for the beginning of the Norwegian proposal. Then we have suggested that Russia put up a committee of investigation to look into the transactions of the Bank for International Settlements during the present war. I heard that this proposal has been interpreted as [expressing] a very aggressive spirit. I must admit I have been the leader of Norwegian fighting forces, but here I am not in collaboration with my colleagues. What we want here is simply that the functions of the bank shall be investigated. And why is it of interest just for this conference to ask for such an investigation? Because the bodies we are going to set up shall work in the same field, and then we wish that everything that has been done in this field before shall be cleared up. This does not contain any accusation.

I should say the Bank for International Settlements perhaps may be just as interested in this investigation as representatives of the United Nations, and in order to make our position clear, I wish to add [that] Norway and the central bank of Norway, which I now [p. 8] represent, have not had any bad experience during the present war from the Bank [for International Settlements]. It is not with any [ulterior] motive that we claim this investigation, and I would like to add that because we proposed that investigation we refuse to enter into any discussion of any of the items that will come up under such an investigation, because that would be to anticipate, and it would not be fit here of any representative of the Bank for International Settlements to come up and give answer to possible questions. Accordingly, we will only ask for a submission of this proposal of the committee.

Chairman: Any further comments on that proposal?

[Wim Beyen] (Reporter, Agenda Committee): [5. Proposal for an international agreement on maintenance of high levels of employment submitted by the Australian delegation.

"Whereas the raising of standards of living throughout the world must be the primary aim of account policy and the most essential conditions for this and for the achievement of the objectives set out in Article I of the International Monetary Fund of the promotion and maintenance of high levels of employment: and

"Whereas the operations of the International Monetary Fund and other forms of international economic cooperation will have the best prospects of success if member countries by domestic measures maintain high levels of employment and consumption and by doing so enable the accumulation of persistent credit (and debit) balances on international account to be avoided;

"This conference resolves that that the governments which are to be invited to accept an International Monetary Agreement should be invited to accept concurrently an international agreement in which the signatories will pledge themselves to maintain high levels of employment in their respective countries, and to exchange information on measures necessary to prevent the growth of unemployment and its spread to other countries."

The Agenda Committee recommends that this proposal be referred to Committee 3 on "Recommendations on Economic and Financial Policy, the Exchange of Information, and Other Means of Financial Cooperation."]

Australia: I would like to say briefly that the Australian delegation considers that this resolution is a suitable, even an essential subject for discussion by the conference. In the first place, I imagine there will be very little argument that the maintenance of high levels of employment are in fact necessary for the success of any international agreement such as the Monetary Fund that we have before us. We are dubious whether it would be possible to persuade nations not to seize the instruments which seemed like prizes to their hands in order to avoid unemployment, even though those means in fact prove illusory.

Secondly, we feel that some agreement of this kind may [p. 9] prove necessary even to persuading nations to accept agreements such as the Monetary Fund. We have often in the past had proposals brought forward for economic collaboration, and in most cases, almost invariably, they failed to secure acceptance by the nations who first discussed and recommended them. We believe that the reason is that ordinary men and women are apathetic to proposals which are too complicated for them to understand. In most circumstances, these interests become clamorous in opposition, and support from ordinary men and women is lacking. If proposals such as the International Monetary Fund are to have even a reasonable prospect of acceptance, we feel they must be set in some framework which the ordinary men and women will feel is essential to certain vital interests which would be regarded as needs. We consider that this is a proper matter for international agreement, because levels of employment in one country react on international trade and on levels of employment in other countries. Therefore we feel a subject of this kind is suitable for discussion at a conference of this kind.

Chairman: Any further comments?

[Wim Beyen] (Reporter, Agenda Committee): [7. Proposal concerning the use of members' gold contribution to the Fund as coverage for note issuance, submitted by the Norwegian delegation:[574]

"Member States whose note issue, according to their monetary legislation, bears some relation to the holdings of gold and/or gold convertible exchange of their central bank or some other institution, are advised to allow their gold contribution of the Fund to be regarded as part of the gold coverage of the note issue."]

Chairman: Is there any further comment?

Norway ([Wilhelm Keilhau]): Mr. Chairman, may I be allowed one brief remark. We have here in a way a technical proposal, because it deals with a technical relation between the Fund and the international monetary systems. I will only draw your attention [p. 10] to this fact that in some countries, it might be argued against the Fund that it places new and heavy burdens upon the nation because of the gold contribution. If this resolution should be passed, it would be very easy to answer that rather dangerous argument.

Chairman: May I hear any further remarks?

[Wim Beyen] (Reporter, Agenda Committee): (Continues to read Proposal 7.) ["Member states possessing rules limiting their note issue are advised to regard notes held by the Fund as additional fiduciary money, which should not be included in the amount of notes bearing any required relation to prescribed legal coverage."

The Agenda Committee recommends that this proposal be referred to Committee 3 on "Recommendations on Economic and Financial Policy, the Exchange of Information, and Other Means of Financial Cooperation."]

Chairman: Any discussion?

[Wim Beyen] (Reporter, Agenda Committee): [8. Proposal concerning a political prerequisite for admission of Germany and Japan to membership of the Fund or Bank, submitted by the Norwegian delegation:

"Be it resolved that the United National Monetary and Financial Conference is of the opinion that neither Germany nor Japan should be

---

574 The Reporter has skipped Proposal 6, which apparently is not discussed here because it was not new; rather, it had originally been submitted to Commission I but was then referred to Commission III. It was listed in the report of the Agenda Committee (Document 235, p. 331). It was a proposal by India to include among the purposes of the IMF the following: "To promote and facilitate the settlement of abnormal indebtedness arising out of the war."

admitted to membership of the United and Associated Nations Monetary Fund or Bank for Reconstruction and Development until the country in question has been admitted to the planned Political World Organization."[575]

The Agenda Committee recommends that this proposal be referred to Committee 3 on "Recommendations on Economic and Financial Policy, the Exchange of Information, and Other Means of Financial Cooperation."]

Chairman: Any discussion?

Norway ([Wilhelm Keilhau]): I should like to say one remark, that the Norwegian delegation considers the treatment of Germany and Japan as a wholly political question that should be resolved by the highest political authorities, and it should not be left to difficult consideration of technical bodies like the Fund and the Bank to make any decisions here.

United Kingdom: I agree with Dr. Keilhau: this is primarily a political question. May I ask him if he does not think singling out Germany and Japan and leaving out other enemy countries—is it our intention to cover merely them, or all of the enemy countries?

Norway: Mr. Chairman, may I suggest that this question be submitted to the committee [Committee 3] for consideration.

Mexico: Another point in connection with this: may we not in some manner or some other way affect the actions that the proposed political organization may desire to carry [p. 11] out to preaching what these countries are to do in other circumstances—may we not handicap the judgment of the others? That is one point, to determine what type of political organization we are to have in the postwar world. One other point is to remember [that] with respect of [to] any resolutions or determination to be made here, Germans and Japanese have still to live in the world whether they are out of the Fund or in the Fund, in the political organization or out of it; they will still be in the world.

USSR: The USSR supports the motion moved by the United Kingdom delegate, but considers [that] this question is purely political and to be decided in a like manner, and [desires] not to discuss this question here and leave this question for the discussion in the respective political organization of different governments.

Chairman: May I hear some comments?

India: The Indian delegation asserts itself with the view that this is not a subject appropriate for the monetary conference. It is very much wider and we cannot dispose of it, in our opinion, in the time that is left to us.

---

[575] The United Nations.

Chairman: The Commission will decide whether this point should be decided right away or whether we would wait until we hear the report of the committee. Those that favor that it goes to the committee first for a report, please say "aye." [p. 12]

("Ayes.")

Those that favor the contrary proposition, please say "no."

("Noes.")

Norway: In this assembly as in others, where there may be a doubt whether the "ayes" or "noes" have it, every nation should be named in alphabetical order.

Chairman: Those delegates that propose the motion—that it be sent to the committee of this delegation—that want this matter to be discussed by the committee and a further discussion will take place here in the Commission when you hear the report of the committee, please raise hands.

Unidentified: I did not get the motion.

Chairman: The question before the Commission is this: whether we reject the proposal right away, or whether we send it before the committee for further consideration. Those delegations that think this proposal should be rejected right away, please raise their hands.

(Hands counted.)

Those delegations that think this proposal should be taken before the committee for further discussion before the Commission, raise their hands.

(Hands counted.)

The "noes" got the decision. So, the proposal is withdrawn.

May I call upon the Reporting Delegate?

[Wim Beyen] (Reporter, Agenda Committee): [9. Proposal for a conference on commercial policy submitted by the delegation from Peru:

"Whereas the International Monetary Fund is devised to maintain orderly exchange arrangements and to lend help to member countries by supplying their needs of foreign exchange of a temporary nature not due to fundamental disequilibrium in their international balance of payments;

"Whereas the Fund is not meant to deal with the basic economic factors which affect the rate of employment and production in the world at large;

"Whereas the Bank will, as its name implies, act only in the fields of Reconstruction and Development;

"Whereas the successful operation of these two institutions is dependent on the smooth development of economic phenomena free from crises of a disruptive nature; and,

"Whereas this condition requires the relaxation of artificial trade barriers to attain greater freedom of commerce; the provision of adequate markets for staple products on which so many national economies depend; and the attainment and maintenance of a high degree of employment and production which will raise the standards of life and conditions of labor everywhere, which must be one of the primary objects of economic policy;

"Resolved that for the successful attainment of the objects to be pursued by the International Monetary Fund and the Bank for Reconstruction and Development a conference of the United and Associated Nations on commercial policy be called to make recommendations for the achievement of greater freedom of commerce and for the orderly marketing of staple products; and that, in the sense of this conference, the nations here assembled should pursue policies to promote the fuller employment of the nations' resources both of men and materials."

The Agenda Committee recommends that this proposal be referred to Committee 3 on "Recommendations on Economic and Financial Policy, the Exchange of Information, and Other Means of Financial Cooperation."]

Chairman: We have heard the report of the Agenda Committee [on this proposal]. Is there any discussion? [p. 13]

Bolivia ([René Ballivián]): I wonder, Mr. Chairman, if it would be possible to bring before the Commission a proposal of the Bolivian delegation, which we did not have enough time to submit before, and has not therefore been considered in the report just read.

Chairman: The motion asks whether [it] allows the Bolivian proposal to be considered before consideration of the Agenda Committee. Those delegations against, raise their hands.

Greece: May we know the proposal?

Chairman: I was asking the Commission whether they accepted the motion by the Bolivian delegate to present a proposal before the committee.

Greece: I would like to know what is the proposal. What is the subject?

Chairman: I think the proposal of the Bolivian delegation [can] be referred to the committee. Is there any discussion of the report of the Agenda Committee?

Brazil: The Bolivian delegation has a proposal to submit. I would take the opportunity to ask whether [there] is still time for the Brazilian delegation to submit a proposal which is very simple. [It] simply refers to the question of prices of primary products. In the introduction of the United States proposal for the International Monetary Fund, it is stated that an international stabilization fund is only ["to promote exchange stability"[576]]. The Brazilian proposal, which might be, if the Commission agrees, distributed [p. 14] and handed to the Chair this afternoon, simply proposes that a conference be called of the United and Associated Nations to deal with prices and commodities.

Chairman: If the Commission has no objection, I will refer to that proposal to Commission III—Committee 3 ["Recommendations on Economic and Financial Policy, the Exchange of Information, and Other Means of Financial Cooperation"]—proposed by the Agenda Committee.

Brazil: Although we have not a proposal to make, but only an amendment to the proposal already presented by the Peru delegation, I want to mention it here in order that it be referred to the same committee to which the Peruvian proposition will go for study.

Chairman: The amendment presented by the Peruvian delegation will be referred to Committee 3, if the Commission has no objection.

Bolivia ([René Ballivián]): I would like to know what is the course that it should follow. If it is going to be considered in the Commission, then the Commission will undoubtedly right now decide which committee it will be referred to, but I would not like to leave the thing pending in the air without knowing where it will go and where it will be considered.

Mexico: May I move that the Bolivian proposal be taken up by the Agenda Committee, and that the Agenda Committee could remit it to whatever committee it seems fit to take it up. I have read the proposal, and if I am not wrong, it refers to commercial matters, so probably Committee 3 would be the proper place, but I think the Agenda Committee should make the final decision. I move, therefore, that [p. 15] this be remitted to the Agenda Committee and that the Agenda Committee should in turn remit it to one of the three committees which are established.

Unidentified: Mr. Chairman, I second the motion of the delegate.

---

[576] The delegate seems to be referring to the Joint Statement, not the earlier U.S. proposal. He may have read more of the article from the Joint Statement on the purposes of the IMF than we have inserted here.

Greece: Could not we briefly be informed of the content of the proposal?

Chairman: I understand the proposal was distributed this afternoon. If the Commission has no objection, the Bolivian delegate might read it.

Bolivia ([René Ballivián]): That is what I have been trying to do since I came here. It is a very short proposal, so you need not be afraid.[577]

["Whereas the full and efficient development of all countries is the prerequisite of an expanding economy;

"Whereas a vastly increased purchasing power in the economic areas over which the produce of the industrialized powers must find its outlet is one of the fundamental elements of future prosperity and well-being;

"Whereas such an increased producing power can only be obtained if the raw materials of countries importing finished products can be sold abroad under conditions and at prices capable of maintaining a high level of domestic productivity;

"Whereas the success and stability of such international mechanisms of economic cooperation, such as the [International] Monetary Fund, will be further insured if supported by policies of international cooperation in other fields of economic activity;

"Be it resolved that the United Nations Monetary and Financial Conference recommends the adoption by its members of the following principles in their international trade policies:—

"1. Whenever contracts have been entered into covering the purchase and delivery of certain materials supporting the economy of the supplying country, the expiration of such contracts should be a matter of mutual concern, and policies should be devised to arrange for the orderly and gradual termination of those contracts in a manner designed to avoid serious disruptions of the economy of the supplying country;

"2. The development and use of synthetic products and of substitute materials should not be encouraged by the granting of subsidies, or by any other protective fiscal policy such as high import duties, et cetera. However, if materials of this type have already been developed and are in use, all conditions being equal, the natural product should always be preferred;

"3. Cooperation in the organization and implementation of international commodity agreements designed to maintain fair and stable prices, and provision for the orderly distribution of raw materials

[577] The transcript merely says, "(Reads proposal)." We have reproduced the proposal from Document 265, pp. 431-432.

throughout the world, whether or not a member country is a party such agreement;

"4. Abstention from—except under abnormal political, social or economic circumstances—any form of trade barriers or discriminatory practices, such as import or export quotas, high tariffs, subsidies, et cetera."]

Greece: Mr. Chairman, I should like to make a proposal with regard to the proposal. We are here delegated by our governments to discuss the Monetary Fund and possibly the Bank for Reconstruction and Development. I don't think that we are entitled her to commit our governments in any way with respect to any other subject. It has been decided that besides the two principal commissions, which will deal with the principal subjects before us, the third commission will be established to examine any other interesting purported questions which might interest our countries. It will be decided, perhaps, that ad hoc subcommittees will be established to examine the proposals which have been or may be submitted to this Commission. May I suggest that we direct this committee to examine these proposals in the light that we have stated [p. 16] before this, to see that our authority here is limited, and we cannot in any way commit ourselves, even as experts, or commit our governments further than the authorizations which we have assumed.

Bolivia ([René Ballivián]): I am of the understanding that no one is committing his government at this conference in any matter.

Cuba: As the new proposal has several indications regarding this proposal—proposal recommending an international commercial conference has been told[578]—the Cuban delegation wants to present to the committee a proposal that may be considered as an amendment or alternative to the Peruvian proposal. I will read the alternative and, as it is clearly stated, I will leave discussion for the Commission. Explanation of our proposal:

["Resolved, that to implement the aims and objects of the International Monetary Fund and the Bank for Reconstruction and Development a Conference of the United and Associated Nations be convened in order to consider the necessary measures to insure higher standards of living and full employment through greater freedom and expansion of trade and the orderly marketing of staple commodities."][579]

---

578 Transcribed as in the typescript. Either the speaker or the stenographer garbled the words here.

579 Document 288, p. 484.

Peru: Mr. Chairman, I move that the motion of the delegate from Cuba be referred to the respective committee.

Chairman: If the Commission has no objections, I will refer all those proposals to the Third Committee [Committee 3, "Recommendations on Economic and Financial Policy, the Exchange of Information, and Other Means of Financial Cooperation"] of this Commission.

The Reporting Delegate will continue reading his report. Is there any comment?

Wim Beyen (Reporter, Agenda Committee): [10. Proposal on status of earmarked gold submitted by the Mexican delegation:

Whereas the practices of earmarking gold might not coincide in all particulars in difference countries;

"Whereas earmarked gold is part of the monetary reserve of such counties and therefore should be free from all restrictions as to its use, transfer, and transportation;

"Whereas, in order to avoid unnecessary movements of gold and thereby reduce to a minimum the cost and risks involved, it would be convenient to adopt a common international policy with respect to such gold;

"Resolved that the countries represented at this Conference agree to extend to earmarked gold the same treatment and immunities they may agree to give to the gold and other assets of the International Monetary Fund."

The Agenda Committee recommends that this proposal be referred to Committee 3 on "Recommendations on Economic and Financial Policy, the Exchange of Information, and Other Means of Financial Cooperation."]

Chairman: Any comment on the proposal?

United Kingdom: Have we come to the end of the resolutions? Is that the last one?

Chairman: This is the last one. [p. 17]

United Kingdom: I would like to make a motion which is in [[accord with?]] that which Mr. Ronald(?) said, that the committees which will pass a resolution in considering all these proposals and proposed resolutions should bear in mind the necessity of acting within the terms of reference of the conference and within the powers of instructions which the delegates have from their governments.

Unidentified: I second that motion.

Netherlands ([Wim Beyen?]): May I draw your attention to the fact that instructions which the delegations have received are to be promptly referred to any resolution here.

USSR: On behalf of the Soviet [Union], we second the motion of the representative of the United Kingdom and think that it would be rather hard to restrict our discussions to those problems which have a direct bearing on the Commission, this conference, being a monetary and financial conference, is confined to discuss; and all other programs [problems], although appreciated by ourselves, should be referred to the organizations which would take care of them instead of this Commission, which is limited in time for the discussion of the Commissions. [p. 18]

Peru: Mr. Chairman, I think it quite appropriate what the delegate for [the] United Kingdom has done and the Soviet delegate has just seconded—that motion to restrict its work to those programs with which it has a direct bearing with the main business of the Commission. But I am in agreement with the delegate from Norway that I don't see how they could very well take into account all instructions which the different governments have issued their delegates in determining what the Commission should study and should not study. I think that whether it has a direct bearing on the problem or not, I fail to see how the instructions of the different delegates would be taken into account.

Ecuador: The very fact that the preamble of Section 1 of the draft of the Fund Agreement speaks of the prevention of unemployment and associated problems shows that these various proposals, particularly those which have been referred to Committee 3 of Commission III, are in a general way contained in the agreement. The plenary session on the very first day created a Commission III to deal with these problems. To my mind, this indicates that we are entitled to study these proposals in Committee 3 of Commission III. What we eventually decide as a result of that study is a different matter, and that would be for the committee to resolve.

Countries like mine [have] contributed to the war [p. 19] effort to the extent of giving up many materials which [they] needed for [themselves]. One example, quinine: we have given our entire production of quinine to combat malaria in the tropical regions, and our own people in Ecuador who require it have had to use substitutes. We have increased our production of [[cinchona]][580] and we are in danger of meeting competition [from] synthetic products after the war which will curtail our production of these two materials, which in turn produces unemployment

580 Our inference. Cinchona is the tree from whose bark quinine is made.

and all other ills. For that reason, I support the idea to submit to Committee 3 of Commission III the various proposals, particularly those of the delegations of Bolivia and Peru, which deal most intimately with what I have tried to explain in these few words.

Chairman: Any further discussion? I suggest that the committees, in sending their report to the Commission, will present their views as to whether the subject presented before them comes within the general scope of the purposes of this conference. If the Commission has no objection, we will consider the resolution as stated.

May I call upon the Reporting Delegate?

[Wim Beyen] (Reporter, Agenda Committee): [Mr. Chairman, all of the proposals received to date by the Agenda Committee have now been placed before Commission III together with the recommendations of the Agenda Committee, namely, that there be established in this Commission three ad hoc committees to consider these proposals and to make recommendations to the full Commission concerning action to be taken at this conference with respect to the general subject assigned to each committee.]

Chairman: We have now heard a full report of the Agenda Committee. Is there any discussion? [p. 20]

France: Mr. Chairman, allow me to complement the Agenda Committee on the fine manner in which they have discharged their responsibility. We have due regard to the judicious observations made by the delegates of the United Kingdom and the Soviet Union and of Greece. I feel that the selection of the remaining subjects submitted for study to the three ad hoc committees is justified. I therefore move that the report of the Agenda Committee be accepted, and that the Chairman of this Commission be empowered to appoint three ad hoc committees to consider and make recommendations with respect to use of silver for international and monetary purposes; enemy assets, looted property and related matters; and exchange of information and other means of financial cooperation.

Peru: I second the motion of the French delegate for the appointment of three committees.

Chairman: Those in favor, say "yes."

Those opposed, "no."

Proposition is carried. In accordance with the recommendations of the Agenda Committee, I appoint the following committee:

Committee 1: Chairman, Peru; Reporter, China; United States; USSR; Ethiopia; Canada; Mexico; Norway; Bolivia. I will ask [the] United Kingdom and India whether they want to be members of this committee.

India: I think that question I must reserve until I discuss it with other members of the delegation. [p. 21]

United Kingdom: We should like to do the same.

Chairman: Committee 2: Chairman, France; Reporter, Norway; USSR; China; Belgium; Holland; Egypt; Netherlands; Dominican Republic; Uruguay; Yugoslavia.

Committee 3: Chairman, Chile; Reporter, Iraq; Greece; Australia; Nicaragua; United States; Czechoslovakia; Ecuador; [El] Salvador; Free French ([André] Istel); United Kingdom.

Bolivia ([René Ballivián]): May I request that Bolivia be changed to the Third Committee [Committee 3].

Chairman: If there is no other subject before the Commission, we adjourn for the day.

(Adjourned.)

40

Commission III
Other Means of International Financial Cooperation
Third (final) meeting: transcript
July 20, 1944, 2:00 p.m.[581]

Report of Committee 1 • Use of silver • Report of Committee 2 • Liquidation of Bank for International Settlements • Looted property • Report of Committee 3 • International agreement on maintaining high employment • Abnormal balances arising from war • Gold as cover for note issues • Earmarked gold • Trade and its relation to other financial policies • Defeat of Australian resolution on agreement to maintain high employment

In its third and final meeting, Commission III considers the reports of the committees it has designated and the proposals they have deliberated. (A remark in the third meeting of Commission I suggests that its chairman, Harry Dexter White, had hoped for Commission I to operate as Commission III did, limiting itself to three or four meetings rather than the nine it actually held.)

Te-Mou Hsi of China gives the report of Committee 1, whose subject was "The Use of Silver for International Monetary Purposes." Hsi was the representative of the Chinese ministry of finance in Washington and previously general manager of the Central Bank of China. The committee recommends that Commission III report to the Plenary Session, the group of all delegations, which gave final approval or disapproval of all proposals, that a lack of time prevented the Commission from making any definite recommendations, but that the subject merits further study. The Commission approves Committee 1's report. Eduardo Suárez of Mexico momentarily steps out of his role as the chairman of Commission III to speak as the chairman of the Mexican delegation. He gives a long speech arguing for a role for silver in the international monetary system. Mexico at the time was both a large producer of silver and a large user of silver coins, which many Mexicans preferred to paper money.

---

581 Summarized in Document 496, pp. 1043-1044. The transcripts also contain minutes of this session, which we have not reproduced because they are almost the same as Document 496.

Wilhelm Keilhau gives the report of Committee 2, whose subject was "Enemy Assets, Looted Property, and Related Matters." Before World War II, Keilhau had been a lawyer and professor of economics in Norway, writing a number of publications on monetary policy. After the German invasion of Norway in 1940, he fled, becoming part of the exile government in London as director in exile of Norway's central bank. Committee 2's first proposal, originated by Norway, is to recommend the liquidation of the Bank for International Settlements (BIS). There were allegations that the BIS was giving Germany cover for assets looted from occupied countries. Wim Beyen of the Netherlands, whose term as president of the BIS had ended soon before World War II began, offers his country's support for the recommendation and adds that it would welcome an investigation into the BIS's wartime conduct, a provision that had been in the original Norwegian proposal but had been deleted from the version now before the Commission. The Commission approves the resolution. Ultimately, the BIS would survive to the present. It would benefit from the change in attitude of the United States; the administration of Franklin Roosevelt favored liquidation, but after Roosevelt's death in 1945, the administration of his successor Harry Truman would favor preserving the bank.

The second item Keilhau reports on for Committee 2 is a resolution recommending that governments of the conference participants take steps to locate enemy assets and looted assets, and to call upon governments of neutral countries to prevent the transfer of looted assets or other assets of the Axis powers. The Commission approves the resolution.

Ibrahim Al-Kabir of Iraq gives the report of Committee 3, on "Recommendations on Economic and Financial Policy, the Exchange of Information, and Other Means of Financial Cooperation." Al-Kabir was a high-ranking official in the Iraqi ministry of finance. The chairman then presents the committee's recommendations for the Commission's consideration. One is an announcement by Egypt and the United Kingdom that they will work on a solution to Egypt's wartime accumulation of pound-sterling assets. Another recommendation is a decision to leave to the IMF and World Bank a proposal by Norway concerning the use of a gold accounting unit for their accounts, much as the Bank for International Settlements for many years used the gold Swiss franc as its accounting unit. Yet another recommendation is that the governments participating in the Bretton Woods conference reach agreement on several other ideas related to promoting economic growth and postwar development. The Commission approves the recommendations. It rejects Australia's proposal for an international agreement on employment policy, apparently on the grounds that the matter is sufficiently covered by the recommendation just mentioned about ideas on promoting economic growth.

Chairman ([Eduardo Suárez, Mexico]): The meeting will come to order.

The Secretary has noted here that he finds there is a quorum.

At the last meeting of Commission III, held on July 10, 1944, three committees were appointed pursuant to the decision of the Commission to consider and make recommendations with respect to the following general fields: first, the use of silver for international monetary purposes; second, enemy assets, looted property, and related matters; third, recommendations on economic and financial policies, exchange of information, and other means of financial cooperation.

I am informed that the three committees have now completed their work and are prepared to report the results of their deliberations. Before calling upon any of the reporters, I would like to point out that, except for Committee No. 2, copies of the respective reports have been given general distribution. However, if any delegate does not have copies of the two reports, will he please raise his hand and copies will be distributed to him.

(Distribution of copies was made.)

I would also like to suggest that the person speaking from the floor clearly announce his name and delegation so that the reporters and members of the Commission will know who is speaking.

I will now call upon the Reporter, Mr. Te-Mou Hsi of the Chinese delegation, to read the report of Committee No. 1.

Te-Mou Hsi (China, Reporter, Committee 1):[582] [At the second meeting of Commission III held at five o'clock on July 10, 1944, Committee 1 was appointed to consider the proposal on silver submitted by the Mexican delegation. The proposal is designated as No. 1 in the Report of the Agenda Committee (Document No. 235).

It is the recommendation of Committee 1 that Commission III report to the Plenary Session as follows:

"The problems confronting some nations as a result of the wide fluctuations in the value of silver were the subject of serious discussion in this Commission. Due to the shortage of time, the magnitude of the other problems on the agenda, and other limiting considerations, it was impossible to give sufficient attention to this problem at this time in order to make definite recommendations. However, it was the sense of the Commission that the subject should merit further study by the interested nations.][583] [p. 2]

Chairman: Is there any discussion?

---

582 The transcript merely says, "(Mr. Te-Mou Hsi read his report.)" We have reproduced the report from Document 235, pp. 326-333.

583 Document 425, p. 713.

Peru (Manuel Llosa): Mr. Chairman, as one of the four greatest producers of silver of the world, Peru is much interested in the lot of this metal. The historical background of the use of silver as a monetary metal cannot be forgotten and must not be underestimated. The psychological prestige of silver cannot be denied, nor its popularity among the less favored classes throughout the world.

Several countries, including Peru, use silver as a part of their legal monetary reserves. Outstanding representatives of the silver-minded opinion have formally claimed that unless a place is assigned to silver in monetary stabilization, there would be an insufficiency of media for the settlement of international balances, and the use of silver as money will be undermined. Backed with enough expert opinion to be realistic, it has been recently suggested, too, as a platform for the mining industry, a general support of hard money philosophy, a policy that Peruvian miners are willing to adopt.

On account of these considerations, the Peruvian delegation supports the approval of the report submitted by Committee 1 of this Commission III, meaning that the subject of value of silver and of the monetary uses of this metal deserve further study by all the interested nations.

Brazil: The Brazilian delegation supports the proposal of the committee and of the delegation of Peru.

United States (Ansel Luxford): Mr. Chairman, the United States wants to add its support to this proposal.

Chairman: We will, then, proceed to take a vote on the report read by the Reporter of the First Subcommittee [Committee 1]. Those in favor of the report, please raise their hands. [p. 3]

(Show of hands.)

Those contrary minded?

(Show of hands.)

The "ayes" carry it. The report is adopted.

I will ask my friend, the Vice President, to take the chair in order to make some remarks and to explain the sense of the vote of the Mexican delegation. [p. 4]

Mr. Chairman, fellow delegates:

The Mexican delegation wishes to make this statement to put on record its position regarding Mexico's approval of the report submitted by Committee I.[584]

---

584 The speech that follows was issued with minor changes as Press Release No. 36, Document 459, pp. 1187-1190.

The Mexican delegation realizes that it is difficult to find a definite solution to the silver problem in this conference. But it considers that a great step has been taken in recognizing the importance that silver has for some countries as a monetary metal. The Mexican delegation expresses the hope that in the near future, countries interested in silver, either as producers or consumers, shall find, after unbiased and technical consideration of the problem, a way to stabilize the value of silver.

Upon creating an International Monetary Fund, the United Nations are tacitly invited to recognize that the fair and just price for gold is $35 an ounce. Henceforth, each of them will accept an ounce of gold whenever they have a right to receive $35, or the equivalent, from another nation.

As for Mexico, her position is clear and definite. During the past few years of tribulations, Mexico has, of her own accord, accepted, in unlimited amounts, an ounce of gold for every $35 due her. She has done so in spite of the hardships of inflation, and even realizing to the fullest extent the risk involved in these transactions, inasmuch as no nation has ever committed itself to buy that gold from Mexico at the same price she has paid for it. Throughout this most difficult period, she has also issued Mexican currency at a fixed rate of [p. 5] 4.85 pesos to the U.S. dollar, or about 169.75 pesos for each ounce of gold, although she has had no assurance or guarantee that other nations will give her and commodities and services a fair equivalent to her investment in gold. Mexico has done all this mainly because of her full unselfish devotion to a higher cause: helping her allies to win this war.

Mexico and other silver-using countries are entitled to expect in return for their cooperation to maintain the present price of gold the assistance of other countries to stabilize the price of silver at a just and fair level.

The history of the past seventy years, according to those who oppose silver, should contradict Mexico's expectation. They claim that silver has no place in the monetary structure of the world.

As if to spite those that like to say the last word on an intricate subject such as silver, humanity insists not to behave according to pure theoretical reasoning. It takes an emergency or a catastrophe, such as we are living today, to realize the importance of silver as a monetary metal. Is it not true, for instance, that in this hour of anxiety the Mexican masses have found in silver what they believe to be the best, most secure value as against all the uncertainties that the future may hold? Is it not also true that many other Latin American countries have tried to buy silver in order to allay the fears of their own populations? Who can deny that the Allied armies have found more willing traders in the East and Near East when the soldiers were provided with silver coins instead of an up-to-date, fully guaranteed gold [p. 6] note? Would it be absurd, besides, to anticipate that in the aftermath of this diabolic nightmare, the peoples of many invaded countries will find hoarding silver is better than many other forms of saving, as it has been proved in the past?

The answers are obvious to all but the prejudiced. Humanity—that is, the larger and poor part of humanity—continues to believe in silver, even if only because it is not their lot to believe in gold or in any of the so-called higher forms of wealth.

If this plain truth be accepted, that it must be evident that any monetary scheme designed to meet the needs of all the peoples of the world is incomplete unless it takes into account silver is one of the component factors of the whole picture.

A nation whose monetary system will henceforth operate in accordance with the plan we will submit to our governments will accept gold at the proposed world price of $35 an ounce, only because she has the assurance that the other member countries of the system will likewise accept gold at the same price, when the former becomes a debtor to them. But that particular nation might well be a silver-minded country whose people want neither bills nor bank deposits backed with gold reserves, but prefer and demand plain silver coins from their monetary authorities. In the latter case, that country would naturally be forced to invest part or all of its gold reserve in silver, in order to meet the demand of its people. When that same nation becomes a debtor, because, for instance, of a serious depreciation of her [p. 7] exports in the world markets, how can she turn the silver coins into gold, in order to meet an unfavorable balance? The only way, of course, will be to sell her silver stocks in a forced market, at whatever price the buyers want to pay for them.

We hold and we shall strive in the future to look upon, as a solution of this problem, a relative stabilization of the international price of silver. We feel that this solution is feasible. Just as the United States government decided that gold was worth $35 an ounce, and was therefore able to establish that price in the world markets, so did that same government decide to maintain silver at a fixed price in the outside world markets, and has been able to do so for a long time. The pegging of both metals in terms of the dollar has brought about, as far as it is possible to find out, none of the calamity with which the traditional enemies of silver like to scare credulous people. If a single nation has been able to do so much both for gold and silver without disrupting its monetary equilibrium, internal or external, why should it not be possible through international cooperation to undertake the same task, without depending entirely on the willingness of one nation to carry forever the whole weight of the stabilization of both metals?

The Mexican delegation is aware of another argument against recognizing silver as a component part of the monetary pattern of the world. Nobody who is anybody, it is said, should give a thought to the silver problem, since it only affects a few of the so-called backward peoples of the Earth, whose international trade added together is but a minor, negligible fraction of the world [p. 8] trade. If this same or a similar attitude were to be applied to all the problems of the postwar world, it is difficult to see how that world could be happy. For how can we brush aside so lightly the economic habits of millions upon millions of humble people, just because they are poor and cannot thus "belong" amongst the economic "elite" of this earth?

In closing, it is most fitting that the Mexican delegation should quote the wise words which His Excellency the President of the United States said to Congress in a special message on January 15, 1934:

"The other principal precious metal—silver—has also been used from time immemorial as a metallic base for currencies as well as for actual currency itself. It is used as such by probably half of the population of the world. It constitutes a very important part of our own monetary structure. Is such a crucial factor in much of the world's international trade that it cannot be neglected."

Mexico feels certain that a monetary problem, small and economic dimensions the large in human implications, will receive due consideration in the future, as envisaged by the report we have just approved. [p. 9]

Chairman: May I call upon the Reporter of the Second Committee [Committee 2] to read his report?

Wilhelm Keilhau (Norway, Reporter, Committee 2): Mr. Chairman, I have to begin by telling a story. I shall try to make it as short as possible. You will have seen before you Document No. 470,[585] which was distributed, I think, this morning and which was prepared last evening when the Reporting Delegate thought that the meeting of this Commission should take place after dinner yesterday.

If you have studied that report you would notice that it in very explicit words gives expression to the fact that all members of the Committee agreed on the two main realities placed before the Committee, but that there was a certain difference of opinion concerning the wording.

[585] Document 470, pp. 861-864. See also Document 481 (470), pp. 919-922.

As for the first two items dealt with by this Committee, namely, the Bank for International Settlements in Basel, two members criticized the formula adopted by the majority. I regret that I didn't get the opportunity of including a definite proposal from those two members in the report, but as a matter of fact during that rush hour, I had before me some documents, and I did not know just which was the right one and I did not find any of those delegates, so that I could be certain which would be used. However, there was a strong feeling within the Committee that if we agreed, in reality it would be a pity if those disagreements concerning the minor point of formulation really should give birth to any debate in this Commission, and our most energetic Chairman called us again together at twelve o'clock today to try to bring about a complete reconciliation, and we succeeded. So, I have here to withdraw the wordings of that first report and place before you a unanimous report from the Committee. [p. 10]

I shall take first the question of the Bank for International Settlements. The proposal here is very short. I shall read it aloud to you, but I have also had typewritten copies of it made, which I shall distribute as soon as I have read the conclusion. This is a proposal submitted jointly by the Norwegian and the Netherlands delegation, and it reads thus:

"The United Nations Monetary and Financial Conference recommends the liquidation of the Bank for International Settlements at the earliest possible moment."

I shall send that around.

(Distribution was thereupon made.)

Chairman: Discussion is open on this part of the report of the Second Committee [Committee 2].

Netherlands (Wim Beyen): On behalf of the Netherlands delegation, I want to make a statement with regard to the proposal for the liquidation of the Bank [for] International Settlements on which the Second Committee of this Commission has acted. Originally the Norwegian delegation had placed before this Commission a proposal that the United Nations Monetary and Financial Conference recommend the liquidation of the Bank at Basel. It was suggested that the liquidation would begin at the earliest possible date, and that the governments of the United Nations now at war with Germany appoint a committee of investigation in order to examine the management and transactions of the bank during the present war.

The Netherlands delegation wants to state that it has always been willing to accept the resolution in its original form. It considers the liquidation of the Bank for International Settlements as inevitable. The

Bank for International Settlements should not continue to function side [p. 11] by side with the International Monetary Fund. But quite apart from that, its statutes and its financial structure are the outcome of the world situation that after the victory of the United Nations will no longer exist. An investigation into the management and transactions of the bank during the present war can only be welcomed by all those who think that it would be in the interest of the future of cooperation in the monetary field if the truth about the bank's conduct should at last be made available to a public whose judgment can now only be based on current stories borne out of ignorance of the true facts. Whether or not this conference is the suitable body to pass the original motion is another matter, about which the Netherlands delegation does not wish to express an opinion. But it never had objections against its contents and would not have objected to the motion on any formal grounds.

The resolution was presented in a different form when the Second Committee [Committee 2] met for the first time. The Norwegian delegation had in the meantime deleted that part of the resolution which deals with the investigation of the management and transactions of the bank during the present war. The Netherlands delegation expressed its regret at that meeting at the deletion of the sentence dealing with the investigation.[586]

Chairman: Any further remarks?

United States (Ansel Luxford): Mr. Chairman, since Committee 2 has unanimously reported this resolution to us, I move that the Commission adopt the resolution.

Belgium (Camille Gutt): I second the motion. [p. 12]

Chairman: That part of the report of the subcommittee is before the Commission for a vote. Those in favor of the report, please say "aye."

Delegates: Aye.

Chairman: Those against, say "no."

(None.)

Chairman: The "ayes" carry. That part of the report is adopted.

May I call on the Reporter of the Second Subcommittee to continue his report?

Wilhelm Keilhau (Reporter, Committee 2): Mr. Chairman, the second item which was referred to this Committee 2 deals with looted

[586] The typescript notes that this remark refers to Document 477, pp. 915-916. Beyen had been alternate president of the Bank for International Settlements from 1935 to 1937 and president from 1937 to 1939.

property. There were, as stated in Document 470,[587] originally one Polish and one French proposal, which both were withdrawn in favor of a proposal from the United States. However, as I have already mentioned, there was a reservation from the delegation of the United Kingdom, but this reservation was not a reservation on substance but more on the formulation, because the United Kingdom felt that the form would not pay sufficient attention to what had already been done in this field, and that which you would call the political side of the formulation was not just 100 percent correct.

Now, we have in the Committee adopted a new formulation, which I regret has not been typed yet. I shall read it out to you very slowly but, to begin with, I shall just state one fact. The delegation of the Soviet Republics [USSR] have not had in their minds a sufficient time to study the physiology, the exact wording, of this resolution. They are in favor of it in substance, but they think there are many delegations which will be in the same position here as they are, and also the fact exists [p. 13] that we cannot present it in typewritten form. Accordingly, the Soviet Republics delegation has suggested to us that there be appointed a special drafting committee in case, what [i.e., as] we sincerely hope, the Commission adopts the proposal, and that this drafting committee shall go through the wording and then send the resolution direct to the conference. All the other members of the Committee have accepted that suggestion from the Soviet delegation, and it has been agreed that in case a member should be the United States, United Kingdom, and the Soviet Republics, the Soviet Republics will join in reporting delegates as additional members.[588]

I shall now read to you the resolution:

"The United Nations Monetary and Financial Conference:

"1. Notes with satisfaction the establishment by the United Nations of machinery designed to assist the nations of the world in

"(a) uncovering, segregating, controlling and making appropriate disposition of enemy assets;

"(b) locating in tracing ownership and control of located property and taking appropriate measures to make restoration to its lawful owners.

"2. Recommends that all governments represented at this conference, and particularly those already participating in the operation of this machinery, call upon governments of neutral countries

---

[587] Document 470, p. 862.

[588] The meaning of the last part of the sentence is unclear to us. Perhaps it means that the drafting committee shall have the United States, United Kingdom, and USSR among its members.

"(a) to take immediate measures to prevent any disposition or transfer within territories subject to their jurisdiction of any

"(i) assets belonging to the government or any individuals or institutions within those United Nations occupied by the enemy; and

"(ii) looted gold, currency, art objects, [p. 14] securities, or other evidences of ownership in financial or business enterprises and all other assets located by the enemy, as well as to uncover, segregate and hold at the disposition of the post-liberation authorities in the appropriate country any such assets within the territory subject to their jurisdiction;

"(b) to take immediate measures to prevent the concealment by fraudulent means or otherwise within countries subject to their jurisdiction of any

"(i) assets belonging to, or alleged to belong to, the government of any individuals or institutions within enemy countries;

"(ii) assets belonging to, or legend to belong to, enemy leaders, their associates and collaborators, and to facilitate their ultimate delivery to the post-armistice authorities."

As you will notice, gentlemen, there are differences between this last unanimous recommendation of the Committee and the formulation given in Document [470].[589] The first one is that we now note with satisfaction the establishment of the machinery. We say, particularly after having ascertained what has already been done, that it is only proper to note this with satisfaction and to give our support to what has already been done. And, second, we do not call upon directly the neutrals—and I quite agree with the United Kingdom's delegation in this, certainly, as the more appropriate way of expressing ourselves.

I have, accordingly, the pleasure to present a unanimous draft resolution on behalf of the Committee to the Commission.

Chairman: Discussion is open on the report of the Second Subcommittee [Committee 2]. [p. 15]

United States (Ansel Luxford): Mr. Chairman, I wanted to be sure—I take it that Committee 2 is recommending the "whereas" clauses also, is it not? The only change was made in the "now, therefore" clause.

Chairman: Any remarks?

Wilhelm Keilhau (Reporter, Committee 2): That is so.

South Africa: Mr. Chairman, I have only one suggestion to make. Of course, I heartily approve. I would suggest a certified copy with the "whereases" be transmitted to Messrs. Hitler, Goering and Goebbels.

---

[589] In Document 470, pp. 862-864. The typescript says "Document 417R2," a mistake.

(Laughter.)

Chairman: Any further comments?

United States (Ansel Luxford): Mr. Chairman, I would like to move that we accept the principles of this resolution and that we instruct a drafting committee to be named by you to go over the document for style and form that maintain the principle of this document.

(The motion was seconded.)

Chairman: Those that are in favor of the motion, please raise their hands.

(Show of hands.)

Those contrary minded, raise their hands, please.

(Show of hands.)

The motion is carried. Therefore, in accordance with the suggestion made by the Reporting Delegate and the motion just approved by the Commission, I will appoint a Drafting Committee composed of USSR, the United Kingdom, the United States, and the president [chairman] and the Reporter of the Second Committee [Committee 2]. [p. 16]

France (André Istel): Mr. Chairman, as chairman of Committee 2, I would like to make a short reservation. I do not think that the Reporting Delegate in his excellent report revealed a secret when he mentioned that the two subjects which were recommended by this Committee were of a controversial nature, and that [at] the origin, there was not complete unanimity, so I would like to pay tribute to the very fine spirit shown by all members in the Committee in joining unanimously [[to approve the resolution?]].

Chairman: May I call upon the Reporter of the Third Committee [Committee 3] to read his report?

Ibrahim Al-Kabir (Iraq, Reporter, Committee 3): The substance of the report of the Third Committee appears in Document No. 428,[590] which is already been distributed. May I read it?

(Document No. 428 was read in part, as follows:)

"At the second meeting of Commission III, held at 5:00 p.m. on July 10, 1944, Committee 3 was appointed to consider proposals for action which had been assigned to it in accordance with the recommendations of the Agenda Committee and to make recommendations to the full Commission concerning action to be taken at this conference with respect thereto.

[590] Document 428, pp. 729-732.

"Committee 3 wishes to report as follows concerning its decisions and recommendations with respect to the various proposals submitted to it: The full texts on the proposals are set forth in the report of the Agenda Committee (Document No. 235)."[591]

Before proceeding further with the reading of this report, I would ask the Chair to give a decision on a point of procedure. In view of the very different nature of the recommendations and the resolution taken by the Committee, it will appear to be more appropriate if the [p. 17] various proposals are made one after the other and considered by the Commission separately. May I ask, Mr. Chairman, for a decision on this point?

Chairman: If the Commission has no objection, I will present for the consideration of this Commission, one by one, the recommendations made by the Third Subcommittee [Committee 3].

Ibrahim Al-Kabir (Reporter, Committee 3): Now, proposal no. 1 appeared in Document No. 218.[592] The proposal refers to an international agreement on the maintenance of high levels of employment submitted by the Australian delegation and designated as no. 5 on the report of the Agenda Committee. It was the subject of much discussion. (Reading.) "In view, however, of a basic disagreement concerning this proposal, it was the consensus of the Committee that no recommendation should be made, but that the Australian delegation might raise the matter before the full Commission."

Australia (Arthur Tange): Mr. Chairman, the Commission has in front of it Document No. 467,[593] which contains the views of the Australian delegation on their proposal for an international employment agreement and indicates the reasons why we were unable to regard the recommendation of Committee 3 as a substitute for the Australian proposal. I do not propose to read this statement fully, but I would like to go through it and select what we regard as the main elements in it.

You will notice that the two essential features of the proposal are, first, that there should be a resolution calling for an international agreement to maintain high levels of employment; and, secondly, that that agreement should be reached at a specified time. [p. 18]

Their reasoning has been that domestic policies directed to the maintenance of high levels of employment are far more significant than measures which can be taken in the international field alone, ignoring the

---

591 Document 235, pp. 326-333.

592 Document 218, p. 279.

593 Document 467, pp. 834-837.

domestic policies. We argue that domestic policy is properly a matter of international concern for three reasons. First, because the initial source of demand of trade lies in domestic policy, and chiefly in those policies which affect employment and the level of income. Secondly, we argue that domestic levels of employment are of international concern because we believe that unless domestic policies are directed to maintenance of full employment, other forms of international collaboration have very limited prospects of success. And our third argument is that the achievement of agreement on international arrangements for economic collaboration—the prospects will be very much greater of having them accepted by the various communities of the world if they can see those closely tied up with policies which are of vital concern to them as ordinary people—in other words, policy affecting their daily bread and butter.

Finally, I should like to draw attention to our remarks at the bottom of page 2 of the document. We did not envisage that domestic policy should become a concern of international authority in the sense that it will be free to direct policies are in any way to interfere with the right of the country to determine in its own way how it would maintain high levels of employment. Our stress is on its obligation by whatever means it sees fit to maintain high levels of employment.

United Kingdom: Mr. Chairman, on a point of procedure, might I make a suggestion? It is this: that instead of [p. 19] proceeding with the discussion of the Australian motion now, we should first have discussion on the longer resolution dealing with commercial policy [[as it relates to the orderly marketing of staple products?]] and economic policy [submitted by Peru as proposal no. 9]. The point of my suggestion is this. I think as the discussion on the Australian proposal proceeds, it will be found that it will be purely arguable, and it is unnecessary to proceed with the Australian proposal because the point covered in the Australian proposal is already covered in the longer proposal. I suggest that it, therefore, might be of convenience to all of us and shorten the discussion if we broke off the discussion on the Australian proposal and proceeded to the longer resolution which relates to a commercial policy and economic policy. After that, we shall all see more clearly what we really think about the need for a proposal along the lines suggested by the Australian delegation.

Chairman: If the Australian delegation has no objection, we will proceed as suggested by the delegate of Great Britain, or may I call upon Mr. Al-Kabir to continue his report.

Ibrahim Al-Kabir (Reporter, Committee 3): Paragraph 2. The first proposal, referred to Commission III from Commission I, concerns the settlement of abnormal indebtedness arising out of the war and designated as no. 6 in the report of the Agenda Committee. It was withdrawn after the following exchange of views which took place between the Egyptian and the United Kingdom delegations. They are inserted verbatim in the record by specific request. I will read the two statements:

"Mr. G.F. Bolton of United Kingdom delegation said, 'In due time, the British government will invite the Egyptian government to send their representative to London to arrive at a satisfactory solution of the problem.' [p. 20]

"On behalf of the Egyptian delegation, Mr. Sany Lackany said, 'It gives me great pleasure to hear the statement of the delegation of the United Kingdom, who are our great friends and allies. We are aware of the difficulties involved, but we feel we are entitled to see some evidence of goodwill on the part of the United Kingdom. Now that a reassuring statement has come from the delegation of the United Kingdom, I would like to place the fact on record and acknowledge it with thanks.'"

Now we pass to paragraph 3. A proposal concerning the use of a member's gold contribution to the Fund as a coverage for note issue, submitted by the Norwegian delegation and designated as no. 7 in the report of the Agenda Committee, was discussed, and it was the decision of the Committee that the subject is not a matter on which the conference should make any recommendation.

Shall I proceed?

Chairman: Yes.

Ibrahim Al-Kabir (Reporter, Committee 3): Paragraph 5 appeared in Document No. 187.[594] The proposal concerned the status of earmarked gold, submitted by the Mexican delegation, and [was] designated as no. 10 in the report of the Agenda Committee. It was considered, and it was the decision of the Committee that no action should be taken with respect to this matter.

Now, paragraph 5: "After discussion [of] the proposal concerning the use of a gold unit in keeping the books of the Fund and of the Bank, submitted by the Norwegian delegation"—that appeared in Document No. 256[595]—"and designated as no. 11 in the report of the Agenda Committee, the Committee decided that no action should be taken with

---

[594] Document 187, p. 227.
[595] Document 256, p. 429.

respect to this proposal, but that decision as to this matter could best be [p. 21] made by the Fund and the Bank at the time of their establishment."

A similar suggestion, although not quite the same, appeared in Document No. 153[596] and it was submitted by the Egyptian delegation. The proposal was considered by the Committee, and the Committee decided that no action should be taken with respect to this proposal, but that decision as to this matter could best be made by the Fund and the Bank at the time of their establishment.

Norway (Wilhelm Keilhau): I rise to state on behalf of the Norwegian delegation that we have no objection to this. We take it that it means one very important thing, namely, that the idea of an international monetary unit is not bad. We may fight for it in the time before the first meetings of the Fund and the Bank, and we are satisfied with that.

Ibrahim Al-Kabir (Reporter, Committee 3): Now, proposal no. 6 [for an international conference on commodities], the last proposal. There have been several proposals submitted by several delegations on the subject, one from Peru, one from Brazil under Document No. 287, one from Chile under Document No. 289, one from Bolivia under Document 265, and one from Cuba under Document 288.[597] The Committee decided that the several proposals submitted by Peru, Brazil, Chile, Bolivia and Cuba, containing recommendations for international consideration and action with respect to other specified international economic problems, should be consolidated into one document which might be an appropriate resolution to be adopted by this conference. Accordingly, the following resolution was drafted and adopted by the Committee. Representatives of the delegations of Bolivia and Peru expressed [p. 22] a preference for certain alternative language, and requested this fact to be noted in the record. However, it is the recommendation of this Committee that Commission III recommended the adoption by the full conference of the following resolution. I now read the resolution as passed by the Committee:

"Whereas in Article I of the Articles of Agreement of the International Monetary Fund it is stated that one of the principal purposes of the Fund is to facilitate the expansion and balanced growth of international trade, and to contribute thereby to the promotion and maintenance of high

596 Document 153, pp. 164-165.

597 Peru's proposal was item no. 9 in Document 235, p. 332; Brazil's was Document 287, pp. 482-484; Chile's was Document 289, p. 484; Bolivia's was Document 265, pp. 431-432; and Cuba's was Document 288, p. 484.

levels of employment and real income in the territories of all members as primary objectives of economic policy." (This paragraph [is modified from Document] 235 in the light of action taken by Commissions I and II.)

"Whereas it is recognized that the complete attainment of this and other purposes and objectives stated in the agreement cannot be achieved through the instrumentality of the Fund alone;

"Therefore the United Nations Monetary and Financial Conference recommends to the participating governments that, in addition to implementing the specific monetary and financial measures which were the subject of this conference, they seek, with a view to creating in the field of international economic relations conditions necessary for the attainment of the purposes of the Fund and of the broader primary objectives of economic policy, to reach agreement as soon as possible on ways and means whereby they may best:

"(1) reduce obstacles to international trade and in other ways promote mutually advantageous international commercial relations;

"(2) bring about the orderly marketing of staple commodities [p. 23] at prices fair to the producer and consumer alike;

"(3) deal with the special problems of international concern which will arise from the cessation of production for war purposes; and

"(4) facilitate by cooperative effort the harmonization of national policies of member states designed to promote and maintain high levels of employment and progressively rising standards of living.

"It is the further recommendation of the Committee that the Chairman of the Commission be empowered to make appropriate modifications in the two 'whereas' clauses to incorporate any changes made in the draft Articles of Agreement of the International Monetary Fund, as well as appropriate reference to the Bank for Reconstruction and Development, in the light of action taken by Commission II."

Cuba: Mr. Chairman, the Cuban delegation moves that the proposal of the committee be adopted by the Commission. We think that this resolution contains a very important principle: that is to say, the recognition that without other international action in solving other international economic problems, the Fund and the Bank cannot successfully operate. The wording in this resolution has not only recognized this fact, but it is recommended that agreement be reached in four main fields, in four main lines: that is to say, the reduction of barriers to trade, the orderly marketing of staple commodities, and the special problems created by the cessation of war production. And, furthermore, this resolution contains in a somewhat denuded and not so strong form, but it nevertheless contains, the principles defended by the Australian delegation, in the sense that there is no possibility of successful international [p. 24] economic relations if each nation within its borders, within its internal economy, does not provide and try to do its best effort to attain full employment for its population within its borders. So, Mr. Chairman, I move that this proposition be adopted.

Allan Fisher (New Zealand): Mr. Chairman, before this is seconded, I would like to take this opportunity for reaffirming what has already been stated as a conviction of the New Zealand delegation by the chairman of the New Zealand delegation, who is not here today: that without the fullest possible utilization both of human and physical resources by member countries, the [International] Monetary Fund cannot be successful in carrying out its aim.

It is, therefore, the view of the New Zealand delegation that to enable the Fund to function to the best advantage, the member countries should come to an agreement that they will explore the best means of promoting the highest possible level of employment and real income. Our view would be largely met if subparagraph (4) on page 5 of the document we are considering were amended by leaving out the words "facilitate by cooperative efforts the harmonization of national policies of member states designed to," and merely making (4) "promote and maintain high levels of employment and progressively rising standards of living."

At first sight, it might seem that does not achieve anything at all, because the promotion of the high level of employment in real income has already provided for there, but it is very greatly qualified inasmuch as it says, "facilitate by cooperative efforts the harmonization of national policies of member states designed to promote." That means if they are already designed to or if they come to be designed to [pp. 25, 26 & 27] promote a high level of employment and real income, then they would be harmonizing national policies, but the ones that did not have that attitude and did not do all they could to promote high levels of employment and real income would not come into the picture. That is why I recommend that the clause should be amended to read "promote and maintain high levels of employment and progressively rising standards of living."

Canada: Mr. Chairman, I should like to second the motion of the delegate from Cuba, and in doing so I should like to make some comments. The Minister of Justice in the government of Canada, Mr. L.S. St. Laurent, wished to speak to this resolution but, unfortunately and unexpectedly, he was called back to Ottawa, and I should like to make some comments on his behalf.[598]

[The resolution, which is now before this conference, brings together a number of resolutions put forward by different countries. The reduction of barriers to trade, the mitigation of fluctuations in the prices of staple primary products and the promotion of high levels of employment are subjects which are highly relevant to the work of this Monetary and Financial Conference. Time forbids that we should here embark on the work of drafting plans through which our countries might cooperate in effective action to achieve these ends. Yet it is of the highest importance to the welfare of the world of such work should be put forward as early as possible. On behalf of the Canadian delegation I welcome the resolution which is before us and the opportunity which it gives to stress the urgent need for action.

In the work of the past few weeks an important beginning has been made in the broad scheme for meeting the international economic problems which will confront the world at the end of the war. Nevertheless it is only a beginning. If plans of international monetary organization and international investment are to be fully successful, other problems—by no means less difficult or less important—will also have to be faced himself by joint international action. It would indeed be unwise to attach to much importance to what has been planned here, if thereby we were led to neglect other problems or to rest on a misguided faith that with new forms of international monetary and investment organizations, the other problems would solve themselves. The problems of commercial policy, the instability of primary product prices, the coordination of national employment policies, must be attacked frontally and on the same wide international basis. No such monetary and investment organizations, however perfect in form, can be expected to long survive the economic distortions of high tariffs, restrictive trading arrangements, or enormous fluctuations in food and raw material prices such as marked the years between the wars.

In presenting in the Canadian House of Commons the "Joint Statement by Experts on the Establishment of an International Monetary Fund," and after expressing sympathy with the particular objects to which that statement was directed, the prime minister said that the Canadian government "is equally anxious that's coming views should be reached on

[598] The transcript merely says, "(The speaker read Document No. 485)." The speech that follows was issued as Press Release No. 40, Document 485, pp. 1194-1196, which we have reproduced here.

other parts also other general plan of international economic cooperation, particularly on the reduction in the barriers to trade expansion, the reduction vital to Canada's welfare and necessary if conditions favorable to stable monetary arrangements are to be achieved."

The other parts of such a general plan of international economic organizations are perhaps less intricate than those in which so much defective work has been done here, but the present problems even more stubborn and those with this conference has been facing. Approached in the same spirit, with the same ingenuity, the same sense of urgency in the same willingness to work together, which have been witnessed here, these problems can be solved.

It is because we believe in the possibility of solving them through international collaboration and because we believe in the urgent need for action that the Canadian delegation support this resolution.]

United Kingdom: Mr. Chairman, on behalf of the United Kingdom delegation, I should say that the United Kingdom also wishes to record their support for the motion as drafted, but they would not be in favor of the alteration of clause (4) as suggested by the New Zealand delegation.

In their view, that clause, (4), quite definitely deals with one aspect of the problem raised in the Australian resolution. In our view, there is a field of transactions which is international in character, and another field for action which is domestic in character. The resolution before you relates to the action in the international field. The United Kingdom delegation support the Australian motion that certain things should be taken up by each government in the domestic field, but that in itself, while necessary, is not enough. Over and above what is done by governments in the national domestic field to promote employment, [there are] arrangements to coordinate the policy adopted by [p. 28] each government, and the result that what one government does in the matter of employment policy does not react unfavorably on another government. It is the coordination—perhaps the "conciliation" may be a better word—of the various national policies directed toward the promotion of employment with which part (4) of the resolution before us is concerned.

In the view of the United Kingdom delegation, both provisions are necessary; that is, the inclusion of point (4) in the resolution before you and as a natural appendment to it the Australian resolution, which addresses itself to what is to be done international sphere. The Australian resolution in effect says, "Yes, while we agree that all this has got to be an international field, that will take more time. Here's something that all of us can be getting on with at home here and now." Each of the governments represented here is recommended to adopt a domestic policy designed to promote higher levels of employment within the territories under its jurisdiction. That is something to be got on with at once. The overflow from that will be international in character. That overflow will be dealt with under (4) of the resolution that you have before you.

The United Kingdom government, therefore, hopes that you will accept the comprehensive resolution which you have before you, and they further hope that when the discussion proceeds to the details of the Australian resolution, you will immediately accept it.

Netherlands: The Netherlands delegation wishes to support the Cuban proposal in its original form.

Peru (Manuel Llosa): Mr. Chairman, may I ask if Article I of the Fund is in final form and whether we can know now what changes have to be made on the two "whereas" clauses to bring it in harmony with the wording of Article I of the Fund? If I am right, the [Section] 2 of Article I ["Purposes"] of the Fund [p. 29] reads practically the same as the first "whereas," almost word for word, with the exception of the words "to the development of the productive resources," which could be very well added to the first "whereas," although I don't know whether it is really important.[599] The second "whereas" I don't think is affected in any way by the changes that may have been made in Article I. I would like to know if the Secretary could tell us something about the changes which he thinks should be introduced in a motion.

Secretary (Orvis Schmidt, United States): Mr. Chairman, it was the feeling of the committee that drafted this that if Commission II agrees upon the Bank, that possibly some mention should be incorporated in the two "whereas" clauses about the Bank as well as the Fund; and furthermore, the change which the delegate from Peru has suggested concerning the addition in the light of any change in the agenda—any change in Article I of the Articles of Agreement. I am not quite clear as to the final form of the Articles of Agreement now, but I would suggest that the matter of the consideration of the precise language be deferred at this point until Commission I and Commission II have finished their meeting

---

[599] Commission I had approved the final agreement on the IMF the previous day. Article I read, "The Purposes of the International Monetary Fund are:...(ii) To facilitate the expansion and balanced growth of international trade, and to contribute thereby to the promotion and maintenance of high levels of employment and real income and to the development of the productive resources of all members as primary objectives of economic policy." See Document 448, p. 768.

today, and changes could be considered when the resolution is reported to the plenary session, where all of the delegates will be represented.

Peru (Manuel Llosa): In other words, I take it that if there are any further changes they will be minor matters, which will not really affect the substance because we all seem to be in agreement with it.

Secretary (Orvis Schmidt): That's right.

Peru (Manuel Llosa): [On] behalf of the Peruvian delegation, I also want to welcome the motion.[600] I think it will strengthen the results of the conference and the conference itself to a [p. 30] very large extent, this motion, because by passing this motion we will be boldly facing an aspect of the economic problem which, unless taken care of, could very well destroy the two organizations which this conference is going to set up. We have discussed the Fund and we have discussed the Bank. They are both meant to tackle very special problems—very special problems which are of great importance for the future prosperity of the world, but problems which the two institutions will not be able to solve by themselves if things are not done which would prevent the problems in those two particular fields from growing beyond the scope of the institutions themselves.

We have witnessed during the last few years before the war permanent disequilibrium in the balance of payments of the different countries in the world. We all know that the Fund is not meant to and could never cope with such permanent disequilibrium. And therefore, one of the major problems to achieve orderly exchange arrangements in the world is to prevent such a permanent disequilibrium from developing again after the war. Nothing that has happened during the war can lead us to believe that the problem will be less serious after the cessation of hostilities. Some people even think that it may be more and more difficult to solve it than before the war, that the trend may be more pronounced, that the disequilibrium may be even deeper. And, therefore, if the conference had not boldly faced this issue, [we would be vindicating] the critics outside who are telling us all the time that we are dodging the real economic problem of the next two years and that in a way we are working up in the clouds, thinking about small aspects of a big problem, and not realizing that unless the big problem is tackled, nothing can be done successfully. Those critics now will [p. 31] not be able to advance their arguments, because here we are saying definitely that certain conditions are necessary for the achievement of the purposes of the Fund itself. In other words,

---

[600] The speech that follows was issued with minor changes as Press Release No. 48, Document 501, pp. 1205-1206.

we are supporting what the chairman of the conference [Henry Morgenthau, Jr.] said in his opening address, when he said specifically that even the problem of achieving exchange stability would not be attained without these other matters being taken care of.

Because it is so important to attack those other problems, because it is necessary to set up the right conditions, the Peruvian delegation has been gravely disappointed that the committee [Committee 3, "Recommendations on Economic and Financial Policy, the Exchange of Information, and Other Means of Financial Cooperation"] hasn't seen its way to go one step further and recommend some definite action. We are here saying that certain things should be done, that they are necessary for the success of the two main organizations which will come out of this conference, but we are not setting up machinery so that that will be done within a reasonable time. We know how often purposes of this sort have been had in view, how often the world has been aiming wishing to do things and yet has not done them because the appropriate machinery had not been set up to start working. In the original motion of the Peruvian delegation, we actually asked for a conference to be called to take up these other problems. Unfortunately, the other members of the committee thought that such a thing could not be done by this conference, that all this conference could do was to recommend a thing and make it clear that in its opinion those other steps were necessary. We are greatly disappointed that they didn't see their way to go a step further because we are very much afraid that unless the matter is taken up at once it may be forgotten, and the world may risk the Fund [p. 32] and the Bank without first of all creating the conditions which are necessary for the success of the Fund and of the Bank, and we are greatly worried by this because these are the first true attempts at world cooperation that are made with a view to the future. Up to now, those local and other agreements have been worked out to take care of the temporary conditions arising out of the war. But here we have the first two definite attempts at permanent world cooperation, and we all know very well that if they were to fail, we might not be able to attempt again world cooperation for very many years to come. Therefore, the world should be more than careful to be sure that it is treading on very firm ground before attempting anything of the sort.

We have set out our views at length in a statement which has been circulated[601] and which I daresay you all have, and I only hope that our disappointment will not prove to be a permanent disappointment, and

[601] Apparently Document 435, pp. 739-748.

that in the very near future we may see the countries which have taken the lead in calling this conference together also taking the lead in calling some sort of a conference or international gathering which may take up the study of the solution of these fundamental problems on which not only the general prosperity of the world relies, but also the very success of these two institutions.

As for the amendment moved by the delegate from New Zealand, for the same reasons that were expressed by the delegate from the United Kingdom, we don't feel that the motion could go as far as he suggests, although we fully sympathize, as it is obvious from what I have said, with the end, as we think, the motion itself makes quite clear. [p. 33]

[New Zealand?]:[602] Mr. Chairman, I wish to add a few words to the statement of the chairman of the Peruvian delegation. As has been stated, the delegation from Peru recognizes that the draft resolution which has been read covers the issues of the Peruvian proposal with regard to the enumeration of the course which must be pursued to assure the attainment of the objective sought by the International Monetary Fund and the [International] Bank for Reconstruction and Development, and the other primary objectives of economic policy. which not only the general prosperity of the world relies, but also the very success of these two institutions.

However, said draft resolution fails to mention a practical method by which to achieve these objectives, whereas the Peruvian resolution does not. We continue our belief in the conference of the United and Associated Nations on commercial policy may be one of such practical means it could not help [but] start major meetings with one or more regional conferences on related subjects. For instance, an American conference which may deal with the special problems which will arise for many American countries on the cessation of production for war purposes, endeavoring to adopt resolutions for an orderly return to peace conditions from the necessary economic mobilization of America for the defense of the continent, which was enacted at the third meeting of the ministers of foreign affairs held in Rio de Janeiro after Pearl Harbor.

We are not going to specify the agenda that might be assigned to such an international commercial conference, already outlined in the Peruvian proposal, but we would like to mention now a sample of the subjects to be tackled at such a conference, which should aim at elimination of

602 The typescript attributes these remarks to Arthur Tange of Australia, whereas we think they were more likely made by a delegate from New Zealand, perhaps Allan Fisher.

discriminatory practices in the field of international trade. [p. 34] A great many practices of that kind, which particularly arise in the relations of small countries with international cartels or other worldwide organizations, will not be taken into consideration outside a conference because they belong to the jurisdiction of moral rather than positive law, namely, the dumping and underselling to destroy legitimate activities of similar industries, the discriminatory rates on transportation and communication and always [destructive] practices which impede the development of orderly commercial and sound economic life. A conference on economic policies seems to be the most suitable institution to take care of these practices, by drafting provisions which could be submitted for the approval of the nations represented, and in which universally sound principles and sound commercial practice should be adopted and the unfair practices that should be condemned should be clearly defined. It may be taken for granted that the existence of such a court, if it happens to be approved, will not eradicate those undesirable practices, but it is hoped that it will constitute a court for the commercial enterprises inclined to employ that sort of means and which would seek to estimate the high moral standard of those who do not employ those means and help the new countries in that way to obtain higher levels of employment and better standards of living.

That is why we place our confidence in the fact that, although not specifically mentioned in the draft resolution among the means with which the resolution will be implemented there will be one or more international conferences, as has been suggested by the Peruvian delegation.

Mr. Chairman, I would like my words to be included in the records of the proceeding. [p. 35]

Australia: The Australian delegation would be unable to support the report of the committee [Committee 3] for the reasons that I gave earlier, in particular because we feel that, as I think the delegate from the United Kingdom pointed out, these are matters of international relations, and clause (4) in that sense is quite consistent with clauses (1), (2), and (3). Our difficulty is that we feel it adds very little to what is already in clauses (1), (2), and (3). Our feeling is that to "facilitate by cooperative effort the harmonization of national policies of member states designed to promote and maintain high levels of employment and progressively rising standards of living" can hardly be brought about through the medium of these other sorts of international collaboration which are set down here.

Our feeling, therefore, is that very little would be added by having this clause included. At the same time, we have the greatest sympathy toward the suggestion of the New Zealand delegation that the emphasis should be shifted from the international aspect of employment to the domestic aspect, by calling for ways and means of promoting and maintaining high levels of appointment, but our position is we feel it does not go far enough, and we still stand on our position that we require a recommendation that governments agree to maintain high levels of employment.

I would like these remarks to be quoted in the record of this meeting.[603]

Unidentified: Mr. Chairman, this seems to be developing into a general debate, and just for my guidance I would like to know how is it that the plenary session of the conference which is been set for this afternoon—are we having a session here while the plenary session is gathering already, or what is the situation? [p. 36]

Chairman: Well, inasmuch as the Cuban delegation has moved for the approval of the report by Committee No. 3 and it has been seconded by many delegations, I will put in a vote the report of the Third Committee before this Commission.

Those in favor of approving the report of the Third Committee, please say "aye."

Delegates: Aye.

Chairman: Those contrary minded, please say "no."

Delegates: No.

Chairman: The "ayes" have it. The report is adopted.

Gentlemen, you have heard the reports of the three committees and you have passed upon them. Mr. E.C. Fussell of the New Zealand delegation, who has been acting as Reporter of this Commission, will present his report to the plenary session of the Commission.

Australia: Mr. Chairman, do I understand that the Australian resolution of foreign policy is still before the Commission, the resolution by the Australian delegation proposing that Document 235[604]—

Chairman: Do you want a vote taken on your proposition?

Australia: Yes.

Chairman: The proposal of the Australian delegation is before the Commission for a vote. Those in favor, please say "aye."

Delegates: Aye.

---

[603] Document 467, pp. 834-837, expresses Australia's reservations.

[604] In Document 235, pp. 330-331, item no. 5 in the report of the Agenda Committee of Commission III.

Chairman: Those against, please say "no."

Delegates: No.

Chairman: Well, I am afraid it will be difficult. We will take a vote by raising hands. Those in favor please, raise their hands. [p. 37]

(Show of hands.)

Those contrary minded?

(Show of hands.)

The proposal of the Australian delegation is rejected.

Before adjourning, I would like to complement the officers of the committees for the splendid work they have done. If there is no other business to be transacted, we adjourn the meeting of this Commission.

(Whereupon, at 3:45 p.m., the Commission meeting was adjourned.)

No transcripts are available for the meetings of the committees of Commission III. The minutes in the conference proceedings are as follows: Committee 1, sole meeting (Document 425, p. 713); Committee 2, sole meeting (Documents 470 and 481 (470), pp. 486-863, 919-922); Committee 3, sole meeting (Document 428, pp. 729-732).

APPENDICES

Appendix A

Conference Participants

The names of participants in the Bretton Woods conference come from several lists in the conference proceedings.[605] We have followed the conference documents in typically listing members within delegations by rank. The previously unpublished conference telephone directory, Document 114 of the conference, lists some other people whose participation in the conference was less important. The previously unpublished biographical summaries in Document 159 contain information ranging from brief to detailed on many delegates from countries other than the United States. Photographs of the directory and of the biographical summaries are available on the page for this book at the Web site of the Center for Financial Stability.

The conference proceedings list the given names of many participants only as initials. We did research to fill in many given names for easier identification. We also added brief biographical highlights about many participants to give the reader an idea of how important they were at the time of the conference and how many later became top officials in the IMF, the World Bank, or national governments. Our main sources were Document 159 of the conference, the IMF's official history of the period,[606] and Internet research of biographical articles and obituaries. Information on the membership of certain subcommittees and ad hoc committees is scattered through the conference volumes and is often incomplete. The countries of committee chairmen and reporters (also

---

[605] See Document 156, pp. 166-181; Document 201 (156), pp. 242-258; Document 291 (156), pp. 242-253; Document 231, pp. 291-306; Document 247 (201), pp. 403-421; Document 279, p. 445; Document 443, pp. 754-760; Document 492, pp. 927-937; Document 1½, pp. 1130-1133.

[606] J. Keith Horsefield, *The International Monetary Fund 1945-1965: Twenty Years of International Monetary Cooperation; Volume I: Chronicle* (Washington, D.C.: International Monetary Fund, 1969), pp. 620-640, 649-654. The World Bank's official history, on the other hand, is shorter and provides much less biographical information on its officials: Edward S. Mason and Robert E. Asher, *The World Bank Since Bretton Woods* (Washington, D.C.: Brookings Institution, 1973).

called "reporting delegates" in the transcripts) were also always members of committees.

Latin American family names sometimes include the mother's family name. So, for Carlos Lleras Restrepo, a delegate from Colombia, Lleras was his father's family name, not his middle name, and Restrepo was his mother's family name. Adding the mother's family name helps distinguish people whose names are otherwise common. Chinese names are listed as given name first, then family name, as is often done in English-speaking countries but not in China. Chinese names are apparently transliterated according to the old Wade-Giles system. No uniform method existed in 1944, or exists today, for transliterating Arabic names.

Some delegates are identified as ministers resident or members of legations to the United States. A legation was a diplomatic representative office lower than an embassy. It is a minor inaccuracy to call the ministers "ambassadors," as we denote them in parentheses, but it is more in accord with present usage, which no longer distinguishes between embassies and legations or between ambassadors and ministers resident.

Bold indicates participants who were especially active or important in the transcripts.

Delegations

AUSTRALIA

Chairman: **Leslie Galfreid Melville,** Economic Adviser to the Commonwealth Bank of Australia; later Executive Director, IMF (1950-1953); Executive Director, World Bank (1950-1953); Alternate Governor, IMF (1951-1952)

Other delegates

James Bristock "Jim" Brigden, Financial Counselor, Australian Legation, Washington; economist noted for contributions to trade, national income, and statistics in Australia

Frederick Henry Wheeler, Commonwealth Department of the Treasury; later Secretary (top career official), Commonwealth Department of the Treasury (1971-1979)

Arthur Harold Tange, Commonwealth Department of External Affairs; later Secretary (top career official), Commonwealth Department of Defense (1970-1979)

Secretary: Morris A. Greene, Australian Legation, Washington

BELGIUM

Chairman: **Camille Gutt,** Minister of Finance and Economic Affairs; previously Chief of Cabinet to Prime Minister Georges Theunis (1921-

1924); later architect of post-liberation currency stabilization in Belgium (1944); Governor, IMF (1946); Executive Director, IMF (1946); first Managing Director, IMF (1946-1951)

Other delegates

Georges Émile Léonard Theunis, Minister of State (ambassador-at-large to the United States) and Governor of the National Bank of Belgium; previously Minister of Finance (1920-1921); Prime Minister (1921-1925, 1934-1935); Minister of Defense (1932)

Baron Hervé de Gruben, Counselor, Belgium Embassy, Washington; later Secretary General (top career official), Ministry of Foreign Affairs (1945-1953); Alternate Governor, IMF (1946)

Baron René Boël, Counselor of the Belgium Government; prominent banker and industrialist; later delegate to first meeting of IMF and World Bank (1946); President, European League for Economic Cooperation

Legal Adviser: Joseph Nisot, Legal Adviser, Belgian Embassy, New York; later a Belgian ambassador

Financial Adviser: Boris Serge "Ben" Chlepner, Professor, Free University of Brussels; monetary economist and economic historian of Belgium

Secretary: Ernest de Selliers de Moranville, Financial Attaché, Belgian Embassy, Washington; previously Chief of Cabinet, Ministry of Finance (1941-1944); later Alternate Executive Director, IMF (1946-1948); Executive Director, IMF (1948-1954); Alternate Executive Director, World Bank (1950-1953)

BOLIVIA

Chairman: René Ballivián Calderón, Financial Counselor, Bolivian Embassy, Washington

BRAZIL

Chairman: **Artur** (English "Arthur") **de Souza Costa,** Minister of Finance

Other delegates

Francisco Alves dos Santos Filho, Director of Foreign Exchange, Banco do Brasil; later Executive Director, IMF (1946-1948); Governor, IMF (1946-1950); Governor, World Bank (1946-1950)

Valentin Bouças, Commission of Control of the Washington Agreements and Member, Economic and Financial Council; wealthy businessman; sometime financial adviser to the President of Brazil

Eugênio Gudin, Economic and Financial Council and Economic Planning Committee; later Governor, World Bank (1950-1951, 1955-1956); Minister of Finance (1954-1955)

Octávio Gouvea de Bulhões, Chief, Division of Economic and Financial Studies, Ministry of Finance; later Alternate Executive Director, IMF (1946-1947); Minister of Finance (1964-1967)

Victor Azevedo Bastian, Director, Banco da Provincia do Rio Grande do Sul

Secretaries

Aguinaldo Boulitreau Fragoso, Assistant to the Minister of Foreign Affairs; later Minister of Foreign Affairs

Roberto de Oliveira Campos, Second Secretary, Brazilian Embassy, Washington; later ambassador to the United States (1961-1964); Minister of Planning and Economic Coordination (1964-1967); ambassador to the United Kingdom (1975-1982); member, Chamber of Deputies (parliament) (1991-1998)

Zeuxis Ferreira Neves, Technical Assistant to the Commercial Counselor, Brazilian Embassy, Washington

Charles Freligh, Brazilian Embassy, Washington

Santiago Fernandes, Banco do Brasil (state-owned quasi-central bank)

R. R. Vieira, Brazilian Treasury Delegation, New York

Daniel Maximo Martins, Private Secretary to the Minister of Finance

CANADA

Chairman: James Lorimer Ilsley, Minister of Finance; later Governor, IMF (1946); Governor, World Bank (1946)

Other delegates

Louis Stephen Saint Laurent, Minister of Justice; later Prime Minister (1948-1957)

Douglas Charles Abbott, Member of Parliament and Parliamentary Assistant to the Minister of Finance; later Governor, World Bank (1946-1954); Minister of Finance (1946-1954); Justice, Supreme Court of Canada (1954-1973)

Lionel Chevrier, Parliamentary Assistant to the Minister of Munitions and Supply; later Minister of Transport (1945-1954); Minister of Justice (1963-1964)

Joseph-Adéodat Blanchette, Member of Parliament

Walter Adam Tucker, Member of Parliament

William Clifford "Clif" Clark, Deputy Minister of Finance; later Alternate Governor, World Bank (1946)

Graham Ford Towers, Governor, Bank of Canada (1934-1954); later Alternate Governor, IMF (1946-1950, 1953-1954); Alternate Governor, World Bank (1946-1947)

William Archibald Mackintosh, Special Assistant to the Deputy Minister of Finance; later Director, Bank of Canada

Louis Rasminsky, Chairman (alternate), Foreign Exchange Control Board; later Executive Director, IMF (1946-1962); Executive Director, World Bank (1946-1962); Alternate Governor, IMF (1950, 1955, 1958, 1960-1968); Deputy Governor, Bank of Canada (1955-1961); Governor, Bank of Canada (1961-1973)

(Arthur FitzWalter) Wynne Plumptre, Financial Attaché, Canadian Embassy, Washington; later Alternate Governor, World Bank (1953-1965); Assistant Deputy Minister, Department of Finance (1953-1965); Executive Director, IMF (1962-1965)

John James Deutsch, Special Assistant to the Under Secretary of State of External Affairs; later Alternate Governor, World Bank (1952-1953); senior official in multiple positions, including Chairman, Economic Council of Canada (1963-1967)

Secretary: Paul Tremblay, Third Secretary, Canadian Embassy, Washington

CHILE

Chairman: Luis Álamos Barros, Director, Central Bank of Chile; later Minister of Interior (1945); Minister of Finance (1946)

Other delegates

Germán E. Riesco, General Representative of the Chilean Line, New York

Arturo Maschke Tornero, General Manager, Central Bank of Chile; later President, Central Bank of Chile (1953-1959); Minister of Finance (1946, 1950)

Fernando Mardones Restat, Assistant General Manager, Chilean Nitrate and Iodine Sales Corporation

Alfonso Fernández Martorell, General Manger, Amortization Bank of Chile

Secretary: Carmen Señoret, Consul of Chile, Boston

Assistant Secretaries

Frank Ledesma, Secretary to the Chairman of the Delegation

Herman Max Coers, Technical Adviser, Central Bank of Chile; Professor, University of Chile

Luis Aguirre

CHINA

Chairman: Hsiang-Hsi "Daddy" K'ung, Vice President of Executive Yuan; Minister of Finance; and Governor, Central Bank of China

Other delegates

Tingfu Fuller Tsiang, Chief Political Secretary of Executive Yuan; previously ambassador to the USSR (1936-1938); later Permanent Representative of China to the United Nations

Ping-Wen Kuo, Vice Minister of Finance

Victor Chi-Tsai Hoo, Administrative Vice Minister of Foreign Affairs

Yee-Chun Koo, Vice Minister of Finance; later Executive Director, IMF (1946-1950); Treasurer, IMF (1953-1966)

Kuo-Ching Li, Adviser to the Ministry of Finance; General Manager, Wah Chang Trading Corporation, New York

Te-Mou Hsi, Representative of the Ministry of Finance in Washington; later Alternate Executive Director, World Bank (1951)

Tsu-Yee Pei, Director, Bank of China

Ts-Liang Soong, General Manager, Manufacturers Bank of China; later Alternate Governor, World Bank (1946-1950)

Advisers

Hu Shih, former Chinese Ambassador to the United States

Kia-Ngau Chang, High Adviser to Executive Yuan; formerly Deputy Governor, Central Bank of China (1935); Minister of Communications (1937-1942); later author, *The Inflationary Spiral: The Experience in China, 1939-1950* (1958)

Ming Li, Chairman, Chekiang Industrial Bank

Ting-Sen Wei, Member, Legislative Yuan

Secretary General: Chao-Ting Chi, Secretary General, Foreign Exchange Control Commission, Ministry of Finance and Research Director, Economic Research Department, Central Bank of China

Secretary: Edward Bing-Shuey Lee, Editor, *Chinese Republic* weekly

Technical Experts

Chi-Ling Tung, Vice Chairman, Foreign Trade Commission

Y.C. Wang, Secretary, Central Bank of China; later an IMF official

Cho-Ming Li, Professor of Economics, Southwestern Associated Universities, Kunming

Chih Tsang, Director, Shanghai Commercial and Savings Bank

Tsung-Fei Koh, Secretary, International Department, Directorate General of Posts

Vung-Yuen Woo, Chief of Monetary Section, Currency Department, Ministry of Finance

C.T. Yen, Director of Department, Central Bank of China

Technical Consultants

Arthur Nichols Young, Financial Adviser to the Chinese Government; American citizen; later adviser on Saudi Arabian monetary reform (1951-1952); brother of John Young, conference Secretariat

Carl Neprud, Commissioner of Customs, Ministry of Finance

Secretaries

Yen-Tsu Chen, Secretary, Central Bank of China

Daniel S.K. Chang, Secretary, Central Bank of China

Ping-Yeh Tcheng, Secretary, Central Trust of China

Bing-Shuey Lee, First Secretary, Chinese Embassy, Washington

Kien-Wen Yu, Second Secretary, Chinese Embassy, Washington

I.C. Sung, Assistant Treasurer, Universal Trading Corporation

Wan-Sen Lo, Secretary to the Representative of the Ministry of Finance in Washington

Ta-Chung Liu, Secretary, Office of Commercial Counselor, Chinese Embassy, Washington; later an IMF official

Yu-Chung Hsi, Secretary to the Representative of the Ministry of Finance in Washington

COLOMBIA

Chairman: **Carlos Lleras Restrepo,** former President of the Chamber of Deputies, Minister of Finance, and Comptroller General; later President of Colombia (1966-1970)

Other delegates

Miguel López Pumarejo, Manager, Caja de Crédito Agrario, Industrial y Minero; previously ambassador to the United States (1938-1939); Minister of National Economy (1940)

Victor Dugand, Banker

Technical Advisers

Antonio Puerto, Banker

Salvador Camacho Roldán, Banker, and Vice President, Bogotá Stock Exchange

COSTA RICA

Chairman: Francisco de Paula Gutiérrez Ross, Ambassador to the United States; previously Minister of Finance and Commerce

Other delegates

Luis Demetrio Tinoco Castro, Dean, Faculty of Economic Sciences, University of Costa Rica; previously Minister of Finance and Commerce; later Minister of Foreign Relations (1958-1961)

Fernando Madrigal A., Member of Board of Directors, Chamber of Commerce of Costa Rica

Counselor: José Rafaël Oreamuno, Vice Chairman, Inter-American Development Commission; previously minister (ambassador) to the United States

CUBA

Chairman: Eduardo I. Montoulieu, Minister of Finance

Technical advisers

Oscar García Montes, Professor of Political Economy, University of Havana

Ramiro Guerra y Sánchez, Technical Adviser of the Ministry of Finance; later director of *Diario de la Marina,* an influential newspaper

Miguel A. Pirez, Assistant to the Minister of Finance

Juan M. Menocal, Professor of Taxation, University of Havana, and Adviser to the Office of the Prime Minister

Felipe Pazos y Roque, Commercial Attaché, Cuban Embassy, Washington; later an IMF official

Luis Machado, Lawyer and Economist; later Executive Director, World Bank (1946-1948, 1952-1971)

Eduardo Durruthy, Director General of Statistics of the Ministry of Finance
Secretary: Calixto Montoulieu, Minister of Finance
Technical Secretary: Irving Gordon

CZECHOSLOVAKIA
Chairman: Ladislav Feierabend, Minister of Finance
Deputy Chairman: Jan V. Mládek, Ministry of Finance; later Executive Director, IMF (1946-1948); Governor, IMF (1946-1947); senior IMF official (1953-1977), including head of Paris office (1953-1961) and Director, Central Banking Service (1964-1977?)
Other delegates
Antonín Basch, Department of Economics, Columbia University; previously an official of the Czechoslovak National Bank; later Chief Economist, World Bank (1947?-1957)
Josef Hanč, Director of the Czechoslovak Economic Service in the United States of America; later Alternate Governor, World Bank (1946-1948)
Ervin Paul Hexner, Professor of Economics and Political Science, University of North Carolina; later Senior Counselor and Assistant General Counsel, IMF (1946-1958)
Technical Adviser and Secretary: Ernest Sturc, Czechoslovak Economic Service in the United States; later an IMF official (1946-1970s?), including Director, Exchange and Trade Relations Department (1965-1970s?)

DOMINICAN REPUBLIC[607]
Chairman: Anselmo Copello, Ambassador to the United States; previously Director, Banco de Reservas (1941-?)
Delegate: José Ramón Rodriguez, Minister Counselor, Embassy of the Dominican Republic, Washington; later Alternate Governor, World Bank (1946-1947)
Secretary: J.M. Sanz Lajara, First Secretary, Embassy of the Dominican Republic, Washington

ECUADOR
Chairman: Esteban F. Carbo, Financial Counselor, Ecuadoran Embassy, Washington; previously employee and branch manager, Banco Central del Ecuador (1927-1937); later Governor, IMF (1946); Governor, World Bank (1946); Alternate Executive Director, World Bank (1950)

---

[607] Roberto Despradel, minister counselor at the Dominican embassy in Washington and formerly Secretary for Finance, is also listed as a member of the delegation in a preconference list in the unpublished Document 159 but nowhere else.

Other delegate: Sixto Enrique Durán Ballén, Minister Counselor, Ecuadoran Embassy, Washington; previously Minister of Finance (1929-1931); later Alternate Governor, World Bank (1946-1947)

EGYPT
Chairman: Sany Lackany Bey
Other delegates
Mahmoud Saleh el Falaky (also transliterated "al Falaki"); later Alternate Executive Director, IMF (1946-1951); Alternate Governor, IMF (1946-1953); Alternate Governor, World Bank (1946)
Ahmed Selim; later Alternate Governor, IMF (1946); Alternate Governor, World Bank (1946-1947)
Adviser: James I. Craig, Commissioner for Customs, Ministry of Finance; British subject
Technical Secretary: Leon Dichy; sometime State Controller of Public Debt
Secretary: Mrs. F. Carritt

EL SALVADOR
Chairman: Agustín Alfaro Morán, Coffee Plantation Owner; sometime board member, Banco Central de Reserva de El Salvador
Other delegates
Raúl Gamero Calderón; later Foreign Minister (circa 1960)
Víctor Manuel Valdés

ETHIOPIA
Chairman: Blatta Ephrem Tewelde Medhen, Minister (ambassador) to the United States; previously Vice Minister of Foreign Affairs (1942-1943)
Other delegate: George Albert Blowers, Governor, State Bank of Ethiopia; American citizen; later Governor, IMF (1946-1948); Governor, World Bank (1946-1948); first Governor, Saudi Arabian Monetary Authority (1952-1954); IMF official
Secretary: Helen Willard

FRANCE (FRENCH COMMITTEE OF NATIONAL LIBERATION)
Chairman: **Pierre Mendès-France,** Commissioner of Finance; later Minister of the National Economy (1944-1945); Executive Director, IMF (1946); Governor, IMF (1946-1957); Alternate Governor, World Bank (1946-1958); Executive Director, World Bank (1946-1947); Prime Minister (1954-1955); holder of numerous other political positions
Other main delegate: **André Istel,** Technical Counselor to the Department of Finance; prominent banker; previously coauthor of a Free French plan for international monetary cooperation (1943)

Assistant delegates

Jean Rioust de Largentaye, Finance Inspector; previously translator of John Maynard Keynes's *General Theory of Employment, Interest and Money* into French (1942); later Alternate Executive Director, IMF (1946); Executive Director, IMF (1946-1964)

André Paul Maury

Robert Mossé, Professor of Economics, New School for Social Research, New York; later Professor of Economics, School of Law, University of Grenoble, and author of books on international monetary issues

Raoul Aglion, Legal Counselor; previously Professor of Economic History, École des Hautes Études Sociales (1930)

Secretaries

Jean Lambert

Gaston Mallet

Georges Roncales

GREECE

Chairman: **Kyriakos Varvaressos,** Governor of the Bank of Greece and Ambassador Extraordinary for Economic and Financial Matters; later Executive Director, World Bank (1946-1948)

Other delegates

Alexander Argyropoulos, Minister Resident; Director, Economic and Commercial Division, Ministry of Foreign Affairs

Athanase (Athanasios) Ioannu "A.J." Sbarounis, Director General, Ministry of Finance; later Governor, World Bank (1946-1947)

Technical Advisers

Alexander Loverdos, Ministry of Finance

André (Andreas) Papandreou; later Prime Minister (1981-1989, 1993-1996)

GUATEMALA

Chairman: Manuel Noriega Morales, Postgraduate Student in Economics, Harvard University; previously Professor of Accounting, University of Guatemala; later Governor, IMF (1946-1954); Governor, World Bank (1946-1954); Secretary of Economy and Labor; Governor, Bank of Guatemala

HAITI

Chairman: André Liautaud, Ambassador to the United States; previously Under Secretary of State for Finance, Commerce, and National Economy (1942-1943)

Other delegate: Pierre Chauvet, Under Secretary of State for Finance

HONDURAS

Chairman: Julián R. Cáceres, Ambassador to the United States; previously departmental governor (1926, 1928); later Governor, IMF (1946-1948); Governor, World Bank (1946-1948)

ICELAND

Chairman: Magnús Sigurðsson, Manager, National Bank of Iceland; later Governor, World Bank (1946-1947)

Other delegates

Ásgeir Ásgeirsson, Fishery Bank of Iceland; previously Minister of Finance (1931-1934); Prime Minister (1932-1934); later President (1952-1968)

Svanbjörn Frímannsson, Chairman, State Commerce Board; previously Head Cashier (a top manager), National Bank of Iceland (1937); later Governor, Central Bank of Iceland (1971-1973)

Secretary: Martha Thors, Secretary, Icelandic Legation to the United States

INDIA

Chairman: **Sir (Abraham) Jeremy Raisman,** Member (minister) of Finance, Government of India; British subject

Other delegates

Sir Theodor Emanuel Gugenheim Gregory, Economic Adviser to the Government of India; sometime Professor of Banking and Currency, London School of Economics and Political Science; British subject

Sir Chintaman Dwarakanath Deshmukh, Governor, Reserve Bank of India; later Governor, IMF (1946-1955); Governor, World Bank (1946-1947, 1950-1956)

Sir Ramasamy Chetty Kandasamy Shanmukham Chetty; previously President, Central Legislative Assembly (1933-1935); later Minister of Finance (1947-1949)

Ardeshir Darabshaw (A.D.) Shroff, Director, Tata Sons, Ltd.

Adviser: Sir David Burnett Meek, Trade Commissioner, London; British subject

Assistant Adviser: Mrs. A.A. Henderson

Secretary: Bal Krishna (B.K.) Madan; later Alternate Executive Director, IMF (1946-1948); Alternate Executive Director, World Bank (1947-1948); Executive Director, IMF (1948-1950, 1967-1971); Alternate Governor, IMF (1957, 1961, 1964, 1967, 1968); Deputy Governor, Reserve Bank of India (1964-1967)

IRAN

Chairman: Abol Hassan Ebtehaj, Governor, National Bank of Iran; later Governor, IMF (1946-1949); Governor, World Bank (1946-1950); Director, Middle East Department, IMF (1953-1954)

Other delegates
A.A. Daftary, Counselor, Iranian Legation, Washington
Hossein Navab, Consul General, New York
Taghi Nassr, Iranian Trade and Economic Commissioner, New York; previously Director General, Ministry of Finance (1940)

IRAQ[608]
Chairman: Ibrahim Kamal, Senator; previously Minister of Finance (1937-1938)
Other delegates
Lionel Maynard Swan, Adviser to the Ministry of Finance; British subject
Is Ibrahim Al-Kabir, Accountant General, Ministry of Finance
Claude E. Loombe, Comptroller of Exchange and Currency Officer; British subject; previously banker with the Chartered Bank of India, Australia and China (1930s); exchange control officer, Reserve Bank of India (1942?)

LIBERIA
Chairman: William E. Dennis, Secretary of the Treasury
Other delegates
James F. Cooper, previously Secretary of the Treasury (1916-1917)
Walter F. Walker, Consul General, New York
Secretary: K. Jefferies Adorkor, Jr.

LUXEMBOURG
Chairman: Hugues Le Gallais, Minister to the United States; later Alternate Governor, IMF (1956-1958); Alternate Executive Director, IMF (1956-1958); Alternate Governor, World Bank (1946-1948)

MEXICO
Chairman: **Eduardo Suárez Aránzolo,** Minister of Finance
Other delegates
Antonio Espinosa de los Monteros, Executive President, Nacional Financiera, and Director, Banco de México; later Governor, IMF (1946-1947); Governor, World Bank (1946-1948)
Rodrigo Gómez, Manager, Banco de México; later Executive Director, IMF (1946-1948, 1958-1960); Alternate Governor, IMF (1946-1947, 1953-1956, 1960-1968); Governor, IMF (1957-1959)

---

[608] Ali Al-Ayyubi Jawdat, Iraqi minister (ambassador) in Washington and previously Prime Minister (1934-1935), is also listed as a possible member of the delegation in a preconference list in the unpublished Document 159 but nowhere else.

Daniel Cosío Villegas, Chief, Department of Economic Studies, Banco de México

General Secretaries

Salvador Duhart, First Secretary, Mexican Embassy, Washington

Julián Sáenz, Mexican Consul, New York

Technical Secretary: Victor Urquidi, Economist, Department of Economic Studies, Banco de México

NETHERLANDS

Chairman: **Johan Willem "Wim" Beyen** (also spelled "Beijen"), Financial Adviser to the Netherlands Government; Director, Unilever; previously Alternate to the President, Bank for International Settlements (1935-1937); President, Bank for International Settlements (1937-1939); later Executive Director, World Bank (1946-1952); Executive Director, IMF (1948-1952); Minister of Foreign Affairs (1952-1956)

Other delegates

Daniël Crena de Iongh, President, Board for the Netherlands Indies, Surinam, and Curaçao in the United States; previously President, Nederlandsche Handel-Maatschappij (Netherlands Trading Company) (1934-1939); later Alternate Executive Director, IMF (1946); Alternate Executive Director, World Bank (1946-1947); Treasurer, IMF (1946); Treasurer, World Bank (1947-1953); Executive Director, IMF (1953-1955); Executive Director, World Bank (1953-1955)

Hendrik Riemens, Financial Attaché, Netherlands Embassy, Washington

Adriaan Hendrick Philipse, Member, Netherlands Economic, Financial, and Shipping Mission in the United States

Experts

A. Andriesse, Private Banker

Anton Dirk Bestebreurtje, President, Netherlands Chamber of Commerce in New York, Inc.

Jacques Jacobus Polak, Economist, Netherlands Economic, Financial, and Shipping Mission to the United States; previously a League of Nations official; later a senior IMF official (1947-1979); originator of the "Polak model" of the monetary approach to the balance of payments (1957); Executive Director, IMF (1981-1986)

C.H. Schoch, Representative, Netherlands Indies Exchange Control

Advisers to the Chairman

J. Jerome Williams, Netherlands Embassy, Washington

J.H. Capriles, Manager, Maduro & Curiel's Bank

W.J.A. de Heer, Secretary, Netherlands Antilles Foreign Exchange Commission

Secretary: Aron "Ronnie" Broches; later a World Bank official (1946-1979), including General Counsel (1959-1979)

NEW ZEALAND

Chairman: **Walter Nash,** Minister of Finance; later Prime Minister (1957-1960)

Other delegates

Bernard Carl Ashwin, Secretary to the Treasury

Edward C. Fussell, Deputy Governor, Reserve Bank of New Zealand

Allan George Barnard Fisher, Counselor, New Zealand Legation, Washington; economist who developed the idea of service industries as a distinct economic sector; later an IMF official and the first editor of the economics journal *IMF Staff Papers*

Adviser and Secretary: Bruce R. Turner, Second Secretary, New Zealand Legation, Washington

NICARAGUA

Chairman: Guillermo Sevilla Sacasa, Ambassador to the United States; later Governor, World Bank (1946-1947, 1949-1979)

Other delegates

León DeBayle, formerly Ambassador to the United States and lawyer for Banco Nacional de Nicaragua

J. Jesús Sánchez Roig, Vice Chairman, Board of Directors, Banco Nacional de Nicaragua; later Governor, World Bank (1948); Alternate Governor, World Bank (1953-1953)

NORWAY

Chairman: **Wilhelm Christian Ottesen Keilhau**, Director, Norges Bank (Bank of Norway), pro tempore, London; previously Professor of Economics, University of Oslo

Other delegates

Ole Colbjørnsen, Financial Counselor, Norwegian Embassy, Washington; previously member of Norwegian parliament (1936-1940); Director, Norges Bank (Bank of Norway) (1940); later Alternate Governor, IMF (1946-1955); Alternate Governor, World Bank (1946-1955)

Arne Skaug, Commercial Counselor, Norwegian Embassy, Washington; formerly Assistant Professor of Economics, University of Wisconsin; later Governor, World Bank (1955-1961)

Technical Adviser: Kaare Petersen, Norwegian Shipping and Trade Mission, New York

Secretary: Torfinn Oftedal, First Secretary, Norwegian Embassy, Washington

PANAMA

Chairman: Guillermo Arango, President, Investors Service Corporation of Panama; formerly Comptroller General of Panama (1940-?)

Other delegate: Narciso E. Garay, First Secretary, Panamanian Embassy, Washington

PARAGUAY

Chairman: Celso R. Velázquez, Ambassador to the United States; previously Under Secretary of the Treasury

Other delegate: Néstor M. Campos Ros, First Secretary, Paraguayan Embassy, Washington

PERU

Chairman: Pedro G. Beltrán Espantoso, Ambassador-designate to the United States; formerly a banker; later Prime Minister (1959-1961)

Other delegates

Manuel B. Llosa, Second Vice President of the Chamber of Deputies; later Minister of Economy (1948)

Andrés F. Dasso, Senator from Lima; later Minister of Economy and Finance (1950-1952)

Juvenal Alvarez Calderón, Senator from Lima

Juvenal Monge, Deputy from Cuzco; previously Professor of Engineering and Economics, National School of Engineering

Juan Chávez Dartnell, Minister, Commercial Counselor, Peruvian Embassy, Washington

Technical Adviser: Emilio G. Barreto

Secretary: Alvaro Rey de Castro, Third Secretary, Peruvian Embassy, Washington

PHILIPPINE COMMONWEALTH

Chairman: Colonel Andrés Soriano, Secretary of Finance

Other delegates

Jaime Hernandez, Auditor General; formerly Professor of Law and Accounting, Far Eastern University

Joseph H. Foley, Manager, Philippine National Bank, New York Agency; American citizen; later Alternate Governor, IMF (1946); Alternate Governor, World Bank (1946)

Technical Adviser and Secretary: Ismael Mathay, Technical Assistant to the Auditor General

POLAND

Chairman: Ludwik Grosfeld, Minister of Finance

Other delegates

Leon Baránski, Director General, Bank of Poland; later Executive Director, World Bank (1946-1950)

Zygmunt Karpinski, Director, Bank of Poland; later Alternate Executive Director, IMF (1946)

Stanislaw Kirkor, Director, Ministry of Finance

Janusz Zółtowski, Financial Counselor, Polish Embassy, Washington; later Alternate Governor, World Bank (1946-1950)

Experts

Michal (Michael) A. Heilperin, Associate Professor of Economics, Hamilton College; writer on international monetary economics

Wladyslaw Malinowski, Assistant Financial Counselor, Polish Embassy, Washington

Secretary: Gustaw Gottesman, Secretary to the Minister of Finance

UNION OF SOUTH AFRICA

Chairman: S. Frank N. Gie, Minister to the United States

Other delegates

John Edward "Jack" Holloway, Secretary (top career official) for Finance; previously Lecturer and Professor of Economics, Gray University College (1917-1925); later Governor, IMF (1946, 1948); Governor, World Bank (1946); Alternate Governor, World Bank (1948); Alternate Governor, IMF (1949-1951, 1954)

Michiel Hendrick de Kock, Deputy Governor, South African Reserve Bank; author, *Central Banking* (1939); later Governor, South African Reserve Bank (1945-1962); Alternate Governor, IMF (1946-1948); Alternate Governor, World Bank (1946-1948, 1949-1963); Governor, World Bank (1948)

Adviser: Willem Christiaan Naudé, Attaché, South African Legation, Washington; later South African ambassador to the United States

UNION OF SOVIET SOCIALIST REPUBLICS (USSR)

Chairman: Mikhail Stepanovich Stepanov, Deputy People's Commissar of Foreign Trade

Other delegates

Pavel Andreyevich Maletin, Deputy People's Commissar of Finance

Nikolai Fyodorovich Chechulin, Assistant Chairman, State Bank of the USSR

I.D. Zlobin (also transliterated "Slobin"), Chief, Monetary Division of the People's Commissariat of Finance

A.A. Arutiunian, Professor; Expert-Consultant of the People's Commissariat for Foreign Affairs

A.P. Morozov, Chief, Monetary Division of the People's Commissariat for Foreign Trade

Aleksei Mikhailovich Smirnov, Professor, Institute of Foreign Trade; later author, *Normalization of World Trade and the Monetary Problem* (1952)

P. Titov

N. Ivanov
A. Borisov
L. Andreev
N. Checkmarev
N. Kuznetzov
N. Panchenko
Mrs. L. Gouseva
Experts
M.M. Idashkin, Financial Adviser, People's Commissariat for Foreign Trade
F.P. Bystrov, Professor of Finance, Institute of Foreign Trade
Secretaries
M.I. Chibisov, Assistant to the Chairman
N.I. Kuzminsky, Private Secretary to the Chairman

UNITED KINGDOM
Chairman: **John Maynard Keynes,** Lord Keynes, Economic Adviser to the Chancellor of the Exchequer; Director, Bank of England; most influential economist of the 20th century; created Lord Keynes, Baron of Tilton (1942); later Governor, IMF (1946); Governor, World Bank (1946); Vice President, World Bank (1946); died 1946
Other delegates
Robert Henry Brand, United Kingdom Treasury Representative in Washington; previously Managing Director, Lazard Brothers and Company; Director; Lloyd's Bank; later created Baron Brand of Eydon (1946); Alternate Governor, IMF (1946); Alternate Governor, World Bank (1946)
Sir (Crawfurd) Wilfrid Griffin Eady, Joint Second Secretary (second-highest career official) and head of Overseas Finance, United Kingdom Treasury; highest-ranking British official at Bretton Woods; previously Deputy Under Secretary of State, Home Office (1938-1940)
Nigel Bruce Ronald, Assistant Under Secretary of State for Foreign Affairs, Foreign Office; later (1947-1955) ambassador to Portugal; knighted
Dennis Holme Robertson, United Kingdom Treasury; second only to Keynes in the British delegation in his contributions to the Bretton Woods conference; previously and later Cambridge University monetary economist; later knighted; the best writer economics has ever produced
Lionel Charles Robbins, War Cabinet Office; Professor, London School of Economics and a leader in its rise to international eminence; later created Baron Robbins of Clare Market (1958)
Redvers Opie, Counselor, British Embassy, Washington; economist
Advisers
(William) Eric Beckett, chief Legal Adviser, Foreign Office; chief British legal expert at Bretton Woods; later knighted (1948)

George Lewis French Bolton, Adviser, Bank of England; later Executive Director, IMF (1946-1952); Alternate Governor, IMF (1952-1956); Executive Director, Bank of England (1948-1957); Director, Bank of England (1957-1968); knighted

Charles H. Campbell, First Secretary, British Embassy, Washington

John W. Russell, Second Secretary, British Embassy, Washington

Ralph H. Thomas, Second Secretary, British Embassy, Washington

Secretaries

H.E. Brooks, United Kingdom Treasury

Arthur Wendell "Peter" Snelling, Dominions Office; later ambassador to South Africa (1970-1973); knighted

Richard T.G. Miles, Third Secretary, British Embassy, Washington; later Adviser, British Delegation to the United Nations

UNITED STATES OF AMERICA

Chairman: Henry Morgenthau, Jr., Secretary of the Treasury

Vice Chairman: **Frederick Moore "Fred" Vinson,** Director, Office of Economic Stabilization; previously member, U.S. House of Representatives (1929-1929, 1933-1938); federal judge (1938-1943); later Secretary of the Treasury (1945-1946); Governor, IMF (1946); Governor, World Bank (1946); Chief Justice, U.S. Supreme Court (1948-1953)

Other delegates

Dean Gooderham Acheson, Assistant Secretary of State; previously Under Secretary of the Treasury (1933); Acting Secretary of the Treasury (1933); later Secretary of State (1949-1953); a major drafter of the World Bank agreement at Bretton Woods

Edward Eagle "Ned" Brown, President, First National Bank of Chicago; President, Federal Advisory Council, Board of Governors of the Federal Reserve System; a major drafter of the World Bank agreement at Bretton Woods

Leo Thomas Crowley, Administrator, Foreign Economic Administration; Chairman, Federal Deposit Insurance Corporation; Alien Property Administrator

Marriner Stoddard Eccles, Chairman, Board of Governors of the Federal Reserve System

Mabel Newcomer, Professor of Economics, Vassar College

Brent Spence, U.S. House of Representatives, Democrat from Kentucky; Chairman, House Committee on Banking and Currency

Charles William Tobey, U.S. Senate; Republican from New Hampshire; Member, Senate Committee on Banking and Currency; previously Governor of New Hampshire (1929-1931)

Robert Ferdinand Wagner, U.S. Senate; Democrat from New York; Chairman, Senate Committee on Banking and Currency

Harry Dexter White, Assistant to the Secretary of the Treasury; chief American negotiator on international monetary matters during World War II; main originator of the ideas in the IMF agreement; previously Professor of Economics, Lawrence College (1932-1934); later Assistant Secretary of the Treasury (a Senate-confirmed position) (1945-1946); Executive Director, IMF (1946-1947); passed secrets to USSR; died 1948

Jesse Paine Wolcott, U.S. House of Representatives; Republican from Michigan; Member, House Committee on Banking and Currency

Technical Advisers

James Waterhouse Angell, Foreign Economic Administration; a major drafters of the World Bank agreement at Bretton Woods; previously and later Professor of Economics, Columbia University

Edward Morris "Eddie" Bernstein, Assistant Director of Monetary Research, Treasury Department, Executive Secretary of the Delegation; the most important contributor to Bretton Woods conference other than Harry Dexter White and John Maynard Keynes; later Director, Research Department, IMF (1946-1958)

Malcolm Bryan, First Vice President, Federal Reserve Bank of Atlanta

Emilio Gabriel "Peter" Collado, Chief, Division of Financial and Monetary Affairs, Department of State; a major drafter of the World Bank agreement at Bretton Woods; later Executive Director, World Bank (1946-1947)

Henry Edmiston, Vice President, Federal Reserve Bank of St. Louis

Walter Gardner, Board of Governors, Federal Reserve System; an important drafter of the World Bank agreement at the Bretton Woods conference

Emanuel Alexandrovich Goldenweiser, Director of Research and Statistics, Board of Governors, Federal Reserve System; previously President, American Statistical Association (1943); one of the most influential career officials of the Federal Reserve

Alvin Harvey Hansen, Board of Governors, Federal Reserve System; previously and later Professor of Economics, Harvard University; introduced the economics of John Maynard Keynes in the United States

Frederick Livesey, Adviser, Office of Economic Affairs, Department of State

Walter Louchheim, Jr., Securities and Exchange Commission

August Maffry, Department of Commerce; later consultant, Economic Cooperation Administration (which administered the Marshall Plan) (1948-1951)

Norman T. Ness, Treasury Department; later a senior official for economic affairs at the Department of State

Leo S. Pasvolsky, Department of State; a major drafter of the United Nations charter; in charge of postwar planning for the Department of State

Warren Pierson, Export-Import Bank of the United States

Chauncey William Reed, U.S. House of Representatives; Republican from Illinois; Member, House Committee on Coinage, Weights and Measures

Andrew Lawrence Somers, U.S. House of Representatives; Democrat from New York; Chairman, House Committee on Coinage, Weights and Measures

Menc Stephen "Matt" Szymczak, Board of Governors, Federal Reserve System

Legal Advisers

Ansel Frank Luxford, Treasury Department; Chief Legal Adviser; later a senior World Bank official (1946-1951), including Assistant General Counsel (1948-1951)

Ben Cohen, Stabilization Board

Oscar Cox, Foreign Economic Administration

Ethan B. Stroud, Vice President, Federal Reserve Bank of Dallas

Secretary General of the Delegation: Charles S. Bell, Treasury Department

Assistants to the Chairman

Henrietta S. Klotz, Treasury Department

Margaret McHugh, Treasury Department

Frederik Smith, Treasury Department

Arthur Sweetser, Office of War Information; previously public information officer, League of Nations; later public information officer, United Nations

Technical Secretaries

Elting Arnold, Treasury Department

Richard B. Brenner, Treasury Department; later Assistant General Counsel, IMF (1946-1955)

Isador Lubin, Department of Labor; later U.S. representative to the Economic and Social Council of the United Nations (1950-1953)

George Luthringer, Department of State; later Alternate Executive Director, IMF (1946-1948); Director, Far Eastern, Middle Eastern, and Latin American Department, IMF (1950-1953); Director, Western Hemisphere Department, IMF (1953-1955)

Emanuel E. Minskoff, Treasury Department; later Director, Division of Foreign Assets Control, Treasury Department

Dorothy F. Richardson, Treasury Department; later married Solomon Adler (1945), a member of the Silvermaster spy ring (see just below); Richardson was not accused of being a member

(Nathan) Gregory Silvermaster, Director, Labor Division, Department of Agriculture; born in Russia; detailed to War Production Board; Chief Planning Technician, Procurement Division, Treasury Department; leader of a spy ring that passed secrets to the USSR

URUGUAY

Chairman: Mario La Gamma Acevedo, Expert, Ministry of Finance; Professor of Finance, University of Montevideo; later Governor, World Bank

Other delegate: Hugo García, Financial Attaché, Uruguayan Embassy, Washington; later Governor, IMF (1946-1947); Governor, World Bank (1946-1947)

VENEZUELA

Chairman: Rodolfo Rojas, Minister of the Treasury; formerly a banker

Other delegates

Alfonso Espinosa, President, Permanent Committee of Finance, Chamber of Deputies

Cristóbal L. Mendoza, Legal Adviser to the Banco Central de Venezuela; formerly Minister of Finance (19137-1938)

José Joaquín Gonzáles Gorrondona hijo, President, Office of Import Control; Director, Banco Central de Venezuela

Secretary: Manuel Pérez Guerrero, Chief, Office of the Committee for the Study of Post-War Questions, Ministry of Foreign Affairs; Professor of Economic and Social Sciences, Central University of Venezuela

YUGOSLAVIA

Chairman: Vladimir Rybar, Counselor, Yugoslav Embassy, Washington

Observers

DENMARK

Observer: Henrik de Kauffmann, Danish Minister (ambassador) at Washington

Adviser: Count Benedict Ahlefeldt-Laurvig, Financial Counselor, Danish Legation, Washington

LEAGUE OF NATIONS

Observer: Alexander Loveday, Director, Economic, Financial, and Transit Department

Alternate: Ragnar Nurkse; author, *International Currency Experience: Lessons of the Inter-War Period* (1944); later Professor of Economics, Columbia University

INTERNATIONAL LABOR OFFICE

Observer: Edward Joseph Phelan, Acting Director

Alternates

(Clarence) Wilfred Jenks, Legal Adviser; later Director-General, International Labour Organisation (1970-1973)

Edward John Riches, Acting Chief, Economic and Statistical Section

UNITED NATIONS INTERIM COMMISSION ON FOOD AND AGRICULTURE
Observer: Edward Twentyman, Delegate from the United Kingdom

UNITED NATIONS RELIEF AND REHABILITATION ADMINISTRATION
Observers
Abraham H. Feller, General Counsel
Mieczyslaw Sokolowski, Financial Adviser

Conference Secretariat

Secretary General: Warren H. Kelchner, Chief of the Division of International Conferences, U.S. Department of State
Technical Secretary General: (Virginius) Frank Coe, Assistant Administrator, U.S. Foreign Economic Administration; later Secretary, International Monetary Fund (1946-1952); member of a spy ring that passed secrets to the Soviet Union and was headed by Gregory Silvermaster, who also attended the conference
Assistant Secretary General: Philip Caryl Jessup, Professor of International Law, Columbia University; later U.S. representative to the United Nations (1948-1952); Judge, International Court of Justice (1961-1970)
Secretaries and Assistant Secretaries of Technical Commissions and Committees
Elting Arnold, U.S. Treasury Department; later General Counsel, Inter-American Development Bank
Henry J. Bittermann, U.S. Treasury Department; previously Associate? Professor of Economics, Ohio State University (1930s-1943); secretary, informal drafting committee, Atlantic City conference (1944)
Karl Bopp, Federal Reserve Board; later President, Federal Reserve Bank of Philadelphia
Alice Bourneuf, Federal Reserve Board; later Professor of Economics, Boston College
Richard B. Brenner, U.S. Treasury Department; later Assistant General Counsel, IMF (1946-1955)
William Adams Brown, Jr., U.S. Department of State; economist; author, *The International Gold Standard Reinterpreted, 1914-1934* (1940)
Malcolm Bryan, First Vice President, Federal Reserve Bank of Atlanta
Lauren Casaday, U.S. Treasury Department; labor economist
Eleanor Lansing Dulles, Office of Monetary Affairs, U.S. Department of State; economist; later active in postwar American economic reconstruction efforts in Austria and Germany

Charles Henry Dyson, Colonel, U.S. Army; helped establish administration of Lend Lease Program during World War II; later a pioneer of leveraged buyouts

Mordecai Ezekiel, U.S. Department of Agriculture; agricultural economist; described the "pork cycle"

John Fuqua, U.S. Department of State

Raymond French Mikesell, U.S. Treasury Department; later Professor of Economics, University of Oregon

Emanuel E. Minskoff, U.S. Treasury Department; later Director, Division of Foreign Assets Control, U.S. Treasury Department

Ruth B. Russell, U.S. Department of State; historian; later author of works on the United Nations

Orvis A. Schmidt, Acting Director, Bureau of Foreign Funds Control, U.S. Treasury Department; later a World Bank senior official (1947-1967), including Director, Western Hemisphere Department (1956-1964)

Arthur Smithies, U.S. Bureau of the Budget; later Professor of Economics, Harvard University

Leroy Dean Stinebower, Adviser, Office of Economic Affairs, U.S. Department of State; previously Chief, Division of Economic Studies, Department of State; later adviser or representative to many international economic and political conferences

Janet Sundelson, U.S. Treasury Department; economist

William Ludwig "Lud" Ullmann, Captain, U.S. Army; leading member of a spy ring that passed secrets to the Soviet Union and that was headed by Gregory Silvermaster, who also attended the conference; previously administrative assistant to Harry Dexter White and colleague of Frank Coe, both also conference participants, at the U.S. Treasury Department

Arthur P. Upgren, Federal Reserve Bank of Minneapolis

John Parke Young, Chief, Division of International Finance, U.S. Department of State; brother of Arthur Young, technical consultant to China at conference

Chief Press Relations Officer: Michael J. McDermott, Special Assistant to the U.S. Secretary of State

Assistant Press Relations Officers

Harold R. Beckley, Superintendent, U.S. Senate Press Gallery

George H. Coffelt, U.S. Treasury Department

John C. Pool, U.S. Department of State

Executive Secretary: Clarke L. Willard, Assistant Chief, Division of International Conferences, U.S. Department of State

Liaison Secretaries

Elbridge Durbrow, chief, Eastern European Division, U.S. Department of State; later U.S. Ambassador to South Vietnam (1957-1961)

James H. Wright, Foreign Service Officer, U.S. Department of State

Special Assistants to the Secretary General
Edward G. Miller, Jr., Adviser, Liberated Areas Division, U.S. Department of State
Ivan B. White, Foreign Service Officer, U.S. Department of State; later Deputy Assistant Secretary for European Affairs. U.S. Department of State
Administrative Secretary: Lyle L. Schmitter, U.S. Department of State
Assistant Administrative Secretary: P. Henry Mueller, U.S. Department of State
Chief of the Interpreting and Translating Bureau: Guillermo Suro, Acting Chief, Central Translating Division, U.S. Department of State
Secretary for Transportation and Special Services: M. Hamilton Osborne, U.S. Department of State
Editor of the "Journal": Frances Armbruster, U.S. Department of State

Officers of the Conference

President: Henry Morgenthau, Jr., Secretary, U.S. Department of the Treasury
Vice Presidents
Mikhail Stepanov, Deputy People's Commissar of Foreign Trade, USSR
Artur de Souza Costa, Minister of Finance, Brazil
Camille Gutt, Minister of Finance and Economic Affairs, Belgium
Leslie Melville, Economic Adviser to the Commonwealth Bank of Australia
Secretary General: Warren Kelchner, Chief, Division of International Conferences, U.S. Department of State
Technical Secretary General: Frank Coe, Assistant Administrator, U.S. Foreign Economic Administration
Assistant Secretary General: Philip Jessup, Professor of International Law, Columbia University

Organizational committees

COMMITTEE ON CREDENTIALS
Chairman: Eduardo Montoulieu (Cuba)
Wim Beyen (Netherlands)
Frank Gie (South Africa)
William Dennis (Liberia)
Wilhelm Keilhau (Norway)

COMMITTEE ON RULES AND REGULATIONS
Chairman: Hsiang-Hsi K'ung (China)
Guillermo Sevilla Sacasa (Nicaragua)
Ludwik Grosfeld (Poland)
Leslie Melville (Australia)

Ibrahim Kamal (Iraq)
Secretary: Philip Jessup

COMMITTEE ON NOMINATIONS
Chairman: Walter Nash (New Zealand)
Hugues Le Gallais (Luxembourg)
Julián Cáceres (Honduras)
Magnús Sigurðsson (Iceland)
Pedro Beltrán (Peru)

STEERING COMMITTEE
Chairman: Henry Morgenthau, Jr. (United States)
Camille Gutt (Belgium)
Artur de Souza Costa (Brazil)
James Ilsley (Canada)
Hsiang-Hsi K'ung (China)
Carlos Lleras Restrepo (Colombia)
Pierre Mendès-France (France)
Abol Hassan Ebtehaj (Iran)
Eduardo Suárez (Mexico)
Mikhail Stepanov (USSR)
John Maynard Keynes, Lord Keynes (United Kingdom)

COORDINATING COMMITTEE
Chairman: Fred Vinson (United States)
Artur de Souza Costa (Brazil)
Robert Mossé (France)
Eduardo Suárez (Mexico)
A.A. Arutiunian (USSR)
Lionel Robbins (United Kingdom)

Commission I: International Monetary Fund

Chairman: Harry White (United States)
Vice Chairman: Rodolfo Rojas (Venezuela)
Reporting Delegate: Louis Rasminsky (Canada)
Secretary: Leroy Stinebower
Assistant Secretary: Eleanor Lansing Dulles

COMMITTEE 1: PURPOSES, POLICIES, AND QUOTAS OF THE FUND
Chairman: Tingfu Tsiang (China)
Reporting Delegate: Kyriakos Varvaressos (Greece)

Secretary: William Brown, Jr.

COMMITTEE 2: OPERATIONS OF THE FUND
Chairman: Pavel Maletin (USSR)
Vice Chairman: William Mackintosh (Canada)
Reporting Delegate: Robert Mossé (France)
Secretary: Karl Bopp
Assistant Secretary: Alice Bourneuf

COMMITTEE 3: ORGANIZATION AND MANAGEMENT
Chairman: Artur de Souza Costa (Brazil)
Reporting Delegate: Ervin Hexner (Czechoslovakia)
Secretary: Malcolm Bryan
Assistant Secretary: Henry Bittermann

COMMITTEE 4: FORM AND STATUS OF THE FUND
Chairman: Manuel Llosa (Peru)
Reporting Delegate: Wilhelm Keilhau (Norway)
Secretary: Charles Dyson
Assistant Secretary: Lauren Casaday

COMMISSION I, AD HOC COMMITTEE ON DEPOSITORIES
Chairman: Peru
Members: Cuba, Czechoslovakia, France, Netherlands, South Africa, USSR, United Kingdom, United States
Secretary: Henry Bittermann

COMMISSION I, AD HOC COMMITTEE ON EXCHANGE CONTROLS ON CURRENT PAYMENTS
Chairman: China
Members: Canada, Costa Rica, France, Greece, Iran, Netherlands, New Zealand, USSR, United Kingdom, United States, Uruguay
Secretary: William Brown, Jr.

COMMISSION I, AD HOC COMMITTEE ON FURNISHING INFORMATION
(No details available)

COMMISSION I, AD HOC COMMITTEE ON QUOTAS
Chairman: Fred Vinson (United States)
Members: Camille Gutt (Belgium), Brazil, Canada, China, Cuba, Czechoslovakia, Egypt, France, India, Mexico, New Zealand, Norway, USSR, United Kingdom

COMMISSION I, AD HOC COMMITTEE ON RELATIONS WITH NON-MEMBER COUNTRIES
Chairman: Wilhelm Keilhau? (Norway)
Members: Canada, China, Cuba, Czechoslovakia, Iran, Netherlands, USSR, United Kingdom, United States
Secretary: Eleanor Dulles

COMMISSION I, AD HOC COMMITTEE ON SPECIAL PROBLEMS OF LIBERATED AREAS
Chairman: Netherlands
Members: Belgium, China, Colombia, Czechoslovakia, Ethiopia, France, Greece, Honduras, Luxembourg, Norway, Philippines, Poland, USSR, United Kingdom, United States, Yugoslavia
Secretary: John Young

COMMISSION I, AD HOC COMMITTEE ON UNIFORM CHANGES IN PAR VALUE [OF CURRENCIES; ARTICLE IV, SECTION 5]
Chairman: André Istel (France)
Members: Brazil, Canada, Czechoslovakia, Mexico, South Africa, USSR, United Kingdom, United States
Secretary: Karl Bopp

COMMISSION I, AD HOC COMMITTEE ON VOTING ARRANGEMENTS AND EXECUTIVE DIRECTORS
Chairman: Artur de Souza Costa (Brazil)
Members: Belgium, China, Cuba, Czechoslovakia, France, Netherlands, USSR, United Kingdom, United States (Ansel Luxford?)
Secretary: Malcolm Bryan

COMMISSION I, DRAFTING COMMITTEE
Chairman and Reporter: Louis Rasminsky (Canada)
Members: China, France, Mexico, Netherlands, USSR, Dennis Robertson? (United Kingdom), United States
Secretary: Leroy Stinebower

COMMISSION I, SPECIAL COMMITTEE ON UNSETTLED PROBLEMS
Chairman and Reporter: Edward Bernstein (United States)
Members: Brazil, Canada, China, Cuba, Czechoslovakia, France, Mexico, Netherlands, New Zealand, USSR, United Kingdom
Secretary: Leroy Stinebower

COMMISSION I, STANDING COMMITTEE
(No details available)

COMMITTEE 1, DRAFTING COMMITTEE
Chairman: Emanuel Goldenweiser (United States)
Members: Leslie Melville (Australia), Eugênio Gudin (Brazil), Tingfu Tsiang (China), Jan Mládek (Czechoslovakia), Kyriakos Varvaressos (Greece), India, Lionel Robbins (United Kingdom)

COMMITTEE 2, ASTERISK COMMITTEE (LANGUAGE COMMITTEE)
Chairman: United States
Members: China, Ecuador, France, South Africa, USSR

COMMITTEE 2, AD HOC COMMITTEE ON ARTICLE III, SECTION 2, [PARAGRAPH] (3) [PURCHASE OF CURRENCIES]
Chairman: France
Members: Australia, Brazil, Canada, China, Mexico, Netherlands, USSR, United Kingdom, United States

COMMITTEE 2, AD HOC COMMITTEE ON ARTICLE V, SECTIONS 3 AND 4 [CONDITIONS GOVERNING USE OF THE FUND'S RESOURCES]
(No details available)

COMMITTEE 2, AD HOC COMMITTEE ON ARTICLE XIII, SECTION 5 [FIXING INTIAL PAR VALUES]
(No details available)

COMMITTEE 3, AD HOC COMMITTEE ON OFFICERS AND VOTING
(No details available)

COMMITTEE 3, AD HOC COMMITTEE ON LIQUIDATION AND WITHDRAWAL [ARTICLE VIII, SECTIONS 3-4]
Chairman: Camille Gutt (Belgium)
Members: Australia, Mexico, United Kingdom, United States
Secretary: Henry Bittermann

COMMITTEE 3, AD HOC COMMITTEE ON ARTICLE VII, SECTION 2 [EXECUTIVE DIRECTORS]
Chairman: Luis Machado (Cuba)

Members: Camille Gutt (Belgium), Wim Beyen (Netherlands), Sir Wilfrid Eady (United Kingdom), Ansel Luxford (United States)

COMMITTEE 3, SECOND AD HOC COMMITTEE ON ARTICLE VII, SECTION 2 [EXECUTIVE DIRECTORS]
Chairman: Artur de Souza Costa (Brazil)
Members: Belgium, Brazil, Canada, China, Cuba, Czechoslovakia, Netherlands, Poland, USSR, United Kingdom, United States

COMMITTEE 4, AD HOC COMMITTEE ON ARTICLE IX, SECTION 7 [TAXATION OF THE IMF]
Chairman: United States
Members: Cuba, Norway, USSR, United Kingdom

COMMITTEE 4, AD HOC COMMITTEE ON ARTICLE XI, SECTION 7 [PUBLICATION OF REPORTS]
(No details available)

COMMITTEE 4, ASTERISK [DRAFTING] COMMITTEE
Chairman: Cuba
Members: China, Cuba, Ecuador, Poland, USSR, United Kingdom, United States
Secretary: Charles Dyson

Commission II: International Bank for Reconstruction and Development (World Bank)

Chairman: John Maynard Keynes, Lord Keynes (United Kingdom)
Vice Chairman: Luis Alamos Barros (Chile)
Reporting Delegate: Georges Theunis (Belgium)
Secretary: Arthur Upgren
Secretary: Arthur Smithies
Assistant Secretary: Ruth Russell

COMMITTEE 1: PURPOSES, POLICIES, AND CAPITAL OF THE BANK
Chairman: Wim Beyen (Netherlands)
Reporting Delegate: José Rafaël Oreamuno (Costa Rica)
Secretary: John Young
Assistant Secretary: Janet Sundelson

COMMITTEE 2: OPERATIONS OF THE BANK
Chairman: Eduardo Montoulieu (Cuba)

Reporting Delegate: James Brigden (Australia)
Secretary: Henry Bittermann
Assistant Secretary: Ruth Russell

COMMITTEE 3: ORGANIZATION AND MANAGEMENT
Chairman: Miguel López (Colombia)
Reporting Delegate: Michiel de Kock (South Africa)
Secretary: Mordecai Ezekiel
Assistant Secretary: William Ullmann

COMMITTEE 4: FORM AND STATUS OF THE BANK
Chairman: Sir Chintaman Deshmukh (India)
Reporting Delegate: Leon Baránski (Poland)
Secretary: Henry Edmiston
Assistant Secretary: Charles Dyson

COMMISSION II, AD HOC COMMITTEE ON SUBSCRIPTIONS
Chairman: Fred Vinson (United States)
Members: Belgium, Brazil, Canada, China, Cuba, Czechoslovakia, Egypt, France, India, Mexico, New Zealand, Norway, USSR, United Kingdom

COMMISSION II, AGENDA COMMITTEE
Chairman: United Kingdom (John Maynard Keynes)
Members: Brazil, Canada, China, Cuba, Czechoslovakia, France, India, USSR, United States

COMMISSION II, DRAFTING COMMITTEE
Chairman: United States (Dean Acheson)
Members: Brazil, Canada, China, Cuba, Czechoslovakia, France, India, USSR, United States, others

COMMISSION II, SPECIAL COMMITTEEE ON UNSETTLED PROBLEMS
Members: Belgium, Brazil, Canada, China, Czechoslovakia, France, India, Mexico, Netherlands, USSR, United Kingdom, United States

COMMITTEE 1, SUBCOMMITTEE 1A, AD HOC COMMITTEE (MEMBERSHIP IN THE FUND AND BANK)
Chairman: Wim Beyen (Netherlands); Emanuel Goldenweiser (United States), acting
Members: Australia, India, Norway, United Kingdom
Reporter: José Rafaël Oreamuno (Costa Rica)
Secretary: John Young

COMMITTEE 1, SUBCOMMITTEE 1B, AD HOC COMMITTEE (SUBSCRIPTIONS TO THE BANK)
Chairman: Wim Beyen (Netherlands)
Members: Wynne Plumptre (Canada), Te-Mou Hsi (China), André Istel (France), Anton Bestebreurtje (Netherlands), Nikolai Chechulin (USSR), George Bolton (United Kingdom), Norman Ness (United States)
Reporter: José Rafaël Oreamuno (Costa Rica)
Secretary: John Young

COMMITTEE 2, AD HOC COMMITTEE ON LOANS
Chairman: Eduardo Montoulieu (Cuba)

COMMITTEE 2, AD HOC COMMITTEE ON LOANS, SUBCOMMITTEE A
(No details available)

COMMITTEE 2, AD HOC COMMITTEE ON LOANS, SUBCOMMITTEE B
(No details available)

COMMITTEE 3, AD HOC COMMITTEE 3A
Reporter: Willem Naudé (South Africa)

COMMITTEE 3, AD HOC COMMITTEE 3B
Chairman: Miguel López Pumarejo (Peru)
Members: Belgium, Brazil, Canada, Colombia, China, Cuba, France, Netherlands, Norway, South Africa, USSR, United Kingdom, United Sates
Reporter: Michiel de Kock (South Africa)
Secretary: Mordecai Ezekiel

COMMITTEE 3, AD HOC COMMITTEE 3B: SPECIAL SUBCOMMITTEE
(No details available)

COMMITTEE 3, AD HOC COMMITTEE 3C
Chairman: Camille Gutt (Belgium)

COMMITTEE 4, AD HOC COMMITTEE: SUBCOMMITTEE 4A
Chairman: Sir Chintaman Deshmukh (India)
Members: Cuba, Czechoslovakia, Poland, United Kingdom, United States

Commission III: Other Means of International Financial Cooperation

Chairman: Eduardo Suárez (Mexico)
Vice Chairman: Mahmoud Saleh el Falaky (Egypt)
Reporting Delegate: Allan Fisher (New Zealand)
Secretary: Orvis Schmidt

COMMITTEE 1: THE USE OF SILVER FOR INTERNATIONAL MONETARY PUROPSES
Chairman: Andrés Dasso (Peru)
Members: Bolivia, Canada, Ethiopia, India, Mexico, Norway, USSR, United Kingdom, United States
Reporter: Kuo-Ching Li (China)

COMMITTEE 2: ENEMY ASSETS, LOOTED PROPERTY, AND RELATED MATTERS
Chairman: André Istel (France)
Members: Belgium, China, Dominican Republic, Netherlands, Poland, USSR, United Kingdom, Uruguay, Yugoslavia
Reporter: Wilhelm Keilhau (Norway)

COMMITTEE 3: RECOMMENDATIONS ON ECONOMC AND FINANCIAL POLICY, THE EXCHANGE OF INFORMATION, AND OTHER MEANS OF FINANCIAL COOPERATION
Chairman: Fernando Mardones (Chile), Germán Riesco (Chile)
Members: Australia, Bolivia, Brazil, Cuba, Czechoslovakia, Ecuador, Egypt, El Salvador, Greece, Iceland, Iraq, New Zealand, Nicaragua, Peru, South Africa, United Kingdom, United States
Reporter: Is Ibrahim Al-Kabir (Iraq)

COMMISSION III, AGENDA COMMITTEE
Chairman: Ludwik Grosfeld (Poland)
Members: Fernando Mardones (Chile), George Blowers (Ethiopia), Hugo García (Uruguay)
Reporter: Wim Beyen (Netherlands)

COMMISSION III, DRAFTING COMMITTEE ON LOOTED PROPERTY RESOLUTION
Chairman: André Istel (France)
Members: USSR, United Kingdom, United States
Reporter: Wilhelm Keilhau (Norway)

Appendix B

Schedule of Meetings

The schedule of meetings during the Bretton Woods is compiled from issues of the daily journal published for delegates to the conference and from other mentions in the conference proceedings or the transcripts. Some scheduled meetings never happened; other meetings happened outside the published schedule.

* Indicates meetings included in the transcripts.

Saturday, July 1, 1944

1200 Executive Meeting of the Chairmen of the Delegations / Banquet Room
1500 Inaugural Plenary Session / Auditorium
1700 Reception by the Delegation of the United States / Hemicycle Room
2100 Committee on Rules and Regulations / Hemicycle Room
2200 Committee on Nominations / Room B

Sunday, July 2, 1944

0900 Committee on Credentials / Room A
0900 Committee on Rules and Regulations / Hemicycle Room

Monday, July 3, 1944

1000 Second Plenary Session / Auditorium
1400 Commission I, first meeting* / Auditorium
1530 Commission II, first meeting / Auditorium
1700 Commission III, first meeting* / Auditorium

Tuesday, July 4, 1944

1000 Commission I, Committee 1, first meeting* / Auditorium
1100 Commission I, Committee 3, first meeting* / Hemicycle Room
1130 Commission I, Committee 2, first meeting* / Auditorium
1130 Commission I, Committee 4, first meeting* / Hemicycle Room
1600 Commission I, Committee 1, second meeting* / Auditorium
1600 Commission I, Committee 3, second meeting* / Hemicycle Room
1730 Commission I, Committee 2, second meeting* / Auditorium

1730 (reserved for Commission I, Committee 4, but not used) / Hemicycle Room
2100 Commission I, Committee 1, Drafting Committee / Room A

Wednesday, July 5, 1944
1030 Commission I, second meeting* / Auditorium
1600 Commission I, Committee 1, third meeting* / Auditorium
1600 Commission I, Committee 3, third meeting* / Hemicycle Room
1730 Commission I, Committee 2, third meeting* / Auditorium
1730 Commission I, Committee 4, second meeting* / Hemicycle Room

Thursday, July 6, 1944
1000 Commission I, Committee 1, fourth meeting* / Auditorium
1000 Commission I, Committee 3, fourth meeting* / Hemicycle Room
1400 Steering Committee / Room unknown
1430 Commission I, Committee 2, fourth meeting* / Auditorium
1430 Commission I, Committee 4, third meeting* / Hemicycle Room
1645 Commission II, Agenda Committee / Room 219
2100 Steering Committee / Room unknown
unknown Commission I, Committee 4, Ad Hoc Committee on Article IX, Section 7 / Room unknown

Friday, July 7, 1944
0930 Commission I, Committee 3, fifth meeting* / Hemicycle Room
1000 Commission I, Committee 1, Drafting Committee / Room A
1430 Commission I, Committee 2, fifth meeting* / Auditorium
1430 Commission I, Committee 4, fourth meeting* / Hemicycle Room
afternoon Commission I, Committee 4, Asterisk Committee / Hemicycle Room?
unknown Steering Committee / Room unknown

Saturday, July 8, 1944
0930 Commission I, Committee 1, fifth meeting* / Auditorium
0930 Commission I, Committee 3, sixth meeting* / Hemicycle Room
1130 Commission I, Committee 2, sixth meeting* / Auditorium
1130 Commission I, Committee 4, fifth (final) meeting* / Hemicycle Room
1430 Commission III, Agenda Committee / Room 219
unknown Commission I, Ad Hoc Committee on Election of Executive Directors / Room unknown

Sunday, July 9, 1944
1000 Commission I, Committee 3, unspecified subcommittee / Room unknown

1600 Committee on Special Problems of Liberated Areas / Room B
1700 Commission II, Agenda Committee / Room 219
1800 Commission I, Ad Hoc Committee on Relations with Non-Member Countries / Room B

Monday, July 10, 1944
0930 Commission I, third meeting* / Auditorium
1430 (Reserved for Commission I but not used) / Auditorium
1700 Commission III, second meeting* / Auditorium

Tuesday, July 11, 1944
1000 Commission I, Committee 3, seventh meeting* / Hemicycle Room
1030 Commission I, Ad Hoc Committee on Liberated Areas / Room A
1130 Commission I, Drafting Committee / Room B
1430 Commission I, Committee 2, seventh (final) meeting* / Hemicycle Room
1600 Commission II, second meeting* / Auditorium
1800 Commission I, Ad Hoc Committee on Relations with Non-Member Countries / Room B

Wednesday, July 12, 1944
0930 Commission I, Drafting Committee / Room A
0930 Commission II, Committee 3, Ad Hoc Committee C / Room B
0930 Commission II, Committee 3, Ad Hoc Committee A / Hemicycle Room
0930 Commission I, Ad Hoc Committee on Uniform Changes in Par Value [of Currencies; Article IV, Section 5] / Auditorium
1000 Commission I, Committee 2, eighth (final) meeting* / Auditorium
1130 Commission II, Committee 2, Ad Hoc Committee A / Room B
1200 Commission I, Ad Hoc Committee on Exchange Controls / Hemicycle Room
1430 Commission II, Committee 1, Ad Hoc Committee B / Room B
1430 Commission II, Committee 4, Ad Hoc Committee A / Hemicycle Room
1430 Commission I, Committee 1, sixth (final) meeting* / Auditorium
1630 Commission II, Committee 2, Ad Hoc Committee B / Room B
1630 Commission II, Committee 4, Ad Hoc Subcommittee A / Room unknown
1800 Commission I, Ad Hoc Committee on Exchange Controls and Current Payments / Room unknown
2030 Commission II, Drafting Committee Room A
2100 Commission I, Committee 3, Ad Hoc Committee on Executive Directors and Voting Arrangements / Room A

Thursday, July 13, 1944
0930 Commission II, Committee 3A / Room A
1100 Commission I, Drafting Committee / Room B
1130 Commission II, Committee 3B / Room A
1430 Commission I, fourth meeting* / Auditorium
1700 Commission II, third meeting / Auditorium
2030 Commission III, Committee 3 / Room A
2030 Commission II, Drafting Committee / Room unknown

Friday, July 14, 1944
0930 Commission II, Committee 3B / Room A
1000 Commission I, fifth meeting* / Auditorium
1100 Commission II, Committee 2, Ad Hoc Committee / Room B
1200 Commission III, Committee I / Room A
1430 (Reserved for Commission I but not used) / Auditorium
1430 Commission II, Committee 3B Hemicycle / Hemicycle Room
1430 Commission I, Committee 2, Ad Hoc Committee / Room B
1730 Commission III, Committee 2 / Room B
2030 Commission III, Committee 3, Drafting Committee / Room A

Saturday, July 15, 1944
0830 Commission I, Special Committee on Unsettled Problems / Room A
0930 Commission II, Ad Hoc Committee 3B / Auditorium
0930 Commission II, Ad Hoc Committee 3C / Hemicycle Room
1000 Commission I, Quota Committee / Room W-1
1000 Commission II, Committee 2, ad hoc Subcommittee / Room B
1000 Commission II, Drafting Committee / Auditorium
1130 Commission I, sixth meeting* / Auditorium
1600 Commission I, seventh meeting* / Auditorium?
1600 (Reserved for Commission II but not used) / Auditorium
2030 Commission I, Special Committee on Unsettled Problems / Room A?

Sunday, July 16, 1944
0930 Commission II, fourth meeting / Auditorium
1430 Commission II, Ad Hoc Committee 2 / Room B
1430 Commission II, Drafting Committee / Hemicycle Room
1500 Commission II, Ad Hoc Committee 3B / Room A
1800 Commission II, Ad Hoc Committee 3B / Room unknown

Monday, July 17, 1944
1000 Commission II, Committee 3C / Room A
1100 (Reserved for Commission I but not used) / Auditorium

1430 Commission II, Committee 2 / Room B
1700 (Reserved for Commission III but not used) / Auditorium

Tuesday, July 18, 1944
0930 Commission I, Special Committee on Unsettled Problems / Room A
1100 Commission II, Committee 2 / Room B
1130 Commission I, eighth meeting* / Auditorium
1630 Commission II / Auditorium
unknown Commission II, Committee 3C / Room unknown

Wednesday, July 19, 1944
0930 Commission II, Committee 2 / Room A
1130 Commission II, fifth meeting / Auditorium
1430 Commission II, Committee 2 / Room B
1530 (Reserved for Commission I but not used) / Auditorium
1630 Commission II, sixth meeting / Auditorium
2030 (Reserved for Commission III but not used) / Hemicycle Room
2100 Steering Committee / Room unknown
2115 Commission I, ninth (final) meeting* / Auditorium?

Thursday, July 20, 1944
0930 Commission II, Special Committee / Room A
1000 Commission II, seventh meeting / Auditorium
1400 Commission III, third (final) meeting* / Hemicycle Room
1530 Executive Plenary Session / Auditorium
1700 (Reserved for Commission II but not used) / Auditorium
unknown Commission II, Drafting Committee / Room unknown

Friday, July 21, 1944
0900 Commission II, Special Committee / Room A
1100 Commission II, eighth meeting / Auditorium
1400 Coordinating Committee / Room W-3
1800 Commission II, ninth (final) meeting / Auditorium?
1900 Executive Plenary Session / Auditorium

Saturday, July 22, 1944
1800 Coordinating Committee / Room unknown
1930 Farewell Dinner / Dining Room?
2145 Closing Plenary Session / Auditorium

Appendix C

List of Conference Documents

The list below of documents of the Bretton Woods conference, taken from the conference proceedings,[609] includes all conference documents, not just those mentioned in the transcripts. The code "SA" after some documents indicates that they were part of the Secretariat Agenda, meaning that they were alternatives to the preliminary draft Articles of Agreement for the IMF and World Bank that had been drawn up at a preliminary conference at Atlantic City, New Jersey, from June 15-30, 1944. Numbering such as "26 (21)" indicates that a later document, in this case Document 26, superseded an earlier one, in this case Document 21, because of later developments or corrections to printing errors.

Certain types of documents that occur frequently in the list deserve a short explanation. *Alternatives* were proposed amendments to the draft IMF or World Bank agreements or to the draft resolution of Commission III. The *order of the day* was a list of the major meetings and other events scheduled for a day. It was posted on its own and included in the *journal,* a daily newspaper of key conference documents and announcements. *News bulletins* summarized the progress of the war. *Press releases* marked the ceremonial aspects of the conference, especially its opening and closing, and allowed delegations to express their views to the world immediately for purposes of domestic politics or international diplomacy. The conference proceedings were not a suitable vehicle to let the world know a delegation's views because they would not be published for several years and because as a general rule they did not specify who said what in meetings. *Secretariat notices* concerned matters related to the operation of the conference.

Readers who refer to the two-volume conference proceedings should be aware that the volumes do not order documents strictly by number. Volume 1 orders its documents by number, but excludes from the sequence what the editors considered the less important documents. Volume 2 contains certain pre-conference documents; almost all press releases; and other material, listed at the end of this appendix. Volume 2

[609] Appendix II, pp. 1520-1534.

orders documents by group, and then by number within groups. All printed documents listed are in volume 1 unless otherwise noted.

Material in brackets is our addition to the list in the conference proceedings. For documents printed in the proceedings, our additional material comes from the proceedings themselves; for documents not printed in the proceedings, our material comes from copies of the unpublished source volumes of the proceedings.

Dates in brackets are the dates listed in the documents, or, if they have question marks after them, our guesses; the dates of publication may have been different. Page numbers in brackets indicate where documents fit into the preliminary draft agreements for the IMF or World Bank. The core document for the IMF agreement was Document 32;[610] the core document for the World Bank agreement was Document 245.[611] They and other especially important documents are **bolded.**

A notation of "not printed" means that a document is not separately printed in the conference proceedings. Some documents were printed more than once at the conference, but only once in the proceedings. The proceedings exclude news bulletins for delegates and notices of the conference secretariat about conference logistics. We have looked through copies of the unpublished source volumes of the proceedings, described in the introduction, and have photographed the documents we found there that were not printed in any form in the proceedings. They appear in an online companion file on the page for this book at the Web site of the Center for Financial Stability. A notation of "not found" means we found no copy in our search of the unpublished documents.

Documents

1 General Information [pre-conference; v. 2]
1½ Delegation of the United States of America [pre-conference; v. 2]
2 Provisional List of Members of the Delegations and Officers of the Conference (not printed) [not found]
2½ Officials of the Conference [pre-conference; v. 2]
3 Memorandum on Participation, Organization and Functions of Conference Officers and Units [pre-conference; v. 2]
4 Minutes and Résumés [pre-conference; v. 2]
5 Documents [pre-conference; v. 2]
5½ Regulations and Special Arrangements Covering Informational Cable, Radio, and Telephone Communication Facilities [pre-conference; v. 2]

610 Document 32, pp. 21-60.
611 Document 245, pp. 365-402.

6 Journal No. 1 [July 1]
7 Agenda [of the Conference]
8 Inaugural Plenary Session (Agenda) [July 1]
9 Press Release No. 1. Statement by Henry Morgenthau, Jr. [July 1; v. 2]
10 Press Release No. 2. Message from President Roosevelt to the Conference (not printed) [part of Document 40]
11 Inaugural Plenary Session (Agenda) [July 1]
12 Press Release No. 3. Program for the Inaugural Plenary Session [July 1; v. 2]
13 Draft Regulations of the Conference [July 1]
14 Regulations of the Conference [July 1]
15 Press Release No. 5. Response to President Roosevelt's Message by Ladislav Feierabend, Chairman of the Delegation of Czechoslovakia (not printed) [July 1; part of Document 40]
16 Press Release No. 4. Response to President Roosevelt's Message by Hsiang-Hsi K'ung, Chairman of the Delegation of China (not printed) [July 1; part of Document 40]
17 Press Release No. 6. Address by Eduardo Suárez, Chairman of the Delegation of Mexico (not printed) [July 1; part of Document 40]
18 Press Release No. 7. Address by Arthur [Artur] de Souza Costa, Chairman of the Delegation of Brazil (not printed) [July 1; part of Document 40]
19 Press Release No. 8. Address by J.L. Ilsley, Chairman of the Delegation of Canada (not printed) [July 1; part of Document 40]
20 Provisional Telephone Directory (not printed) [July 1; in online companion file]
21 Notice of Meeting of Committee on Rules and Regulations [July 1]
22 Notice of Meeting of Committee on Nominations [July 1]
23 Notice of Meeting of Committee on Credentials [July 1]
24 Press Release No. 9. Address by M.S. Stepanov, Chairman of the Delegation of the Union of Soviet Socialist Republics (not printed) [July 1; part of Document 40]
25 Document Registration and Order Form (not printed) [not found]
26 (21) Notice of Meeting of Committee on Rules and Regulations [corrected version of Document 21; July 1]
27 Order of the Day, July 2 (not printed) [part of Document 28]
28 Journal No. 2 [July 2]
29 Press Release No. 10. Message from Secretary of State Cordell Hull to Henry Morgenthau, Jr., Chairman of the United States Delegation [July 2; v. 2]
30 Secretariat Notice (not printed) [Package—Room No. (Form); July 2; not found]
31 Secretariat Notice (not printed) [Record Sheet; July 2; not found]

32 **Preliminary Draft of Suggested Articles of Agreement for Establishment of an International Monetary Fund** [July 1; preliminary draft IMF agreement; contains Joint Statement plus alternatives; core document for Commission I]
33 Secretariat Notice (not printed) [July 1; Numbering Duplication; in online companion file]
34 Regulations of the Conference [July 1]
35 Room Directory of the Chinese Delegation (not printed) [not found]
36 Committee on Nominations [minutes, July 1]
37 Press Release No. 11. Statement by Senator Robert F. Wagner, Delegate of the United States [July 2; v. 2]
38 Order of the Day, July 3 (not printed) [in Document 43]
39 Secretariat Notice (not printed) [July 1?; Maplewood-Mount Washington Bus Schedule; in online companion file]
40 Inaugural Plenary Session (Verbatim Minutes) [July 1]
41 Secretariat Notice (not printed) [Courier Service for Conference Mail; not found]
42 Provisional Telephone Directory (not printed) [not found]
43 Journal No. 3 [July 3]
44 Press Release No. 12. Address of Senator Charles W. Tobey, Delegate of the United States (not printed) [July 2; part of Document 63]
45 Secretariat Notice (not printed) [Special Note on Hotel Registration and Conference Directory; not found]
46 Notice to Chinese Delegation (not printed) [not found]
47 Opening Remarks of Lord Keynes at First Meeting of the Second Commission on the Bank for Reconstruction and Development [July 3]
48 Press Release No. 13. Addenda Committees for Commissions II and III [July 3; v. 2]
49 Press Release No. 14. Remarks by Eduardo Suárez, Chairman of Commission III, at First Session [July 3; v. 2]
50 Secretariat Notice (not printed) [Representations of the Delegates on Commissions and Committees; in online companion file]
51 Commission I, Committee Assignments
52 Report of the Committee on Rules and Regulations [July 1]
53 Minutes of the Committee on Rules and Regulations [July 1]
54 Secretariat Notice (not printed) [July 3; Attendance List of Committees; in online companion file]
55 Journal No. 4 [July 4]
56 Proposal on Voting Changes in Rates of Member Currencies [submitted by Mexico, July 3; p. 17a of IMF draft]
57 Order of the Day, July 4 (not printed) [part of Document 55]
58 Minutes of Meeting of Commission I, July 3

59 Opening Remarks of Harry D. White at First Meeting of the Commission of the International Monetary Fund [July 3]
60 Minutes of Meeting of Commission II, July 3
61 Minutes of Meeting of Commission III, July 3
62 Conferencia Monetaria y Financiera de las Naciones Unidas. Reglamento [translation of Document 14; v. 2]
63 Verbatim Minutes of Second Plenary Session [July 3]
64 List of Correspondents [July 4; v. 2; registration form in online companion file]
65 Press Release No. 15. Statement by Hsiang-Hsi K'ung, Chairman of the Delegation of China [July 4; v. 2]
66 Agenda of the Conference (Spanish translation) [v. 2]
67 Secretariat Notice (not printed) [July 4; Emergency Transportation of U.S. Group to Crawford House; in online companion file]
68 Secretariat Notice (not printed) [July 4; Luncheon Arrangements for Members of Conference in Residence at Crawford House; in online companion file]
69 Report of Committee on Credentials [July 2]
70-99 (numbers not used)
100 Order of the Day, July 5 (not printed) [part of Document 101]
101 Journal No. 5 [July 5]
102 Minutes of Meeting of Commission I, Committee 1, July 4
103 Minutes of Meeting of Commission I, Committee 3, July 4
104 Minutes of Meeting of Commission I, Committee 2, July 4
105 Minutes of Meeting of Commission I, Committee 4, July 4
106 Secretariat Notice (not printed) [July 4; Procedure for Handling Correspondence; not found]
107 Alternative E (SA/1/1) [July 4; p. 6d of IMF draft]
108 Alternative B (SA/1/2) [July 4; p. 18a of IMF draft]
109 Alternative H (SA/1/3) [July 4; p. 1d of IMF draft]
110 Alternative E (SA/1/4) [July 4; p. 11b of IMF draft]
111 Minutes of Meeting of Commission I, Committee 1, July 4
112 Minutes of Meeting of Commission I, Committee 2, July 4
113 Minutes of Meeting of Commission I, Committee 3, July 4
114 Directory of the Conference (not printed) [July 4; telephone directory; in online companion file]
115 News Bulletin No. 1 (not printed) [July 5; in online companion file]
116 Proposal on Silver (Mexican Delegation) [July 5?; relates to p. 6d of IMF draft]
117 Memorandum Submitted by the Egyptian Delegation Requesting Certain Additions to Joint Statement [Article] I, "Purposes and Policies of the Fund" [July 5?; p. 1 of IMF draft]

118 Proposal on Voting a Uniform Change in the Gold Value of Member Currencies (Mexican Delegation) [July 5?; p. 18 of IMF draft]
119 News Bulletin No. 2 (not printed) [July 5; in online companion file]
120 Joint Statement (SA/1/5) [July 5; p. 41 of IMF draft]
121 Joint Statement (SA/1/6) [July 5; p. 43 of IMF draft]
122 Report of Drafting Committee of Committee 1, Commission I, on Matters Referred to it at Meeting of Committee 1 on July 4 [July 5]
123 Mensaje del Excelentissimo Señor Franklin D. Roosevelt, Presidente de los Estados Unidos de America, a la Conferencia [July 1; translation of part of Document 40; v. 2]
124 Joint Statement, VIII, 2 and 3 (SA/1/7) [July 5; pp. 36-36a of IMF draft]
125 Report of Committee 1 on Purposes, Policies and Quotas of the Fund to Commission I [July 5]
126 Report of Committee 3 on Organization and Management of the Fund to Commission I [July 5]
127 Report of Committee 4 on Form and Status of the Fund to Commission I [July 5]
128 Report of Committee 2 on Operations of the Fund to Commission I [July 5]
129 Report of Special Committee on Furnishing Information of the Pre-Conference Agenda Committee [June 28]
130 News Bulletin No. 3 (not printed) [July 5; in online companion file]
131 (7) Agenda of the Conference (corrected copy) [July 5?; corrected version of Document 7]
132 Minutes of Meeting of Commission I, July 5
133 Secretariat Notice (not printed) [Requests for Documents; in online companion file]
134 Secretariat Notice (not printed) [Notification for Prospective Arrivals and Departures; not found]
135 Press Release No. 16. Statement by the Delegation of Mexico [July 5; v. 2]
136 Press Release No. 17. Statement by the Delegation of Uruguay [July 5; v. 2]
137 Journal No. 6 [July 6]
138 Minutes of Meeting of Committee I of Commission I, July 5
139 Order of the Day, July 6 (not printed) [part of Document 137]
140 Minutes of Meeting of Committee 2 of Commission I, July 5
141 Minutes of Meeting of Committee 3 of Commission I, July 5
142 Minutes of Meeting of Committee 4 of Commission I, July 5
143 Joint Statement (SA/1/8) [July 6; pp. 14-14a of IMF draft]
144 Alternative B (SA/1/9) [July 5; p. 9a of IMF draft]
145 Alternative C (SA/1/10) [July 5; p. 2b of IMF draft]
146 Alternative D (SA/1/11) [July 5; p. 4b of IMF draft]

147 Alternative F (SA/1/12) [July 5; p. 6c of IMF draft]
148 Alternative F (SA/1/13) [July 5; p. 11c of IMF draft]
149 Alternative B (SA/1/14) [July 5; p. 10a of IMF draft]
150 Alternative D (SA/1/15) [July 5; p. 25g of IMF draft]
151 Alternative C (SA/1/16) [July 5; pp. 25d-25f of IMF draft]
152 Combined Alternatives A and B for Joint Statement VII, I, 2, and 3, and Additional Material on P. 27 of Document SA/1 (32) [July 5?; pp. 26-26c of IMF draft]
153 Memorandum [on Par Values] to be Submitted to Commission I, Committee 2 (Egyptian Delegation) [July 5?]
154 News Bulletin No. 4 (not printed) [July 6; in online companion file]
155 Secretariat Chart [for Committee Reports] (not printed) [in online companion file]
156 Representation of Delegations on Commissions and Committees [July 5?]
157 Address Delivered Before Committee 2 of Commission I, by Antonio Espinosa de los Monteros, Mexican Delegate, in Support of Mexico's Proposal on Silver [July 5]
158 Declaración Conjunta de los Peritos sobre el Establecimiento de un Fondo Monetario Internacional [translation of Joint Statement by Experts on the Establishment of an International Monetary Fund; v. 2]
159 Biographic Data (not distributed) (not printed) [in online companion file]
160 (25) Document Registration and Order Form (not printed) [supersedes Document 25; not found]
161 Alternative I (SA/1/18) [July 6; p. 1b of IMF draft]
162 Revised Amendment to Joint Statement I, Subdivision 2, proposed by Indian Delegation [July 6?; p. 1 of IMF draft]
163 Secretariat Notice (not printed) [July 6?; Crawford House Bus Service; not found]
164 Alternative C (SA/1/19) [July 6?; p. 18b of IMF draft]
165 News Bulletin No. 5 (not printed) [July 6; in online companion file]
166 Joint Statement IV, 1 (SA/1/20) [July 1; p. 16 of IMF draft]
167 Statement by Mahmoud Saleh el Falaki [Falaky], Delegate for Egypt, in Support of Alternative H, Article I, "Purposes and Policies of the Fund," Made Before Committee 1, Commission I [July 6]
168 Journal No. 7 [July 7]
169 Proposal for a Bank for Reconstruction and Development [July 7]
170 Order of the Day, July 7 (not printed) [part of Document 168]
171 Minutes of Meeting of Committee 2, Commission I, July 6
172 Minutes of Meeting of Committee 1, Commission I, July 6
173 Minutes of Meeting of Committee 3, Commission I, July 6
174 Minutes of Meeting of Committee 4, Commission I, July 6
175 Procedural Decisions of the Steering Committee [July 6]

176 News Bulletin No. 6 (not printed) [July 7; in online companion file]
177 Alternative B (SA/1/21) [July 6; p. 16a of IMF draft]
178 Alternative C (SA/1/22) [July 6; p. 26d of IMF draft]
179 Alternative D (SA/1/23) [July 6; p. 26e of IMF draft]
180 Alternative B (SA/1/24) [July 6; p. 36b of IMF draft]
181 Alternative D (SA/1/25) [July 6; p. 29b of IMF draft]
182 Alternative C (SA/1/26) [July 7; p. 14c of IMF draft]
183 Alternative B (SA/1/27) [July 7; p. 17b of IMF draft]
184 (canceled) [issued as Document 190 (184)]
185 Press Release No. 19. Bond Wagon Tour [July 7; v. 2]
186 Status of Business before Committee 3, Commission I [July 7]
187 Agreement on Earmarked Gold (Mexican Delegation) [for Commission III; July 7?]
188 Press Release No. 20. Statement by J.E. Holloway, Delegate of the Union of South Africa [July 7; apparently a statement to Commission I, Committee 2; v. 2]
189 Mexico's Proposal on Silver [to Commission III; July 7?]
190 (184) Press Release No. 18. Address by H.H. K'ung, Chairman of the Delegation of China [July 7; v. 2]
191 Alternative A (SA/1/29) [July 7; p. 43b of IMF draft]
192 Second Report of Drafting Committee of Committee 1, Commission I [July 7]
193 News Bulletin No. 7 (not printed) [July 7; in online companion file]
194 Alternative B (SA/1/28) [July 7; p. 43a of IMF draft]
195 Alternative J (SA/1/30) [July 7; p. 1f of IMF draft]
196 Alternative C (SA/1/31) [July 7; p. 40a of IMF draft]
197 Esbozo Preliminar de un Proyecto de Banco de Reconstrucción y Fomento de las Naciones Unidas y Asociadas [translation, but does not seem entirely based on Document 169; v. 2]
198 Report of the Subcommittee (Committee 4, Commission I) to Consider Article IX, Section 7; Report of the Asterisk Committee [July 7]
199 Journal No. 8 [July 8]
200 Minutes of Meeting of Committee 3, Commission 1, July 7
201 (156) Representation of Delegations on Commissions and Committees [July 7; updates Document 156]
202 Commission I, Status of Committee Assignments [July 7]
203 Alternative D (SA/1/32) [July 7; p. 14e of IMF draft]
204 Minutes of Meeting of Committee 4, Commission I, July 7
205 Minutes of Meeting of Committee 2, Commission I, July 7
206 Order of the Day, July 8 (not printed) [part of Document 199]
207 Substitute Alternative A (SA/1/33) [July 7; pp. 23b-23c of IMF draft]
208 Alternative A (SA/1/34) [July 7; pp. 17a-17aa of IMF draft]
209 Joint Statement (SA/1/35) [July 7; p. 48 of IMF draft]

210 Joint Statement (SA/1/36) [July 7; p. 35 of IMF draft]
211 Joint Statement (SA/1/37) [July 7; pp. 37-37b of IMF draft]
212 Final Alternative Submitted by the Special Subcommittee Appointed to Consider All Proposals Relative to the Executive Directors [July 8?]
213 News Bulletin No. 8 (not printed) [July 8; in online companion file]
214 Alternative E (SA/1/38) [July 8; p. 26f of IMF draft]
215 Proposed Amendment to Article IX, Section 2, Gold Purchases Based on Parity Prices [July 8?; proposed by Colombia; p. 2 of Document 192 and refers to p. 39 of IMF draft]
216 Alternative K (SA/1/39) [July 8; p. 1g of IMF draft]
217 Alternative C (SA/1/40) [July 8; p. 17c of IMF draft]
218 Draft Resolution [on Employment] Submitted by Australian Representatives [for Commission III; July 8?]
219 Alternative D (SA/1/41) [July 8; p. 40b of IMF draft]
220 Alternative C (SA/1/42) [July 8; p. 37c of IMF draft]
221 Report Submitted to Committee 3, Commission I, by the Special Subcommittee Appointed to Consider the Various Proposals Relative to the Organization, Election and Powers of the Executive Directors [July 7]
222 News Bulletin No. 9 (not printed) [July 8; in online companion file]
223 Journal No. 9 [July 9]
224 Minutes of Meeting of Committee 1, Commission I, July 8
225 Minutes of Meeting of Committee 2, Commission I, July 8
226 Minutes of Meeting of Committee 3, Commission I, July 8
227 Minutes of Meeting of Committee 4, Commission I, July 8
228 Order of the Day, July 9 (not printed) [part of Document 223]
229 News Bulletin No. 10 (canceled)
230 Conférence Monétaire et Financière des Nations Unies. Règlement [translation of Document 14; v. 2]
231 Officers of the Conference, Members of the Delegations, Officers of the Secretariat [July 8?]
232 Secretariat Form (not printed) [not found]
233 Second Report of Committee 4, Commission I [meeting of July 5]
234 Second Report of Committee 2 on Operations of the Fund to Commission I [July 9]
235 Report Submitted to Commission III by the Agenda Committee Appointed to Receive and Consider Proposals Submitted for Consideration in Commission [July 10; core document for Commission III]
236 Alternative B (SA/1/43) [July 9; p. 39a of IMF draft]
237 Alternative G (SA/1/44) [July 9; p. 26g of IMF draft]
238 Report of the Reporting Delegate of Committee 1, Commission I, on Purposes, Policies, and Quotas of the Fund [July 9]

239 Report of Committee 3, Commission I, on Organization and Management of the Fund [July 9]
240 (202) Commission I, Status of Committee Assignments [July 9; updates Document 202]
241 Alternative B (SA/1/45) [July 9; p. 37bb of IMF draft]
242 Alternative C to Article VIII, Section 3 (SA/1/46) [July 9; pp. 36-36f of IMF draft]
243 Report of Subcommittee of Committee 3, Commission I, on Liquidation and Withdrawal
244 Journal No. 10 [July 10]
245 Preliminary Draft of Proposals for the Establishment of a Bank for Reconstruction and Development (SA/3) [July 10; preliminary draft World Bank agreement; core document for Commission II]
246 Order of the Day, July 10 (not printed) [part of Document 244]
247 (201) Representation of Delegations on Commissions and Committees [July 10; updates Document 201]
248 News Bulletin No. 10 (not printed) [July 10; in online companion file]
249 Report of Ad Hoc Committee of Commission I on Voting Arrangements and Executive Directors [July 10]
250 United Kingdom Delegation Memorandum to Commission I [on capacities and immunities of the IMF; July 10?]
251 Speech of A. D. Shroff, Delegate for India, before Committee 1, Commission I, on July 6, Supporting the Egyptian Amendment to Article I, "Purposes and Policies of the Fund"
252 Press Release No. 21. Proposals by the Norwegian Delegation [to Commission III; July 10; v. 2]
253 (canceled) [not found]
254 Press Release No. 23. Proposal of the Bolivian Delegation to Commission III [on commodities; July 10; v. 2]
255 Second Report of Committee 4, Commission I [meeting of July 5]
256 Report Submitted to Commission III by the Agenda Committee Appointed to Receive and Consider Proposals Submitted for Consideration in Commission III [on Norway's proposal for a gold unit; July 10]
257 Press Release No. 22. Statement on Behalf of the United States Delegation at Meeting of Commission I [July 10; v. 2]
258 Press Release No. 24. Statement by Lord Keynes on Behalf of the Delegation of the United Kingdom at Meeting of Commission I [July 10; v. 2]
259 Press Release No. 25. Statement by A.D. Shroff, Member of the Indian Delegation, at Meeting of Commission I [July 10; v. 2]
260 Press Release No. 26. Statement by Mr. Istel, French Delegate, at Meeting of Commission I [July 10; v. 2]

261 Conférence Monétaire et Financière des Nations Unies [translation of Document 7; v. 2]
262 Press Release No. 27. Norwegian Proposal to Commission III [on a gold unit; July 10; v. 2]
263 News Bulletin No. 11 (not printed) [July 10; in online companion file]
264 Statement by the Cuban Delegation on Article III, Section 2(c) [July 10?; p. 6 of IMF draft]
265 Proposal of the Bolivian Delegation to Commission III [on trade; July 10?]
266 Alternative C (SA/1/47) [July 10; p. 39 of IMF draft]
267 Minutes of Third Meeting of Commission I, July 10
268 Journal No. 11 [July 11]
269 Secretariat Notice (not printed) [Transportation Form—Estimate of Special Trains Space; not found]
270 Secretariat Notice (not printed) [Transportation Form—Pullman Sleeper Space on Special Trains; not found]
271 Order of the Day, July 11 (not printed) [part of Document 268]
272 Alternative J (SA/3/1) [July 11; p. 15f of World Bank draft]
273 Alternative C (SA/3/2) [July 11; p. 20a of World Bank draft]
274 Alternative E (SA/3/3) [July 11; p. 22e of World Bank draft]
275 Alternative C (SA/3/4) [July 11; p. 24a of World Bank draft]
276 Alternative B (SA/3/5) [July 11; p. 15a of World Bank draft]
277 Combined Alternatives A and B (SA/1/48) [July 11; p. 13a of IMF draft]
278 Section 5. Fixing Initial Par Values (SA/1/49) [July 10; p. 50 of IMF draft]
279 Minutes of Meeting of Commission III, July 10
280 Text of Provisions Recommended by Committees (Working Paper for Drafting Committee of Commission I) [July 10]
281 Use of Currencies Held by the Fund (Memorandum to Committee 2) [July 11?]
282 News Bulletin No. 12 (not printed) [July 11?; not found]
283 Press Release No. 28. Statement by the Delegation of Panama [on the Bretton Woods conference; July 11; v. 2]
284 Alternative D (SA/1/50) [July 11; p. 18c of IMF draft]
285 Minimum Percentage Charges Payable by a Country on Fund's Holdings of Its Currency in Excess of Its Quota [July 11?; p. 13a of IMF draft]
286 Memorandum Submitted to Commission II by United Nations Interim Commission on Food and Agriculture [July 11?]
287 Proposal for a Conference to Promote Stability in the Prices of Primary International Commodities [submitted by Brazil to Commission III; July 11?]

288 Draft Resolution Submitted to Commission III by Cuban Representatives [on an international conference on trade and staples; alternative to proposal No. 9 of Document 235; July 11?]
289 Draft Resolution Submitted to Commission III by Chilean Representatives [on promoting production, including staples, in weaker countries; alternative to proposal No. 9 of Document 235; July 11?]
290 Proposed Amendment to Draft, Commission II (Mexican Delegation) [July 11?; p. 2 of World Bank draft]
291 News Bulletin No. 13 (not printed) [July 11; in online companion file]
292 (114) Revised Directory of the Conference (not printed) [updates Document 114; in online companion file]
293 Alternative G (SA/3/6) [July 11; p. 2d of World Bank draft]
294 Alternative A (SA/1/52) [July 11; p. 50b of IMF draft]
295 Revised Wording of Article II, Section 5, Suggested by the Drafting Committee of Commission I and Submitted to Committee 1 [July 11?; p. 4 of IMF draft]
296 Proposals Put Before Committee 2, Commission I, July 11
297 Alternative H (SA/3/7) [July 12; p. 2d of World Bank draft]
298 Commission II, Schedule of Work Assignments to Committees and Subcommittees of Bank Commission [July 11?]
299 Journal No. 12 [July 12]
300 Minutes of Meeting of Commission II, July 11
301 Order of the Day, July 12 (not printed) [part of Document 299] [in online companion file]
302 Minutes of Meeting of Committee 2, Commission I, July 11
303 Minutes of Meeting of Committee 3, Commission I, July 11
304 Alternative A (SA/1/53) [July 11; p. 51 of IMF draft]
305 News Bulletin No. 14 (not printed) [July 12; in online companion file]
306 Press Release No. 29. Statement by Delegation of Mexico at Meeting of Commission II, July 11 [on the proposal in Document 290; v. 2]
307 Third Report of Drafting Committee of Committee 1, Commission I [July 11]
308 Discurso Pronunciado por el Señor Henry A. Morgenthau, Jr., Secretario de Hacienda de los Estados Unidos de America, al Aceptar la Presidencia de la Conferencia en la Sesión Plenaria Inaugural del 1° de Julio [translation of part of Document 40; v. 2]
309 Proyecto Preliminar de Proposiciones Para Establecer un Banco de Reconstrucción y Fomento [partial translation of Document 245; v. 2]
310 Alternative J (SA/I/54) [July 12; p. 26j of IMF draft]
311 Ad Hoc Committee of Commission I on Relations with Non-Member Countries [July 11; p. 38 of IMF draft]
312 News Bulletin No. 15 (not printed) [July 12; in online companion file]
313 Alternative J (SA/3/8) [July 12; p. 2e of World Bank draft]

314 Alternative C (SA/3/9) [July 12; p. 12a of World Bank draft]
315 Alternative E (SA/1/55) [July 12; p. 25h of IMF draft]
316 Joint Statement (SA/1/56) [July 12; p. 43c of IMF draft]
317 Amendment to Article VII, I, of Joint Statement (Egyptian Delegation) [July 12?; p. 25d of IMF draft]
318 Third Report of Committee 3 to Commission I [July 12?]
319 Journal No. 13 [July 13]
320 Report of Drafting Committee of Commission I—Annex I [July 13?; outline of the intermediate, "New Testament" draft that formed the basis of later deliberations]
321 Report of Drafting Committee of Commission I—Annex II [July 13?; text of the intermediate, "New Testament" draft that formed the basis of later deliberations]
322 Order of the Day, July 13 (not printed) [part of Document 319]
323 Alternative A (SA/1/57) [July 12; p. 44a of IMF draft]
324 Alternative B (SA/3/10) [July 12; p. 31e of World Bank draft]
325 Minutes of Meeting of Committee 2, Commission I, July 12
326 Minutes of Meeting of Committee 1, Commission I, July 12
327 Alternative C (SA/3/11) [July 12; p. 14a of World Bank draft]
328 Alternative K (SA/1/58) [July 12; p. 26m of IMF draft]
329 Report of Ad Hoc Committee of Commission I [on Article X, Section 4, exchange controls on current payments; July 12]
330 Report of Subcommittee 1a, Committee 1 of Commission II [July 12]
331 Report of Subcommittee 1b, Committee 1 of Commission II [July 12]
332 Alternative B (SA/3/12) [July 12; p. 31e of World Bank draft]
333 Report of Committee 2 to Commission I Concerning Meetings of July 11 and 12
334 Report of Ad Hoc Committee of Committee 3 on Executive Directors and Voting Arrangements to Commission I [July 12]
335 Report of Ad Hoc Subcommittee A of Committee 4, Commission II [July 12]
336 Report of Subcommittees A and B of Committee 2, on Operations of the Bank, to Commission II [July 13]
337 Text of Provisions Recommended by Committee 2A and Committee 2B (Working Paper for Drafting Committee of Commission II) [July 12]
338 Report of Ad Hoc Committee 3C of Commission II [July 12]
339 News Bulletin No. 16 (not printed) [July 13; in online companion file]
340 Report of Drafting Committee, Commission II [July 13]
341 Article XVI—Amendments (Addition Proposed by U.K. Delegation) [July 13?; p. 26 of Document 321 on IMF articles]
342 First Report of Drafting Committee of Commission I [July 13]
343 Third Report of Reporting Delegate of Committee I, Commission I [July 13]

344 Article XVI—Amendments (Addition Proposed by U.K. Delegation) [July 13?; p. 26 of Document 321 on IMF articles]
345 Addition to Alternative C (SA/1/59) [July 13; p. 14c of IMF draft]
346 Alternative L (SA/1/60) [July 13; p. 26n of IMF draft]
347 (278) Alternative B (SA/1/61) [July 13; pp. 50c-50e of IMF draft]
348 Alternative D (SA/3/13) [July 13; p. 1b of World Bank draft]
349 Memorandum from Delegation of EI Salvador to Assistant Secretary General and Technical Secretary General [July 13; refers to p. 1 of World Bank draft]
350 (314) Alternative C (SA/3/14) [p. 12a of World Bank draft; corrected version of Document 314]
351 Initial Par Values (Addition to Article XIX, Section 4, of Document 321 on IMF articles) [July 13]
352 Report of Ad Hoc Committee 3B to Commission II [July 13]
353 Press Release No. 30. Statement by Antonio Espinosa de los Monteros, Mexican Delegate, before Commission I, July 14, on Changing the Gold Parities of Currencies [July 14; v. 2]
354 Report to Commission II on Actions by Ad Hoc Committee 3A [July 13]
355 Discours Prononcé le 1er Juillet 1944 par M. Henry A. Morgenthau, Jr., Secrétare du Trésor des États-Unis d'Amérique, à l'Occasion de la Séance d'Ouverture de la Conférence Monétaire et Financière des Nations Unies, à Bretton Woods, New Hampshire [translation of part of Document 40; v. 2]
356 News Bulletin No. 17 (not printed) [July 13; in online companion file]
357 Article VIII—Amendments (Recommended by Drafting Committee) (SA/3/15) [July 13; p. 53a of World Bank draft]
358 Article IX, Interpretation of the Agreement (SA/3/16) [July 13; p. 54a of World Bank draft]
359 Article VII, Status, Immunities and Privileges of the Bank (SA/3/17) [July 13; pp. 49a-52a of World Bank draft]
360 Commission II, Second Report of Drafting Committee [July 13]
361 Journal No. 14 [July 14]
362 Statement by the Polish Minister in Commission II Meeting [July 13]
363 Article I; Substitute for Alternatives A to G (SA/3/17) [July 13; p. 2f of World Bank draft]
364 Article III (1); Substitute for Alternatives A, B, and C (SA/3/18) [July 13; p. 12ba of World Bank draft]
365 Article IV (8); Substitute for Alternative A (SA/3/19) [July 13; pp. 26a-26b of World Bank draft]
366 Article IV (9); Substitute for Alternative A (SA/3/20) [July 13; p. 27a of World Bank draft]
367 Article IV (10); Substitute for Alternative A (SA/3/21) [July 13; p. 28a of World Bank draft]

368 Article V (9); Substitute for Alternative A (SA/3/22) [July 13; p. 37a of World Bank draft]
369 Order of the Day, July 14 (not printed) [part of Document 361]
370 Minutes of Meeting of Commission I, July 13
370 (Correction) Correction to Minutes of Meeting of Commission I, July 13
371 Text of Provisions Recommended by Ad Hoc Committee 3C of Commission II (Working Paper for Drafting Committee of Commission II) [July 13]
372 Text of Provisions Recommended by Ad Hoc Committee 3B of Commission II (Working Paper for Drafting Committee of Commission II) [July 13]
373 (canceled)
374 Report of Special Committee of Commission I [July 14]
375 News Bulletin No. 18 (not printed) [July 14; in online companion file]
376 Alternative D (SA/1/63) [July 14; pp. 37d-37e of IMF draft]
377 (363) Article I; Substitute for Alternatives A to G (SA/3/23) [July 14; p. 2f of World Bank draft; corrected version of Document 363]
378 Alternative B (SA/3/24) [July 14; p. 52b of World Bank draft]
379 Message de M. Franklin D. Roosevelt, Président des États-Unis d'Amerique, Addressé le 1er Juillet 1944 aux Membres de la Conférence [translation of part of Document 40; v. 2]
380 Supplemental Report of Ad Hoc Subcommittee A of Committee 4, Commission II [July 13]
381 Minutes of Meeting of Commission II, July 13
382 News Bulletin No. 19 (not printed) [July 14; in online companion file]
383 Press Release No. 31. Statement by Sir Shanmukham Chetty, Indian Delegate, before Commission I [July 14; v. 2]
384 Text of Provisions Recommended by Ad Hoc Committee 3B of Commission II (Working Paper for Drafting Committee of Commission II) [July 14]
385 Report of Committee 3B, Commission II [July 14]
386 Statement of Sir Shanmukham Chetty, Indian Delegate, Before Commission I [July 14; v. 2]
387 Commission II—Status Report [July 14?]
388 Journal No. 15 [July 15]
389 Third Report of Drafting Committee, Commission II [July 14]
390 Order of the Day, July 15 (not printed) [part of Document 388]
391 Commission II—Fourth Report of Drafting Committee [July 15]
392 (canceled)
393 Minutes of Meeting of Commission I, July 14
394 Report of Ad Hoc Committee 2, Commission II [July 15]
395 Report of Quota Committee of Commission I [July 15]
396 News Bulletin No. 20 (not printed) [July 15; in online companion file]

397 International Monetary Fund (Purposes, Methods, Consequences) [July 8]
398 Commission II, Documents to be Considered at Meeting [July 15]
399 Report of Meeting of Ad Hoc Committee 2, Commission II [July 15]
400 Article VI: Alternative D (SA/3/25) [July 15; p. 45a of World Bank draft]
401 Minutes and Report of Reporter, Subcommittee 3C, Commission II [July 15]
402 (canceled)
403 Alternative E (SA/1/65) [July 15; p. 29c of IMF draft]
404 News Bulletin No. 21 (not printed) [July 15; in online companion file]
405 Alternative C (SA/1/66) [July 15; pp. 50c-50e of IMF draft]
406 Order of the Day, July 16 (not printed) [part of Document 408]
407 Tentative Suggestion from Special Subcommittee to Ad Hoc Committee 3B (Committee 3, Commission II) [July 15]
408 Journal No. 16 [July 16]
409 Minutes of Meeting of Commission I, July 15
410 Minutes of Meeting of Commission I, July 15
411 News Bulletin No. 22 (not printed) [July 16; in online companion file]
412 Alternative G (SA/1/67) [July 16; pages 11d-11e of IMF draft]
413 Working Draft—Fund Agreement [July 16]
414 Report of Special Committee on Unsettled Problems of Commission I, July 15
415 Report of Special Committee on Unsettled Problems of Commission I, July 16
416 Article I, Alternative L (SA/1/68) [July 16; p. 1h of IMF draft]
417 Alternative A (SA/1/69) [July 16; pages 47-47b of IMF draft]
418 News Bulletin No. 23 (not printed) [July 16; in online companion file]
419 Report of Ad Hoc Committee 2, Commission II, July 16, 1944
420 Journal No. 17 [July 17]
421 Commission II, Fifth Report of Drafting Committee [July 17]
422 Order of the Day, July 17 (not printed) [part of Document 420]
423 Minutes of Meeting of Commission II, July 16
424 Commission II, Report of Ad Hoc Committee 3B [July 16]
425 Report Submitted to Commission III by Committee 1 on Use of Silver for International Monetary Purposes [July 17]
426 Draft Proposals for Establishment of a Bank for Reconstruction and Development [July 17; shows progress toward the final World Bank agreement; not discussed in the transcripts because no transcripts exist for the meetings of Commission II near this date]
427 News Bulletin No. 24 (not printed) [July 17; in online companion file]

428 Report Submitted to Commission III by Committee 3 on Recommendations on Economic and Financial Policy, the Exchange of Information, and Other Means of Financial Cooperation [July 10]
429 Proposal of the Czechoslovakia Delegation to Commission III [on credit to liberated countries; July 17?]
430 (389, 391) Commission II, Addenda to Third and Fourth Reports of Drafting Committee [July 17; addendum to Documents 389 and 391]
431 (410) Commission I, Addendum to Minutes of Meeting of July 15 [addendum to Document 410]
432 Press Release No. 32. Remarks Made by Mexican Delegation on Veto Power of Lending Countries Before Commission II [July 17; v. 2]
433 Press Release No. 33. Date of Adjournment of Conference [July 17; v. 2]
434 Draft Proposals for the Establishment of a Bank for Reconstruction and Development [July 16]
435 Statement of the Delegation From Peru on Definite Economic Action Required to Create Conditions Necessary to Make Possible Attainment of the Specific Purposes of the Fund and of the Bank [July 17]
436 Press Release No. 34. Telegram from President of Bretton Woods Company [July 17; v. 2]
437 Report of Subcommittee 3C of Commission II [July 17]
438 News Bulletin No. 25 (not printed) [July 17; in online companion file]
439 Order of the Day, July 18 (not printed) [part of Document 440]
440 Journal No. 18 [July 18]
441 News Bulletin No. 26 (not printed) [July 18; in online companion file]
442 News Bulletin No. 27 (not printed) [July 18; in online companion file]
443 Final Act (Draft Text) [July 20]
444-445 Proyecto de Proposiciones para el Establecimiento de un Banco de Reconstrucción y Fomento [translation of Document 426; v. 2]
446 News Bulletin No. 28 (not printed) [July 18; in online companion file]
447 Report of Special Committee of Commission I [July 18]
448 Second Report of Drafting Committee of Commission I—Annex I [July 18?; shows progress toward the final IMF agreement]
449 (424) Commission II, Report of Ad Hoc Committee 3B [July 16 and July 18; supersedes Document 424]
450 Journal No. 19 [July 19]
451 Press Release No. 35. Statement by Carlos Lleras Restrepo, Chairman of Delegation of Colombia, Before Commission I [July 18; v. 2]
452 Report of Committee 2, Commission II [July 18]
453 Order of the Day, July 19 (not printed) [part of Document 450]
454 (437) Report of Subcommittee 3C of Commission II [July 18; supersedes Document 437]
455 Minutes of Meeting of Commission I, July 18
456 Commission II, Documents to Be Considered at Meeting, July 19

457 News Bulletin No. 29 (not printed) [July 19; in online companion file]
458 (canceled)
459 Press Release No. 36. Address by Eduardo Suárez, Mexican Minister of Finance, Before Commission III [July 19; v. 2]
460 Report of Committee 2, Commission II [July 19; not distributed]
461 Acuerdo Sobre el Fondo Monetario Internacional (Traducción Preliminar) [20 July; translation of Document 413; v. 2]
462 Press Release No. 37. Draft Resolution Approved by Committee 2 and Recommended to Commission III for Adoption [July 19; v. 2]
463 Press Release No. 38. Draft Resolution Considered by Committee 2 and Recommended to Commission III for Adoption in Principle and Reference to a Drafting Committee to Make Certain Technical Changes [regarding enemy assets and looted property; July 19; v. 2]
464 News Bulletin No. 30 (not printed) [July 19; in online companion file]
465 Journal No. 20 [July 20]
466 Report No. 6 of the Special Committee of Commission I [July 20]
467 Statement by the Australian Delegation on Report of Committee 3 to Commission III Dated July 10, 1944 (Document 428) and on Australian Resolution on Employment Agreement (Document 235) [July 20]
468 Report of Drafting Committee of Commission II—Annex I [July 19; shows progress toward the final World Bank agreement]
469 Minutes of Meetings of Commission II, July 19, 1944
470 Report Submitted to Commission III by Committee 2 on Enemy Assets, Looted Property, and Related Matters [July 20]
471 Order of the Day, July 20 (not printed) [part of Document 465]
472 Report of Commission I (International Monetary Fund) to the Executive Plenary Session, July 20—Louis Rasminsky, Canada, Reporting Delegate
473 Minutes of Meeting of Commission I, July 19
474 (omitted) [not found]
475 News Bulletin No. 31 (not printed) [July 20; in online companion file]
476 (canceled)
477 Statement by the Netherlands Delegation to Commission III [on liquidation of the Bank for International Settlements, July 20]
478 Additional Material Approved by Committee 2, Commission II [July 20]
479 Resolution to Be Introduced at Executive Plenary Session, July 20 [regarding initial deposits for the IMF]
480 (468) (426) Commission II, Amendments to Document 468 Proposed by USSR Delegation [July 20; Document 468 itself refers to Document 426]
481 (470) Report Submitted to Commission III by Committee 2 [July 20; supersedes Document 470]
482 Report of the Steering Committee [July 20]

483 Press Release No. 39. Statement by Mahmoud Saleh el Falaki [Falaky], Delegate of Egypt [July 20; v. 2]
484 Supplemental Report of Drafting Committee of Commission II [July 20]
485 Press Release No. 40. Statement by L.S. St. Laurent on Behalf of the Canadian Delegation at Meeting of Commission III [July 20; v. 2]
486 News Bulletin No. 32 (not printed) [July 20; in online companion file]
487 Press Release No. 41. Statement by Lord Keynes at Executive Plenary Session, July 20 [v. 2]
488 Press Release No. 42. Statement by Kyriakos Varvaressos, Chairman of the Greek Delegation, at Executive Plenary Session, July 20 [v. 2]
489 Press Release No. 43. Statement by Vladimir Rybar, Chairman of the Delegation of Yugoslavia, at Executive Plenary Session, July 20 [v. 2]
490 Press Release No. 44. Statement by H.H. K'ung, Chairman of the Delegation of China, at Executive Plenary Session, July 20 [v. 2]
491 Press Release No. 45. Statement by Pierre Mendès-France, Chairman of the French Delegation, at Executive Plenary Session, July 20 [v. 2]
492 Final Act [July 22; contains the IMF and World Bank Articles of Agreement]
493 Press Release No. 46. Statement by Fred M. Vinson, Vice Chairman of the Delegation of the United States, at Executive Plenary Session, July 20 [v. 2]
494 Order of the Day, July 21 (not printed) [part of Document 497]
495 Final Report of All Committees to Commission II [July 20]
496 Minutes of Meeting of Commission III, July 20
497 Journal No. 21 [July 21]
498 Minutes of Executive Plenary Session (not distributed) (not printed) [July 20; largely covered by Documents 487-491, 500, 504-505, and 514; script prepared before the meeting and minutes in online companion file]
499 News Bulletin No. 33 (not printed) [July 21; in online companion file]
500 Press Release No. 47. Remarks of Fred M. Vinson, Vice-Chairman of the Delegation of the United States, toward the close of the Executive Plenary Session, July 20 [v. 2]
501 Press Release No. 48. Remarks by Manuel B. Llosa, Delegate from Peru, before Commission III on the Creation, in the Field of International Economic Relations, of Conditions Necessary for the Attainment of the Purposes of the Fund and the Bank, and Other Broader Primary Objectives of Economic Policy [July 21; v. 2]
502 Press Release No, 49. Motion of Manuel B. Llosa, Delegate From Peru, on the Subject of Silver, Before Commission III [July 20; v. 2]
503 Secretariat Notice (not printed) [in online companion file]
504 Press Release No. 50, Statement by M.S. Stepanov, Chairman, Delegation, Union of Soviet Socialist Republics, at Executive Plenary Session, July 20 [v. 2]

505 (495) Report of Commission II to the Executive Plenary Session—Annex I [July 21; supersedes Document 495]

506 Articles de l'Accord du Fonds Monétaire International (not printed) [not found]

507 Minutes of Meeting of Commission II, July 20

508 Press Release No. 51. Memorandum on the International Monetary Fund (International Monetary Fund (Purposes, Methods, Consequences)) [July 21; v. 2]

509 Report of the Coordinating Committee [July 21]

510 Resolution, Recommendations, and Statement Submitted to the Conference by Commission III [July 21?]

511 Commission II, Report of Subscriptions Committee [July 21?]

512 News Bulletin No. 34 (not printed) [July 21; in online companion file]

513 Press Release No. 52. Remarks of André Istel, Delegate of France, at Executive Plenary Session, July 21 [v. 2]

514 Press Release No. 53. Remarks of Lord Keynes at Executive Plenary Session, July 20 [v. 2]

515 Order of the Day, July 22 (not printed) [in Document 523]

516 Press Release No. 54. Remarks of Georges Theunis, Delegate of Belgium, at Executive Plenary Session, July 21 [v. 2]

517 Press Release No. 55. Remarks by Dean Acheson in Executive Plenary Session, July 21 [v. 2]

518 Acta Final (Traducción Preliminar) [translation of Document 492; v. 2]

519 (473) Corrected Minutes of Meeting of Commission I, July 19 [supersedes Document 473]

520 Press Release No. 56. Remarks by the President of the Conference, Secretary Morgenthau, Before Executive Plenary Session, July 21, and the Reply of the Mexican Delegate, Eduardo Suárez [v. 2]

521 Press Release No. 57. Concluding Remarks by the President of the Conference, Henry Morgenthau, at Executive Plenary Session, July 21 [v. 2]

522 Press Release No. 58, Address of Henry Morgenthau, President of the Conference, at Closing Plenary Session, July 22 [v. 2]

523 Journal No. 22 [July 22]

524 Report of Commission III to the Executive Plenary Session, July 21

525 Minutes of Meetings of Commission II, July 21

526 Verbatim Report of Executive Plenary Session (not distributed) (not printed) [July 21; largely covered by Documents 517, 520-521, and 527]

527 Report of Commission II (International Bank for Reconstruction and Development) to the Executive Plenary Session, July 21

528 Secretariat Notice (not printed) [Memo on Issuance of Per Diem Checks; not found]

529 Secretariat Notice (not printed) [not found]

530 News Bulletin No. 35 (not printed) [July 22; in online companion file]
531 Closing Plenary Session (Agenda)
532 Press Release No. 59. Comment by Edward E. Brown (United States) on Announcement by the Secretary of State of the Forthcoming Conversations on the General Subject of International Security Organization [July 22; v. 2]
533 Press Release No. 60. Statement by Charles W. Tobey (United States) on Announcement by the Secretary of State of the Forthcoming Conversations on the General Subject of International Security Organization [July 22; v. 2]
534 Press Release No. 61. Comments by Fred M. Vinson on Announcement by the Secretary of State of the Forthcoming Conversations on the General Subject of International Security Organization [July 22; v. 2]
535 Press Release No. 62. Address by Arthur [Artur] de Souza Costa, Chairman of the Brazilian Delegation, at the Closing Plenary Session, July 22 [v. 2]
536 (withdrawn) [issued as Document 542 (536)]
537 Press Release No. 64. Statement by Ludwik Grosfeld, Minister of Finance of Poland [July 22; v. 2]
538 Press Release No. 65. Message from the President of the United States to the Conference at the Closing Plenary Session, July 22 [v. 2]
539 Press Release No. 66, Address by Pierre Mendès-France, Chairman of the French Delegation, at the Closing Plenary Session, July 22 [v. 2]
540 Press Release No. 67. Address by J.L. Ilsley, Chairman of the Canadian Delegation, at the Closing Plenary Session, July 22 [v. 2]
541 Press Release No. 68. Address by Eduardo I. Montoulieu, Chairman of the Cuban Delegation, at Closing Plenary Session, July 22 [v. 2]
542 Press Release No. 69. Address by Lord Keynes, Chairman of the Delegation of the United Kingdom, at Closing Plenary Session, July 22 [v. 2]
542 (536) Press Release No. 63. Remarks of H.H. K'ung, Chairman of Delegation of China, at Dinner Given by Henry Morgenthau, Jr., July 22, 1944 [v. 2]
543 (withdrawn) [not found]
544 Press Release No. 70. Statement by the President of the Conference, Henry Morgenthau, Jr., at Opening of the Final Plenary Session, July 22 [v. 2]
545 Press Release No. 71. Statement of the Chairman of U.S.S.R. Delegation, Michael [Mikhail] Stepanov, at the Closing Plenary Session, July 22 [v. 2]
546 Journal No. 23 [July 23]
547 Verbatim Minutes of Closing Plenary Session, July 22
548 Texte de l'Acte Final (Traduction Préliminaire) [translation of Document 492; v. 2]

Overview of conference proceedings[612]

Volume 1. [Major Documents]
Preface
Introduction
Proceedings and Documents Issued at the Conference [most of the documents listed above]

Volume 2. [Minor Documents and Index]
Appendix 1. Miscellaneous
1. Pre-Conference Documents
2. Press Releases
3. List of Correspondents [journalists]
4. Translations of Certain Documents into French and Spanish

Appendix II. List of Documents Issued at the Conference
Appendix III. Key to Symbols Used on Documents
Appendix IV. Related Papers
1. Preliminary Draft Outline of Proposal for a United and Associated Nationals Stabilization Fund [White plan]
2. International Clearing Union [Keynes plan]
3. Letter from Secretary Morgenthau to the Ministers of Finance of Thirty-Seven Countries
4. Tentative Draft Proposals of Canadian Experts for an International Exchange Union
5. Preliminary Draft Outline of a Proposal for an International Stabilization Fund of the United and Associated Nations
6. Preliminary Draft Outline of a Proposal for a Bank for Reconstruction and Development of the United and Associated Nations
7. Joint Statement by Experts on the Establishment of an International Monetary Fund of the United and Associated Nations

Index
- Commission I: International Monetary Fund
  - A. Articles of Agreement: Deliberations
  - B. History of Committees
  - C. Commission I (subject cross reference)
- Commission II: International Bank for Reconstruction and Development
  - A. Articles of Agreement: Deliberations
  - B. History of Committees
  - C. Commission II (subject cross reference)
- Commission III: Other Means of International Financial Cooperation
  - A. Proposals

---

612 Taken from the conference proceedings, v. 1, p. iv; v. 2, p. iii.

B. Resolutions
C. Committees
D. Subject Cross Reference
Conference: General
A. Organization of Conference
B. Participation by Countries and Organizations Attending

Appendix D

Glossary

Alternate director: Official serving as Executive Director in the absence of the primary director.

Alternative: A proposed amendment to the Articles of Agreement.

Appointed directors: Executive Directors chosen by and representing single countries having large quotas, rather than elected by coalitions of countries each having a small quota.

Articles of Agreement: The IMF and World Bank agreements, especially in their final versions.

Atlantic City: Site of a preliminary conference on the IMF and World Bank just before the Bretton Woods conference.

Bank for International Settlements: Organization with headquarters in Basel, Switzerland, originally established in 1930 to handle German reparation payments for World War I, but later serving mainly as a forum for central bank cooperation.

Bank for Reconstruction and Development: Name used early in the Bretton Woods conference to designate the International Bank for Reconstruction and Development (World Bank).

Board of Governors: Highest authority of the IMF and World Bank, composed of officials appointed by every member government. Delegates day-to-day supervision to Executive Directors.

"Bible": A loose-leaf binder containing the preliminary draft IMF agreement, the "Old Testament," to which delegates could add and subtract pages as they were amended.

Capital transactions: Payments for capital-account transactions, that is, those involving financial assets or other investments, as opposed to current payments.

Charges: Interest rates and fees on purchases (loans).

Commission: The three main bodies for conducting the work of the Bretton Woods conference. Commission I considered the IMF; Commission II, the World Bank; and Commission III, other means of international financial cooperation.

Committee: A particular subdivision of the Bretton Woods conference (plenary session > commission > *committee* > subcommittee, ad hoc committee, special committee, etc.), but often used by delegates to refer to any subdivision, whatever its official name.

Current payments: Payments for current-account transactions, that is, those involving goods and services, as opposed to capital transactions. Given a precise definition in the IMF Articles of Agreement.

Depository: Place where the IMF and World Bank hold gold and other assets.

Drafting Committee: Committee charged with devising language to express accurately provisions agreed by a committee. Refers especially to the Drafting Committees of Commissions I and II.

Drawings: See "purchases."

Exchange controls: Restrictions on the use of a currency in international payments.

Elected directors: Executive Directors elected by coalitions of countries each having a small quota, rather than chosen by and representing single countries having large quotas.

Executive Directors: A small body of officials supervising the day-to-day affairs of the IMF and World Bank. Includes some appointed directors and some elected directors.

Gold-convertible exchange: Financial assets that can be sold for gold, which implies that the assets are denominated in currencies that do not have exchange controls on capital transactions.

Joint Statement: "Joint Statement by Experts on the Establishment of an International Monetary Fund," also known as the Joint Statement of Principles, a draft proposal for the IMF published in April 1944.

Managing Director: Top manager of the IMF. The top manager of the World Bank is called the president.

Multilateral clearing: Use of a currency for payments with countries other than the issuing country.

"New Testament": Intermediate draft of the IMF agreement, Document 321 of the conference.

"Old Testament": Preliminary draft of the IMF agreement, Document 32 of the conference, containing the Joint Statement plus alternatives proposed before the Bretton Woods conference began.

Par (parity) value: Value, expressed in terms of gold, at which a country promises to maintain the exchange rate of its currency.

Purchases: The IMF's term for loans. In economic reality, the same as loans; in terms of legal treatment, different in some respects.

Quotas: Capital subscription. Voting power at the IMF and World Bank is linked to quotas.

Repurchases: The IMF's term for repayments of loans.

Remittances: Payments not in exchange for goods and services, especially payments by immigrants to family members in their country of origin.

Reporter (Reporting Delegate): Delegate charged with summarizing the proceedings of a committee meeting.

Scarce currency: A currency whose stock at the IMF is exhausted. The IMF Articles of Agreement provided that the IMF could declare such a currency to be scarce and that member countries would then be allowed to discriminate against the issuing country in their trade policies and exchange controls.

Silver-hoarding country: A country where silver coins are a large share of the currency. A term used by the Mexican delegation.

Special Committee: Special Committee on Unsettled Problems, a committee of Commission I that addressed many of the most contentious issues related to the IMF Articles of Agreement. Commission II also had a committee with the same name, but it does not appear in the transcripts.

Sterling balances: Assets denominated in pounds sterling, which at the time of the Bretton Woods conference and for many years thereafter could not be freely exchanged for U.S. dollars.

Transitional period: Period during which an IMF member country could continue to apply exchange controls on current payments.

Uniform changes in par values: Simultaneous changes in the value of all currencies against gold.

United and Associated Nations: World War II Allies and associated countries. Included governments in exile for many countries occupied by German and Japanese military forces; excluded the Axis powers and neutral countries.

Appendix E

Concordances for Articles of Agreement

The Bretton Woods conference did not develop the agreements for the IMF and the World Bank from zero. A conference among a smaller group of countries at Atlantic City, New Jersey just before the Bretton Woods conference devised preliminary draft agreements. The preliminary draft agreement for the IMF was published as Document 32 of the conference proceedings.[613] It consisted of the Joint Statement by Experts on the Establishment of an International Monetary Fund,[614] which had been published a few months previously, plus material added at Atlantic City. Conference participants occasionally referred to page numbers of the "Joint Statement," but what they meant was Document 32. When they referred to section numbers in Document 32, it was usually the section numbers of Alternative A, the material added at Atlantic City. Document 51 of the proceedings summarizes those section numbers and titles.[615] Document 32, the preliminary draft, was dubbed "Old Testament." In some later meetings of Commission I, delegates referred to an intermediate draft, dubbed the "New Testament"; it was Document 321.[616] Document 320[617] summarizes the contents of Document 321. The first preliminary draft agreement for the World Bank, published as Document 169, was never used in meetings because it was quickly superseded by Document 245.[618] The final agreements (Articles of Agreement) for both the IMF and the World Bank were published as Document 492 of the conference proceedings.[619]

Participants in the conference kept the draft agreements in loose-leaf binders. Pages in the preliminary drafts were organized so that each proposed section of the preliminary draft had its own page number. The conference Secretariat gave page numbers to proposed amendments

---

[613] Document 32, pp. 21-60.

[614] Appendix IV, part 7, pp. 1629-1636.

[615] Document 51, pp. 88-91.

[616] Document 321, pp. 518-537.

[617] Document 320, pp. 515-518.

[618] Document 169, pp. 191-215; Document 245, pp. 365-402.

[619] Document 492, pp. 927-1015.

consisting of a number keyed to the preliminary draft plus a letter. So, for example, Article IV, Section 1 of the preliminary draft articles of the IMF was on page 16 of the Joint Statement, and Alternative B to the section was printed as Document 177, numbered page 16a. Participants could easily add and delete pages to their binders to reflect changes to the draft agreements.

Participants referred to page numbers, articles, and sections of the agreements as they were numbered in the drafts, not in the final agreements. The tables below will help readers follow how the numbering of articles and sections changed between the preliminary drafts and the final agreements. Readers who wish to perform further comparisons should see the spreadsheet workbook we have posted on the page for this book at the Web site of the Center for Financial Stability. The workbook allows users to choose their own sorting criteria.

International Monetary Fund

Here is a key to the table below.

Document:

Joint Statement (J.S.): Appendix IV, part 7, pp. 1629-1636 of the conference proceedings.

Preliminary (Prelim.): Document 32, pp. 21-60.

Intermediate (Int.): Document 321, pp. 518-537.

Final: Document 492, pp. 927-1015.

Pages: Pages are keyed to the page numbers of the original Document 32 as distributed at the conference. Several references in Document 321 referring to Document 32 are absent or seem incorrect to us, and in such cases we have placed what we consider the correct references in brackets.

Title: Roman numerals identify articles, Arabic numerals identify sections, lower-case letters identify paragraphs (subsections), and capital letters identify supplementary schedules to the agreement. **Bold** indicates titles of articles and supplementary schedules.

Document	*Page*	*Title*
J.S.	none	None
Prelim.	none	None
Int.	new	**Introductory Article**
Final	n.a.	**Introductory Article**
J.S.	1	**I. Purpose and Policies of the Fund**
Prelim.	1	**I. Purposes and Policies of the Fund**
Int.	1	**I. Purposes**
Final	n.a.	**I. Purposes**
J.S.	2	**II. (part) Subscription to the Fund**
Prelim.	2	**II. (part) Subscription to the Fund**
Int.	2	**II. Membership**
Final	n.a.	**II. Membership**
J.S.	none	None
Prelim.	2	II.1. (part) Countries eligible for membership
Int.	2	II.1 Original members
Final	n.a.	II.1 Original members
J.S.	none	None
Prelim.	2	II.1. (part) Countries eligible for membership
Int.	2	II.2 Other members
Final	n.a.	II.2 Other members

Document	*Page*	*Title*
J.S.	2	**II. (part) Subscription to the Fund**
Prelim.	2	**II. (part) Subscription to the Fund**
Int.	2	**III. Quotas and Subscriptions**
Final	n.a.	**III. Quotas and Subscriptions**
J.S.	2	II.1 [Quotas]
Prelim.	2	II.2 Quotas
Int.	2	III.1 Quotas
Final	n.a.	III.1 Quotas
J.S.	none	none
Prelim.	2	**A. [Quotas—placeholder]**
Int.	2	**A. [Quotas—placeholder]**
Final	n.a.	**A. Quotas**
J.S.	none	none
Prelim.	2	II.3 Time and place of payment
Int.	2, 5	III.3(a) Subscriptions: time, place and form of payment
Final	n.a.	III.3(a) Subscriptions: time, place and form of payment
J.S.	3	II.2 [Adjustment of quotas]
Prelim.	3	II.4 Adjustment of quotas
Int.	2 [3]	III.2 Adjustment of quotas
Final	n.a.	III.2 Adjustment of quotas
J.S.	4	II.3 [Gold subscriptions]
Prelim.	4	II.5 Initial payments
Int.	2, 5 [4]	III.3(b-c) Subscriptions: time, place and form of payment
Final	n.a.	III.3(b-c) Subscriptions: time, place and form of payment
J.S.	none	none
Prelim.	none	none
Int.	none	none
Final	n.a.	III.3(d) Subscriptions: time, place and form of payment
J.S.	none	none
Prelim.	4	II.6 Payments when quotas are changed
Int.	2, 5 [4]	III.4 Payments when quotas are changed
Final	n.a.	III.4 Payments when quotas are changed
J.S.	5	**III. Transactions with the Fund**
Prelim.	5	**III. Transactions with the Fund**
Int.	5	**V. Transactions with the Fund**
Final	n.a.	**V. Transactions with the Fund**

Document	*Page*	*Title*
J.S.	5	III.1 [Agencies dealing with the Fund]
Prelim.	5	III.1 Agencies dealing with the Fund
Int.	5	V.1 Agencies dealing with the Fund
Final	n.a.	V.1 Agencies dealing with the Fund
J.S.	6	III.2 (part) [Conditions upon which any member may purchase currencies of other members]
Prelim.	6	III.2 (part) [Conditions upon which any member may purchase currencies of other members]
Int.	6a	V.3 Conditions governing use of the Fund's resources
Final	n.a.	V.3 Conditions governing use of the Fund's resources
J.S.	6	III.2 (part) [Conditions upon which any member may purchase currencies of other members]
Prelim.	6	III.2 (part) [Conditions upon which any member may purchase currencies of other members]
Int.	6a	V.4 Waiver of conditions
Final	n.a.	V.4 Waiver of conditions
J.S.	none	none
Prelim.	6	III.2a Conditions governing purchases for capital transfers
Int.	6a	VI.2 Special provisions for capital transfers
Final	n.a.	VI.2 Special provisions for capital transfers
J.S.	none	none
Prelim.	6	III.3 Declaring members ineligible to use the resources of the Fund
Int.	6b	V.5 Ineligibility to use the Fund's resources
Final	n.a.	V.5 Ineligibility to use the Fund's resources
J.S.	7	III.3 [Limitation on the Fund's operations]
Prelim.	7	III.4 Limitation on the operations of the Fund
Int.	7	V.2 Limitation on the Fund's operations
Final	n.a.	V.2 Limitation on the Fund's operations
J.S.	8	III.4 [Measures to replenish the Fund's holdings of scarce currencies]
Prelim.	8	III.5 Operations for the purposes of preventing currencies from becoming scarce
Int.	6a [8]	VII.2 Measures to maintain the Fund's holdings of scarce currencies
Final	n.a.	VII.2 Measures to replenish the Fund's holdings of scarce currencies

Document	***Page***	***Title***
J.S.	9	III.5 [Multilateral international clearing]
Prelim.	9	III.6 Multilateral international clearing
Int.	9	VIII.3 Multilateral clearing
Final	n.a.	VIII.4 Convertibility of foreign held balances
J.S.	10	III.6 [Purchases of currencies from the Fund for gold]
Prelim.	10	III.7 Acquisition by members of currencies of other members for gold
Int.	10	V.6 Purchases of currencies from the Fund for gold
Final	n.a.	V.6 Purchases of currencies from the Fund for gold
J.S.	11	III.7 [Other acquisitions of gold by the Fund]
Prelim.	11	III.8 Other acquisitions of gold by the Fund
Int.	11	V.7 Other acquisitions of gold by the Fund
Final	n.a.	V.7 Repurchase by a member of its currency held by the Fund
J.S.	none	none
Prelim.	none	none
Int.	none	none
Final	n.a.	**B. Provisions with Respect to Repurchase by a Member of Its Currency Held by the Fund**
J.S.	none	none
Prelim.	12	III.9(a) Transferability and guarantee of the assets of the Fund
Int.	12	IX.5 (part) Freedom of assets from restrictions
Final	n.a.	IX.6. (part) Freedom of assets from restrictions
J.S.	none	none
Prelim.	12	III.9(b) Transferability and guarantee of the assets of the Fund
Int.	12	VIII.4 Acceptance of currency purchased from the Fund
Final	n.a.	IX.6 (part) Freedom of assets from restrictions
J.S.	none	none
Prelim.	12	III.9(c) Transferability and guarantee of the assets of the Fund
Int.	12	XII.3 Guarantee of the Fund's deposits
Final	n.a.	XIII.3 Guarantee of the Fund's assets
J.S.	none	none
Prelim.	13	III.10 Charges and commissions
Int.	13	V.8 Charges and commissions
Final	n.a.	V.8.Charges

Document	*Page*	*Title*
J.S.	none	none
Prelim.	14	III.11 Furnishing information
Int.	14c	VIII.5 Furnishing of information
Final	n.a.	VIII.5 Furnishing of information
J.S.	none	none
Prelim.	15	III.12 Consideration of representations of the Fund
Int.	15	XI.8 Communication of views to members
Final	n.a.	XII.8 Communication of views to members
J.S.	16	**IV. Par Values of Member Currencies**
Prelim.	16	**IV. Par Values of Member Currencies**
Int.	16	**IV. Par Values of Currencies**
Final	n.a.	**IV. Par Values of Currencies**
J.S.	16	IV.1 [Par values of the currencies of members]
Prelim.	16	IV.1 Par values of the currencies of members
Int.	16	IV.1 Expression of par value
Final	n.a.	IV.1 Expression of par values
J.S.	none	none
Prelim.	none	none
Int.	17a	IV.4(a) Obligations regarding exchange stability
Final	n.a.	IV.4(a) Obligations regarding exchange stability
J.S.	17	IV.2 (part) [Changes in par values]
Prelim.	17	IV.2 (part) [Changes in par values]
Int.	17a	IV.4(b) Obligations regarding exchange stability
Final	n.a.	IV.5(a) Changes in par values
J.S.	17	IV.2 (part) [Changes in par values]
Prelim.	17	IV.2 (part) [Changes in par values]
Int.	17a	IV.5 (preamble) Changes in par values
Final	n.a.	IV.5(b) Changes in par values
J.S.	17	IV.3 [Action by the Fund on proposed changes]
Prelim.	17	IV.3 [Action by the Fund on proposed changes]
Int.	17aa	IV.6 Action by the Fund on proposed changes
Final	n.a.	IV.5(d-f) Changes in par values
J.S.	17	IV.4 [The Fund and changes in par values]
Prelim.	17	IV.4 [The Fund and changes in par values]
Int.	17a	IV.5(a-c) Changes in par values
Final	n.a.	IV.5(c) Changes in par values

Document	***Page***	***Title***
J.S.	none	none
Prelim.	none	none
Int.	17aa	IV.7 Effect of unauthorized changes
Final	n.a.	IV.6 Effect of unauthorized changes
J.S.	18	IV.5 [Uniform changes in par value]
Prelim.	18	IV.5 Uniform changes in par values
Int.	18	IV.8 Uniform changes in par values
Final	n.a.	IV.7 Uniform changes in par values
J.S.	none	none
Prelim.	19	IV.6 Protection of the assets of the Fund
Int.	19	IV.9 Maintenance of gold value of the Fund's assets
Final	n.a.	IV.8 Maintenance of gold value of the Fund's assets
J.S.	none	none
Prelim.	20	IV.7 Separate currencies within a member's territories
Int.	20	IV.10 Separate currencies within a member's territories
Final	n.a.	IV.9 Separate currencies within a member's territories
J.S.	21	**V. Capital Transactions**
Prelim.	21	**V. Capital Transactions**
Int.	21	**VI. Capital Transfers**
Final	n.a.	**VI. Capital Transfers**
J.S.	21	V.1 [Use of the resources of the Fund for transfers of capital]
Prelim.	21	V.1 Use of the resources of the Fund for transfers of capital
Int.	21	VI.1 Use of the Fund's resources for capital transfers
Final	n.a.	VI.1 Use of the Fund's resources for capital transfers
J.S.	22	V.2 [Limitation on controls of capital movements]
Prelim.	22	V.2 Limitation on controls of capital movements
Int.	22	VI.3 Controls of capital transfers
Final	n.a.	VI.3 Controls of capital transfers
J.S.	23	**VI. Apportionment of Scarce Currencies**
Prelim.	23	**VI. Apportionment of Scarce Currencies**
Int.	23	**VII. Scarce Currencies**
Final	n.a.	**VII. Scarce Currencies**
J.S.	23	VI.1 [General scarcity of currency]
Prelim.	23	VI.1 General scarcity
Int.	23b	VII.1 General scarcity of currency
Final	n.a.	VII.1 General scarcity of currency

Document	*Page*	*Title*
J.S.	23	VI.2 [Scarcity of the Fund's holdings]
Prelim.	23	VI.2 Scarcity of the Fund's holdings
Int.	23b	VII.3 Scarcity of the Fund's holdings
Final	n.a.	VII.3 Scarcity of the Fund's holdings
J.S.	none	none
Prelim.	none	none
Int.	23c	VII.4 Administration of restrictions
Final	n.a.	VII.4 Administration of restrictions
J.S.	none	none
Prelim.	none	none
Int.	23c	VII.5 Effect of other international agreements or restrictions
Final	n.a.	VII.5 Effect of other international agreements or restrictions
J.S.	24	**VII. Management of the Fund**
Prelim.	24	**VII. Management of the Fund**
Int.	24	**XI. Organization and Management**
Final	n.a.	**XII. Organization and Management**
J.S.	24	VII.1 (part) [Structure of the Fund]
Prelim.	24	VII.1 Board of Governors
Int.	new	XI.1 Structure of the Fund
Final	n.a.	XII.1 Structure of the Fund
J.S.	24	VII.1 (part) [Structure of the Fund]
Prelim.	24	VII.1 Board of Governors
Int.	24	XI.2 Board of Governors
Final	n.a.	XII.2 Board of Governors
J.S.	25	VII.1 (part) [Structure of the Fund]
Prelim.	25	VII.2 Executive Directors
Int.	26 [25]	XI.3 Executive Directors
Final	n.a.	XII.3 Executive Directors
J.S.	26	VII.2 [Voting]
Prelim.	26	VII.3 (part) Voting
Int.	26	XI.5 (part) Voting
Final	n.a.	XII.5(a-c) Voting
J.S.	none	none
Prelim.	none	none
Int.	none	none
Final	n.a.	**C. Election of Executive Directors**

Document	*Page*	*Title*
J.S.	26	VII.3 [Majority voting]
Prelim.	26	VII.3 (part) Voting
Int.	26	XI.5 (part) Voting
Final	n.a.	XII.5(d) Voting
J.S.	none	none
Prelim.	27	VII.4 The General Manager
Int.	27	XI.4 Managing Director and staff
Final	n.a.	XII.4 Managing Director and staff
J.S.	28	VII.4 [Publication of reports]
Prelim.	28	VII.5 Publication of reports
Int.	28	XI.7 Publication of reports
Final	n.a.	XII.7 Publication of reports
J.S.	none	none
Prelim.	29	VII.6 Depositories
Int.	29	XII.2 Depositories of the Fund
Final	n.a.	XIII.2 Depositories
J.S.	none	none
Prelim.	29	VII.7 Form of holdings of currency
Int.	29	III.5 Substitution of securities for currency
Final	n.a.	III.5 Substitution of securities for currency
J.S.	none	none
Prelim.	30	VII.8 Relationship to other international organizations
Int.	30	**X. Relation with Other International Organizations**
Final	n.a.	**X. Relations with Other International Organizations**
J.S.	none	none
Prelim.	none	none
Int.	none	none
Final	n.a.	**XI. Relations with Non-Member Countries**
J.S.	none	none
Prelim.	none	none
Int.	none	none
Final	n.a.	XI.1 Undertakings regarding relations with non-member countries
J.S.	none	none
Prelim.	none	none
Int.	none	none
Final	n.a.	XI.2 Restrictions on transactions with non-member countries

Document	*Page*	*Title*
J.S.	none	none
Prelim.	31	none
Int.	31	**XII. Offices and Depositories**
Final	n.a.	**XIII. Offices and Depositories**
J.S.	none	none
Prelim.	31	VII.9 Location of offices
Int.	31	XIII.1 Location of offices
Final	n.a.	XIII.1 Location of offices
J.S.	none	none
Prelim.	32	VII.[10] [Distribution of net income of the Fund]
Int.	32	XI.6 Distribution of net income
Final	n.a.	XII.6 Distribution of net income
J.S.	none	none
Prelim.	none	none
Int.	none	IX.1 Purposes of Article
Final	n.a.	IX.1 Purposes of Article
J.S.	none	none
Prelim.	33	VII.11 Miscellaneous powers
Int.	33	IX.2 Status of the Fund
Final	n.a.	IX.2 Status of the Fund
J.S.	34	**VIII. Withdrawal from the Fund**
Prelim.	34	**VIII. Withdrawal from the Fund**
Int.	34	**XIV. Withdrawal from Membership**
Final	n.a.	**XV. Withdrawal from Membership**
J.S.	34	VIII.1 [Right of members to withdraw]
Prelim.	34	VIII.1 Right of members to withdraw
Int.	34	XIV.1 Right of members to withdraw
Final	n.a.	XV.1 Right of members to withdraw
J.S.	none	none
Prelim.	35	VIII.2 Suspension of membership or compulsory withdrawal
Int.	35	XIV.2 Compulsory withdrawal
Final	n.a.	XV.2 Compulsory withdrawal
J.S.	36	VIII. 2 [Settlement of accounts with countries ceasing to be members]
Prelim.	36	VIII.3 (part) Settlement of accounts with countries ceasing to be members
Int.	36	XIV.3 (part) Settlement of accounts after withdrawal
Final	n.a.	XV.3 Settlement of accounts with members withdrawing

Document	*Page*	*Title*
J.S.	36	VIII.3 [Fund's disposal of currency of a withdrawing country]
Prelim.	36	VIII.3 (part) Settlement of accounts with countries ceasing to be members
Int.	36	XIV.3 (part) Settlement of accounts after withdrawal
Final	n.a.	**D. Settlement of Accounts with Members Withdrawing**
J.S.	none	none
Prelim.	none	none
Int.	none	none
Final	n.a.	**XVI. Emergency Provisions**
J.S.	none	none
Prelim.	none	none
Int.	none	none
Final	n.a.	XVI.1 Temporary Suspension
J.S.	none	none
Prelim.	none	none
Int.	none	none
Final	n.a.	XVI.2 Liquidation of the Fund
J.S.	none	none
Prelim.	37	VIII.4 Liquidation of the Fund
Int.	37	**XV. Liquidation of the Fund**
Final	n.a.	**E. Administration of Liquidation**
J.S.	38	**IX. (part) Obligations of Member Countries**
Prelim.	38	**IX. (part) Obligations of Member Countries**
Int.	38	**IX. Status, Immunities and Privileges of the Fund**
Final	n.a.	**IX. Status, Immunities and Privileges**
J.S.	38	**IX. (part) Obligations of Member Countries**
Prelim.	38	**IX. (part) Obligations of Member Countries**
Int.	38	**VIII. General Obligations of Members**
Final	n.a.	**VIII. General Obligations of Members**
J.S.	none	none
Prelim.	38	IX.1 Purpose and scope of additional undertakings
Int.	38	VIII.1 Introduction
Final	n.a.	VIII.1 Introduction
J.S.	38	IX.1 (part) [Gold purchases based on parity prices]
Prelim.	38	IX.2 Gold purchases based on parity prices
Int.	38	IV.2 Gold purchases based on parity
Final	n.a.	IV.2 Gold purchases based on par values

Document	*Page*	*Title*
J.S.	39	IX.2 [Foreign exchange dealings based on par values]
Prelim.	39	IX.3 Foreign exchange dealings based on par values
Int.	39	IV.3 Foreign exchange dealings based on par values
Final	n.a	IV.3 Foreign exchange dealings based on parity
J.S.	39	IX.1 (part) [Gold purchases based on parity prices]
Prelim.	39	IX.3 Foreign exchange dealings based on par values
Int.	none	none
Final	n.a.	IV.4(b) Obligations regarding exchange stability
J.S.	40	IX.3 [Exchange controls on current payments]
Prelim.	40	IX.4 Exchange controls on current payments
Int.	40	VIII.2 Exchange controls on current payments
Final	n.a.	VIII.2 Avoidance of restrictions on current payments
J.S.	none	none
Prelim.	none	none
Int.	none	none
Final	n.a.	VIII.3 Avoidance of discriminatory currency practices
J.S.	none	none
Prelim.	none	none
Int.	none	none
Final	n.a.	VIII.6 Consultation between members regarding existing international agreements
J.S.	none	none
Prelim.	41	IX.5 (part) Immunity of assets of the Fund
Int.	12	IX.5 Freedom of assets from restrictions
Final	n.a.	IX.6 (part) Freedom of assets from restrictions
J.S.	none	none
Prelim.	41	IX.5 (part) Immunity of assets of the Fund
Int.	41	IX.4 Immunity from other actions
Final	n.a.	IX.4 Immunity from other action
J.S.	none	none
Prelim.	42	IX.6 Immunity from suit
Int.	41 [42]	IX.3 Immunity from judicial process
Final	n.a.	IX.3 Immunity from judicial process
J.S.	none	none
Prelim.	none	none
Int.	none	none
Final	n.a.	IX.5 Immunity of archives

Document	*Page*	*Title*
J.S.	none	none
Prelim.	none	none
Int.	new	IX.7 Immunity of officers and employees from restrictions
Final	n.a.	IX.8(ii) Immunities and privileges of officers and employees
J.S.	none	none
Prelim.	none	none
Int.	new	IX.8 Privilege for communications
Final	n.a.	IX.7 Privilege for communications
J.S.	none	none
Prelim.	none	none
Int.	new	IX.9 Privilege of officers and employees in respect of travel
Final	n.a.	IX.8(iii) Immunities and privileges of officers and employees
J.S.	none	none
Prelim.	none	none
Int.	41 [42]	IX.6 Immunity of officers and employees from suit
Final	n.a.	IX.8(i) Immunities and privileges of officers and employees
J.S.	none	none
Prelim.	43	IX.7 Restrictions on taxation of the Fund, its employees and obligations
Int.	43a	IX.10 Immunities from taxation
Final	n.a.	IX.9 Immunities from taxation
J.S.	none	none
Prelim.	none	none
Int.	43a	IX.11 Application of article
Final	n.a.	IX.10 Application of Article
J.S.	44	**X. Transitional Arrangements**
Prelim.	44	**X. Transitional Arrangements**
Int.	[44]	**XIII. Transitional Period**
Final	n.a.	**XIV. Transitional Period**
J.S.	44	X.1 [Exchange restrictions and currency arrangements and practices retained]
Prelim.	44	X.1 Exchange restrictions and currency arrangements and practices retained
Int.	[44]	[XIII.1. Introduction]
Final	n.a.	XIV.1 Introduction

Document	*Page*	*Title*
J.S.	44	X.2 [Withdrawal of exchange restrictions]
Prelim.	44	X.2 Withdrawal of exchange restrictions
Int.	[44]	[XIII.2 Exchange restrictions]
Final	n.a.	XIV.2 Exchange restrictions
J.S.	44	X.3 [Policy of the Fund during the transition period]
Prelim.	44	X.3 Policy of the Fund during the transition period
Int.	[44]	[XIII.3 Action of the Fund relating to restrictions]
Final	n.a.	XIV.3 Notification to the Fund
J.S.	none	none
Prelim.	none	none
Int.	none	none
Final	n.a.	XIV.4 Action of the Fund relating to restrictions
J.S.	44	X.4 [Nature of transitional period]
Prelim.	44	X.4 [Nature of transitional period]
Int.	44	[XIII.4 Nature of transitional period]
Final	n.a.	XIV.5 Nature of transitional period
J.S.	none	none
Prelim.	45	**XI. Amendments**
Int.	45	**XVI. Amendments**
Final	n.a.	**XVII. Amendments**
J.S.	none	none
Prelim.	46	**XII. Interpretation of the Agreement**
Int.	46	**XVII. (part) Interpretation**
Final	n.a.	**XVIII. (part) Interpretation**
J.S.	none	none
Prelim.	46	XII.1 Interpretation
Int.	46	XVII. (part) Interpretation
Final	n.a.	XVIII. (part) Interpretation
J.S.	none	none
Prelim.	47	XII.2 Definitions
Int.	47	XVIII. Definitions
Final	n.a.	XIX. Explanation of Terms
J.S.	none	none
Prelim.	48	XII.3 Effect on other international commitments
Int.	48	VIII.6 Consultation of members regarding existing international agreements
Final	n.a.	XVIII. (part) Interpretation

Document	*Page*	*Title*
J.S.	none	none
Prelim.	49	**XIII. Final Provisions**
Int.	51	**XIX. Final Provisions**
Final	n.a.	**XX. Final Provisions**
J.S.	none	none
Prelim.	49	XIII.1 Entry into effect
Int.	51a	XIX.2 Entry into force
Final	n.a.	XX.1 Entry into force
J.S.	none	none
Prelim.	49	XIII.2 Effective date of the Agreement
Int.	51	XIX.1 Signature
Final	n.a.	XX.2 Signature
J.S.	none	none
Prelim.	49	XIII.3 Calling the initial meeting of the Fund
Int.	51a	XIX.3(a) Inauguration of the Fund
Final	n.a.	XX.3(a) Inauguration of the Fund
J.S.	none	none
Prelim.	49	XIII.4. Agenda of the initial meeting
Int.	51a	XIX.3(b-c) Inauguration of the Fund
Final	n.a.	XX.3(b-c) Inauguration of the Fund
J.S.	none	none
Prelim.	49	XIII.5. Fixing initial par values
Int.	51b	XIX.4 Initial determination of par values
Final	n.a.	XX.4 Initial determination of par values

International Bank for Reconstruction and Development (World Bank)

Pages are keyed to the page numbers of the original Document 245 as distributed at the conference (pages 365-402 of the conference proceedings). As with the table for the IMF agreement, Roman numerals identify articles, Arabic numerals identify sections, lower-case letters identify paragraphs (subsections), and capital letters identify supplementary schedules to the agreement. **Bold** indicates titles of articles and supplementary schedules. The table is keyed to the order of sections in the preliminary draft. With a few readily apparent exceptions, the order in the final agreement was almost the same.

Page	*Preliminary draft (Doc. 245)*	*Final agreement (Doc. 492)*
1	**Title**	**Introductory Article**
2	**I. Purposes of the Bank**	**I. Purposes**
3	**II. Membership in and Capital of the Bank**	**II. Membership in and Capital of the Bank**
3	II.1 Countries eligible for membership	II.1 Membership
4	II.2 Authorized capital	II.2 Authorized capital
5	II.3 Subscription for stock	II.3 Subscription of shares
6	II.4 Availability of subscribed capital	II.5 Division and calls of subscribed capital
7	II.5 Payment of subscription	II.8 Time of payment of subscriptions
none	none	II.9 Maintenance of value of certain currency holdings of the Bank
8	II.6 Issue price of shares	II.4 Issue price of shares
9	II.7 Limitation on liability	II.6 Limitation on liability
none	none	II.7 Method of payment of subscriptions for shares
10	II.8 Disposal of shares limited	II.10 Restriction on disposal of shares
11	II.9 Return of subscriptions	none; V.14 is the closest similar provision
12	**III. General Provisions Relating to Loans**	**III. General Provisions Relating to Loans and Guarantees**
12	III.1 Use of resources restricted	III.1 Use of resources

Page	*Preliminary draft (Doc. 245)*	*Final agreement (Doc. 492)*
13	III.2 Agencies dealing with the Bank	III.2. Dealings between members and the Bank
14	III.3 Limitation on loans and guarantees	III.3 Limitations on guarantees and borrowings of the Bank
15	III.4 Conditions on which Bank may guarantee or make loans	III.4 Conditions on which the Bank may guarantee or make loans
16	III. between Sections 4 and 5. [Exclusion of loans that can be placed through private channels]	none
17	III.5 Provision of currencies for loans	IV.3 Provision of currencies for direct loans
18	III.6 Use of loans guaranteed, participated in or made by the Bank	III.5 Use of loans guaranteed, participated in or made by the Bank
19	**IV. Operations**	**IV. Operations**
19	IV.1 Methods of facilitating provision of loans	IV.1 (part) Methods of making or facilitating loans
20	IV.2 Loans from subscribed capital	IV.2 Availability and transferability of currencies
21	IV.3 Loans from borrowed funds and guarantees	IV.1 (part) Methods of making or facilitating loans
22	IV.4 Payment provisions for direct loans	IV.4 Payment provisions for direct loans
23	IV.5 Participations	IV.1 (part) Methods of making or facilitating loans
24	IV.6 Guarantees	IV.5 Guarantees
none	none	IV.6 Special reserve
25	IV.7 Order of meeting obligations	IV.7 Methods of meeting liabilities of the Bank in case of defaults
26	IV.8 Miscellaneous operations	IV.8 Miscellaneous operations
27	IV.9 Warning to be placed on securities	IV.9 Warning to be placed on securities
28	IV.10 Political activity prohibited	IV.10 Political activity prohibited
41	IV.11 Miscellaneous powers	VII.2 Status of the Bank
29	**V. Management**	**V. Organization and Management**
none	none	V.1 Structure of the Bank
29	V.1 Board of Governors	V.2 Board of Governors

Page	*Preliminary draft (Doc. 245)*	*Final agreement (Doc. 492)*
30	V.2 Voting	V.3 Voting
31	V.3 The Executive Directors	V.4 Executive Directors
none	none	V.5 President and staff
32	V.4 Advisory Council	V.6 Advisory Council
33	V.5 Loan committees	V.7 Loan committees
34	V.6 Relationship to other international organizations	V.8 Relationship to other international organizations
35	V.7 Location of offices	V.9 Location of offices
none	none	V.10 Regional offices and councils
36	V.8 Depositories	V.11 Depositories
37	V.9 Form of holdings of currency	V.12 Form of holdings of currency
38	V.10 Protection of the assets of the Bank	VII.6 Freedom of assets from restrictions
39	V.11 Publication of reports	V.13 Publication of reports and provision of information
40	V.12 Allocation of income	V.14 Allocation of net income
42	**VI. Withdrawal and Suspension of Membership and Liquidation**	**VI. Withdrawal and Suspension of Membership; Suspension of Operations**
42	VI.1 Right of members to withdraw	VI.1 Right of members to withdraw
43	VI.2 Suspension of membership	VI.2 Suspension of membership
44	VI.3 Financial assistance to be withheld	no similar provision
45	VI.4 Cessation of membership in International Monetary Fund	VI.3 Cessation of membership in International Monetary Fund
46	VI.5 Settlement of accounts with countries ceasing to be members	VI.4 (part) Settlement of accounts with governments ceasing to be members
47	VI.6 Assessments to meet losses	VI.4 (part) Settlement of accounts with governments ceasing to be members
48	VI.7 Liquidation	VI.5 Suspension of operations and settlement of obligations
49	**VII. Additional Undertakings on the Part of Member Countries**	**VII. Status, Immunities, and Privileges**
49	VII.1 Purposes and scope of undertakings	VII.1 Purposes of article

Page	*Preliminary draft (Doc. 245)*	*Final agreement (Doc. 492)*
50	VII.2 Immunities of the Bank	VII.4 Immunity of assets from seizure
51	VII.3 Suits against the Bank	VII.3 Position of the Bank with regard to judicial process
none	none	VII.5 Immunity of archives
none	none	VII.7 Privilege for communications
none	none	VII.8 Immunities and privileges of officers and employees
52	VII.4 Restrictions on taxation of the Bank, its employees and obligations	VII.9 Immunities from taxation
none	none	VII.10 Application of Article
53	**VIII. Amendments**	**VIII. Amendments**
54	**IX. Interpretation**	**IX. Interpretation**
55	IX.1 Interpretation	IX. (part) Interpretation
56	IX.2 Definitions	IX. (part) Interpretation
57	IX.3 Approval deemed given	X. Approval Deemed Given
58	**X. Final Provisions**	**XI. Final Provisions**
none	none	XI.1 Entry into force
none	none	XI.2 Signature
none	none	XI.3. Inauguration of the Bank
none	none	**A. Quotas**
none	none	**B. Election of Executive Directors**

Appendix F

Selected Conference Documents (Note)

In the electronic versions of the book, this appendix includes conference documents cited in the transcripts, accessible by hyperlinks from the footnotes in the main text. We have excluded the conference documents from the print edition because they would have doubled the length and price of the book. Almost all of the documents were published in the conference proceedings.[620] Readers who wish to consult the documents may search or download the conference proceedings at the page for the book on the Web site of the Center for Financial Stability. The Web site also contains some previously unpublished conference documents.

---

[620] United Nations Monetary and Financial Conference, *Proceedings and Documents of the United Nations Monetary and Financial Conference, Bretton Woods, New Hampshire, July 1-22, 1944,* 2 v. (Washington, D.C.: Government Printing Office, 1948).

Index to the Transcripts

The index is limited to the transcripts themselves; it excludes the introduction (chapter 1) and the appendices. It is brief because the electronic versions of the book offer the capability for word searches. The conference proceedings published in 1948 (cited in the footnote on the previous page; available in some research libraries and online) contain multiple indices at the end, which will be useful to readers who wish to make a deep study of the conference. Readers who do not find a topic listed in the index should also consult the table of contents. We have tried to list all delegates identified by name in the transcripts; Appendix A lists still more delegates. The glossary in Appendix D defines key terms.

www.ingramcontent.com/pod-product-compliance
Lightning Source LLC
Chambersburg PA
CBHW070944150426
42812CB00066B/3295/J

* 9 7 8 1 9 4 1 8 0 1 0 1 7 *